HEARING THE MOVIES

HEARING THE MOVIES
Music and Sound in Film History

SECOND EDITION

James Buhler
The University of Texas at Austin

David Neumeyer
The University of Texas at Austin

New York · Oxford
OXFORD UNIVERSITY PRESS

Oxford University Press is a department of the University of Oxford.
It furthers the University's objective of excellence in research,
scholarship, and education by publishing worldwide.

Oxford   New York
Auckland   Cape Town   Dar es Salaam   Hong Kong   Karachi
Kuala Lumpur   Madrid   Melbourne   Mexico City   Nairobi
New Delhi   Shanghai   Taipei   Toronto

With offices in
Argentina   Austria   Brazil   Chile   Czech Republic   France   Greece
Guatemala   Hungary   Italy   Japan   Poland   Portugal   Singapore
South Korea   Switzerland   Thailand   Turkey   Ukraine   Vietnam

For titles covered by Section 112 of the US Higher Education
Opportunity Act, please visit www.oup.com/us/he for the
latest information about pricing and alternate formats.

Published by Oxford University Press
198 Madison Avenue, New York, New York 10016
http://www.oup.com

Library of Congress Cataloging-in-Publication Data
Buhler, James, 1964-
   Hearing the movies : music and sound in film history / James Buhler,
David Neumeyer. -- Second edition.
      pages cm
   ISBN 978-0-19-998771-9 (alk. paper)
   1. Motion picture music--History and criticism. 2. Motion picture music--Analysis,
appreciation. 3. Film soundtracks--Production and direction--History. I. Neumeyer,
David. II. Title.
   ML2075.B84 2015
   781.5'42--dc23

                                                        2014044921

Printing number: 9 8 7 6 5 4 3 2

Printed in Canada

Contents

Preface

This book is about music in cinema, with music in the context of the film sound track, and with the sound track in the context of a history of film technology. We proceed from the view that "hearing the movies" involves skills that are different from listening to music for its own sake. Film is a technology-dependent medium that relies on reproduced sound, and the aesthetics of film sound have changed over time with changes in technology.

Approach

Our goal is to facilitate critical viewing and listening within the framework of an appreciation of the history of film and sound technology over the past 120 years. The book is designed to teach a general method for analyzing and interpreting the sound track and its music and to take advantage of those skills to position individual films and practices within a technological history. *Hearing the Movies*, in other words, is not intended primarily as a film music or sound track "masterworks" history, although we have worked at achieving a reasonably open level of coverage of repertoires, in addition to making ample use of films that are commonly taught. One can find simple chronological narratives for film music in many sources, from trade books and textbooks to online sites. We regard it as more important for students to understand the history of sound in the twentieth and early twenty-first centuries and to situate their film-viewing experiences within that context.

Organization

Hearing the Movies is laid out in three parts and fifteen chapters, a design intended to facilitate use on its own as the textbook for a semester course on film music and film sound. The book may also serve effectively as a substantial supplementary or reference text in introductory film courses, courses on sound design and aesthetics, courses on film music composition, courses on twentieth-century and contemporary music, courses on music and media, or even seminar courses on specific repertoires—for example, science fiction films after 1970, composers (such as Bernard Herrmann or John Williams), or periods (Hollywood in the 1930s, film and rock and roll in the 1950s and 1960s, etc.). We have mapped out basic syllabi for many of these options in files on this text's companion website, where we have also made suggestions for adapting the book to 10 week term formats. The URL is www.oup.com/us/buhlerneumeyer.

Part I is an introduction whose three chapters encourage development of basic listening and viewing skills. The overall goal is to position music within the sound track as one of its elements, as a peer (and partner) of speech and effects, and to introduce terms that are essential to the analysis of spatial and temporal aspects of sound and music. Chapter 1 introduces the sound track elements and the concept of an integrated sound track, Rick Altman's notion of *mise-en-bande*, the aesthetic standard for sound film since the 1930s. The emphasis here is on general relations of sound and image, in particular, the narrative functions of sound. In Chapter 2, we stress the musicality of the sound track by introducing musical terms (such as tempo and timbre) that can also be used to describe speech or sound effects or the sound track as a whole. Chapter 3 turns to sound and music in relation to narrative space and time, with special attention to commonly used oppositions, including diegetic/nondiegetic, synchronization/counterpoint, and empathetic/anempathetic.

Parts II and III, then, lay out a history of music and film sound organized around technological innovations and their role in film production and exhibition. The stages of that history discussed in Part II include the remarkably varied practices of the early cinema (Chapter 4), the rapid series of technological and aesthetic changes in the first few years of sound film (Chapter 5), the settling in and standardization of practices for sound film in the studio era (Chapter 7), and the shifts in aesthetics (especially with respect to musical styles) but relative conservatism in sound technology in the two subsequent decades (Chapters 9 and 10). Each chapter includes sections on film style and film form that continue to make direct use of the concepts from Part I and to develop the associated listening skills.

Part III considers the revolution in sound technology (and birth of modern sound design) that took place with the introduction of Dolby stereo and the consequences of that change for the New Hollywood generation (Chapters 11 and 12), and the characteristics of digital sound production and postproduction (including music) in the most recent decade, including the current—and prospective—situation for music and sound in film production and in other venues, particularly those that are Internet-based (Chapters 13 and 14).

The chapters not yet listed (Chapters 6, 8, and 15) combine the historical and the analytical, and in that sense also contribute to the work of Part I, but now with respect to methods and motivations for writing about films in terms of their sound tracks, particularly their musics. Chapter 6 presents basic terminology for film form and then provides step-by-step instructions for the analysis of a scene from *The Broadway Melody* (1929), a major film of the transition era that was already discussed in some detail in Chapter 5. Chapter 8 maps out the construction of an analysis report or response paper based on a cue list for an entire film, using *Mildred Pierce* (1945) as the example. The closing sections of Chapters 10 and 12 give information about writing compare/contrast papers, but all of Chapter 15 continues and expands the work to essays of analytic appreciation and interpretation, including essays of critical and ideological analysis.

Features

- The book's design integrates a chronological historical narrative with the development of critical listening and analysis skills.
- Copious examples and screen stills help bring film music into the context of sound, and sound into the context of the whole film.
- Detailed sample analyses, many with timings and shot descriptions, tie the image track to the sound track.
- Students can get full benefit from the book without the ability to read music notation (the authors have taught courses based on this material to general undergraduate audiences successfully for more than 10 years), but some musical examples have been included to enhance understanding for those who can read them.
- We have made every effort to bring together the broadest range of scholarship on film music currently available, spanning both music scholarship and film/media studies.
- Sidebars and text boxes augment the historical narrative with summaries and quotes from source material keyed to Mervyn Cooke's *The Hollywood Film Music Reader* (also published by Oxford University Press).
- Other sidebars and text boxes offer additional behind-the-scenes commentary from historical and contemporary industry professionals.
- Key terms are included in a glossary at the back for easy reference.
- Three chapters embedded in the historical sections provide guidelines and templates for writing about films in terms of their sound and music.
- A companion website at http://www.oup.com/us/buhlerneumeyer offers basic syllabi for 10 and 15 week courses in which *Hearing the Movies* is the principal textbook, along with suggestions for using the book in other courses. The site also contains electronic copies of many of the screen stills (but not other graphics) from the book, a list of the DVD editions we used, additional timings for scenes with music in the films discussed here, annotated film music

bibliographies, commentary on articles we particularly recommend for class readings, links to relevant film and film music websites, supplementary scene analyses, and suggestions for assignments and projects.

- The authors have established and continue to maintain a companion blog at http://hearingthemovies.blogspot.com.

A Note on the Films

As a practical matter, films were chosen on the basis of availability in DVD format with region coding for North America. Timings for specific scenes are given in the usual DVD player format: 0:00:00 (= hours:minutes:seconds). Many films have multiple DVD editions, some of which feature quite different versions of the film (for example, the theatrical release versus the director's cut). Wherever possible, we have used editions readily available through major distributors at the time this book was written.

A Note on the Second Edition

This second edition integrates the two halves of *Hearing the Movies* more closely while maintaining a design that permits flexibility in emphasis. Part I has been streamlined and updated, but its focus on careful listening/viewing and analysis of the soundtrack is intact. The historical section from the first edition—Part III—has been expanded into two. The new Part II covers early cinema through the end of the studio era, and Part III covers the period since. Another way to put it is that Part II is "pre-Star Wars" and Part III is "Star Wars and later"—or still another is "pre-Dolby" and "Dolby to digital."

The scene analyses and style generalizations about music usage in Part II of the first edition have been moved into appropriate places in the historical chapters. The writing "interludes" have been revamped and expanded into full-fledged chapters, also embedded in Parts II and III. As a group they continue to develop the strong audioviewing skills from Part I.

A majority of the material of the original book has found its way into this second edition, and instructors can be assured not only of continuity with respect to concepts but also of finding that many of the same films are discussed. A few analyses were removed, and we have posted some of them to the *Hearing the Movies* website.

The website also has a detailed table collating passages or sections from the first edition with their new placements in this second edition. This is for the use of instructors who might wish to organize the material more along the lines of the first edition.

Acknowledgments

We would like to thank Richard Carlin for initiating the idea of a revised second edition, along with Emily Schmid, Editorial Assistant for Music and Art; Lori Bradshaw, production editor; and Harvey L. Gable Jr., indexer. We are also happy to acknowledge six reviewers for their valuable input: J. Drew Stephen, C. Michael Porter, Donald C. Meyer, Matthew McDonald, Timothy A. Labor, and Rika Asai. For various advice and assistance in pedagogical and practical matters, we are grateful to Dan Goldwasser, Charles Leinberger, Michael Pisani, Bethany McLemore, Alex Newton, Joel Love, Cari McDonnell, and Rob Deemer, our co-author for the first edition. For graphics materials and help with permissions, we again thank Dan Goldwasser, who supplied the series of Hollywood session photographs, and John Waxman, for images of his father.

Introduction

In the opening minutes of *Citizen Kane* (1941), low orchestral instruments and percussion create an eerie atmosphere for a series of exterior images of Xanadu, Kane's ruined mansion—music more appropriate to a horror film than a drama. Out of this eventually emerges, during an extreme close-up of Kane's mouth, the famously enigmatic word, "Rosebud." In Akira Kurosawa's *Rashômon* (1950), four witnesses tell markedly different versions of an event involving (perhaps) a rape and a murder. It was a samurai who died, and throughout his wife's account, as she justifies her own actions, a repetitive music strongly resembling Ravel's *Bolero* pushes the scene toward a trance-like or even hallucinatory state, seeming to undermine her veracity. During the main title sequence in the recent film *Atonement* (2007), we hear the quiet chirping of birds as we see one of the studio logos, then the sound of a manual typewriter, which types out the film's title. Both the rather loud typing and the quiet bird sounds continue into the first scene, during which the camera pans slowly from an interior wall to the outside wall of a child's room. At the end of this, we see an adolescent girl at the machine; we never see the birds, but the windows are open and, thanks to their chirping, it is easy to understand those birds as existing in an outdoors that extends the film's physical space beyond what the camera has framed for us.

Films achieve their effects with sound as well as images. Although people usually speak of "watching a movie," in fact speech, music, and noise fundamentally and routinely influence our understanding of what we see. (Speech is often called *dialogue*; the term used for noise is *sound effects* or just *effects*.) To achieve that influence, the sound track is as carefully constructed as the image track. Since the 1930s, production personnel have referred to this work as *sound editing*, by which they mean the process of creating and blending the sound track elements. Since about 1970, the commonly used term for the same process is *sound*

Although the feature film is perceived as a visual medium, 50 percent of the motion picture experience is aural. As the sound track reaches the audience via the theater sound system, it creates the illusion that the sound for a film has been captured by a single, magical microphone which records dialogue, sound effects, and music on-set in perfect balance. The fact is, just as every visual component in a film is designed and executed by the writer, director, cinematographer, and design team, each single sound in a film is carefully conceived, chosen, recorded, edited, and mixed by an array of sound artists and technicians.
—Vincent LoBrutto (Sound Designer)[3]

Knowing more of what goes into the scoring of a picture may help the movie listener to get more out of it.
—Aaron Copland (Composer)[5]

design. In recent years, some scholars have begun using the term *soundscape*—the aural complement to the image's "landscape"—to refer to this aspect of film.

Thus, it would be better to say that we "watch and listen to a movie"—unfortunately, this expression is clumsy, as are terms such as *audioviewing* or *viewing-hearing.* In short, we do not (yet) have an easy way to point in language to this complex interplay of hearing and seeing in the experience of a film (or a television show, or commercials, or Internet content with an auditory component).

In some types of films, the importance—and foregrounding—of sound is obvious, but sound design is important to all movies. As film music scholar Robynn Stilwell writes, "In the film industry, sound seems to be of greatest concern to those who produce big movies; we have come to expect teeth-rattling explosions and bombastic scores in modern blockbusters. However, sound can be even more intensely felt in intimate, quiet films, where the slightest whisper or silence can have a marked effect."[1] Similarly, director David Lynch said that "[Although] half the film is picture, the other half is sound . . . [and] they've got to work together."[2]

In some respects, music stands in a special place within sound design: we tend to take speech and effects sounds, such as footfalls or airplane noises, for granted because they are understood as natural, or what we would expect to hear if we found ourselves in the environment depicted on the screen (on a city street, in a forest or jungle, in the middle of a sports event, in a house with persons in conversation, etc.), but music is only "natural" when someone is performing or when a radio—or other mechanical sound source—is shown onscreen. Yet "background music," or music that has no apparent natural placement, has been a part of film exhibition from its beginnings in the 1890s, long before the sound film replaced the "silent" film in most countries by the early 1930s. Surprisingly, perhaps, this practice of accompanimental music has continued in the sound tracks of almost all films down to the present day, and it does mean that music poses a special problem for film viewing—or, as another film music scholar, Claudia Gorbman, puts it, "an issue central to film music aesthetics is the question of music's place in the hierarchy of the spectator's attention."[4]

Our goal in this book is to offer an historical account that brings music into the context of sound, and sound into the context of whole films. Broadly speaking, we try to avoid isolating music from the whole of the film experience. Instead, we concentrate on showing how filmgoers integrate music and sound, sound track and image track, and have done so from the early years of film exhibition. Thus, the book's chapters are designed to help you learn to appreciate the interdependence of technology and aesthetics throughout the course of film history, to hear the musicality of the sound track as a whole, to grasp the structuring principles of the sound track, to recognize that the sound track is rendered ("designed"), and to understand contemporary production methods and priorities. In the chapters of Part I, terminology, concepts, and examples are introduced to enable you to analyze and describe a film's sound track, including its music, in relation to narrative, both broadly (in terms of the film as a whole) and down to detail (the sound within a scene, or even the sound within a shot). The seven chapters in Part II begin the historical account of sound within film production and exhibition—an account that necessarily pays attention to technological change and the way it has affected sound and music throughout film history. One could argue—we *do* argue—that the great innovation, the watershed moment that influenced contemporary feature films more than any other, was the introduction of Dolby stereo in the early 1970s. Therefore, the break between Parts II and III is there: Part II covers early film, the transition to sound film, the classical studio era, its break-up and immediate aftermath; Part III covers the emergence of modern sound design, music and sound in the New Hollywood, and the impact of digital technologies over the past decade and more.

A decade ago, in the wake of the invention of "computer literacy," some authors began to refer to an analogous "visual literacy," which builds on our everyday visual capacities, or how we handle understanding what we see. Because basic visual literacy is a skill learned in the everyday, not through specialized training, we all have the ability needed to understand films. Increasing visual literacy starts by making us aware of those skills and employing them self-consciously. In that way, we become (and remain) aware of how images and editing methods construct meaning; that is, how they are rhetorical (they try to make us believe or accept an idea, a point of view, a particular way of understanding a story or a character). It is not difficult to extend the range of this sort of critical viewing to include the constructedness of sound. In studying film sound tracks or writing about them, then, it can be helpful, but is by no means necessary, to have a specialized knowledge of music history, music theory, or film history or theory. This book is designed for students with any background—musical, film studies, film production, or simply avid filmgoer—and it can be readily and productively used by readers with a wide range of backgrounds. The main requirement is a willingness to listen carefully and to articulate what you hear.

By the end of the book, then, you should have reached the stage where you can not only watch but also listen to historical and contemporary films and write productively about them with the support of a rich historical context.

When I write music for a film I try to imagine what the sound of that music will be in a theater, what it will sound like in relation to the dialogue and the action.
—Franz Waxman (Composer)[6]

HEARING THE MOVIES

ONE

The Sound Track and Film Narrative

BASIC TERMS AND CONCEPTS

Introduction to Part I

Catch Me If You Can (2002) tells the story of Frank Abagnale, Jr. (played by Leonardo DiCaprio), who runs away from home rather than face the trauma of his parents' divorce and his father's slow financial ruin. Frank is a risk taker who discovers that he has innate talent for imitating professionals (airline pilots, doctors, and lawyers), and he develops great skill in forging checks. The story, told mostly in flashback, is about FBI agent Carl Hanratty's (Tom Hanks) campaign to capture Frank, who spends several years in prison but eventually, thanks to Hanratty's advocacy, works for the FBI cracking check forgery cases.

In one scene, midway through the film, Carl is working alone on Christmas Eve (DVD timing 1:03:38); a radio sits on his desk and resonates weakly in the large empty room of desks and metal fixtures (see Figure I-1: Carl is turning the volume knob). From the radio, we hear Bing Crosby singing "Mele Kalikimaka" (Hawaiian for "Merry Christmas") as Carl examines some evidence. The phone rings; Frank is calling from his hotel room. Very near the end of their conversation, Carl tells Frank that he will be caught eventually, and orchestral music enters with a melancholy theme that was associated earlier in the movie with Frank's feelings about his father.

In this book's general introduction, we asserted that "Films achieve their effects with sound as well as images." The image track of a sound film in fact is not complete and autonomous in itself—if that were true, any added sound could do no better than to mimic or duplicate emotions, rhythms, and other information already apparent in the image. Although all of those uses of sound do happen in films, it is even more common that sound "adds value" to the image (according to sound designer, composer, and film theorist, Michel Chion).[1] In other words, the three components of the sound track—speech, music, and

Figure I-1. *Catch Me If You Can* (2002). Carl works on Christmas Eve.

sound effects—transform the image. According to Chion, sound and image achieve what he calls an "audiovisual contract," according to which film viewers intuitively accept the notion that image and sound mutually influence one another (that, of course, is what allows sound and image to add value to each other).[2]

In the phone conversation from *Catch Me If You Can*, the radio transforms what is visually a stark, even forbidding, environment into something like an everyday workplace—Carl keeps the radio on as background while he does his repetitive work tasks. The music on the radio tells us something about Carl's character as well—because he chose this station, we can reasonably assume that his tastes are middlebrow and a bit out of date for the mid-1960s. Similarly, when the orchestral music enters while we see a close-up of Frank's face, by convention we understand that the music is representing Frank's emotions, which are not immediately obvious in his face (Figure I-2).

It works the other way around, too. A sound track is changed—transformed—by the image, a point that can be easily demonstrated by listening to a popular song, then watching a music video with that song as the sound track, and perhaps then a film scene that uses the same song as part of the orchestral underscore. Imagine the difference between listening to "Mele Kalikimaka" on the radio yourself and listening to it while watching this scene. What has happened to that music because it was included here? We cannot say that it suddenly acquired meaning where it had none before: any music will have a collection of cultural meanings gathered around it (here, at the very least, Bing Crosby as a radio performer, Bing Crosby as a star, and "Hawaiian" style popular music in the 1930s and early 1940s). "Mele Kalikimaka," however, has also acquired some specific meanings in relation to Carl Hanratty's character—and, as it happens,

Figure I-2. *Catch Me If You Can*. Frank listens as Carl talks.

Christmas music becomes an aural motif in *Catch Me If You Can*, a motif that has substantial dramatic significance later in the film as Nat King Cole sings the "Christmas Song" while Frank stands outside his mother's house in the snow and the police and FBI appear to arrest him for the final time.

Although the three sound track elements usually work together to transform the image track, each also has unique capacities for "adding value." The ability to supply voluminous and specific information is an obvious property of speech ("dialogue"), and the naturalizing or realistic effect of speech and sound effects is equally evident. (Note that the privileged role of speech is so strongly assumed that we did not even comment on it in our discussion. As it happens, sound effects are minimal.) Music's role is more complicated, or perhaps we should say more flexible. Music is sometimes very much involved with speech, as in a song performance or, less obviously, in dialogue underscoring (music that accompanies speech, playing "under" it). At other times, music interacts with sound effects, as in many science fiction and action-thrillers, where music and effects dovetail to create what often seems like a single continuous strand of sound. Music can also mimic sound effects (for example, percussion instruments were routinely used to generate sound effects during silent-film performances). Finally, music can float in its own sphere, in effect outside the story and the physical world of the images: "background music" (like the orchestral music that reflects Frank's suddenly dejected mood) can affect a film in a manner very much like that of the voice-over narrator, an unseen person who comments on characters and action.

It is important to understand, however, that film music is not just the symphonic underscore that has been a part of cinema practice since the late 1920s (and has its roots in music played for silent films before that), nor is film music restricted to this accompanimental role (no matter what musical style it may be). *Film music is any music used in a film.* In this respect, film music follows the changing social and cultural patterns of music over the past century. In the present day, it can be difficult to recognize that, before the sudden rise of commercial radio and the mass-market phonograph in the early 1920s, access to a variety of musical styles was difficult for almost anyone to achieve. From that time forward, music making of all kinds has drawn to a wholly unprecedented degree on a variety of historical and cultural sources. Every sort of music can find its way into a film score, from the latest song by Radiohead to medieval Gregorian chant, from modernist concert composer Gyorgy Ligeti's *Atmospheres* to a Balinese gamelan. A music's functions are not restricted stylistically: any of the four radically different kinds of music named in the previous sentence could be part of the underscore, heard on a radio, or be part of an onscreen performance. In Figures I-3 to I-7, we have gathered five other examples from the enormous range of possibilities: Figure I-3 shows a traditional Texas dancehall scene in *Hope Floats* (1998); Figure I-4 is a contemporary photo of a Hollywood studio orchestra recording a musical cue; Figure I-5 is an eighteenth-century orchestra from a country dance scene in *Pride & Prejudice* (2005); in Figure I-6, Robert Redfords's character, Denys Finch Hatton, adjusts the gramophone he is presenting as a

Figure I-3. *Hope Floats* (1998). Dancehall scene: in the background (right center) Jack Ingram sings "Coming Back for More" (the scene begins at 1:00:50 or DVD chap. 12).

Figure I-4. Studio orchestra in recording session (photo: Dan Goldwasser).

Figure I-5. *Pride & Prejudice* (2005). An eighteenth-century orchestra plays for a country dance (the dance begins at 5:00).

gift to Karen Blixen (Meryl Streep) in *Out of Africa* (1985); and in Figure I-7, Chico Hamilton's jazz quintet is just finishing a number in *Sweet Smell of Success* (1957; Hamilton is the drummer).

A description of a film in terms of its sound and music must inevitably deal with the way the sound track is organized and the effects it makes, how it adds to (or detracts from) the film, and how it helps to tell the story. In preparation for the work of the historical narrative in Parts II and III, the chapters of Part I cover this ground by first introducing terms and concepts associated with the

Figure I-6. *Out of Africa* (1985). Denys presents Karen with a gramophone (the scene begins at 1:19:20 or DVD chap. 11).

Figure I-7. *Sweet Smell of Success* (1957). The Chico Hamilton Quintet plays at a nightclub (the scene begins at 7:15 or DVD chap. 2).

narrative functions of sound and general sound–image relations (Chapter 1), then emphasizing the sound track as an entity by invoking musical terms that can also be used to analyze sound (Chapter 2). Chapter 3 turns attention to the physical world of the narrative (because sound always presupposes space) and to aspects of film sound and time.

The Sound Track and Narrative

Introduction

Even in the digital age, a sound film consists of two separate components: image track and sound track (or "audio track"). This is a technological division: the image track appears on the screen, the sound track comes through the speakers. Consequently, this division also requires a technology to synchronize image and sound track. Today, just as in the earliest days of commercial film exhibition, almost all films are narrative films; that is, they tell stories. In this chapter, we discuss in general terms the ways the three sound track components interact to inflect and influence the image track and, with it, to form and enrich narrative. In addition to many short examples, scenes from *Sleepless in Seattle* (1993) and *Good Will Hunting* (1997) provide detailed case studies.

Basics: Image Track, Sound Track, Narrative

The film we discussed in the introduction to Part I, *Catch Me If You Can* (2002), tells the story of Frank Abagnale, Jr.—a "true story," as the image track informs us during the opening credits. Stories are essentially reports that involve time, persons, and events. It is important, however, to distinguish between time of the events and time in the telling—that is, we need to make a basic distinction between the terms story and plot. *Story* is the chronological series of events; *plot* is the order in which those events are presented to us in the film. Thus, the story of *Catch Me If You Can* begins when Frank's father meets and marries his mother in France during World War II (this is the earliest event mentioned in the film) and continues into the present (the final intertitle informs us that Frank and his FBI captor and mentor, Carl Hanratty, remain close friends). All these events happen in "linear time" (clock time or calendar time).

Note, first, that this story is selective; it does not include *all* events between World War II and the present, only those that are relevant to the life and career of Frank Abagnale, Jr., and even then only a small selection of those. Second, note that the story is independent of the film *Catch Me If You Can*—it is the story of Frank Abagnale, Jr., whether that story was ever made into a film or not. Plot, however, belongs to *this* film because the term *plot* means the order in which the events of the story are presented. The film begins with Frank's appearance on the TV show *To Tell the Truth* and then flashes back from there to his release from a French prison—both of these events occur much later in his life than most of those shown later. Although much of the film occurs in linear time thereafter, occasional short scenes in the airplane as Carl and Frank return to the United States suggest that the plot of the film is an elaborate flashback, a recollection of past events from the vantage point of the present. In this case, the "present," or present time, is a particular moment late in the story because the film's plot continues in a linear fashion past the plane flight, as Frank escapes through the airplane's toilet, is later apprehended, goes to prison, and finally begins to consult for the FBI on bank fraud cases.

Narrative feature films inevitably are concerned with the actions and inter-actions of persons, but the aesthetic product of the sound film is very complex—it throws a great deal of visual and aural information at the viewer-listener. As psychologist Annabel Cohen puts it, "In the language of cognitive psychology, cinema is a multisensory stimulus that, millisecond by millisecond, impinges on sensory receptors and excites networks of neuronal activity in the mind of every film spectator. [This is] the daunting perceptual-cognitive challenge that cinema presents to each member of the audience."[1] Therefore, much of the work in film postproduction is ordered toward adjusting all the film's elements to make its points or tell its story as clearly as possible. The sound track's three components, which are normally recorded as separate tracks and then mixed, are heavily implicated in this process.

Most of us, of course, do not think much about technique or technology when we watch a movie. Filmmakers can be more or less adept at using them, but for the viewer it is the narrative that counts: technique and technology are a means to an end. Indeed, they seem most effective when we are not aware of their presence, when we are absorbed by a convincing narrative. Such a narrative resonates—it clarifies our experience of the world: what we endure as more or less random or contingent events becomes suddenly coherent and significant when woven into a narrative. Thus, the "realism" of a successful narrative film is not a product of its fidelity (the actual contingency of our world) but of its clarity (its construction of a world that makes sense to us).

This substitution of clarity for fidelity extends down to basic elements of cinematic technology and technique. With respect to sound, this might seem counterintuitive. We tend to think of recording as "reproducing" sound; we also tend to think that we evaluate the quality of a recording by how faithfully it has reproduced the sound, but fidelity has not historically been a value in and of itself in the cinema; rather, fidelity is pursued only to the extent that it enhances the clarity of the narrative.

Microphones, for example, are designed and positioned to record the voice clearly, without distortion, and to minimize noises other than the voice. To accomplish this, microphone technology has developed along two lines, neither of which is related primarily to fidelity. First, manufacturers worked to increase the range so that the microphone could be placed outside of the view of the camera. Second, the sensitivity was focused so that the microphone could isolate the voice from its surroundings; that is, from the extraneous noises of the camera and soundstage. Sound mixing works on the same principle: dialogue is almost always rendered clearly, whatever the represented acoustical setting. The isolation of the voice when the microphone records it ensures that the dialogue can remain intelligible in postproduction because mixing can elevate its level no matter what else may be contained on the sound track.

The historical privileging of the voice also suggests that a primary way in which the principle of narrative clarity is realized on the sound track is through hierarchy: dialogue occupies the sonic foreground, and music and effects occupy the background. The image track is set up similarly, of course, in the familiar foreground/background distinction of visual staging (although it is important to understand that the levels of the sound track do not have to match those of the image track). The foreground/background structure ensures that narratively important figures are placed in the foreground, less important ones in the background. In other words, image and sound tracks are arranged in such a way that we know what to pay attention to, what is important in order for us to understand the narrative. Foreground clarity thus gives us a sense of omniscience: we know what is important in a way that those inhabiting the world of the film do not.

If the foreground shows us where to direct attention, the background provides a sense of presence, of a continuous, uniform space that joins the sound and image edits into the appearance of a unified physical place, a "world." A background sound common to a series of shots helps convince us that each piece of dialogue comes from the same space—although, in fact, dialogue is typically edited along with the images and is often rerecorded after the fact. The background obscures the production space (sound stage) and transforms it into the fictional world represented on film; this constructed background is therefore precisely what allows the fictional world to appear to us as something "real." Establishing such continuity is one of the main functions of both music and ambient sound.

Thus, in the usual experience of audio-viewing a film, the sound track shapes or interprets the image track for us: it encourages us to look at the images in a certain way, to notice particular things, and to remember them. As Figure 1-1a suggests, the distinctions between the sound track components are clear enough: we know the difference between human speech and the sound of footfalls, or between a saxophone playing and an airplane flying overhead. On the other hand, that clarity of definition is not absolute: there are quite a number of

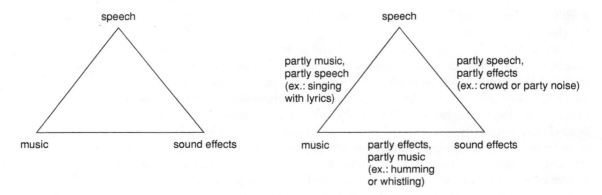

Figure 1-1. (a) The three sound track elements. (b) The elements with combinations.

familiar, intermediate effects that have the potential to enrich and complicate the sound track and its relation to the image track. These additional categories have been added along the sides of the triangle in Figure 1-1b along with an example for each. In the following sections, we discuss each of the sound track components in turn in relation to narrative design, touching on the intermediate categories where they are relevant.

Sound Track Components and Narrative

SPEECH

The most obvious way in which the sound track serves narrative is through speech, whose semantic dimension supplies a great deal of information that we either cannot get from the image track or could get only with considerable difficulty. In *Catch Me If You Can*, for example, we learn about the courtship of Frank Abagnale's father and mother through dialogue. Speech, however, can also organize (clarify) and interpret the frame for us. If we see a crowd on the screen, but the voice we hear is the voice of a person who is one of several standing in the foreground, our attention is turned to that person—the sound of speech interprets the image, telling us where to focus. From speech we also often get a sense of the emotion of the speaker, which may confirm or supplement what we see in his or her face or bodily movements. This emotional confirmation is a basic narrative function of sound in feature films. (A lack of such emotional confirmation is one reason silent film, especially when screened without music, can seem quite disorienting.)

Consider this short scene from *The Fellowship of the Ring* (2001): After a harrowing journey, Frodo awakens in Rivendell and talks with the wizard Gandalf; the scene ends as Sam enters (DVD Chapter 18). At the outset, in bright white light, we see a close-up of Frodo's head on a pillow; Frodo speaks in a muffled voice—"Where am I?"—and Gandalf's voice (we do not see him) answers, first clouded by reverberation then in natural acoustics as all traces of the white light

Figure 1-2. *The Fellowship of the Ring* (2001). Gandalf hems and haws.

disappear and Frodo awakens. A conversation between the two is shown in a typical way, with the camera jumping back and forth, staying on the speaker (this method is called shot/reverse shot). Frodo asks questions, and Gandalf supplies information about recent events. Partway through this conversation, Frodo asks why Gandalf did not arrive to help his friends escape from their pursuers (ghostly horsemen of the evil Sauron), and Gandalf hesitates to answer, saying only, "I was delayed" (Figure 1-2). This brief comment prompts a flashback that briefly recounts how Gandalf escaped from the traitorous Saruman (the flashback itself includes speech that explains the reason the two wizards are now enemies). We return to the conversation in Rivendell, and shortly thereafter Frodo's companion, Sam, enters (we first hear his voice offscreen) to greet his friend warmly. Thus, it is speech that interprets the opening (awakening), which is obviously the point of the conversation scene and that invokes the flashback. Only once is speech missing—at the end of the flashback, as Gandalf speeds away on the eagle's back and orchestral music is foregrounded in the sound track.

The example shows that speech can supply new information, offer clues to emotion, and explain and direct plot elements (as with the flashback). The extreme case for the control of speech is voice-over narration (or just "voice-over"): a person we cannot see (and who may not belong to the physical world shown in the film) talks directly to us, and the image track shows us the story he or she is telling. On the other hand, although speech typically controls scenes (that is to say, it is foregrounded), it can be moved to the background, literally by the reduced volume of persons speaking in the distance, or by the only partially grasped speech of guests at a party or of persons in a crowd (partly speech, partly sound effect—this is called "generic sound" or "generic noise"). Early sound films often used this procedure as a means of introducing human speech without the added difficulty of close synchronization. Two examples are the diners in *Coffee Dan's* night club just before Al Jolson sings his first songs in *The Jazz Singer* (1927) and the noise of people entering a train station, then on the street

The voice-over not only clarifies but can even determine our understanding of a sequence. In Letter from Siberia *(1957), for instance, an identical sequence is shown three times but with different narration. In each case, the narration frames the sequence of images, marking certain details for attention, and encouraging us to interpret them in a particular way—for the first, celebration; for the second, demonization; and for the third, a more measured response.*

outside a hotel, and then the diners in the hotel restaurant in Hitchcock's *Blackmail* (1929), starting at about 10:50.

Because speech occupies such an important place in the narrative feature film, its absence is often notable. For example, in the Rivendell scene, Gandalf hesitates before answering Frodo's question about Gandalf's late arrival—we hear only the non-speech sounds of Gandalf's hemming and hawing—and this, more than anything, triggers the "visual" answer of the flashback sequence.

SOUND EFFECTS

Sound effects ("sfx" or "fx") can also supply new information. This is sometimes in the simple form of non-speech human noises such as crying, groaning, or laughing (recall Gandalf's "hmm's"). More often, effects are used to "create" objects, animals, or even persons that we can hear but cannot see—an offscreen sound whose source we are able to identify: the bird sounds at the beginning of *Atonement* (2007); the call of the eagle that rescues Gandalf in an earlier scene; the bark of a dog and the croaking of frogs in a night scene from *Impromptu* (1991) as George Sand walks across a yard, returning, bruised, from a riding accident. Ambient sound (or generic noise) can create this same effect: in *The Big Sleep* (1946), the sound of (many) crickets in the nighttime as Philip Marlowe (Humphrey Bogart) walks up to the door of a casino club situated outside of town (DVD 1:05:56; see Figure 1-3), or the noise of waterfall or stream and birds during

Figure 1-3. *The Big Sleep* (1946). Marlowe approaches Eddie Mars's casino at night.

the conversation between Gandalf and Frodo discussed earlier. In this way, ambient sound extends the physical space depicted in the frame.

Ambient sound can be offscreen, as in the examples cited in the previous paragraph, or onscreen, as with typical daytime urban noises while we see their usual sources onscreen (cars, trains, crowd noises, etc.). In this way, the ambient sounds are not "creating" objects but confirming their expected characteristics. Sound effects operate primarily within the conventions of the sound film by confirming rather than creating physical space and significant action. In classical Hollywood sound film, sound effects were carefully marshaled and sparingly used. If you watch a typical scene from that period, you may be surprised at how infrequently you hear the body movements (footsteps, clothes swishing) of even the foregrounded actors. Background speech (except for crowd noise) is rare, and even ambient sounds in outdoor scenes are limited. The result is that the sound track contains only those sounds we are supposed to hear, those that give us significant narrative information.

In classical Hollywood cinema, in other words, sound effects are generally governed by pertinence to the narrative. We might put it this way: synchronized sound cues us that some object or some person is important. This is obvious with dialogue. When Sam wheels his piano over to Ilsa's table in *Casablanca* (1942), we hear neither squeaking of the piano wheels nor Sam's footfalls—we hear only speech from the two actors, and as soon as their conversation gets underway in earnest, voices and sounds from the rest of *Rick's Café Américain* drop away. Advancements in sound technology have made it possible for the sound tracks of films in the past 30 years to be much more "live"—filled with sounds, especially ambient noise—but the same principle applies: sound effects help to extend or confirm the physical environment of the scene and to identify the actions, objects, or events important to the narrative. In this scene from *Casablanca*, the absence of sound effects sends a message that dialogue (and music) are the focus—there is, in fact, not a single sound effect in the 4-minute sequence from the point Ilsa asks for Sam (Figure 1-4) until a car engine starts very near the end of the scene, despite a group of four people going to a table, sitting, ordering drinks, getting up, leaving, and (three of them) going outdoors.

The presence or absence of sound effects in itself can be significant, as can their foregrounding or backgrounding—that is, whether effects are prominent or "neutral." In some genres, sound effect "accents" (sharp or sudden loud sounds or *stingers*) are exaggerated for suspense or humor, as in the seemingly unmotivated slamming of doors, crashing of tools or canned goods, and so forth in teenage horror films (such as *Scream* [1996]), or in the enclosed, reverberant metallic environments of spaceships or space stations.

To summarize, sound effects can provide new information, but more often they aid narrative by directing attention to and confirming existing image track elements. (By the way, for our purposes here we are making no distinction between sound effects that are direct recording of the events we see and those that are the result of Foley or library recordings; that is, sound effects created apart

Reel 1, Part 2, just after the refugee realizes his wallet is gone: "Aeroplane imitation" and note: "Somewhat like the Main Title—they'll keep the aeroplane effect down in the dupe room!!"
—Max Steiner, marginal note in his musical sketches for *Casablanca*[2]

Figure 1-4. *Casablanca* (1942). Sam approaches Ilsa's table.

from the filming of the scene and added to the sound track. Indeed, it is the task of the Foley artist to make effects as natural sounding as possible.)

MUSIC

In general, speech and sound effects do a better—or at least a more specific and concrete—job than music can in providing narrative information. Music can provide narrative cues, but these tend to be fairly general and are usually used in an overdetermined way, confirming with the music what we already know from the visuals or dialogue: "Indian" music in the classical western; military marches or national anthems in war films; romantic foxtrots, ballads, or classical *andantes* with violins for love scenes; older popular tunes for nostalgia (as in *Casablanca* or in Nora Ephron's romantic comedies); threatening low strings and brasses for the entrance of the villain; or rapid, rhythmic "hurry" music to accompany a chase. Such uses of conventional music are known as "style topics" or more generally as "musical topics" (see the sidebar for Aaron Copland's comment on how these can be an aid to composers).

When a musical theme (usually short) is created for a film and then developed (varied, reorchestrated) within that film, the theme acquires some of the properties of a word or symbol, with independent meaning or associations

Having to compose music to accompany specific action is a help rather than a hindrance, since the action itself induces music in a composer of theatrical imagination, whereas he has no such visual stimulus in writing absolute music.
—Aaron Copland[3]

that can be called up when the theme is repeated. In such a case, the theme is sometimes referred to as a *leitmotif* (a term associated with nineteenth-century opera composer Richard Wagner). At the simplest level, the information garnered from hearing a leitmotif is redundant, as when two lovers are together and we hear a melody earlier presented as the love theme. On the other hand, a leitmotif can be used to indicate absence rather than presence, as Erich Korngold does in *Captain Blood* (1935), where the love theme occasionally appears to signal Peter Blood thinking about Arabella. The leitmotivic method is mainly associated with early sound film and composers such as Max Steiner, Korngold, and Alfred Newman, but it has remained an essential tool for orchestral underscoring practice to the present day. John Williams is often credited with deliberately reviving elaborate leitmotivic networks in *Star Wars* (1977) and its sequels.

The use of themes for narrative reference shows that music can provide new information under certain circumstances. Although both of the examples here have referred to musical themes, the sound of the music (its timbres, accompaniment figuration, and tempo) is often enough to establish mood, as composer Franz Waxman observes:

> The immediate establishment of a particular mood is one of the most important functions of motion picture music. This usually can be done most effectively through expert orchestration and scoring rather than through melodic and harmonic development, [so that] the same melodic statement may serve many moods through a variety of orchestration and treatment.[4]

In comparison with the other sound track elements, music is especially good at two things: (a) adding emotional specificity and (b) influencing and organizing time. Music can give the underlying or implied emotions of a scene direct expression; this is not mere redundancy—rather, it foregrounds the emotional content of a shot or scene, encouraging us to "read" the image or scene in a particular way. An example is the theme for Frank Abagnale, Jr. in *Catch Me If You Can*—the restlessness of the rhythms, furtiveness of the lowered dynamics, hint of whimsicality, and perhaps even the repetitiousness all portray the character very well (Figure 1-5). These traits in the music are used later in the film to undercut Frank's appearance of self-assurance and daring. Composer Aaron Copland refers to this effect of music as "underlining psychological refinements—the unspoken thoughts of a character or the unseen implications of a situation."[5]

 Music is by no means alone in articulating time in a film (linear time is the foundation of any narrative, after all, and associations can be created by stylistic devices such as showing the same image for the start of each day, returning to locations, etc.). Speech can be repeated or direct references can be made to earlier events. Speech can unify a scene simply by its continuous presence or absence, but in general speech is not deliberately exploited for this purpose. Instead, effects and music (and especially the latter) are used.

Figure 1-5. *Catch Me If You Can.* Frank's theme (transcription from the sound track by Rob Deemer).

Music is particularly good at promoting what Claudia Gorbman calls "formal and rhythmic continuity."[6] In *King Kong* (1933), for instance, the absence of orchestral music under the opening sequence in New York City allows music to emphasize the fantastic Skull Island, Kong's home, as an enchanted place (orchestral music enters when we see the fogbound ship slowly approaching the island). Music is also characteristically used to establish continuity by overlapping and thereby connecting otherwise unrelated scenes. It was a routine practice in early sound films to extend the main-title music into the first few seconds of the film's first scene to smooth the viewer's path from the formal frame of the opening credits to the world of the film. The reverse—a sound advance—can function in the same way. Early in *Casablanca*, Sam's performance of "It Had to Be You" begins while we see the café sign from outdoors, as customers enter (06:30); it takes more than 30 seconds before Sam finally comes onscreen. This long, slow visual path makes the viewer familiar with the café and comfortable with the transition to it.

It is important to distinguish between "background music" and foregrounding or backgrounding of visual or aural elements. Although background music is a common term, other terms used for the same musical effect include "underscoring," "accompaniment," "commentative music," "dramatic scoring," or just "scoring." The basic characteristic of this music is that it belongs to a film's narrative register (like a voice-over narrator) rather than the fictional (diegetic) world. To avoid confusion, from this point on, we refer to either "underscoring" or "nondiegetic music," the term commonly used by film music scholars (it means music not belonging to the physical world shown in the film). Underscoring can be foregrounded, as when we hear loud, dramatic music accompanying a chase, battle, or ceremony, but it can also be backgrounded—indeed, this is perhaps the most common situation for underscoring, to which we as viewers generally pay little attention but in which narrative cues, mood setting, themes, and so forth are often embedded. Onscreen performances, of course, can be foregrounded, but they, too, can be backgrounded, as when a band plays in a club but the sound track's attention is given to a conversation between customers sitting in a booth.

To summarize, music can provide new information through narrative cues or through themes and leitmotifs. It can also define emotional states and situations, as well as influence and direct our perception of time in the experience of a film. Music moves easily between foreground and background and can take over the screen entirely during onscreen performances.

De-Lovely (2004). Illustration of shot types. (a) Extreme Long Shot (ELS). (b) Medium Long Shot (MLS). (c) Medium Shot (MS). (d) Medium Close-Up (MCU). (e, f) Shot/ Reverse-Shot (S/RS) pair, in typical over-the-shoulder fashion. Note that Cole is presented Close-Up (CU), whereas Linda is shown in MCU. This places the emphasis on Cole. An Extreme Close-Up, or ECU, would have been even tighter, little more than the face itself: Figures I-2 and 1-2 are examples. (g) 2-Shot. The 2-shot is often used in conjunction with S/RS pairs, especially at the beginning and ending of the sequence. When used at the end of a sequence, it can also serve as a sign of reconciliation or the pair coming to a point of resolution. This is the case here, the 2-shot emphasized by moving to a tighter shot. (In this case, it is done by dollying in; it can also be done by zooming.)

Example for Sound Track Components and Narrative (1): *Sleepless in Seattle*, Second Botched Meeting

Sleepless in Seattle, a romantic comedy directed by Nora Ephron and released in 1993, stars Tom Hanks as Sam Baldwin and Meg Ryan as Annie Reed. Annie has recently become engaged, but remains uncertain about the relationship; she

Figure 1-6. *Sleepless in Seattle* (1993). Annie (end of Shot 4).

hears Sam, a widower, talk about grieving for his wife on a call-in radio show, and Annie becomes obsessed with meeting him, convinced that he may be her "destiny." Eventually, she travels to Seattle, where he lives with his young son. After at least two "close calls" (botched attempts to meet Sam) she returns home; in the meantime, her friend Becky (Rosie O'Donnell) has mailed a letter that is intercepted and answered by Sam's son, who in turn sets up a meeting that finally takes place in New York, on the observation deck of the Empire State Building.

The sequence we are interested in here is the second—and more embarrassing—of the botched meetings in Seattle. In the preceding scene, Annie is in a hotel room talking by phone to her friend Becky; Annie has decided she will certainly meet Sam the next day.

For reference, here is a shot list. (Note: For definitions and illustrations of shot types, such as "point-of-view shot" or "medium close-up," please see the glossary that follows Part III and the discussion of *De-Lovely* in the textbox on p. 19.)

0. Hotel room, Annie falls back on bed after hanging up phone (DVD 1:10:30)
1. Cut outdoors; car moves into a parking place, seen from across the street (shot lasts 8 seconds).
2. Annie inside car, seen from outside front.
3. Point-of-view shot: She sees Sam's vehicle arrive at marina.
4. Annie gets out of car (Figure 1-6).
5. Back to 3.
6. Long shot of Annie, seen from across the street.
7. Medium close-up of Annie.
8. To 3, but seen from behind Annie's back.
9. Sam and Jonah (his son) seen a bit closer; "wife" (actually his sister) enters frame from the left.
10. Medium shot of Annie.
11. To 9, but closer still.
12. To 10.
13. Medium shot of Sam and sister: "Where's Greg?"
14. Cut back to medium long shot of the two; truck horn sound starts during this shot; music out briefly.
15. Truck.
16. Medium close-up of Annie.

17. To 14.
18. To 16.
19. Truck.
20. Sam and sister, with truck passing by in foreground (blurred).
21. Street from more straight-on, with truck going off left; truck horn finishes during this shot.
22. Annie; ambient sounds mostly gone.
23. Cut back to long shot of Annie; music in again.
24. Sam and sister; he approaches.
25. Medium shot of Annie.
26. Annie, from behind; Sam approaches (Figure 1-7).
27. To 25.
28. Medium shot of Sam: "Hello."
29. Medium shot of Annie: "Hello."
30. To 28.
31. To 29—car horn noise.
32. She looks offscreen.
33. Cab.
34. Cab from over Annie's shoulder.

Figure 1-7. *Sleepless in Seattle.* Annie and Sam (Shot 26).

First, we describe the sound track elements, their balance (foreground and background), and the dominant or striking events (or *accents*). (The term *dominants* is Michel Chion's.)[7] A concise version of the description can be given in the form of a list:

0:00	Music enters with the cut outdoors; music actually started in the final second or two of the previous scene, but a new *scherzando*—playful, upbeat music—comes in with this cut (Figure 1-8). Outdoor sound effects: automobile noises. Music, however, dominates. (The sound level of passing cars is reduced to an improbably light "swish.")
0:50	The volume of the music comes down (Figure 1-9), but sound effects do not replace it—the general level of sound is reduced.

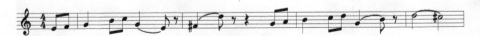

Figure 1-8. *Sleepless in Seattle.* Music at beginning of the "Second Botched Meeting" scene (transcription from the sound track by Rob Deemer).

Figure 1-9. *Sleepless in Seattle.* Music in the middle of the "Second Botched Meeting" scene (transcription from the sound track by Rob Deemer).

0:55	Speech—a few words from Sam, Jonah, and sister. These words "poke out" of the music, as if they are fragments heard by Annie from a distance.
1:07	Truck horn (loud)—a stinger or *hit* (Figure 1-10, left).
1:20	Music in again, even softer and slower than before; sound effects out.
1:30	"Hello"—Sam and Annie speak one word, in turn.
1:40	Scene out with another stinger, this time a taxi screeching to a halt (Figure 1-10, right); music immediately answers with its own stinger over the cut, and speech follows closely with the suddenly foregrounded voice of Becky offscreen (a sound advance for the next scene).

This is a modern, multitrack stereo sound track: live, active, with wide low- and high-frequency definition. The first and most obvious thing to notice about the balance of the three elements is that speech plays a small—if narratively crucial—role in this scene. Even in genres like romantic comedy, which tend to have a lot of talking, speech does not necessarily dominate in every scene. Because this is a modern sound track, "speech is no longer central to [the composition of the sound track]," as Michel Chion has put it. "Speech tends to be

a | b **Figure 1-10.** *Sleepless in Seattle.* "Second Botched Meeting": two strong sound effects stingers.

reinscribed in a global sensory continuum that envelops it, and that occupies both kinds of space, auditory and visual."[8] Simple although our scene is, it is a good example of what Chion describes. Certainly, the two "Hellos" are weak, tentative speech very much "enveloped" by their sound environments, but also impossibly quiet given that environment; and, of course, for the sake of the narrative, that is exactly how we are supposed to hear them, as "weak and tentative" but also establishing an intimate connection.

As we think back over it, it is not hard to recognize that the three sound track elements in this typical scene from *Sleepless in Seattle* were woven together in a detailed, careful way—"composed," as it were—that is the essence of sound design. To bring out this "compositional" quality of the sound track, let us imagine for a moment that it is a piece of concert music or a CD track. Our "musical composition" consists of two main sections with an introduction: The introduction is the phone conversation, which leads into a more substantial musical section with clear design (music that easily enfolds the rhythmic swishing we guess belongs to passing cars); the section seems to slow down rather than stop, as if making a transition rather than a clear cadence (that is, a formal musical close)—it is interrupted by the huge articulation of the blaring truck horn and the sounds swirling quickly and loudly around that; the second part of the scene is characterized by a much duller sound environment with most of the ambient noise gone or greatly reduced in volume; the two accents in this section are the two "Hellos"; and this scene has an ending that is parallel to the first scene—this time, a car horn and its attendant quick crescendo of sounds. Tom Hanks's voice is heard in both sections: "Where's Greg?" is balanced by his "Hello"; Meg Ryan is mute in the first section—her "Hello" gives her a voice and allows the scene to finish once it is rounded off by Hanks's answer. Mood and expression in the two sections are sharply different—positive, rhythmic, *allegretto* in the first (Figure 1-8); subdued, slow, tentative in the second (Figure 1-9).

If we want to add more detail to our description of the sound track, we can pay attention to the physical sources of the sounds in this scene. This matching of sound and source can be very specific (locating speech in Tom Hanks's body as we see it onscreen or connecting the sounds of passing cars to cars we see onscreen), or it can relate more generally to a category of sources (in this scene women's voices, a man, automobiles, horns), or even more generally to a category of sound classes (swishing, harsh and loud, white noise), or to a temporal "history" of a sound's evolution regardless of category or class (for example, the truck horn, which is relatively long and changes quality and level over time).

The music, on the other hand, is clearly nondiegetic (there is no orchestra standing behind Meg Ryan or hiding in the boats behind Tom Hanks), and we need to describe the music in terms of how it functions in relation to the characters and events. One of the most obvious things to notice is that composer Marc Shaiman's music follows closely in tempo and mood the changing feelings of Meg Ryan's Annie Reed character, but the slowing tempo and more tentative affect in the moments before the truck horn tell us something the image track does not do very well—we see in Ryan's face and posture a few doubts or questions but no sharp collapse of her positive mood equivalent to what we hear in the music. This mood change is new; music supplies it and so "adds value" to the image track that helps us interpret it the way the filmmakers want us to. This focus on mood, or empathic treatment of music, was typical of classical Hollywood film, and it obviously survives as a basic element of contemporary practice, too. Matching mood does not mean that music has to be closely synchronized to action, as in a cartoon; instead, it can create an overall mood for a scene, or, as it does here, follow shifting moods or feelings as they unfold.

Another way in which music clearly adds value is in the move from an external reality to subjective or internal sound. Once the truck horn blares, much of the outside world is shut out. This happens not in the image track, where we are seeing the same things (there are no close-ups of Ryan or Hanks—the usual cue for what is called point of view); it happens in the sound track, where the ambient sound—the outdoor noises—almost disappear, and we are there, perhaps in Ryan's mind, perhaps in the momentary private world she and Hanks share. Then comes the cab horn and, "poof," we are back in reality, almost as physically startled as Annie. It is the sound track that creates the impression of that subjective world.

Finally, the pacing of the shots in the image track is quite fast—almost the whole scene is in a flurry, rushing by us. There are thirty-four shots in 1 minute and 40 seconds—that is an average of just over 3 seconds each. The pacing matches the emotional excitement, the uncertainty, and the disruption in the story during this scene. We are set up for it by a long take in the hotel scene beforehand, and we remember it in the following scene, whose first four shots last 15, 10, 11, and 56 seconds, respectively. What music accomplishes here is to slow down the pace, especially in the second part of the scene, so that the chaos of the quick sequence of shots for the truck and cab horns, and the quick rhythms of scene change, music stinger, and offscreen voice, stand out even more.

Music adds affect, empathy, and subjectivity while slowing down the pacing of the sequence; and sound (the truck horn) strongly articulates a scene whose parts are not all that different—in the second part, we are still on the street, we are seeing the same characters, and shots are still from the same angle, although the camera has moved in somewhat closer.

Example for Sound Track Components and Narrative (2): *Good Will Hunting*, Boston Common Scene

The Boston Common scene from *Good Will Hunting* uses a conventional pattern of framing that is used to streamline narrative priorities in dialogue scenes. Discussing this conventional design will not only help refine terms like "long shot" and "medium close-up" but will also relate sound to those image track conventions.

Good Will Hunting (released in 1997) was jointly written by Matt Damon and Ben Affleck. Damon and Robin Williams are the principal actors; Affleck, Minnie Driver, and Stellan Skarsgård play the main supporting parts. The film combines qualities of romantic comedy, the coming-of-age film, and character drama, as it follows a series of parallel plot lines whose common factor is Will Hunting (Damon). The basis of romantic comedy is the formation of the couple, and *Good Will Hunting* ends appropriately as Will follows Skylar (Driver) west (she has gone to California for graduate school). At the same time, Will's drive west is the final step in his coming of age, his outgrowing of his childhood environment, the south Boston embodied especially in his group of young male friends. The trip also represents his overcoming the psychological obstacles posed by the dissonance between his background and the situations he finds himself in due to his uncanny mathematical abilities—here, his therapist, Sean (Williams), and a math professor (Skarsgård) are the principal figures. In all areas of his life, Will finds it hard to make positive decisions and act on them.

Will has been assigned to therapy as part of probation. After some false starts, his therapist, Sean, decides to take Will out of the office and talk to him in a neutral setting. The preliminaries to the scene (in Sean's office) begin at about 46:00, the scene proper at 47:00, with a simple cut to the outdoors—although not identified as such, it is the Boston Common (a large park in the center of the city) on a pleasant autumn afternoon. Will and Sean are seated on a park bench, and they talk. The scene goes out a few seconds after 51:00.

Prologue:

1. Indoors; Will coming down stairs (backlit); camera moves down to show him entering Sean's office.
2. Sean in medium shot (as if point-of-view shot: what Will sees), grabs jacket, and walks past the camera.
3. Back to 1, with Sean walking behind Will.

Establishing shot:

4. Two on park bench, seen from behind; pond beyond them (Figure 1-11).

Reverse angles or shot/reverse-shot sequence (Figure 1-12):

5. Close-up of Sean.
6. Close-up of Will.
7. Back to 5; later in the shot, camera pans very slightly to the left, then to the right, stopping as part of Will comes into the extreme right side of the frame (this shot is unusually long, at 2:43).
8. Back to 6, but now with part of Sean's face at the extreme left side of the frame (this shot lasts a bit over 1 minute).
9. Back to 7 (as it stood at the end).
10. Back to 8 (music enters quietly near the end of this shot and continues to the end of the scene).

Figure 1-11. *Good Will Hunting* (1997). Will and Sean on Boston Common.

11. Back to 7 and 9.
12. Back to 8 and 10.
13. Back to 7 and 9; Sean stands up and walks out of the frame; camera adjusts slightly to show more of Will's face.

Reestablishing shot:
14. Back to 4, but Will sitting alone.

Consider this note on scene design: The prototypical scene design begins with a general view of the physical space; this is referred to as an establishing shot. Then a series of transitions moves gradually inward to close views of the conversing persons—a master shot (normally showing a room for indoor scenes) is the frame of reference to which we return occasionally after a series of closer shots, and a medium 2-shot (or set of them) focuses in on a pair of characters but

a | b   **Figure 1-12.** *Good Will Hunting.* Will and Sean on Boston Common: shot/reverse-shot sequence.

in an emotionally neutral way (the medium shot shows characters from below the knees—or sometimes from below the waist—to the tops of their heads).

In this case, the first three shots, marked "prologue," are actually a miniature scene unto themselves that makes reference to a preceding scene and motivates the change of venue for the therapy session. The establishing shot is Sean and Will seen from some distance on the park bench; this lets us know that the scene will take place in the park and positions them in that physical space. Both master shot and medium 2-shots are missing, however. When you watch it, notice how abruptly the film cuts directly from the establishing shot to a standard (collar bone–up) close-up of Sean. After a shot/reverse-shot series, all carried out in close-up with some small but telling horizontal shifts by the camera, a scene commonly closes as this one does, by briefly pulling back out to the establishing shot (or at least to the master shot).

The complete series, then, is as follows: establishing shot, master shot, medium 2-shot, medium close-up (or close-up) in alternation, and reestablishing shot to end. In the section on description and evaluation that follows, we link common features of sound to this scene design schema.

Sound in the prologue section is muted: we hear a little speech and faint indoor ambient sounds, the most distinctive being the click of the office door opening. With the cut outdoors and the establishing shot of the two sitting on a park bench, outdoor sounds are strong—traffic, dogs, birds, and the faintly heard speech of adults and children. With the close-up, dialogue takes over. Not surprisingly, in dialogue scenes the dominant element is usually speech, in terms of sheer amount, prominence (loudness and accent), and narrative significance.

The Boston Common scene is an extreme case because it is essentially a monologue by Sean; after his initial sarcastic remarks, Will is mostly silent (the few words he speaks are almost all offscreen as well [during Shot 7]). Sean speaks for some time as a sharp foreground/background distinction is maintained in the sound track; an essential element of this moment is that the background sounds, although by no means loud, do not decrease in volume either (as they typically would in a classic film to ensure clarity of the dialogue). Near the end of Shot 7, the sound of a low-pitched motor (airplane?) is added to the ambient sound under Sean's reflections on his wife's losing fight against cancer. Shortly thereafter, Shot 8 reverses to a close-up of Will with Sean at the edge of the screen, as Sean begins to home in on Will's vulnerabilities; in the background, we hear car horns and sirens throughout this segment, until a reverse again in Shot 9.

As Sean connects and Will is clearly affected, an emotive but not tuneful orchestral music enters very quietly (50:25; in Shot 10; the music is by Danny Elfman, who appears in another context in Figure 1-13) and gradually displaces most of the ambient sounds except that of birds, which fill the silences between Sean's sentences (Figure 1-14). He leaves at 50:52, and speech is gone; music takes over as Will sits silently, then overlaps into the next scene and dominates through its 2-minute montage of the following day(s?). (We hear only occasional sound-effect accents and little, if any, speech until the final segment): A friend

Figure 1-13. *Meet the Robinsons* (2007) director Stephen Anderson with composer Danny Elfman (photo: Dan Goldwasser).

picks Will up for work, a brief view of the construction site, a phone call in the rain, the interior of a car with Will and his friends. During the phone call, speech, music, and effects (rain noise) are equal, but music goes out as Will climbs into the car.

The physical sources of sounds are kept very clear throughout the prologue and the park scene proper. The effect of this, paradoxically, is to support the

a
b

Figure 1-14. *Good Will Hunting.* Will and Sean on Boston Common: nondiegetic orchestral music near the end of the scene (transcription from the sound track by Rob Deemer).

concentration on close-ups by isolating the characters from their environment—we are made continually aware that the two men are having a very private conversation in a public space (the "stereo" effect of the relatively crisp background sound and somewhat muffled close miking on the two characters only exaggerates this contrast). Another result is that, when the music enters, its role as depicting Will's rising emotions is unmistakable, not only because its nondiegetic status is so blatantly obvious, but also because the opposition of external sound to the music's "internal sound" of emotion is so stark. Thus, sound supports a sense of distance yet emotional connection that is this scene's contribution to the larger narrative: Sean has figured out how to reach the well-barricaded psyche of his reluctant patient, who is talkative and seems self-confident at the beginning, but who is silent and brooding at the end. The foreground/background opposition serves to sharpen the unexpected intensity of the conversation, and the music confirms the emotion that begins to register in Will's face in Shot 13.

In the typical dialogue scene, we expect effects and music to drop off gradually, in line with the gradual movement into the physical space and toward the intimacy of the characters' conversation, at which point, of course, speech takes over and continues to dominate throughout, until the reestablishing (or other closing) shot, where conversation might cease and music or effects might make a final comment, a final spatial or narrative reference, or a transition into the next scene. In this scene from *Good Will Hunting*, as we have seen, effects do not drop back as much as they would normally, but we have also seen the narrative motivation for that atypical usage. The music, on the other hand, does serve a role as transition into the next scene (which it dominates, as is typical of montage sequences). Music, in fact, more often than not will enter at the emotional crux of a conversation and then serve a double role: representing emotion but also acting in the formal function of transition sound.

Hearing the Sound Track as Music: Masking

The final two sections of this chapter present simple tools that you can use to explore the characteristics of the image track and sound track and the effects of different kinds of musical styles and tempos.

The first of these is masking, which Michel Chion promotes to prove his point about added value.[9] Powerful though it is, the idea is simple: masking just means watching the image track of a scene without the sound, or, vice versa, listening to the sound track of a scene without the images.

Seeing the image track alone can alert one to both the richness and the ambiguity of the frame, but also to the rhythms of action within the frame and the rhythms of cutting (relative shot lengths and the transitions between shots). (See the sidebar for a composer's take on this exercise.) Similarly, hearing the sound track by itself can bring out its "musical" qualities, the shifting of volume (loudness) in toto or relatively among the three sound track elements, textures (sharp, soft, metallic, dull, etc.), register (high, middle, low) emphases, and sound track rhythms.

When well contrived, there is no question but that a musical score can be of enormous help to a picture. One can prove that point, laboratory-fashion, by showing an audience a climactic scene with the sound turned off and then once again with the sound track turned on.
—Aaron Copland[10]

When we return to normal audio-viewing after a masking exercise, we can see how, for example, many image track rhythms tend to be suppressed by sound track rhythms but others stand out when the rhythms are in sync, how (previously) disembodied speech is anchored by the images of people, how some sound effects are anchored by their sources (such as telephones), how effects or speech can create offscreen space, how visual and auditory backgrounding and foregrounding interact, and so on.

Because you have probably watched the conversation scene from *Catch Me If You Can* and the "Second Botched Meeting" from *Sleepless in Seattle* several times already in the course of reading this chapter, a masking exercise using them would not be very effective. In any case, recall that we already asked you to consider the sound track for the scene as if it were a piece of concert music or a CD track. You might try audio and video masking for the next scene in each of the films: Hanratty discovers an important clue (DVD timing 1:06:29–1:07:50); Annie continues her conversation with Becky (DVD timing 1:12:03–1:14:45).

You can also turn masking into something of a game by choosing a DVD chapter at random from a movie you have not seen before and trying to guess how the sound track is shaped from the clues in the image track, or how the image track editing is likely to feel after the rhythms and balance (foregrounding/backgrounding) of the sound track are added.

Masking, curiously, reproduces certain conditions of early film exhibition. Although music and effects were both important from the earliest years of the cinema, there was no guarantee that you could enter a theater in, say, 1913 and be assured of hearing music throughout the film. Stories abound of pianists or even entire orchestras taking breaks, during which the film would continue silently for one or even two reels (a reel is roughly a 10-minute segment). Although such episodes were extremely rare in the picture palaces (large urban theaters) in the 1920s, they were still possible—even likely—in small neighborhood or rural theaters.

Experimenting with Music and Image: The Commutation Test

Another very useful tool in addition to masking is the commutation test, which is very closely allied in its method and even in its goals to the spotting process that is used to decide on music for a film. There is no easier way to confirm our explanation of music's role in the sound track and its narrative functions in a scene than by seeing (hearing) what happens when we substitute other music. Another way to put it is that you can feel much more comfortable that you "got it right" by considering alternatives.

Commutation tests are easily made for any film by simply playing music on a CD player or through computer audio while the film runs without sound.[11] The disadvantage is that you lose the dialogue and effects, so that the overall character of the sound track is altered (unless you have editing software available, of course). You might try an experiment with main titles, which are often accompanied by music only. For scenes without music, on the other hand, you can judge what music does by playing both music and film audio simultaneously. Occasionally nowadays, DVDs are even released with alternate tracks, for example *Dracula* (1931) with a new string quartet score by Philip Glass, or with historical alternatives, such as the French audio track for *Casablanca*, which offers substitutes for some of the music.

Suppose that we removed the quiet, slightly nervous music from the bedroom scene in *Psycho*, where Marion Crane packs her suitcase before running off with her employer's money (Figure 1-15). Now, replace that music with a much more obviously ominous cue from a recent horror film. The empathy we feel for Janet Leigh's character as she mulls over an all-too familiar human dilemma about how to balance behavior and desire would be lost—we would immediately be sharply distanced from her ("Is she about to become a victim *already*?") but still wanting to communicate, to warn her about the danger that awaits her in a closet, perhaps, or in the shower we see in the background (yes, the director Alfred Hitchcock intended that intimation of the subsequent murder scene). What this substitution confirms, by negative example, is how effectively Bernard Herrmann's music makes us empathize with Marion, despite its rather sparse and understated quality.

More radically, if we substituted a popular song sung by a woman, such as the classic 1970s-era "Get It While You Can" (Janis Joplin) or the more recent "Cornflake Girl" (Tori Amos), there would suddenly be an extra semantic layer whose meanings we would take to be emanating from Marion (because the

Figure 1-15. *Psycho* (1960). Marion hesitates for a moment about whether to take the money.

Figure 1-16. *Psycho.* Marion takes the money.

soloist is a woman) or else from the singer as a confidante or mentor for Marion. This substitution confirms, again by negative example, that Bernard Herrmann's music emphasizes the immediate problem of desire in Marion—"Should I take the money or not?"—rather than the sexual desire that is the root motivation for her stealing the money (Figure 1-16). (Sexual desire here is best understood in the more abstract sense of wanting to establish the couple: Marion steals the money so that she and her lover, Sam, can move away and establish a life for themselves.) Alternatively, the stylistic anachronisms provoked by these songs might seem to put the singers at a distance from Marion, encouraging an interpretation of them as narrators or commentators (voice-over narration or "Greek chorus") and perhaps unsympathetic commentators at that.

Finally, if we used an electronic dance track (say, early 1990s house, with volume level set lower than normal—for its style—although still prominent in the sound track), the music would pass over and ignore the very subtle shifts of emotion that occur every few seconds in this scene. What such an overbearing but neutral music confirms is that Bernard Herrmann's cue is firmly set in the classical tradition of empathetic, synchronized music. That in itself is an important observation about film style, as Herrmann is not necessarily known for closely adhering to that tradition, especially in his later film scores.

Note that the issue is not whether the music we substitute has an effect on the scene—thanks to the cognitive process that Chion calls the "audiovisual contract," *any* music added to the sound track will have *some* kind of effect, leading us to draw connections among the things we see, even if those connections provoke confusion and therefore "play against" (what if we tried the opening of Beethoven's Fifth Symphony?).[12] The issue is the narrative coherence of those connections—our ability to judge easily the appropriateness of the music to the characters, emotions, and actions of a scene and our understanding of its narrative contexts.

Summary

Almost all films are narrative, and their elements are ordered to present the narrative in particular ways. The classical model, which continues to dominate contemporary filmmaking, favors narrative clarity over fidelity to the real world. This preference extends to sound, as well as image, with the result that the sound track is often called on to shape our understanding of the image track, to interpret it for us. The individual sound track elements—speech, effects, and music—typically work in concert, but each has characteristic or conventional ways in which it contributes to narrative.

The Musicality
of the Sound Track
Concepts and Terminology

Introduction

As you may have discovered from doing a masking exercise or during class discussion of sound track details, describing what you hear is often difficult, not just because the task of sorting out the various elements can be exacting but because, for the most part, we lack a common vocabulary for talking about sound. Sound designer Mark Mangini notes that even among professional sound personnel, communication often relies on onomatopoeia: "boink, boing, twang, squidge, zip, rico, whibble, wobble, wubba—I can go on for hours. There's thousands of them, and every sound editor uses different ones."[1]

The fact that every sound editor uses different terms suggests the limits of an onomatopoeic vocabulary. This is where music terminology can be of value to the student of the sound track: musical terms are limited in number and well understood by everyone who uses them. Musical terminology also has an added benefit: like the image-masking exercise, it draws our attention to the many ways the sound track itself is organized along musical principles.

Language has certain limiting factors in terms of sound. Describing a blooming explosion may not mean anything to you but sounds bloom. They are strident, they have a rizzz quality, they have a boomy quality, they have a piercing quality, they have a stinging quality.
—Wylie Stateman (Sound Designer)[2]

Music and Sound

Music in the broadest sense is an art of sound (not just an art of musical notes or musical performance), and a complex set of terms has been developed to describe it. For those without formal training in music, these terms can seem daunting, perhaps even a little mysterious. Some of them are, in fact, difficult to understand without the ability to read music, but a great many are readily accessible to any listener. For instance, most of us have a good idea of what words like *melody, tempo, dynamics, range,* and *beat* mean. These terms may seem relatively basic, but they do divide the material of music into specific categories that allow us to highlight certain attributes.

The same can be said for sound. Take the terms mentioned earlier. *Melody* certainly seems to be a specifically musical term, but the others extend easily to the domain of sound in general. Footsteps, for example, can be described in terms of tempo as fast or slow (as in running vs. walking), in terms of dynamics as loud or soft (stomping vs. tiptoeing), and in terms of range as high pitched or low (the crunch of gravel vs. the heavy thud of unseen footsteps on wood floors overhead). Beat is related to tempo but designates some kind of regular pattern; thus, walking might be fitful (involving repeated stops, as might happen when two characters engage in conversation while walking in a garden or along a street), but the marching of soldiers is obviously highly regular, as are the pistons of a train or the ticking of a clock.

Musical terminology helps us focus on the abstract qualities of sound so that we can draw distinctions of this sort. This terminology does not cover all aspects of sound, of course, but it does give us a general strategy for proceeding: instead of following the basic mode of human cognition to look for the causes or sources of the sounds, as much as possible we try to describe the sound itself. As this suggests, in cinema the causal relation between image and sound can be broken; that is, it is not necessary always to insist on realistically anchoring a sound in a physical source or requiring a particular naturalistic sound to represent an onscreen object in the sound track (Jack Warner makes a point about this in the sidebar).

To cite one very common example, footsteps on a quiet street can be rendered by all sorts of sounds: music for a highly stylized effect, coconuts for a humorous effect, or a highly "realistic" tap-tap-tap. In addition, realistic footsteps might sound loud or soft, heavy or light, dull or hollow; they might have an echo added; the echo might be subtle or pronounced, and so forth. Each of these choices will affect our understanding of a scene. Louder footsteps, for instance, will emphasize the act of walking, encouraging us to follow the moving figure and underscoring that character's importance. Likewise, through their use especially in *film noir*, echoing footsteps have accrued connotations of loneliness and even existential despair. Thus, something as seemingly mundane as the sound of a footstep can be raised to the level of a thematic element of the narrative.

Once we recognize the extent to which the sound track presents filmmakers with choices, we will realize that the sound track is crafted, that is, designed in a more or less conscious way. We might even think of the sound track as "composed," much like a piece of music. Applying musical terminology can help us hear a continuity between the design of a sound track and music. In essence, it allows us to hear, recognize, and describe how musicality—an artful organization of sound—extends beyond a film's music to the sound track as a whole.

Music has, among the arts, the most, perhaps the only, systematic and precise vocabulary for the description and analysis of its objects.
—Stanley Cavell[3]

The real sound is not necessarily the right sound. Sound is an element that is easy to apply abstractly. Once you realize the capability, you're really painting with sound.
—Jack Warner (Supervising Sound Editor)[4]

The varying tempi and volumes of each set of footsteps render the nearness of the respective threats, and carry essential information about each of the steppers. Their bodily dimensions, their gender, and even their fearful mental states are rendered through pitch and irregularities of rhythm—stumblings, shufflings, trippings, and the segueing of walking-into-running. The patterning of the footsteps also renders the surfaces of these cinematic streets.
—Helen Hanson, writing about 1940s horror films[5]

TEMPO

Tempo is the perceived rate (beat or pulse) of sound or musical events. (In non-musical contexts, tempo is often used interchangeably with pace.) Recognizing the beat is fundamental to the way we organize and hierarchize musical sounds in consciousness. Cognitive scientists who have studied how humans recognize tempo differences have found that an "average" or "moderate" tempo lies in the typical range of the (resting) human heartbeat, or from about 60 to 75 beats per minute. A "slower" tempo has fewer than 60 beats per minute, a "faster" tempo more than 75 beats per minute. It should not be surprising to find that the same is true for sound in general.

A persistent, foregrounded sound can strongly focus a scene and increase tension, often dramatically, as in the creation scene of *The Bride of Frankenstein* (1935), where gradually louder drumbeats are heard as a sound effect representing the beating of the Bride's heart. Regularly recurring sounds can also be put into the background, in which case foreground elements determine the overall tempo of the sound track. For example, if we are outdoors or near an open window at night, the chirping of crickets creates a lively tempo—their sound dominates because, more than likely, other sounds will be intermittent and irregular (a car drives by, an owl hoots, a dog barks, etc.). In a film sound track, on the other hand, the cricket sounds may in fact be rather quick, yet the overall tempo of the nighttime environment may seem relaxed, almost slow. This effect is a function of context. Typically, the ambient sound of crickets is isolated, especially at the beginning of a scene that uses them to establish an atmosphere of pastoral night. Other sounds that do occur are generally sparse, meaning not just that there are few of them but that they tend to be relatively spread out in time. As a result, the ambient sound of the crickets tends to fade into the background (because it is continuous), and it is the pace of those other sounds that determines the perceived tempo.

The musical conception of tempo encourages more precise description of the sound track, although more often than not there is not a clear, regular beat of the kind we find in music. Even without that, we can profitably think in terms of gradations of tempo: just how fast or slow do the sounds seem to be coming in this scene? How do these affect the way(s) we are asked to interpret characters' actions and narrative unfolding?

Dialogue, for example, establishes a tempo that generally conforms to the tempo of the rest of the sound track (or else determines that tempo if dialogue is especially dominant). A moderate tempo of speech suggests the "everyday," or a calm but attentive mood. Rapid (and perhaps overlapping) speech can be either excited and happy or tense and nervous, depending on the situation—a condition that also applies to slow speech, which can be relaxed and inviting or sad and detached. In addition, characters are frequently defined by the tempo of their speech. In *Star Wars IV: A New Hope* (1977), Luke Skywalker and Han Solo deliver dialogue at relatively quick tempos, whereas the tempo for Obi-Wan and Darth Vader is relatively staid. In addition, through the course of the *Star Wars* films, Luke's delivery becomes slower, suggesting that measured dialogue is associated with command of the Force.

Actors, too, usually have tempos that define their voice. Jimmy Durante, for instance, spoke at a relatively rapid tempo. The characteristic pace of John Wayne, on the contrary, was much slower. Some of the humor of the films of Jerry Lewis and Dean Martin comes from the marked difference in tempo (and pitch) between the actors. Indeed, the exasperation of Martin's characters at the antics of Lewis's has the effect of accelerating the tempo and raising the pitch of Martin's voice toward that of Lewis as he tries to gain control of the situation. The same can be observed in many other classic comedic pairings, such as Abbott and Costello or Lucy and Ricky in *I Love Lucy* (1951–1957). Something similar happens between Cary Grant and Katharine Hepburn in *Bringing Up Baby* (1938)—both of these actors were masters at modulating the tempo of their voices.

Finally, a useful pair of musical terms related to tempo is *accelerando* and *ritardando*, a smooth, usually gradual speeding up or slowing down of tempo. Returning again to the example of footsteps, changing from walking to running produces the effect of an accelerando, although a fairly rapid one. A train pulling away from a station is an example of a more gradual one. Action sequences often consist of a series of accelerandos, each marking an intensification of the action. Scenes can also be initiated through an accelerando or ritardando before settling into a basic tempo.

RHYTHM AND METER

Closely related to tempo is the concept of "meter." Meter is a regular, recurring unit of time corresponding to groups of beats—in other words, meter is a higher level organization of beats. Musicians distinguish two basic types of meter, duple and triple, reflecting the number of beats in each group. Each repetition of the group is called a measure or bar. Most popular music is written in duple meter, as are marches. The waltz, by contrast, is the prototypical example of triple meter.

Because of the way it organizes beats, meter can be an important factor in determining tempo. Music can produce meter almost effortlessly. In fact, the effects of meter are so strong that music can easily alter the perceived pace of a scene significantly. When directors count on music to "save" a scene, they often have in mind music's ability to affect the pacing through the strong patterning of meter.

Rhythm is closely connected with meter, but it usually refers to distinctive groupings of notes rather than to the regular groups of meter (the famous da-da-da-da-duh that opens Beethoven's Fifth Symphony is a rhythmic figure, not a meter). Rhythms can produce a metrical feel if they repeat at regular intervals, as they often will in dances: genres such as the tango, the Charleston, and swing are defined through recurring characteristic rhythms, as well as an underlying meter.

Rhythm and meter in general are important for other aspects of sound as well, even when they are not strictly defined. The cadence and beat of dialogue,

There's a lot you can do very subtly with sound tracks. It doesn't have to be in-your-face, traditional, big sound effects. You can especially say a lot about the film with ambiences—the sounds for things you don't see. You can say a lot about where they are geographically, what time of day it is, what part of the city they're in, what kind of country they're in, the season it is. If you're going to choose a cricket, you can choose a cricket not for strictly geographic reasons. If there's a certain cricket that has a beat or rhythm to it, it adds to the tension of a scene. In Rush *(1991) some bad guys break into Jason Patric's house. They get into a fight and break a window. Once the window's broken, there's a cricket sound that comes in. It's this really rapid, machine gun-paced cricket chirp, very low on the sound track. The audience doesn't have to be aware of it, but it adds a subtle, emotional, sense of tension to the scene.*
—Gary Rydstrom
(Sound Designer)[6]

$\frac{3}{4}$ ♩ ♩│♩ ♩│♩ ♩│

Figure 2-1. Machine rhythm.

At the beginning of
Love Me Tonight
(1932), Paris slowly
awakens in rhythm.
We hear the sound of
a bell chiming the
early hour, a lone
bicyclist, then the
sound of a pick ax, all
laying down a basic
rhythm. The ham-
mering of cobblers,
beating of rugs, and
sounds of a factory
all join in rhythm,
suggesting the vital-
ity and common pur-
pose of the city. This
symphony of sound
ultimately dissolves
into Maurice Chevalier
singing "That's the
Song of Paree."

Something similar
occurs in **Shall We**
Dance *(1937), where*
Pete Peters (Fred
Astaire) is sailing to
America to make his
debut as "Petrov,"
purportedly a Russian
ballet dancer. To con-
ceal his identity, Pete
must refrain from
openly dancing in the
vernacular "jazz"
style that he prefers.
He descends to the
engine room, where
the pistons of the
ship's engines

for instance, set up a basic framework within which vocal rhythm works. Timing is intimately bound up with rhythm: whether to stay ahead of the beat, on the beat, or behind it; and whether and where to increase or decrease the tempo. We might also speak of the "rhythm" of a machine, where the meter is triple but the recurring rhythm is long-short|long-short|long-short . . . , as shown through musical notation in Figure 2-1. Approached from the standpoint of meter and rhythm, each repetition here defines a measure. In terms of sound, such regularity is usually associated with machines and manual labor.

The placing of sound effects is determined as much by rhythm as by the need for synchronization. In a martial arts fight sequence, for instance, the choreography of the sounds is as important as the choreography of the images. Indeed, Michel Chion suggests that many of these fight sequences are comprehensible only because sound helps us parse a visual image that is moving too fast for the eye.[7] Moreover, many such scenes and action scenes in general have a substantial amount of offscreen sound. This allows considerable freedom in making decisions about how to render the sound track. Sound designer Gary Rydstrom notes the interplay between image and sound rhythm in gun battles:

> Guns are hard. You do have to follow along with how they've designed the scene. The rhythm or pattern to a scene is due to the picture editor, but a lot of the action in a gun battle takes place offscreen, so that gives the sound people more flexibility to give it shape and rhythm. You can use it just like music. I always think of film sound in terms of rhythm. That's sound happening over time, so it's the rhythm of the sound effects over time that people remember.[8]

VOLUME

Volume is the physical strength of the sound we perceive, its loudness. Strictly speaking, volume is defined by amplitude, which is the power of sound (normally as measured in decibels). The correlations between perceived loudness and amplitude are inexact, however, so decibel levels are only approximations for our impressions of volume. In any case, it is usually sufficient to distinguish three levels: normal, loud, and soft. Extremes are rendered as "very loud" and "very soft." Musical terminology uses eight generally accepted sound levels, the two basic ones being *p* (*piano*)—soft—and *f* (*forte*)—loud.

In recording, dynamics are often referred to as "levels," quantified in decibels (dBs). The dB is a logarithmic measure, where +10 dBs signifies ten times the amplitude. This means that perceived volume of sound doubles approximately every +3 dBs. The standard dynamic range of mixing for cinema is 0 to 105 dB (0 is threshold of hearing), although in practice the full range is rarely if ever used (see Walter Murch's comment in the sidebar). By way of comparison, normal conversation is about 65 dB; dialogue in a film is mixed at roughly 75 dB.

Considerations of dynamics and recording level come into play at nearly every stage of sound production, from the object that first makes the sound to the sound as it leaves the loudspeaker in the theater. At a minimum, there are four points along the way where the volume of the sound can be altered: (a) the initial unrecorded sound, (b) the recording of that sound, (c) the mixing of that recording to the print (see Richard Portman's comment on this in the sidebar), and (d) its output through the speakers of the theater. In practice, there are actually several additional, intervening steps where the sound is mixed down to intermediate tracks before the final mix.

Dynamic levels can be altered at any one of these stages. A whisper might be mixed at a very high level (as occurs during Galadriel's Elvish narration that opens *The Fellowship of the Ring* [2001]), or a ninety-piece orchestra might be recorded or mixed at a much lower level. A good example of the latter is the music in the sound track for *Foreign Correspondent* (1940): despite an extensive and complex orchestral score rich in referential melodies, the music is mixed so low that its complexities are mostly lost. For a more recent example, most of the orchestral underscoring is mixed unusually low in *Four Weddings and a Funeral* (1994). On the other extreme, music is mixed very high in the so-called spaghetti westerns that feature music by Ennio Morricone (such as *A Fistful of Dollars* and *The Good, the Bad, and the Ugly,* both U.S. releases in 1966).

In addition, volume need not remain constant—and historically it has not. In classical Hollywood, a device known as the "up-and-downer" automatically raised and lowered music levels inversely with the presence of dialogue. Musicians use the terms *crescendo* and *diminuendo* or *decrescendo* to refer to the gradual increase or decrease in the volume of sound (for one use of this device, see Figure 2-2). In

establish the rhythm so that the song "Slap That Bass" seems to emerge from it.

We've actually got too much dynamic range. We have to control it in the mixing or else we will blast people out of the theaters.
—Walter Murch (Sound Designer)[9]

It's very simple: you play the music up when they kiss, down when they talk.
—Richard Portman (Rerecording Mixer)[10]

Figure 2-2. *Das Boot (The Boat,* 1981). Pursued by a destroyer, the crew listens as the sound of the enemy ship's propeller slowly increases in volume. The crescendo here is an effective means of raising the tension, and it culminates in the explosion of depth charges and the resulting aural confusion on the ship.

mixing, the fader is the device that changes the levels for a recording. Fading up and fading down refer to increasing and decreasing from one volume level to another; fading in and fading out, by contrast, take the beginning and end level, respectively, as zero. As with the relation between dynamics and sound levels previously mentioned, fading need not coincide with a crescendo or decrescendo of the recorded sound source. The aesthetic effect of the fade out of a pop song, for instance, depends in large measure on the fact that the musical performance maintains its dynamic level while the actual sound of the recording dissipates. In this way, we are left with the impression that the song has passed out of the range of hearing rather than ended.

The clichéd fade out of the typically constant-volume pop song points to one of the most important practical questions in using preexisting music in film: How is the music to be introduced onto and removed from the sound track? When the music is played by a band or is heard from a radio, there is usually no problem because the story world justifies the entry and exit of the music. On the other hand, when it is treated as underscoring, the music will sound like a fragment, and, unless carefully controlled, the effect can be awkward. In *There's Something About Mary* (1998), Danny Wilson's "Mary's Prayer" covers the transition between Ted talking with his friends and his arrival at Mary's for their date (Figure 2-3). The entrance and exit of the music here is handled in a very clumsy manner, the fragment seemingly chosen only as a forced method of knitting the two scenes together while also using another song with "Mary" in its title. On the other hand, this awkwardness might be justified as underscoring the awkwardness of the "first date."

Figure 2-3. *There's Something About Mary* (1998). Awkward Ted.

Timbre

Think of the difference between a baseball hit by a wooden bat and by an aluminum one. Although it might begin with a "crack," the wooden bat gives a relatively round sound. The metal bat produces a sharp ping, full of high frequencies. Musicians call such distinct coloring of sound *timbre*. Timbre is also one of the most important categories for describing the sound track.

FILTERS AND "DISTORTION"

Common effects such as the fade out are examples of purposeful recording distortion, which might be defined as the difference between the sound produced by the original output (for example, the orchestra in the recording studio) and the sound produced in its final reproduction (the speakers in the movie theater). Any departure is, by this definition, a distortion of the original.

Despite the negative connotation of the word, distortion is basic to sound editing. Telephone sound, for instance, is generally represented by compressing the frequency response. The same is true for the cinematic representation of the sound of television, radio, or public address. Such filtering marks the technological mediation as distinct from sounds present in the physical space depicted in the frame. The effect is to reinforce the appearance of presence, so that face-to-face dialogue is clearer and more direct (and therefore seemingly more "authentic") than communication through technological media. In this sense, the lack of distortion in "real" sound is symbolic.

A change of level in mixing will also produce a change in tone color. In particular, sound that is output at a level below that at which it was recorded will lose disproportionate strength in the lower frequencies; and, vice versa, sound output at a higher level will increase it. These transformations are part of what effects a change in tone color. Microphone placement has similar timbral effects. A close microphone placement will emphasize direct sound and high frequencies. A more distant placement will capture more reflected sound and fewer high frequencies. Due to the presence of the reflected sound, distant placement also gives a better sense of the space in which the sound was produced. Different types of microphones also have different response characteristics and so capture different timbres, most subtle but some very pronounced.

Similarly, the sound of the same "sound" varies with the dynamic level at which it was produced in the first place. For instance, the tone color of a trumpet playing *fortissimo* (very loud) is quite different from the trumpet playing *piano*. If we compare the sound of the subdued trumpet under the credits of *Glory* (1989) or in the opening scene of *Saving Private Ryan* (1998) to the brash sound of a trumpet signaling "Charge," we can get some sense of what volume contributes to tone color.

Overt signal processing is often used for timbral effects. Adding artificial reverb (an echo effect; short for reverberation) is one common device used to render the illusion of a large space. Somewhat differently, *Laura* (1944) manipulates the recording of a piano playing the main theme; here the reverb alters and unsettles the familiar sound of the instrument. This distortion accompanies Detective McPherson's passage into dream, whereas the musical theme itself suggests that his thoughts are on Laura. In *The Social Network* (2010), the recurring piano tune is treated with increasing amounts of reverb and recorded at greater distances to represent Mark's growing social isolation. In still another treatment, a trumpet motive in *Patton* (1970) is processed through an Echoplex to produce a distinctive, almost unworldly timbre that helps endow General Patton with a seemingly mythical status.

PITCH

The musical measure of frequency is called "pitch." Particular ratios of frequency define intervals as between pitches, and these intervals in turn fix the positions of pitches as notes within a musical scale. Most musical systems recognize the octave as the primary interval that contains the scale, meaning that once the octave is reached, the scale seems to repeat, only at a higher pitch level twice the original frequency.

To hear how pitch affects timbre, try an experiment. Play two notes on the piano relatively close in pitch, and you will find that they sound more or less the same (except for the frequency difference). Now play a low note on the piano and another in the same position within the octave but several octaves higher (the higher the better), and you should find that they sound quite different (except that they are octaves). The similarity you hear in the first case and the difference in the latter are the domain of what musicians generally refer to as timbre, whereas the difference you hear in the first case and the similarity in the second are the domain of pitch. You can hear a similar effect by speaking in a very low voice or in a very high voice (*falsetto*) and then comparing that to your normal voice. The timbre characteristic of pitch levels is called "tessitura," which in typical usage is divided into registers: high; middle or normal; low.

Another element that colors sound is harmony, which is the sounding of more than one pitch at the same time. We call any groups of simultaneous notes *chords* or *sonorities*, although musicians tend to restrict these terms to complexes of three or more notes. If you hear any two notes played simultaneously, you should recognize a difference: some of these combinations will sound "sweet," some "hollow," whereas others will seem "harsh." These differences are also timbral, but they are so important to music that musicians have special terms for them: "consonance" refers to the first two categories and "dissonance" to the last. As more notes are played together, you will hear that some combinations seem very consonant, others very dissonant indeed, but there will also be many gradations in between. For our purposes, the main thing to pay attention to is how each combination gives a particular color to the sound.

Individual sounds are constructed along similar principles to harmony. Musical sounds tend to sound musical on the basis of their harmonious quality, that is, they vibrate with primarily consonant intervals—so-called "harmonic" overtones—beyond the basic note we perceive. This series of overtones consists of simple ratios of that basic note, which is called the "fundamental." Noise, by contrast, is characterized by jumbled, "inharmonic" overtones, so that noises sound "harsh" by contrast to a musical pitch. An intermediate stage would be represented by a "humming" motor, which would have some discernible pitches but not the clarity of a musical sound (the sounds of many percussion instruments are similar).

As suggested earlier, volume also affects timbre because the strength of the individual harmonics does not always vary equally with volume. This is particularly true at the extremes of the dynamic range. It is important to recognize that this is true of most sounds: the timbre of a shouting voice differs from that of a normal voice, although much of the difference may be attributable to a markedly different way of using the vocal instrument. We know that this difference is timbral rather than simply a product of mere volume because these voices sound quite different when recorded and played back at the same volume.

ORCHESTRATION

Another, more characteristic example of timbre would be something like the difference between the sound of the oboe and that of the flute. In its middle register, the flute has a sweet, rather smooth sound, whereas the oboe is more nasal. As the instruments go higher in their range, the flute becomes brighter, almost piercing. The oboe, on the other hand, generally mellows in its upper register, especially at moderate dynamic levels.

The timbres of musical instruments can be mixed. We might have a flute and oboe playing the same tune in unison, for instance. Such combinations often blend to produce a tone color quite different from the timbres of each taken individually. In this sense, combining instruments is somewhat analogous to blending paints, where colors mix in ways that nonprofessionals might not expect they would. The traditional symphony orchestra (the model for a studio orchestra) can produce a surprising variety of timbral combinations (see Figures 2-4 and 2-5 for orchestral images).

"Orchestration" is the term musicians use to designate this art of choosing and combining instruments to produce a particular sound. Tone color in music is not used indiscriminately any more than is pigment in painting (indeed, orchestration is regarded as a specific professional skill in the commercial film industry—see Figures 2-6 and 2-7). Timbre sets an underlying "mood" to the music, much as the palette does for painting. In addition to differences in sound, the instruments carry many connotations inherited from opera, operetta, melodrama, program music, and so forth: the oboe and flute, for instance, are pastoral instruments; the trumpet is associated with military and heraldic functions; the horn suggests

Figure 2-4. Recording studio, view from within the orchestra (photo: Dan Goldwasser).

Figure 2-5. Composer George S. Clinton conducts a studio orchestra (photo: Dan Goldwasser).

Figure 2-6. Orchestrator Brad Dechter and composer James Newton Howard (photo: Dan Goldwasser).

Figure 2-7. *Firewall* (2006) orchestrator Conrad Pope, director Richard Loncraine, and composer Alexandre Desplat (photo: Dan Goldwasser).

hunting; and so forth. These connotations are not always obvious—in fact, generally they are not—but they are always latent, so that something will seem wrong when for no apparent reason the orchestration calls for an instrument to play too far against type.

TIMBRE AND SOUND

Much like the sound of a flute differs from that of an oboe, footsteps on gravel sound markedly different than those on grass or concrete. Likewise, the sound of the footstep of a large animal in the distance differs from that same footstep in close-up, even if the sound levels remain the same. (This has to do with the fact that distant sounds have primarily low frequencies, whereas the close-up contains many more high frequencies as well—the strength of high-frequency sound diminishes greatly with respect to distance.) Also like musical instruments, many sounds have specific associations. A low rumble is often ominous, suggesting a distant danger (such as the previously mentioned large animal); a bright, crunchy sound puts us on alert, indicating close proximity and danger (the close-up of the large animal); crickets have pastoral associations, suggesting a calm, peaceful night; a dull thud often fills us with dread (body hitting floor); and so forth.

As Walter Murch explains, the particular timbre of a sound is often chosen with extreme care to ensure an appropriate filmic effect:

> The image of a door closing accompanied by the right "slam" can indicate not only the material of the door and the space around it but also the emotional state of the person closing it. The sound for the door at the end of *The Godfather* (1972), for instance, needed to give the audience more than correct physical cues about the door; it was essential to get a firm, irrevocable closure that resonated with and underscored Michael's final line: "Never ask me about my business, Kay."[11]

Tessitura also can serve as an important concept for thinking about the sound track in general, especially issues of the voice. As we noted earlier, the regular speaking voice, *falsetto*, and whisper are quite different in timbre. Furthermore, if we listen to how an angry voice sometimes grows shrill as it stretches into the upper register, we can start to hear that "raising a voice in anger" is more than a matter of a change in volume. Tessitura arguably plays as great a role in characterization as dialogue. Voices themselves have characteristic tessituras. Jimmy Stewart's voice was generally placed relatively high in its range and Jerry Lewis's very high; whereas John Wayne's voice was pitched much lower. Similarly, Ginger Rogers and Betty Grable both had voices that were placed in the upper range; whereas Lauren Bacall, Marlene Dietrich, and Greta Garbo all had relatively low voices.

Finally, as in the orchestration of music, sounds can be produced through blending a number of individual sounds together. For instance, a tiger's roar was added to jet sounds of *Top Gun* (1986), giving the fighter jets a ferocious personality. The sounds of the dinosaurs in *Jurassic Park* (1993) are also composites created by combining various animal sounds. Such "sweetening" of sounds through combination is extremely common.

Texture

In music, texture designates the functional relation of musical lines to one another. This concerns the number of musical strands or layers occurring simultaneously and the type and nature of the connections among them.

DENSITY AND LIVELINESS

A "thick" texture refers to a relatively large number of strands, but the strands are fairly well coordinated, like a thick string of yarn. The strands in a "busy" texture, by contrast, are generally more active and more discrete, the effect being that they compete for attention.

In music, a texture can be thickened by doubling a strand (as by adding an instrument), especially at intervals other than the octave or unison. Thickness is also influenced by spacing. When strands occur in approximately the same register, the sound will be thicker than if the strands are separated by register. The impression of thickness is also influenced by registral placement, as lower notes seem to have more "mass" than higher ones and so create a much denser aural impression.

In recording and editing, the creation of sound texture is often called "layering," each layer being more or less equivalent to a musical strand. The thickness of the texture in this sense would be determined by the number of discrete layers but also by the overall volume. We might call this thickness the "density" of the mix. As with music, low-frequency sounds tend to increase the impression of density. Busyness, by contrast, is a measure by the total amount of activity. We might term this busyness the "liveliness" of the mix. In this respect, liveliness does not refer to the absolute number of layers but to the perceived level of activity (and, secondarily, the amount of high frequencies).

Density and liveliness of the mix do not necessarily correlate with scene type. Walter Murch notes that "Sometimes, to create the natural simplicity of an ordinary scene between two people, dozens and dozens of sound tracks have to be created and seamlessly blended into one. At other times an apparently complex 'action' sound track can be conveyed with just a few carefully selected elements."[13]

Density and liveliness are useful terms for describing a sound track mix, but they offer little help in determining the functions of the various layers of a mix. Musicians, however, do have terms that refer to the means of controlling functional relations among various lines, especially in terms of foreground and background. We describe and illustrate these four textures next: (a) monophony, (b) homophony, (c) melody and accompaniment, and (d) polyphony. To these four categories, we add a fifth that is understandably rare in music but common in film: (e) accompaniment without melody (or "a-melodic"). As we see, each of these textures has important correlates in sound design.

If something is clear but isn't dense enough, if it doesn't have any heft to it, I try to find something to make it have heft. If something is as dense as you want it but you can't understand anything in it, what do I have to take out to make it clear? So I'm always looking for that balance point between density and clarity.
—Walter Murch[12]

MONOPHONY

Monophony is the simplest texture. Strictly speaking, it consists of a single melodic line. Obviously, this melodic line will occupy the foreground, as the "background" is absent, consisting only of silence. A familiar example is the singing of medieval chant. In film, a person singing without any accompaniment creates a monophonic texture, as do several persons all singing the same melody. In most writing, the meaning of the term *monophony* is expanded to include a single melody against a pedal point, that is, a pitch or sonority held without change in the background. A good example would be the drones of bagpipes or of certain types of Tibetan chant.

In terms of sound, a monologue—even a dialogue—can be considered "monophonic" if it occurs with no sound effects (see Figure 2-8 for an example with commentary). When the ambient sound field is relatively thin and inactive, the overall effect might still be considered to be monophony. In other words, the important consideration for a monophonic sound design is that the background be absent or minimally defined. When dialogue is rendered with a monophonic sound design, the emphasis falls squarely on the words, allowing for maximum clarity. That is one reason this texture was commonly used for dialogue sequences, especially in the 1930s and 1940s, whenever clarity of dialogue was the absolute value of the sequence. On the negative side, a lack of well-defined background cues to establish time and place is the primary drawback of this kind of sound design.

HOMOPHONY

In music, a strict homophonic texture consists of more than one line, but each line moves with more or less the same rhythm. This is a style you may be familiar with from hymns. In homophony, the tune is supported by the other lines, so in that sense there is a separation into foreground and background function.

a | b **Figure 2-8.** *Trois Couleurs: Bleu* (*Three Colors: Blue*, 1993). Olivier (Benoît Régent) and Julie (Juliette Binoche) talk on the phone. The lack of ambient sound in the sequence places strong "monophonic" emphasis on dialogue in the scene. The silence of the sound track here also underscores the long gaps of silence between the lines.

The fact that the lines do not have distinct rhythms, however, considerably diminishes the differentiation of the functions. For this reason, homophonic texture is not frequently encountered as a textural component of sound design— although it may, of course, be used for music within the sound track. One instance of such a texture might be when two or more sounds are causally connected, such as punches and grunts in fight scenes of martial arts films, or in military charges, where a single voice (the commander's or sergeant's) nevertheless needs to emerge above the others.

MELODY AND ACCOMPANIMENT

Probably the most common texture in music is that of melody and accompaniment. As the name implies, the tune is supported by its accompaniment, making for a strong functional separation of melodic foreground and background accompaniment. Because the accompaniment is rhythmically distinct from the melody, foreground and background functions are better defined than in homophony.

One of the most powerful functions of accompaniments is establishing the "setting" (genre) or "mood" (affect) in which the melody will appear. Tunes certainly have generic and affective qualities in themselves, but an accompaniment can augment, diminish, or even transform the character of a melody.

If we think about how filmmakers distinguish foreground and background on the sound track, we should quickly recognize that melody and accompaniment is also the texture that dominates in sound design. In almost any dialogue scene, the voice will be set off as foreground. Music and ambient sound typically serve as a background that supports the voice, clarifies meaning of the dialogue, and gives a scene direction by "setting" the mood, establishing location, providing emphasis, and so forth.

POLYPHONY

In music, polyphony is characterized by an independence of musical lines. In other words, polyphonic texture exhibits a relatively shallow hierarchy between foreground and background. The term *polyphony* is often used as shorthand for imitative counterpoint, such as a fugue or canon, where musical lines achieve musical independence through imitation. Familiar examples of imitative counterpoint include the rounds "Row, Row, Row Your Boat," and "Are You Sleeping, Brother John?" The independence of line in the case of these simple canons is clearly not between the lines themselves, which are identical; rather, the independence refers to the lack of functional differentiation between the lines: the lines do not establish a clear hierarchy but rather compete for our attention. Which line is primary? As a rule of thumb, the more we feel obliged to ask this question, the more likely it is that we are dealing with a polyphonic relation.

It should be remembered, however, that polyphony is not restricted to imitation. For our purposes, polyphony is a measure of hierarchy: the shallower the hierarchy between foreground and background layers, the more polyphonic or "contrapuntal" it will be.

Polyphonic textures are quite common in sound design. Action sequences, for instance, often set music and sound effects off against one another in such a way that neither seems to dominate the other—at least not over long stretches. Even at moments when sound effects mask the music almost to the point of obliteration—for example at the beginning of *Star Wars IV: A New Hope* where laser blasts in the corridors often make it impossible to hear the music—the sound design does not set up a real hierarchy between the elements. It is more like they are set one against the other in a somewhat antagonistic manner (*counterpoint* literally means "point against point"). As with music, the sounds need to be controlled if they are not to simply produce cacophony. Sound designer Skip Lievsay puts it this way:

> When you attack a film with a volume of work, it tends to muddy up the issue unless you're trying to create something [that] is a conflagration of sounds. Even then it is almost always more meaningful to isolate certain sounds that will play on a given shot in a very succinct way, and will go ten times farther psychologically and emotionally than all of the ninety-seven other elements that you're not listening to.[14]

Overlapping dialogue—for instance in screwball comedies—is also a form of counterpoint. As the name implies, the beginning of one line of dialogue begins before another line ends, and at times several people may be speaking entire sentences simultaneously (see Figures 2-9 and 2-10 for examples with commentary).

A-MELODIC (ACCOMPANIMENT WITHOUT MELODY)

The a-melodic texture is similar to monophony in that it diminishes the foreground/background distinction, but whereas monophony occupies only a foreground, an a-melodic texture has only background. In music, the a-melodic

Figure 2-9. *M*A*S*H* (1970). Radar O'Reilly (Gary Burghoff) closely echoes—sometimes even anticipates—Col. Blake's (Roger Bowen) commands, suggesting dialogue in close canon. This gives the effect that Radar is running the unit as much as Col. Blake.

Figure 2-10. *Brigadoon* (1954). Dialogue is heard simultaneously from two conversational groupings, one on the left and one in the center, as well as a man on the phone toward the right. As the camera moves through the crowd, other conversations are briefly isolated. With ambient sound of background chatter mixed at an extremely high level, the impression is one of utter confusion, underscoring the disorientation and alienation of the modern city that the film opposes to the pastoral utopia of Brigadoon.

texture occurs most commonly at the beginning of a piece or section where it serves to introduce an accompaniment pattern. In musical theater, jazz, and popular music, this is called a "vamp" (as in "vamp till ready") and functions to set tempo, mood, and genre or occasionally just fill time between melodic statements. The primary characteristic of the vamp is that the reduction to background alone is only temporary; that is, it presumes the eventual appearance of melody and so also a restoration of the foreground/background distinction. (In the past two decades, certain types of "ambient" music styles can hold a-melodic textures over the course of an entire track.)

Something akin to introductory vamping is common in sound design. It is not at all unusual for scenes to begin with background alone. This observation applies to sound as a whole as much as to music (see Figure 2-11 for an example with commentary). Ambient sound especially is often used this way. One reason for using an a-melodic texture as an introduction is that it permits us to concentrate on the details of the background, allowing us to absorb the details of setting and place, which can be particularly useful if we need to orient ourselves to a marked change of tempo and mood. Like the establishing shot, it "sets the scene" before initiating action or dialogue.

The a-melodic texture is occasionally used as an ending as well, where the return to background serves as a means to disperse the energy of the scene, to allow reflection, and to buffer the transition to the next scene. In *Impromptu* (1991), for instance, George Sand (Judy Davis) rushes into the woods on a horse as Chopin's Prelude in G# Minor plays on the underscore. She is ultimately thrown from the horse, and the scene ends with a thud (00:24:38) and then only

a | b   **Figure 2-11.** *Rashômon* (1950). The sound of rain is prominent at the beginning of each episode under the ruined Rashômon gatehouse. In each case it serves as a prelude to the scene (a), where it settles into the background for the generally sparse dialogue (b). Although it is a-melodic in itself and serves consistently as an introductory figure, rain—along with sunlight and the baby—is a prominent symbol, marked not simply through recurrence but also through the length of each introductory sequence and its continued presence as background for the dialogue.

ambient sounds. This is followed immediately (00:24:44) by a slow dissolve to George stumbling back to the house at night, again with only ambient sound accompanying the shot. The ambient sound in this case is a kind of "reverse" or "mirror" vamp: it comes after the main part of the sequence; it serves as a transition; and its mood contrasts quite markedly with the scene that precedes it. (For another example, see the graphic with commentary in Figure 2-12.)

TEXTURE AND FOREGROUND/BACKGROUND FUNCTIONS

Texture offers a useful way of thinking about and describing the functional relations among components of the sound track. The terms should not, however, be taken as absolutes—for our purposes, making a correct identification is less important than using the terms to make sense of foreground and background; and, in any case, scenes frequently fluctuate from one texture to another as the dramatic action plays out.

Monophony emphasizes foreground to such an extent that background cues to setting are all but eliminated. Homophony offers a richer texture but is little different in function. Melody and accompaniment occupies a middle point between monophony and polyphony. What separates it decisively from the other textures and what makes it the most common texture is that it establishes a clear hierarchy between foreground and background and thus allows the formation of strongly demarcated functions. Polyphony introduces multiple conflicting foreground elements that confuse the foreground/background distinction. Finally, the a-melodic texture

Figure 2-12. A-melodic musical texture plays a role in the opening scene of *Aguirre, der Zorn Gottes* (*Aguirre: The Wrath of God*, 1972). After a brief set of explanatory titles with no sound, the film opens with a shot of people snaking their way along a narrow mountain pass (0:36). Atmospheric synthesizer music evocative of voices enters and continues throughout the scene, which plays silent (that is, there is no diegetic sound). A voice-over narration is added (0:49), suggesting that the music has been functioning as a vamp because the voice-over establishes a foreground relationship with respect to the synthesized music. Yet, when the voice-over ends 15 seconds later, the music continues alone until the beginning of the next scene (4:53). Because the voice-over is comparatively brief and the music is amorphous, the latter ultimately seems to function as an extended accompaniment lacking melody (i.e., the voice-over). In a sense, the long continuation of the music serves as a rejection of the foreground/background hierarchy and, therefore, also of the clarity offered by the voice-over.

asks us to pay attention exclusively to the details of the setting; that is, it directs attention to background but without fully transforming that background into a foreground: it leaves an unfilled space.

In distinguishing between monophony and melody and accompaniment, setting and mood are paramount. The more redundant or less narratively pertinent information the background conveys, the more the texture will seem monophonic. In distinguishing a-melodic texture from melody and accompaniment, the delineation of a foreground figure against the background is most important. When a foreground is well defined against a background, we will understand the figure as significant. In short, melody and accompaniment situates the foreground within a context determined by the background. Polyphony differs from melody and accompaniment in terms of clarity. The relative lack of hierarchy coupled with a multiplicity of layers creates confusion, which need not be construed negatively. Action sequences, for instance, often benefit from such aural confusion because the aesthetic of spectacle that drives these sequences depends on sensory overload.

Few scenes rely exclusively on one texture or another except in a broad sense. As noted earlier, accompaniment alone often functions as a vamp, that is, an introduction to a scene that will be characterized primarily by the foreground/ background relation. As in this case, texture generally fluctuates; it will typically be centered on melody and accompaniment so long as dialogue dominates, for instance, but drifting now and then toward the other textures. Likewise, chase scenes may fall more on the polyphonic side, but there will inevitably be moments where, say, dialogue comes forward accompanied by a suspension of the "contrapuntal" field.

Finally, we need to bear in mind that we can apply the idea of texture to different levels of the sound track. For example, an a-melodic musical texture— music without a strong melodic component—might easily function as an "accompaniment" to dialogue. The repetitions of the distinctive marimba figure at the beginning of *American Beauty* (1999), for instance, are essentially an a-melodic texture. On the larger level of the sound track, however, they serve as an accompaniment to Lester's voice-over. Something similar happens between the music and voice-over in *Double Indemnity* (1944). Each time Walter Neff begins to narrate, an agitated musical figure accompanies his speech.

Example for Sound Track Analysis Using Musical Terms: *Atonement*, Main-Title Sequence, and First Scene

In *Atonement* (2007), the first sounds are effects—birds chirping, heard against the last two of four studio credits and quickly joined by a sharp mechanical sound (something like "zzzzt"), which viewers recognize in retrospect as the carriage return of a manual typewriter. The letter-by-letter presentation of the main title against the sounds of typing is no surprise, then, nor is the typing out of "England" during the "establishing shot" of a large English country house (the house is a scale model of the actual house in which the action takes place). Typing, strongly rhythmic and foregrounded, continues as the camera pans slowly across what is clearly a child's room until it reaches Briony (Saoirse Ronan; see Figure 2-13). The typewriter sounds continue undiminished and unchallenged, then music enters to compete, in the form of a single repeated piano note not rhythmically synchronized with the typing (an obvious counterpoint).

Figure 2-13. *Atonement* (2007). Briony types.

As the scene continues, the typing stops, Briony gathers her papers and walks out of the room in a determined, march-like gait. As soon as the typing stops, the music takes over (moving at a similar pace) and we hear Briony's theme over her procession through the house to her mother's drawing room. All the while, typing sounds continue, now synchronized with the music (indeed, the typing forms rhythms within the music—note that the melody moves at a slower pace than the elements of the accompaniment [including the typewriter], suggesting a certain disjunction in mood). All stop abruptly with two loud chords, both stingers tightly synchronized, the first with a door closing, the second with a jump cut to Briony and her mother seated inside the room.

The charming anachronism of the manual typewriter does help to suggest time and place before the opening titles are past, and the volume and tempo are plausible. The typewriter is also strongly linked to the character of Briony herself: single-minded, brisk, and one might imagine slightly "brittle," like the sound of the typewriter key striking. Like the disparity between melody and accompaniment, this brittleness suggests both the charming and the slightly disturbing, a premonition of the flaws that have tragic consequences not only for Robbie (James McAvoy) and Briony's older sister Cecilia (Keira Knightley) but also for others in the household, including Briony herself.

Summary

Musical terminology is much more specific and concrete than most terms for sound analysis. In this chapter, we introduced a number of musical terms, defined them, and then extended their meanings to sound in general. The terms cover broad distinctions in musical materials, including rhythm, meter, volume, timbre, and texture.

Music, Sound, Space, and Time
Concepts and Terminology

Introduction

The basic human cognition of sound is to "anchor" it in an object—a person speaks, a door creaks, a dove coos, the radio plays. Those objects necessarily reside in some physical space (the space of the real world). Narrative complicates matters, however. A storyteller speaks and in that sense is the object-source of that speech, but he or she also conjures up a fantasy world whose own "objects" can be the sources of sound, as when the storyteller attributes dialogue to a character ("Then Francesca said, 'I know what you mean'").

The cinematic narrative complicates things still further because it directs attention to that conjured-up fantasy world. The primary vehicle of narrative is no longer the storyteller's speech but the representation of the story world. In film, the role of a storyteller is sometimes taken over by voice-over narration, someone unseen who speaks on the sound track, but there is always an "implied narrator" (because narrative films tell stories, there must be a storyteller "somewhere"). Therefore, the viewer-listener's cognition of sound is obliged to operate at two levels: the level of the narration (implied or spoken) and the level of sound in the fantasy or screen world.

Background and *source*, respectively, are terms commonly used for sound in these two levels, but as we noted in Chapter 1, "background" is too easily confused with the subordinate element in the foreground/background pair. You'll understand what we mean if we assert that in voice-over narration background sound is foregrounded. The terms *onscreen* and *offscreen* do not solve the problem: *screen* refers simply to the part of the film world that is within the camera's frame at any particular moment. "Offscreen" is whatever part of that filmic world we cannot see in the frame but may already have seen or may imaginatively project from the part we can see (recall those chirping bird sounds in the opening minute or so of *Atonement* [2007]). Partly to solve this problem, but also partly to draw attention to the fundamental importance of visual representation in film, scholars have borrowed the term *diegetic* from literary theory to refer to the world of the narrative, the screen world or world of the film. Thus, *non-diegetic* refers to the level of narration: voice-over narration is nondiegetic—and so is underscoring.

In addition to physical space, we need time: the basis of any narrative is the story, or the chronological ordering of a series of related events; the plot presents a particular arrangement—again temporal—of these events. The temporalities of story and plot can be set against one another. At the level of the scene, time can interact with image and sound in multiple ways.

This chapter is divided into two main sections, the first dealing with space, the second with time. We begin with the diegetic/nondiegetic pair, which is essential to the analysis and interpretation of sound and music in film but from which all kinds of ambiguities arise. Then, we cover a number of specific traits and devices of diegetic sound related to the onscreen/offscreen pair and to sound perspective. Finally, we discuss some specialized but commonly used devices that exploit the boundaries between diegetic and nondiegetic space. The second main division of the chapter discusses three distinct but related ways that sound impacts the perception of time in and between scenes: the formal treatment of transitions, synchronization (or "playing with the film"), and counterpoint (or "playing against the film").

Space (1): Diegetic/Nondiegetic Sound and Narrative

Diegetic sound refers to everything that can be heard by characters in the film. By contrast, *nondiegetic sound* cannot be heard by the characters. Consider, for example, the conversation scene from *Catch Me If You Can* (2002) that we discussed in the Introduction to Part I and have mentioned several times since. The radio on Carl Hanratty's desk produces sounds (Bing Crosby singing "Mele Kalikimaka") that Carl can hear and that Frank also hears through the telephone receiver. The melancholy underscoring near the end of the scene, on the other hand, is heard only by the audience—if we understand this music as mimicking Frank's mood, we do not assume that it is literally going through his mind at the time (in fact, that would be highly unlikely because the music continues when Frank speaks).

The typewriter sounds in *Atonement*, on the other hand, pose a problem. We can assume in retrospect that Briony can hear the diegetic sounds that actually first appear behind the opening titles, but what about the typewriter sounds that continue after she stops and walks away? Have they simply been transferred to the underscoring, or are they sounds of typing still mentally resounding in Briony's ears? The music's march-like gait, which seems synchronized with her walking,

Figure 3-1. *Das Testament des Dr. Mabuse* (1933). A distressed Hofmeister (Karl Meixner) tries to think amidst the din of the machinery in the Forger's factory.

If we are not bothered by music that lacks anchoring in the diegesis, equally we are not bothered by music that begins onscreen and then wanders off. This is business-as-usual in musicals: in Meet Me in St. Louis *(1944), for example, Judy Garland sings a verse and chorus to accompaniment of a piano that we see, but then she sings a second chorus with an invisible orchestra. Film sound scholar Rick Altman refers to this shift from diegetic to non-diegetic accompaniment as an* audio dissolve. *See the discussion of the audio dissolve later in this chapter.*[1]

also threatens to lose its nondiegetic independence and join in the action, so to speak—not to mention the stinger chords at the end, which are not so much music as stylized sound effects.

It is by no means uncommon for ambiguities of this kind to arise, especially in connection with rhythmic mechanical sounds such as a typewriter. Furthermore, underscoring can move with both ease and speed between diegetic and nondiegetic functions. In one striking instance from early sound film, *Das Testament des Dr. Mabuse* (1933), very dissonant music over the title quickly dissolves into the oppressive rhythm of a machine stamping out a triple beat. The opening scene, furthermore, begins *in medias res*: Hofmeister has slipped into the Forger's factory and has been forced to hide in a room (Figure 3-1). The scene plays essentially as silent film, the machine being the only noise on the sound track.

EXAMPLE FOR DIEGETIC AND NONDIEGETIC MUSIC: *GLORY*, BOSTON PARTY SCENE

A scene from early in the Civil War film *Glory* (1989) will illustrate the distinction between diegetic and nondiegetic music as well as the ambiguities that can arise from them. The city (Boston) is the same one depicted in *Good Will Hunting* (treated in Chapter 1) and the scene is probably just a few blocks away at most from the Common (because both films use location shooting, this could be literally true), but in *Glory* the time is about 130 years earlier. A party is underway to honor officers who fought in the recent battle of Antietam (September 1862). It is one of the few non-military scenes in the film, which stars Matthew Broderick, Denzel Washington, and Morgan Freeman and recounts the early history of the 54th Massachusetts Infantry, the first regularly formed African-American regiment in the United States Army.

The party scene begins at about 09:30, lasts just over 5 minutes, and is heavily scored—only about 30 seconds are without music. Up to this point, more than half the film has had nondiegetic orchestral music: music begins with the opening titles and runs about 3½ minutes until the beginning of the Antietam battle scene; a second cue begins at 05:30, as Captain Robert Gould Shaw (Broderick) rises from the ground after the battle, and continues until he enters the field hospital (1 minute and 45 seconds in all).

The extended party scene that follows breaks down readily into three parts, the first being Shaw's self-conscious entry into the party, the second a conversation with the Governor and others about forming the regiment, and the third a conversation with his friend Forbes (Cary Elwes) carried on outdoors. We will be concerned here only with the first part and its transition into the second.

The scene opens with a shot of a rose window, which is quickly revealed as a skylight providing illumination to the upper end of a staircase (top frame in Figure 3-2). Music is heard from a piano, a pastoral piece stylistically appropriate for the era (by early nineteenth-century composer Franz Schubert; Figure 3-3). Our first reaction, then, is to regard the music as belonging to the physical environment, as diegetic, but the volume level is quite unrealistically high. Eventually we learn that the music *is* meant to be diegetic—we see a pianist (and harpist) briefly in the general shot of the room (Figure 3-4), but sound levels are never quite appropriate (even when we see the piano and harp close by in the background of segment two). The transition to this scene was achieved by a short lap dissolve (overlapping images) from an Army field hospital where,

Figure 3-2. *Glory* (1989). Boston a
Party Scene: (a) Dissolve from b
previous scene; (b) Shaw descend- c
ing the staircase; (c) entering the
main room of the party.

Figure 3-3. *Glory.* Boston Party Scene: Franz Schubert, *Drei Klavierstücke*, D.946, No. 2.

Figure 3-4. *Glory*. Boston Party Scene: A pianist and harpist play on the far side of the room.

among other things, an amputation was being performed—sound participates, as the hospital sounds mingle briefly with the music. In the course of the shot, the camera pulls back and moves down and to the left to reveal Shaw (in medium shot) descending the stairs (middle frame of Figure 3-2). He is in his parents' upper-class Boston house on his way to join the large party in progress.

After a point-of-view shot (from the staircase looking down on people below and traveling across them as if Shaw is scanning what he sees below him) and a sudden, inserted close-up of a plate of food, with a woman and an older man talking (the man takes and is about to eat a small tomato), comes what we will take as an establishing shot, a general view of a large room with partygoers. Sound, on the other hand, is oddly unsettled. The piano music does provide a suitable aural counterpart to the establishing shot: its unrealistic sound levels and broad stylistic-chronological reference would work just as well as nondiegetic music. A generalized sound of party conversation is appropriate, but it is also undermined by unusually loud laughter and whispering during the close-up mentioned earlier. We begin to suspect the sound is subjective—specifically, it is ambient sound as filtered through Shaw's mind and emotions. It is still diegetic—unlike the generalized sense of emotion in the scenes from *Catch Me If You Can* and *Good Will Hunting*—we are hearing diegetic sounds as filtered, distorted, by Shaw's own hearing and attention.

All this is confirmed in subsequent shots: (1) Shaw in medium shot as he walks through the doorway (lower frame of Figure 3-2) (at this point, the crowd sounds begin to mingle with a wordless [and nondiegetic] boys' chorus [as the piano fades out]—this music continues, mixed with bits of conversation, and gradually grows louder); (2) another extreme close-up, now of two women talking

Figure 3-5. *Glory.* Boston Party Scene: (a) Shaw is deep in thought, disconnected   a | b
from the party; (b) Thomas greets Shaw.

as they look at Shaw; (3) cut back to a close-up of Shaw (another soldier enters the room behind him), then (4) away to another close-up of a woman laughing, (5) again back to Shaw, (6) then a medium shot of an officer in a wheelchair entering the room, (7) back to one last close-up of Shaw before the nondiegetic music goes abruptly out and the diegetic piano and harp music returns as Thomas (Andre Braugher) addresses him.

Until the greeting from Thomas, Shaw maintains his distance from the crowd, the shot/reverse-shot series emphasizes that distance (it jumps back and forth between close-ups of him and of people who seem to be at some physical distance), and the disjointed quality of the sound track corresponds. The uncertain diegetic status of the piano (and harp) music is followed by Shaw's mental filtering of room sounds, and the intrusion of nondiegetic music over them. The crux of the scene is reached, not in conversation, but in Shaw's rapidly increasing discomfort (Figure 3-5a). Rather than concluding and making a transition to another scene, this first part is simply cut off by Thomas's greeting (Figure 3-5b). There is a strong sense in which this moment explains everything before it as subjective: with a sudden return to the real world comes a normal mode of hearing.

The basic categories are defined easily enough: the piano and harp, crowd, and speech are all diegetic; the wordless chorus is nondiegetic. Before Thomas's greeting, however, the diegetic sounds, including the music, were interpreted, filtered, as if they were sounds "narrated" for us by Shaw. (Narrative theorists call this process of subjective filtering "focalization.")

Space (2): Onscreen/Offscreen Sound and Music

Diegetic and nondiegetic are not the same thing as onscreen/offscreen, which refer specifically to everything that is within the frame (onscreen) or not (offscreen). By combining the terms in these two pairs, we can create a list of basic relations between image and narrative space.

The first of these combinations, diegetic-onscreen, is certainly the default case: we see within the frame what we expect to see in the film world (Will and Sean talking on a park bench, not a view of Sean's empty office or an insert of, say, the Voyager I spacecraft while they talk). Diegetic-offscreen is also common: a room is shown onscreen but we hear someone speaking or music playing with the correct volume and other sound qualities that would match another room connected to the one we see. Nondiegetic-onscreen, on the other hand, is much less common but is likely to be invoked when an onscreen character imagines or remembers speech or music and the performance of that music is visualized, or a character speaks in direct address, as the title character frequently does in *Ferris Bueller's Day Off* (1986). Nondiegetic-offscreen is the default case for voice-over narration and underscoring, but it can perhaps also apply to characters such as ghosts whose voices can be heard but who have no definable place in the physical world.

In this section, we will first stress offscreen sound and then several ways in which offscreen and onscreen sound interact.

OFFSCREEN SOUND

Without evidence to the contrary, we will take offscreen sound as simply an extension of onscreen space. For example, dialogue scenes that utilize the shot/reverse-shot syntax will often cut away at some point in the conversation to the non-speaking character. During this reaction shot, clearly, the speech that continues will be offscreen. The reaction shot is so common that we seldom pay attention to the fact that the shot itself creates offscreen sound, which has the effect of also binding offscreen and onscreen space more tightly together.

A brief but narratively important scene late in *The Big Sleep* (1946) provides a simple example (1:43:54). Phillip Marlowe and Vivian Greenwood, characters played by Humphrey Bogart and Lauren Bacall, have escaped from one dangerous encounter and are heading toward another. They are shown in a car (Figure 3-6), and they discuss their situation. In the course of the scene they admit, for the first time, genuine romantic feelings.

The scene lasts less than 2 minutes and consists of twelve shots, three of which are 2-shots of Vivian and Marlowe: at beginning and end, as well as one in the middle. The others are alternating close-ups. At several points one character is shown in close-up while we hear the other speaking. The effect is not only to bind offscreen and onscreen space but also to highlight the emotional resonance in this newly forming couple. (See Figure 3-7 for another example of offscreen sound.)

When offscreen sound is localizable as an object that *could* be shown but is not—that is, a sound that suggests an object is more than simply background—we refer to it as "sound-off" (short for "sound offscreen"). Examples include doors, footsteps, telephones, and so forth. Such noises are commonly used as a

This overrunning of one person's image with another person's voice is a method peculiar to the talkies; it is one of the devices which help the talkies to tell a story faster than a silent film could tell it, and faster than it could be told on stage.
—Alfred Hitchcock, on the significance of offscreen sound to the reaction shot.[2]

Figure 3-6. *The Big Sleep* (1946). Second car scene, Vivien and Marlowe.

Figure 3-7. *Trois Couleurs: Bleu* (*Three Colors: Blue*, 1993). Julie (Juliette Binoche) listens as a man, evading thugs, runs through her building knocking on doors (34:48–36:04); the scene is rendered primarily in offscreen sound.

means of establishing a scene, either at the beginning of the sequence itself, where an offscreen sound can motivate a cut to the location, or to introduce new characters (and so also a new direction) to the scene. Offscreen bomb sounds, for example, are used this way in *Lawrence of Arabia* (1962) (at 37:58). The sound of the bombs interrupts a conversation between Lawrence and Colonel Brighton; a cut to an encampment of Arabs being attacked by Turkish planes follows. (This is also an example of a sound advance; see the section on that device later in this chapter.)

As a "noise" in the diegetic world, music can also be used in this manner. In the opening of *The Broadway Melody* (1929), for instance, music wafts from a window of a music store before a cut shows the interior of the shop. In *The Bride of Frankenstein* (1935), the monster hears the sound of a violin and gradually finds his way to the house of its blind player; and the main-title sequence of *The Birdcage* (1996) includes (apparently) nondiegetic underscoring that is revealed as a stage performance of "We Are Family" after the camera moves gradually across the water, beach, and street into the interior of the club.

The voice-off is similar to the sound-off, except that it highlights the voice. A simple voice-off will occur with a cut to a reaction shot. More characteristic, perhaps, are introductory words, like "hello," that announce the presence of a new character before we see him or her. A voice-off will sometimes involve a clear mismatch in sound scale (that is, linking sound volume and timbre to shot scale).

ONSCREEN/OFFSCREEN SOUND INTERACTION: *THE APARTMENT*

Filmmakers are very sensitive to the play between onscreen and offscreen sound. One of many striking examples we could cite occurs in *The Apartment* (1960). Bud (Jack Lemmon) has just been promoted and is settling into his new office (43:00). As he is hanging up his overcoat, an offscreen voice offers congratulations. He finishes putting away his jacket, and responds, "Hi, fellows." Only at this point is there a cut to four men entering his office. This, then, initiates the scene proper where the men remind Bud that he is beholden to them for his promotion.

As everyone moves further into the office, the camera reframes to incorporate Bud into the group. In a sense, the camera here entertains the perspective of the men: "all for one and one for all." Nevertheless, the desk intervenes to keep Bud somewhat apart from the group (Figure 3-8a). When he is accused of not having the right "attitude," he is separated from the group with a cut for his response. There is another accusation, this time delivered completely offscreen with the camera locked on Bud through his response. A reverse shot of the four men brings a third accusation. The shot is reversed again for Bud's response. Another accusation begins offscreen before cutting back to the man to complete his line. One of the men complains of the trouble he's been having because Bud no longer lets him into the apartment. Bud's response occurs in another reverse shot.

Next comes a cut back to the full group, with the four men now clearly separated from Bud, and one of the men delivers a threat. Bud responds briefly, but this is followed by a more pointed threat. At this moment (44:03) Jeff (Fred MacMurray) enters, he and Bud begin to converse, and the other men leave. Bud closes the door and returns to his desk, sits down, and a relatively uncomplicated shot/reverse-shot sequence follows, but without reaction shots and off-screen sound. One exception is an odd moment with the close-up of a mirror (45:01): Bud delivers a line while being somewhat out of focus (Figure 3-8b) and Jeff's face appears in the broken mirror for his response (Figure 3-8c). The lack of departure from onscreen sound emphasizes the strangeness of this particular exchange, the distorted image of each man suggesting each character's relation to the mirror—or rather to Fran (Shirley MacLaine), its owner.

AMBIGUITY OF OFFSCREEN SOUND: UNDERDETERMINATION OF SOUND

Sound is often underdetermined, that is, not defined down to all its possible naturalistic details. Depending on how it is rendered, a waterfall, for instance, sounds very much like applause, which is also similar to the rustling of leaves or the crackle of fire. Crumpling paper might likewise be mistaken for fire or fallen leaves in autumn. The crack of a baseball bat can sound like a tree branch snapping; the buzz of an insect like an electric saw or a malfunctioning radio tube. Indeed, the production of sound effects often depends on misrecognitions of just this sort: the hitting of high tension wires for the sound of a laser blast, or coconuts for horses' hooves. Figures 3-9 and 3-10 give examples from two films, along with commentary.

POINT-OF-VIEW SOUND

Point-of-view sound, sometimes called *point-of-audition sound*, is rendered from the perspective of a character in the film. The effect is generally to increase our identification with that particular character whose hearing the sound track mimics. A very common example is a conversation heard over the telephone when a shot/reverse-shot structure is not used. The filtering of the voice to render a realistic telephone sound underlines the distance between the characters and in so doing increases our focus on the character we can see.

The first part of the Boston party scene from *Glory* is a clear instance of point-of-view sound, as we hear speech and music filtered through Captain Shaw's ears and mind. A more recent film, *Lost in Translation* (2003), contains a short example that effectively illustrates point-of-view sound. Bob (Bill Murray) is swimming laps while a water aerobics class is also taking place. The short

Figure 3-8. *The Apartment* (1960). Sound and the dynamic play of onscreen and offscreen space.

a
b
c

Figure 3-9. *Lawrence of Arabia* (1962). After a beating at the hands of the Turkish army, Lawrence (Peter O'Toole) has gone to Jerusalem, abandoning his Arab comrades and vowing to be nothing more than a regular man. The establishing shot shows a marching band. As Lawrence enters the military compound, a cut to the interior coincides with music that echoes significantly, to the point where the echo separates into its own channel. Lawrence himself is almost stooping as he walks, while the echo separates further and further from the source. The complex sound seems to represent Lawrence's own divisions and self-doubts. Music continues as Lawrence moves through the building, going out when he reaches the office where General Allenby (Jack Hawkins) and Prince Feisal (Alec Guinness) are waiting.

Figure 3-10. *The Apartment.* Ambiguity of offscreen sound: Near the end of the film, Fran (Shirley MacLaine) has come to realize that she loves Bud. As she is rushing up the stairs to his apartment, she hears what sounds like a gunshot coming from Bud's apartment (2:03:11). Fearing the worst, she rushes to the door. Bud opens it to reveal a bottle of bubbling champagne. Here, Fran's reaction to the offscreen bang allows us to see just how deeply she feels for Bud.

scene all takes place from Bob's aural perspective, with the characteristic tone of his gentle sound and music dulled.

"Imagined sound" is a special case of point-of-view sound. Here, the sound track presents what a character is hearing in his or her head. A good example of this occurs in *The Bourne Ultimatum* (2007), where Jason Bourne's numerous flashbacks are presented with distorted sound (and image). Such imagined sound may be a dream, memory, or hallucination; an internal monologue; or hearing something like music in one's head. For obvious reasons, the latter case is especially common in films about musicians. Another typical use is for an individual reading a message, letter, or passage from a book silently. A potentially more complex instance occurs when a character in a film also acts at one or more points as a voice-over narrator. Once we have associated the voice-over narration with a character in the diegesis, the sound can no longer be unambiguously nondiegetic. Instead, we hear a simple imagined sound if the character is onscreen, not shown speaking but nevertheless speaking in imagination.

Space (3): Offscreen Sound and Music in Relation to the Diegesis

In the following sections, we discuss three of the most common conventions of sound design that take advantage of the ambiguity in diegetic/nondiegetic and onscreen/offscreen relations. These are voice-over narration, the audio dissolve, and Mickey-Mousing as "sweetener" for sound effects.

VOICE-OVER

Along with music, narration also serves to direct viewer attention and, through intonation and pacing, lets the audience know how they are supposed to understand the image. The voice-over is often used in documentary film, where it serves to provide context for the images as well as to fill in other pertinent information that is either not present or not obvious in the image. Morgan Freeman's work for the English language version of *March of the Penguins* (2005) is an excellent recent example of straightforward, detached narration. In this film, the narrator seems simply to relate to us the information we need to make sense of the sequence of images. Because documentary is the genre most likely to be dominated by the voice-over, narrative films frequently exploit an audience's knowledge of this convention to create a documentary "atmosphere."

In fictional film, as we might expect, voice-over generally serves the function of narration. *Laura* (1944) and *The Name of the Rose* (1986) are examples of films in which the narrators are intimately connected with the story. In the former, Waldo Lydecker (Clifton Webb) is a rather unreliable narrator (as he tries to conceal his own responsibility for what he mistakenly thought was Laura's murder); in the latter, Adso of Melk (Christian Slater) is recounting an episode in his life. Many voice-overs operate under this conceit of describing a significant

Figure 3-11. *Good Night and Good Luck* (2005). The sound track is notable for the exclusive but sparing use of a jazz combo evoking the film's setting in the 1950s. Six songs are performed once each by the combo and a female singer. "When I Fall in Love" plays during the prologue and opening credits, as very faint chatter is heard from the party scene in the background. Throughout the film, the musicians act like a quasi-Greek chorus, as they perform four songs in a television studio: in each case, the camera cuts back and forth between the principal actors and the musicians, while the lyrics of the songs link to action. End credits roll with the sixth song, "One for My Baby"; a brief reprise of "When I Fall in Love" comes at the very end.

episode of the narrator's life. This does not mean that the narration need be "realistic." Fiction works by its own rules: both *Sunset Boulevard* (1950) and *American Beauty* (1999), for example, feature dead narrators. For a recent example of diegetic music performances used for a similar narrative function as the voice-over narrator, see Figure 3-11 and its commentary.

Voice-over can also be used to establish character or as a plot device. Cher's irreverent monologue at the beginning of *Clueless* (1995) immediately captures her self-centeredness but also her charming naiveté. In *Million Dollar Baby* (2004) (Figure 3-12), the voice of Morgan Freeman's character, Eddie "Scrap-Iron" Dupris, is very prominent as a voice-over narrator in the first 20 minutes—even when he is also onscreen—but then appears only intermittently in the remainder of the film, until the very last moments, when his final words in voice-over reveal that the entire film has been an elaborate visualization of a letter he is writing to the estranged daughter of Frankie (Clint Eastwood).

In addition to delineating character and structuring the plot, the voice-over is frequently used for informational prologues. In these cases, the voice-over does not belong to a character in the story but to some unknown, extra-diegetic individual who relates the general background that allows us to understand the

Figure 3-12. *Million Dollar Baby* (2004). Frankie and Eddie ("Scrap") talk in the office of Frankie's gym.

significance of the actions in the story. Good examples include the prologue to *Casablanca* (1942) and *King of Kings* (1961). *Le Fabuleux Destin d'Amélie Poulain* (*Amélie*, 2001) demonstrates that such detached voice-over narration can be used for comedic effect as well.

AUDIO DISSOLVE

A dissolve is a means of joining two shots, the one briefly overlapping the other so that we momentarily see both shots simultaneously, one fading as the other becomes visible. Generally, the dissolve is used to signify an ellipsis, that is, a marked change of time and (usually) place. By analogy, the "audio dissolve" can function as a transition from the primary level of the diegesis to another level (such as a dream), but it finds its most characteristic treatment in the musical, where it serves as a transition to song and dance.

Rick Altman proposed the term *audio dissolve* to describe how musicals operate on principles that are distinct from other narrative films, in particular, the fact that song in a musical generally does not lend itself to strict interpretation in terms of diegetic or nondiegetic. The character seems to know very well that he or she is singing, and thus (especially with musicals written specifically for the screen rather than close adaptations of stage musicals) the song begins diegetically, just as it normally would in any other narrative film (one very common device in classical Hollywood musicals is to show one or more characters gathered around a piano). As the song progresses, however, nondiegetic orchestral accompaniment enters, replacing the piano. It is this displacement, or dissolve of one accompaniment into another, that Altman defines as the audio dissolve.

This formal feature of the musical sets it apart from other narrative films. Musicals do not maintain the clear separation of diegetic and nondiegetic registers and so cannot rigorously enforce the boundaries of the diegetic world, which seems to constantly dissolve under the force of song. For Altman, this is the very point of the musical: the world of song is a world apart from mundane reality.[3] We should remember, however, that, aside from the song performances, musicals are essentially romantic comedies and so are generally governed by the "normal" strictures of narrative film. The function of the songs, then, is to intensify the romance to the point where it can constitute and sustain an idealized world. The audio dissolve is the process by which this transformation occurs.

For Me and My Gal (1942) provides an exceptionally clear example of the audio dissolve, because it takes place fairly slowly and in distinct stages (the scene begins at 19:54 or DVD ch. 8). It begins with Harry (Gene Kelly) clumsily pounding out the title song at the piano (Figure 3-13a). Jo (Judy Garland) then comes over to the piano and relieves him (b). As she sings the verse, the orchestra comes in under the piano, which at first remains audible. By the end of the verse, although the orchestra has completely taken over, she continues to play at the piano. Harry then joins her as they sing a duet on the second chorus, with Jo still at the piano (c). She stands up (d) and they stroll across the room still singing. Finally, they move into dance (e). (Curiously, part of the dance itself is accompanied by a solo piano.) Of course, the orchestra continues through to the end of the song, when Jo and Harry sit down at the table and laugh (f). The laughter itself serves as a transition, reversing the dissolve and bringing the characters back into the mundane world.

Although the audio dissolve appears most frequently in the musical, it can occur in other sorts of narrative film, where it generally retains the function of a bridge, or a passage to a different, usually idealized world. As we might expect, in non-musicals (and especially in classical Hollywood cinema), the audio dissolve requires strong narrative and psychological motivation. That motivation is perhaps easiest in romantic comedies, which occasionally deploy the gesture of the audio dissolve to help define the world of their romance, especially, interestingly enough, to help signify blockages to it. In *The Apartment*, for instance, a piano begins to play as Bud and Fran leave their table (40:51). The piano continues until they reach the door, at which point nondiegetic strings enter under the piano (41:16). Once in the street, the tune continues in the strings until the cut to Bud standing in front of the theater, where he is waiting for Fran to join him to see *The Music Man* (41:44). The lonely saxophone associated with Bud enters with this cut—Fran has broken their date. Here, the collapse of the audio dissolve represents the deflation of Bud's hopes.

Another, more complex example occurs during the "Sacrifice of Faramir" sequence of *The Return of the King* (2003). Denethor, Faramir's father, has ordered Faramir to lead a suicidal attack on Osgiliath. As Faramir begins the attack, there is a cut back to Denethor eating noisily with Pippin standing in attendance. Denethor demands that Pippin sing. As Pippin does, the scene cuts back to Faramir's attack in slow motion. With a return to Pippin on the climactic phrase "on the edge of night," his voice is given more reverberation. The charge is depicted once again as Pippin returns to the original vocal register, quieter dynamic but continued reverberation. After two brief shots of Orcs, there is

Figure 3-13. *For Me and My Gal* (1942), title song. An illustration of an audio dissolve.

a	b
c	d
e	f

another of the charge, this time with the prominent whinnying of a horse. Strings sneak in under this, at first seeming simply a part of the reverberation of Pippen's voice. This accompaniment grows more dissonant and intense across a series of cuts—Denethor, Faramir, Orcs, Denethor, Orcs, Faramir, Pippin, and Orcs—reaching its peak as the Orcs unleash a flight of arrows.

Then comes a surprise: a sharp cut to Denethor coincides with the sound track falling shockingly silent as Pippin takes a dramatic pause for the end of his song. What emerges from this silence is nothing but Denethor's chewing, relieved only when Pippin haltingly intones the final word of the song, "fade," once again without accompaniment. Throughout the song we hear sound effects—horses, Faramir drawing his sword, the shooting of the arrows, and most of all Denethor's eating—but no voice other than Pippin's, although both Faramir and the Orc captain are shown yelling. In that sense, the "dissolve" here is a transition to anything but an idealized world. Instead, it would seem to represent a fall from an idealized world into the hostile, fully mundane world of things. Pippin's song is a lament, and this case suggests that the audio dissolve in the context of the lament can serve an inverse function to that of the musical.

MICKEY-MOUSING: MUSIC AS EFFECTS "SWEETENER"

The voice-over and audio dissolve generally affect our perception of film form and narrative at the level of a performance scene, scene transition, or even the plot design of an entire film. At times, however, the ambiguity of the diegetic and nondiegetic can be felt at the opposite extreme, at the level of close synchronization within a shot or short series of shots, when music closely mimics screen action, cartoon style, blurring the boundary between music and sound effects. This is called Mickey-Mousing, and, although generally denigrated as a gimmick by most composers and theorists of film music and tolerated only in comedy, it can be extremely effective in dramatic contexts.

Mickey-Mousing was employed on a regular basis in Hollywood film scores during the 1930s and 1940s. Of the composers who were fond of this device, Max Steiner stands out. *The Informer* (1935), for instance, makes extensive use of Mickey-Mousing. In one scene, Gypo has informed on a friend, a member of the Irish resistance, to get money to help his destitute girlfriend. Wracked with guilt, Gypo moves through the neighborhood, his every step falling heavily to the beat of the music. The Mickey-Mousing here seems like a metaphor for the weight of his conscience.

We can also construe Mickey-Mousing as a way of sweetening a sound effect, thereby making the world "other," or different from our own. By sweetening, we mean that a sound is rendered so that it seems to violate the conditions of verisimilitude. Increasing volume above expected levels, adding unmotivated distortion, and otherwise altering the expected timbre of the sound effect are some of the ways in which sound can be sweetened. As might be expected, this device is useful for emphasizing a particular action or thing, especially one that is fraught with significance but might otherwise go unmarked and so unnoticed. Generally

Figure 3-14. *The Apartment*. Near the beginning of the film, Bud (Jack Lemmon) watches his electronic accounting machine as it moves through its task. As Bud's head bounces up and down to the stuttered rhythm of the carriage movement, the music Mickey-Mouses those movements with a series of low-pitched notes that are almost noise, thus sweetening the sound effect, drawing our attention to the curious rhythm of the odd work task and setting the comedic tone of the film.

the effect is humorous (see Figure 3-14 for an example with commentary). Often the very idea is one of mismatch, an absurd sound that matches the absurd world of slapstick comedy, as in the substitution of a timpani glissando or a cymbal crash for a fall, for instance.

Sweetening is often coupled with a verisimilar close-up. Although this might seem overly redundant, in fact the disjunction between the realistic image and the less-than-realistic sound allows us to understand that we are aware of a significance that is not apparent to those in the diegetic world. See Figure 3-15, where

Figure 3-15. *Shakespeare in Love* (1998). Will's manuscript burns in the fire.

Figure 3-16. *Casablanca* (1942). The stinger chord that sounds when Rick first sees Ilsa (transcription from the sound track).

A stinger can be used melodramatically, especially as a means of demonization. An example of this occurs near the opening of Hangmen Also Die *(1945), where a particularly harsh stinger chord accompanies a shot of a portrait of Hitler. The dissonant stinger that underscores Darth Vader's initial entrance in* Star Wars IV: A New Hope *(1977) serves a similar function.*

Will (William Shakespeare, played by Joseph Fiennes) throws his manuscript on the fire. To signify its importance, the sound of the fire is sweetened by introducing it offscreen, placing it in the center channel, and mixing it at an abnormally high level. The sound increases in intensity (crackling of the paper) and volume once the manuscript ignites.

A special case of this sort of sweetening effect is the stinger, a sharp, usually dissonant musical chord (although we should note that effects, such as doors slamming or gunshots, can be used the same way). Stingers are particularly common in underscoring as a means of punctuating dialogue, but they can also provide multiple sound accents in action sequence. When used under speech, stingers can be thought of as psychological sound effects. In other words, they serve as audible metaphors of particular psychological states and as such greatly aid in reading expressions, especially facial ones. Composers are precise about the timing of stingers so as to "catch" just that right moment that opens the expression of the face to the fullest. Stingers are also used as a means of emphasizing psychological shock. As such, they are often reserved for turning points in dialogue and scenes. An excellent example of this technique occurs at a critical moment in the reunion scene from *Casablanca*, where Rick first sees Ilsa. The stinger here renders his absolute shock of recognition, whereas the fact that the chord is held manages to convey in a short span of time the extent of attraction between the two (Figure 3-16).

THE *ACOUSMÊTRE* (ACOUSTICAL BEING)

Michel Chion notes that sound film makes possible a special kind of character, one who exists in the diegetic space but is placed consistently offscreen. He calls such a character an *acousmêtre*, a French neologism that means "acoustical being."[4] Being heard but not seen, such a character is defined wholly in terms of diegetic sound. This situation is distinct from narration because the voice of the acoustical being is taken to occur in the same timeframe as the diegesis, whereas narration is necessarily after the fact, even when the voice of the narrator is also that of a character in the diegesis. The acousmêtre is also distinct from a radio voice, which may be defined solely through sound and in that sense is "acousmatic" but lacks any expectation of being visualized: the world of radio is an acousmatic world consisting only of sound, and so no character can have other than an acoustical presence.

Whereas the typical film character lives by the rules of psychological realism, the acoustical being lives outside them. In particular, a typical character has no awareness of and so no control of the camera and what the camera shows. The acoustical being, on the contrary, seems aware of the camera inasmuch as it has the mysterious ability to avert the camera's gaze, to be always just outside the frame. This ability to sense the frame so as to avoid being shown seems to endow the character with almost god-like powers. On the other hand, the acoustical being is generally represented as malevolent. The loss of its powers, through revelation of its body onscreen (what Chion calls *de-acousmatization*), undoes and destroys the malevolent *acousmêtre*. Chion points to such pathological or even psychotic characters as the child murderer in *M* (1931), the Mother in *Psycho*, and Mabuse in *The Testament of Dr. Mabuse* as the common type of acoustical being. Mabuse is a prototype of the evil genius that appears frequently in later films. Those films in the James Bond series dealing with threats of world domination or destruction often have antagonists who are revealed and gradually lose power through the process of de-acousmatization (becoming visible). Likewise, horror films often introduce their monsters as acoustical beings, and the more we see the more vulnerable they become—it is the unseen monster that is most terrifying.

Acoustical beings are not absent from musicals or comedies, where they often appear as authority figures who rule or assert control despite absence. In such cases, the process of de-acousmatization is often the process by which comedic deflation, subversion, or inversion of authority occurs, allowing the individual to escape the determinations of authority. Although represented by a giant head floating translucently in space among flames and smoke, the Wizard in *The Wizard of Oz* (1939) is in many respects an acoustical being; certainly, the revelation of the "man behind the curtain" is a particularly direct example of de-acousmatization.

Time (1): Transitions between Scenes

The sound bridge and the hard cut may be understood as opposed terms: the sound bridge effects a smooth transition by means of different kinds of overlaps, whereas the hard cut is a simple, direct cut from one scene to the next in which the change in the sound track is as abrupt as it is in the image track, sometimes disconcertingly so.

A hard cut uses sound to further mark an abrupt shift from one place and time to another. Because such moments tend to be memorable, the hard cut will probably seem familiar to most film viewers, as will the fact that sound often contributes. The alarm clock that abruptly shifts a nighttime or dream sequence to the next morning, the loud factory or ship horn that suddenly shifts location, the scream of jet plane engines on take-off or landing, a diegetic musical performance (or radio or phonograph) that enters without warning and probably *in medias res*—all these are common treatments of the hard cut intensified by sound.

The sound bridge is obviously related to the very brief overlaps that arise from an editing rule of thumb: image and sound should not be cut at the same point unless a particular effect is called for. The sound bridge can be understood as simply a longer version of these overlaps, long enough to reach the immediate consciousness of the viewer, sometimes even long enough to focus one's main attention on the overlap, thus raising questions about its narrative function. Like a simultaneous cut of image and sound, in the system of continuity editing the bridge and the hard cut are specialized devices, for both draw attention to the act of editing and therefore cannot be used freely: they need to be motivated by the needs of filmic narration or its principle of stylization.

Sound bridges are now a relatively common way to make a transition from one scene into the next. Generally speaking, bridges are most striking when they are diegetic, especially when they consist of dialogue. Nondiegetic music and voice-over narration often perform a similar function, but perhaps because they have a long history of doing so, the effect is usually less noticeable. Montage sequences, for instance, almost always use music to organize a disparate set of images into a single unit, and even films that otherwise have no music will typically employ its bridging effects for montage.

In the following sections, we distinguish between four different kinds of bridges and discuss each in turn: the advance, the lag, the link, and the match.

SOUND ADVANCE

A sound advance occurs when we hear a sound before we see its associated image. This device can be used equally well in connection with a cut or a dissolve into a new scene and may be anywhere from less than 1 second up to several seconds—in unusual cases (like two discussed later), the advance may run much longer.

Although rare before the 1960s, advances used as transitions between scenes have since become a fairly frequent occurrence. Nevertheless, the most famous single example is from the 1930s: in Alfred Hitchcock's *The Thirty-Nine Steps* (1935), a woman discovers a dead body and screams, but a train whistle is substituted for her natural voice. With a hard cut, the scene changes and we see a train blowing its whistle. Because music has commonly been used as a transition device, it was also not unusual in classic Hollywood sound film for diegetic music to appear in anticipation of the scene with which it was associated. The rehearsal scene for "It Must Be Spring" in *42nd Street* (1933) begins with the chorus singing over black briefly before the images appear. Likewise, the introduction to Kathy (Debbie Reynolds) recording "Would You" in *Singin' in the Rain* (1952) occurs over the end of the preceding scene where Don (Gene Kelly), Cosmo (Donald O'Connor), and R. F. (Millard Mitchell) devise a plan to save "The Dueling Cavalier" by turning it into a musical, "The Dancing Cavalier."

You may have noticed, in connection with the "Second Botched Meeting" from *Sleepless in Seattle* (1993), which we discussed in Chapter 1, that the map-like graphic insert that appears just after the scene ends is accompanied by speech that anticipates the next scene. The first scene ends with the cut to the graphic at 1:12:02; within 1 second or so, we hear Rosie O'Donnell's voice asking, "So then what happened?" followed by Meg Ryan's answer; at 1:12:06, the graphic "rolls up" as if it were on a map stand; the screen is black for 1 sec, then cuts to the two getting out of a car—their conversation continues at the same sound level. The suggestion created by this sound advance, combined with the dialogue, is that the "Second Botched Meeting" scene itself was a visualization of Annie's account as she told it to Becky in the car before they stopped and got out. The effect, then, is to smooth over what is, after all, a considerable break in temporal continuity (Annie had to leave Seattle and fly back to Baltimore, of course, before the conversation in the car with Becky could take place).

The opening of *Atonement* (2007) offers a lengthier instance in its bird sounds and typing noises during the opening credits. Both of these anticipate diegetic sounds: in the one instance, Briony's typing, in the other, birds heard (but not seen) singing or chirping outside the open windows to Briony's room. Note that it is possible, therefore, to have a sound advance for what eventually turns out to be offscreen diegetic (even ambient) sound.

SOUND LAG

A sound lag occurs when sound from one scene lingers over into the next. Lags are much less common than advances, probably because they tend to retard the plot rather than push it forward. The continuation of the sound across a scene change makes a connection between the scenes, to be sure, but it seems to force us to retain the old scene even as the new scene appears, creating a sense of nostalgia for the "lost" scene.

The lag is particularly effective when used to color the following scene. In *De-Lovely* (2004), the applause following "Let's Fall in Love" carries over into a scene at the Murphys' house (39:14). This scene also ends with a performance ("True Love") and applause, but the song and setting are much more domestic. Here the bridge ties these two scenes together, in the process asking us to draw a comparison between the public Cole Porter (played by Kevin Kline) and the private Cole. This is made evident by the stylistic juxtaposition of "Let's Fall in Love," which is one of his most distinctive tunes, and "True Love," a simple waltz about which Cole says, "It doesn't sound like me."

Near the end of the film, applause is once again used in a sound lag, this time moving from Cole's success with *Kiss Me Kate* to Gabe (Jonathan Pryce) and old Cole watching the scene play out in front of them (1:41:23). The old Cole's reaction to Gabe's insistence that they "move on" underscores the nostalgic aspect of the sound lag: "Please, please, let me enjoy this." (The "So in Love" sequence that precedes this [1:34:19–1:40:48] is particularly rich in the sound track qualities and devices explored throughout this chapter. Note especially the frequent use of various kinds of sound bridges and the complicated play between diegetic and nondiegetic music occasionally mediated by audio dissolves.)

SOUND LINK AND SOUND MATCH

A sound link is the use of sound to bridge a series of cuts, transforming what might otherwise seem a collection of unrelated shots. *Emma* (1996) contains an excellent example of this procedure. Emma is speaking with Mrs. Weston (Greta Scacchi) about how to tell Harriet about Mr. Elton's marriage. At the end of the scene (44:26) she says, "I suppose I'll just say, 'Harriet,'" where there is an immediate cut to the next scene with Emma and Harriet. Emma's line simply continues across the cut, "I have some bad news about Mr. Elton."

Links are quite common with music. We are already familiar with the stereotyped use of music behind montages in classical cinema. As one of many possible examples, *The Glenn Miller Story* (1954) uses a continuous rendition of "Pennsylvania 6-5000" over a montage of the band playing at various venues. Here the device is used rather simply to represent the band on tour. So-called passed-along songs in musicals, such as the opening title number from *Meet Me in St. Louis* (1944) or "Isn't It Romantic" from *Love Me Tonight* (1932), work similarly. Radio is often used in this way as well. In *American Graffiti* (1973), the radio broadcast is a ubiquitous presence, often continuing across cuts from one scene of action to another. The effect in this instance is to stitch these scenes together in terms of time: Although the scenes happen in different places, they occur at the same time.

A similar effect occurs when a sound belonging to one scene can be followed by a similar or identical sound belonging to the next. We call this a sound match. For instance, near the beginning of *The Big Broadcast* (1932), Mr. Clapsaddle (George Barbier) complains to George (George Burns), the owner of a radio station, that Bing Crosby has failed to appear for the show Clapsaddle sponsors. He demands that Crosby be fired and emphasizes his point by pounding on the desk three times. A cut to a taxi driver sounding his horn three times (in the same beat) immediately follows. The continuity of sound serves to bridge the two scenes in an unequivocal way and adds an element of humor as well.

Sound matches are not only used for comedy. In *De-Lovely*, Cole and Linda finish singing "You'd Be So Easy to Love." During the applause that follows, the sound of a galloping horse is faded in, which serves as a brief sound advance to the next scene, where Cole has a rendezvous with Boris, a dancer in Diaghilev's *Ballet Russe*. The match between the applause and the horse serves to tie the two scenes together as his two different loves.

For another example, see Figure 3-17. Early in the film, Cole sits at the piano and begins playing the introduction to "In the Still of the Night" (a). As he lands on the chord to begin the song proper, a substitution match brings a shot of hands (b) and a sound match that acts as a bridge to what appears to be a rehearsal (c). The cut here is the first of many confusions where Cole looks back on his life as though it were a musical.

a
b
c
Figure 3-17. *De-Lovely* (2004). An example of a substitution match: the hands in the middle frame, although motivated by the first image, belong to the younger Cole of the third image.

Time (2): Synchronization ("Playing with the Film")

The default case for sound in relation to the image is *synchronization*, or the appropriate temporal linking of sound to image. Synchronization plays an important role in the process of sealing our identification with a film: it aids the impression that the sound emanates from the world of the screen. This function is very similar to the carefully managed fluctuations of onscreen and offscreen sound, which also reassure us that the diegetic world exists and that the space beyond the edge of the frame can be represented. Synchronization thus stitches the diegetic world together, convincing the film viewer that it might be possible to see all of that world and to hear the sounds within it, even if the camera frame limits what we can see at any particular time.

Synchronization is also a basic means of enabling clarity. The correspondence of image and sound aids us in determining pertinence because, as a general rule, characters and objects with narrative significance (whether at the local or global level) are synchronized. We most likely wouldn't care if seagulls in the distance failed to be synchronized with the sounds of their squawking, but we would care if performers in a foregrounded musical performance or conversation are not in sync.

The degree of synchronization can vary depending on circumstances, however. Loose synchronization is usually adequate for groups of people talking at a party or in a crowd (the generic sound or generic noise we mentioned in Chapter 1). Given the mechanical limitations of recording in the early years of sound film, generic sound often lacked any attempt at close synchronization, as, for example, in the boat arrival scene early in the Greta Garbo synchronized silent film *Wild Orchids* (1929) or the previously mentioned conversation of café customers and the silverware tapping in advance of Al Jolson's first two songs in *The Jazz Singer* (1927). On the other hand, we expect close synchronization in dialogue scenes, that is, a match on the movements of a character's mouth and the words that we hear. It is true that, once rerecorded dialogue (ADR or automated dialogue replacement) became common practice, standards for dialogue syncing relaxed a bit (films in the 1950s and 1960s, in the United States and in Europe as well, sometimes test the limits of this relaxation), but the principle of close synchronization remained in force—indeed, in recent years, with digital editing technology that allows sound editors to stretch and compress the length of phonemes at will, synchronization is generally extremely tight, even with rerecorded dialogue.

Occasionally, a film uses effects of synchronization as part of its narrative theme. *Singin' in the Rain*, to cite one of the most famous examples, acknowledges the fictional unity of synchronization and foregrounds the technical work that is required to obtain that synchronization. Both technology and technique falter in Don and Lina's first attempt to make a talking picture. In terms of technology, the recording apparatus proves inadequate and at the screening the film slips out of synchronization. In terms of technique, the screenplay is inappropriate, and Lina (Jean Hagen) has difficulty mastering the microphone. These deficiencies prove to be inspirational. When Cosmo lip-syncs Kathy singing "Good Morning," he demonstrates that "faulty" synchronization can be used to create its own fiction. Cosmo's "performance" allows us to recognize that the technology does not in any sense compel a body to sing with its own voice. Nothing in the technology in and of itself constrains a particular relation between image and sound.

The surprising ability of technology to split body and voice only to reassemble them otherwise is demonstrated in the sequence built around the song "Would You." The song opens with a sound advance from the previous scene, which motivates a cut to Kathy singing. This moment of synchronization initiates a series of links: Kathy records the song, her performance is displaced to a phonograph record to which Lina attempts to synchronize her lips, and the perfect mating of Lina's body to Kathy's voice as the filming dissolves into the finished film. The continuity of the sound track, in this case the song, serves as a means of tying together into a single thread the discontiguous space and time of the images. In other words, Kathy's voice must be disembodied before it can be placed on Lina's body, thereby creating the heroine of "The Dancing Cavalier." Despite this feat, the film ultimately suggests that *proper* synchronization must rather exclude the appearance of this phantasmatic body; the unity of body and voice in the character should naturally reproduce that of the actor. In other words, the fact that Kathy's voice can be moved and shifted into Lina's body to produce the splendid appearance of that phantasmic body, the perfect success of the synchronization in "The Dancing Cavalier" (the first talking picture with Lina and Don), poses an ethical problem. If technology allows the voice and body to be separated and reassembled in essentially any way, *Singin' in the Rain* ultimately asserts a *moral* obligation to reproduce a proper, natural unity. (The moral point of the film is extremely ironic given that Hagen rather than Reynolds looped in Lina's character's spoken lines in "The Dancing Cavalier" and that "Would You" was sung not by Reynolds, but by Betty Noyles.)

Another way of thinking about synchronization is in terms of empathy, or emotional engagement. When the sound track is coordinated with the image track, following and emphasizing the mood of onscreen characters and action, we can describe the effect as empathetic or engaged. Like synchronization itself, the empathetic is the default case for most narrative cinema. Certainly we expect that voices will speak in ways appropriate to the apparent emotions of the characters and that ambient sounds will help rather than hinder (quiet effects in subdued scenes, accents in scenes of tension, etc.).

Overwhelmingly, music in both classic and contemporary Hollywood sound film is empathetic and coordinated with the scene. In one now very familiar example, the "Second Botched Meeting" from *Sleepless in Seattle* follows closely in tempo and mood the changing feelings of Meg Ryan's character (note, however, that dialogue synchronization is questionable for the other characters in that scene—do Tom Hanks's lips move at all when he says "Hello"?).

On the other hand, music can be empathetic yet threaten to lead us out of the scene by adding new information or, more likely, by so exaggerating its presence that it defamiliarizes the action, turning mythic. In *Empire of the Sun* (1987), for example, the final scene at a Shanghai stadium, as British citizens prepare to depart "upcountry" near the end of World War II, brings the death of one of their number, a Mrs. Victor (Miranda Richardson), and the young Jim (Christian Bale) at that moment sees a bright light flash across the sky. He takes this to be Mrs. Victor's soul departing into the ether, and the music does nothing to dissuade us from believing him. Not long thereafter, we learn that the light came from the second of the American atom bombs dropped on Japan. This suggests that irony is not only the property of music that "plays against" but can emerge in an even more powerful way from (deceptive) empathy.

Time (3): Counterpoint ("Playing against the Film")

If sound can play "with" a scene, in synchronization, then one has to assume that it also has the potential to play "against" a scene, an effect that is sometimes referred to by the term *counterpoint* (not to be confused with the same word used for texture: we prefer to reserve *polyphonic* for references to a lively, complex texture). As with synchronization, we can think of counterpoint in two different ways: either the *failure* of temporal synchronizing of image track and sound track elements, or the creation of an emotional *distance* of sound from image.

The first of these—inadequate temporal synchronizing—is amusingly familiar from overdubbed, translated dialogue in Japanese horror films of the 1950s; but "failed" synchronization of dialogue and mouth movements can also be used to defamiliarize speech, as in Elia Kazan's *East of Eden* (1954) and, rather later, in Clint Eastwood's spaghetti westerns, such as *The Good, the Bad, and the Ugly* (1966) and, especially, *Once Upon a Time in the West* (1968).

These two effects—humor and defamiliarization—are the two primary results of failed synchronization at this level. Music and sound effects can do this, too, but they require unusual emphasis and perhaps for that reason are employed for this purpose far less often than speech. Examples include inappropriate sound effects (a sheep quacking), a delayed rimshot for humor, and an obvious and prolonged mismatch of a performer's physical motions and the resulting music (although this last is perhaps more often the result of production failures—the inability of actors to imitate performers' motions accurately—than it is a deliberate device). Consider the sound advance from *The Thirty-Nine Steps* that we mentioned earlier in this chapter: the initial moments, while we see the woman screaming but hear the train whistle, are counterpoint: the image and the sound don't match, even if the latter is similar to what we would have expected naturally. Jean-Luc Godard often uses sounds in this way, as when an apparently unmotivated boat horn blares out against a shot of a young woman on a Paris street (it turns out this is a sound advance, but we do not realize that until 30 seconds later) in *À bout de souffle* (*Breathless*, 1960), or when we hear sounds of seagulls' cries against an image of a nighttime Paris street in *Prénom Carmen* (*First Name: Carmen*, 1983).

Sounds or music that are emotionally distanced are anempathetic, or not in empathy with the image track. A simple example would be a sad or distraught person in the midst of a happy, celebrating crowd—clearly, the generic sounds of the crowd do not match the mood of the character. A nondiegetic pop song in a mood, or with lyrics, that contradict a character's feelings or speech would be another common example. Near the end of *Catch Me If You Can* (2002), Frank has escaped from the airplane as it lands in New York and has made his way to his mother's house, where she lives with her second husband and their young daughter. It is Christmas, and Frank approaches the house in the snow; inside, the house is well-appointed, and out of its warmth the daughter gazes at him with silent curiosity. He sees his mother sitting on a couch, and her contented pleasure when the spouse enters. Christmas music plays, rather too loudly; with one barely noticed exception, the camera jumps back and forth between inside and outside views, as if to emphasize Frank's isolation. Here, the music plays strongly against Frank's emotions, but it is important to note that the sharp dissonance between music and image is closely tied to narrative, as he (and we) quickly realize that his mother is happy and that he cannot be a part of her new life.

This example from *Catch Me If You Can* shows the active sense of "playing against" the image: the music not only contradicts Frank's feelings but seems to mock them. It is also possible to have "neutral" music, or music that is indifferent to the scene, neither significant to its narrative nor emotionally engaged—in other words, music that functions much like ambient or environmental noise. A band playing in the background of a club scene will often act neutrally (as in those parts of the casino scene from *The Big Sleep* [1946] other than Bacall's numbers, or many of the numbers in the lengthy first part of *Casablanca*, which consists of a series of scenes all taking place in one evening at Rick's *Café Américain*).

A neutral music, whether diegetic or nondiegetic, can continue without paying any heed to emotional nuance; if it continues long enough, we are encouraged to ignore it as a kind of aural wallpaper. On the other hand, neutral music can turn in a flash into aggressive counterpoint with the image or close empathy. For example, neutral carnival (circus) music can suddenly turn empathic if a melody strongly associated with a character or couple appears, or intrusive and even unnerving if the volume suddenly rises substantially or if a familiar and upbeat melody is played against some emotional anguish in a character or couple or against physical violence. For some treatments of music in circus scenes, see *A Streetcar Named Desire* (1951), *Strangers on a Train* (1951), *Tarnished Angels* (1958), and *Der Himmel über Berlin* (*Wings of Desire*, 1987).

During [a] cabaret scene, while the jazz orchestra is playing, if the daughter is notified of her father's death, it would be absolutely wrong to change from the hot tune in progress to music appropriate to her mood. We must consider the jazz orchestra as actual music, not as underscoring; and, in order to make this sequence realistic, we should contrive to make the music as happy and noisy as possible. For, in the first place, the orchestra leader does not know what has happened, and would, therefore, have no reason to change his music; and, second, no greater counterpoint has ever been found than gay music underlying a tragic scene, or vice versa.
—Max Steiner[5]

Writing Task #1: How to Write a Synopsis

The chapters and exercises of Part I have supplied some tools for basic analysis of the sound track, and Part II provides two additional chapters to guide you to write effectively about it. One skill that is absolutely essential to writing about film is the ability to formulate succinct synopses of the films. This section presents advice and models for producing synopses.

In a paper on a film, an effective, well-written synopsis does not serve merely to summarize a film, although it needs to do that as well; like any summary, a synopsis should also introduce the film on the terms you want to discuss it. The opening statement of a synopsis should get across basic information about the film (director, title, date of film, actors' names) and anticipate an important theme:

> **Opening Template**   Directed by <NAME OF DIRECTOR>, <NAME OF FILM> (<YEAR OF FILM>) tells the story of <BRIEF SYNOPSIS>.

For a model, let's use that template to create an opening sentence for a synopsis to *Catch Me If You Can*. This statement is from the synopsis that opens the general introduction to this book.

> **1**   Directed by Steven Spielberg, *Catch Me If You Can* (2002) tells the story of Frank Abagnale, Jr. (Leonardo DiCaprio), who runs away from home rather than face the trauma of his parents' divorce and his father's (Christopher Walken) slow financial ruin.

Note, first, that this statement attempts to summarize rather than recount, and, second, that it already hints at a complex of general themes of the film: Frank's close, if troubled, relationship with his father and his penchant to run away from trouble. This statement also leaves the implication that these two themes are related and that the film will work through them.

If the film focuses on a central character, as in the case of *Catch Me If You Can*, one effective strategy for the second sentence is to move from the general thematic level to specifics of that character. This statement is again drawn from the synopsis that opens the general introduction.

> **2**   Frank is a risk-taker, who discovers that he has innate talent for imitating professionals (airline pilots, doctors, and lawyers), and he develops great skill in forging checks.

By focusing on Frank's character in this sentence, the synopsis suggests that the theme of the film is intimately connected with the development of Frank's character. We learn that Frank's running away has, by the time of the main action of the film, become an integrated element of his character, as he is an expert at the illegal activities of impersonation and forgery. This film, in other words, is a character-driven drama, and the film's theme will take shape through the transformations of Frank's character traits and his relationships with other characters.

The next sentence will typically convey something about the general narrative arc or goal of the film and perhaps mention anything remarkable about the storytelling. This statement is based on the one that opens the general introduction but gives a somewhat different emphasis by shifting the character name from Hanratty to Carl.

> | 3 | The story, told mostly in flashbacks, is about FBI agent Carl Hanratty's (Tom Hanks) campaign to capture Frank, who spends several years in prison; but eventually Carl persuades the FBI to hire Frank to solve check forgery cases.

The mention of flashbacks acknowledges a distinctive aspect of the way this story is told. Although not explicitly mentioned in the synopsis, the technique of flashback is closely related to Frank's character development: the trauma of his parents' divorce, his running away, and illegal activities are all shown in flashbacks, whereas his capture, recognition of family issues, and ultimately his reform as he bonds with Carl are all shown in normal temporal order. The connection of this part of the story to the larger theme—Carl taking the place of Frank's father, allowing Frank to reset his moral compass—is stated only implicitly here. You may want to keep the theme implicit for papers that are primarily descriptive, since an explicit statement of the theme generally promises some interpretation based on it, which may detract from your descriptive aims.

> | 4 | Aside from the flashbacks, the storytelling is generally straightforward rather than ambitious, and [in this paper I argue that] the sound track follows suit in being dominated by speech and music.

A full synopsis might then run:

> Directed by Steven Spielberg, *Catch Me If You Can* (2002) tells the story of Frank Abagnale, Jr. (Leonardo DiCaprio), who runs away from home rather than face the trauma of his parents' divorce and his father's (Christopher Walken) slow financial ruin. Frank is a risk-taker, who discovers that he has innate talent for imitating professionals (airline pilots, doctors, and lawyers), and he develops great skill in forging checks. The story, told mostly in flashbacks, is about FBI agent Carl Hanratty's (Tom Hanks) campaign to capture Frank, who spends several years in prison; but eventually Carl persuades the FBI to hire Frank to solve check forgery cases. Aside from the flashbacks, the storytelling is generally straightforward rather than ambitious, and the sound track follows suit in being dominated by speech and music. (131 words)

An interpretive paper, by contrast, requires a thesis statement that draws in the theme more overtly:

| 4A | [In this paper I argue that] Carl's changing place in Frank's life is reflected in the handling of music over the course of the film. |

Or:

| 4B | [In this paper I argue that] John Williams's score contributes significantly to representing the transformation of the relationship between Frank and Carl, where Carl's role changes from being Frank's antagonist to becoming a substitute father figure. |

We can abstract templates for presenting a basic interpretive thesis:

| Thesis Templates | <THEME> is reflected in the handling of the music over the course of the film. |

<COMPOSER'S> score contributes significantly to representing <THEME>.

A full synopsis that sets up an interpretation based on music underscoring the changing relationship between Frank and Carl is shown here:

> Directed by Steven Spielberg, *Catch Me If You Can* (2002) tells the story of Frank Abagnale, Jr. (Leonardo DiCaprio), who runs away from home rather than face the trauma of his parents' divorce and his father's (Christopher Walken) slow financial ruin. Frank is a risk-taker, who discovers that he has innate talent for imitating professionals (airline pilots, doctors, and lawyers), and he develops great skill in forging checks. The story, told mostly in flashbacks, is about FBI agent Carl Hanratty's (Tom Hanks) campaign to capture Frank, who spends several years in prison; but eventually Carl persuades the FBI to hire Frank to crack check forgery cases. John Williams's score contributes significantly to representing the transformation of the relationship between Frank and Carl, where Carl's role changes from being Frank's antagonist to becoming a substitute father figure. (136 words)

A Note on Writing about the Sound Track

As with any other kind of writing, the way an essay on film sound or film music is shaped—in its design, in the information it provides, and in its argument—will vary according to the author's goals. In general we can say that essays will usually fall into one of three broad categories: analysis, criticism, or interpretation. For a class, you might be asked to produce a scene analysis (see Chapter 6) or a screening report that characterizes the sound track for a whole film (see Chapter 8). Or you might write a short response paper (similar to an essay question on an exam) that summarizes music's narrative functions in a film (see Chapter 8 for this, too) or that compares the treatment of sound or music in two films or two scenes (see Chapter 10). (Less likely is a response paper that asks for your personal opinion of a film—but we do explore that in Chapter 10 as well.) In Chapter 15, we bring all of these steps together to show how you can develop an interpretive essay on a film's sound track.

The published critical literature includes evaluative reviews of sound track CDs and, occasionally, significant mention of sound and music in journalistic film reviews. The general literature also includes interviews with sound designers, composers, and other film professionals. Finally, scholarly articles range from archive studies to historical narratives to interpretive essays that may be informed by theoretical, literary, or narratological models. The advanced student who wants to make sound or music the focus of his or her work needs to know something of narratology, literary theory, and the historical and interpretive traditions of film studies and music studies.

There are many readily available examples of reviews and journalistic writing on film music, but fewer on film sound in general. In that connection, it is important to understand that the term *soundtrack recording* or *soundtrack album* does not in fact refer to a recording of the film's sound track but to a recording of some or all of its music. When LP recordings of film sound tracks became common in the early 1970s, they normally consisted either of a film's nondiegetic orchestral music or of its songs in popular or jazz idioms, but rarely both. In more recent years, the contents of soundtrack CDs have become more diverse, consisting sometimes of the orchestral cues, as in earlier decades, sometimes of a mixture of orchestral cues and songs (or older recordings quoted in the film) that were used either diegetically or nondiegetically, and sometimes only of songs and related performances.

The purpose of a CD review of a soundtrack recording is the same as a film reviewer's task in a review of current theater or video offerings: to give a lively, brief account of the contents, to assess the technical quality of performance and recording, and to offer an evaluation that might guide the reader's decision to purchase the item. One of the curious features of CD reviews is that they often make little mention of the film from which the music is derived. Although that may seem strange at first, it becomes understandable if you remember that the average fan does not need a review of the recording—he or she will buy a soundtrack CD based on a liking for the film. It is the soundtrack collector who typically reads CD reviews, and he or she buys sound tracks for reasons that might include fondness for the film but are more likely to be related to building a broad-based or carefully specialized but comprehensive collection, or else preference for a composer, genre, or even orchestra and conductor (in the case of newly performed suites or re-recorded classical sound tracks).

We will not discuss the writing of CD reviews further in this book. Instead, we will concentrate on class reports and papers, including descriptive and interpretive essays that approach their topics in ways similar to the articles found in scholarly journals.

Summary

In this chapter we covered sound in relation to the physical space of the filmic world and then turned our attention to the temporal relations of sound and image. In the three sections on space, we paid particular attention to the (surprisingly complex) relations between sound in the sound track and the physical world or diegesis represented through the narrative. The distinction between diegetic and nondiegetic refers to this anchoring of sound in the filmic world (or, in the nondiegetic, the failure to be anchored in that world). Another pair, onscreen/offscreen, refers more narrowly to sound anchored in what the camera frames for us at any given moment (onscreen) or that we can reasonably assume belongs to space we can extend from what we see (offscreen). In the three sections on time, we discussed the formal effects of scene transitions that manipulate sound (sound bridge) and the close (or loose) coordination of sound and image (synchronization)—and its opposed term, the deliberate juxtaposition of sound and image (counterpoint). We also discussed synchronization and counterpoint in terms of what we might call narrative or emotional dissonance (another common meaning of "playing with" or "playing against" the film). We concluded with advice on writing a synopsis and with an overview of types of papers you might be asked to produce.

TWO

Music and the Sound Track

FROM THE BEGINNING TO 1975

Introduction to Part II

Music has been in the movies forever. Or, at least since 1895, the traditional date for the beginning of the cinema. In December of that year, the Lumière brothers in Paris gave a public showing of a film projected on a screen, and that showing was apparently accompanied by a piano, though we don't know what music was performed. Photography, of course, was invented much earlier in the century, but the celluloid backing that allowed one to make reliable long strips of photos for projection was only invented by George Eastman in the late 1880s. It was natural for the Lumiére brothers to assume that their film would have musical accompaniment—they wanted it to be taken seriously, as a theatrical event, and since music was a standard component of stage productions it was also used for higher class photographic shows and similar events. Music is required in opera and operetta, of course, but it's easy to forget that melodrama and serious dramatic stage plays in the late 1800s routinely had music, too. For example, one of the most familiar pieces of nineteenth-century concert music—the two *Peer Gynt* suites of Edvard Grieg—originated as incidental music for Ibsen's play of that name.

The dramatic feature film developed after World War I, in a firmly established studio system that enabled the production of 1- to 2-hour long films with well-developed stories. These films used continuity editing, that complex art of framing and editing of many shots that we all take for granted but which requires the skills of the cinematographer and picture editor, the artistic control and vision of a director, and the financial resources gathered by a producer. That system also enabled a flourishing music composition and publication industry that supplied works for performances, which were not only remarkably varied in the kinds of music that were played but also in the ensembles, which could range from a solo pianist or a violin-piano duo to a forty-piece orchestra. Experiments with reproduced sound—playing recorded music with a gramophone—were made repeatedly throughout this period but were hampered by inadequate amplification, even in small theaters.

Sound was added to the mix in the late 1920s, and it was in this "transitional cinema" that studio producers, directors, composers, and sound technicians worked out the basic practices in film sound and film music that remain largely in force today. The transition years are usually taken to be 1927 to 1932: in 1927, the first feature film was released with at least some synchronized sound, Warner Brothers' *The Jazz Singer* (in which Al Jolson says "You ain't heard nothin' yet" and sings "Toot, Toot, Tootsie, Goodbye"); and by 1932 sound engineers had invented effective postproduction mixing and rerecording technology. For music, we should expand the range just slightly, from 1926 to 1935: in 1926, Warner Brothers released *Don Juan*, a silent film with a complete, recorded orchestral music track, mixed with very few sound effects, and the program also included a number of shorts with synchronized sound; in 1935, Max Steiner's music for John Ford's *The Informer* won the first Academy Award for Best Original Score for a Dramatic Picture. Therefore, the year 1935 might be taken as the inauguration of the modern era of feature film: cinematography and postproduction film editing had already matured in the 1920s; by 1935, both of cinema's basic elements—image track and sound track—were functioning together in the now familiar manner.

Thus, the heterogeneous venues and practices of the early cinema (which we discuss in Chapter 4) gave way to a rapid series of technological changes in the first few years of sound film (Chapter 5) and an aesthetic "follow-up" in the standardization of studio practices for sound film (Chapter 7). Chapter 6 is the first of the book's three chapters that combine readings of important films with instruction in analysis and writing. Here we discuss film form and show how to analyze and write up a description of a film scene, for which we use as our example *The Broadway Melody* (1929), which won the second Academy Award and the first for a sound film. Chapter 8 expands the analysis to an entire film—*Mildred Pierce* (1945)—and shows how to build on that information to write a response paper on music and narrative or a compare/contrast paper that focuses on music. (Chapter 15 in Part III is the last of the three writing chapters.) Chapters 9 and 10 pick up the story of the classical studio era again, tracing events in the immediate post–World War II era and into what is referred to as the "post-classical" era. Beginning no later than 1950, major shifts in film aesthetics occur, partly driven by the adoption of widescreen ratios, partly by competition with television, which drove studios to make greater and greater efforts to distinguish their products, and partly by economics, as the largest studios were forced to divest themselves of the theater chains on which they had depended for reliable income streams. With these changes also came some marked shifts in the range of musical styles—especially the introduction of jazz and contemporary atonal musics into the underscore. Surprisingly, however, the treatment of sound technology remained conservative, despite advances such as magnetic tape and stereo sound. Another important factor in this period is the internationalization of sound film production. Part II stops at the early 1970s, just before a major development in sound technology—the introduction of Dolby stereo—quickly stimulated practices that we recognize as modern sound design and that led eventually to the characteristics of contemporary digital sound production and postproduction.

From 1895 to 1929
Music and Sound in Early Film

Introduction

Irving Thalberg's remarks in the sidebar reflect a very common viewpoint: it has often been asserted that silent film was never truly silent. Presentations from the earliest days typically included some form of musical accompaniment, although the manner of that accompaniment varied widely, depending especially on place of performance and time of day. For example, a vaudeville theater, the dominant venue for exhibiting motion pictures before the rise of the nickelodeon, would be more likely to have musical accompaniment than would a tent show, which might have only an automated drum for ballyhoo—if that; but even in theaters dedicated to motion picture exhibition, the first show of the day and the dinner show would occasionally be run without accompaniment even as late as the 1920s. As another example, early sound practice was more likely to include substantial sound effects than was later practice, which tended to restrict effects to key narrative moments (thunderclaps, the fateful knock on the door, etc.). Finally, it was common for certain films, such as the popular travel documentaries, to be accompanied by live narration, a mode of presentation that did not disappear until as late as the 1960s; and, although we usually think of 1927 as the initiating moment of the sound film, successful, if commercially unviable, attempts to synchronize film and recorded sound go back to the earliest days of film.

The sound practice of the silent era divides into roughly three phases: (1) early cinema, 1895–1905, where the sound practice was extremely heterogeneous, almost wholly determined locally and by venue; (2) the nickelodeon, 1905–1915, a transitional phase when sound was first institutionalized as a specifically cinematic practice and determined more and more by the institutions of cinema exhibition; and (3) the picture palace, 1915–1929, the mature period of the silent film, when relatively homogeneous performance was expected, as

There never was a silent film. We'd finish a picture, show it in one of our projection rooms and come out shattered. It would be awful. We'd have high hopes for the picture, work our heads off on it, and the result would always be the same. Then we'd show it in a theater, with a girl pounding away at a piano, and there would be all the difference in the world. Without that music, there wouldn't have been a movie industry at all.
—Irving Thalberg (Producer)[1]

determined by the multireel feature film and a sound practice weighted heavily toward music; also in this period the theaters were highly stratified into various levels of performance, for each of which specific kinds of musical performances were required.

The Early Years

In early cinema, sound practice was mediated by venue, which is another way of saying that the cultural and commercial institutions of cinema did not yet exist to regulate its own sound practice. Consequently, music and sound were used in a manner in keeping with the place where an individual film was shown. A vaudeville theater, for instance, would treat a film as an "act," and, insofar as we can tell, the music was generally chosen to accord with similar, live vaudeville acts (see Figure 4-1; here the picture is a dance act). A speaker in a lecture hall, by contrast, might use film as a substitute for magic lantern slides, and music would be adapted to this situation; most probably it would be used in the familiar

Figure 4-1. This ad is for a vaudeville exhibition of the Vitagraph in 1896. The conductor is watching the screen, the orchestra is clearly playing, and it seems likely they would have been playing music appropriate for the dance act depicted. As such acts would have been usual vaudeville entertainment, this scene does not tell us how, or whether, a vaudeville orchestra would have accompanied a scenic—say, a film of a train or pictures of the seashore.

manner of the popular stage melodrama—for introductions, entr'actes, exit music, and so forth. Traveling lecturers such as Lyman Howe, on the other hand, placed great emphasis on the realistic use of sound effects. So did Hale's Tours, an early, dedicated film exhibition venue introduced at the St. Louis World's Fair in 1904 and made up to look like a train car. Effects included hydraulic lifts to simulate motion, realistic train sounds, and in some cases even a short run of track to help create the illusion of actual train travel. With this conceit of a train ride, Hale's Tours obviously left little room for musical practice. This attraction, which was generally positioned in amusement parks and theatrical districts, proved quite popular until the rise of narrative films. The nickelodeons, which quickly eclipsed other venues for cinema, were cheaper to build and more adaptable to the narrative film, whereas Hale's Tours seemed best suited to the exhibition of travelogues, especially, of course, those shot from trains.

The Nickelodeon

The nickelodeon's origin was the storefront theater; these first began appearing in appreciable numbers around 1905 and were often located, as were the vaudeville theaters, near transportation hubs at the edges of major retail areas. Indeed, in the early days the shows were often known as "mechanical vaudeville." Figure 4-2 shows a basic floor plan for a small nickelodeon. The typical

Figure 4-2. Nickelodeon theaters. (a) Plan for a typical storefront theater, c. 1911.   a | b
(b) Photograph of a storefront theater as seen from the back of the room. Note that the piano in the corner is not well positioned to see the screen.

theater held between two hundred and three hundred spectators (the plan shown in Figure 4-2 accommodates 192), and a characteristic program consisted of two or three reels of film (each reel was one thousand feet long and might take anywhere from 10 to 18 minutes to run, depending on the projectionist, the size of the crowd outside, and the policy of the theater); the intervals between reels were usually filled with some form of live entertainment, such as a brief illustrated lecture or an illustrated song.

Illustrated songs were a particularly common part of the program. Film historian Richard Abel notes that many theaters featured their live singers as prominently as films in advertising for their shows.[2] As the name implies, illustrated

Figure 4-3. These images are from paper proofs of an illustrated song slide set for "In My Merry Oldsmobile" (1905) sent to the U.S. Copyright Office in 1907. The actual lantern slides used for exhibition would likely have been hand colored, and a slide with the full chorus would have been included at the end. Many theaters would sell sheet music of the day's songs, and song publishers would pay for the singer in larger theaters as a means of plugging the song.

songs were popular songs accompanied by a set of lantern slides, which were often richly colored. The singer would sing two verses and two choruses, and then the audience would be encouraged to join in on a final chorus (see Figure 4-3). Frequently criticized as shoddy and indecent, the illustrated song nevertheless maintained a strong presence on the program until the mid-1910s, when the emergence of the multireel feature encouraged most theaters to invest in a second projector. The added equipment facilitated the film showing by eliminating the interval for changing reels but therefore also eliminated the performance niche for illustrated songs.

In addition to the singer, the musical forces were usually a pianist, occasionally a small orchestra in larger theaters, or sometimes just a phonograph in smaller ones. Many theaters featured large phonographs or mechanical pianos at the entrance specifically to hail passersby (ballyhoo); in the smallest theaters this might be the only music. Besides the illustrated song, music within the theater was also used as entrance and exit music to distract the audience as it filtered in and out of the crowded theater before and after the films, and as an attraction in its own right. Music was also commonly—but not always—played while the film was screened (see Figure 4-4). Initially, then, music was not understood so much as an accompaniment to the film as an "added attraction." In most theaters the

Figure 4-4. *Those Awful Hats* (1909). Notice the piano player in the lower right corner. This film is a humorous short reminding women to remove their hats. It is akin to contemporary trailers reminding us to turn off our cell phones.

music would have consisted of a series of popular hits in ragtime style; but other theaters used classical music as a way of attracting a particular class of patronage. In either case, music was considered foremost a diversion for the ear that complemented the screen's entertainment for the eye. The musicians sought to engage the audience by offering variety to the program. Consequently, except when music was used as a sound effect, such as to accompany a scene of a dance, coordinating music to the film was not a high priority.

Sound effects, which had already been used to accompany films in vaudeville houses and on lecture programs such as those of Lyman Howe, became more common in theaters specializing in motion picture exhibition as the size of these theaters and their number began to increase around 1908. In a period when demand for films far outstripped supply, theaters across the street from one another might easily end up with the same film on their programs. Along with special musical offerings, the illusion of synchronized sound effects was one way for a theater to distinguish its shows from those of other nearby theaters (see Figure 4-5).

"PLAYING THE PICTURE"

Although nickelodeons included all sorts of pictures on their programs, narrative film was the mainstay. Over the period, these films grew both longer and more complex in their storytelling. In 1905, stories rarely filled a single reel; by 1915, the production of feature films of modern length was already becoming standardized. As the films became more ambitious, theater owners realized that audiences appeared more engaged when music and sound seemed attuned to the story. (Another way to put this might be that film viewers were intuitively recognizing—or being encouraged to recognize—the validity and force of Chion's notion of an audiovisual contract.) Although it was admitted that the audience might prefer the sounds of ragtime music in general, this amusement now became something of a problem if it served to distract the audience from the story and made the musician seem indifferent (anempathetic) to the plight of the characters. Simply put, music that did not support the narrative often made it difficult to follow the story, and, consequently, musicians were increasingly urged to "play the picture."

This radical aesthetic change shifted priority from entertaining the audience to accompanying the film: conceptually, music now played to the screen rather than to the audience. Previously, attracting notice (drawing the audience into the theater) had been one of the primary goals, but now, to keep that audience, the music could not be allowed to become an obstacle by distracting attention away from the pictures. Over and over again, trade papers criticized musicians for giving concerts rather than "fitting" or "synchronizing" music to the film. As the poem in the text box illustrates, the trade papers were merciless in ridiculing musicians who seemed indifferent to the film, especially those who played nothing but ragtime. Whereas ragtime and popular song had dominated

A Practical Demonstration

of the simplicity and effectiveness of the Yerkes'
Sound Effects for Moving Pictures

Audience delighted with the absolute realism
of the show

YERKES & CO.

53 West 28th Street   **New York City**

Phone 594 Madison Square

SEND FOR ILLUSTRATED SOUND EFFECT LIST

Figure 4-5. Ad for Yerkes' Sound Effects. The three sound effects operators (they were usually called "drummers") are working behind the screen, where their equipment would be out of sight. This was the recommended placement for sound effects. The musicians, by contrast, were almost always placed in the theater, where they would remain, to some extent, visible to the audience. In the 1920s, the bigger theaters placed the musicians on hydraulic lifts that could lower the orchestra into the pit below the sightline for screening the film but also raise them to stage level for highlighted performance opportunities such as the overture.

in the early nickelodeon years, light classical and melodramatic mood music were now seen as the creative solution to playing the pictures, especially for the multireel dramatic features that became the main attraction by the mid-1910s. This is not to say that popular music disappeared from the program; its use was widespread in comedies, for instance, where musicians frequently drew on the frenetic pace of popular dance music to match the action. Any scene featuring contemporary dancing would almost certainly require popular music, and films set in a modern urban environment were amenable to such treatment as well. Thus, that variety of musical expression that we characterized early on in this book with the assertion that "film music is any music used in a film" can be seen to have been a characteristic trait of commercial film exhibition from the beginning.

> Lizzie plays at the nickelo—
> Plays for the moving picture show,
> All the time her fingers go
> With an endless whirl and a rhythmic flow
> And a ceaseless flitting to and fro;
> She fakes and vamps till her hands get cramps
> And there is no tune that she does not know;
>
> With a tum-te-tum and an aching thumb
> She keeps the time with her chewing gum,
> She chews and chaws without a pause,
> With a ragtime twist to her busy jaws,
> And her fingers fly as the hours go by;
> She pounds the keys with a languid ease
> Till the folks go home and the pictures cease;
>
> But Lizzie plays like a grim machine,
> And she never thinks what the measures mean,
> For she's played them oft and the notes don't waft
> Any thought to her that is sweet and soft. . . .
> —Wilbur D. Nesbit, "Lizzie Plays for the Pictures" (1911)[3]

Coordinating music and story was by no means a simple task. Some musical selections were obvious—soldiers suggested the style topic of a march, a dance scene suggested a waltz, tango, or one-step—but it was not always so clear what to play in other, less strongly profiled situations, especially as most theaters continued to favor a repertory of popular song where possible. Three methods were tried—using song titles as "links" to film content, classical music for drama, and musical topics and moods borrowed from stage melodrama. As we shall shortly see, the last of these proved most effective—although all three continued as practices into the sound era.

One method was to select music on the basis of appropriate titles. For the film *Statue Dog* (1910), for example, one writer made the following musical suggestions: "When the title 'A Rah Rah Boy' comes on you play 'He's a College Boy' or 'College Boys,' then comes a title '2 A. M.,' you can play 'We Won't Go Home Until Morning,' and when the title 'Kelly' comes on you can play 'Has Anybody Here Seen Kelly?'"[4] This remained a standard approach to accompany comedies throughout the silent era. It was a different matter with dramas, where such choices often had the unfortunate effect of parody. One trade paper, reasonably enough, was very critical of a pianist's decision to play "No Wedding Bells for Me" to accompany a scene where a man mourned his wife's death.[5] This parodic practice was known as "funning" or "guying" a film and, although common, was generally reproved, because it ran contrary to the intention of the film. More often, however, the problem was that the title in the song seemed irrelevant to the event on screen: playing "Where the Shannon River Flows" when a character named Molly Shannon appeared on screen, for example, made little sense even for those who knew the lyrics, because the character and the river have nothing but a name in common. The result of that choice might be confusion, because attention would be focused on unimportant details.

Dramas, especially tragedies, and historical pictures posed even more of a challenge to song title accompaniment. In the case of tragedy, the bright, up-tempo sound of ragtime was deemed inappropriate if not outright callous to the sentiment of the sorrowful stories; in the case of a historical setting, the contemporary sound contradicted the image in a way that many found bothersome. Some observers, including musicians, saw such films as opportunities for "bettering" the musical taste of the audience and therefore urged the use of classical music. Generally speaking, then, the music for main features was typically heavier (more classical), as was felt appropriate for dramatic action, but it was also more disjointed because of the increased responsibility to synchronize with the unfolding action.

Besides classical music, stage music based in the melodrama tradition offered another obvious alternative to song titles as a guide to accompaniment choices, and in fact that repertory would ultimately prove the basis for the dominant practice (or what we referred to as the principle of synchronization in Chapter 3). The number of musicians with requisite experience was quite limited in the early 1900s, however, and the exceedingly rapid expansion of the nickelodeons thus insured that the vast majority of theaters would be staffed by musicians with little or no training in theater music. This deficiency was addressed in a number of ways. Beginning in 1909, the Edison Company began releasing "musical suggestions" to help pianists and musicians with the difficult job of finding suitable music. Each film was broken down into scenes, with appropriate music listed for each. Table 4-1 gives an example of the *Edison Kinetogram*'s suggestions for *Frankenstein* from March 1910.

When trade papers began adding columns on music soon after, cue sheets of this sort featured prominently there as well. Although programs on the whole

Table 4-1 *Frankenstein* (1910). Musical suggestion from The *Edison Kinetogram*, 15 March 1910 (vol. 2, no. 4).

Note in particular how the cue sheet associates music from Weber's *Der Freischutz* with the monster. "Annie Laurie" is likewise connected with the heroine. The way these two themes are used suggests a rudimentary leitmotivic conception. Stage melodramas often followed a similar strategy, and such simple associations of themes with characters remained a common means of devising accompaniments throughout the silent-film era.

At opening.	Andante ([Balfe] "Then You'll Remember Me")
Till Frankenstein's laboratory.	Moderato ([Rubenstein] "Melody in F")
Till monster is forming.	Increasing agitato
Till monster appears over bed.	Dramatic music from [Weber] *Der Freischutz*
Till father and girl in sitting room.	Moderato
Till Frankenstein returns home.	Andante ([Scott] "Annie Laurie")
Till monster enters Frankenstein's sitting room.	Dramatic (*Der Freischutz*)
Till girl enters with teapot.	Andante ("Annie Laurie")
Till monster comes from behind curtain.	Dramatic (*Der Freischutz*)
Till wedding guests are leaving.	Bridal chorus from [Wagner] *Lohengrin*
Till monster appears.	Dramatic (*Der Freischutz*)
Till Frankenstein enters.	Agitato
Till monster appears.	Dramatic (*Der Freischutz*)
Till monster vanishes in mirror.	Diminishing agitato

changed too frequently during the nickelodeon period for cue sheets to have practical value on a large scale, they proved pedagogically useful in that they taught players how to think of music in terms of dramatic classification, that is, in terms of the style topics or musical "moods" that we discussed in Chapter 1. In particular, these cue sheets frequently used terms such as *hurry, lively, plaintive,* and so forth, which alerted musicians not trained in the stage tradition to the existence of this sort of functional music, and by extension how to recognize these functions in music not specifically written for the stage. Regular tempo indications likewise carried melodramatic conventions. In the *Frankenstein* cue sheet, for instance, *moderato* and *andante* suggest functions of "neutral" music and "heroine" (or "love theme"), respectively; these are common tempo designations for these functions. So, among other things, the cue sheet for the 1910 *Frankenstein* tells us that Rubinstein's Melody in F can be construed as a species of neutral music. Similarly, many allegros could be substituted for a hurry— indeed, sometimes a hurry was simply listed as an allegro on a cue sheet.

By necessity, the musical suggestions tended to be rather general, focusing on broad functional categories, or naming extremely well-known exemplars (Liszt's

"Liebestraum," for instance). The point of these suggestions was not to insist that other musicians follow them slavishly; rather the idea was that the individual musician could use them as a general guide, substituting suitable numbers from his or her own library for the sake of variety, taste, or accessibility. Clearly, this system required that players have a well-rounded library catalogued by dramatic function. Around 1910, one writer offered the following advice for compiling such a library:

> A few marches and waltzes, though these are indispensable, are not sufficient. Long *andantes* such as [Schumann's] "Träumerei," [Lange's] "Flower Song," [Braga's] "Angel's Serenade" and the like are useful. The intermezzo, valse lento and gavottes make convenient "fill-ins" where the scene is neutral yet the general character of the picture is subdued or pathetic. Religious music, national airs (of different countries), Oriental music and dances are frequently called for. Popular songs are useful, especially in sentimental pictures and comedies. . . . Your library should also include some melodramatic music, such as mysterious, *agitato*, "Hurrys" for combats, storms, fire scenes, etc.[6]

The size and refinement of an adequate library grew quickly. About this same time, music written specifically for use in movie theaters began appearing, as did catalogues of pre-existing music, much of it from the standard classical repertory, organized according to dramatic function. Figure 4-6 shows the first few entries for two categories in Lyle C. True's *How and What to Play for Moving Pictures: A Manual and Guide for Pianists* (1914). Note especially the mixture of classical composers like Mendelssohn, Beethoven, and Chopin, with composers whose music was popular at the turn of the century, such as Benjamin Godard and Anton Rubinstein. Note also that the publishers are listed at the right (C. F. is Carl Fischer, for example) to facilitate ordering the music.

"Playing the picture" usually meant using a compilation of such pieces. Musicians favored music that was sectional, with frequent cadence articulations, and amenable to repetition of sections. This form was preferred because it allowed the music to be adapted more easily to the varying length of film sequences. Most music composed for silent film was structured in this way. Figure 4-7 is an example of a hurry from 1913.

Some players favored improvisation to playing from score, in part because it offered obvious advantages in terms of matching music to the scene. At the same time, improvisational skills were not easily acquired. Some theaters also preferred performances of classical music because it helped to draw a particular kind of audience; improvisation, by contrast, lacked the same force of cultural prestige. Most players had a repertory of memorized music they could draw on—and more easily modify—when they needed careful coordination with the picture. In practice, improvisers frequently quoted folk tunes, national airs, and similar familiar works, whereas those playing from score limited themselves to improvising transitions from one piece to the next.

Very Dramatic or Agitated Scenes
Heavy Drama

The Flight No. 24. Song without wd's	Mendelssohn	Wood
The Wanderer, No. 10 " "	"	"
Le Cavalier Fantastique	Godard	C. F.
Chaconne	Durand	C. F.
Crescendo	Lasson	C. F.
Bedouin Love Song	Pinsuti	Cent.
Over the Steppes	Schytte	C. F.
Pensiero Lugubre	Coop	C. F.
I Love Thee. Song	Sobeski	D. Co.
1st Movement Sonata Pathetique	Beethoven	Cent.
Prelude, op. 2, E min.	Chopin	Cent.
Erl King	Schubert	Cent.
Brooklet in the Woods	Spindler	C. F.
Istorietta	Lack	C. F.
L'Automne	Niedermeyer	Sch.
Le Lac	"	Ash.
Marcel	Godard	C. F.
Czardas	Delibes	C. F.
Commotion op 47 No. 5	Heller	C. F.
Bolero de Concert	Vivien	C. F.
Non e ver	Mattei	C. F.
Polonaise, op. 26, No. 1	Chopin	Cent.
The Fleecy Cloud op 53 No. 2	Mendelssohn	Wood

Plaintive or Romantic Music for
Love Dramas

Placida. Tone Poem	Keiser	W. W.
Thou Art Like Unto a Flower. Song	Rubinstein	Cent.
Nachtstuck, op. 23, No. 4	Schumann	Cent.
Lost Melody	Bell	Wit.
Song of the Soul. Song	Breil	Chop.
On Wings of Love	T. Bendix	Witt
Cavatina	Raff	T. P.
It Was a Dream. Song	Lassen	Cent.
Prelude, op. 28, 3 and 4	Chopin	Cent.
Good Bye. Song	Tosti	Cent.
Still As The Night. Song	Bohm	Cent.
Traumerei & Little Romance	Schumann	Cent.
Serenade	Schubert-Heller	Wood
Farewell	"	G. S.
Ave Maria	"	G. S.
Warum (Why)	Schumann	Cent.
It Was Not Thus To Be. Song	Nessler	Cent.
Evening Hour	Kussner	K.
Don't You Mind The Sorrows. Song	Cowles	D. Co.
Au Matin'	Godard	Cent.
Solvejg's Song, op. 55, No. 4	Grieg	C. F.
Chanson de Florian	Godard	Cent.
Love Song	Henselt	Cent.

Figure 4-6. Lyle C. True, *How and What to Play for Moving Pictures: A Manual and Guide for Pianists* (San Francisco: The Music Supply Co., 1914). The first few entries in two categories. True lists seventeen pages of music for different topics and scenes. He concludes by saying that "there is so much good music of this type that the improvising of the average pianist would suffer by comparison."

Figure 4-7. J. S. Zamecnik, "Hurry Music." This is a typical piece of cinema music from 1913. Note that the music is modular, which gives it great flexibility in terms of how it might be performed. It not only contains an opening repeat and reprise (*D. C.* means "go back to the beginning") but also a number of other internal stopping points (cadences), which are indicated by the arrows. These are places a pianist might easily use to jump to a different piece when a scene changed—or the pianist might play through the piece (or one of its sections) more than once for added length. Most music written for the silent cinema was composed with this sort of modular structure to allow for easier synchronization with the action.

The job of "playing the picture" was a strenuous one. Programs rarely stayed longer than a week. In smaller theaters, the entire program was commonly changed daily to encourage—and reap the profits of—habitual patronage. The standard program during the period was three reels of film, an illustrated song or two, and perhaps a vaudeville act, which required music to cover entrance and exit even in those cases where the act itself did not need support from the theater musician(s). The piano player was expected to play as necessary for the film, the songs, and the acts, to provide entrance and exit music between the shows, and even to have music ready to dissipate audience panic in case of an incident (fires were a common occurrence in theaters at the time, and nickelodeons were particularly susceptible to panics because of highly flammable nitrate film stock as well as narrow aisles and inadequate exits).

Throughout this era, musicians complained bitterly that they did not have sufficient time to prepare the shows, that they would only infrequently have an opportunity to screen the program before they had to play it, and that consequently requiring them to play the picture in anything but the most rudimentary fashion was simply demanding the impossible. The following account from 1914 illustrates how a typical small-town program was put together:

> We try to "play to the picture" so far as we are able and manage to play a pretty fair class of music as well. But it is a pretty hard matter sometimes to fit the picture as we know it should be done, for the reason that there is so little time. Our house gives evening shows only. Four reels—usually three shows nightly. Change the bill every day. The first show we "dope out" the music—roughly of course, that is more in the nature of a rehearsal than anything else. The second show is played just about as we first laid it out. The third show we smooth up the rough spots—and then it is time to go home. Just about the time we are ready to play the picture the way we think it ought to be played, it is time to quit.[7]

As film companies began shifting toward the long multireel feature, the situation grew worse, as the practice of a daily change remained in place in most small theaters but the film program seemed to grow ever longer. Depending on the venue, the singer was displaced by extra reels of film, by vaudeville, or by intricate stage shows, and the whole program grew steadily in length toward the 2- to 2½-hour standard of the picture palace era.

SPECIAL SCORES

Throughout the period when the nickelodeon dominated film exhibition, decisions about music and sound were in the hands of the theater owners and staff, rather than the studios. Nevertheless, the studios recognized the importance of the accompaniment, and the dissemination of cue sheets was one way they attempted to influence how their films were presented. Some film companies went a step further and even tried distributing music along with the films. In 1908, Camille Saint-Saëns composed an intricate score to the art film *L'Assassinat du duc de Guise*. Its premiere in Paris anticipated the careful, fully worked out scores of the 1920s, and the original performance itself followed Wagner's custom in concealing the orchestra from view, a device that deluxe picture palaces would attempt to imitate in the 1920s. The precedent of the Saint-Saëns score had no direct impact on American exhibition practice, however, as, for unknown reasons, the film circulated without the score in the United States. More typical was the Kalem studio's experiments, beginning in 1911, with the regular release of what came to be known as "special scores" composed for its major films. These were modest piano scores of discrete pieces; the effect was similar in many respects to an accompaniment based on a cue sheet.

Special scores never became the dominant means of providing films with music during the silent era, as they posed a number of difficulties to theaters. Three sorts of challenges were particularly significant. First, the musical ensembles of nickelodeons were by no means standard. Even in those places dedicated to playing the picture, one theater might have only a pianist, whereas another had an orchestra—and the music would have to be quickly adaptable to any group. Second, censorship was not uniform across the nation, meaning that scenes might have to be omitted in some locales. Scores would have to be modified accordingly. Finally, as mentioned earlier, rehearsal time was practically non-existent during the nickelodeon period. It was far easier for musicians to work with pieces in their own library than to learn music that they would be able to use only for a single film; this would particularly be the case for any theater working with a daily change of program.

Toward the end of the nickelodeon period, long, multireel features began to appear regularly. These films were for the most part not distributed through nickelodeons, however; they were more likely to be treated as road shows to be played in legitimate or standard theaters with larger orchestras, special scores, and prices scaled according to the venue. This was the case, for instance, with *The Birth of a Nation* (1915). Unlike the intense pressure on musicians in the nickelodeons, the road show offered, from the musicians' point of view, a more familiar and amenable mode of work, very similar to a theatrical show or opera. Joseph Carl Breil's score for *The Birth of a Nation* set the standard for this sort of production. The music is partly original and partly compiled, and the whole is carefully coordinated with the film. Breil borrowed traditional songs and marches but also such orchestral excerpts as Weber's *Freischütz* Overture and Wagner's "Ride of the Valkyries." Breil himself considered the score Wagnerian because he composed a number of themes that he used as leitmotifs for many of the characters. The musical roots of Breil's themes, however, often lay closer to popular song than to classical music or melodrama. Indeed, as Figure 4-8 shows, his love theme was close enough to a sentimental ballad that it was fit with lyrics and became a hit as "The Perfect Song." A number of the other cues in Breil's score were also drawn from such popular song genres as waltzes and tangos.

Figure 4-8. Sheet music for Joseph Carl Breil's "Perfect Song." This is the leitmotif Breil composed as the love the theme for Elsie and Ben. It proved to be a significant hit and is an early example of music being used as a source of ancillary income (note that the music is copyright by David W. Griffith Corporation). As the cover indicates, the piece was available in six separate arrangements: song, piano solo, cello and piano, small orchestra and piano, large orchestra and piano, and band. The song would later be resurrected to serve as the theme for the immensely popular *Amos 'n' Andy* radio show in the late 1920s.

a
―
b

The Picture Palace

STRATIFICATION OF EXHIBITION

When most of us think of silent-film exhibition, we probably have in mind the picture palace—a large, well-appointed theater with a large orchestra and a Mighty Wurlitzer organ. In fact, these venues dominated exhibition only in major metropolitan areas, and many of the largest and most famous theaters did not appear until the very end of the silent era, when most were built, paradoxically enough, already wired for sound. Although by the late 1920s picture palaces were responsible for capturing the majority of the revenues for film exhibition, the absolute number of deluxe theaters was quite small compared to the vast number of smaller, more modest theaters located in outlying neighborhoods and small towns. In these venues many of the exhibition practices of the nickelodeon, with at best a small "orchestra" of a handful of players or perhaps nothing more than a phonograph, continued well into the 1920s. Something along the line of deluxe performance was achieved by the occasional employment of small-time vaudeville acts, in addition. The relatively small size (and modest revenues) of such theaters, however, made actual deluxe performance prohibitively expensive. The result was that neighborhood and, even more so, rural theaters were hardly able to compete effectively with large downtown theaters for the middle-class audience that was the key to leveraging large profits.

Exhibition practices thus became more and more stratified as the size of the theater—and so also the expenses that it could support—increased rapidly through the 1920s. This trend toward increasing largess of the deluxe theaters culminated in the 5,920-seat Roxy Theatre in New York, run by its namesake, Samuel L. "Roxy" Rothafel; this included among its musical features fourteen grand pianos spread throughout the building and three separate organs: a massive theater organ and two smaller organs to provide music in the lobbies and foyers. The main theater organ had three separate consoles, which would appear to rise spectacularly out of the abyss of the orchestra pit on hydraulic lifts. Radio City Music Hall, another theater built to the specifications of Rothafel, was in many respects the swansong of the picture palace era, as the conversion to mechanical sound and the upheaval of the Great Depression made the economics of live acts in large movie theaters less and less tenable.

THE SHOW

Modeled on high-class vaudeville houses, the picture palace began emerging around 1910, at the same time that "playing the pictures" gained ascendancy. During the first half of the 1910s, theaters routinely changed back and forth between featuring vaudeville and film exhibition as the primary attraction; and it was out of this intersection that the picture palace aesthetic, which combined film and live performance, was born.

If the illustrated song had largely disappeared as an expected part of exhibition practice with the arrival of the multireel feature and a second projector, live performance—really an extension of the vaudeville aesthetic—continued to dominate in that the "show" was often considered more important than the picture. The firm of Balaban and Katz, which would grow from a modest set of theaters in 1916 into a widely imitated large chain of picture palaces that formed the basis of Paramount Publix in 1926, established the high reputation of its theaters through the production of elaborate shows. Prior to its merger with Lasky-Famous Players (Paramount), Balaban and Katz was unaffiliated with any of the major film production companies, and because it could not guarantee the quality of the pictures in its theaters, the firm devised an exhibition strategy that minimized the importance of any particular film. In a Balaban and Katz theater, it was not the picture per se, but the distinctiveness of the "show"—which included the picture only as a part in the whole. The audience attended for the entire experience—in addition to the performances, the look of the façade and marquee, the appointments of the lobby and auditorium, and the smart discipline

Table 4-2 The Rules of Conduct for Orchestra Members from the *Manual of Instructions and Information for Publix Theatres Employees* (1926).

Music Department

Orchestra

Members of the orchestra are under the direct supervision of the Orchestra Contractor who is held responsible for the conduct of the personnel. In most cases the Conductor or Orchestra manager is the Contractor.

1. All conversation in the orchestra pit is forbidden.
2. No musician is expected to be looking at the stage or screen at any time while the orchestra is playing.
3. Members of the orchestra are expected to refrain from all noise-making during the performance.
4. The chewing of gum, tobacco, or smoking while in the pit will not be tolerated.
5. No pencil other than a soft black lead pencil will be used for marking music.
6. A prompt response to the bell for rehearsals or performance is expected from each member of the orchestra.
7. When the tuning bell is struck, get the pitch immediately, preluding or improvising is absolutely forbidden.
8. Every member of the orchestra must be ready to play when the performance or rehearsal is called. All tuning or fixing of instruments must be done before this period. This applies especially to wood wind players and to string players.
9. No one is to leave the orchestra pit or rehearsal room during a performance or rehearsal without obtaining the permission of the Conductor.
10. In entering and leaving the pit be exceptionally careful to prevent the creating of any noise or unnecessary disturbance.

of the ushers and other theater personnel were all crucial components of the "show." (Table 4-2 is a section of the Publix Theaters training manual applying to the music department.)

The model for Balaban and Katz's success was Rothafel (Figure 4-9), better known simply as "Roxy," who had in many respects pioneered this approach while managing a series of theaters in New York City during the 1910s, most notably The Strand, the Rivoli, and Rialti. Among other things, Roxy emphasized lush interior decoration of both theater and lobby space, a trained, uniformed, and courteous staff, and many amenities, all of which were specifically

Figure 4-9. Samuel L. Rothafel, better known as "Roxy."

designed to make the spectator feel pampered. Already in 1910, even before moving to New York, he had declared:

> The secret of the successful motion picture theatre of the future will be the ability of the management to make the people forget that they are witnessing a motion picture, to make them forget that they only paid you five or ten cents to witness the performance.[8]

Roxy believed that a proper musical atmosphere was the key to such "forgetting," and thus to the success of any show. He therefore continually improved his theaters by investing first and foremost in music, adding elaborate theater organs, hiring top-flight musicians, and increasing the size of the orchestra to the limits of what theater attendance could support. (Both the Roxy Theatre and Radio City Music Hall were his.) The idea was to be able to present a musical program that could serve as a feature in its own right. Roxy was known particularly for his staging of spectacular finales, what became known as the "Roxy finish."

Although, strictly speaking, the central piece of such exhibition remained the long feature, the "show" was based around a program where that feature was balanced by live performance and shorter films. The basic aesthetic of the program was variety, consistent with the idea of the elaborate and popular revues of impresarios such as Florenz Ziegfeld. The programs often, although not always, followed a theme drawn from the feature (see Figure 4-10). A typical program would consist of an overture, the feature, several short films (usually including a comedy and a newsreel), and a variety of live performances.

MUSIC AND SOUND PRODUCTION IN THE PICTURE PALACE

Music was fundamental to the picture palace, perhaps more so than even the film itself. For music was present not only for the film: it also accompanied most of the live acts and often served as an act in its own right. The importance of music can be measured in its cost to the theater: in the late 1920s theaters expected expenses for musicians' salaries alone to equal that of the film service.

Music featured prominently in the architecture of the theaters as well. The pit was a major architectural consideration, and by the 1920s the pits were generally placed on hydraulic lifts, which would allow the orchestra to be raised or lowered depending on the portion of the program—stage level for the overture, below eye level for the film, and so forth. Organ consoles—often there were multiple consoles—were treated similarly. One common theatrical trick was to have the Mighty Wurlitzer emerge from the depths of the pit, with lighting effects adding to the spectacle. These organs were often exceptionally large and were equipped not only with standard organ stops but a whole battery of sound effects as well. Beyond the music in the auditorium, some theaters had pianos or occasionally even a small organ installed in the lobby to provide music for patrons as they waited to be seated.

Because of the importance of music to the show, the position of music director was a powerful one in the picture palace, perhaps more powerful than any

Hugo Riesenfeld was lauded for his ability to choose the right music for the right mood. The process was laborious: along with the conductor and a pianist, he would painstakingly select music segment by segment, trying various tempos against the film. For him, the key to finding the perfect music was "having an ear for subjugation," or knowing which pieces were pleasing but not so striking as to distract from the image. Riesenfeld would then spend several hours splicing film and fiddling with frame speeds so that the picture would fit his accompaniment appropriately.
—See Scott T. Buhrman, "Photoplays De Luxe," in Cooke, *The Hollywood Film Music Reader.*

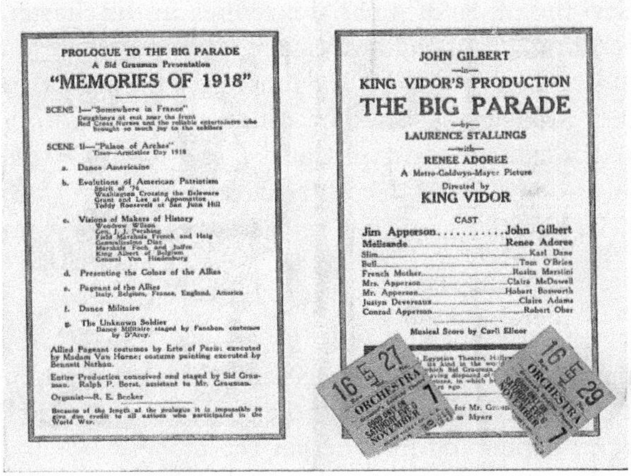

PROLOGUE TO THE BIG PARADE
A Sid Grauman Presentation
"MEMORIES OF 1918"

SCENE I—"Somewhere in France"
Doughboys at rest near the front
Red Cross Nurses and the reliable entertainers who brought so much joy to the soldiers

SCENE II—"Palace of Arches"
Time—Armistice Day 1918

a. Dance Americaine

b. Evolutions of American Patriotism
Spirit of '76
Washington Crossing the Delaware
Grant and Lee at Appomattox
Teddy Roosevelt at San Juan Hill

c. Visions of Makers of History
Woodrow Wilson
Gen. J. J. Pershing
Field Marshals French and Haig
Generalissimo Diaz
Marshals Foch and Joffre
King Albert of Belgium
General Von Hindenburg

d. Presenting the Colors of the Allies

e. Pageant of the Allies
Italy, Belgium, France, England, America

f. Dance Militaire

g. The Unknown Soldier
Dance Militaire staged by Fanchon, costumes by D'Arcy.

Allied Pageant costumes by Erte of Paris: executed by Madam Van Horne; costume painting executed by Bennett Nathan.

Entire Production conceived and staged by Sid Grauman. Ralph P. Borst, assistant to Mr. Grauman.

Organist—R. E. Becker

Because of the length of the prologue it is impossible to give due credit to all nations who participated in the World War.

JOHN GILBERT
—in—
KING VIDOR'S PRODUCTION
THE BIG PARADE
—by—
LAURENCE STALLINGS
—with—
RENEE ADOREE
A Metro-Goldwyn-Mayer Picture
Directed by
KING VIDOR

CAST

Jim Apperson	John Gilbert
Melisande	Renee Adoree
Slim	Karl Dane
Bull	Tom O'Brien
French Mother	Rosita Marstini
Mrs. Apperson	Claire McDowell
Mr. Apperson	Hobart Bosworth
Justyn Devereaux	Claire Adams
Conrad Apperson	Robert Ober

Musical Score by Carli Elinor

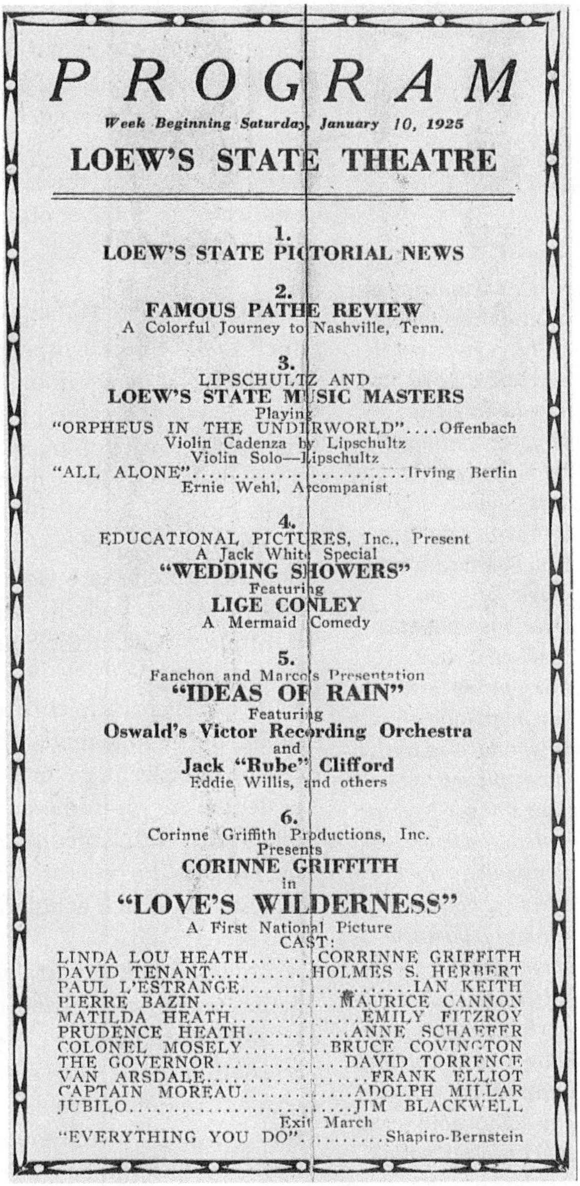

PROGRAM
Week Beginning Saturday, January 10, 1925
LOEW'S STATE THEATRE

1.
LOEW'S STATE PICTORIAL NEWS

2.
FAMOUS PATHE REVIEW
A Colorful Journey to Nashville, Tenn.

3.
LIPSCHULTZ AND
LOEW'S STATE MUSIC MASTERS
Playing
"ORPHEUS IN THE UNDERWORLD"....Offenbach
Violin Cadenza by Lipschultz
Violin Solo—Lipschultz
"ALL ALONE"........................Irving Berlin
Ernie Wehl, Accompanist

4.
EDUCATIONAL PICTURES, Inc., Present
A Jack White Special
"WEDDING SHOWERS"
Featuring
LIGE CONLEY
A Mermaid Comedy

5.
Fanchon and Marco's Presentation
"IDEAS OF RAIN"
Featuring
Oswald's Victor Recording Orchestra
and
Jack "Rube" Clifford
Eddie Willis, and others

6.
Corinne Griffith Productions, Inc.
Presents
CORINNE GRIFFITH
in
"LOVE'S WILDERNESS"
A First National Picture
CAST:

LINDA LOU HEATH	CORRINNE GRIFFITH
DAVID TENANT	HOLMES S. HERBERT
PAUL L'ESTRANGE	IAN KEITH
PIERRE BAZIN	MAURICE CANNON
MATILDA HEATH	EMILY FITZROY
PRUDENCE HEATH	ANNE SCHAEFER
COLONEL MOSELY	BRUCE COVINGTON
THE GOVERNOR	DAVID TORRENCE
VAN ARSDALE	FRANK ELLIOT
CAPTAIN MOREAU	ADOLPH MILLAR
JUBILO	JIM BLACKWELL

Exit March
"EVERYTHING YOU DO".........Shapiro-Bernstein

Figure 4-10. (a) Program for the Egyptian Theatre's presentation of *The Big Parade* (1925). Although the film had a special score prepared by William Axt and David Mendoza, Sid Grauman, like many silent-film impresarios, preferred to have a score put together by his theater's musical staff. Grauman, like Roxy, was renowned for his elaborate programs, and Grauman was especially known for his extended prologues. This one, as was usually the case for Grauman, was linked topically to the film. The two attached ticket stubs indicate that the theater used reserved seating much like live theater. (b) Program for Loew's State Theatre in Eureka, California. The program here is much more modest than the Egyptian's, and there is a far greater proportion of film on the program—two newsreels and a short (two-reel) comedy in addition to the feature. Fanchon and Marco was a production company that supplied dance acts to vaudeville and movie theaters, particularly on the West Coast.

a | b

other than the general manager. Indeed, music directors frequently served as managers. Hugo Riesenfeld, for instance, was in charge not only of the music but also of general operations of the Rialto, the Rivoli, and the Criterion in New York. Often, the conductor had final authority over projection speed—the podium was usually equipped with a signal to the booth that allowed the conductor to call for a change in projection speed—and could even mandate editing of the film to insure proper synchronization between music and film.

The music director oversaw the range of musical activities in the theater. These activities included rehearsing, acquiring and cataloguing music, fitting music to the film, laying out the musical portion of the program in consultation with the general manager, hiring musicians, assistant conductors, and librarians. The size of the music staff was dependent on the size and nature of the theater. In the most prestigious theaters, the staff consisted of multiple assistant conductors, arrangers, organists, librarians, and the musicians of a large symphony orchestra.

FITTING THE PICTURE

Much as was the case in the nickelodeon period, compilations and improvisation were by far more common than original scores, and these different approaches often shared the same program, depending on whether the orchestra or the organist was playing. In general, an organist would play the lunch, dinner, and late night shows. Even during the regular shows, the organist would assume duties during the union-mandated break times. Not only would the orchestra and organist split duty over the various shorts (comedy, newsreels, etc.), but quite often they would share responsibility for scoring the feature as well. One common division of labor was having the orchestra begin and end the film but take a 30-minute break in the middle where the organ would assume the duties of accompanying.

The basic principles of accompanying films with compilations or improvisation did not change markedly from the nickelodeon era. Compilations continued to enjoy the advantages of cultural prestige, a more predictable accompaniment not dependent on immediate inspiration, and a wider range of coloristic possibilities (although large theater organs could by the 1920s rival and in some ways even surpass the orchestra in this respect). Improvisation, by contrast, promised the ability to match action far more precisely than an orchestra playing a compiled score could.

Quite apart from differences in the precision of synchronization, the compilation and improvisation methods addressed the film with somewhat different aesthetic emphases. Because a compilation score was assembled from pre-existing music, the chance of consistently matching action at a close level of detail was remote; consequently, pieces were chosen primarily on the basis of the appropriateness of the mood for that particular sequence. Following the fluctuation of these moods was the aesthetic foundation of the compilation score; matching action, especially using thematic variations to underscore changes in the situation of the main character, was the foundation of improvisation. Nevertheless, in practice, improvisation and compilation did not lead to radically different results. The musical language of both was derived from popular song, waltzes, marches, melodramatic, and other incidental music. In the case of the compilation score, the choice of mood was most often based on considerations of character; and, in the case of improvisation, one of the major considerations in working out a variation was fitting the theme to the proper mood.

Max Winkler was an early entrepeneur of the cue sheet (he even claimed to have invented it). Los Angeles filmmakers relied heavily on music publishing companies on the East Coast to supply music for them, a relationship that reached its apex when producers began making efforts to standardize the music played with their films. Given the high demand and companies' rapid rate of production, Winkler's business boomed and he was able to outsource work to various little-known American and European composers. The establishment of synchronized sound technology led to a swift collapse of the cue sheet industry in the late 1920s.
—See Max Winkler, "The Origin of Film Music," in Cooke, The Hollywood Film Music Reader.

THE SYNCHRONIZER
By M. L. Lake

SIX SYNCHRONIZING SUITES FOR MOTION PICTURE SETTINGS IN LOOSE LEAF FORM
A complete library of Incidental Music in six volumes. Each Suite provides all the necessary material for any given picture. Individual movements of any Suite may be used independently for any motion picture situation.

THE PLAN OF THE SYNCHRONIZER

Suite No. 1. General Use   Suite No. 4. Spanish-Mexican   **EACH OF WHICH CONTAIN**
Suite No. 2. General Use   Suite No. 5. General Use   **FIVE MOTIFS AS FOLLOWS:**
Suite No. 3. Oriental-Indian   Suite No. 6. General Use

MAJOR LOVE MOTIF
To announce the entrance of the Heroine or Hero; also to predominate in normal (or joyous) scenes wherein these characters appear.

MINOR LOVE MOTIF
To announce the entrance of the Heroine or Hero; to predominate in pathetic scenes wherein these characters appear.

SINISTER MOTIF
To announce the entrance of the "Heavy" (Villain).

AGITATO (based on Sinister Motif)
To predominate in scenes wherein the Heavy appears.

HURRY OR FURIOSO (based on Love and Sinister Motif)
To predominate in scenes wherein the Heavy and the Heroine or Hero appear.

PRICE OF EACH SUITE: Piano Part, 40c; All Other Parts, 20c Each; Piano Solo, 75c

Figure 4-11. Ad (from the 1920s) for music especially composed to be used in silent-film performances. Each suite not only presented the basic motifs as themes but also developed them into hurries, agitatos, and pieces of other melodramatic function. This would allow the music director to create a score that seemed better integrated musically. According to the ad copy, music for any one of these suites would be sufficient to accommodate the needs of most feature films of its type—though the scores would still require filling out with other numbers.

By the 1920s, compilation had become a fine art, and a whole industry had developed around the practice. An ever-increasing amount of "photoplay" music was commissioned and published in appropriately catalogued collections and series—see Figure 4-11 for a characteristic example. The music here is offered in suite form, as a single-volume collection, and each suite includes "all the necessary material for any given picture." The major music publishers produced catalogues of their music—not just "photoplay" music—organized by appropriate moods. The facsimile from the first page of Erno Rapee's *Encyclopedia of Music for Pictures* (1925; see Figure 4-12) is similar to Lyle True's catalogue from a decade earlier, but note that classical composers are now missing and that many of the pieces obviously belong to series ("Agitato no. 20," "Furioso no. 11"). Rapee has parsed his list by three specific functions: "heavy" for the most serious situations, "light" for those that tend to the comedic, and "medium" (others use the word *neutral*) for general accompaniment without a specific emphasis. This additional level of categorization, meant to reflect differences in the intensity of mood in a scene, was very common throughout the silent era.

AGITATO

(H)	Before Titles — means	"HEAVY"
(L)	" " "	"LIGHT"
(M)	" " "	"MEDIUM"

Title		Composer
(H)	AGITATO No. 37 (For Fights and Riots)	*Andino*
(M)	AGITATO ALLEGRO No. 8.	"
(M)	DESCRIPTIVE AGITATO..	*Boehnlein*
(M)	AGITATO IN D MINOR	"
(L)	RHYTHMIC AGITATO	"
(M)	AGITATO No. 20	*Borch*
(L)	LIGHT AGITATO	"
(H)	TURBULENCE	"
(M)	AGITATO No. 10	"
(H)	HEAVY AGITATO No. 12 ..	"
(H)	MOURNFUL AGITATO	*Hilse*
(M)	DRAMATIC AGITATO No. 1 (For General Use)	*Hough*
(L)	ALLEGRO AGITATO No. 1 (For General Use)	*Kiefert*
(M)	AGITATO No. 6 (Angry Discussion or Riot)	"
(H)	FURIOSO No. 11	"
(M)	TREMBLING AGITATO ...	*Kilenyi*
(H)	FURIOSO No. 1	*Levy*
(L)	AGITATO No. 69 (Scenes of Tumult)	*Minot*
(H)	FURIOSO No. 60	*Shepherd*
(M)	AGITATO No. 49 (For General Use)	"
(H)	DRAMATIC AGITATO	*Ketelbey*
(H)	AGITATO FURIOSO	"
(H)	MOLTO AGITATO	*Breil*
	(A) STORMS—AGITATOS, FIRES—EXPLOSIONS,	
	(B) CONSEQUENT MOB EXCITEMENT, followed by	
	(C) VICTORY OR RESCUE.	
(H)	ALLEGRO AGITATO	"
	A—Hurry For Races, Runways, Speeding Trains with	
	B—Sudden Crash or Stop...	
	C—Consequent Disaster or Quieting of Excitement	
(M)	MOLTO AGITATO	"
(H)	MOLTO AGITATO No. 5 ...	"
(L)	MISTERIOUS FURIOSO	*Langey*

Figure 4-12. Erno Rapee, *Encyclopedia of Music for Pictures.* This is an excerpt from the section "Agitato."

In conjunction with the studios, those same publishers offered cue sheets, which suggested appropriate music from that particular publisher's catalogue. These cue sheets would be distributed with the picture or published in various trade papers and were the primary way studios attempted to assert some control over the musical accompaniment. Figure 4-13 is the first page of a cue sheet for *Coney Island* (1928). In this case, the film's distributor, FBO, which sent films mainly to unaffiliated theaters in the midwestern United States, was responsible for the cue sheet. Note the mix of popular songs and characteristic pieces: a new foxtrot by Irving Berlin (1), a "galop" (an old dance) that could have been called a hurry or comic hurry (2), an agitato (3), a one-step (a more rapid late-nineteenth-century dance that could also be a hurry) (4), a "grotesque" or mysterioso also marked as a theme (5), a schottische (old-fashioned dance that could be "comic") (6), the love theme, a waltz and also a recently copyrighted song (7), and another light comic cue (8).

The *Coney Island* cue sheet is more complex than most, but with its recently copyrighted Irving Berlin numbers, it does participate in one of the music promotion practices common in this period: the "theme song," an early attempt to realize synergies between the film and music industries. In this practice, the compiler of the cue sheet suggested a theme, sometimes something classical, sometimes an original theme written specifically for the film. If a theme proved popular, it might be fitted with lyrics and sold as sheet music that made an explicit tie-in to the film.

Tensions between the music and film industries in the late 1910s and 1920s prevented full exploitation of the potential synergies. The American Society of Composers, Authors and Publishers (ASCAP) had won a ruling in 1917 that required theaters to pay a "music tax" if they wanted to use music by any of its members—and these included the best known song composers of the day, such as Irving Berlin and Victor Herbert. Theaters could avoid the tax by using music that was out of copyright or by buying music from publishers who sold music with performance rights included. The ASCAP "tax" therefore prevented many theaters from using music specifically associated with the film. Nevertheless, the financial success of the title song to *Mickey* in 1918 suggested that linking film and popular music systematically could be very profitable, and many songs from the time featured covers with pictures of stars or a

Figure 4-13. The first page of a studio-issued cue sheet for *Coney Island* (1928). Note that someone (music director, pianist, or organist) has marked dates of performance in pencil at the upper left.

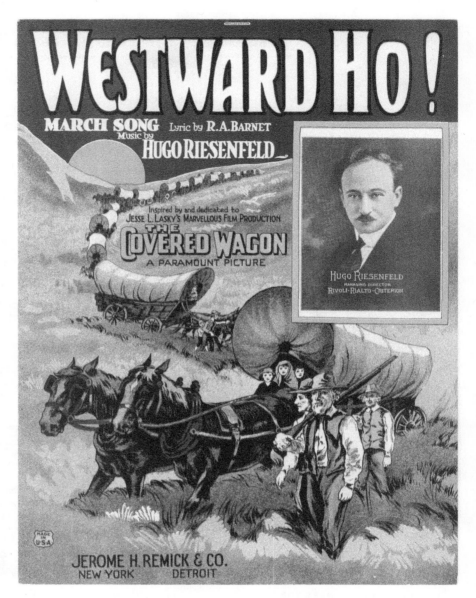

Figure 4-14. Hugo Riesenfeld was hired by Rothafel to conduct the Rialto orchestra. When Rothafel left to take over the Capitol Theatre, Riesenfeld assumed Rothafel's role as general manager of the theater as well as the Rivoli. Later he added the Criterion. Riesenfeld provided scores, usually a combination of compilation and original composition, for a number of major films, including *Covered Wagon* (1923) and the American release of *Siegfried* (1924). His scores for both these films were recorded and distributed using the Phonofilm process. With the coming of sound, Riesenfeld went to Hollywood as music director of United Artists, where he arranged music for films such as *Hell's Angels* (1930) and *Abraham Lincoln* (1930).

scene from the film as a selling point (see Figure 4-14). In the 1920s, most film studios purchased chains of theaters to serve as guaranteed exhibition outlets for their films, and one way they managed the risk of this so-called vertical integration of their business was to acquire music publishers so that they would have better control of the music as well. It was at this point, toward the end of the silent era, that theme songs proved immensely profitable. Erno Rapee's "Charmaine" from *What Price Glory?* (1926) sold well over a million copies, as did his theme for *Seventh Heaven* (1927).

Cue sheets were often less than optimal: compilers usually worked for music publishers, and their suggestions reflected this fact. Many complained that the cue sheets often were nothing but a form of advertisement (the *Coney Island* cue sheet raises that suspicion). Also, especially in the early years, compilers sometimes worked without having had a chance to see the film, meaning they had to rely on timings and a synopsis provided by the studio. Given that the interest of the compiler was not always in making the best accompaniment for the film, it is hardly surprising that many theaters simply disregarded the suggestions, although the music directors probably found the timings useful as a starting point.

In the larger theaters, the music staff took great pride in assembling accompaniments. This was an arduous task. Rapee was Rothafel's music director at the Capitol, the Roxy, and at Radio City Music Hall, and he proposed that creating an accompaniment should begin with a simple analysis. "Firstly—determine the geographic and national atmosphere of your picture,—secondly—embody every one of your important characters with a theme. Undoubtedly there will be a Love Theme and most likely there will be a theme for the Villain."[9] (Recall that this was exactly the case in the *Coney Island* cue sheet.) The staff would then go painstakingly through the film with the timings. For each sequence, among other things they would consider the mood, the length, what appropriate music the theater had in its library, and how recently that music had been used. Riesenfeld made the following observation about choosing music:

> There are millions of ways of selecting music to serve as accompaniment for a picture, but there are only two ways that a good musician would choose. One is to select beautiful music that is appropriate for the scenes of the picture, and the good musician, inexperienced in motion picture presentation would undoubtedly follow this course. The second course, and the one that requires the hardest work, is to select music such as would be chosen in the first mentioned way, but with an ear to its subjugation. There may be half a hundred waltzes that would go prettily with certain scenes, but the experienced scorer of motion pictures will, after listening to the piece, know whether it is too striking—or even too beautiful.[10]

Once selected, the pieces would be run against the film, the speed of which could be increased or decreased to make the musical selection fit better. In some circumstances, the film might even be re-cut to better fit the musical selection. Someone from the staff would be assigned to write short transitional passages

The organ, specifically the Mighty Wurlitzer, became the emblematic musical instrument of the silent film era. In the larger theaters, organists often filled in for orchestra musicians so that they might have intermittent breaks during performances. The organ itself was often the centerpiece in the pit and was conceived of as part of the cinematic spectacle. Some picture palaces even sported organ elevators—organs on hydraulic lifts so that the instrument could seemingly rise out of the depths to "picture level."
—See Rudy Behlmer, "An Interview with Gaylord Carter, 'Dean of Theater Organists,'" in Cooke, *The Hollywood Film Music Reader.*

Erno Rapee's Encyclopaedia of Music for Pictures categorized its lists of musical cues according to musical topics and possible narrative situations. Rapee also offered practical advice on the main functions of film music, including how to choose various themes, and how to keep those themes interesting throughout the picture. He provided information on how to store and maintain music in a theater library, and even on what to do in case of a fire in the film booth—a common event given the high flammability of early celluloid-backed film.
—See Erno Rapee, "Musical Accompaniment to the Feature Picture," in Cooke, The Hollywood Film Music Reader.

where needed; occasionally new music might be composed if nothing appropriate could be found in the library. All of this was then collated into a *score* that could easily exceed one hundred pieces for a feature film.

SPECIAL SCORES IN THE 1920s

By the 1920s, any film with ambition—one where an extended run was expected or the film was to be distributed through a road show—would likely have a commissioned score of some sort. Fully original scores were relatively rare until the coming of sound. Some notable examples of original scores include Victor Herbert's *The Fall of a Nation* (1916), Mortimer Wilson's *Thief of Bagdad* (1924), Edmund Meisel's *Battleship Potemkin* (1925), and William Axt's *La Boheme* (1926). Most scores, however, continued to be at least partially compiled. This was true even of such spectacles as *The Big Parade* (1925), *Ben-Hur: A Tale of Christ* (1925), and *Wings* (1927). The special scores were used when the film was exhibited in a road show, and they were available to those theaters who wanted to rent them through syndication. In addition, individual chains often circulated scores through their theaters. All of this is to say that, although studios may have gone to the expense of commissioning a special score, the existence of that score in itself could not guarantee anything like a standardized exhibition of the film.

ROAD SHOWS

Only films that were distributed exclusively through road show engagements that reproduced all aspects of a production, as was the case with *The Big Parade* (which followed the New York City Astor Theatre production) and *Ben Hur* (the Embassy), could be sure of having a relatively uniform exhibition. Road shows had been used regularly for film exhibition since the mid-1910s, when the enormous success of *The Birth of a Nation* had ensured that the musical score became a fixed part of the production. Only a handful of pictures per year went on the road, however, in large part because a successful road show required a large theater where the film could remain for an extended run. That is to say, rather than the common movie theater practice of continuous performance and general admission, road shows ran by the principles of regular theater with reserved seating and typically two shows per day. The prices were on par with, and often exceeded those of, legitimate theater. This meant that road shows were geographically restricted to large urban centers. Moreover, each urban center had only a small number of theaters appropriate for producing such shows, a fact that placed an absolute limit on the number of films that could be exhibited through road shows at any one time. If theaters were not available when a film was ready for distribution, the film would either have to wait or go immediately into regular release. Even films exhibited first through road shows would eventually go through a regular release, and at that time they were unlikely to be accompanied by their original score.

MUSIC ON THE SET

Music was often used as part of film production during the silent era. Many actors and directors felt that performance before the camera improved with music that set a proper mood. The practice has a long history. Already in 1907, one trade paper reported:

> In order to add to the reality of the moving pictures, music is always played while the actors pose. A very fine phonograph is one of the important properties of the factory. When there is a picture where quick motion is needed, a lively record is played by the phonograph; where pathos or emotion is to be expressed, some of the plaintive music from [Bizet's] Carmen or [Grieg's] Peer Gynt is used; and where there is a dream scene mysterious music is played. It is wonderful help to the actors in throwing themselves into the part.[11]

The use of music on the set grew more and more common over the course of the silent era, and by the 1920s it was standard practice. The phonograph recordings were replaced by live musicians, who played more or less the same sort of mood music that patrons would hear in the theater. Generally, these ensembles were small, consisting of a violinist or pianist, say, but for large-budget pictures it was not unheard of to have a much larger ensemble; Cecil B. DeMille, for instance, reportedly hired a thirty-piece orchestra to provide military music during the filming of the Exodus scene in *The Ten Commandments* (1923). Although miniscule in comparison to music expenses at theaters, the cost for studio music was not small. In 1927, MGM spent more than $50,000 for musicians on the set; by way of comparison, this was roughly equivalent to the yearly cost of a modest-sized orchestra (sixteen players) or the Roxy's live entertainment budget for one week (which included the orchestra, organists, corps de ballet, and Roxyettes, as well as other contract soloists and headliners).

Characteristic Music Practices in the Later Silent Era

Despite the great variety of practices in early film exhibition, music was, for the most part, used in characteristic and predictable ways (at least, after about 1910). This was especially true with respect to dramatic or emotional codes that were themselves inherited from the nineteenth-century theater. From the melodrama in particular came the conventional musical topics of the hurry for action scenes, the love theme for romantic scenes, the fanfare or overture for the main-title sequence, the mysterioso for suspense, and so on.

In this section, we look more closely at the way music participates in the characterization of time and place and the representation of individuals through the style topic (conventionally coded types of music) and the recurrent theme (short musical phrases that, through repetition, become associated with important narrative elements, such as individuals, specific locales, and even narrative situations).

Film scholar Claudia Gorbman refers to these two types as "cultural musical codes" and "cinematic musical codes," respectively. As we shall see, in many instances the stylistic and thematic properties are combined in a single musical cue.

Neither characterization nor thematic association is entirely new: we have already referred to both categories in previous chapters. In Chapter 1, we described the use of stereotyped music for particular characterizations ("Indian" music in the classical western; military marches or national anthems in war films, etc.), and we have mentioned such uses in many of the discussions of films or film scenes since. The device of the recurrent theme (sometimes called "leitmotif") was also discussed in the context of the ways music provides narrative information and compares with speech and effects in that task.

THEME, MOTIF, AND MOTIVE

The word *theme* in literature is a concise general statement about a story or poem that says what it is about. This could be an extremely brief description of action ("*King Kong* is about a great ape who comes to and devastates New York, but dies in the end") but is usually a characterization of what we understand as its essential idea or focus ("*Romeo and Juliet* is about tragic love" or "*Romeo and Juliet* is about the ways culture can interfere with and damage healthy expressions of human love"). In music—especially in purely instrumental music—this essential idea or focus is taken to be the most clearly defined melodies (or "themes") that are "developed" (or altered and commented on) in the other, more figural or dramatic sections of a composition. This distinction is important to us here, because when instrumental music is moved into the realm of the film sound track, the theme really functions like a motif; that is, the theme is no longer the "idea" of a piece but a significant recurring sound element. (A narrative motif is usually defined as a significant recurring element; in film, visual motifs are very common, perhaps the most famous instance being the pervasive bird motif in Hitchcock's *Psycho* [1960].) As we shall see later, the leitmotifs of Richard Wagner's operas are also sound motifs in this sense.

The very common musical term *motive* is essentially synonymous with *motif* because it refers to a short, recurring musical fragment. Motive and theme are used interchangeably when referring to a short theme, that is, a phrase or shorter—normally 2 to 5 seconds. Once you reach 10 to 15 seconds, the limit of short-term memory, a melodic unit is most likely a fully presented theme of at least two phrases.

THE LEITMOTIF

As we noted in Chapter 1, a theme used to refer consistently to a character, as in the case of the love theme and the heroine, is called a *leitmotif,* a term that derives from the music dramas of nineteenth-century German composer Richard Wagner, where it designates musical themes or motifs associated with people, objects, and even ideas. The device is used most consistently in *Der Ring des*

Nibelungen (*The Ring of the Nibelung*), a cycle of four music dramas (or operas) based on Germanic and Scandinavian myths. The Sword, the Ring, and the Rhine River all have their own themes, as do characters such as Loki, Thor, and Wotan. Some of the principal characters, such as Siegfried, have several. The signification is somewhat more complex than is suggested here, however. For instance, the leitmotif that is generally associated with Wotan also designates his spear, which in turn stands for a contract he is bound to uphold. (This contract is the cause of much tragedy in the drama.) Likewise, some of the leitmotifs refer to rather abstract ideas such as Fate or the so-called Redemption through Love theme. Throughout the cycle, the leitmotifs undergo variation and transformation that reflect the dramatic situation.

Wagner's influence on music for the theater in the decades after his death in 1883 can hardly be overstated, and therefore it should be no surprise that film composers also adopted the technique of the leitmotif, albeit generally in a much simplified form (at its most basic, in fact, it is no different than the use of a recurrent theme). Most telling is just the number: whereas Wagner juggles dozens and dozens of motifs across his music dramas, film composers usually restrict themselves to only a handful. Often, they will use only two or three themes: the main title for the hero, a love theme for the heroine, and perhaps recurring music for a place, villain, or something or someone else of particular narrative importance. Even such sprawling multi-film epics as *Star Wars* (1977–2005) or *Lord of the Rings* (2001–2003), although in many respects quite close to Wagner's complex usage otherwise, do not attempt abstract signification to the same degree.

Leitmotifs in films also tend to be much more direct in signification, the theme appearing only when the character does or, occasionally, when the character signified by the motif is clearly referred to in the dialogue. As music scholar Justin London says, "In filmic contexts the introduction of musical leitmotifs is highly conventionalized. Usually this introduction involves the simultaneous presentation of the character and his or her leitmotif, especially when we are given a striking presentation of both early on in the film."[12]

The leitmotif does not just signify its referent, that is, the character, thing, place, or idea. It is also modified to reflect its context. This is done through musical variation. Such variations can be subtle—changing the orchestration, adjusting the tempo or dynamics, or the key—but they can also be quite substantial—altering the meter, rhythm, mode (for example, from major to minor), accompaniment, and so forth.

MUSICAL TOPICS

In Chapter 1 we defined *topics* as "uses of conventional music." Here, we offer a more elaborate definition: topics are conventional musical figures that evoke, represent, or signify a particular mood, place, emotion, or some other character trait in the narrative. When we speak of a "love" theme, for instance, we are dealing with a musical topic. The music has a certain quality—a "style"—that allows us to recognize it as a love theme even if we have not heard it in a narrative context (such as a film) that would allow us to specify that meaning. The meaning does not reside just in the melody: love themes, for instance, are typically scored for strings with the melody in the violin, and the texture places a strong emphasis on melody with flowing accompaniment. In addition, the tempo is generally on the slow side of moderate (often andante, roughly at or just a bit slower than the average resting heartbeat rate). The overall effect is one of a deeply felt lyricism. Love themes are generally very prominent in films that make use of them, and, as might be expected, they are typically associated with the heroine.

Writing in the "picture palace" era, Erno Rapee described the importance of the love theme as follows:

> The choice of the Love Theme is a very important part of the scoring—it is a constantly recurring theme in the average run of pictures and as a rule will impress your audience more than any other theme. Special care should be taken in choosing the Love Theme from various angles. If you have a Western picture dealing with a farmhand and a country girl you should choose a musically simple and sweet ballad. If your Love Theme is to cover a relationship between society people, usually portrayed as sophisticated and blasé, choose a number of the type represented by the compositions of such composers as Victor Herbert or [Cecile] Chaminade.[13]

Like love themes, most leitmotifs are also usually instances of musical topics. This is because topics are an effective means of musical characterization. Fanfares, military calls, and hunting calls are specific musical topics. Another topic oftentimes associated with these or used in conjunction with them is the march. The signifying properties of a musical topic very often affirm our understanding of a scene. Most obviously, national anthems are used in this way. In these cases, the music comes culturally determined, through lyrics and other uses, but signification is similar for other music, even if the meaning will be more difficult to fix than with anthems and other national songs. We have already noted how love themes have a style that allows us to identify the sort of situations or characters they are associated with. In fact, much film music works this way. For instance, music for battles, storms, deaths, pastoral scenes, and the West—each of these has a relatively distinctive sound that allows us to make a fairly good judgment of the sort of scene a certain type of music will accompany without even seeing the images. The same holds true for mood: mysterious, agitated, grotesque, action—each of these, too, has a characteristic sound. Of course, it is seldom the case that we can make an exact determination—the same music may well be acceptable for both a battle scene and a storm—but a certain type of music has a limited range of scenes for which it will fit comfortably. It would be highly unlikely to hear soft pastoral music accompanying the height of a battle, or battle music accompanying a quiet pastoral scene. Such music would seem utterly inappropriate—unless it seemed plausible that playing against the situation in this way had a narrative purpose.

The Villain ordinarily can easily be represented by any Agitato, of which there are thousands.
—Erno Rapee[14]

Location and Stereotype

Musical topics are a particularly good means of marking locale. This conflation of place with ethnicity was common in silent-film accompaniment and it continued through the classic studio era. "Chinese" music—inevitably centered on a pentatonic scale—might be used either for a place or a character. "Arabian" music—or, as it was usually called in the silent era, "Oriental"—likewise has its distinctive figures, typically flowing, ornamented melodies using scales featuring the augmented second or lowered second scale degree, as well as percussion. Most of the stereotypical elements are evident in this citation from the middle section of Tchaikovsky's "Arabian Dance" (*The Nutcracker* ballet): Figure 4-15a. We see later renderings of the topic in music for the native Blue Parrot café in *Casablanca* (Figure 4-15b) and in themes from *Lawrence of Arabia* (Figure 4-15c & d).

Such music could be used for a wide range of locations, including North Africa, Egypt, the Middle East, and some places in Southeast Asia. The same is true for the open fifths or beating tom-toms of the "Indians" (see Figure 4-16a for the contents list of a silent-film era collection and Figure 4-16b for the opening of its "Indian Music" selection). In a different context, such music could be used to signify the "primitive" in general. Indeed, markers of the exotic and primitive are often quite malleable (reflecting a general cultural conflation of the terms).

As these examples make clear, musical topics often work by means of stereotypes.

These sorts of musical topics, which remained part of film music practice at least through the 1970s (and in somewhat altered ways even after that),

Figure 4-15. (a) Tchaikovsky, ballet *The Nutcracker*, Arabian Dance (middle section); (b) *Casablanca* (1942), music for the *Blue Parrot* café (transcription from the sound track); (c) & (d) *Lawrence of Arabia* (1962), two examples of "exotic" style topics: the main theme and music associated with the Arab army (transcription from sound track).

Figure 4-16. (a) A table of contents of an early collection of music written specifically to accompany silent film. Note that the contents are organized along the lines of musical topics. (b) The opening of "Indian Music." Note the minor key and stereotypical open fifths in the left hand.

a
—
b

SAM FOX MOVING PICTURE MUSIC

By J. S. ZAMECNIK

VOL. I   PRICE 50 CENTS

CONTENTS

	Page
Festival March	2
Indian Music	3
Oriental Veil Dance	4
Chinese Music	5
Oriental Music	6
Mexican or Spanish Music	8
Funeral March	9
Death Scene	9
Church Music	10
War Scene	
Part 1 (In Military Camp)	11
Part 2 (Off to the Battle)	12
Part 3 (The Battle)	12 and 13
Cowboy Music	14
Grotesque or Clown Music	15
Mysterioso-Burglar Music	16
Mysterioso-Burglar Music	16
Hurry Music (for struggles)	17
Hurry Music (for duels)	17
Hurry Music	18
Hurry Music (for mob or fire scenes)	19
Storm Scene	20
Sailor Music	21
Fairy Music	21
Plaintive Music	22
Plaintive Music	23

Copyright MCMXXIII by Sam Fox Publishing Co., Cleveland, Ohio. (International Copyright Secured)

Published by Sam Fox 🦊 Pub. Co. *Cleveland, O.*

originated in nineteenth-century practices. Figure 4-17 reproduces the sidebar from Rapee's *Motion Picture Moods* (1924), a collection of music meant to serve as a single anthology for a theater pianist's or organist's use. This particular sidebar is printed on every page of music in his book to allow the keyboardist to note pages and flip quickly to an appropriate topical category for a new scene or situation. The headings cover the whole range of categories we have discussed in this chapter, from mood or affect indicators (grotesque, happiness, horror,

Table 4-3 Julius S. Seredy, *Carl Fischer Analytical Orchestra Guide* (1929), headings showing conflation of mood and style.

Agitatos—for General Use—see also Furioso, Battle, Storm, Hurries

Dramatic—for longer dramatic scenes, trials, etc., see also . . . Anger, Argument, Foreboding, Grief, Passion, Pulsating, Regret, Resignation, Tragic

Hurries—General Use—see also Agitatos, Excitement, Furiosos, Chase, Dramatic Pursuit, Exotic and Comic Hurries

Love Scenes—see also Love Themes and Dramatic Love Scenes for Lighter Courtship Numbers, see Garden Scenes

Mysteriosos for General Use [with its subcategories], "Mysteriosos—Comic (Burlesque)—see also Mystic Suspense in Comedy," "Mysteriosos—Grotesque—Spooky—see also Comic Mysteriosos, Exotics," and "Mysteriosos—Heavy Dramatic."

---

joyfulness, mysterioso, passion, quietude, sadness, sinister, but also neutral) to characteristic music for objects (aëroplane), groups (children, national, oriental, western), or scenic situations (battle, chase, festival, love-themes, parties, race, sea-storm), to musical sound effects (birds, calls, chatter). Dances are listed separately—whereas some would be strongly marked (*mazurkas* for Poland, eastern Europe, Russia, or gypsies; *minuets* for eighteenth-century high society; *tangos* for Latin American society, but also for strong sensuality), others could serve a variety of purposes (for example, marches, but also waltzes, which in the silent-film era still were markers of a traditional popular music).

Perhaps because of their necessary brevity, the labels in Figure 4-17 do not reflect the conflation of mood and topic that was central to musicians' planning and performance for feature films in the silent-film era. In the *Carl Fischer Analytical Orchestra Guide*, compiled by Julius S. Seredy and published in 1929, we find clearer indications of these combinations in headings such as those shown in Table 4-3.

Analysis: Silent Film with Historically Appropriate Music: *Lady Windermere's Fan*

Released in 1925, during the "picture palace" era, the heyday of the silent feature film, *Lady Windermere's Fan* was a major production of the Warner Bros. studio and, fortunately for them, was also very successful at the box office. The most prominent member of the production team, however, was not an actor, but the

Figure 4-17. Erno Rapee, *Motion Picture Moods* (1924). This sidebar ran on every page of the book, giving the player a quick index of topic categories.

Aëroplane	2
Band	5
Battle	10
Birds	21
Calls	273
Chase	599
Chatter	28
Children	31
Chimes	259
Dances	39
Gavottes	39
Marches	102
Mazurkas	48
Minuets	54
Polkas	61
Tangos	94
Valses lentes	78
Valses	65
Doll	129
Festival	140
Fire-Fighting	151
Funeral	160
Grotesque	165
Gruesome	169
Happiness	202
Horror	173
Humorous	174
Hunting	186
Impatience	194
Joyfulness	202
Love-themes	209
Lullabies	231
Misterioso	242
Monotony	250
Music-box	254
National	261
Neutral	467
Orgies	487
Oriental	496
Parties	523
Passion	571
Pastorale	564
Pulsating	587
Purity	591
Quietude	591
Race	599
Railroad	608
Religioso	616
Sadness	621
Sea-Storm	651
Sinister	663
Wedding	671
Western	665

director, Ernst Lubitsch, who took the remarkable step of removing most of the dialogue from this film version of Oscar Wilde's play. These would otherwise have been displayed on multiple intertitles, but Lubitsch explained that "playing with words is fascinating to the writer and afterward to the reader, but on the screen it is quite impossible."[15]

The play is part comedy of manners and part domestic melodrama, and Lubitsch successfully maintains the balance between these two aspects. The best known actor is Ronald Colman, who plays Lord Darlington, infatuated with the married Lady Windermere (May McAvoy). Her husband, Lord Windermere (Bert Lytell), has agreed to pay money to Mrs. Erlynne (Irene Rich) to keep quiet the fact that she is Lady Windermere's mother (presumably the child was born out of wedlock). After starting an affair with Lord Augustus Lorton (Edward Martindel), Mrs. Erlynne insists on an invitation to Lady Windermere's birthday party. Lady Windermere finds the check intended for Mrs. Erlynne, misunderstands its significance, and agrees to go away with Lord Darlington, but she is intercepted in the latter's apartment by Mrs. Erlynne. Having hoped to break into society through the birthday party (which she had attended with great success), Mrs. Erlynne now sacrifices her chances by staying in the apartment as her daughter escapes unnoticed. In the end, the Windermeres are re-united and so are Mrs. Erlynne and Lord Augustus.

The film is readily divided into three parts, or acts. In the first, the characters are introduced and the central narrative problems are presented in a series of four scenes. The second act (beginning at 32:27 or DVD ch. 5) could be understood as one large scene because it concerns the events of a single day and a specific place, but it is probably better to think of it as an act comprised of two sequences: the preliminaries to Lady Windermere's birthday party and the party itself. The third act (beginning at 1:11:30 or DVD ch. 11) takes place at Lord Darlington's apartment, as Mrs. Erlynne arrives to find Lady Windermere already there, the men arrive to continue the festivities after the party, and Mrs. Erlynne diverts attention while her daughter escapes but permanently ruins her reputation in the process, as the men find Lady Windermere's fan and she is obliged to claim that she took it by mistake. The final scene, the film's denouement, takes place the next morning (1:23:04 or DVD ch. 13), as Mrs. Erlynne visits Lady Windermere to return the fan and explain as much as she can (without divulging her parental status). As she leaves, she encounters Lord Augustus on the street, and the two go off together.

We will focus here only on the first act, whose four scenes are as follows: (1) the Windermere's house (conversations between Lady Windermere, Lord Darlington, and Lord Windermere); (2) Mrs. Erlynne's apartment (including a conversation with Lord Windermere); (3) the racetrack; and (4) Mrs. Erlynne's apartment (including a conversation with Lord Augustus). Each of the scenes begins with an intertitle. Figures 4-18a through 4-18d show the first image that follows in each scene.

Figure 4-18. *Lady Windermere's Fan* (1925). Initial images for each of the four scenes in Act 1: (a) Lady Windermere's home, establishing shot; (b) Mrs. Erlynne's apartment; (c) the race track; (d) Lord Augustus arrives at Mrs. Erlynne's apartment.

a	b
c	d

For the recent DVD release of *Lady Windermere's Fan*, silent-film music scholar and performance specialist Martin Marks provided a piano accompaniment closely aligned with silent-film era performance practices. As he explains, "I created a compilation score, using preexistent music of the sort that a pianist or an orchestra could have played at the time of the film's original release. I also employ the silent-film pianist's methods for varying and developing this music in accordance with the story." In keeping with that spirit, the seventeen pieces of music played, quoted, or alluded to in Act 1 include only one that is Marks's own: the "fan motive" that first appears in the main title sequence. All the other music, except for an anachronistic reference to *My Fair Lady*, could very well have been performed by a theater pianist or organist in 1925.

Table 4-4 *Lady Windermere's Fan*. **Establishing sequence and Act 1, first scene, cue list and timings.**

TIME STAMP	ACTION	MUSIC PLAYED BY MARTIN MARKS
0:00:00	Credits	1. J. S. Zamecnik *The Sacrifice* beginning. (see music in Figure 4-19) [with the main title] Marks Fan Motive ad lib (see second half of Figure 4-19)
0:00:33		2. V. Herbert *The Only Girl* Overture Waltz
0:01:15	T. *Lady Windermere faced . . .*	3. Trad "Oh, Dear, What Can the Matter Be?"
0:01:27	Scene in Drawing Room	4. Thomas *Mignon* Gavotte beginning (see Figure 4-20)
0:02:47	Lord Darlington enters	5. Mozart *Don Giovanni*: "*Là ci darem la mano*"
0:03:38	Lord Windermere at desk	Variation of #1 (*The Sacrifice*) (from Figure 4-19)
0:04:24	Lady W enters	Fan Motive ad lib (from Figure 4-19)
0:04:35	Lord D enters	Continuation of #4, strain 2 etc. (*Mignon* Gavotte; see Figure 4-20)
0:06:12	Lady W & Lord D alone, long shot	New version of #5 ("*Là ci darem la mano*"), leading to
0:06:32	T. "*Lady Winderemere, I have . . .*"	6. W. Goodell, *Dreaming* until pause at fade

Music that plays continuously throughout a 2-hour long feature is necessarily complex and varied, but the unifying associations that come with recurring themes and motives remain typical of classical sound-film practice, where music is only very rarely continuous throughout. Unlike the later practice of the fixed sound track, Marks's performance tends to emphasize the film's temporal articulations much more consistently, a tendency that makes sense not only because a continuous music needs some articulation (which the film aids) but also because the film, in turn, lacks dialogue and effects and thus relies more heavily on music.

The lead character in the story is clearly Mrs. Erlynne, not Lady Windermere, and Marks immediately presents her theme in the opening credits: see the cue list with timings for the opening credits and the first scene in Table 4-4; and see the melody in Figure 4-19a (the "fan motive" is near the end of the example). The theme presented here is the first section, a long introduction to the piece titled *The Sacrifice*, which was taken from a silent-era music anthology of the sort mentioned previously, in this case, the *Sam Fox Photoplay Edition: A Loose Leaf Collection of High Class Dramatic and Descriptive Motion Picture Music*, Vol. 2, published in 1922. The piece is classified under "Deep Emotion, Sorrow": see the advertisement text in the sidebar. As Marks explains, the theme is "intense [and] conveys the emotions Mrs. Erlynne displays from scene to scene. . . . I like to imagine that [its composer] had such a woman in mind when he composed (or at least titled) his piece—especially because her 'sacrifice' of social position for her daughter's sake is the climactic action in the film."

Both *The Sacrifice* as we first hear it and Marks's "fan motive" reappear in the first and second scenes (and, of course, at a number of other significant moments later in the film as well), but it is the major-key melody of the second strain of *The Sacrifice* that really dominates: see Figure 4-19b.

Of the other music, Marks says that the works he chose "speak in accents of wit and romance. Several are stylized dances that bring to mind comic images of formal behavior and ritualized social interactions, such as constrain the film's aristocratic characters." Among these are a gavotte, which was an old-fashioned dance already before 1800, from a nineteenth-century French opera, *Mignon* (first entrance at 1:27; see Figure 4-20 for the melody). It came from Rapee's *Motion Picture Moods* and was catalogued under "Dances," a very broad category that includes historical,

3. **CONSPIRACY** (Intrigue, Evil Purposes)
4. **VIOLENCE** (Great Confusion, Struggles)
5. **SHADOWED** (Mystery, Horror, Gloomy Scenes)

(continued)

Figure 4-19. Two melodies used by Martin Marks to accompany *Lady Windermere's Fan*: (a) J. S. Zamecnik, *The Sacrifice*, opening melody (mm. 1–8), plus Marks, "Fan Motive" (mm. 8–12); (b) the middle section of *The Sacrifice*.   a / b

Figure 4-20. Ambroise Thomas, "Gavotte" from *Mignon*: (a) melody only for the first section; (b) melody for the second section.   a / b

(continued)

6. *A GRUESOME TALE (Fear, Dreary Situation)*

7. *THE FURIOUS MOB (Great Disturbance, Riot, Mob Scene)*

8. *GRIEF (Despair, Dramatic Emotion)*

9. *CONFESSION (Sorrowful Emotion)*

10. *THE TEMPEST (Storm at Sea, Shipwrecked)*[16]

contemporary, and national dances of different character. The other music in the main-title sequence is an upbeat waltz from a Victor Herbert operetta overture. In the first scene are a humorous reference to a traditional waltz-song "Oh, Dear, What Can the Matter Be?" and "Dreaming" from the *Robbins-Engel Series of Moviemusic for Piano or Organ,* Folio 1, published in 1927. The quotation from Mozart is a somewhat unusual love theme that would have struck opera fans in the audience as a humorous allusion: in the opera, Don Juan is trying to seduce a young woman and the two sing; in the film, Lord Darlington enters and the two talk: we learn through their conversation that he is in love with Lady Windermere.

Music in the second scene is dominated by *The Sacrifice.* Another serious theme is introduced, however: *Madeleine,* the second melody associated with Mrs. Erlynne (at 13:48; see Figure 4-21 and Table 4-5). As Marks explains, "Mrs. Erlynne is too complex a character to be pictured by only one piece of music. . . . This I took from [a] 1921 set of *Sam Fox Motion Picture Themes,* for female characters only. It plays like a moody fox-trot of the era, although it eventually puts on a happier face."

The third scene gives a full sense of the complexity that was achieved by early film pianists and organists: see Table 4-6. More allusions are tucked in between several restatements of the associative themes we heard earlier. The Offenbach "Can Can" is a clichéd hurry, and "With Catlike Tread" is a fast march that also functions as a hurry in this situation. Two new piano pieces similar in character to the *Mignon* gavotte and used for "wit" or elegant comedy were originally meant to be played in the home but are equally suitable to film

Figure 4-21. J. S. Zamecnik, *Madeleine,* melody.

Table 4-5 *Lady Windermere's Fan.* **Establishing sequence and Act 1, second scene, cue list and timings.**

TIME STAMP	ACTION	MUSIC PLAYED BY MARTIN MARKS
0:07:29	*[beginning of DVD Chapter 2]* T. After a life of adventure	Continuation of #1 (*The Sacrifice*), several strains ad lib (from Figure 4-19)
0:13:48	Lord W takes out checkbook	7. Zamecnik, Theme "*Madeleine*" (see Figure 4-21)
0:15:12	Photograph of Lady W	#1 (*The Sacrifice*) final strain to cadence at fade (from Figure 4-19)

Table 4-6 *Lady Windermere's Fan*. Establishing sequence and Act 1, third scene, cue list and timings.

TIME STAMP	ACTION	MUSIC PLAYED BY MARTIN MARKS
0:16:42	*[beginning of DVD Chapter 3]* T. *Thanks to Windermere's cheques . . .*	8. Allusion to Loewe *My Fair Lady* "Ascot Gavotte"
0:16:56	Racetrack scenes	9. Offenbach "Can Can" as 6/8 march
0:17:08	Scottish band marching	10. A. Sullivan *Pirates* "With Catlike Tread"
0:17:25	Mrs. Erlynne surrounded by men	11. Allusion to Arne *Rule, Britannia*
0:17:47	Mrs. E leaves, ascends stairs	12. Herbert, *The Only Girl*: Overture March
0:18:02	Montage: looking at Mrs. E	Variation of #7 ("*Madeleine*")
0:18:51	Ladies sitting in box	13. A. Czibulka *Stephanie* Gavotte strains 1 & 3 (see Figure 4-22)
0:20:46	T. *The Duchess of Berwick . . .*	14. L. Gautier *Le Secret*, strains 1–2 (see Figure 4-23)
0:21:54	Duchess looks at Mrs. E.'s hair	13a. *Stephanie* strain 2 ad lib (from Figure 4-22)
0:22:47	After T. "*She is getting gray*"	14a. *Le Secret* strains 3–4 ad lib (from Figure 4-23)
0:24:11	After T. "*Why gossip about a woman*"	Variations of #13 & #13a (*Stephanie* Gavotte) (from Figure 4-23)
0:26:04	Horse race	Ad lib
0:26:18	Mrs. E followed by Lord Augustus	Variation of #12 (*The Only Girl*: Overture March) as tango, cadence at fade

accompaniment. These are *Stephanie* (another gavotte; at 18:51; see Figure 4-22), and *Le Secret* (at 20:46; see Figure 4-23).

Music in the fourth scene, the last in the film's first act, consists of statements and restatements of two new themes: an ironic love song for Mrs. Erlynne and Lord Augustus (taken from *Metzler's Original Cinema Music*, published in 1920) and a waltz written specifically for use in "photoplays" (at 28:12; see Figure 4-24). See Table 4-7.

All of the five combinations of musical topics and moods listed in Table 4-3 are clearly represented in the first act of *Lady Windermere's Fan*. The style topics of agitato and hurry overlap, the former referring more often to dramatic or dangerous events such as battles or storms or to psychological agitation, the latter to action scenes such as races, chases, and games. The Offenbach "Can Can" obviously fits the latter as it introduces the racetrack scene. The milling crowd is equally well represented by the fast march that follows. As Martin Marks explains, the score is filled with romantic themes whose modes run the gamut from light or comic to neutral and occasionally to heavy or fraught. Several are associated with one or another of the couples, as we have seen: *Mignon* and "*Là*

Figure 4-22. Alphonse Czibulka, *Stephanie* (gavotte).

Figure 4-23. Léonard Gautier, *Le Secret*, melody of section A.

Figure 4-24. Frank C. Dougherty, *Waltz* (*for General Use*).

Table 4-7 *Lady Windermere's Fan*. Establishing sequence and Act 1, fourth scene, cue list and timings.

TIME STAMP	ACTION	MUSIC PLAYED BY MARTIN MARKS
0:26:51	*[beginning of DVD Chapter 4]* T. *A gentleman's relation to a lady*	15. G. Clutsam *Billet-doux*, Intro & strain 1
0:27:54		Ad lib
0:28:12	Maid leaves, Lord A alone	16. F. Dougherty *Waltz* (Eb) (see Figure 4-24)
0:29:05	Maid returns to Lord A	Ad lib & Variation of #15 (*Billet-doux*)
0:29:50	T. *But when the relation becomes*	16a. *Waltz*, strain 2 & ad lib (c#) (from Figure 4-24)
0:0:53	CU Cigar, Lord A becomes jealous	16. *Waltz* strain 1 (E)
0:31:25	T. *"If you really loved me"*	16a. Variation of *Waltz* strain 2 (c#)
0:31:45	Mrs. E. goes over to Lord A with cigar	Ad lib with Variation of #15 (*Billet-doux*)
0:32:27	T. *"I am sorry my maid forgot"* scene ends	

ci darem la mano" in scene 1, *Madeleine* in scene 2, and *Billet-doux* in scene 4. Other similar themes are used more generally for social interactions, such as *Stephanie* and *Le Secret* in scene 3. *The Sacrifice*, of course, is a dramatic theme whose first section fits such heavy moods as grief and whose second strain is appropriate to regret or resignation. Marks varies the second strain to create lighter and darker moods, as appropriate to the situation. The mysterioso topic appears in scene 3, as the Duchess investigates the "mystery" of Mrs. Erlynne's hair color. At that point the music shifts to a comically spooky mood, with short staccato notes, little tremolos, and a minor key.

Summary

In this chapter we offered a historical narrative for sound and music in the early decades of cinema, roughly 1890 to 1927, tracing a path from the earliest stages through the nickelodeon to standardization of exhibition practices in the 1920s.

Timeline

1894   Edison introduces the Kinetoscope commercially in New York City.

1895   Lumière Brothers introduce the *Cinematographe*, a camera and projection system. For the first decade, film will be exhibited primarily in vaudeville theaters, in tents at fair grounds, and by traveling exhibitors booking local theaters.

1904   St. Louis World's Fair. One of the first theaters dedicated to film exhibition, Hale's Tours, is introduced here.

1905   The nickelodeon craze begins. The story film establishes its dominance.

1908   Camille Saint-Saëns composes original score to *L'Assassinat du duc de Guise.*

1909   The *Edison Kinetogram* releases suggestions of musical selections to use with the company's films.

1910   Music practices begin to change as music columns appear in trade papers and music publishers begin to offer music written specifically for motion picture needs.

1911   The Kalem film company releases "special scores" to accompany its films.

1913   The first volume of J. S. Zamecnik's *Sam Fox Moving Picture Music* is published.

1915   Larger and better motion picture theaters are built. These theaters are equipped with space for more musicians and often a theater organ. The long (multireel) feature becomes the dominant form of film. *The Birth of a Nation* travels around the country with a special score composed by Joseph Carl Breil.

1917   ASCAP wins the right to collect a fee from theaters for the performance of music by its members.

Early on, the exhibition venues varied widely, and sound practices varied with them. After about 1905, the nickelodeons—storefront film theaters—came to dominate exhibition, and with them a gradual process began that tended toward a common sound practice for feature film presentation. (This common practice was only achieved in the sound-film era.) Films were part of a program that featured considerable amounts of live musical performance as well. Once feature films expanded to four reels or more (about 1915), the demand for music that was appropriate to the picture's character and mood became stronger. Feature films and theaters expanded dramatically thereafter, and in larger cities theaters became "picture palaces" that could often marshal considerable resources to music (as well as effects).

1920	The "deluxe" exhibition style becomes common in large urban theaters. The film industry becomes vertically integrated, with major film companies controlling production, distribution, and exhibition.
1924	Erno Rapee publishes *Motion Picture Moods*.
1925	*Lady Windermere's Fan.*
1926	Paramount acquires Balaban & Katz Theatre corporation.
1927	The Roxy Theatre opens in New York City with Samuel "Roxy" Rothafel as impresario. The Roxy is one of the many very large and opulent theaters that are built in most major cities in the late 1920s. These theaters feature grand organs, ample stages, and orchestra pits that could hold full symphony orchestras.
1928	*Coney Island.*
1930	Hollywood studios have all but ceased the production of silent films. Musicians are dismissed by theaters as quickly as contracts expire.
1932	Radio City Music Hall, one of the last of the picture palaces, opens in New York City under Rothafel.
1936	Charlie Chaplin makes his last silent film (*Modern Times*).
2011	*The Artist* wins the Oscar for Best Picture. This is the first time since *Wings* that a silent film has won the Best Picture Oscar.

The music that was played during a film showing varied widely, from popular songs and ragtime early on, to a complex mixture of classical music, popular and traditional song, and dance music. "Playing the film" relied heavily on musical topics, or categories of musical types that were familiar to the film's intended viewing audience. Recurrent themes (motives or leitmotifs) formed short, usually melodic, gestures that became associated with characters, places, or situations in the course of the film. Such conventional musical figures were used in a variety of ways: to add additional information missing in the image, to "certify" or over-determine what was already available in the image, to provide or qualify emotional qualities in individuals or social situations, to lend humor or make a critique through ironic juxtaposition, or even to deceive with incorrect information.

A Note on the Music for Silent-Film Releases to VHS and DVD

At least as long ago as Morodor's 1984 electronic score for *Metropolis* (1927), silent films have been released in VHS or DVD with newly composed accompaniments. Some of these have been sensitive to historical styles and practices of silent-film exhibition, but many have not. In principle there is nothing wrong with a newly composed score that uses musical styles not typical of the first quarter of the twentieth century, but for the purposes of a course based on this textbook, it will be more useful to study films with scores that were actually composed for the film or that are newly composed and fit the era. The obvious exception, of course, is the commutation test from Chapter 1: you could very profitably use two or more versions of silent films to make the same kinds of "spotting" comparisons.

We highly recommend the series *Treasures from American Film Archives* (2000–2009), which now has five multi-DVD volumes: "Treasures from American Film Archives" (2000), "More Treasures from American Film Archives: 50 Films, 1894–1931" (2004), "Treasures III: Social Issues in American Film, 1900–1934" (2007), "Treasures from American Film Archives, Avant Garde" (2009), and the recently released "Treasures 5: The West, 1898–1938" (2011). All accompaniments in the first volume are by pianist Martin Marks, who is also the music curator for the other volumes, which make use of a wider range of instrumental groups. (*Lady Windermere's Fan* [1925] is on "More Treasures.")

In the 1980s and early 1990s, Carl Davis also composed a series of orchestral scores for well-known silent films. Where they are still available, we recommend *A Woman of Affairs* (1928), *The Crowd* (1928), *Napoléon* (1927), *Ben-Hur: A Tale of the Christ* (1925), *The Phantom of the Opera* (1925), *Greed* (1924), *The Thief of Bagdad* (1924), and *Intolerance* (1916).

From 1926 to 1932
The Transition to Sound Film

Introduction

Sound and music were both very much involved in the performance practices of the silent-film era. By the early 1930s, however, the program of an American movie theater was dominated by film projection, not by performances, and almost all of those films—and certainly all features—included a recorded and edited optical sound track. The path from one film exhibition culture to another was a long one, and it started as soon as the moving picture was invented. This chapter traces that history but focuses on the final segment, the transition to the sound film, a period that ends in 1932 as the basic procedures for sound film began to codify after the development of a reliable method of rerecording, an advance that allowed much work on the sound track to be moved out of production and into the postproduction phase of filmmaking.

Issues of Technology and Economics

Sound synchronization was attempted almost from the time Thomas Edison invented the apparatus for taking moving pictures. Indeed, Edison's guiding idea from the start was to combine film with the phonograph—he conceived his Kinetograph (the motion picture camera) as doing for the eye what the phonograph did for the ear. He wanted to bring great performers and artistic works to those who could not afford to attend concerts or who lived too far away from urban centers. His specific stated goal—to distribute grand opera to the masses—very much embodied the American ethos of cultural uplift of one's class position through education and the arts. William K. L. Dickson, Edison's assistant on the Kinetograph and Kinetoscope (the latter was used to view the

Figure 5-1. *The Dickson Experimental Sound Film* (c. 1894). W. K. L. Dickson, Edison's main assistant in developing the motion picture camera, plays a selection from Jean Robert Planquette's opera, *The Chimes at Midnight*, on the violin while two lab assistants dance. The need to have the recording horn close to the sound source was one of the obstacles to synchronized sound film. One common solution was to prerecord the sound and then perform the action for the camera to playback. The horn is visible in this film because it was never intended for commercial release. The film was restored by Walter Murch and Richard Schmidlin.

moving pictures), did in fact manage to produce a number of short experimental films with synchronized sound as early as 1895. A screen grab of one of these films is shown in Figure 5-1. Some models of Edison's original peepshow-style Kinetoscope were also outfitted with ear tubes, although these pictures were not shot as synchronized sound films: they were coupled with a cylinder having more or less appropriate music (Figure 5-2).

Over the years a number of schemes were proposed to provide what was portrayed at the time as "the missing voice" of the picture. Devices such as the Cameraphone, the Picturephone, the Cameragraph, the Faceagraph, the Auxetophone, the Theatrephone, the Biographon, the Synchronoscope, the Cinephone, and so forth all promised a means of synchronizing film and phonograph. The first really serviceable system of mechanically synchronized sound was the Gaumont Chronophone, introduced in 1902 and frequently exhibited as a novelty in vaudeville houses beginning around 1905 before it moved into the

Figure 5-2. The Edison Kinetophone was a Kinetoscope outfitted with a phonograph and ear-tube headphones.

nickelodeons around 1908. The Chronophone had limited success in the United States but had a longer run in European countries, especially in France.

As with most early sound synchronization schemes, the Chronophone's most serious defect was not in the synchronization, which a capable operator could master reasonably well, but in amplification. The volume of standard commercial phonographs was insufficient for a theater any larger than the most

If details and effects are to be brought out in talking pictures, the actors and actresses must use judgment in regard to placing the voices of the character in speaking from the center of the drop. The line should be read directly behind the character that he or she is impersonating. This will apply either to the right or the left of the center. At all times, in talking from behind a drop, try to keep as near to where the character is standing as possible. All letters and titles, before scenes, should be taken out, so that the story will not be told before the actors and actresses have read their lines, as this will have a tendency to kill the dramatic climax.

The operator must also be drilled carefully and thoroughly in regard to the running speed of films, of struggles, horses galloping, battles scenes, which must be run very fast, while scenes in offices and homes must be run at a certain speed to bring out the desired
(continued)

modest nickelodeon, and the use of compressed air as a device for amplification tended to make the sound excessively tinny. In addition, the frequency response of phonographs of the time was limited, especially in the upper range (sibilants [s-sounds] were a particular problem), which negatively affected the intelligibility of dialogue. Theater acoustics were usually optimized for live musical performance rather than for reproduced sound, and this tended to muddy dialogue even further. Still worse, the length of a sound disk (or the cylinder in Edison films) could not be pushed much past 4 minutes, which meant that a system of dual phonographs needed to be employed for longer films. These, of course, were also susceptible to both mechanical failure and operator error. Finally, it was virtually impossible to edit sound recordings. Invariably, recordings were made first and the action was then lip-synced to the recording, a technique that would be rediscovered when the industry turned to sound film on a large scale after 1927, especially for the production numbers of musicals. Therefore, it is hardly surprising that most of the sound films in these early years were short musical performances; in the United States, singers from the musical and vaudeville stage predominated.

The failure of the Chronophone in America nevertheless seems to have come about not because of these very real technological limitations, but rather primarily for economic reasons. Apparently, the cost of the special equipment was simply too dear for most theaters, the great majority of which were run on very tight budgets. The sound films ran about twice the price of regular films, but the demand for the former was still relatively low. The cost of keeping the films in good repair, which was absolutely essential to effective performance, was also much higher than for regular films. Ultimately, costs were simply too high to make sound synchronization a going proposition for theaters that were small enough for the phonographic sound to be adequate for the space.

Perhaps the most successful early scheme for providing films with speech, especially in the larger theaters, was the so-called "talking picture." This involved placing a troupe of three or four actors behind the screen to speak lines of dialogue and provide sound effects. The sidebar provides one account of how this was done. This method, although evidently popular with audiences at first, suffered from high production, labor, and transportation costs because a film would need to be specially edited, the actors rehearsed, and both film and company moved from theater to theater on a circuit. The novelty soon wore off, and the costs, as with the contemporary systems of mechanical synchronization, proved too high to remain viable.

Another major push toward synchronized dialogue occurred in 1913, when Edison introduced a new system of mechanical synchronization that included a number of innovations, such as longer and larger cylinders and improvements in microphone technology that allowed the recording of dialogue and filming at the same time (Figure 5-3). This system was not a success, however, due to inadequate amplification and difficulty in maintaining synchronization, problems that were only compounded by the increasing popularity of multireel features.

Figure 5-3. *Nursery Favorites* (1913) was one of the films Edison made using the second version of the Kinetophone. This new effort at sound pictures proved no more profitable than the first. The films suffered from the familiar problems of amplification and synchronization, but the introduction of the long, multireel feature pushed down the demand for other sorts of film-based novelties. When a fire destroyed the studio equipped for making sound pictures in December 1914, Edison chose not to rebuild it. For more than a decade, Edison's failure with the Kinetophone made filmmakers very skeptical about the potential of sound film.

SOUND RESEARCH IN THE 1920s

The amplification problem was finally solved by developments in radio, or, specifically, by the technology of the radio tube. Electronic public address systems based on the radio tube were introduced in 1919, but it wasn't until the later 1920s that some further improvements to amplification and loudspeaker technology, along with the public's growing familiarity with amplified sound through radio, set the stage for a successful introduction of sound film. In addition, better sound recording was enabled in the electrical pickup as the recording industry shifted from the recording horn to the microphone for commercial releases in 1925. Finally, theaters found an incentive for a change-over to sound synchronization in the devastating effect that commercial radio quickly was having on the size of theatrical audiences. (The Keith and Orpheum circuit of vaudeville went so far as to ban its performers from appearing on radio for a period in the

effect of the character, and to give the necessary illusion.

But many will ask, How can this be brought about? The answer is in rehearsing and drilling the people, not alone by explanation, but by having everyone act the character thoroughly, as if he were appearing on the stage, without being hidden by the drop. As an example, take a woman in tears. She should go through the same action that she would if it were happening to her in real life, using the handkerchief and hands and all gestures that accompany it. Struggles should be gone through in the same manner. To make the effect more complete, the breaking of a glass or the shooting of a revolver or a gun, or slapping the hand on a table to bring out a convincing point in an argument should always be done by the person speaking the line.
—James Clancy (Impresario) (1909)[1]

mid-1920s, a tactic the company would repeat briefly with sound film a few years later. Ironically, the Keith and Orpheum circuit would be bought out by Radio Corporation of America [RCA] as part of the deal to create RKO Pictures.) In the mid-1920s, RCA (a subsidiary of General Electric), which owned a number of useful amplification patents from its radio technology, and AT&T, with its work in public address systems, phonograph recording, and radio, competed to develop a workable solution to amplification and synchronization. In 1926, the two companies agreed to cross-license their patents for use in amplification. This allowed rapid development of sound-film recording and exhibition technology without fear of a major lawsuit.

Industrial research pursued two basic approaches to sound film: (a) sound-on-disk and (b) sound-on-film; and it focused in three areas: (a) "nonsynchronous sound" for adding recorded musical accompaniments to features; (b) short features of music and vaudeville; and (c) newsreels. Each of these placed somewhat different demands on technology, but all three required the development of a suitable means of amplifying sound in the large theaters.

Work on nonsynchronous sound centered on increasing the time length available in the recording medium to equal a reel of film and on improving the fidelity of recording and reproducing equipment, particularly with respect to the sound of a full orchestra. Most research on sound film prior to the 1920s had used a sound-on-disk (or, in the case of Edison, sound-on-cylinder) method, but the longest standard commercial phonograph recording format at the time was only about 5 minutes—less than half the length of the usual one-thousand-foot reel of film. This did not prevent theaters from using phonograph records as a substitute for live musicians; many small theaters employed phonographs when musicians were either unavailable (such as on dinner break) or too expensive. The short duration of the recording, however, meant that the records would have to be changed independent of the reels, which made coordination with the image both labor intensive and unreliable. To distribute a recorded score efficiently with a film would require a recording format that matched a reel of film. Although variable in the silent era, average projection speed increased over time and, by the late 1920s, ninety feet per minute (twenty-four frames per second) was considered about normal. At that rate—which became the standard in the sound-film era—a reel of film ran about 11 minutes. Any sound-on-disk method would need to increase the length of the record accordingly. This could be done by increasing the size of the disk (or cylinder), by increasing the density of the grooves, or by reducing the speed of rotation; each of these posed distinct technological challenges in preserving the quality of the recording.

Sound-on-film, by contrast, was limited in terms of time only by the length of the reel. A sound-on-film technology had been developed around 1905 by Eugene Lauste (a former Edison employee), although it proved infeasible for commercial exploitation at that time. Nevertheless, the minimal restriction on length was attractive, especially to those working in radio, who were looking for a reliable way to record longer material for broadcast. This was one of the

Figure 5-4. Phonofilm produced primarily short films of such musical and vaude- a | b
ville acts as (a) Sissle and Blake, but also included films of famous people such as
this one (b) of President Coolidge (1924). This latter film, the first sound picture of a
U.S. president, was heavily promoted, but de Forest neglected to credit Case's
contribution to the device. Case consequently withdrew from the partnership and
worked with William Fox to develop Movietone.

important reasons that Lee de Forest, an early radio pioneer, began working with
sound film, but he quickly realized that he could also use his improvements in
recording sound on film to make synchronized sound pictures. Developed in
conjunction with Theodore Case, de Forest's Phonofilm system (Figure 5-4) was
demonstrated in 1923 and placed in limited circulation thereafter. Hugo Riesenfeld was a principal sponsor of de Forest's research and featured Phonofilm frequently at his Rivoli Theatre. Although Phonofilm specialized in short films, de
Forest also recorded scores for features such as *The Covered Wagon* (1923) and
Siegfried (1924), both (not coincidentally) with scores by Riesenfeld. Although de
Forest made significant improvements on the sound-on-film process, he never
adequately solved the amplification problem. Phonofilm reportedly also suffered
from pronounced "wow and flutter," which reflects a basic incompatibility in
sound-on-film: whereas projecting the image requires an intermittent action,
where the film must start and stop at the projecting head, reproducing sound
requires a continuous action, where the film moves past the projecting head at a
constant rate.

Western Electric, a subsidiary of AT&T, was responsible for the Vitaphone,
a sound-on-disk system developed for Warners that would prove to be the first
commercially viable system for synchronized sound. Although Western Electric had also considered sound-on-film—like de Forest, Western Electric was
heavily involved with radio research—the company opted eventually to work on
a disk-based system. Because the company had been largely responsible for developing electrical recording for the phonograph, its personnel knew that disk

recording, unlike sound film, was a mature technology, relatively inexpensive with a very reliable manufacturing procedure. Sound-on-film, by contrast, remained experimental, with uneven quality and much higher production costs throughout the 1920s.

The Vitaphone system consisted of a special phonograph mechanically coupled to a projector. The real advantage that it enjoyed over Phonofilm and other earlier attempts at sound film lay not in the medium, however, but in the amplification. Indeed, as amplification systems improved in general in the later 1920s, many theaters turned to phonographs as a means of supplementing (or replacing) their live musicians. Nonsynchronous scores did not require the special synchronizing equipment that sound films did, and theaters that could not afford the installation by AT&T or RCA or were judged to be of insufficient importance to have synchronized sound systems installed immediately often turned to regional theater sound companies, which installed an amplification system connected to a phonograph that allowed for effective but nonsynchronous sound. Collections of records catalogued by mood could then be used to construct a full orchestra score for a film, in the already familiar manner of the compiled score for live performance (although, of course, without the finesse that was possible in a synchronized live performance).

Short features of musical and vaudeville acts were another area of sound research, and Vitaphone proved particularly appropriate for such use (Figure 5-5). Just as the recording of the nonsynchronous score could substitute for the live musicians, so too these recorded musical and vaudeville shorts could replace live stage acts and prologues. These films were shot as performances in a theater; they provided a method to present a theatrical act from the perspective of a good seat from the orchestra section (the main floor) of the theater. In a sense, such films could be considered visualized sound recordings as much as they were sound motion pictures. In any case, the important thing was that the performance was staged for the camera and microphone in a highly controlled environment, and the phonograph was perfectly suited to exhibition of such films.

Newsreels were the final area for sound research, and these posed a completely different set of challenges to sound than those of vaudeville or musical acts, which were filmed in a studio, theater, or some similar acoustically controlled environment. Newsreels had to capture news where it happened, on location. Consequently, they required a production system that was highly efficient, relatively mobile, and with a robust recording mechanism rather than one focused on capturing the highest possible fidelity of sound. Intelligibility of speech was far more important than the fidelity of the recording for the needs of the newsreel. Because a newsreel was made by splicing together a variety of short strips of film so that a series of events could be shown in short vignettes, the ability to edit the footage was another crucial factor to creating a sound newsreel.

Sound-on-disk and sound-on-film each held distinct advantages during the period of development. The sound-on-disk process, based on the phonograph,

Figure 5-5. *The Voice From the Screen* (1926). This was a film made to demonstrate the technical aspects of the Vitaphone. The camera records from the soundproof booth; here with the side removed for the purposes of illustration. The recording engineer is visible at the left; again the sides of the recording booth have been removed for illustration.

At sixteen inches, the Vitaphone disk was far larger than the largest commercial records (twelve inches) and it rotated at 33⅓ rather than 78 rpm. This allowed for sufficient recording time to accompany a standard reel of film. For improved playback, the material used in the production of the Vitaphone disk was softer than commercial disks, which meant that each disk could be used only twenty times before it needed to be replaced.

initially had a higher (or at least more reliable) level of sound fidelity than did the sound-on-film process, and therefore it is not surprising that Western Electric's Vitaphone, which pursued the idea of recording performances, should have developed a sound-on-disk method. Vitaphone was well adapted to use for nonsynchronous scores and short films of performances. It was not, however, well adapted to location work. Movietone, the sound-on-film process Case perfected for Fox after he broke with de Forest, was by contrast extremely portable (Figure 5-6). Although Fox dabbled a bit in recorded vaudeville as well, he saw a much greater opportunity in recording newsworthy events, thus capturing for the cinema some of the radio-like immediacy of events as they happen. The early Movietone newsreels thus emphasized synchronized sound through the presentation of short

Figure 5-6. *The King of Spain* (1927). Frame enlargement of a Movietone sound film release print. The variable density sound strip runs along the left side between the sprockets and the image. Note that the area available on the film strip for the image was necessarily reduced, and the resulting picture has a squarer aspect ratio (roughly 1.19:1). Many filmmakers disliked the square format, and in 1932 the Academy of Motion Picture Arts and Sciences stepped in and established the standard 1.37:1 (known as the Academy ratio). (Because the sound track of the Vitaphone was on a record, the full filmstrip was available for the image and its aspect ratio was the standard 4:3 [1.33:1] of silent film.)

speeches and other public activities that might feature sound. The recording apparatus for Movietone was much less bulky and, because it did not involve a delicate needle cutting grooves, was less affected by the rough handling that was an inevitable part of recording on location (Figure 5-7).

SOUND FILM AND THE STANDARDIZATION OF EXHIBITION

In all of these cases, the synchronized sound film was a "short" meant to supplement the feature on a theater's program. The primary impetus for the development of the sound film in the 1920s was in fact the standardization of exhibition, not the development of a feature-length talking picture (with synchronized dialogue).

As we noted in the previous chapter, the business of movie exhibition became more and more stratified in the 1920s. The deluxe theaters in large urban areas presented films with lush orchestral accompaniment and improvisation played on majestic organs, and they featured entr'acte performances such as vaudeville headliners, chorus lines, singers, and so forth. From the standpoint of the movie studios, which by the end of the 1920s owned large theater chains, the deluxe theaters, although profitable, were also expensive.

Figure 5-7. The commercial potential of sound newsreels was made particularly evident with the recording of Charles A. Lindbergh's departure for his historic Atlantic flight on 20 May 1927. The Movietone footage and sound of the take-off created a sensation at the Roxy Theatre when it was shown that same evening.

At the same time, the smaller neighborhood theaters and, even more so, the rural theaters could not afford to compete on anything like the same scale. At best, such theaters might have an "orchestra" with five or six players, and they could support some small-time vaudeville. At their worst, small theaters used only a mechanical piano (with piano rolls) or a phonograph. A lack of standardization in accompaniment therefore made it difficult for the studios to calculate accurately how a film might play. A good accompaniment could make an otherwise indifferent film seem remarkable, whereas an indifferent accompaniment could make an otherwise fine film seem flat and unremarkable. Recorded sound therefore offered a way to standardize exhibition that would control both labor costs (at the large theaters) and quality (at the small theaters). The studios could offer a standardized product to be distributed nationally, thus giving all spectators a more or less uniform film experience that could be calculated in advance by the studios. The patrons of smaller theaters would enjoy access to the same sort of deluxe show available in the downtown picture palaces; and the studios would gain huge economies of scale in their quickly expanding theater chains, economies of scale that would allow them to put intense competitive pressure on the independents.

VITAPHONE PRELUDE

Will H. Hays (President of Motion Picture Producers and Distributors of America)
Welcome

New York Philharmonic Orchestra, Henry Hadley Conducting
Wagner, *Tannhäuser* Overture

Marion Talley
Verdi, "Caro Nome," from *Rigoletto*

Roy Smeck
"His Pastimes"

Anna Case
"La Fiesta"

Mischa Elman, violin, accompanied by Josef Bonime
Dvorak, "Humoresque"

Giovanni Martinelli
Leoncavallo, "Vesti la guibba," from I *Pagliacci*

INTERMISSION

Don Juan, starring John Barrymore
Musical score by Major Edward Bowes, David Mendoza and Dr. William Axt. Played by the New York Philharmonic Orchestra, Herman Heller, conducting.

Figure 5-8. Inaugural Vitaphone Program. John Barrymore starred in *Don Juan* (1926), the first feature-length Vitaphone film. With a recorded orchestra score, occasional hard synced sound effects, but no sync dialogue, it was what would later be called a "synchronized" film.

a
―
b

The gala program Warner Bros. used to premiere Vitaphone gives a good indication of how the company initially understood the technology. The program contained an introductory film of Will Hays talking, a series of short musical films, and, after an intermission, *Don Juan* (1926), a big-budget John Barrymore feature (Figure 5-8). Although *Don Juan* had been produced as a regular silent-film feature, Warner Bros. decided to add a few synchronized sound effects and a complete synchronized orchestral score by composers David Mendoza, conductor of Loew's Capitol Theatre in New York, and William Axt, who had written a number of special scores, including one for *The Big Parade* (1925). The score was even recorded by a prestigious classical symphony orchestra, the New York

Philharmonic. Although it was the Vitaphone shorts that received the bulk of the attention in the press, the program overall remained a traditional one: a series of presentation acts and a long silent feature. Fox's approach was similar: the first Movietone feature was *Sunrise* (1927), a silent film with a synchronized score by the musical staff of the Roxy Theatre.

SOUND AND THE FEATURE FILM, 1927: *THE JAZZ SINGER*

By the beginning of 1927, both Warner Bros. and Fox had established regular production of sound pictures, Warners specializing in short musical and vaudeville acts with an occasional silent feature with synchronized music and effects and Fox in newsreels. The other studios followed Warners' and Fox's experiments but were not ready to commit themselves to production because sound film was by no means on solid economic footing. As often happens, the problem was circular: there were not yet a sufficient number of wired theaters to absorb the cost of production, and therefore no possibility of enough high-quality productions to fill the need for weekly, or even biweekly, program changes. These issues were addressed to some extent when both Warners and Fox made agreements with Western Electric so that films from either company could be shown at any theater having a Western Electric sound installation; previously, the company would wire theaters for one system or the other (Figure 5-9). Despite the agreement, the rate of installation remained painfully slow.

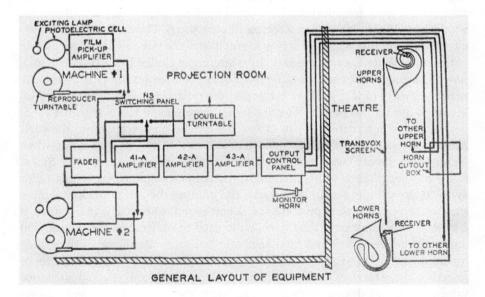

Figure 5-9. Schematic for Western Electric sound installation. The projection room is equipped for both sound-on-film and sound-on-record reproduction, giving theaters the ability to play films in either format.

Moreover, already by Spring 1927 interest in the Vitaphone had begun to flag—a number of recently wired theaters canceled their service. In a bid to maintain or rebuild public interest, Warners announced they were making a feature film with Al Jolson that would have some synchronized sound sequences. The success of this film, *The Jazz Singer*, proved to be a turning point in the history of the sound film, as it demonstrated that synchronized sound could be effectively incorporated into a feature presentation, offering an entertainment that was something more than simply a canned vaudeville act or a silent film with synchronized score and sound effects. Apart from this, the film did not mark a definitive break with silent-film practice, however, although it is often portrayed that way. Indeed, even a casual look will show that *The Jazz Singer* was conceived as a silent with a few synchronized sound sequences added. In fact, it was received by many in its contemporary audience as a series of Vitaphone shorts inserted into what remained a silent film (like *Don Juan*, *The Jazz Singer* has a complete synchronized orchestral score in addition to the performances). The sound sequences, in other words, were supplementary rather than essential: that the film was perfectly intelligible without them is attested by the fact that a purely silent print of the film also circulated and did a reasonable box-office business.

The sound sequences were, however, chosen to reinforce the general rhetorical thrust of the film, which aligns the new technology of synchronized sound with the youthful hero and the hip urban life (and secondarily with canting in the synagogue), whereas the silent sequences are used primarily for old-fashioned family melodrama. The initial synchronized sequence shows the young Jakie illicitly singing in a saloon (Figure 5-10a). The extremely loose synchronization of this sequence serves to emphasize the placement and regulation of the voice. When we next see Jack, he is singing at Coffee Dan's (Figure 5-10b), now to perfect synchronization. Between these two scenes, there is a synchronized sequence of Jack's father canting in the synagogue. In this way, the film seems to ask: is the proper place for Jack's voice on the stage or in the synagogue, and who has the right to determine it? The one exception to the basic pattern is also the only speech outside of the context of a performance: when Jack's father shouts "stop" as he finds Jack singing Irving Berlin's "Blue Skies" to his mother (Figure 5-10c). Strikingly, the father's word (46:53) brings Jack's synchronized singing to an abrupt halt and plunges the sound track into more than 20 seconds worth of pure silence. When sound returns, it is in the form of a synchronized orchestra music, which is used to underscore the subsequent argument between Jack and his father over tradition, the theme of the family melodrama (Figure 5-10d). In this way, the score seems to follow Jack's father in rejecting the sound of Jack's (synchronized) singing, and the old-fashioned values of the melodrama also seem to accrue to the sound of the silent-film orchestral score. Even here, however, the film hedges its bets because the two synagogue scenes (as well as a performance by cantor Josef Rosenblatt)—moments that should rightly be classed with the melodrama—are also given with synchronized sound (Figure 5-10e).

Figure 5-10. *The Jazz Singer* (1927). (a) Young Jakie sings "My Gal Sal" at the saloon. Even in long shots, the synchronization is poor. (b) Jack sings "Dirty Hands, Dirty Faces" at Coffee Dan's. After finishing this song, Jack banters with his audience, using Jolson's famous tag line: "You ain't heard nothing yet." (c) Jack's father says, "stop." This is in fact the only actual piece of spoken dialogue in the entire film. The other spoken lines consist of Jack addressing the audience at *Coffee Dan's* and his odd monologue to his mother (including Jack sitting at the piano vamping) that immediately precedes this scene. (d) Jack and his father argue over singing "jazz." This sequence is accompanied by an orchestral score (Tchaikovsky's *Romeo and Juliet Overture*). (e) Jack sings the Kol Nidre as the spirit of his father hovers behind him. According to production records, Jolson lip synced the scene to an edited playback recording of Cantor Josef Rosenblatt. As Donald Crafton notes, this proves that rerecording and filming to playback were already in use in 1927.[2]

Figure 5-11. Al Jolson and Davey Lee in *The Singing Fool* (1928). Although less well known today than *The Jazz Singer*, *The Singing Fool* enjoyed greater commercial success— it would remain the highest grossing film until the release of *Gone with the Wind* (1939)—and carried more weight in the other studios' decisions to invest in feature sound-film production.

The commercial success of *The Jazz Singer* encouraged other studios to think seriously about the possibility of the sound picture as a "talking picture," but we should be wary about attributing too much influence in such matters to any one film. MGM in particular remained cautious, even after *The Jazz Singer* was held over for extended runs. After all, three earlier films, *Four Horsemen of the Apocalypse* (1921), *The Big Parade* (1925), and *Ben-Hur* (1925), all had runs that exceeded the box-office performance of *The Jazz Singer*. It was actually the huge success of the decidedly mediocre *The Lights of New York* (1928), the first all-talking film, and *The Singing Fool* (1928), Jolson's follow-up to *The Jazz Singer*, that finally convinced Hollywood to the convert to sound (Fig. 5-11). Seeing the returns from these films, the studios changed course and committed to the production of sound film.

THE TRANSITION FROM SILENT TO SOUND FILM

The passage from silent film to sound film took roughly five years, from 1926 through 1930; but many of the technical and aesthetic issues were still not satisfactorily settled until 1933, some even later than that. The studios themselves did not complete the changeover in production until the fall of 1929. The theaters would not be completely wired until the early 1930s: by the end of 1927 only 157 theaters in the United States had been wired for sound (although these included most of the important urban venues); by the end of 1928, after RCA began competing with Western Electric to wire theaters, roughly four thousand theaters (including most of those owned by the major studios) had installed sound, and a year later more than eight thousand theaters were so equipped (or about 40 percent of the country's roughly twenty thousand theaters). By spring of 1931, the total had risen to 60 percent.

Partly because of cost and partly because equipment was in short supply, many smaller rural and neighborhood theaters were not converted to sound even in 1931. Although production of silent films had largely ceased by the end of 1929, new films were released in two prints, sound and silent with intertitles as late as the end of 1930, by which time a sufficient number of theaters had converted to sound to make the market for sound film viable—but even then nearly a quarter of the theaters in the United States remained unwired. (Many of these theaters would never convert to sound.) Not surprisingly, theaters owned by studios were among the first to be converted, and this placed them at a distinct competitive advantage. Their profits were positively affected in two ways. First, because of the novelty factor, theaters with sound did proportionally better in ticket sales. Second, theaters with sound were considerably more cost-efficient than theaters without sound because they saved on musicians' salaries.

Although much has been written about the devastating effect the changeover to sound had on Hollywood stars, the effect was even more acute for musicians. As theaters were wired for sound, they had less need for live musicians, and large numbers of musicians were laid off. The elimination of orchestras and organists occurred quickly (musicians' salaries typically totaled $3,000 per week in the largest theaters), and the union ran an ad campaign designed to win continued support for live music (Figure 5-12), but without notable success. In Minneapolis and St. Paul, for instance, only a single theater retained an orchestra by the end of 1929. National unemployment in the musicians' union (the American Federation of Musicians) was about 50 percent in the 1930–31 season. A number of the deluxe theaters kept their musical programs for a period after the coming of sound, but the challenges of the Depression made it more and more difficult for even these theaters to attract sufficient patronage to meet expenses. Wiring costs became a problem once the Depression hit because wiring for sound was typically financed, and the declining audience after 1931 meant many theaters struggled to meet the debt payments. Soon, the deluxe theaters, too, lost their musicians or at least reduced the number on the payroll. In addition, many of the prominent musical directors, as well as the best musicians, had relocated to Hollywood or moved to radio, so that the programs lost some of their luster and prestige. Riesenfeld, for example, left his post as director of the Rivoli, Rialto, and Criterion theaters in New York to become musical director of United Artists in Hollywood. When the music library of the Capitol Theater was

Figure 5-12. "Canned Music on Trial" was part of an ad campaign in 1929 against wired theaters. The collapse of the vaudeville circuit around the same time only exacerbated the problem for musicians. Some were able to find work in Hollywood and radio stations; and the large number of idle musicians undoubtedly contributed to the proliferation of big bands, since the economic conditions and general oversupply of musicians helped hold down the labor cost of running a touring band with a large number of musicians.

transferred to the New York studio to form the basis of the MGM music library, it became absolutely clear that the time of musicians in the movie theater was drawing to a close.

Finally, we should note that many theaters and theater chains invested in sound-on-disk hardware during the first sound conversions in 1928. The optical sound track eventually won out, but between 1928 and the end of 1931, the major studios—not just Warner Bros.—released their feature film sound tracks in both disk and optical-on-film format. The reason was not a matter of aesthetics but of finance: virtually all theaters wired for sound had disk systems, but only gradually did they either acquire dual sound systems or convert to optical-only.

TYPES OF EARLY SOUND FILM

In 1929, sound film was understood to fall into one of three types: synchronized (recorded orchestral accompaniment and sound effects); part-talkie ("synchronized" recorded orchestral accompaniment interspersed with talking sequences); and the 100-percent talkie. This terminology can be confusing because a "synchronized" film in this typology is what we would now call a silent film; "synchronization" here refers to the fact that the *music* has been fit to the action. (Recall that in contemporary usage the term refers to a general principle of sound and image coordination—"playing with the film"—and is opposed to counterpoint, or "playing against the film"; see Chapter 3.)

"Synchronized" films often make use of sound effects, both hard and loosely synchronized as was the case in "live" performances. A fateful knock on the door, for instance, was likely to be closely synchronized in live performance either by the drummer or by a supernumerary backstage—and so such synchronization in *Don Juan* was fully typical. Swordplay and other more atmospheric noises, on the contrary, were treated more casually (as they would continue to be in later sound film), and this was also the case in *Don Juan*. The loosely synchronized opening sequence of MGM's *Wild Orchids* (1929) is likewise fully in keeping with silent-film practice (see Figure 5-13a). *Wings* (1927) supplemented its live orchestra and sound effects personnel with a synchronized optical sound track of airplane and machine gun noises to heighten the spectacle of the battle sequences; this arrangement also made for efficient road show exhibition (although the technology was anything but flawless). In all of these cases, sound effects were used as an element of spectacle, much as was color during the silent era; the "synchronized" sound film was simply a means of mechanizing these effects, just as the recorded score mechanized the orchestra.

A fully synchronized sequence would, in these terms, simply be a way of *heightening* the spectacle. Ideally, such scenes could add to the experience of the film without being absolutely necessary to understand it, so that the films could play at those theaters that had sound installed as well as those that did not. *The Jazz Singer* followed this strategy of supplemental synchronized sound, which seems to have been one motivation for the part-talkies. In fact, audiences soon proved resistant to the part-talkie, at least when presented as such (critics derided the part-talkie as a "goat gland," preferring either the all-talkie or the

The Mexican film Redes (1936) is a part-talkie, a hybrid of silent and sound film common in the early transitional years, but increasingly rare in commercial filmmaking after 1930. In a part-talkie, the juxtaposition of scenes treated in silent film fashion with scenes of talking is often stark. Audiences today, acclimated to smooth aural modulations between scene types, are liable to attribute the abruptness to technical shortcomings and discount its aesthetic effect. In the best part-talkies, however, it matters when the film talks, when it does not, and how it passes from one state to the other. The scenes with music in Redes present an image where hope for a better world is mixed with grief over a world that would allow such suffering. Silvestre Revueltas' music is beautifully composed to sound as though it must labor mightily against the technology, a straining that is central to its affective character.

a | b   **Figure 5-13.** *Wild Orchids* (1929). (a) The opening sequence contains a flurry of sound effects, most prominently the blaring horns on the wild car ride to the ship and the crowd noises on the dock. Yet these sounds are atmospheric: they are not closely synchronized to the image but rather suggest a basic soundscape. Indeed, they seem to float uncannily above the scene. This fact is heightened by the continuation of the sound over the intertitles. Compare the treatment of sound here with the hard synchronization of the exotic, "native" dance sequence later in the same film. (b) This latter scene is pure sonic spectacle, with numerous crisp claps used to show off the precision of the synchronization. There is nothing in this synchronized sequence necessary to understand the narrative, however, so the film was easily adaptable to exhibition in those theaters not wired for sound (a different music might be used or the scene might be deleted).

The first generation of Hollywood composers for the sound film were mostly of European origin. Two American composers who stand out as exceptions are Alfred Newman and his protégé, David Raksin. Raksin is best known for his score to Laura *(1944), but he began his career working with Charlie Chaplin on* Modern Times *(1936). Raksin's detailed and colorful account of his time with Chaplin reveals details about collaboration on films and film scoring.*

—See David Raksin, "Life with Charlie," in Cooke, *The Hollywood Film Music Reader.*

"pure" silent film. A film like *Wild Orchids*, however, which was essentially a "synchronized" film, could still effectively contain a number of sequences with hard sync, perhaps because (like those in *The Jazz Singer*) they were framed as performances (Figure 5-13b).

The 100-percent talking film, by contrast, could be shown only in a theater equipped for sound. The first such feature film was *Lights of New York*, which Warner Bros. released in 1928, but only 1 year later, when MGM, which had long been the holdout on the talking picture, won the Academy Award for Best Picture for *The Broadway Melody*, it was clear that talking film was quickly becoming synonymous with sound film. By 1930 in Hollywood, production of silent film had essentially ceased, with a few notable exceptions such as Charlie Chaplin (see Figure 5-14 and its commentary; also see the sidebar for a summary of composer David Raksin's recollections of working with Chaplin). Europe took somewhat longer to make the transition, and a film such as *Le Million* (1931) resembles a part-talkie in the way it plays talking and silent sequences off of one another. Even outside the United States, however, going to the movies was quickly coming to mean going to the talkies.

Figure 5-14. *City Lights* (1931). Charlie Chaplin took an extreme position with respect to sound film, remaining almost fully committed to the silent-film aesthetic through the mid-1930s. He composed and closely supervised the placement of the music, which was "synchronized" and ubiquitous in silent-film fashion. Yet he drew on the resources of recorded sound to give the muteness characteristic of the silent film a new, albeit financially untenable, eloquence in the sound era; that is, he was able to use the control that synchronized sound allowed and even demanded but in some degree to turn it against the realistic aesthetic of sound film.

Moments in his films that gesture toward synchronized speech tend to emphasize the monological quality of the discourse, especially the political power that comes along with the control of speech. This happens, for instance, early in *City Lights*, where the voices of the public officials are presented as voices, but represented as noise: their speech is unintelligible. The effect is wonderfully deflating of the pretensions of public speech even as it illustrates, in its miscarriage, the way that such speech carries the voice of authority. *Modern Times*, released in 1936 and Chaplin's last film featuring his trademark figure of the Tramp, likewise remains almost entirely silent. Many sound effects are hard synced, as are snippets of dialogue (even some nonsensical bits and the Tramp's climactic song performance that concludes the film). Here, too, the power of speech is associated with abusive, arbitrary authority.

MUSICALS IN EARLY SOUND FILM

Early sound films were predominantly musicals—"all singing, all dancing, all talking" was standard advertising copy. The reasons are several. First, musicals offered an easy means of exploiting popular music. Much of the vaudeville recorded in Vitaphone shorts was based in popular song, and, as mentioned earlier, *The Jazz Singer* was understood initially at least as a silent film with added Vitaphone shorts of Al Jolson singing popular songs. These songs were a commodity in their own right, and Warner Bros. had invested in acquiring music publishing firms around the same time as the studio was developing Vitaphone. Clearly, Vitaphone and the music publishing concerns were intended to be mutually reinforcing from the standpoint of producing profits. Although hardly a film lacked a theme song in the late 1920s, musicals exploited popular music in a highly efficient manner. In any case, the preponderance of musicals in the early sound film meant that popular music helped define *the* music of the sound film.

Musicals offered a further advantage: the narrative was understood as being punctuated by the spectacle of musical performances. In that respect, the production process of a sound musical differed little conceptually from that of *The Jazz Singer*, which could therefore serve as a model (much as that film also served as the model for the part-talkie). The difference was mainly that the narrative was carried by recorded dialogue rather than by intertitles. All-talking dialogue films ("talkers") were another entity altogether, as it was not clear where or even whether music should be introduced in such films, an aesthetic problem that simply points to another advantage of musicals: they gave a diegetic motivation for the presence of music and offered opportunity for staged spectacle—most musicals included at least one production number filmed in two-color Technicolor, usually a final production number.

Confining music to performance had the further benefit of minimizing the need for rerecording. Although it had been technically possible to dub sound tracks since at least 1927 (*The Jazz Singer* used some rerecording), the process was risky due to the significant loss of fidelity in the process. Consequently, rerecording did not become standard until after 1930. Even filming to playback—that is, recording the sound and playing it back as the scene was acted out—was seldom done (Figure 5-15). Any voice doubling that did occur—in musical numbers at least—usually occurred on the set, with the voice double positioned outside the frame but in proximity to the actor. In general practice, then, sound tracks were recorded live, along with the film. In terms of the musical practice this meant that scenes with dialogue and music required that the musicians be assembled on the same soundstage as the scene being shot. The musicians would then play for every take of the scene. (As mentioned in the previous chapter, the practice of musicians on the set to help actors catch the pace and mood of a scene went back to the silent-film days, but, of course, the stakes of this music-making became much higher when the music became part of the film.)

Figure 5-15. *The Broadway Melody* (1929). The production number "Dance of the Painted Doll" was initially recorded and filmed at the same time. After it was decided that the scene needed to be reshot, Douglas Shearer, who would become the long-time head of the sound department at MGM, suggested they keep the audio, which was excellent, shoot to playback, and resynchronize in postproduction. Although this was not the first instance of shooting to playback, its success helped make the practice standard for production numbers.

Obviously, such an arrangement was inefficient from the standpoint of labor time. Moreover, watching the balances in this real-time recording was a challenge for the sound personnel. Because the early microphones were weak in sensitivity, fidelity, dynamic range, and directionality, music often had a detrimental effect on the intelligibility of dialogue, which was understood then as now as the primary consideration in making an effective sound film. Many of these problems could be mitigated when music was treated as a performance—as, again, would be the case with musicals. Thus, until technology advanced sufficiently that it was possible to rerecord reliably—that is, to record dialogue, music, and effects separately and then mix them down later—music tended to be used only when it was deemed indispensable. (Warner Bros., which used sound-on-disk recording, developed effective rerecording early and many of their films before 1930 feature extensive music behind dialogue. The company's use of such musical underscoring dropped considerably when they changed to recording sound on film, though it is not clear whether the shift in scoring practices was related primarily to the change in technology or to the general industry preference for less music in the years between 1930 and 1933.)

Production

PRODUCTION PHASES

During the early sound era, most of the work on the sound track needed to be accomplished during the production phase—indeed, getting a good recording became just as important as getting film footage. In any case, the introduction of sound directly affected the visual sphere. Before effective sound insulation was devised for the cameras, scenes would typically be shot with multiple cameras, each enclosed in a sound-proof booth, so as to allow for cutting while ensuring that the sound would remain in sync. Because each of the cameras was required to remain out of the visual field of the others, this arrangement severely limited the number of possible set-ups for each scene. With fewer shots to choose from, directors and editors tended to use longer takes, often in medium and long shot. The need for a controlled acoustic environment also meant that most shooting was done on soundproofed soundstages rather than on location or even in the back lot (Figure 5-16).

By 1932 engineers had devised solutions to most of the pressing technological problems: better microphones with increased sensitivity, fidelity, dynamic range, and directionality; improved film stock and development timing for sound film; the microphone boom; improvements in lighting to make the apparatus

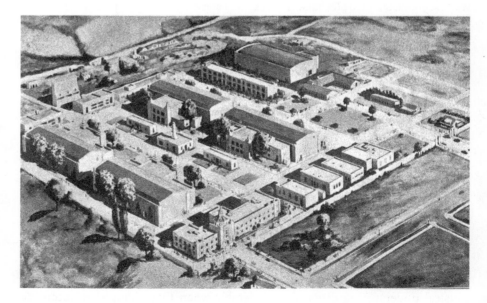

Figure 5-16. Fox Movietone Studio, Los Angeles, c. 1929. Increasingly, sound stages took the place of the back lot.

quieter; effective sound insulation for the camera; and so forth. Most important, these improvements made it feasible for rerecording or dubbing to become a normal part of postproduction. This meant that music and effects no longer needed to be recorded during principal shooting, and the recording engineer would thereafter only have to be concerned with capturing dialogue. Music and effects, if needed, could be recorded separately and added later; the three components—dialogue, music, and effects—could then be mixed together before the final sound track was added to the release print. The importance of this development was already lauded by recording engineer K. F. Morgan in 1929, well before it was fully realized: The post-production rerecording process "has been instrumental in supplying a unity and finesse as well as rhythm and continuity to the sound picture. There are some who believe that as the technique of sound recording is developed to a high degree, the need for dubbing will be diminished or even eliminated. However, dubbing has contributed largely to the success of recent sound pictures and the indications are that, in all probability, its application will expand with the development of the art."[3]

This change greatly simplified the making of sound film, both saving money and giving filmmakers much more flexibility. It also greatly facilitated dialogue replacement or looping, the rerecording of dialogue to an existing segment of film, a technique that could be used to fix flubbed lines but, more important, to dub dialogue in foreign languages, the key to Hollywood maintaining its dominance of the world film market. Prior to rerecording, films would need to be re-shot completely in a foreign language—a procedure that was normal practice in the early years of the sound era.

MUSIC DEPARTMENT

The music personnel for the early sound pictures were drawn from two primary sources: the large deluxe theaters and the popular music industry, especially the part associated with musical theater. Their duties were divided along predictable lines. The deluxe theater musicians (many of whom also began in music theater), primarily well-known musical directors such as Riesenfeld, Rapee, or Mendoza, were at first assigned to provide scores for the "synchronized" silent films. These scores would be prepared much like any other silent feature. The main difference lay in distribution. Rather than scores being available to theaters for live performance, the music would be recorded by an orchestra with sound effects added (when appropriate). It is worth pointing out that for these synchronized silents, music and effects were thus added in the postproduction phase—exactly as they would be for regular sound film once rerecording became standard.

Because the films with dialogue were primarily musicals, music for these films was provided by those who worked in the music theater industry. Song writers were an obvious necessity, and studios quickly placed large numbers of them under contract. Songs of a musical were essentially part of the script, and they needed to be composed in the preproduction phase, that is, prior to the filming. Beyond that, they needed to be arranged and orchestrated in a fashion suitable for recording prior to the filming as well. Arrangement and orchestration were considered specialized

If Walt Disney is the father of the cartoon, Carl Stalling is the father of cartoon music. He got his start with Disney through the Silly Symphony series (1929–1939) and may have been the first to use a click track—or what he referred to as the "tick method"—when recording for Disney's **The Skeleton Dance** *(1929). In a manner reminiscent of the silent-era compilation score, Stalling also incorporated pre-existing music as a sort of commentary on his cartoons, drawing on a wide variety of classical music and even popular music of the time.*
—See Carl Stalling, "Conversations with Carl Stalling," in Cooke, *The Hollywood Film Music Reader*.

One of the chief jobs of an orchestrator was arranging and filling out musical themes provided by the composer. For André Previn, some orchestrations were easier than others depending on the expertise of the composer. When he worked for Georgie Stoll, Previn went to every rehearsal to interpret the score, due to the composer's limited musical literacy. Other composers, like Hugo Friedhofer, got their start as orchestrators and would provide such detail that Previn found himself merely cleaning up the music notation for the copyists.
—See André Previn, "No Minor Chords," in Cooke, *The Hollywood Film Music Reader.*

skills in the music industry at the time (and arranging for microphone was an even more specialized skill), so it is hardly surprising that musicals also drew many experienced professional arrangers and orchestrators to Hollywood.

Especially after 1929, songs were generally prerecorded and then the scene was shot silent to playback—a practice that remains dominant in filming musical numbers to this day. Such prerecording gave the cinematography of these numbers, nowhere more than in production numbers (many of which were originally also in color), a vividness and liveliness lacking in dramatic scenes dominated by dialogue.

Many of the music professionals who started on film musicals would in fact make the jump to feature film scoring. Louis Silvers, for instance, received initial acclaim for his Broadway work on Gus Edwards's revues in the 1910s and early 1920s. His best known piece was "April Showers," which he wrote for Al Jolson's appearance in the 1921 show. This number was included in Jolson's first Vitaphone short, *A Plantation Act* (1926), and Silvers's work on that film led to his being assigned the score for *The Jazz Singer*. He went on to supervise, arrange, and compose numerous feature films in the 1930s and served as music director at Columbia and Twentieth Century Fox. Alfred Newman, who would succeed Silvers at Twentieth Century Fox, likewise began on Broadway; he came to Hollywood in 1930 at the bidding of Irving Berlin. Max Steiner also worked on Broadway for a decade before coming to Hollywood in 1929 to score an adaptation of Florenz Ziegfeld's *Rio Rita*. In Germany, Franz Waxman began his career in a jazz band, where he arranged some numbers for Frederick Hollander, a highly regarded and exceptionally well-connected German cabaret and music theater composer. When Hollander was asked to write the music for Josef von Sternberg's *Der blaue Engel* (*The Blue Angel*, 1930), Waxman was called to orchestrate and conduct the score. That in turn led to work on a score for Fritz Lang's *Liliom* (1934) and then to arranging Jerome Kern's music for *Music in the Air* (1934).

During the transitional period, music departments tended to be organized on a somewhat ad hoc basis. This was simply a reflection of the fact that the nature of sound film was in constant flux. The standardization that would allow the formation of a regular music department would come only after rerecording had developed to the point that most music work could be moved into postproduction.

SOUND DEPARTMENT

Early on, most of the personnel working on sound were technical specialists, drawn primarily from the telephone and radio industries, because Western Electric and RCA were the two primary companies involved. Those working on sound, unlike those in music, understood their tasks as more technical than artistic in nature, and in the early years, at least, both progress and accomplishment were measured mostly by advances in technology: noise reduction, increased dynamic and frequency response, better directionality, and so forth. Because almost all of the sound that would end up on the sound track of a

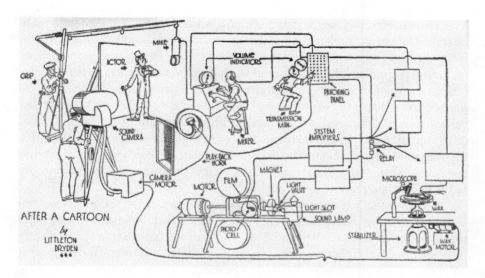

Figure 5-17. This cartoon diagram of the Western Electric System (1929) shows distinct duties for the grip, mixer, and transmission man. Note the presence of the playback horn, suggesting that music was occasionally prescored. A disk recording was often made even when primary recording was sound-on-film for the purpose of checking the sound on the set. The wax masters would be replaced by acetate transcription disks in the 1930s.

talking picture was at first recorded on the set, there was not much need for postproduction sound editing. (Figure 5-17 shows some of the jobs on a sound stage.) The sound track was cut along with the picture (or, more often, the picture was cut to the sound track). Only toward the end of the period, when rerecording became common, did dialogue editing begin to emerge from picture editing as a separate job with its own particular set of responsibilities.

In terms of sound, the situation with synchronized silent films was, like music, somewhat different in that the work was from the beginning done in the postproduction phase. The synchronized silent features would in that sense become important models (and the training ground) for the postproduction of sound in general.

Dubbing is acoustic cutting.
—Joe W. Coffman, Motion Picture Engineer (1929).[4]

Mastering the Sound Track and Elements of Style

SOUND TRACK COMPONENTS AND THE PRINCIPLE OF CLARITY

During the late 1910s and 1920s, Hollywood had developed a filmmaking system that was dominated by editing, whose fundamental commitment therefore was to a narrative assembled from various shots in postproduction. The transition to the sound film briefly challenged this commitment inasmuch as it offered the alternative of recorded performance. Then, too, early sound film often needed to be staged for the microphone, which took precedence in choosing camera angles, blocking, lighting, vocal delivery, and so forth. As Hollywood developed its recording technology, however, it did so in directions that reasserted its commitment to the narrative built through editing. In particular, the technology was pushed to facilitate the expression of narrative clarity (a priority that we discussed early in Chapter 1). Microphone techniques ensured a preponderance of direct sound, and the basic mixing strategy heavily favored dialogue, but the key innovation was the development of a reliable system of rerecording, as it permitted a conception of the sound track not as a simple reproduction but as an entity to be built in postproduction through editing.

What eventually emerged from this was a clear separation and functional differentiation in the sound track components. Sound film became a talking film, that is, a film centered on dialogue. This made sense from the standpoint of story centered on character because dialogue is, like the visual close-up, the most overt aural expression of character. Dialogue was usually further emphasized by being presented in synchronization, departures from which were generally motivated by an appeal to narrative hierarchy—for instance, reaction shots or use of off-screen sound to motivate a cut. Filmmakers went to great lengths to make sure that nothing on the sound track interfered with the intelligibility of dialogue.

The central practical question revolved around the fact that the three components of the sound track—dialogue, sound effects, and music—must contend for aural space. As Rick Altman puts it, sound film is governed by an "intermittent" rather than a continuous system.[5] Sound film contrasts markedly with silent film in this respect. In the latter, music is ubiquitous, the determining sound element of the performance. In the mature silent cinema, for instance, verbal narration might occasionally be used, although by all accounts infrequently in the United States and Europe (the practice of using a narrator continued longer in the Japanese cinema), whereas sound effects often appeared to mark narratively pertinent details or to add to aural spectacle in a particularly pitched scene (such as a battle). Once exhibition practices stabilized around the long feature in the mid-teens, sound effects became supplementary to the music, much as sound effects from the stage are understood as supplementary to the music in opera. Even in comedy, which permitted a more raucous style of accompaniment with extensive use of humorous effects, sound effects never really eclipsed music.

In the sound picture, by contrast, sound effects and dialogue became tied very strongly to image; and unlike the silent period, where the decision on whether to render a sound effect could be overridden for musical purposes, in the sound era it became extremely rare that a noticeable visual event, such as moving lips or, say, a glass being placed on a table, was not rendered with synchronized sound. Indeed, any moments of non-synchronization under those circumstances would be fraught with significance in the sound era.

Another particular challenge for early sound design was how to understand nonsynchronous sound. Synchronized sound clearly belonged to the image.

Synchronized dialogue, for instance, had its (obvious) source in the figure depicted speaking. By contrast, the source of nonsynchronous sound and so also its relation to the image was unspecified. In particular, it was not clear whether such sound should be considered as coming from offscreen space or from somewhere else, and if it was coming from somewhere else, where that place was located.

In general, early sound film managed this ambiguity by approaching the filming as though it were a recording of a performance. Nonsynchronous sound, unless it was a mistake—such as ambient set noise or perhaps the sound of the camera itself—was then simply conceived as the sound of offscreen space. Offscreen dialogue, for instance, would be simply dialogue where the speaking character was not visible but was still presumed present in the scene. The conception of nonsynchronous sound in this case presumes an identity between nonsynchronous sound and offscreen diegetic space. This identity made it easy to rationalize nonsynchronous sound, but it left little room for music. Recorded silent-film music accompaniment was certainly not diegetic; but neither was it music of the theater in the way that live orchestral music would be. It seemed to belong nowhere. Finding a place for such music therefore required breaking down the identity between nonsynchronous sound and offscreen space. In short, it required conceptual work: the division of nonsynchronous sound into diegetic and nondiegetic spheres.

The identity between nonsynchronous sound and offscreen space obtained its interpretive stability by reducing film to a species of recorded theater. This worked so long as sound film remained a novelty, but when audiences complained of "staginess" filmmakers spent considerable time pondering the status and potential of nonsynchronous sound, realizing that its non-redundancy with the image offered sound film possibilities not present with the stage. Nonsynchronous sound, in other words, was a trait of sound film that was particular to it, that potentially distinguished it from the stage but also from the silent screen.

At the same time, intimate scenes, especially love scenes featuring close-ups, were making audiences feel uncomfortable in a way that a similar scene in a silent film would not. In 1928, one reviewer wrote, "Having so much smoldering sexiness, [*The River*] is occasionally liable to laughter. . . . Coming from the women mostly there may have been a factor of overflowing tension expressing itself as tittering."[6] A similar sentiment was expressed the next year: "Some of the love scenes [in the talkies] aren't so effective when the actors are putting their emotions in words. This is especially true when the hero pleads with the heroine for her love. While she is deciding what the answer will be, we hear nothing but the whispering, coughing audience and the suspense is terrible."[7] In 1930, a reviewer went so far as to call for a return to playing such scenes as silent film: "An old observation has it that nothing seems so silly to a man as another man's love letters. But there is something sillier, it would seem; not only public, but audible, love making. It appears to be the consensus of opinion that all love scenes should be silent—unless comedy is intended."[8]

<table>
<tr><td>a</td><td>b</td></tr>
<tr><td>c</td><td>d</td></tr>
</table>

Figure 5-18. The love scenes from (a) *Dance, Fools, Dance* (1931) and (b) *Queen Christina* (1933) both minimize dialogue and feature stylized, pantomimic acting to prominent background music. The effect in each case is highly reminiscent of silent film. Two similar scenes from (c) *Behind Office Doors* (1931) and (d) *Red Dust* (1932) are both driven by dialogue, and neither uses music. (*Red Dust* features a constant background sound of rain here as in much of the film.) These two scenes share an ambiguity with respect to how receptive a character is to a sexual advance. As a comparison of these four scenes demonstrates, music was particularly effective at unobtrusively resolving such ambiguity.

Figure 5-18 shows love scenes from four films, two of which use music, two of which do not. A comparison of these scenes suggests that music apparently helped authorize the physical proximity by seeming to give the audience emotional proximity to the characters' feelings, thus illuminating the intention of a scene. This suggests that the construction of nondiegetic space offered a means of improving narrative clarity by giving filmmakers an additional dimension for presenting information.

FOREGROUND AND BACKGROUND

The sound film of the studio era maintained a consistent distinction between audible foreground and background with dialogue most commonly occupying the foreground. As David Bordwell notes, "classical sound technique articulates foreground (principal voice) and background (silence, 'background' noise, music 'under' the action) with the same precision that camera and staging distinguish visual planes."[9] As with the image track, such hierarchy was effective in rendering a clear narrative representation. The sidebar refers to an attempt from the time to draw a theoretical analogy between the sound and image tracks: where the image used lighting and contrast to create depth and narrative focus, the sound track attempted the same thing with volume and reverberation (reflected sound). All things being equal, something relatively loud with a high degree of direct sound will be taken as foreground. Not surprisingly, in classical Hollywood film the foreground usually consisted of dialogue, and it was usually synchronized to a visible body.

The system of regulating sound is functionally defined, meaning that different components of the sound track—dialogue, music, or effects—can serve different functions intermittently. The background, for instance, can be formed by any of the components, although dialogue only rarely is placed there, and, when it is, it is most often construed as a sound effect such as crowd noise. Music, sound effects, or dialogue can all occupy the foreground position, which will be determined by narrative salience. When Lola Lola (Marlene Dietrich) sings a song in *Der blaue Engel* (*The Blue Angel*, 1930), music is obviously treated as a foreground event. When she is talking to Professor Rath in her dressing room with the door open, dialogue occupies the foreground, and music, in the background, is understood as ambient sound, as emanating from the diegetic world beyond the door.

The hierarchical stratification of the sound track is correlated with but not determined by volume. Foreground events, especially dialogue, are generally closely miked with a high degree of direct sound and mixed at higher levels than background sound when both occupy the sound track simultaneously. On the other hand, background sound is typically mixed at a higher level in the absence of foreground events; thus, nondiegetic music, for instance, can become very prominent at moments when foreground sound is largely suspended, as in establishing shots, for example, or when the film brackets off the unfolding of "normal" diegetic time and sound, as in montage sequences. It is also noteworthy that both establishing shots and montage sequences often appear mute, without diegetic sound, and thus offer a throwback, as it were, to the silent film practice. More important, such scenes also tend to be associated with filmic spectacle.

At any moment, any of the three sound track components may or may not be present as well. This intermittent quality offered filmmakers useful flexibility and choice: music or sound might be used for ambience; dialogue or music might express character feeling; offscreen dialogue ("hello") or effect (knock at the door) might serve to motivate a cut; and so forth.

With the two-dimensional camera, which bears the same psychological relation to the eye as the monaural sound does to the ear, the illusion of depth can be achieved by the proper use of lighting and contrast, just as by the manipulation of loudness and reverberation with the microphone. And just as the eye can be drawn to particular persons or objects by the adjustment of focal length, so can the ear be arrested by the intensification of important sounds and the rejection of unimportant ones. If in a scene we wish to draw the attention of the audience to a child's toy in the center of the floor, we can, by employing an appropriate lens, focus sharply on the toy and blur the background. But if we want to draw attention to a music-box, and yet keep the other props in focus at the same time, we can have the music-box play a tune, which will arrest the ear and draw the eye.
—Leon S. Becker, Sound Engineer, Warner Bros. (1942)[10]

The presence of a strong hierarchy between foreground and background was almost as important to establishing narrative clarity as making a clean recording of the dialogue. Filmmakers controlled the hierarchy of the sound track in various ways. First of all, the foreground was louder, generally with low reverberation. Background sound, by contrast, was usually treated nonsynchronously, and one of the important functions of that lack of synchronization was to allow foreground events—dialogue and sound effects—to emerge as important and narratively marked by virtue of their synchronization. Synchronized bodies are narratively important bodies: this was a fundamental premise of classical Hollywood sound design (and remains fundamental to all cinema to the present day). The audience came to know that a character was important because the sounds that his or her body (dialogue, sound effects) made as it moved through the diegetic world seemed to demand synchronization. Many crowd scenes were shot silent and fit with non-synchronized sound later, not just to save money but also because a lack of close synchronization encouraged spectators to read the noise as background. When synchronization did occur in such scenes, it served generally as a figure of individuation: focus fell on the bodies that the sound track granted individuated representation through synchronization.

In early sound film, the audio background consisted primarily of silence, perhaps due to the conceptual and technological challenges of mixing. Conceptually, silence was the simplest background: through mere presence, foreground sounds stood out against a background of silence. In such a "monophonic" context, whatever was heard would occupy the foreground by default. Because this basic hierarchy of presence and absence was simple, it was often used, particularly early in the era, as, for example, in *The Testament of Dr. Mabuse*—see Figure 5-19 and commentary. Although effective, this hierarchy was also drastic. Because silence established no basic sound level against which narrative pertinence could be measured, every sound was fraught with significance; and it was only with great difficulty that the relative importance of sounds could be established against a background of silence. Therefore, other sounds had to be carefully managed. Silence was also wholly undifferentiated and thus ineffective at marking place (room, outdoors, etc.) as characteristic. Consequently, it could not be used to distinguish one sequence from another or to set up a hierarchy among the shots on the basis of the unity of place.

A silent background was also extremely difficult to cut dialogue against. Subtle changes between shots and takes, variation in microphone placement, and so forth were accentuated when the only background was silence. Indeed, negotiating the cut with a simple background of silence proved a particular aesthetic and technological challenge. The most obvious solution to managing the relation of sound and image across a cut in this situation—matching a cut in image with a cut in sound—has the effect, as film sound historian James Lastra points out, of emphasizing the autonomy of the shot at the expense of the coherence of the sequence.[11] The opening of *The Broadway Melody* (1929) will demonstrate—see Figure 5-20. The first shot (a) presents the exterior of the

Figure 5-19. *Das Testament des Dr. Mabuse* (1933). A conversation between Prof. Dr. Kramm (Theodor Loos) and Prof. Dr. Baum (Oscar Beregi, Sr.): The silent background allows for better intelligibility of dialogue, but it can neither distinguish one place from another nor distract from the prominent hiss of the sound track.

building, and we hear the blending of several musical performances. The second shot (b) moves to the interior, and we hear some distant lines of dialogue spoken by Eddie (Charles King, *left*, at the piano) amidst the general musical din. Shot 3 (c) moves inside one of the practice rooms, the sound of the woman's singing voice now treated clearly and without disruption from the noisy musical background. Shot 4 (d) returns to the outer room, the background just as noisy as before despite the closer framing. The fifth shot (e) and the seventh (g) are treated analogously to (c); whereas the sixth (f) likewise goes back to (d). Finally, shot 8 (h) starts again with the loud background, which is mitigated slightly for the move to a medium shot (i), during which Eddie's dialogue is somewhat elevated with respect to the general noise of the background.

With no background but silence to mediate the cuts between shots—and with the background silence masked by the extensive foreground sounds—the sound in this sequence is guided by what is happening immediately in the shot rather than by the coherence of the overall sequence. Although this might seem

<table>
<tr><td>a</td><td>b</td><td>c</td></tr>
<tr><td>d</td><td>e</td><td>f</td></tr>
<tr><td>g</td><td>h</td><td>i</td></tr>
</table>

Figure 5-20. *The Broadway Melody,* In the opening sequence, each cut in image is matched by a cut in sound; the sound exactly matches the image.

like a perfectly natural way of proceeding—the sound of each shot is "realistic"— the effect in fact is narratively quite disorienting and runs counter to what became codified as classical Hollywood sound practice, which insists on a structured relationship between foreground and a generally audible background. The prohibition against cutting sound and image at the same point within a sequence was one way of forcing filmmakers to conceptualize sound in terms of narrative sequence rather than image, to conceive background sound vis-à-vis foreground, and, ultimately, to think about sonic continuity across the cut.

SCORING PRACTICES

As we noted earlier, under the heading "Music Department," the nature and status of music was in flux throughout the transition years. Although different approaches were taken by individual studios, as an overall historical process non-diegetic music came early, as a simple continuation of silent-era accompaniment practices (*The Jazz Singer*; some sequences in *The Lights of New York* and other Warner Bros. films before 1930), then was greatly reduced (as in *The Broadway Melody* and many other films between about 1929 and 1931), and finally made a slow, irregular, and only partial recovery that accelerated after 1932, thanks in part to improvements in postproduction technologies made during that year.

Studio music departments adopted a variety of approaches to sound film. One, of course, was to focus heavily on performances and other diegetically motivated music, whether on- or offscreen. One might, for example, hear an offscreen band, or music understood to be coming from a radio or phonograph, whether onscreen or off. From the latter, it was a simple step to introduce an arrangement—perhaps a new version of a chorus from a song already heard—or even an underscore cue, which might be something out of a silent film music library (a hurry or pastorale) but might also be original. The particular attraction of this last option is that one could introduce and develop associative themes.

As noted in Chapter 3, neither onscreen diegetic nor offscreen nondiegetic music or sound poses any real obstacle to our attempts to make sense of what we see and hear. Onscreen diegetic sound testifies to the reality of the diegetic world. As typically used, offscreen nondiegetic sound (especially music) testifies to the inner psychology of the character. One of the most common functions of nondiegetic music, for instance, is to give us some sense as to how a particular piece of dialogue or incident affects a character. "Underscoring" thus operates in two senses: technically, it is music that is scored under dialogue; but figuratively, it is also music that *underscores*—that is, emphasizes—gestures and moments that are particularly psychologically fraught and revealing.

For nondiegetic underscore, then, two basic methods evolved, but both were actually inherited directly from the silent era: playing the overall mood of a scene, which had been associated especially with the orchestral practice of the picture palace, and playing to the details, which had been associated with improvising keyboard players. Both methods continued in the sound era, with overall mood being favored for establishing, spectacle, and montage sequences and playing to details being favored for underscoring dialogue, especially in melodramatic scenes.

Playing to details had an advantage in dialogue sequences in that the music was carefully composed to fit between and around the lines of dialogue, whereas playing to the overall mood—say, a love theme—necessarily simply went on as written. The conductor might be able to coax the music around the dialogue somewhat by judiciously pushing the performance forward or holding it back, and proper orchestration could mitigate masking, allowing the music to sound somewhat louder without affecting the intelligibility of the dialogue. In general, however, the balance with the dialogue had to be accomplished primarily through mixing.

Russian composer Leonid Sabaneev was one of the first to write about the recently developed compositional norms of sound film and offered crucial advice, both on balance between dialogue and underscoring as well as spotting. Not only does Sabaneev write on sound film compositional practice, but he also offers succinct explanations of how the two chief sound film technologies of the 1930s worked.
—See Leonid Sabaneev, "Music for the Films," in Cooke, The Hollywood Film Music Reader.

Composers also followed silent-film practice in favoring the leitmotif as a principle in constructing their scores. Indeed, the device was probably more common in the sound film, if for no other reason than the score was specifically composed for the film. (Special scores of the silent era also tended to be leitmotivic.) As in the silent era, leitmotifs tended to be conceived as well-rounded themes, and composers would usually restrict themselves to only a handful, usually associated with the principal characters (main theme for the hero, love theme for the heroine) but sometimes referring to more abstract ideas.

CHARACTERISTIC MUSIC PLACEMENTS

Because the sound track is a physical part of the film, it had to be fixed permanently, and, thus, as we have already seen, careful decisions and a great deal of creative effort needed to go into the work. In the context of production, making decisions about the placement of music is referred to as "spotting." In the context of reception (watching or analyzing a film), we match our expectations against the decisions made by the director, sound designer, and composer. (Except as backstory, it does not matter to the viewer-listener which of these three might have been responsible for the spotting.) For the feature film, the standard practices that were fully realized by the early 1920s under the regime of continuity editing were the guide during the transitional period, even if a great deal of experimentation went on as well.

For music, two of the most characteristic—and predictable—categories of placement were in connection with the establishing sequence and the end credits. In addition to those formal framing segments and to diegetic performances, music early on in the sound era acquired conventional functions for scenes within the narrative proper, in particular for dialogue scenes (to underscore speech), action scenes (to provide both momentum and unity), montages (to unify the rapid series of shots), and love scenes (usually to provide an additional element of emotion). Music was—and is—by no means obligatory in any of these types. Practices varied widely and continue to do so even in the present, within recognized national schools and studios, over decades, and in the work of individual directors; but when music *is* used, a relatively restricted set of musical topics and sound track treatments does prevail.

In this section, we discuss each of the seven categories named previously in turn, understanding them as frameworks within which we expect to position music and interpret its functions in film narrative.

Establishing Sequence

One of the most powerful roles for music is in the formal framing of opening titles and end credits. These conventions, inherited directly from the theater, have been manipulated in many ways over the years—see the sidebar for one suggestion for a dramatic opening. The function of music as a buffer between the outside world and the diegetic world (time, space) of the film, however, has remained constant. The traditional "overture" of the musical theater was central to exhibition practices of the silent-film era, when live concert-style or song performances were normally also part of the program and, in theaters that could afford orchestras, overtures were often played before the main feature. (Appropriately to the occasion, these overtures frequently were taken from nineteenth-century operas.) The grand orchestral music making associated with these moments was transferred to music for the main-title sequences in sound films as a way to frame the feature film that followed but also to give it due prominence in the theater's program.

Alternatively, the opening credits might be covered with a recorded performance of a popular song, especially likely for musicals but also common in films whose contemporary and "real-life" aspects were to be highlighted. The opening titles could even be linked to the first scene of the film by means of music (other linking devices include prologue intertitles and background shots or drawings that anticipate the action of the film). Although the technique is far more common in the classical Hollywood sound film after about 1935, one occasionally finds it in the transitional period as well. In order to cover all the variants, we conflate the "main-title sequence" (the opening credits) with the first shots of the film's diegetic world in what we will call an "establishing sequence."

The establishing sequence begins with the studio logo (if there is one). In *The Broadway Melody*, MGM's famous lion is there to start the show, but he roars silently as the nondiegetic orchestra begins with a dramatic introductory flourish, which continues into a fade to black and then shifts to the title song, so that we hear its first phrase before we see the main title—see Figure 5-21a & b. The song continues and cadences during the second credits card, after which the music changes to "Give My Regards to Broadway" in a bright fox-trot arrangement. With the arrival of music functioning as the song's bridge we see the first of several aerial shots of New York against which the reprise phrase is heard (Figure 5-21c). The music concludes at 1:24, and a simple cut shows the exterior of the music publishing house (Figure 5-21d) along with offscreen sound emanating from within. With the cut inside the first scene begins (Figure 5-21e).

The components, then, are the studio logo, the main title, two additional credits cards, and the introduction and gradual narrowing of the physical space from city to building to interior. The appearance of the title card is the single most important event in an establishing sequence, and thus the music (or other sound) played against it is always carefully planned. It is unusual for the main theme to start before the main title appears, but the device makes sense here: "The Broadway Melody" was brand new, having been written for this film, and for a moment all attention goes to it because the screen is black. "Give My Regards to Broadway" then confirms the topic and locale, as George M. Cohan's song was already well known (it's also heard at the beginning of *The Lights of New York*, for example) and it creates an immediate association of music with place, whereas the first scene turns attention back to the title song by focusing the narrative on a build-up to and subsequent performance of the new song.

I [have] found the following a very satisfactory plan—start your prologue with offstage singing drawing nearer and interrupting some kind of pantomime on stage—this will prove particularly effective if done behind the scrim and when the picture [starts] let the singing and dancing continue by dimmed lights until the picture on the screen occupies the complete attention of your audience and your orchestra has drowned the singing on stage.

—Erno Rapee[12]

Figure 5-21. *The Broadway Melody*, establishing sequence: (a) studio logo; (b) main title; (c) aerial shot of New York; (d) exterior of music publisher's office; (e) interior.

End Credits

End credits in early sound cinema were usually just two titles: "The End," followed by a cast list. The former might have music but was just as likely to be silent, whereas the music for the latter was typically not related to the film. Here again, a silent-era practice continued on into the sound film. Most often, one heard a piece in a bright foxtrot tempo that encouraged the audience to shift their attention away from the film quickly and therefore, presumably, prompted them to get up out of their seats as well.

The Broadway Melody uses a slightly different model that in fact is the most common one throughout the following decade or so of the classical studio era. There is no cast list, only a card "The End." Nondiegetic music—an instrumental arrangement of "You Were Meant for Me"—enters nearly 2 minutes earlier (at 1:38:10), fading in and staying fairly low under conversation. A minute later a cut to an exterior street view prompts "Broadway Melody," again in an instrumental setting. As before, the music continues under conversation, but on a final cut to the street view the music quickly rises in volume and concludes against the end card. This final flourish—an up-and-out effect—is so common in the classical sound cinema that it has become one of Hollywood's best known clichés.

Performance Scene

In addition to the establishing sequence and end credits, certain scene categories involving music also have what might be called "formal" properties. First among these are musical performances, especially any highlighted or foregrounded performances. Another category is the montage or fantasy scene. Music enables montages to provide clear information while nevertheless rapidly shifting time and sometimes place, and dream or fantasy scenes to retain a sense of continuity in what is otherwise usually a disjointed visual sequence. Both performance and montage scenes are quite distinctive, set off from the "everyday," clock-time depiction of conversation and action.

The simplest example of music shaping a scene is a direct onscreen performance. Music is unquestionably foregrounded, and the form of the music dictates the form of the scene. Such radical presence is routinely expected in musicals, of course, but occurs in dramatic feature films and comedies, too, as in *Casablanca* and many, many other historical and contemporary films.

Musical forms are sometimes superimposed on film segments—the most obvious case being the diegetic performance of a song or other piece, where scene (or scene segment) and musical form can coincide. We will see instances of both types, but in general film music adapts itself to cinematic form. Musical performances naturally take over and structure a film's timeline, superimposing the music's design on the scene. It is possible, of course, to continue action over a performance, especially if the music is in the background (as neutral music such as a diegetic café band), but even then classical practice tends to situate articulations of scene segments and music together.

The Broadway
Melody (MGM, 1929).
Producers: Irving
Thalberg and Law-
rence Weingarten.
Director: Harry
Beaumont. Story:
Edmund Goulding.
Sound: Douglas
Shearer. Original
Music: Nacio Herb
Brown with lyrics by
Arthur Freed. Leads:
Charles King, Anita
Page, Bessie Love.

Act 1: A vaudeville
sister act, Hank and
Queenie Mahoney,
have come to New
York to assist Hank's
fiancé Eddie Kearns
with his number for a
stage revue. Kearns
introduces his new
song, "The Broadway
Melody," to a group
in a music publish-
er's office. The scene
changes to "A theat-
rical hotel on 46th
St., New York" [inter-
title], where we learn
more about the two
women, then to
"Zanfield's Theatre,
during the rehearsal
of the latest revue,"
where they struggle,
and to "The final
dress rehearsal of
Zanfield's Revue,"
where they are cut
out of the number in
favor of dancers.

(continued)

The extreme case is the highlighted performance, where musical design controls all the film's elements. As Claudia Gorbman puts it, "The stanzaic form
of popular song, the presence of lyrics to 'compete' with the viewer's reception
of film narrative and dialogue, and the cultural weight and significance of
the stars performing the songs all work directly against classical Hollywood's
conception of film music as an 'inaudible' accompaniment."[13]

Musicals, of course, have many such highlighted performances, in the form of
songs, instrumental numbers, songs with dance, or large-scale production numbers. Dramatic feature films often have performances, too, but in musicals the
narrative typically stops for performances (that is, we learn little if anything new
about characters and narrative action is not forwarded, although the status of relationships may be confirmed, intensified, or undermined). In the dramatic film
performances may structure the time of a scene segment but usually are obliged to
share the viewer's attention with some kind of narrative-forwarding action.

Needless to say, there are multiple performances in *The Broadway Melody*.
They run the gamut of types, from casual and incomplete to highlighted production numbers. The opening scene, for example, includes several short fragments
of music played or sung in the music publisher's office, but it ends with the group
surrounding Eddie and musicians assisting him as he presents the title song
(this performance is analyzed in detail in the next chapter). Performances are
frequently interrupted during the rehearsals in the latter half of Act 1 (see the
sidebar for a plot summary), but then we are given a complete stage performance,
with dancers, again of the title song (this scene is also analyzed in detail in the
next chapter), and a second one, "Love Boat," whose rehearsal had been interrupted earlier by an accident. Both numbers, of course, are motivated by the
backstage musical narrative, but in Act 2, Eddie sings "You Were Meant for Me"
entirely out of the personal motivation of expressing his feelings for Queenie
(Anita Page). In the hotel scene near the end of Act 2, "You Were Meant for Me"
is played by the band and is meant both associatively (to remind us of Queenie's
relationship with Eddie) and ironically (because she is now with Jock Warriner
[Kenneth Thompson])—see Figure 5-22a. The scene also has a pure revue
number, as a guitar quartet performs "Truthful Parson Brown" (Figure 5.22b).
Act 3 goes a step further in the direction of the revue with the production number
"The Wedding of the Painted Doll," which, like the guitar quartet's piece, has no
integral connection to the narrative at all. Immediately following, however, is
another revue number—"The Boy Friend"—that *does* have ties to the story, as
Hank and Queenie are finally successful, an event that propels them in opposite
directions, however, as Hank (Bessie Love) goes on the road again, and Queenie
marries Eddie.

Montage or Fantasy Scene

Many musical performances, especially those that are carried out onscreen with
minimal narrative interruption (from cutaways or panning, with or without superimposed dialogue), are capable of lending the formal properties of the music

Figure 5-22. *The Broadway Melody*, hotel scene: (a) dancing as the band (at left)   a | b
plays; (b) revue-style featured performance.

to the image track, in many cases because the film is in fact edited to the music (this was especially true of performances in film musicals). Although the procedure of editing may be the same and one will normally hear continuous music, the narrative effect of montage or fantasy scenes is quite different: the focus is not so much on the music "as music" as it is on its formal capacities: music is added on top of a diverse, weakly connected collection of images to lend a degree of temporal or spatial coherence that the images themselves cannot manage well (or manage at all).

The term *montage* can be synonymous with continuity editing or simply film editing, but its alternate meaning is more familiar in everyday speech: a short scene with a series of brief shots (often combined with inserts or graphics) that are either related to one another, in the manner of a gallery of images, or that advance the narrative quickly by compressing time (and frequently changing locations as well). This technique is sometimes used for dream sequences as well. In the classical Hollywood cinema, music was always present in such scenes and functioned in much the same way as in action scenes, simultaneously keeping up strong rhythmic movement and giving a sense of cohesion to the series of rapid shot changes. Claudia Gorbman describes one very well-known instance in a later film, *Citizen Kane* (1941):

> Montage sequences often use nondiegetic music to bridge gaps of diegetic time. The famed breakfast-table sequence in *Citizen Kane*, for example, showing Kane and his first wife sitting at progressively greater distances from each other as the years pass, visually signaling the emotional distance that grows between them, has a theme-and-variations music—as well as equally symmetrical shot compositions—to simultaneously bridge and demarcate the temporal discontinuities in the narrative.[14]

Act 2 (at 0:49:50) opens in "The girls' apartment. Two weeks later." A lecherous society man, Jock Warriner, one of the financial backers of the revue, has set his eyes on Queenie. She, in turn, realizes that Eddie is falling for her, too, when he sings "You Were Meant for Me," and she does her best to put him off. Complications continue through "The birthday party at the girls' apartment" and a hotel restaurant/club scene where Queenie dances with Jock.

Act 3 (at 1:12:48) begins with a formal glimpse of the revue

(continued)

(continued)
through two numbers: "The Wedding of the Painted Doll" and "The Boy Friend," in which Hank and Queenie are featured. In the wings, Eddie tells Queenie he loves her. An argument ensues in the dressing room, and Queenie leaves. Jock has given her an apartment, Eddie confronts Jock there and is thrown out. Queenie leaves with Eddie. The final scene shows the couple returning from their honeymoon and Hank departing for a road tour with a new partner.

There are no montage scenes of this type in *The Broadway Melody*. The first part of the opening scene could qualify in the image editing, but the music actually *enhances* the visual disruption rather than mitigates it. We will therefore look back to *Lady Windermere's Fan*, which has a montage in the third scene of Act 1, as discussed in Chapter 4. When Mrs. Erlynne leaves the track level and walks up the stairs to the spectators' seats (at 17:47), a number of people, both scandalized and interested, look at her through small binoculars (from 18:02 to 18:51). Several shots jump about the space of the stands, and we see her framed in each of them. The pianist Martin Marks plays a single piece with little variation of texture or volume to hold together this spatially diverse montage.

Dialogue Scene

So far we have looked at the framing segments at beginning and end of a film (establishing sequence and end credits) and the special cases of the performance, where music must necessarily be foregrounded, and the montage or fantasy sequence. Music is sometimes—but by no means always—used in segments that commonly appear internally within films, are strongly focused on narrative, and tend (even in modern films) to make both substantial and very specific use of thematic references and style topics: these are dialogue scenes, action scenes, and love scenes.

Music in relation to dialogue underscoring has a complex history. As we have seen, in the transition period, technological problems in both recording and playback, plus a bias toward realistic depiction, at first sharply limited the use of music in dialogue scenes. Creative experimentation, some successes with audiences, and improvements in rerecording by 1932 made underscoring dialogue practical. Increasingly throughout the decade, then, more and more dialogue was underscored as part of a general trend toward covering a very large percentage of a film with music (examples from 1939 include *Gone with the Wind, Dark Victory*, and *The Hunchback of Notre Dame*; from 1940, *Rebecca* and—somewhat surprisingly—the espionage film *Foreign Correspondent*). Film sound historian Rick Altman describes the evolving aesthetic priorities in the 1930s: "Like atmospheric effects, the music thus remains continuously present, even when its volume is reduced to assure maximum dialogue comprehension. This system has two functions: to guarantee comprehensible dialogue and to confect a sound track with virtually constant total volume."[15]

Films in the transition period can only hint occasionally at this. By far the most common method is to place diegetic—or at least plausibly diegetic—music in the background while characters speak in the foreground. In *The Broadway Melody*, an extended example occurs during the first rehearsal scene (at 24:30 and following), as the producer Zanfield talks with performers or his assistants, then Eddie and Queenie talk, while the rehearsal pianist is heard offscreen. Others include the hotel restaurant/club scene (1:02:50, especially after 1:06:30) and the apartment scene and fight (1:28:42).

There are also interesting examples of the difficulties that diegetically implausible music could cause. A notable one is when Eddie sings "You Were Meant

Figure 5-23. *The Broadway Melody*, Eddie sings "You Were Meant for Me" to Queenie.

for Me" to Queenie (54:42). They are in the women's apartment, and we see the couple in a tightly framed medium two-shot—see Figure 5-23. An unseen orchestra intervenes with an introduction, and then Eddie sings to its accompaniment. The foreground presence of orchestra and singer is identical to the performances we have heard earlier in the film, yet the orchestra must be nondiegetic. Although this kind of fluid and ambiguous spatiality becomes a common feature of musicals, it is disruptive here, the more so because, once Eddie finishes the song, the orchestra keeps on and he talks in a slow rhythmic patter that maintains the rich presence of the recorded performance, not the flatter and thinner sound of dialogue recorded directly on the sound stage. We can clearly hear the difference when Hank suddenly arrives, the orchestra is cut off, and the three characters talk.

All told, *The Broadway Melody* has 34 minutes of music out of 100 minutes runtime. It is primarily a "talkie" and, with the exceptions just noted, it carefully isolates scenes dominated by music from those dominated by speech.

Action Scene

Music has a long history of association with action scenes in the theater—as early as the eighteenth century a type of music had evolved for this purpose out of rapid-tempo dances. In the nineteenth-century melodrama, these pieces became known as "hurries." As we noted in Chapter 4, they retained that designation throughout the silent-film era, although one frequently finds the musical term *agitato* applied to them as well. Hurries were used for chases, lively crowd scenes, trains, airplanes, and—in their more serious or "heavy" forms—for battles.

In the classical Hollywood cinema, music was almost obligatory for action scenes. Music is still common in such scenes today, although sound effects typically are foregrounded in the sound track, with music frequently struggling for attention or merely providing a bit of additional emotional "edge."

There are no action scenes of this type in *The Broadway Melody*. A fight between Eddie Kearns and Jock Warriner, who are competing for Queenie's affections, might qualify (1:31:00–1:32:00). It is not long, however, and it involves only two short pieces of action in between foregrounded dialogue and generic noise from the partiers in the apartment (a lavish place that Jock has given to Queenie but which she now rejects)—see Figure 5-24a–c. Adding music on top of that would certainly have strained the resources of the sound department in the transition era, and to no obvious purpose: the confusion of generic sound and raised voices does very well on its own. In fact, any music added here might have undermined the scene by turning it into something comic or even farcical, which would contradict the narrative: Eddie is made to look foolish and weak, true, but his determination to rescue Queenie is what finally convinces her to choose him (Figure 5-24d). (When they next appear on the screen, they are returning from their honeymoon.)

Love Scene

Of all the categories we have discussed in this section of the chapter, the love scene is the most difficult to pin down generically. That may be true in large part because the love scene in its simplest definition—a scene focused on the erotically charged interactions of a couple—is ubiquitous in the movies: overwhelmingly, both classical and modern film narratives serve the basic theme that scholars call "creating the couple," a process that typically works itself out in one or more attraction–repulsion cycles that motivate the twists and turns of the narrative. Even where the main theme of a film is something else—as in war films, westerns, or films about large political events—the progression of an intimate relationship (normally of the lead characters) is typically the most important subplot.

Despite the difficulties posed by the genre, we can still make some practical distinctions. When most people think of a love scene, they think of the moment in which two people not only realize they are attracted to one another but accept the consequences of that attraction (if not always completely at first). If the attraction is immediately played out in a physical coupling, then the love scene is foreplay; otherwise, it establishes the emotional bond that influences the characters' further actions. Although many other encounters of couples may be erotically charged (as in flirting or in an established couple's arguing), we use the commonplace idea of the love scene as our definition here.

Figure 5-24. *The Broadway Melody*, in the apartment Jock Warriner gave to Queenie: (a) crowd talking and dancing (piano at back left not visible in this shot); (b) Eddie attacks Jock; (c) Eddie is thrown out; (d) Queenie goes out to Eddie in the corridor.

Because "music itself signifies emotion,"[16] as Claudia Gorbman points out, it is not surprising that music usually plays a role in love scenes, if not necessarily always in the form of the classical cliché of soaring violins. In *The Broadway Melody*, as we have seen already (under "Performances"), Eddie sings "You Were Meant for Me" to Queenie while the two are shown together, as he woos her through the song and she resists her own feelings (recall Figure 5-23). Jock Warriner attempts the same with "You Were Meant for Me" as orchestral background, but he is rebuffed. When Eddie and Queenie do finally admit that they love one another, it happens in the wings of the theater stage while the diegetic orchestra plays "You Were Meant for Me" offscreen (motivated as the introduction to Eddie's number; the music starts just after 1:20:00). In this last case, however, the very fact that we can anchor the music in the diegesis distances it somewhat emotionally.

Timeline

1877   Edison invents phonograph.

1895   *The Dickson Experimental Sound Film.*

1902   Gaumont introduces Chronophone. The company begins widespread commercial exploitation around 1905.

1905   Eugene Lauste develops system to record sound on film.

1913   Edison introduces the new Kinetophone.

1919   The first amplified public address system is introduced.

1920   Regular radio broadcast begins.

1923   Theodore Case and Lee De Forest have limited success with Phonofilm system.

1925   The major record labels begin electrical recording of phonograph records. Western Electric releases improved condenser microphone.

Summary

In this chapter we continued the historical narrative for sound and music that was started in Chapter 4, beginning with early experiments in sound reproduction and leading up to the role of radio technology (and competition from commercial radio broadcasts) in the 1920s. By the late 1920s, the transition from silent-film performance practices to the film with a reproduced sound track was well underway, but a range of problems occupied both the technicians and film artists. The crucial technical issues were synchronization, fidelity of sound in recording and theater reproduction, and the effective mixing of the sound track elements. To these were added aesthetic issues: how to manage the "intermittent" sound track (and the hierarchy of sound track elements), how to understand nonsynchronous sound, and how to manage sound in relation to the physical space depicted in the image track. Music continued some silent-film practices while gradually finding its place in the newly fixed sound track.

1926   Warner Bros. signs contract with Western Electric for Vitaphone. Fox hires Theodore Case to develop Movietone. *Don Juan* is released.

1927   Warner Bros. releases *The Jazz Singer*, which has several synchronized songs.

1928   Warner Bros. releases *Lights of New York*, the first feature-length talking picture.

1929   Major studios all but end production of silent films in the fall of 1929. MGM releases *The Broadway Melody*.

1930   *Der blaue Engel* is released.

1931   *Le Million* is released.

1933   *Gold Diggers of 1933* and *Das Testament des Dr Mabuse* are released.

The Broadway Melody, Gold Diggers of 1933, and Le Million

Runtime Segmentation and Scene Analysis

Introduction

Throughout Part II we direct attention especially to music's contributions to film form and film style. Film form refers to the overall design of a film, or the temporal articulations of its running time in relation to the deployment of conventional units such as establishing sequences, scenes, chapters (or acts), and so forth. It addresses how these units are structured and how they themselves work to articulate higher (or lower) levels of structure. One of the key concepts for understanding the sound track's contribution to film form is audiovisual phrasing, which treats the coordination of image and sound track through an analysis of sync points. Audiovisual phrasing and sync points are discussed later in this chapter.

Film style also refers to the treatment of conventional expectations, but the basis of film style is the collection of techniques, practices, aesthetic preferences, and cultural and cinematic expectations that constitute the distinctive way narrative is "delivered" in any individual film. The treatment of film form, which varies historically, by national cinema, by genre, by studio, and even by director, is an important aspect of film style. Film style can also be generalized to groups of related films: in that broader sense, film style means the various conventions and figures that have evolved over the course of time as films have been made by production teams, exhibited in theaters and via home media, and responded to by audiences. By calling on these conventions and figures (and the codes they form), film scholars can develop descriptions of the ways that film elements, including the sound track, are presented and manipulated, and can make comparisons of the ways these basic materials are treated in different national or regional cinemas or how they are distinguished from other audiovisual media such as television or video games. Using these comparisons, one can also construct style histories, that is, accounts of the ways these treatments have changed over time within a single tradition (or, on a grander scale, multiple cinematic traditions).

The term *film style*, thus, can apply to any level of discussion and analysis. We can refer to national or regional styles (Hollywood, European, etc.), to movements (Italian Neo-realist, New Wave, etc.), to genres (film noir, musicals, etc.), to studio styles (Warner Bros. or MGM in the 1930s), or to individual directors, sound designers, or composers. In the same way as other components, the approach filmmakers take toward music or sound participates in and helps shape film style.

This chapter gives an overview of ways to mark the units of film form and to position music in relation to them. Three films—*The Broadway Melody* (1929), *Gold Diggers of 1933* (1933), and *Le Million* (1931)—provide extended examples. These films are all musicals, and musical performances receive extensive attention in this chapter because such sequences feature audiovisual phrasing where music plays an unusually prominent role. Focusing on these scenes allows us to identify certain principles that underlie audiovisual phrasing in general but usually in much more attenuated form (and musical form more typically follows and adjusts itself to film form than the processes traced in this chapter).

Music in Film Form

The time of a film rarely coincides with the time of the story that the film tells. This is true whether a film is fictional or documentary. The action recorded by the camera and microphone may be manipulated in many ways, as story elements are reordered, given more or less emphasis, or even deleted, but the most basic experience of watching a film is the same as it is with a piece of music: movement through linear or clock time. A symphony may last 45 minutes, a CD album may last 1 hour, a feature film may run 2 hours. Articulating or segmenting that time line is the process of breaking down the continuous flow of clock time into graspable units. By convention we refer to this as analyzing form in music and as segmentation in film. Although terminology differs, the articulation of musical form and film segmentation work in much the same way. The units do not correspond in terms of clock time (for example, we do not have a simple equivalent in musical form to the scene in film), but both modes of analysis segment time hierarchically, that is, into smaller units contained inside successively larger units. Of course, because narrative is the driving force in all traditional feature films, the test for descriptions of film form at any level is how well they fit plausible narrative units.

RUNTIME SEGMENTATION

In music, the smallest significant time unit is the measure (or bar), a group of two to four beats with an initial accent (recall from Chapter 2 that it is the recurring patterns of musical meter that make the measure or bar-length units recognizable). Measures provide a kind of metrical grid against which other temporal units of music are defined. A motive, which can vary from a single note to several measures in length, is a short, yet distinctive, musical idea. A basic idea is the set of motives, usually two measures in length, that opens a theme or melody. Beyond the basic idea, measures are grouped by articulation into increasingly larger segments: phrases, periods, sections, movements. The most familiar of these terms is probably *phrase*. More or less aligned with short-term memory, phrases are typically 6- to 10-second segments articulated by means of devices such as a clichéd cadence, a slight slowing down, a drop downward or stop on a long note in the melodic line, or starting over with the same melodic figure in the immediately following bar.

Consider George M. Cohan's song "Give My Regards to Broadway" that is heard during the main title sequence of *The Broadway Melody*. Strictly speaking, this melody is the chorus of a verse-chorus structure, the most common design of popular songs from the late nineteenth century up through at least the 1960s. As was often the case, the chorus opens with the title line, which serves as the basic idea of the chorus. This basic idea is then answered by another figure of the same length ("Remember me to Herald Square") but with a different rhythm and shape, ending with a long-held note, a vocal cadence—see Figure 6-1. This entire unit, which most people would sing in 7 to 8 seconds, is a phrase (in the bright, upbeat instrumental arrangement used in *The Broadway Melody*, it takes less time). Thus, the musical phrase is more like a sentence in language than like a spoken or written phrase, which usually refers to a shorter, incomplete grammatical unit; and there is a sentence-like "grammar" to the musical phrase: it is composed of

Figure 6-1. "Give My Regards to Broadway," used in the establishing sequence for *The Broadway Melody* (1929).

smaller units (the motives or ideas), and it typically concludes with punctuation (cadence, in musical terms) that effects closure. Like language, which offers commas, semi-colons, periods, etc., the strength of a musical closure can vary. The opening phrase from "Give My Regards to Broadway" includes a very weak stop (after the title line) and a somewhat more conclusive stop at the end of the next line ("Remember me to Herald Square").

As the song continues, the second phrase starts with a new idea, though the opening motive is the same ("Tell all the gang at 42nd Street"), which then leads to another idea ("That I will soon be there") that ends with an even more pronounced cadence. These two phrases together, lasting roughly 13 seconds, form the first half of an ABAC design, one of the two standard forms for choruses of popular songs (and many numbers in musical theater as well) from the late nineteenth century until about 1960. (The other form is AABA, sometimes called 32-bar song form.) At this point, the melody of the opening phrase returns with new lyrics ("Whisper of how I'm yearning/To mingle with the old time crowd"). As is typical of ABAC designs, the music for the fourth phrase is more distinct, here opening at a new melodic high point (and then pushing even a note higher) before falling back to a more conclusive sounding ending (or final cadence). Altogether this chorus runs about 25 seconds.

In the film, this chorus is followed by new music—this is the cue that we hear with the cut to the aerial shots of New York. This music consists of a pair of phrases, each half the length of the phrases in the chorus. These are not, in fact, from the George M. Cohan song, but here they serve the function of a bridge (the B section of an AABA song), since they lead back to a reprise of the second half of the chorus to "Give My Regards to Broadway," which concludes just before the cut to the building exterior. This interpolated bridge has the effect of stretching the song out, as if converting it into a common AABA form (ab ac B ac).

Both of the principal songs in *The Broadway Melody*—the title song and "You Were Meant for Me"—are also cast in the verse-chorus design. (See the sidebar for the verse-chorus design of "You Were Meant for Me.") In the case of the title song, the chorus follows the same ABAC form as Cohan's original "Give My Regards to Broadway." The title song is first introduced in the credits, where, after the opening fanfare flourish, the second half of the chorus plays while the title of the film is onscreen. It also appears in the opening scene, after the din of the music publishing shop has been established. The formal breakdown of the song is as follows:

> Verse: 0:02:43 ("There may be streets . . .")
> Chorus:
> A (phrase 1): 0:03:08 ("Don't bring a frown . . .")
> B (phrase 2): 0:03:16 ("Your troubles . . .")
> A (phrase 3): 0:03:24 ("A million lights . . .")
> C (phrase 4): 0:03:32 ("No skies of gray . . .")
> Chorus 0:03:40: repeat with altered text for the opening two phrases

The Broadway Melody, *"You Were Meant for Me"*: Eddie Kearns' first performance of the song (to Queenie, in her apartment). Because of the slow tempo and held notes, the phrases are longer than usual.

Verse: 0:54:50 ("Life was a song . . .")
Chorus:
A, phrase 1: 0:55:10 ("You were meant . . .")
B, phrase 2: 0:54:25 ("Nature patterned . . .")
A, phrase 1: 0:55:38 ("You're like a . . .")
B, phrase 2: 0:55:53 ("For I'm content . . .")

Chorus: instrumental with some speech/almost-singing by Eddie; breaks off early in the first phrase B when Hank enters.

After a brief piano introduction, Eddie (Charles King) opens the song at a relaxed tempo singing a short verse, two rhymed couplets that set up the chorus. The first three lines are set to variations of the same basic phrase and so give the impression of being repetitious. Although such lack of musical differentiation was common in verses of the time, since the point of the verse was the delivery of the words, the repetitious musical form here also fits with the idea of the verse, which suggests that most "streets," most locations in the world, are trapped in a cycle of sorrow. People, the lyric suggests, may find moments of happiness, but they are always left with "a tear tomorrow." The final line of the verse breaks out of this pattern to mark an exception, the existence of another street that curiously "tells the same old story," but not, it seems, of a tragic descent into sorrow.

For the chorus, the most recognizable part of any popular song from this era, the tempo picks up markedly, and Eddie moves away from the piano and encourages the clarinetist and guitar player to join him. The chorus does not begin with the title but with the premise of distraction and entertainment ("Don't bring a frown to old Broadway"), and the chorus is organized around discarding trouble ("your troubles there are out of style") through the entertaining distraction of upbeat comedic action (clowning, "wearing a smile," "A million lights, they flicker there/A million hearts beat quicker there"). These parts then are assembled into the title, "The Broadway Melody," the closing line of the chorus.

Unfortunately, there is no simple analogue to the term *phrase* in film analysis. The *shot* is the basic unit of continuity editing, but the length of a shot can vary greatly, from 1 to 100 seconds (or more). For instance, the single long take of the first performance of "The Broadway Melody" just discussed runs 98 seconds, from 2:31–4:09, and similarly the first performance of "You Were Meant for Me" is also done in a single long take that lasts 93 seconds, from 54:39–56:12. In both cases, the shot that contains the performance, though long, is part of a larger scene.

A scene is a number of shots gathered together in terms of unity of time and space. In a scene, we understand clock time in the diegetic world as corresponding roughly to the clock time in our viewing of it, and usually a scene will take place in a single location, such as a room, a garden, and so forth, along with a unified, cause-and-effect–based narrative progress. Screenwriting textbooks typically dictate that a new scene starts whenever there is a change of either time or place (or preferably both). Thus, scenes, like shots, can vary greatly in length, although we can still venture to say that, on average, scenes typically last from 1 to 5 minutes.

A series of shots related as a narrative unit is a *sequence*. The term is generally reserved, however, for large segments encompassing several short scenes that have stronger than usual narrative connections (e.g., action sequence), a set of short scenes unified by technique, function, or meaning (e.g., montage sequence, establishing sequence), a self-contained segment within another scene (e.g., a performance sequence), or scenes edited together through parallel editing

Essentially, the logic here is the logic of the screen, which happily does not preclude musical logic. Poets manage to think within the sonnet form, philosophers within the essay. So composers can think within the film scene.
—Lawrence Morton[1]

(cross-cutting). Strictly speaking, "sequence" is short for "sequence of shots" and thus can refer to any series of shots that are related by some criteria that is important to the person doing the analysis. Such a series could be five contiguous shots of a face, a dialogue scene in a room or café covering twenty shots, or a major segment of the film running 10 minutes with perhaps one hundred shots. The last of these is still the most common way to use the term, not only in reviews and similar writing about films but also in most scholarly writing. We will follow this usage and, thus, the sequence is a "sequence of scenes" roughly equivalent to a chapter in a book—and just as the number (and length) of chapters in a book can vary widely, so can sequences.

The term *act* is used to gather several sequences in a common broad narrative grouping, using the same general criterion of unity of time and place. Typically, a film would not have more than three or four acts. (Here again, screenwriting conventions refer to "three-act," "four-act," or even "five-act" models.) It is not absolutely necessary to use the word "act," because most 2-hour films can easily be understood in terms of a relatively small number of sequences (perhaps 10–12), but many films naturally fall into a smaller number of major narrative units.

Film scholar Kristin Thompson has proposed a four-part design consisting of set-up, complicating action, development, and climax-plus-epilogue. She analyzed a large number of films and additionally found that each of these four units tends to be roughly the same length. Needless to say, these proportions don't *always* hold, but they are surprisingly widespread across the historical record of mainstream feature films from the 1910s to the 1990s. On that basis, she argues that a four-segment model is the most appropriate one for most films (note that she does not call these "acts"). Her calculations include *Casablanca*, for which the numbers are 24, 26 1/2, 24 1/2, and 27. The first of these articulations occurs during the first evening in Rick's Café, just as Ilsa and Laszlo enter the Café for the first time. Just after minute 50, the first evening ends and the cut to the next day prepares for the police interview of Ilsa and Laszlo. At minute 75, the Café has just been closed and Major Strasser confronts Ilsa (after this Laszlo will go to a resistance meeting and Ilsa will come back to the Café to confront Rick about the exit visas). Thompson's analyses of narrative design and trajectory are valuable to keep in mind, but we will not adopt her terminology here because the narrative units do not reliably line up with scene or temporal units. Note that, for *Casablanca*, only the articulation at 50:00 matches a strong time division (end of the first day), whereas those at 24:00 and 75:00 are scene boundaries within the first or second day, respectively.

Finally, although the term *chapter* is a synonym of sequence, we suggest avoiding it, because the word is commonly used to designate individual DVD tracks, which are more likely to cover the dimensions of one or two scenes. (The mechanical division of a DVD into chapters, however, can sometimes be a useful place to start in sorting out the segmentation of a film because chapter articulations normally coincide with *some* significant level of film articulation.)

Thus, the filmic analogy to music's hierarchy of motive, basic idea, phrase, section, and movement is shot, scene, sequence, and act, respectively. At all levels from scene through act, the change from one unit to the next is typically demarcated clearly, by a change in the physical location (from town to country, indoors to outdoors, etc.), by a change in time (to the next day, morning to night, flashback), or by a formal marker in the film (fade to black, dissolve, an establishing shot of a different location)—or by any combination of these. These articulations are much more reliable indicators than any temporal marker (such as "scenes equal x minutes," "sequences equal y minutes"), but the latter are still generally applicable: A scene is unlikely to run for more than, say, 10 minutes, and sequences are commonly between 10 and 30 minutes long.

The Broadway Melody provides a good example of this hierarchy. The story moves in strict chronological sequence, and the breaks between its acts represent significant time gaps. In addition, the second act is separated in spatial terms, as events take place entirely outside and away from the theater that dominates Acts 1 and 3—see Table 6-1, which provides a runtime segmentation for the

Table 6-1 *The Broadway Melody*. **Film form and musical cues.**

ACT 1:

ESTABLISHING SEQUENCE AND FIRST SCENE (MUSIC PUBLISHER'S BUILDING)

| 0:00 | Credits sequence |
| 1:24 | Music publisher's building |

SECOND SEQUENCE (HOTEL)

5:15	Intertitle: "A theatrical hotel on 46th St., New York."
	Scene 1: Hank and Queenie's apartment.
	10:00 Scene 2: Uncle Jed arrives
	13:05 Scene 3: Eddie arrives.

THIRD SEQUENCE/SCENE (THEATER; REHEARSAL, PART 1)

| 18:00 | Intertitle: "[rehearsal]." Theater back-stage, with piano music, some speech, dancing. This might be broken up by interruptions to the rehearsal but is really one long scene. |

FOURTH SEQUENCE (THEATER; REHEARSAL, PART 2)

28:35	Intertitle: "The final dress rehearsal of Zanfield Revue."
	Scene 1 cuts back and forth between the stage and Hank and Queenie's dressing room.
34:40	Scene 2: stage; "The Broadway Melody," interrupted early on but then a complete performance with dancing in additional choruses.
40:35	Scene 3: "Love Boat" performance; having seen Queenie in the number, Jock Warriner pursues her.
46:00	Scene 4: Dressing room, Hank and Queenie with Eddie.

ACT 2:

FIRST SEQUENCE (WOMEN'S APARTMENT)

49:50   Intertitle: "The girls' apartment. Two weeks later."

Scene 1, part 1: Warriner appears, then Eddie. Conversation and argument.

53:30   Scene 2: Brief interpolated scene: Uncle Jed's office; he and Hank talk.

54:25   Scene 3: Cut back to Queenie and Eddie; he sings "You Were Meant for Me." Hank enters; conversation.

58:12   Intertitle: "The birthday party at the girls' apartment."

Scene 3: Generic speech; conversations.

SECOND SEQUENCE (HOTEL; EPILOGUE IN WOMEN'S APARTMENT)

1:02:50   Scene 1: Hotel restaurant/club: Warriner woos Queenie; band plays an upbeat version of "You Were Meant for Me."

1:03:50   Interpolated performance: guitar quartet performs "Truthful Parson Brown."

1:06:30   Scene 1 continues: "You Were Meant for Me" starts up again; Queenie dances with Warriner; he gives her a diamond bracelet.

1:09:00   Scene 2: fade to clock showing 5:05 am. Hank awake; Queenie comes in; the two talk.

ACT 3:

FIRST SEQUENCE (IN THE THEATER; TWO PERFORMANCES, TWO ARGUMENTS)

1:12:48   Insert: program "Zanfield Theatre . . ."

Scene 1: production number "The Wedding of the Painted Doll."

1:16:26   Insert: program, unseen person turns page.

Scene 2: Production number "The Boy Friend." Chorus, then dance, then chorus in the orchestra. Scene continues as Eddie and Queenie argue in the wings.

1:22:40   Insert: Jock Warriner's card with note for Queenie.

Scene 3: Hank and Queenie, then Eddie too. At the end, Hank is left alone.

SECOND SEQUENCE (THREE LOCATIONS, ONE FOR EACH OF THE THREE SCENES)

1:28:42   Scene 1: the new apartment Warriner has rented for Queenie. Party; Queenie and Warriner again, Eddie comes in; fight.

1:33:10   Scene 2: women's apartment; Uncle Jed and Hank; Queenie and Eddie arrive, returning from their honeymoon.

1:39:15   Scene 3: cut to street view of Broadway; Hank, Flo, and Uncle Jed in train; back to street view briefly, then music "up and out" to the end title at 1:40:00.

entire film. Within the acts, sequences are marked by a change of location, made more prominent by an intertitle. Scenes are sometimes marked by change of location as well, but more often by the arrival or departure of a character or by the start of a performance.

Formal Screening Notes

Runtime segmentation also provides a useful way to organize screening notes for a film or scene. The segmentation and amount of detail in your notes will depend on whether you are working at the level of the film or the level of the scene. In this section we address making screening notes for the film as a whole. In the next section, we look at notes appropriate for scene analysis.

Begin by preparing a spreadsheet or notebook with a requisite number of columns. Generally, you want six columns: time code, scene description, dialogue, sound effects, music, and general remarks. If you prefer to work on paper, you can also use a set of screening blanks with prompts such as in Figure 6-2. In any event, it is useful to consult a screening blank of this sort for the prompts as you are taking notes. Note that the prompts are arranged so that you can focus on description at the top and on interpretation with respect to the narrative at the bottom. Figure 6-2 does not have time codes because it is designed for use in screenings.

Film:			
Scene:			
Principal characters:		Summary of Action:	
Speech	**Music**	**Sfx**	**General Comments**
Quality	Style	Physical source	Balance
Tempo	Tempo	Ambience	Blurring
Voice-over	Diegetic/nondiegetic	Sweetening	Offscreen sound
Volume	Volume	Volume	Unusual uses of sound
	Narrative functions (leitmotif, mood, emotion, etc.)	Narrative functions (motif, mood, emotion, etc.)	Relationship to narrative including point of view
Transition in:		Transition out:	

Figure 6-2. Screening notes template.

As you watch the film, write in the time code (unless you are watching at a screening) and a descriptor for each scene as it comes. For each scene, you want to list the principal characters present and very briefly describe the general action of the scene. More important, you want to give a general characterization of the sound track in terms of each component (speech, music, and effects), with a special emphasis on unusual usage and places where the sound track intersects with the major thematic concerns of the film. You may find this difficult at first, especially if you are having to do this at a screening and you haven't seen the film before, but it will become easier with practice as you learn how to focus your attention in an efficient manner. For each scene, also listen especially for uses of sound that strike you as unusual (either for the film or for films in general). Also be on the lookout for important sync points, places where sound/music and image, sound/music and narrative, or sound/music and dialogue intersect in a cogent way, especially when this intersection relates a major thematic concern of the film. Sync points are discussed in detail in the next large section.

Following are some questions to ask yourself about each component as you are taking notes. Some questions will be appropriate for each scene; others relate more to the sound track as a whole.

DIALOGUE

Dialogue is ubiquitous in film. For just this reason you need to take special care to note aspects of dialogue that extend beyond the sense of the words being spoken and address the manner in which it is delivered: tempo, rhythm, tessitura, accent, volume, intonation, enunciation, intensity, and so forth.

- Find an adjective or two to describe the dialogue delivery of each of the main actors. Does the delivery change much over the course of the film as the narrative situation changes? What does the delivery of dialogue tell us about the character?
- Dialogue will usually be presented onscreen. What sort of exceptions to this rule do you find? What are the reasons the filmmakers present dialogue offscreen?
- Dialogue will usually dominate most scenes of a film. List any scenes where dialogue is not dominant and the sound track component that is prominent in those scenes. What are the reasons the filmmakers give prominence to music or effects?
- Does the film use any voice-over narration? If so, in what situations? Does one of the characters in the film deliver the voice-over? Is the voice-over accompanied by other sounds and/or music? What are the reasons the filmmakers used voice-over?
- Is any of the dialogue unusual or difficult to categorize? What are the reasons the filmmakers used dialogue in an unusual way?

- **TIP**: Often in the first scene or two after the title sequence, a film will have a relatively extended scene of expository dialogue. This is generally a good scene from which to draw a baseline reading of a film's sound design (how much music and effects will a film typically use when dialogue is present?).

MUSIC

The use of music varies greatly from film to film. In taking notes, you will want to pay particular attention to interactions of music with dialogue, narrative, and image.

- Find an adjective or two to describe your general overall impression of music in film.
- Describe the title music. What style of music is it? Orchestral? Jazz? Rock? Pop? What does it tell you about film?
- Does the film make use of existing songs and recordings? Which ones? Is it a compilation sound track or does it also make use of original music? If it is a mix, is the sound track primarily compilation or original score? What are the reasons the filmmakers used compilation or original score?
- Identify as many recurring themes (leitmotifs) as you can. What does each theme seem to be associated with (a particular character, thing, relationship, situation, etc.)? What is the character of each theme? How does the theme change over the course of the film?
- How much of the music is diegetic? Nondiegetic? Is any of the music unusual or difficult to categorize in these terms? What are the reasons the filmmakers used music in an unusual way?
- Is music used in scenes with dialogue? Which ones? What does music seem to be doing in these scenes?
- Does music establish ambience and underscore the general mood of a scene, or does it seem to react to emotional flux of unfolding action or situation? Whose point of view does the music seem primarily to reflect?
- What percentage of the scenes use music? What style of music seems dominant? How varied is the music?
- **TIP**: The music of the main title sequence is generally associated with the main character of the film. It also usually announces a film's genre.

EFFECTS

Effects, while not as ubiquitous as dialogue, are generally so naturalized that it is easy not to notice them, especially the first time you are watching a film. Vice versa, it is often easy to imagine you heard sound effects that were not in fact present. This is why close attention to sound effects almost always requires multiple viewings, even for experienced analysts of the sound track.

- Find an adjective or two to describe your general overall impression of effects in film.

- Does the film feature any recurring sounds (water, trains, explosions, etc.)? If so, what are the reasons the filmmakers chose this recurring sound?
- How much ambient sound does the film use? Do certain scenes feature ambient sound more than others? What are the reasons the filmmakers chose to feature ambient sound?
- Are effects used in scenes with dialogue? Which scenes? What do effects seem to be doing in these scenes?
- Do any of the effects seem like they were "sweetened" with added music or other sounds? What are the reasons the filmmakers sweetened the sound?
- Are there any nondiegetic or extradiegetic sound effects? What are the reasons the filmmakers used sound effects this way?
- What percentage of the scenes feature sound effects?
- When taking notes, be sure to listen for sound effects that are particularly prominent, notably absent, or unusual in some way. These are the types of things that deserve mention in your paper.
- **TIP**: During a quiet moment of the screening, especially at the beginning of an extended scene, take a minute and note every sound you hear that is neither dialogue nor music.

GENERAL COMMENTS

This is the place to note important relations and interactions among the components as well as how the balance and decisions among the components relate to narrative.

- At the beginning of scenes, before the dialogue starts, which generally receives more emphasis, music or effects? Do the filmmakers use music for certain kinds of scenes and effects for others?
- Are music and effects clearly distinguished? When music and effects are both present, which seems to get preference in the mix?
- Which sound track components seem most prominent in the scene? If it is not dialogue, what are the reasons the filmmakers chose to feature this component in this scene?
- What is the most likely candidate(s) for an important sync point in the scene?
- What is the proportion of onscreen and offscreen sound? Does it change over the course of the scene?
- Does anything strike you as particularly unusual about the sound track in the scene?

TRANSITIONS

Because transitions affect the audiovisual phrasing of higher levels of structure, you will want to pay attention to how filmmakers use the sound track to link scenes together. A typology of sound transitions is presented in Chapter 3.

Table 6-2 contains the runtime segmentation and sample screening notes for the first act of *The Broadway Melody*.

Table 6-2 *The Broadway Melody*. **Act 1: runtime segmentation and screening notes.**

ACT 1:

ESTABLISHING SEQUENCE AND FIRST SCENE

0:00	MGM lion
0:13	Fade to black
0:18	Main title with song in the orchestra; cadences, then overlaps with second title
0:35	Aerial views of New York City, "Give My Regards to Broadway" in bright foxtrot setting
1:24	Cut to exterior of building with offscreen sound, then to interior
2:11	To medium shot of three men
2:40	"The Broadway Melody" verse and chorus (two); out at 4:10. Eddie leaves

SECOND SCENE (HANK AND QUEENIE; UNCLE JED, THEN EDDIE)

5:15	Intertitle: "A theatrical hotel on 46th St., New York." Silent. Then conversation between the two women.
8:53	In the bathroom, Hank briefly sings wordlessly. When asked, identifies it as "Bubble Song" by Gluck. This scene combines effects, singing, and speech.
10:00	Uncle Jed arrives; he leaves at 12:30.
13:05	Eddie arrives. Long close-ups at about 13:30.
16:00	Eddie sings, with an offscreen ?? or nondiegetic orchestra. Combines speech with singing. Out at 17:55; fade to title.

THIRD SCENE (REHEARSAL, PART 1)

18:00	Intertitle: "[rehearsal]." Theater, with piano music, some speech, dancing. Hank and Queenie speak to Zanfield, do their number (21:55–22:50), which flops, and Hank fights with Flo. At 24:25 dance starts up again, but music is offscreen as Zanfield talks to Flo, then to Queenie. At 26:00 dancing again, then to conversation between Queenie and Eddie. Out at 28:30, speech lags into black.

FOURTH SCENE (REHEARSAL, PART 2)

28:35	Intertitle: "The final dress rehearsal of Zanfield Revue." Theater again. Generic sound against announcement board. At 29:00 cut to Hank and Queenie's dressing room. 30:30 cuts back and forth between stage and dressing room. Stage and music in at 31:25 briefly, then a series of brief comic scenes backstage and onstage. Burrows briefly sings "Love Boat" on his own.
34:40	Stage, verse and first chorus of "The Broadway Melody." Stops when Hank and Queenie are cut out of the number. 36:20: starts up again: chorus and dance, orchestra only; then two choruses of solo ballet-tap by woman dressed as a cat (!); out at 38:50.
40:35	"Love Boat" number; out and curtain down at 42:28. Thereafter Jock [Jacques] Warriner talks with Queenie. At 46:00, to the dressing room, Hank and Queenie with Eddie; fade as the two women dress; back in, then Queenie leaves at 49:00. At 49:10 closing door sound overlaps into fade to black.

Scene Analysis

SYNC POINTS AND AUDIOVISUAL PHRASING

Another way to think of the segmentation of clock time in a film is the temporal coordination of sound and image in terms of points of synchronization, or *sync points* (sometimes spelled "synch point"). Michel Chion defines a sync point as "a salient moment of an audiovisual sequence during which a sound event and a visual event meet in synchrony."[2] By "synchrony" he means the general psychological effect of the combination of sound and image; because this operates at every level of time, from the immediate moment to the level of scene and sequence, there are in fact "thousands of sync points," but for practical purposes of sound analysis, "only certain ones are important, the ones whose placement defines what we might call the *audiovisual phrasing* of the sequence." A simple example is the "stinger chord," a sudden, accented musical chord (or short figure) that "hits" screen action such as a surprised look or a fall. Gunshots, an explosion, a knock on the door, a loud cry, or clapping hands are also natural sound accents or stingers. What counts as a sync point will also depend on the level of structure that an analysis is attending to. The principal sync points of a short scene may fade in significance when we examine a 10-minute sequence, an act, or the whole film. Then, too, at higher levels of structure, sync points might manifest that do not actually appear clearly at the more local level of the shot or scene due to displacements of sound advances, lags, and other devices of offscreen sound that work to expand and complicate the audiovisual phrasing at the local level.

Sync points and audiovisual phrasing refer principally to the dramatic or expressive articulation of a sound film's timeline rather than to its formal segmentation. They may reinforce that formal segmentation or attenuate the joins, but determining the reasons for doing so will require examining issues of dramaturgy, expression, and style. Sync points and audiovisual phrasing nevertheless fall under the general processes of synchronization. The end of a scene is in many ways a *negative* articulation of time—something comes to an end, whether it's a conversation, a cause-and-effect action sequence, a period of time, or an event. The techniques used will reflect this negative articulation: the screen fades to black or dissolves to another time and place, conversations cease and the sound track goes quiet, a musical performance stops, the dynamic level (loudness) of the background music falls. Thus, one can say that the image, music, and plot are synchronized in this "negative" effect of ending. These "low points" are likewise a type of sync point, though the attributes are opposite of our usual meaning of the term, which entails a *positive* articulation of time where image and sound are active, expressive, and usually louder than their temporal surroundings.

Ending and (positive) sync point can coincide (for example, the conventional cliffhanger of the old serials—and some contemporary television shows—almost required punctuation with a tense stinger that underscores the melodramatic situation). The beginning of any scene will likewise usually feature a locally important sync point—a moving object, a piece of dialogue—within the first few seconds that will serve to anchor the sound in the image. In general, however, the most important sync points at a particular level of structure will almost always be distinct from the formal boundaries of the segmentation at that level: at the level of the shot, sound and image are usually edited so they are not cut at the same moment, which greatly attenuates the significance of any sync points at the local level in favor of continuity; at the level of the scene, the major sync point is most likely to coincide with the scene's climax, not its beginning or ending. A sync point, no matter the level, creates a before–after effect: the "before" seems empty as we forget it under the newly raised attention forced by the sync point and an "after" or reaction that follows directly from it.

Beyond the level of the scene, the sync point—as a specific, significant point in time—becomes an increasingly less tangible entity than is the ostensibly more abstract narrative category of the crux or climax: in the case of the latter, tension and narrative complications accumulate to a moment—or segment—of greatest conflict and (usually) resolution, after which the sequence, act, or entire film "winds down" in a denouement or final scene(s). The climax is usually punctuated by an important sync point that marks the turning point, but it is the climax itself, not the sync point that underscores it, that is structurally salient at this level. Besides adding punctuation at higher levels of structure, sync points can also affect these levels through a kind of structural rhyming, so that a punch in one scene is answered by a gunshot in another. The process of deacousmatization that ultimately renders the acousmêtre mundane (see Chapter 3) is another instance of the sync point operating on a higher level, this time with actual structural consequences. Likewise, spotting (whether a scene has music or sound and if so what kind) is another way that the principle of the sync point (music is present in some scenes and not in others) can apply to higher levels of structure.

Without the more specific control afforded by post-production dubbing, films in the transition years rarely structure scenes according to sync points. In *The Broadway Melody*, for instance, sound effects are nearly absent, except for those accidentally captured by direct recording, and thus they are generally not available to create sync points. Several scenes do lead toward performances, and one could argue that the performances themselves—or their beginnings—constitute sync points.

DRESS REHEARSAL SCENE FROM *THE BROADWAY MELODY*

In a number from a musical, the audiovisual phrasing is often determined by the relation of sync points to the formal articulation of the song. We have already analyzed the opening performance of the title song from *The Broadway Melody* and noted that the entire performance is captured in a single long take, with a cut at the very end to punctuate the finish. A similar procedure is followed in the first performance of "You Were Meant for Me," which is also punctuated by a cut at the finish. In both cases, the film form of the segment is determined by the length of the musical performance. This pattern occurs frequently in the film, where performances that are not production numbers have infrequent cuts, presumably to emphasize that what we are seeing and hearing is a recording of an uncut live performance. Although there are no cuts during Eddie's first performance of "The Broadway Melody," the camera moves twice, once to frame Eddie as he moves forward to deliver the verse and a second time as he moves to join the crowd of musicians for the chorus. Thus, both Eddie's blocking and the camera movements create sync points that align with the musical articulations of the verse-chorus structure.

In the dress rehearsal performance of the same song (beginning at 34:40), by contrast, the cutting, although still infrequent, occurs much more often, and it is variable, with editing and song structure not directly aligned even if the choreography still follows the song structure. Table 6-3 provides a shot list of this sequence and places the shots against the lyrics and dialogue to show the relation between the editing and the musical form.

Table 6-3 *The Broadway Melody.* Dress rehearsal for "The Broadway Melody" production number, with shots and lyrics aligned.

Time Code	Shot	Description of Action	Lyrics and Dialogue
34:37	LS	Backstage	(Musical Intro: 34:39)
34:40	ELS1	Curtain rises; Eddie walks on stage	*Broadway, you magic street*
34:48	ELS2		*River of humanity*
			I have trudged my weary feet
			Down your gay White Way
			Dreaming the million dreams of fame
34:54	LS		*Yearning for you to know my name*
			Lord, where you have heard the story
			Of a lot of tears of glory
			But you've always been the same
			Always playing in the game
			Noisy, hurry with your bustle
			Scrambling, dizzy, full of hustle
			Jazzy, frilly, brassy, silly
			Broadway singing
			Broadway music
			Broadway melody.
35:16	ELS1	Enter Hank and Queenie on "to old Broadway"	*Don't bring a frown to old Broadway*
			You've got to clown on

(Continued)

Table 6-3 (*Continued*)

Time Code	Shot	Description of Action	Lyrics and Dialogue
35:22	ELS2		*Broadway*
			Your troubles there are out of
35:27	LS		*style*
			For Broadway always wears a smile
			A million lights they flicker there
			A million hearts beat quicker there
			No skies of gray on the Great White Way
			That's the Broadway melody
			Zanfield offscreen (35:46): Wait a minute, wait a minute, hold it. (begins over "melody "of sung line)
35:50	MS	Zanfield speaks to conductor	Zanfield: That number is too slow. Cut out the Maloney sisters.
			Conductor: Cut out the whole first chorus?
			Zanfield: Yes
35:54	LS	Queenie, Hank, and Eddie onstage	Hank: Well has he cut us out altogether?
35:56	MS	Flo	Flo: Ain't it awful the way they cut out these big stars?
36:01	MS	Queenie and Hank (at end of shot Hank crosses in front of Queenie to reverse positions)	Hank: I'll get to you in a minute. (Turning to Zanfield) Listen here, Mr. Zanfield, you can't cut us out like that. Well, we've got equity contracts.
36:07	MS	Zanfield and conductor	Zanfield: Kearns, go into the dance on the first chorus and end it there.
36:11	MS	Flo	Flo: One more cut for you, dearie, and you'll be holding a spear.
36:14	MS	Hank and Queenie	Hank: And one more crack from you, bimbo, and you'll be holding a lily. (Turns to Zanfield) Now
36:18	LS	Hank, Queenie, and Eddie (Queenie pulls Hank offstage at end of shot)	Hank: you listen to me, Mr. Zanfield, we can't be cut—
			Eddie: Hank, be quiet. Would you cut it out and give me a chance to do my number?
			Hank: Well, I know, but—
			Queenie: Hank, come on.

36:26	ELS2	Eddie. Dance line begins to enter at 36:28.	Intro music then:
			Don't bring a frown to old Broadway
			You've got to clown on Broadway
			Your troubles there are out of style
		Dancers finish entering stage	*For Broadway always wears a smile*
		New dance move for dance line	*A million lights they flicker there*
			A million hearts beat quicker there
			No skies of gray on the Great White Way
			That's the Broadway melody
			Dance Chorus 1 (37:00)
			(Don't bring
37:01	MS	Eddie with dancers in background	a frown to old Broadway)
			(You've got
37:05	ELS2		to clown on Broadway)
			(Your troubles there are out of style)
			(For Broadway always wears a smile)
			(A million lights they flicker there)
			(A million hearts beat quicker there)
			(No skies of gray on the Great White Way)
		New dancer enters	(That's the Broadway melody)
			Dance Chorus 2 (37:34)
			(Don't bring a
37:35	CU	Feet	frown to old Broadway)
			(You've got to clown
37:39	MS	Head and torso	on Broadway)
			(Your troub-
37:43	LS		les there are out of style)
			(For Broadway always wears a smile)
			(A million lights they flicker there)
			(A million hearts beat quicker there)
			(No skies of gray on the Great White Way)
			(That's the Broadway melody)
38:07	CU	Feet	Dance Chorus 3
			(Don't bring a frown to old Broad-
38:11	MS	Head and torso	way)

(Continued)

Table 6-3 (*Continued*)

Time Code	Shot	Description of Action	Lyrics and Dialogue
			(You've got to clown on
38:14	CU	Feet	Broadway)
			(Your troubles there are out of style)
			(For Broadway always wears a smile)
			(A million lights they flicker there)
			(A million hearts beat quicker there)
			(No skies of
38:33	LS		gray on the Great White Way)
			(That's the Broadway melody)
38:41	ELS2	Eddie enters singing	*No skies of gray on the Great White Way*
			That's the Broadway melody

This performance opens not with the simple verse Eddie sang in the shop but with Eddie delivering a long, convoluted verse more spoken than sung. The musical accompaniment is as overwrought as the text, and the lyrics and music, rather than complementing each other, seem to fight for attention. Eddie's enunciation of the words is poor, especially during the verse, and the balance is odd with his voice seeming distant compared to the orchestra. The verse uses three shots—see Figure 6-3. The first is an extreme long shot (ELS1) that shows the complete proscenium opening and covers the introduction and first line of the verse. A slightly closer extreme long shot (ELS2) eliminates the proscenium framing for the next four lines. A much tighter long shot (LS), cut in right after the start of the word "yearning," covers the remainder of the verse. This pattern of editing continues in the chorus: Eddie sings the first line of the chorus framed with ELS1, and Hank and Queenie enter dancing during the second half of the first line. A cut to ELS2 on the last word of the second line is marked by a light cadence. A cut to LS occurs at the end of the third line, and that shot is maintained through the remainder of the chorus. For both the verse and the chorus, the first two shots (ELS1 and ELS2) follow the articulations of the musical form, but the move to LS cuts subtly against it.

At the end of the first chorus, the performance is interrupted by Zanfield, who orders the number reduced in length, and in the dialogue that follows, the cutting is much faster, as the editing follows the flow of conversation, which takes place in three distinct locations in the theater: in front of the stage (Zanfield and the conductor), on stage (Hank, Queenie, and Eddie), and from the wings

(Flo). Only one cut comes inside a line of dialogue, and that is cued by Hank redirecting her speech from Flo (MS) to Zanfield (LS). (The actual cut comes a word after she has begun addressing Zanfield, and the LS is roughly from the position of Zanfield.)

After the conversation, the number resumes with Eddie singing another chorus. This time the performance begins with ELS2 (Figure 6-4a). This shot is maintained through the whole chorus, as the dance line enters behind him during the first half (Figure 6-4b) and executes a new move during the second half (Figure 6-4c), using the last line to get into position for the next chorus. The first (unsung) dance chorus is a tap line routine. This chorus begins continuing the ELS2 from Eddie's chorus, but quickly cuts to a MS of Eddie in the middle of the first line only to return to the ELS2 at the same point in the second line. This shot is then maintained for the remainder of the chorus. A new dancer enters at the end of this chorus and becomes the featured dancer for the next two choruses.

The second dance chorus also continues the ELS2 from the previous chorus and then follows an editing pattern similar to that of the first chorus. Indeed, at roughly the same point in the first dance chorus that cut to the MS of Eddie, the second dance chorus cuts to a CU of the dancer's feet to show her tapping on point. Whereas during the second line the first dance chorus had cut back to ELS2, here the second dance chorus substitutes a matching MS of the dancer's head and upper torso. A new edit point is also introduced during the third line, a LS that is maintained through the rest of the chorus.

The opening of the third dance chorus coincides with a return to the CU of the dancer's feet, the first time since the opening of the number that the beginning of a chorus has been reinforced by a cut (Figure 6-5). The matching MS comes at the end of the first line, which is complemented by a return to the CU of the feet near the end of the second line. This shot continues until the middle

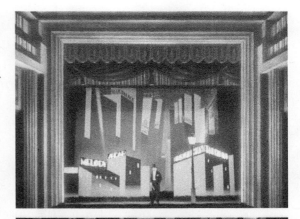

Figure 6-3. *The Broadway Melody,* dress rehearsal for "The Broadway Melody," first section: series of shots cutting in to focus on Eddie.

a
b
c

Figure 6-4. *The Broadway Melody.* (a) Dress <u>a</u>
rehearsal for "The Broadway Melody"; (b) <u>b</u>
Second section: the chorus line enters; (c) ELS <u>c</u>
maintained through a chorus of the song.

of the penultimate line, where a cut to a LS is used to close out the chorus. A return to ELS2 then marks a reprise of the final two lines, used as a closing tag, as Eddie enters singing and then walks off with the dancer, the music comes to a close, and the stage is momentarily empty and silent.

From the preceding analytical description, we can draw several conclusions about the audiovisual phrasing of the sequence. First, the sound track dominates the sequence not just in the two performance segments but also in the dialogue segment. That is, the editing of the visuals follows the articulations of the sound track, whether those fall in the music or the dialogue. Such dominance of the sound track is a common feature of early sound films, because the visuals were often edited to the sound track in order to ensure proper synchronization. Second, the approach to audiovisual phrasing is nevertheless quite different both between the performance segments and the dialogue segment and between the two performance segments. The audiovisual phrasing of the dialogue segment is determined by the principle of showing the speaker of the lines of dialogue from more or less the perspective of the addressee (rather than showing, for instance, reaction shots), and the rate of cutting follows rather mechanically from the speed at which lines are exchanged (with the exception of those who are speaking in the same frame). This principle foregrounds speech as an intentional act, but it also excludes the effect of the speech on the addressee, which must be inferred from the next line of dialogue. That is, this principle of audiovisual phrasing frames speech as a series of one-way broadcasts rather than as a communicative exchange that includes the reaction of the listener as part of the exchange.

The editing in the two performance segments, by contrast, is much slower in pace, being dominated by long takes from a relatively anonymous perspective of an arbitrary seat in the theater. The song form nevertheless plays an important role in

Figure 6-5. *The Broadway Melody.* CU of solo dancer's feet at beginning of second dance chorus.

the editing. With only one exception, the cuts are all grouped near the beginnings of song sections (i.e., verse or chorus), usually one cut per line until the shot that will remain through the duration of that section is reached. Moreover, the editing follows predictable, though slightly different patterns in the two performance segments. In the first, the principle is one of cutting in for a closer view. As noted previously, both verse and chorus move from ELS1 to ELS2 and finish the unit with a long take in LS. The basic pattern is somewhat different in the second performance segment. The opening chorus is simply one long take in ELS2. The first dance chorus then establishes a pattern: (1) start with a relatively distant shot, (2) cut to a detail, then (3) return to a more distant shot for the duration of the unit. A variant of this pattern is offered in the second dance chorus, and the third inverts the pattern to focus on the feet, returning to the more comprehensive view only for the last two lines.

Overall, then, the principle of these two performance segments appears to be guiding the attention of an arbitrary spectator into a staged spectacle set to music. Each trip through the chorus focuses that attention in a slightly different way, and each chorus except the last is bound to the previous one by continuing the shot from the end of the one chorus over into the beginning of the next. The whole of the second segment seems to aim at the synchronized spectacle of the dancer tapping on point, which is featured briefly in close-up during the second dance chorus and then dominates the third dance chorus, with a cut to the close-up of her feet coinciding and producing a strong sync point with the start of the chorus. This, not Eddie's rather anemic singing, is the high point of the scene.

"MY FORGOTTEN MAN," FROM *GOLD DIGGERS OF 1933*

Many song performances in musicals are accompanied by dance, and these scenes will require choreography matched to the music. This was the case with dress rehearsal in *The Broadway Melody*. Typically, the editing of such scenes will also follow the articulations more closely than was the case with the scenes in *The Broadway Melody*, where the editing and camera work were relatively modest.

In "My Forgotten Man," a Busby Berkeley production number that concludes *Gold Diggers of 1933*, both choreography and editing are closely aligned with formal articulations of the music. The overall structure of the sequence is relatively straightforward: an introductory pantomime, a short verse, and then five choruses of the AABA song, the fourth abridged using only the second half (BA). Each of these segments except the verse and opening chorus, which are treated as a unit, is clearly distinguished in terms of musical treatment, choreography, editing, and camerawork. Similar to Table 6-3, Table 6-4 combines a shot list with the lyrics and song structure. Overall, the sequence gives a strong impression of an audiovisual phrasing where the song structure dominates.

Table 6-4 *Gold Diggers of 1933.* "My Forgotten Man," shot list with lyrics aligned.

Time Code	Shot	Description of Camera Movement and Action	Lyrics
1:30:30	MS	Conductor	(Intro music)
1:30:33	ELS1	Deep in audience. Proscenium	
1:30:37	ELS2	On stage; slow dolly in, stops at tight 2-LS on Carol and Forgotten Man.	
1:30:52	2-MCU	Carol and Forgotten Man	
1:30:56	2-MLS	Carol and Forgotten Man; Forgotten Man exits	
1:31:07	MS	Carol, leaning against lamp post.	**Verse**
			I don't know if he deserves a bit of sympathy
			Forget your sympathy; it's alright with me.
			I was satisfied to drift along from day to day
			Till they came along and took my man away.
			Chorus 1
			A
			Remember my forgotten man?

			You put a rifle in his hand, You sent him far away, You shouted hip hooray! But look at him today.
1:31:49	CU		**A** Remember my forgotten man? You had him cultivate the land, He walked behind a plow The sweat fell from his brow But look at him right now.
			B And once he used to love me I was happy then. He used to take care of me Won't you bring him back again?
			A 'Cause ever since the world began A woman's got to have a man Forgetting him, you see, Means your forgetting me, Like my—my forgotten man.
		Offscreen voice singing.	**Chorus 2** **A** *Remember my forgotten man?*
1:32:56	MLS	Forgotten Man walks by, tilt up to woman in window MS woman singing (~1:33:00)	*You put a rifle in his hand, You sent him far away, You shouted hip hooray! But look at him toda- -ay*
1:33:13		Tilt and pan to another window	**A** *Remember my forgotten man?*
		MS woman with baby (1:33:17)	*You had him cultivate the land,*

(*Continued*)

Table 6-4 (*Continued*)

Time Code	Shot	Description of Camera Movement and Action	Lyrics

1:33:25		Tilt down
		  and pan
		MS woman in rocker (1:33:28)
			He walked behind a plow
			The sweat
			  fell from his brow
			But look at him right now.

1:33:35	MS	Woman singing	**B** *And once he used to* *love me* *I was happy then.* *He used to take care*

1:33:47	LS	Carol and Forgotten Man
		Carol walks to door, where a man sleeps on the sidewalk. Camera follows. Policeman enters (1:33:53)
			of me
			Won't you bring him back
			  again?
			
			A
			'Cause ever since the world
			  began
			A woman's got to have a

1:34:02	3-MS	Forgotten Man, Carol, Policeman	*man*
1:34:03	CU	Medal	

1:34:06	3-MS		*For-*
			  getting him, you see,
			Means your forgetting
			  me,

		Exit Forgotten Man (1:34:10) Exit Policeman (1:34:14)	*Like my forgot-* *ten man.*
1:34:16		To black	
1:34:18	ELS	Curtain opens (Men marching right)	**Chorus 3** **A** (Remember my forgotten man?) (You put a rifle in his
1:34:23	ELS	From above. Men marching toward camera	hand,)

1:34:27	MS	Men marching right	(You sent him far a- way.)
			(You shouted hip hooray!)
			(But look at him today.)
1:34:33	ELS	Behind the crowd. Men marching left. Camera cranes up and over	**A**
			(Remember my forgotten man?)
			(You had him cultivate the la- -and)
1:34:40		To black	(He walked behind a plow)
1:34:40	LS	Curtain opens. (Marching toward the camera)	
			(The sweat fell from his brow)
			(But look at him right now.)
1:34:47	MS	Marching toward the camera	**B**
			(And once he used to love me)
1:34:51	LS	Marching toward the camera	(I was happy then.)
1:34:55	CU	Marching toward the camera	(He used to take care of me)
1:34:59	ELS	One set of soldiers marching right, wounded soldiers moving left. Rain	
			(Won't you bring him back again?)
			A
			('Cause ever since the world began)
1:35:06	LS	Wounded soldiers moving left	(A woman's got to have a ma-
1:35:10	MS	Wounded soldier moving toward camera	-an)
1:35:12	2-MS	Wounded soldiers moving toward camera	
			(Forgetting him, you see,)
1:35:15	LS	Wounded soldiers moving left	(Means your forgetting me,)
1:35:18	2-MS	Wounded soldiers moving left	(Like my forgotten
1:35:19	MS	Soldier carrying soldier	man.)

(Continued)

Table 6-4 (*Continued*)

Time Code	Shot	Description of Camera Movement and Action	Lyrics
1:35:22		Black	**Chorus 4 (abridged)** **B** (And once he used to love me) (I was happy then.)
1:35:23	MLS	Opens on food line	(He used to take care of me) (Won't you bring him back again?)
1:35:35	MLS	Another line of men waiting	**A** ('Cause ever since the world be-
1:35:40	MCU	Track past men in line	gan) (A woman's got to have a man) (Forgetting him, you see,) (Means your forgetting me,) (Like my forgotten man.)
1:35:54		Black	**Chorus 5** **A** Women: *Oh bring them back*

	ELS	Curtain opens on silhouette soliders
		Camera slowly dollies back
			Men: *We are the real
			  forgotten men*
			Women: *Then bring them back*
			Men: *Remember, bring us
			  back again*
			Women: *Are they gone*
			Men: *Some who fought and cried*
			Men: *For glory was our pride*
			Men: *But few have glory now!*
			Women: *And guns are mad
			  at my fate*
			A
			Women: *Oh bring them back*

		Camera stops dollying (1:36:17)	Men: *Remember your forgotten men*
			Women: *We want them back*
			Men: *You've got to let us live again*
			Women: *Are they gone*
			Men: *You can't say much for me*
			Men *Still thanks for USA*
			Men: *But where are we today?*
1:36:31	LS	Men in front	Women: *But where are they today?*
		Men turn and get out of the way, revealing Carol in ELS (1:36:33)	**B**
			Carol: *And once he used to love me*
			I was happy then.
1:36:42	MS	Carol	*He used to take care of me*
			Won't you bring him back again?
1:36:49	LS	Chorus of women	Women: *Oh bring him back*
			A
			Chorus: *'Cause ever since the world began*
1:36:57	LS	Carol from above and behind with men around her	*A woman's got to have a ma-*
1:37:01	MLS	Carol. Camera dollies back quickly	*-an*
			Forgetting him, you see,
			Means your forgetting me,
			Like my forgot-
		Ends in ELS of whole stage	*ten ma-*
1:37:18		To black	*-an.*

The sequence opens with the MS of the conductor starting the orchestra. It then shifts to an ELS from the back of the audience before passing to another ELS, now centered on the stage as the curtain opens. The camera then tracks in, stopping on a tight LS of Carol (Joan Blondell) and the first Forgotten Man (Frank Mills) as Carol takes out a cigarette (Figure 6-6a). On a cut to a 2-shot in MCU,

Carol lights the cigarette and places it in the Forgotten Man's mouth. With a cut back to a MLS, he exits and Carol moves to a lamp post as the camera moves to reframe. This whole segment, which serves as an elaborate introduction to the numbers, plays in pantomime to a lush melodramatic orchestral accompaniment. The editing here is primarily based on the action, which is only loosely coordinated with the music. There are no significant sync points in the passage, with the possible exception of the meandering entrance of a pathos-laden string line that serves to plunge the scene into the melancholic representation after a slight dramatic pause for the opening of the curtain.

The lack of close coordination helps emphasize the introductory function of this pantomime, and the shift from pantomime to speech is emphasized by a cut to Carol next to the lamp post, a closer framing that makes apparent the synchronization of speech (Figure 6-6b). The appearance of synchronized speech here serves as a sync point that redirects the action. Once we become aware that Carol is delivering her speech in rhymed couplets and that the musical accompaniment, now more the bluesy gestures of popular song of the period than the conventional melos of melodrama, is shadowing her voice, we also recognize that her words are lyrics to a song (actually the verse) that is not yet sung, an impression that becomes even stronger when the chorus begins and the orchestra begins to play a discernable tune behind the lyrics, which Carol now delivers—or rather performs—close in rhythm and time to the melodic line. Yet the effect of this "performance" here seems to position Carol's speech outside of song, however much the song is nevertheless determining the placement of her words. Lyric and song have not properly synchronized.

This lack of synchronization is furthered in the second chorus when a singing voice enters offscreen, and we see a man walk by as though a new pantomime is beginning to unfold. Instead, the camera begins to move around, first seeking out the singing voice (Figure 6-6c), then a woman with a baby, and a woman in a rocking chair before coming back to the woman singing. These camera movements are all coordinated with the subdivisions of the song. As noted, the song is a traditional 32-bar AABA song, though more elaborate than many. Each of the A sections has five lines, with an aabbb rhyme scheme for the opening two and aabba for the last. The musical form of each A section is similar with each of the opening "a" lines presented with the same 2-bar basic idea, the next two "b" lines presented in compressed and varied 1-bar contrasting idea, and the final line a new 2-bar idea that leads to a cadence. The B section, or bridge, is a simpler abab rhyme scheme, each line set to a 2-bar idea, and the bridge as a whole is structured as a 4-bar phrase and a repetition. The camera movements produce sync points with the lyrics or song structure: passing by the man walking for "forgotten man"; the second statement of the basic idea ("You put a rifle . . ."), where we see the singer; the fall to "forgotten man" to open the second A; and "the sweat fell from his brow" for the woman in the rocker. The bridge of the song (B) coincides with a cut back to the singer, but the repeated phrase ("He used to take care of me") opens a new pantomime that plays out for the rest of the chorus. At the return of the A, Carol intervenes when a policeman starts to harass a man sleeping on the street, by showing the policeman that the man is actually a decorated war veteran (Figure 6-6d). The key point in the intervention coincides with the line "a woman's got to have a man." The end of the chorus, like the end of each chorus after this, is punctuated with the negative sync point of the image going to black.

The third chorus, unsung, opens with soldiers marching (Figure 6-6e), getting ready to go off to war, and the style of performance and orchestration has changed the musical topic of the music from a blues-inspired lament into an aggressive military march. The editing in this chorus does not precisely match up with the section boundaries of the song—a dissolve to black for a scene change even occurs in the middle of the second A—but the cuts are

Figure 6-6. *Gold Diggers of 1933*, "My Forgotten Man."

a	b	c
d	e	f
g	h	i

nevertheless sharp and tend to follow the strong downbeats of the music, which also serve to organize the editing. The bridge, scored and functioning like an abbreviated march trio, shows the march beginning to break down: wounded soldiers begin to pass, moving the other direction (Figure 6-6f), and the rain becomes worse, with peals of thunder that become increasingly disruptive when the aggressive march music returns ironically to accompany only wounded soldiers. Throughout the second half, the editing gets increasingly ragged with respect to the beat.

The fourth chorus begins again with a black screen, and the chorus is abridged, starting with the B section, with the march trio musical topic given even greater emphasis through the new scoring with strings dominating. The scene is now after the war, with men in bread and soup lines (Figure 6-6g). Only three shots are used in this chorus, and all three focus on the men queued in lines, the last a dramatic tracking shot. It is also significant that this chorus, which depicts the material effects of the cultural forgetting of the soldiers, is abridged: the first half of the song is simply forgotten.

The final chorus once again begins on black, and lyrics return in a very elaborate choral arrangement that begins by dividing male and female choruses. The women call for the men to come back, whereas the men demand to be remembered. Yet the chorus opens again with a lack of synchronization, with the female voices announcing the new chorus against the black, and when the curtain parts, the shot shows neither female nor male singers, but silhouettes of marching men (Figure 6-6h). A mass of men begins to form at the back for the stage, gathers numbers, and marches forward, but we cannot really see them singing for most of the shot. As the camera dollies back with the advancing men, women come into view gesturing with their choral responses, but it is only the cut near the end of the second A, as the men hold "today," the final word of the section, that the camera is close enough that we can see the men's faces and make out that they are indeed singing. This close shot, however, comes too late to create the sync point. This sync point is therefore deferred to the next section, as the men turn around and reveal Carol, who now sings the words from the original bridge first in an ELS (Figure 6-6i)—though sufficiently close to see her lips moving—and then in MS, as she sings "He used to take care of me," which definitively establishes the sync point, and marks the Forgotten Man's absence as a social catastrophe: there can be no community so long as the men are not remembered. The final A brings male and female choruses together, but again not in a way that establishes a strong sync point that would lodge these sounds in the community of this chorus. The female chorus does not seem to be singing the words we hear, and when we see the male chorus, the focus on Carol draws attention to her "need" for a man to complete her and the community. As the chorus builds to a mighty climax, the camera again moves back to frame the community as a whole, but Carol remains very much without her Forgotten Man, despite the resounding major chord on which the number ends.

Overall, the large changes in the scene coincide with the song structure, with each chorus offering a new phase in the narrative presented during the number. At lower levels, the editing is more variable, yet it seems deployed purposefully to defer sync points. These deferrals, in turn, relate to the basic thesis of the number: to be forgotten is to be left outside society. The lack of synchronization, in other words, relates to men's loss of voice that marks them as forgotten. Even the women (and instruments) who sing for them cannot easily put image, voice, and song together.

Writing a Scene Analysis Paper

One kind of short essay you might be asked to write is a scene analysis, where you describe how the sound or music works in a scene (or sequence). For example, in this chapter we have analyzed three performance sequences from *The Broadway Melody* as well as part of the title sequence. We have also analyzed "My Forgotten Man," from *Gold Diggers of 1933.* Any of these might have been turned into the body of an essay by adding a synopsis and a conclusion. This would result in the following outline for the paper:

1. A short synopsis of the film including pertinent background information (genre, director, release year, summary of the plot with principal actors) to serve as an introduction to the paper. The end of the synopsis should transition to a short thesis statement making some claim about the sound and music in the scene.
2. A very brief introduction to the scene giving any narrative background necessary to follow the analysis of the scene. This leads directly to the scene analysis itself.
3. A brief summary paragraph to serve as a conclusion at the end.

This basic framework might be expanded into a scene comparison essay by adding a second scene analysis and replacing the summary paragraph with a paragraph that compares and contrasts the scenes. For instance, in a previous section, we explicitly compare and contrast two performance scenes of the title song from *The Broadway Melody* in terms of audiovisual phrasing and make a similar albeit more cursory comparison to the first performance of "You Were Meant for Me."

There are many things you may attend to in a scene analysis other than audiovisual phrasing. For instance, in the analysis of "My Forgotten Man," we attended to song structure, performance style, rhyme scheme, timbre, musical topics, narrative sequence, camera movement, shot composition, and many other things besides sync points and audiovisual phrasing, even if the overall goal was to illustrate an audiovisual phrasing dominated by the song structure on the one hand and a deferral of sync points on the other.

In general, you will want to attend to three large areas in preparing a scene analysis: (a) presence or absence of sound track elements and balance between them, (b) general design of the sound track (that is, how it is mapped out over time or how the balance changes over time), and (c) relation of sound track in the scene to the narrative and/or theme (how sound track elements are tied to characters and action, and how design of the sound track in a scene relates to the articulations of the narrative).

The second section of the paper describes and evaluates the sound track from different angles: these analytical passages tie information together and create something like a "story" of the sound track design. In "My Forgotten Man," the description follows the chronological presentation of the film because the music, which dominates the sound design in this sequence, changes markedly with each chorus. The analytical description here focuses on delineating the differences among the various choruses and abstracting a narrative arc for the number from them. Most non-performance scenes won't lend themselves as readily to this sort of treatment since most scenes are not as autonomous as performance scenes, and the task will often involve coming to some sort of conclusion about how sound and music are working in the scene. That is, it will be analytically more important to address the scene as a whole rather than tracing the sequencing of sounds and music in the scene.

A checklist for scene analysis in terms of sound, then, looks like this:

1. Background, general information, and synopsis: This might include genre, director, release year, principal actors, summary of the plot or story with attention to describing the context of the scene you are analyzing
2. Theme and/or thesis statement
3. Description and synopsis of the scene
4. Shot list
5. Description of the sound track elements and their balance
6. Description and evaluation of the sound track from different angles: physical sources of sounds, music's narrative functions (emotion and characterization, the external–internal opposition), musical structure (if the scene is a performance scene or uses an extensive excerpt of pre-existing music), filmic (or narrative) structure (if the scene breaks down into distinct segments). In this section, we might also look more closely at sound, music, and representation (What does sound or music tell us about the kind of person a character is? Whose feeling does the music seem to be telling us about? etc.)
7. If needed, a summary statement about the sound track in the scene

In the next section, we use this checklist to produce a sample scene analysis.

SCENE ANALYSIS SAMPLE: LEAVING THE OPERA HOUSE, *LE MILLION*

Directed by René Clair with a score by Armand Bernard, Philippe Parès, and Georges Van Parys, *Le Million* (1931) is a musical that tells the story of the pursuit of a jacket containing a winning lottery ticket. Michel (René Lefèvre), an artist deeply in debt and pestered at every turn by creditors, learns of his good fortune only to discover that Béatrice (Annabella), his fiancée, has given away the old jacket containing the ticket to Granpere Tulipe (Paul Ollivier), who uses the jacket to escape the police. Resembling a part-talkie, the film deploys an unusual combination of dialogue, musical numbers, and silent film–style pantomime to trace Michel's desperate attempts to recover the jacket. The plot turns on the frantic (and successful) pursuit of good fortune. The ticket (and jacket that contains it) continually eludes all who know of its existence, but they strive after it, not because the labor of the chase is rewarding or socially useful, but because the ticket represents the only conceivable alternative to a world ruled by economic exchange. (As Michel illustrates, art conceived as labor, in this film, leads only to debt.) The sound track underscores this contrast: talking sequences serve primarily for communication about money, debts, and social obligations; musical choral numbers celebrate community; musical monologues reveal characters' concerns; and silent film pantomime is used for chasing—escape and pursuit— a madcap unsettling and resettling of social boundaries.

A little more than 90 seconds in length, the short scene analyzed here—the last portion of an elaborate sequence at the opera house—takes place near the end of the film when Michel believes he has lost the lottery ticket for good. Table 6-5 contains a shot list and notes about music and sound in the scene. Although pantomime and dialogue alternate in the scene, music runs throughout and provides a dominant line of continuity. We analyze the scene in five short segments based on this alternation.

The first (1:12:57–1:13:19) plays in pantomime, that is, without dialogue or sound effects. The scene starts outside the theater where a group of men are greeted by a clunky fanfare in muted trumpets followed by some clownishly dissonant woodwinds. The prominent music here has the effect of creating unease about these men, who have in fact been interfering with Michel's attempts to retrieve the jacket. Michel and Béatrice then appear. Frustrated by his loss of the jacket, Michel lashes out at Prosper (Jean-Louis Allibert), who has also been repeatedly getting in the way (Figure 6-7). Although everything at the beginning of the scene plays out in pantomime, the music here, aside from the opening fanfare, is not closely linked to the action.

The second part of the scene (1:13:19–1:13:42) begins formally when a taxi pulls up accompanied by a subtle car sound, and a reverse angle cut marks a shift from pantomime to talking film, though music continues, at a lower volume, under the dialogue of the policeman and taxi driver (Raymond Cordy). This segment is dominated by dialogue and also features a few prominent sound effects (car doors opening and closing). The dialogue here consists of the policeman berating the taxi driver for not following the rules and the taxi driver complaining about needing to collect his fare.

The third part (1:13:42–1:13:59) returns to pantomime to show Michel and Béatrice beginning to go back to the theater and the taxi driver intercepting them before they can. Music is again the only sound track element present and the orchestration is now primarily strings.

Table 6-5 *Le Million* (1931). Leaving the opera house, shot list and screening notes.

Time Code	Shot Description	Dialogue (English Translation)	Effects	Music	General Comments
1:12:57	2-MLS third added (1:13:02)	None	None	Muted Trumpet fanfare. Then chattering winds.	Plays silent.
1:13:05	ELS Michel and Béatrice exiting theater with crowd. Camera follows and ends with Michel and Béatrice in MS (1:13:09); joined by Prosper at 1:13:14. Michel chases him away.	None	None	Chattering wind music continues over cut, gradually smoothes out as Michel and Béatrice move into place. Strings enter as though in anticipation of the arrival of Prosper. Flute line begins . . .	
1:13:19	ELS, theater in background. Car enters foreground.	None (Policeman starts to talk but no sound until next shot)	Car sound.	Flute line continues.	
1:13:23	2-MS Taxi driver and police officer.	**Policeman**: You again. What do you take me for? I told you to move on. **Taxi Driver**: I've been around the block a dozen times. I'm waiting for my fare to come out. He's got to pay me. Here he comes now. **Policeman**: Next time I'll hit you with a ticket.	Car door at end of shot when driver gets out of cab. Door sounds punctuate musical cadence.	Music ducks under dialogue but otherwise continues without concern for dialogue or action. Instrumentation varies considerably in this shot. Cadence just as driver gets out of car.	Dialogue. The policeman's speech is very to the point. The taxicab driver's speech is much more loquacious as he tries to explain himself.
1:13:42	2-MS Michel and Béatrice. Add taxi driver (1:13:47).			A new musical idea, mostly strings now, starts as Michel and Béatrice turn and begin walking back toward the theater.	Plays silent.
1:13:53	MS Taxi.		(No sound of doors)	That new idea is repeated and varied.	

1:13:58	MS Taxi (reverse angle); Béatrice, Michel, and taxi driver.	**Taxi Driver**: Where to now? The police station? **Michel**: Not the police station. You can spend your life there. Home! **Taxi Driver**: Home? Where's home? **Michel**: You were waiting there this morning. **Taxi Driver**: Will I get paid this time?	Door slams both near start of shot and near end of shot.	Music ducks under dialogue but otherwise continues without concern for dialogue or action.	Dialogue. Michel stands in front of driver's face with his back turned to the camera. Michel's voice is much louder and more prominent.
1:14:20	2-MLS Third man enters.		None	Music continues. Drum roll starts.	Plays silent.
1:14:22	LS Taxi pulling away turns into 3-ELS.	**Michel**: Sure, sure, you'll get paid. **Taxi Driver**: It's about time. **Michel**: You tire me out. **Taxi Driver**: I tire you out? I just want what's coming to me.	None	Drum roll continues over cut. Second drum roll starts as new car drives up. Musical cadence coincides with end of scene. Immediate crossfade to song that starts with next shot.	

Back at the cab, the fourth part (1:13:59–1:14:20) presents a dialogue between Michel and the taxi driver about whether Michel will pay for the taxi, as music again continues, at a reduced volume, under the dialogue.

The little scene ends (1:14:20–1:14:31) with a cut back to the men shown at the beginning of the scene, again in pantomime, the music once again alone on the sound track. The cab drives off, as the sound of the car is imitated by a snare drum, and the men give chase in a second cab.

Throughout the scene (and indeed the film as a whole), the action associated with the pursuit of the ticket is presented in silent film pantomime style. By contrast, talking film is used to focus on issues of money and law. The two spaces are similarly delineated, with the sidewalk in front of the steps of the theater reserved for pantomime, whereas the space around the taxicab is inhabited by dialogue.

Figure 6-7. *Le Million* (1931): Michel lashes out at Prosper.

The pantomime segments are assembled through editing, whereas the two talking segments are each single shots. Nondiegetic music, on the other hand, accompanies action in both spaces, without the musical structure aligning closely with the shifts from one space to the other. The music does change across the scene from initially being dominated by brass and woodwinds to being dominated by strings at the end, and this musical change accords with a general shift in the focus of the scene from the theater and the hope of the chase to the cab and the crushing reality of Michel's debt. But aside from the imitation of the car engines by the drum at the end, the music seeks to capture the overall mood of the scene rather than picking out and underscoring particular moments in it.

Here, in list form, is a completed checklist for the scene:

- Background, general information, and synopsis: "Directed by Rene Clair with a score by Armand Bernard, Philippe Parès, and Georges Van Parys, *Le Million* (1931) . . ."
- Theme and/or thesis statement: "The plot turns on the frantic (and successful) pursuit of good fortune . . ." "The sound track underscores this contrast . . ." Because the theme is not easy to summarize, it is somewhat longer than is typical.
- Description and scene synopsis: "A little more than 90 seconds in length, the short scene analyzed here . . ."
- Shot list: "Table 6-5 contains a shot list and notes about music and sound in the scene."
- Description of sound track elements and balance: "Although pantomime and dialogue alternate, music runs throughout the short scene."

- Description and evaluation of the sound track from different angles: "The first part of the scene plays in pantomime. . . . The second part of the scene begins when the taxi pulls up. . . . The third part returns to pantomime. . . . Back at the cab, the fourth part presents a dialogue. . . . The scene ends with a cut back to the men shown at the beginning of the scene. . . ." The description here emphasizes the alternation of the filmic structure in order to contrast it with the basic musical continuity.
- Summary statement: "Throughout the scene (and indeed the film as a whole), the action associated with the pursuit of the ticket. . . ."

Summary

The segmentation of a film's running time produces a flexible hierarchy of units: shot, scene, sequence, and act. Listening to concert or other instrumental music also involves a hierarchy of grouping—motive, phrase, section, and movement— but these units do not correspond, one-on-one, to filmic units. Musical motives, for example, are always short (a few seconds), but shots can range anywhere from 1 second to many minutes.

Learning how to make an effective runtime segmentation of a film is an important step to taking effective screening notes on a film. Most films allow for several different convincing runtime segmentations, so the primary consideration should not be on producing a correct segmentation but rather finding the segmentation that allows you to take notes in the most effective way. Music, whether principally diegetic or nondiegetic, is laid out over the segments of a film, and nondiegetic music in particular frequently extends over the boundaries of the film's segmentation determined by action.

The case studies in this chapter from *The Broadway Melody, Gold Diggers of 1933,* and *Le Million* offered opportunity to examine a number of ways the sound track articulates with the image track in films from the transitional era.

From 1932 to 1950
Music and the Sound Track in the Classical Studio Era

Introduction

The late 1920s were a period of extensive experimentation and a wide variation in practices, but by the mid-1930s studios had settled into a regular production system, dominated by genre films. Along with that model necessarily came a rapid codification of the sound track. As in earlier decades, however, both economics and technology were drivers of change. Economically, the Great Depression adversely affected movie attendance, giving film producers every incentive to find formulas to streamline costs. Technologically, the development of an effective system of rerecording was key: it greatly simplified shooting by allowing a large number of tasks to be shifted to the postproduction phase, where they could be handled not only in a more systematic fashion but also with greater finesse. Without question the most important impact of rerecording on the sound track was that production sound could now concentrate on dialogue.

Issues of Technology and Economics
IMPROVEMENTS IN RECORDING TECHNOLOGY

By 1930, sound-on-film (optical sound) had become the accepted standard for both production and distribution. By 1932, the available technologies had improved remarkably in nearly every area. Among the most notable advances were better microphones and speakers, and quieter cameras and lights, as well as several significant refinements in the sound-on-film process.

Two optical sound formats, variable area and variable density, would compete with one another for more than two decades. Not only were they compatible from the standpoint of exhibition, meaning there was little incentive for the studios to standardize, but the competition in fact worked to the studios' advantage.

RCA controlled one method and Western Electric the other, and maintaining both formats helped ward off legal complaints of monopoly while encouraging both companies to invest in further research. Sound-on-film had always been easier to edit and easier to use in location shooting, but enhancements in film stock, the adoption of the double system of recording (separate cameras and film strips for image and sound), the "noiseless" film preparation, and a reduction in the wow and flutter of optical sound projection had increased the fidelity of sound-on-film to the point that it equaled or exceeded that of the disk system. Sound-on-film also had the advantage of being physically attached to the release print and of being more durable, so that the cost advantage of sound-on-disk soon disappeared (see Figure 7-1). By 1930, even Warners, the last studio to insist on distributing its sound tracks via disk, had begun offering optical prints as well. Disk recording continued to have a presence on the movie set, however, as it was a far more efficient means of checking the sound of a scene than developing and printing a proof copy of the optical sound track.

The development of directional microphones was another important technological innovation that eliminated much of the extraneous set and camera

Figure 7-1. *Okay for Sound* (1946). A scene from *Night and Day* (1946) with variable area sound track exposed. Note the two sound tracks, 180 degrees out of phase: originally a means of noise reduction, these were later exploited for stereo reproduction. In the 1970s, Dolby managed to matrix these two tracks in order to encode four channels of stereo sound on them.

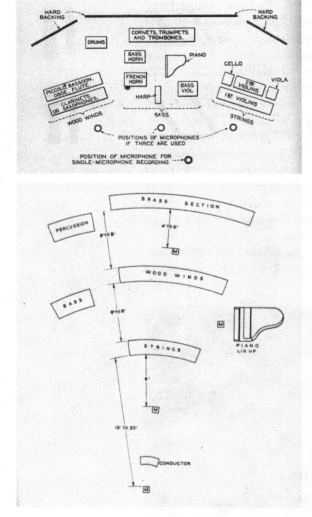

noise. Introduced in 1931, the ribbon microphone, for instance, was bidirectional, meaning that it could be placed between actors, but it was insensitive to sounds coming from the sides (such as camera and crew). In 1936, RCA developed the unidirectional microphone, which allowed for an even narrower focus. This, along with additional soundproofing measures taken on the set and in the camera apparatus, allowed for a much more fluid use of the camera and a return to the standard single camera setup that had been common in the silent era.

The improved fidelity of the recording technology had a direct bearing on music, especially with respect to instrumentation. In the early sound era, much consideration had to be given to scoring that suited the microphones available, but by the mid-1930s the accommodations to the microphone had become minimal. Studio orchestras tended to be smaller than the live orchestras they emulated; they also had fewer strings relative to the other instrumental groups compared to what a live group would need. This imbalance was compensated for by microphone placement, mixing and "sweetening"—the string section, for instance, sometimes played a cue a second time and that recording was mixed with the original take to give a fuller sound. Physical placement also aided microphone setup as much as the musicians: Figure 7-2 shows two common seating arrangements for a studio orchestra.

Figure 7-2. Two common studio set-ups for $\frac{a}{b}$ recording an orchestra in the 1940s. The signals from the multiple microphones were either mixed live at the recording session or recorded separately and mixed later.

RERECORDING

The consistent use of rerecording allowed sound work on the set to focus on capturing dialogue, because the other sounds—effects and music—could be added during postproduction.

Although rerecording had been possible earlier, the process, as we saw in Chapter 5, was difficult and expensive, and the results were often unsatisfactory. The loss of fidelity was such that, in the first few years of sound-film exhibition, the sound track could not even be reliably rerecorded to the release print when using the sound-on-film process. Instead, each shot would simply be reproduced at whatever level the mixer had set, and a cue sheet with instructions on volume adjustment would be sent out with the film. The projectionist was expected to make these changes while the film was shown. As can be expected, the results varied widely depending on the skill and attention of the operator, and complaints about sound levels in theaters were frequent. The problem disappeared once postproduction mixing became standard and the sound track could be set to a master level.

Studios established rerecording as a normal part of postproduction during 1932, and it was at this point that the sound track was divided into its three familiar components—dialogue, music, and effects. Each of these was assigned its own crew of personnel. Dialogue was captured primarily during production, and the sets, microphone placement, and actor positioning and movement were all designed with the idea of capturing dialogue clearly. During postproduction, the editing of dialogue closely paralleled the picture editing and was in many respects simply an adjunct to it. Although some sound effects would also naturally be recorded as part of the production sound, most effects were dubbed in during postproduction. Indeed, filmmakers tried to avoid non-dialogue sounds as much as possible during production, not just because they could easily obscure dialogue, but also because they limited editing possibilities when they were mingled in with the dialogue. Nondiegetic music was almost always recorded after the fact, and onscreen music, more often than not, was prerecorded so that the actors could concentrate on the visual parts of presentation during filming. Once the dialogue, music, and effects tracks were created, they could be combined through rerecording into a final sound track mix, where the elements were placed in (narrative) balance. Through rerecording, the filming of sound film was greatly simplified, giving filmmakers more flexibility and making the whole process more economical.

SOUND IN THE THEATERS OF THE 1930s AND 1940s

Mechanical sound reproduction for films in the 1930s was limited in two important respects: frequency response and volume response. In addition, sound reproduction was forced to contend with the overly reverberant acoustics of most theaters, many of which had been converted from previous uses. The live performance media of silent film, vaudeville, and legitimate stage all demanded a warmer hall, one with a significant amount of reflected sound, but that acoustic property muddied reproduced sound.

The typical theater of the 1930s wired for monaural sound had anywhere from two to six speaker horn placements, depending on the size and configuration of the theater. Once a sonically permeable screen was developed in the late 1920s, the speakers were generally moved behind the screen to reinforce the illusion that the sound emanated from the film world (Figure 7-3). As engineers improved frequency response, they discovered that volume needed to be increased to match, because otherwise the sounds seemed too distant from their apparent sources on the screen. Increased volume could also be used as a means of masking flaws in the auditorium, a strategy that resulted in complaints of excessive volume in theaters, especially after the introduction of the so-called "wide-range" sound systems of the mid-1940s. These wide-range systems shifted

Figure 7-3. Speaker horn designed for placement behind the screen.

from a two-speaker design introduced in the mid-1930s, based on separating low frequency and high-frequency sound, to a three-speaker design that separates out a mid-range of 300–3000 Hz (this setup would also become the standard in home stereos by the early 1960s).

Besides matching increased frequency response and masking flaws in auditoria, a third reason motivating the increased volume was undoubtedly the sonic spectacle that the new systems made possible. The increased fidelity permitted theaters to produce louder sounds without distortion, and this ability became a spectacle in its own right; that is, theaters with the latest sound equipment could distinguish themselves from lesser theaters on the basis of sound reproduction, a fact that led some to emphasize the difference by turning up the volume. Suddenly every word, every note, even a whisper, could boom forth with unmistakable clarity and volume to every corner of the theater. (A similar strategy seems evident today, when theaters seem intent on displaying the power and fidelity of their sound systems by blasting spectators from their seats.)

Yet the larger dynamic range also allowed for a more effective dramatic use of sound, as the obtainable contrast between soft and loud sounds expanded. Loud sounds may have been the most immediately spectacular elements on the new sound systems, but these systems also permitted much more sonic detail at low volume as well; even silences were more effective as the hiss from the apparatus was greatly reduced in the 1940s. (Recall Robynn Stilwell's comment cited in this book's Introduction: "In the film industry, sound seems to be of greatest concern to those who produce big movies; we have come to expect teeth-rattling explosions and bombastic scores in modern blockbusters. However, sound can be even more intensely felt in intimate, quiet films, where the slightest whisper or silence can have a marked effect.")

In general, however, the recording technology available exceeded the reproducing capabilities of even the best theaters. By 1940, film could be recorded at upwards of 8000 Hz and through 60 dB of dynamic range. The weak point remained the amplifying equipment, which required constant maintenance: theaters, economically squeezed during much of the 1930s, were often negligent in replacing radio tubes, with the result that amplifiers would hum or buzz. Even the best equipment in good repair, however, was rarely capable of exploiting the signal captured, and studios wisely adopted protective measures to ensure that sound would remain acceptable in theaters with less than optimal equipment. As the quotation in the sidebar demonstrates, dynamic range in particular was often compressed to no more than 30 dB. Dialogue, of course, was favored in the mix; and an automated balance regulator was developed to keep it well above music and effects (this was the "up-and-downer" that we mentioned in Chapter 2).

THE GREAT DEPRESSION AND THE CONSOLIDATION OF GENRES

Attendance, which had reached eighty million per week in 1930, tumbled to fifty-five million only 2 years later. The revenues from foreign markets were also declining, not only because of the general economic downturn but also because most of the foreign theaters had been wired for sound by this time and naturally were demanding pictures with dialogue in their own languages. With the cost of

The rerecording Mixer . . . should limit the volume range to 30 DB; that is, the difference in level between the lowest signal and loudest signal should be no more than 30 DB, which means the loudest sound will be thirty-two times greater than the lowest. . . . When a picture having more than a 30 DB volume range is shown in a theater, one of two things happen—both of which are detrimental. . . . If the projectionist adjusts the volume so that the high level signals are [toned down, the low level signals are] lost and . . . the sound becomes unintelligible. If the projectionist adjusts the volume [for] the low level signals . . ., then the high level signals will—in many cases—be badly distorted due to the overloading of the sound reproducing system.
—James Cameron, *Sound Motion Pictures* [1947][1]

producing a sound picture running about double that of a silent one, it became difficult for studios to turn a profit. One of the ways that American studios responded was to distribute films with dubbed dialogue (and often different music tracks)—films dubbed in Spanish in particular were important income sources for studios throughout the 1930s. Even more important, the studios turned to genre films, which helped to regularize production and create more predictable attendance numbers. Genres were standardized in as many dimensions as possible, including the use of music and sound.

Production
PRODUCTION PHASES

The sound film became codified with the establishment of the postproduction phase of sound; with the ability to rerecord, studios created three major departments devoted to sound—production, music, and sound (effects). Each department had clearly defined responsibilities. Production sound (all sound on the set) was devoted almost entirely to capturing dialogue. In general, rerecording dialogue was, with the exception of dubbing into foreign languages, avoided until the late 1930s because it was difficult to match microphone perspective in rerecording dialogue. Production sound therefore had to do everything possible to ensure a clear recording of the dialogue. Dialogue might be touched up during postproduction, but initially at least many of the dialogue editing chores were handled by the picture editor, who cut the picture to the sound track during the early years of multicamera shooting and would often follow the master shot for continuity after the return to single-camera filming. Sound edits would be cut in and joined using a bloop so as to avoid pops on the sound track at edit points (Figure 7-4).

Sounds other than dialogue (footsteps, clothing noises, etc.) were minimized on the set because they could inadvertently obscure lines of dialogue or cause continuity problems when shots from different takes were joined. Instead, like music, the vast majority of effects would be added during postproduction where the levels could be carefully balanced to ensure the clarity of dialogue and, even more important, the proper narrative focus of a scene. Footsteps, for instance, could be introduced or not, depending on the perceived needs of the scene. Inevitably, however, the fact that music and effects were added in postproduction reinforced the sense that they were to be considered something added, supplementary rather than primary.

Although optical sound meant that the sound track was physically attached to the image track for purposes of exhibition, this was not the case until the final print was made. Each department produced its own sound strip (indeed, often more than one) and only at the end of postproduction would these be mixed down into a single track, properly balanced for narration and modulated for distribution. This combined track would then be placed beside the image on the exhibition print (see Figure 7-5).

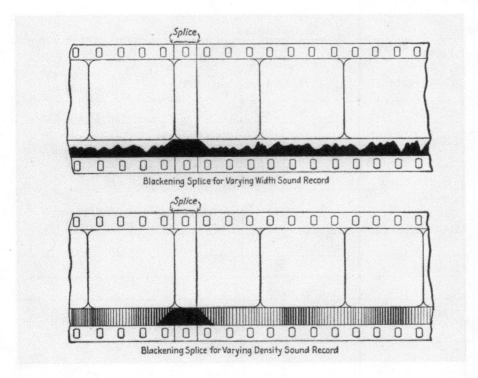

Blackening Splice for Varying Width Sound Record

Blackening Splice for Varying Density Sound Record

Figure 7-4. Blooping. Each edit of the sound track needed to be blooped to avoid a "pop" where the wave forms did not perfectly match up. Blooping involved placing an opaque elliptical or trapezoidal mark across the edit point. This produces the effect of a quick fade out and fade in. A semicircular stroke of a pen would also do the trick.

MUSIC DEPARTMENT

The music department was run by a director, who was responsible for such administrative tasks as budget, scheduling, and assigning composers (and other musical personnel such as orchestrators and music editors); the director might occasionally also perform other tasks such as conducting when the composer was unavailable to do so. Unlike the music director of the silent-era picture house, the job in the studio was generally more managerial than creative in scope. Nevertheless, most music directors were also working composers. Indeed, often they were top-notch composers (for example, Herbert Stothart at MGM, Alfred Newman at Twentieth Century Fox, and Victor Young at Paramount).

Once the task of scoring a film became an accepted part of postproduction in the early 1930s, the basic job of the film composer was to write the underscore and to oversee its performance and recording. (Although the methods and constraints have evolved greatly over the past 85 years, the duties of the composer remain largely the same today). During the studio era, most composers worked

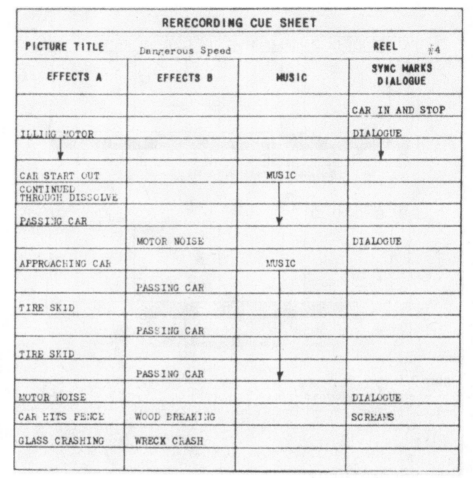

RERECORDING CUE SHEET			
PICTURE TITLE Dangerous Speed			**REEL** #4
EFFECTS A	**EFFECTS B**	**MUSIC**	**SYNC MARKS DIALOGUE**
			CAR IN AND STOP
ILLING MOTOR			DIALOGUE
↓			↓
CAR START OUT		MUSIC	
CONTINUED THROUGH DISSOLVE			
PASSING CAR		↓	
	MOTOR NOISE		DIALOGUE
APPROACHING CAR		MUSIC	
	PASSING CAR		
TIRE SKID			
	PASSING CAR		
TIRE SKID			
	PASSING CAR	↓	
MOTOR NOISE			DIALOGUE
CAR HITS FENCE	WOOD BREAKING		SCREAMS
GLASS CRASHING	WRECK CRASH		

Figure 7-5. Rerecording cue sheet for a final mix. These instructions for the rerecording mixers would typically be prepared by the picture editor in consultation with the music and sound department. In this case there are four sound strips, two for effects, and one each for music and dialogue. Note that the initial car sound effect and screams are contained on the "dialogue" strip. Because the dialogue track accompanies the picture during editing, significant sounds would often be placed on this track at moments dialogue was absent.

The symphonic underscore became commonplace once studios recognized the financial benefits that could accrue. Max Steiner's scores for RKO's King Kong *(1933) and* The Informer *(1935) played a prominent role in this process. Steiner notes that sound film intensified the work of the composer whose painstaking process of spotting, composing, conducting, and recording was often compounded by tight deadlines, as well as last-minute changes in the films.*
—See Max Steiner, "Scoring the Film," in Cooke, *The Hollywood Film Music Reader.*

full-time in the music department of the studio that hired them (although, like stars, directors, and other personnel they were sometimes "lent" to other studios to work on individual projects). The composer was the central creative agent in the music department. Once a picture assignment was made, the composer would meet with the film's director in a "spotting session," compose the music, and usually record the score with orchestra—all within the confines of the studio lot itself. During the spotting session, the composer and director would discuss the general concepts of the entire score as well as specific requirements of certain scenes. This was quite similar to the sorts of discussions music directors and their staffs would have had over how to fit music to the picture in the silent era. (See the commentary for Figure 7-6 for a discussion of structural spotting in *King Kong* [1933].) Although the composer's life during the studio era had a great amount of stability (one could work without worrying where the next job would come from), it also lacked flexibility: generally speaking, composers had limited control over their film assignments, and only the most prominent had much negotiating power in terms of compensation because composers (like almost everyone else, including actors) worked on a salary basis for the studios. Composers typically did not even own the rights to their music, as everything was done on a work-for-hire basis (a practice that became less common in the 1950s but has persisted to a surprising degree even into the present day).

During the studio era, the actual labor of composing film music was always broken down into writing the music and scoring it, or composition proper and orchestration. These were considered two separate occupations, and jobs were most commonly, although not always, filled by separate people. Although this division of labor has struck many—even those in the industry—as illogical, it had a precedent in the theater (where many of the film composers and orchestrators started). In any case, it did increase the speed at which music could be composed, because the composer did not have to worry about writing out music for all of the parts. The orchestrator could also serve as a kind of musical copy editor, catching incorrect clefs, accidentals, and other sorts of errors before they found their way into the parts and disrupted the recording session. (Good music copyists—the person responsible for creating the parts for the orchestral musicians—could serve a similar function.) Moreover, particularly early in the sound era, the microphone posed scoring issues that benefited from specialized knowledge that an experienced orchestrator could provide. In any case, the division of labor between composition and orchestration has proved resilient in the film industry, and it continues to this day.

Typically, the orchestrator was assigned to take the composer's sketch score of each cue (usually written on four to eight musical staff lines) and separate out the individual instrument parts onto a full score (which contained as many as thirty to forty staff lines, each for a different instrument). The sketch score could vary in detail, but it would usually contain at minimum a melodic line and indications for harmonic treatment; often these sketch scores were more or less reductions of the full score, with countermelodies, accompaniment patterns, and instrumentation all present in the sketch. In the latter cases, the orchestrator was responsible for determining the final balance and making sure the music sounded as good as possible given the orchestra that was budgeted. In the former case the orchestrator could play a much more substantive compositional role— for instance, assigning the melody to the violins, clarinets, and horns, devising a countermelody for the violas and English horn, or working out an ostinato

Adolph Deutsch presents one example of film as a collaborative art in his account of the making of Three Strangers *(1946). He attended a screening of the film with the director, producer, and writer; each broadly discussed how the score should function. Deutsch, along with a team of music directors, recordists, and foley artists, then began the laborious task of assembling a sound track that adhered to the wishes of the filmmakers.*
—See Adolph Deutsch, "Adolph Deutsch on *Three Strangers*," in Cooke, *The Hollywood Film Music Reader.*

Figure 7-6. *King Kong* (1933) shows how effective the systematic use of spotting can be. The film breaks down into three large segments determined by locale: New York City, Skull Island, and a return to New York City. The sound is treated in a characteristically different fashion in each segment. In the original sequence in the city (a, b), the sound is very "efficient": dialogue drives almost every sequence; there is no music and little ambient sound. Effects are confined to only the most obvious sounds. Essentially, we hear exactly what we see. This appears as a rationally organized sonic space: Everything in its proper space, but a dearth of sound makes the city

feel lifeless (a). The lack of music means that we are as unsure of Denham's intentions as is Anne during their meeting (b).

The scene on the ship begins, like the initial New York City sequence, with no music. When the ship enters the fog around Skull Island (c), however, music enters, and music continues to be present for almost the entirety of the Island sequence (d–h). Moreover, the music often hovers in an uncertain state—drums are confused with "breakers," the images of the native drummers do not coincide with full orchestra we hear (d), and sound effects are sweetened with music. When the leader descends the stairs (e), for instance, each footstep is rendered by the orchestra. The overall impression of this treatment is that the island is a fundamentally musical place, and that the island is therefore an enchanted space.

The power of dialogue, by contrast, is subverted on Skull Island. It is still present, to be sure, but over the course of the sequence it tends to devolve into the barking of orders, which are nearly always ineffectual, or screams, which places human speech on the same plane as the sounds of the animals encountered (f). Music is present for the entire sequence on the island except the battle between Kong and the Tyrannosaurus rex (g); the exclusive use of effects here is in line with the representation of a regression to pure animality. Music and effects dominate the sound track on Skull Island, then, which leaves the impression that the island is a primitive, pre-rational (because pre-linguistic) aural space. Skull Island is not lifeless like the city, but it lacks any sense of rational control of its sound. In any case, it is significant that dialogue reasserts control over the sound track once Kong has been captured at the end of the sequence (h).

At this point, music is transformed into theater music, which leads to a dissolve back to the city and crowds entering to see an exhibition featuring Kong. With this theater music playing in the background, the impression of the city is quite different from the lifeless image of the opening sequence, but the musical treatment is also distinct from the island, an impression that is furthered during the show when Denham's theatrical speech calls up fanfares and marches on cue: the music here is functional, contained, bound to the image. Music appears diegetically shackled here just as Kong is shackled. This changes when Kong escapes (i): the music breaks free of its theatrical trappings and becomes completely nondiegetic the exact moment Kong bursts his bonds, and the sound track regresses to the effects, screams, and music that had been characteristic of Skull Island. As with the island, music is ubiquitous in the remainder of the sequence, disappearing only for the final battle between Kong and the airplanes (j), which recalls the fight with the Tyrannosaurus rex and suggests a basic inhumanity to the human actions in the scene. This effect is emphasized by the music, which returns, empathetically scoring Kong's pain just as he is mortally wounded. Dialogue takes over again only after Kong is dead, with the music, however, continuing in empathetic mourning.

The spotting of the film for music and sound makes for a clear tripartite, dialectical scheme: The city is initially presented as rational, but mundane and lifeless. The island, by contrast, is presented as teeming with life, but it is irrational and uncivilized. The return to the city seeks to reconcile the lifeless city with the irrational island, but an actual "synthesis" of a city rationally organized and alive comes only at the expense of the sacrifice of Kong.

accompaniment pattern in the cellos, basses, percussion, and piano parts. When time was short, trusted orchestrators often became what might be considered assistant composers, writing cues within the guidelines specified by the actual credited composer. (The practice of "uncredited" music was common—and in fact remains so to this day; especially in B-films, one might find that several staff composers wrote cues for a film, whose music was more often than not credited to the music department director.)

Besides the orchestrator, the composer also worked closely with the music editor. One of the most important initial duties of the music editor was to compile a cue sheet for each scene that would require music. The composer would consult this in working out the score. The cue sheet included a list of exact timings, a detailed description of the action, the type of camera framing and angles used, and every word in the dialogue track. Hugo Friedhofer described the process as Max Steiner used it in the 1930s and 1940s:

> Steiner, after running the picture once—at the most twice—would depend entirely on the cue sheets which were supplied to him by his music editor—who was really not a music editor, in that there were some union restrictions at that time that specified that nobody except a film editor could touch a foot of film at any time. So what he did was simply to time the stuff on the movieola [an editing machine] and make up the cue sheets.[2]

Once the music had been composed and scored, the music editor was responsible for preparing a click track (if needed) and a marked-up, working print of the film itself. The click track was essentially a metronome track that would be played back to the musicians through headphones. It was created by punching holes in the sound track of blank leader and was commonly used in cartoons and those scenes that needed precise timings (such as chases or comedy scenes with "hits" on action). Those scenes not requiring a click track (the majority) would be conducted "to picture": the film was actually shown without sound on a screen positioned behind the orchestra (see Figure 7-7). The music editor would have prepared this print to aid the conductor by marking the various segments with streamers (a diagonal line drawn on the film used to indicate beginnings and endings of sections) or punches (holes punched on the film at regular intervals used to indicate tempo).

The actual recording process obviously required the presence of musicians—conductors and players. The conductor was usually the composer or the head of the music department at the studio. The composer was generally preferred because he—in the studio era composers were almost always men—knew the music best, had the best sense as to how the music was to fit with the film, and could ensure that the (expensive) time in the studio was minimized. Even if not up to the dimensions of a full symphony orchestra, the number of musicians in a studio orchestra was considerable, and they were paid by the hour, so any delays in the studio could prove costly. The job of film studio musician was (and remains) one of the most demanding jobs in the industry. These players have

Figure 7-7. *Okay for Sound*. This is a music recording session for *Night and Day* (1946). The music recording mixer (in the foreground) adjusts the mixing panel according to notations in the score.

legendary reputations. During the studio era, Hollywood attracted many of the best orchestral musicians in the world. They were certainly the best sight readers: they were called upon daily to play anything a composer had written with little rehearsal and no mistakes.

Although most work on music was done in postproduction once rerecording became the norm, an exception was source music (either in drama or in musicals), which required *prescoring*. (Animation often used prescoring as well, although music and image production could also proceed in parallel, both composers and animators working off of detailed cue sheets.) As the term suggests, prescoring involved writing music prior to the shooting. Filming could then be done silent to playback. In the previous chapter, we mentioned that shooting to playback was common in the early sound era (because it gave the cameras more freedom), and it remained the norm for onscreen musical performance throughout the studio era because it continued to give filmmakers more flexibility in terms of editing. By the late 1930s, prescoring usually involved multichannel recording for vocal music. The singer would be aurally isolated from the other musicians, which allowed for much better balance control and permitted the editing of the vocal track. (See Figure 7-8 for an exceptional use of this technique.)

Although the comedic nature and brevity of animated cartoons might suggest a simpler, less refined music, by the 1940s composing for animation was actually quite an involved task. At MGM, Scott Bradley would fill out a "detail sheet" that included music, frame units, and various shorthand symbols concerning the cartoon's narrative, action, and frame speed.
—See Ingolf Dahl, "Notes on Cartoon Music," in Cooke, *The Hollywood Film Music Reader.*

Figure 7-8. *One Hundred Men and a Girl* (1937). This film pioneered massive multi-track recording of music. Eight separate channels were used—six for individual sections of the orchestra, one for the orchestra as a whole, and one for Deanna Durbin's voice. This process allowed the performances themselves to be assembled through editing and with precise control of balance. Durbin was also able to rerecord portions of her numbers, especially some high notes, which were then combined with other takes to produce the edited version of her performances in the film.

Prescoring involved many of the same personnel who would work on the actual scoring—at least the job descriptions were similar. Stylistically, music that was prescored was often in popular style, which required a different ensemble from the studio orchestra. It also often needed to be arranged for a vocalist (or choral ensemble) and choreography. In musicals, the credited composer was frequently well-known—someone like Irving Berlin, Jerome Kern, or George Gershwin—and not under long-term contract to the studio. In this case, the composer was commissioned only to write the songs. The songs would then be dispersed to arrangers, who would work out arrangements suitable to the actors' voices and to any choreography for the scene. These arrangements would in turn be given to orchestrators, who scored the music for the appropriate ensemble. Sometimes, but not always, one person served as both arranger and orchestrator of the song. Orchestrators for prescoring and scoring were no more interchangeable than were song composers and composers who wrote the background score. Some were accomplished at both, but orchestrating popular song was considered

Figure 7-9. *Casablanca* (1942). During Rick's flashback, Rick and Ilsa go dancing at a night club. The dance band music for the scene, an arrangement of the song "Perfidia," segues smoothly out of the preceding orchestral score and will move without a break back into the orchestral at the end of the brief scene. Whereas Max Steiner composed the orchestral score, another Warner Brothers staff member, Frank Perkins, was responsible for arranging the song, which had also been used earlier that same year in *Now, Voyager* (1942), another film Steiner had scored. Perkins wrote many of the diegetic music arrangements for Steiner's films in the 1940s, including a number of the other band arrangements for *Casablanca*.

According to Scott Bradley, the composer for MGM's Tom and Jerry series, scoring cartoons allowed the composer much more liberty with musical style and instrumentation than did live action films. Harmonic language was less limited by melodramatic conventions, and instruments with extreme ranges or palpable timbres. Furthermore, since characters rarely spoke, there was ample room for music to develop and emphasize narrative. —See Scott Bradley, "Personality on the Soundtrack," in Cooke, *The Hollywood Film Music Reader.*

its own specialty and most of these specialists had backgrounds in dance band arrangement (Figure 7-9).

SOUND DEPARTMENT

Sound was usually divided into two departments, one devoted to production sound, the other to postproduction. In the studio era, the production sound department was organized to capture dialogue, and its principal workers—boom operators, mixers, and recordists—reflected that fact: everything they did was predicated on ensuring a technically clean dialogue recording. In postproduction, dialogue continued to be treated separately from other sound, and its editing was closely allied with the picture editing.

Sound effects, by contrast, came under the full jurisdiction of the sound department. Although effects might also be taken from production sound, they were far more likely to come out of libraries. Because most sound effects were physically cut in, simultaneous sounds required a separate sound strip for each sound. It was common to have a half dozen sound strips in use at any one time—even more than a dozen was not all that unusual. Although in principle the number of simultaneous (or near simultaneous) sounds was unlimited, in practice the difficulty of working with large numbers of sound strips was another limiting factor on density.

In general, the sound department was less elaborately organized than the music department in the 1930s; before the rise of sound design in the 1970s, it was understood more as a technical department than an artistic one. This valuation can be seen in the types of screen credit given and the academy awards, both of which centered on departments (or department heads) rather than individuals.

The Sound Track in the Studio Era and Elements of Style

THE CLASSICAL SYSTEM

As we noted in connection with the transition from early film performances to the sound film, the principle of clarity almost immediately came to dominate. Dialogue—human speech—was always given priority, and thus when it came to making decisions about what should be rendered on the sound track, comprehension almost always trumped realism. In the classical system, when this principle was violated, the inversion generally served a clear narrative function. For instance, a loud background such as a raging fire might overpower a character shouting, making the words somewhat inaudible. This heightened the realism of the sequence, to be sure, but more important, the apparent elevation of the sound of the fire served the narrative function of emphasizing its power: the fire threatened to consume the voice and by analogy the character. In this sense, the sound of the fire would be treated almost as a voice, one that transformed the fire, if only for a moment, into something like a character. (See Figure 7-10 for an example and commentary.) The point to be taken from this is that the exception was validated by an appeal back to the story.

Another factor that discouraged using silence as the primary background was that it could not mask the hiss of the sound-reproducing apparatus, a hiss that with optical sound became progressively more audible with wear. Critical complaints about the early talkies, especially dramas, spoke not just to the stilted dialogue that was a product of theatrical projection and the technological shortcomings of early microphones but also to the audibility of the silence between the lines, as opposed to the live situation of the theater; in other words, the hiss revealed talking film as nothing other than recorded drama. So long as the background remained conceived in terms of silence, filmmakers could only conceal the hiss by filling the sound track with diegetically motivated sound, often to cacophonous and narratively disorienting results.

Figure 7-10. *You Can't Take It with You* (1938). The Kirbys, a well-to-do family, make an unexpected visit to the Vanderhofs, the eccentric family of their son's fiancée, Alice. When the visit is interrupted by a police raid, the entire group is hauled off to jail, leading to a courtroom scene that opposes the Kirbys and their lawyers to the Vanderhofs and the larger community that has packed the court in their support. During the proceedings, the crowd grows unruly, all but drowning out the attempts by Mr. Kirby, his lawyers, and even the somewhat bemused judge to impose order. In the this shot, Tony Kirby, the son (played by James Stewart), attempts to reason with Alice (Jean Arthur), but his words are obscured by the crowd noise. In the scene, the crowd itself briefly becomes the dominant character, reflecting the narrative theme that the community of friendship has far more power than wealth in producing happiness.

The invention of the concept of audio background—a ground other than mere silence—was therefore crucial to constituting sound film; and this concept required in turn the availability of rerecording to make its realization feasible. However much clarity of dialogue may have seemed to drive the construction of the sound track, it was the underlying continuity of audible background sound across cuts that encouraged spectators to bind a series of individual disparate shots into longer spans—scenes and sequences. The audio background thus became the constructive equivalent to the early practice of the visual master shot, a medium to long shot of a sequence, filmed uninterrupted from beginning to end, which was used to ensure synchronization and continuity of action and sound across the sequence. Sound would be recorded along with the master shot, and then closer shots, whether taken simultaneously with or separately from the master shot, could be cut in on the basis of that continuity. In the finished film, the visual master shot was generally used at the beginning of the sequence and other points of spatial and narrative redefinition in the sequence, and it established the geography of the place and oriented the figures in relation to a visual background that maintained visual continuity across cuts. Similarly, the audio background served to unify the sequence by means of what might be termed *sonic ambience*, that is, the characteristic sound of the place. (In moving to an audio background, film was moving from a monophonic conceptualization of the sound track to one characterized more akin to melody and accompaniment, with dialogue usually understood to occupy to the place of "melody.") This sonic ambience was generally added in postproduction, where filmmakers could select realistic ambient sound (crowd noises, crickets, water, and so forth) or take the more stylized route of music, a choice that became increasingly common after 1933.

BACKGROUND(ED) MUSIC AND THE SOUND TRACK

Given the limited fidelity of the early optical tracks and the constant concern about the intelligibility of dialogue, music generally turned out to be a more effective medium for the background than did ambient sound itself. The primary

a | b | c   **Figure 7-11.** *The Big Sleep* (1946). In the casino scene, the choice of ambient sound rather than music pertains to the exterior setting of the casino itself, which is marked sonically by the sound of music (heard in counterpoint to the crickets). Understood in terms of sound, the sequence as a whole is structured as a sort of palindrome, moving from (a) sounds of nature in the exterior to (b) diegetic music and performance on the interior and then (c) into the private meeting with casino owner Eddie Mars (John Ridgely), which serves as the central moment of the sequence. The process then reverses, as Marlow (Humphrey Bogart) returns to the casino and watches Mrs. Routledge (Lauren Bacall) win at roulette before leaving, at which point the sound track returns to the footsteps and ambient sound of crickets. The sound in the sequence thus tracks an underlying thematic thread of the narrative: crickets are opposed to music, as exterior is opposed to interior, the innocence but loneliness of nature to the decadence but community of culture.

reason was that, with the exception of a few characteristic "white noise" sounds, such as crowds, waterfalls, engine sounds, and so forth, it was difficult to construct a consistent and continuous background of ambient sound that did not distract from the intelligibility of the dialogue. Although somewhat more common by the 1940s, ambient sound only began to be used as a background regularly in the 1950s, thanks in part to the advent of stereo, which allowed a spatial separation of ambient sound from dialogue, in part to the higher fidelity of magnetic tape recording, which likewise increased the intelligibility of dialogue. Earlier, ambient sound tended to be employed in highly conventionalized contexts; it also tended to be restricted to establishing shots, as in Figure 7-11, because it would not then interfere with dialogue. Music, by contrast, had the advantage of being composed, and a skilled composer could work it in and around dialogue to a degree that ambient sound could not match. This was an important consideration in the relatively low-fidelity environment of early optical sound. Another consideration was that the underscoring, unlike ambient sound, was understood to be fully nondiegetic; that is, it was a representation of ambience rather than making any pretenses toward being a depiction of ambient sound itself. Consequently, the dynamic level of music could be more freely manipulated in the mix without threatening to dissolve the rendering of reality in which the diegetic sound track otherwise engages. These later two situations are discussed in the commentary for Figure 7-12.

Figure 7-12. *The Adventures of Robin Hood* (1938). Two early scenes provide a good   a | b
example of the interplay between dialogue and music. (a) The dubbing volume of Erich Korngold's rousing score is routinely raised and lowered in the first tax collection scene and the meeting of Robin Hood (Errol Flynn) with Sir Guy (Basil Rathbone). (b) The varied orchestration throughout the following court scene allows the score to be played at a consistent level throughout the dialogue between Prince John (Claude Rains) and Maid Marian (Olivia De Havilland).

In 1950, Franz Waxman discussed musical topic and leitmotif in a radio interview with film music critic Lawrence Morton. Choosing musical topics was often "quite obvious," as the setting and genre of the film would suggest topics of their own. Such was the case of the epic war film Operation: Burma! (1945). However, psychological thrillers like Possessed (1947) were more difficult to score as the music was often reflecting a character's mood and state of mind. Waxman argued that the leitmotif was a necessity as it could stand out as a distinct idea yet be repeated in endless recognizable variations throughout a film. Leitmotifs could be related timbrally as well as melodically and rhythmically.
—See Lawrence Morton, "A Radio Interview with Franz Waxman," in Cooke, The Hollywood Film Music Reader.

SCORING PRACTICES

Once symphonic underscoring came to be accepted as an integral part of sound track style, the trend over the decade of the 1930s was toward closer and closer integration of music and image. As we noted in Chapter 5, two basic methods were inherited from the silent era: playing the overall mood of a scene and playing to the details. It is the latter that came to dominate by the late 1930s and continued to do so until at least 1945—and in some genres, long after that.

Playing the overall mood was frequently employed, too, especially in scenes of action, because it held the important advantage of continuity, of presenting well-rounded musical themes and ideas, rather than constantly breaking off into a series of seemingly musically incoherent fragments, fermatas, and stingers, however well motivated those might be dramatically in other kinds of scenes. Musical continuity could also bind a series of otherwise disparate shots together, thereby reinforcing the principle of the sequence. This was the basis for its use covering establishing and especially montage sequences, but it could also be used to emphasize the central idea of a sequence. A love scene, for instance, was often scored through the simple device of playing a love theme under the dialogue. Doing so had the effect of cueing the basic mood of the scene rather than the individual words, which in and of themselves could be trite, mundane, or even ridiculous and, as mentioned in Chapter 5, often caused audiences discomfort. Music in such cases could productively divert attention away from those words to the particular sentiment of the scene (Figure 7-13).

In practice, most composers drew on both methods, and—with the exception of long dialogue scenes—the cues themselves were, often as not, hybrids: based in thematic material, the music would nevertheless follow the dramatic course of a scene and mark especially important turning points with changes in its own direction.

Musical Topics in the Underscore: The Opening of Rebecca

Advances in rerecording technology and sound track aesthetics did not diminish the continued vitality and significance of musical topics or moods throughout the classic studio era. As a characteristic example from a prestige film, let's look at the opening 10 minutes of *Rebecca* (1940).

Like most studio logo cues, the music for the Selznick Studio fits the musical topic of the dramatic and majestic (dramatic cues in the silent era were sometimes labeled alternatively with the traditional Italian musical term *maestoso*). The first few seconds of Franz Waxman's main-title cue just as plainly fit the *mysterioso* (alternatively the *agitato mysterioso* or "grotesque"). With the appearance of the main title, however, a lyrical melody rises in a sumptuous orchestral setting. By convention, we know this is the theme of the woman named—Rebecca—and we also leave open the chance that it is a love theme, although, as in *Mildred Pierce* (1945), the setting is noticeably too strong, too loud and full, so at the very least we would consider this a "heavy" love theme (in the three-level intensity scale of light-medium-heavy). Thus, this film is unlikely to be a straightforward

Figure 7-13. *Yankee Doodle Dandy* (1942). After singing "Mary," a song George (James Cagney) has written for his fiancée (Joan Leslie), the couple engages in a brief, intimate conversation, which is underscored by the song in a light orchestral arrangement. This practice is typical of musicals, where the transfer of the song from diegetic performance to nondiegetic orchestra serves to underscore the ideal of romance. (It resembles an audio dissolve.) But love scenes in dramatic films are often treated analogously, with the love theme being played without musical interruption. (In this case, the song has been shortened but the continuity is unaffected.)

The signifying properties of a musical topic very often affirm our understanding of a scene. Most obviously, national anthems are used in this way. In Casablanca, Rick's flashback in the after-hours scene is inaugurated by the opening phrase of "La Marseillaise," situating it in Paris. The Germans are likewise characterized through "Deutschland über Alles" in distorted form, which marks them as villains.

romance; if romance is involved, it will be in the context of drama and perhaps even to a tragic result. (Eventually, we learn that Rebecca is in fact the acousmêtric villain of the story.)

At about 1:25, the theme suddenly breaks down and we return briefly to the *mysterioso*, but the tempo slows and another string melody enters over a pulsating accompaniment of repeated chords. We will learn in the prologue that this melody is the theme for Manderley (Maxim De Winter's fabled mansion in Cornwall) and that will secure its associations and function. For the present, the topic is hard to pin down—it could fit Seredy's category of "resignation" or Rapee's "sadness" (recall these from Chapter 4). Many cues of this type were simply called "andante," after the musical term for a moderately slow, but not too slow, "heartbeat" tempo. We might call this one a "heavy andante" ("dramatic andante" is another common term), given its minor key and melancholy affect. Note, by the way, that Waxman has maintained the two-theme title cue structure; here, however, the dramatic theme belongs to Rebecca and the lyrical theme to an object that signifies the past for Maxim (Laurence Olivier). In both cases, the formal position helps to confirm our judgment about their affective qualities.

As the prologue begins with Joan Fontaine's voice-over (at 1:44), the melody slows down even further and is heard in a plaintive oboe solo, but layered against it is an obvious return to the suspenseful *mysterioso* mood: the result is wholly appropriate to the dream that Fontaine's character is recounting and would probably fit Seredy and Rapee's category of "reverie." With the entrance of an emotionally more intense version of the Manderley theme on a solo cello (at 2:35) comes a brief turn to a "dramatic andante" again, but the music soon relapses into reverie.

With the dissolve to the first scene and after the loud intrusion of wave sounds, a new *agitato mysterioso* starts up, now suspenseful, sinister, "heavy," and it continues to the moment that Fontaine's "I" shouts, thereby preventing Maxim from following through on his plan for suicide. Their brief conversation (Figure 7-14) is treated musically as dialogue underscoring, and consequently the topical associations are offered only in brief passages that shift as the conversation evolves: first tremolo strings revive the lighter side of the *mysterioso*, then a plainly lyrical melody is hinted at (the love theme for the two of them? Yes, as it turns out). A suddenly soaring version of the Manderley theme is heard after "I" leaves and Maxim turns to look toward the cliffside he had almost thrown himself over.

Figure 7-14. *Rebecca* (1940). Opening scene. Encounter between "I" and Maxim.

With the dissolve to an establishing shot of Monte Carlo, the music at first retains its contemplative mood from the previous cue. With the second establishing shot, an elegant hotel seen from its entrance, we hear the introduction to a classical waltz (actually composed by Waxman, as it happens). In the early twenty-first century, the details of a topical reference like this have been mostly lost: a "Strauss" waltz (like *The Blue Danube* or *Tales from the Vienna Woods*) does connote elegance and upper-class or aristocratic society and thus fits a particular social stereotype, but for an audience in 1940 it would also have specified locale, because the orchestration Waxman uses is that of a hotel orchestra, which would have played similar music at various points through the day in a high class hotel. (In fact, Waxman had previously used this waltz for another hotel lobby scene, in *Lady of the Tropics* [1938].)

The music now adopts a formal role as well: the introduction finishes with the second establishing shot, then the waltz proper begins with the first interior shot (a wealthy older woman, Mrs. Van Hopper, and her paid companion, "I"). The waltz ends and a new one begins with the dissolve to the next scene, the next morning's breakfast. Waltzes play throughout the breakfast scene and cadence, a bit abruptly, with the dissolve (the Terrace, which follows, is discussed later in this chapter as a dialogue scene). Through the entire hotel sequence, the order of the waltzes is: Waxman, Hotel Lobby (Waltz) from *Lady of the Tropics*; Joseph Lanner, *Die Pesther*; Johann Strauss, Jr., *Artist's Life* and *Roses from the South*. The waltzes do not start up again with the return to the hotel after the Terrace scene. Contained in the two initial hotel scenes, then, they signify both elegance and wealth as characteristic of the venue. In the process, they suit Maxim's character quite comfortably but play anempathetically against "I," whose social discomfort is only too obvious (especially in the breakfast scene, where, among other things, she knocks over a vase of flowers).

The hotel scenes—the lobby and breakfast—together are an especially clear example of the way that sound can serve narrative clarity through redundancy. Visual and aural motifs (recurring figures, including musical themes) are obvious devices for this function, but music also routinely serves in this capacity by reinforcing narrative associations and references. The waltzes are historically accurate (even Waxman's!) and appropriate for a fancy European resort hotel in the early twentieth century, but they are not necessary to identify the hotel or its elegance. By confirming these things, the music suggests that the environment is important, as it turns out to be, because the very elegance of the place is upsetting to Joan Fontaine's "I," whose social uncertainties are central to the plot.

CRITIQUES OF HOLLYWOOD UNDERSCORING PRACTICES

As symphonic underscoring became an established practice and underscoring dialogue became common, they became the focus of critical attention. Mainly outside Hollywood, debates on the proper relation of sound and image raged almost from the moment sound feature films were first exhibited. Some critics thought synchronized dialogue was overly redundant and urged using the sound

A Note on Sound Topics. *Many musical topics have correlates in sound. The pastoral is as easily evoked by bleating sheep or a cowbell as by pastoral music. The squeal of a tire announces a chase. A low rumble, such as the Empire's ships in* Star Wars IV: A New Hope *(1977), is ominous; whereas a crisp, bright sound, such as the skull crushed by the robot at the opening of* Terminator 2: Judgment Day *(1991), suggests immediate danger. A loud, resonant clank like the one framing the title sequence of the* Terminator *films or the fall of Sauron's helmet in the prologue of* Fellowship of the Ring *(2001) portends mythic doom.*

Crickets are among the best established sound topics of all. In Close Encounters of the Third Kind *(1977), they suggest a nocturnal setting but also heighten the suspense of the aliens. Preceding each encounter, the ambient sound crescendos, only to disappear immediately for the encounter itself. As Frank Warner, Supervising Sound Effects Editor, explains:*

At the end of each [encounter] I imagined that one little cricket would look up over a rock and another one would look up, I keyed them up the scale and then maybe a dog bark, then the wind would come back. It all happened until finally at the end of the scene, everything came back in and settled down. You only had to do it once, twice maybe. Then throughout the picture, when things would go quiet, in your mind you'd go, "Uh oh, something's going to happen."⁴

track more imaginatively. The Russian director Sergei Eisenstein, for example, thought sound could be most effective when considered in counterpoint to, rather than in synchronization with, the image. He proposed that music be treated similarly. In this way Eisenstein thought sound (and music) could take on the character of montage.⁵ Since the silent era, "synchronization" had always been taken as the goal of film music. Music was understood as a reflection of, or reaction to, the drama. Counterpoint suggested other relations: Music might, for instance, play against the image or remain indifferent to it. In any case, music might be more proactive. Eisenstein found a sympathetic ear in many concert composers because when working with Sergei Prokofiev he had brought the composer in early in the production process and even reversed the usual procedure by cutting some scenes to music.

In the United States, art music composers generally did not participate in film music composition. One early exception was Aaron Copland whose musical style as represented in *Billy the Kid* (1938) and *Appalachian Spring* (1944) came to epitomize the "American sound." Copland had at least two lasting effects on film music practice. First, he disagreed with the prevalent use of nineteenth-century musical style and techniques and introduced his own American and modernist styles, which would influence what is often called the "second generation" of film composers in the 1950s and 1960s. Second, he advocated that composers, musicians, and critics take film music more seriously as an American art form. His book, *Our New Music*, for example, includes an entire chapter devoted to film music in which Copland outlines the strengths and weaknesses of composition for film and details the intricate process of scoring. (For his discussion, see Aaron Copland, *Our New Music* and "Aaron Copland in the Film Studio," in Cooke, *The Hollywood Film Music Reader.* In that same volume, also see Frederick W. Sternfeld's essay on Hugo Friedhofer's music for *Best Years of Our Lives* [1946], a film score that is often cited as influenced by Copland's musical style.)

Another established, if less well-known, composer of avant-garde music, George Antheil, vividly recounts his experiences working in Hollywood, where he struggled. Although he did write symphonic underscore for several Paramount feature films and contributed numerous library cues used in "B" films, he met resistance from the music department, where skepticism about modern composers disrupting "the whole technique of scoring pictures" prevailed. Antheil believed that the movie industry was full of artistry, but that music departments produced bad results due to low budgets and short timelines. Because of this, Antheil worried about American musical taste, because, as he said, "musical tastes become molded by these scores, heard without knowing it." Antheil's writings clearly reflect the tension between commercial and art music, through his critiques of movie scores and in the studio's resistance to his notions of innovation. (See George Antheil, "I Am Not a Businessman," in Cooke, *The Hollywood Film Music Reader.*)

One area where contemporary concert music styles were successful was in the documentary. Around from the earliest days of the film medium, the *documentary* as a term was not coined until the 1920s. These films were particularly prevalent in the United States and Great Britain during the Second World War as the studios essentially worked for the government in producing a large quantity of film-based propaganda. Gail Kubik, who composed for William Wyler's documentaries *The Memphis Belle* (1943) and *Thunderbolt* (1947), urged composers to get involved in the genre, as he saw it as the only place where a composer could truly give voice to his or her own musical style. While producers and directors supposedly restricted composers in other film categories, in the American wartime film the composer was—as Kubik put it—a "symbol of democracy at work" through the freedom of self-expression. (See Gail Kubik, "Music in Documentary Films," in Cooke, *The Hollywood Film Music Reader*.)

Two of the most famous European concert composers of the period between the two World Wars, Igor Stravinsky and Arnold Schoenberg, were among the many cultural and political émigrés in the 1930s. Both settled in Los Angeles, where, although neither wrote any music for a released film, they nevertheless had a profound impact on the area's musical community, inside and outside the studios. Schoenberg reportedly believed that film music was "incredibly bad, meaningless, numbing all expression," although he was willing enough to give lessons to almost any film composer who asked and to write a dozen pages of sketches on speculation for *The Good Earth* (1937). Stravinsky, who did the same for the film *Commandos Strike at Dawn* (1942), let his similar views be known through an article by Ingolf Dahl. Stravinsky believed that using music as a soundtrack to film degraded the music to the equivalent of aural wallpaper, heard but not recognized. (See "Igor Stravinsky on Film Music," in Cooke, *The Hollywood Film Music Reader*.) Not surprisingly, a professional Hollywood film composer stood up to complain about Stravinsky's views. David Raksin, whose credits already included *Laura* (1944) and *Forever Amber* (1947), defended film music as being capable of great expression: rather than merely serving the image, music has the power to transform it. Raksin asserted that "the gulf between [Stravinsky's] own music and that of the films is neither so wide nor so impassable as he would like to imagine." In response to Stravinsky's censure of film music's commercial interests, Raksin appealed to music composers throughout history who had worked on commission. He believed that there is nothing wrong with making a living through composition, and "if film music makes this possible, so much the better." Instead of judging it against the rubric of other "serious" compositions, film music is a musical domain of its own and should be measured for its "essential worth." (See David Raksin, "Hollywood Strikes Back," in Cooke, *The Hollywood Film Music Reader*.)

Two other émigrés who landed in southern California were Hanns Eisler, a former student of Schoenberg, and the philosopher and cultural critic Theodor W. Adorno, who studied with Alban Berg, another student of Schoenberg's. The two collaborated on *Composing for the Films* (1947), a book that resulted from a 3-year Rockefeller research grant awarded to Eisler for his study of film music. Eisler and Adorno went further than Antheil or even Stravinsky: they criticized a set of "bad habits" they claimed were ingrained in film music practice: simplified and ineffective use of leitmotifs and the constant emphasis on simple melodies without regard for cinematic context. They also attacked composers' reliance on stereotypical musical figures which reduced music to "a cheap mood-producing gadget." They noted that, due to technological constraints, dynamic contrast in film music was reduced, but that to compensate, composers exaggerated other aspects. To overcome this last problem, they called for a greater economy of expression. (See Theodor Adorno and Hanns Eisler, *Composing for the Films*, in Cooke, *The Hollywood Film Music Reader*.)

Adding to the litany of harsh criticism were British composer Antony Hopkins and critic Hans Keller. Lawrence Morton, author of some of the most trenchant and insightful film music criticism in the 1940s, offered evidence for the inherent worth of Hollywood film music. Hopkins had voiced concern about the "enormous sums" paid to Hollywood composers, but Morton countered that the average musician was part of the lower middle class. Morton sarcastically deconstructed Keller's insult to Hollywood's "musico-sociological-economical set-up," and insisted on critical distinctions between these aspects. Keller disparaged the use of orchestrators, but Morton said that they serve the practical purpose of speeding up the compositional process. Morton concluded that the overriding issue with Hopkins's and Keller's criticisms was their tendency to overlook music's dramatic function, as they analyzed the music for itself (as if concert music) and failed to consider its crucial role in the film drama. (See Lawrence Morton, "Composing, Orchestrating, and Criticizing," in Cooke, *The Hollywood Film Music Reader*.)

The attention given to symphonic underscore by these several authors is evidence of the important place that this music had gained in the feature film, but it should also remind us of two other things: (1) the ubiquity of film as entertainment and (2) the increasing significance of the feature film as a cultural product. The first of these would be undercut in a dramatic way by television starting in the 1950s. The second, however, would continue as a general trend throughout the second half of the century.

The Sound Track in the Studio Era and Elements of Film Form

Music's role in the integrated sound track, the *mise-en-bande* of the later 1930s, was to help maintain the constant overall volume that was the sound film's primary aesthetic criterion (that is, as we noted earlier, clarity rather than fidelity or acoustic realism). Because sound effects were kept to the minimum necessary, the need for sound material to "fill in" the gaps increasingly favored large amounts of symphonic underscore. At least, this was the case with prestige films, the high-budget productions that reaped the largest profits for the studios, along with the most widespread recognition, since these were the films that were premiered in the flagship urban theaters. Prestige films would often not make it to small town or rural theaters until weeks or even months later. The reverse was often true of low budget ("B") films and sometimes also of "programmers," films with mid-level budgets that might be in a matinee or on the lower end of a double bill in an urban theater but on the higher end for a second-run or small town theater.

In addition to the uniformity of approach that came about because of aesthetic priorities, the industrial style of production that all major American studios engaged in throughout the classical era in order to satisfy the demands of their theaters inevitably led to relatively sharp distinctions of genre, on the one hand, and to a focus on stars, on the other hand. The latter is perhaps the more obvious: a person who had seen and enjoyed a film starring Clark Gable was more likely to return to the theater to see a second film of his. The sound track is not implicated in this process, but in the case of genre it is. The basic group of genres in the narrative film are those of the theater, novel, and short story: romantic comedy, slapstick or farce, heroic drama, social drama, exotic adventure, and so on. In the cinema, these types tended to coalesce into clearly defined genres when one film was particularly successful and inspired both imitators and sequels. The musical, for example, was essentially defined by *The Broadway Melody* and the many films that quickly followed it in 1929 and 1930. The Western drama of action was well-established in popular literature and the early cinema long before sound and remained distinct throughout the studio era, but a separate type, the singing cowboy film, developed after 1935 following on the success of films starring Gene Autry, such as *Comin' Round the Mountain* (1936), *Man from Music Mountain* (1938), and *Mexicali Rose* (1939)—see Figure 7-15. Both gangster films and horror films had similarly evolved from early sound film hits and were even associated with specific studios: the horror film with Universal (*Frankenstein* [1931], *Dracula* [1931], *The Mummy* [1932], *The Bride of Frankenstein* [1935], and others), the gangster film with Warner Bros. (*Little Caesar* [1930], *Public Enemy* [1931], and others throughout the 1930s and early 1940s, including *High Sierra* [1941], merging about that time with detective's films such as *The Maltese Falcon* [1941]). At least one genre that became prominent in the 1940s, the women's film (also called women's melodrama or just melodrama) arose, not from a single hit film, but from the needs and interests of a specific audience (by the late 1930s, women constituted the largest segment of the audience for Hollywood feature films). The genre entered prestige films when Bette Davis took leading roles in *The Sisters* (1938), *Dark Victory* (1939), *All This and Heaven Too* (1940), *The Letter* (1940), *In This Our Life* (1942), *Now, Voyager* (1942), and *Old Acquaintance* (1943), among others.

Figure 7-15. *Down Mexico Way* (1941). Gene Autry sings for a picnic gathering.

A few generalizations can be made about music with respect to film genres, but few hold up beyond the films—such as those just named—that are taken as the best representatives of a particular genre. For example, the gangster and detective films of Warner Bros. are known for having little to no nondiegetic music, but after Max Steiner joined the studio in 1936 that can no longer be said to be true. Romantic comedies and films based on stage plays tended to have relatively little underscore because these films were often dialogue heavy. This is true of films such as *His Girl Friday* (1939) and *Philadelphia Story* (1942) but not of *The Young in Heart* (1938) and *Made for Each Other* (1939), which were produced by Selznick International Pictures, whose chief executive, David O. Selznick, strongly favored large amounts of symphonic underscore. Even the women's films, which relied heavily on the power of symphonic underscore for emotion and the underlining of character psychology, were by no means so heavily scored for the lower ranking productions as they were for the Bette Davis films, largely a reflection of the relative cost of production.

A generalization about the treatment of music in the sound track during the 1930s and 1940s that does hold up is the set of preferences for music placement that had begun to form in the transition period. These preferences crystalized under the pressure of large-scale feature film production in the mid to late 1930s and became very familiar, even clichéd elements of films for 1940s-era viewers. As we did in Chapter 5, we will discuss representative examples for each of the seven categories: establishing sequence, end credit music, performance scene, montage or fantasy scene, dialogue scene, action scene, and love scene.

ESTABLISHING SEQUENCE

With a few exceptions in the earliest years, the opening of a feature film was almost never silent in the classical studio era. On rare occasions, sound effects might dominate the establishing sequence for an action film (in particular, one involving car races or airplanes), but by far the more common treatment was with nondiegetic music. Symphonic cues were favored in prestige productions and some programmers (films that could fill either the A or B position on a double bill, depending the theater), whereas other films, including musicals, were as likely to have a band or orchestral arrangement of a song. Singers or choral groups were rarely used—that is a device much more characteristic of the 1950s and 1960s.

Three Films from 1933 Starring Katharine Hepburn

Christopher Strong, Katharine Hepburn's second film, was directed by Dorothy Arzner. The producer was David O. Selznick; he had moved from MGM to RKO, where he stayed for about a year with the expectation that he would raise the quality of the fledgling studio's offerings. (Recall that RKO was the youngest of the major Hollywood studios and was founded based on its technological prowess, not on any depth of experience in programming.) A "Music Director" credit went to Max Steiner. The establishing sequence, which lasts 1 minute and 20 seconds, reveals a transition-period awkwardness in its treatment of diegetic and nondiegetic music. The opening is a minor-key tango that plays through all the credits and then goes out with the first shot, an insert of Big Ben ringing. Dance band music then starts up, as if offscreen. The low volume and the musical style clearly suggest that the band is indoors as the image keeps us outside a house while cars arrive for a party. With the cut inside, however, we find that the diegetic status of the music is unclear (no band in sight, nor is there a change in volume level), but then the music suddenly cuts out with the first speech, as nondiegetic music would most likely do (though more subtly).

Morning Glory was directed by Lowell Sherman, with "Music by Max Steiner." Hepburn won her first Academy Award for her role. After the RKO logo, with its transmission tower and signal broadcast sound, a fanfare announces the title and continues in the recognizable form of the dramatic introduction to a waltz. (We say "recognizable" because such introductions were ubiquitous in the universally known repertoire of the Viennese waltzes by Johann Strauss, Jr., and others). Somewhat awkwardly, the waltz theme itself appears with the second card, for the director. The waltz music takes up the rest of the titles in an ABAB design. There is no dramatic flourish at the end: instead, the waltz theme overlaps to the first shot (the exterior of a theater) and connects to a short quotation of the familiar tune "Give My Regards to Broadway" already discussed in Chapters 5 and 6. The remainder of the sequence is quite long, effectively an explanatory prologue that only concludes at 3:10. The music continues from the preceding with a new introduction on solo violin, heard as Eva Lovelace (Hepburn) examines actors' portraits in the theater lobby. This music soon turns into the waltz theme again, played more slowly and contemplatively. The theme concludes against brief speech as she is directed to an elevator. A whimsical coda carries on through the elevator ride, a "sound gag" where the music slowly but continuously rises in pitch. Once she is in the office of an agent/impresario, the music quickly disappears under speech of two actors.

The opening of *Little Women* is more complex still. The film was directed by George Cukor, again with "Music by Max Steiner." The first music is the theme for Jo (Hepburn), and it is heard frequently throughout the film. Initially the sound is that of an old square piano, but at 1:15 the orchestral timbre helps segue into a Civil War montage showing winter in a small town and soldiers marching among the citizens. In this case, the music keeps shifting through the montage, starting with "Tramp, tramp" and then several others, including "Silent Night." At 3:24, during a brief scene of an old man being given help by a woman, Jo's theme reappears at her mention of the woman's daughters. Music is out by 3:45.

These three films are obviously closely related, having been produced in a single year at one studio with the same music director. Nevertheless, they represent characteristic attempts to expand the main title music into the film's opening scene, whether that is the first scene itself or a prologue. The goal, clearly, is

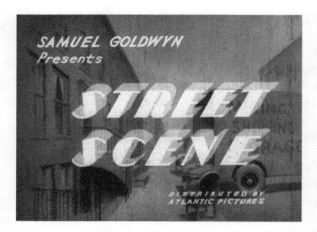

Figure 7-16. *Street Scene* (1931). Main title, against which we hear Alfred Newman's theme.

to integrate the opening "frame" more closely with the film proper, to lead the viewer gradually into the narrative and provide a certain amount of style-topical and other referential information along the way.

Street Scene *and a Theme as Series or Genre Marker*

Alfred Newman was a versatile musician: a concert piano prodigy in New York, he also worked on Broadway before coming to Hollywood among the early wave of East Coast professionals who were imported to bolster music in sound films. Like others, notably Max Steiner and Herbert Stothart, Newman originally was hired as a music director, based on his experience in the musical theater—at this point musicals were still the most important sound genre. But also like others, he soon found himself adding original nondiegetic music for special uses such as main title sequences or dramatic scenes. One of his earliest original cues was the main title music for *Street Scene* (1931). This lyrical theme was a *Rhapsody in Blue* sound-alike and quickly became a hit: it was published in multiple versions for various instrumental ensembles and converted into a song that was recorded frequently throughout the 1930s. Like *Rhapsody in Blue* (which was premiered in 1924), the *Street Scene* theme evoked a contemporary urban atmosphere, syncopated but sophisticated—see Figure 7-16. As such, once Newman became the music department head of Twentieth Century Fox in 1940, the theme was used repeatedly to open what would now be considered early *films noir*, or crime films centered on nighttime urban life. This series of films include, among others, *I Wake Up Screaming* (1941), *The Dark Corner* (1946), *Cry of the City* (1948), and *My Friend Irma* (1949; television 1952).

The last of these is particularly telling, as the *Street Scene* theme became the theme song for an early television series. If classic feature films typically opened with the same musical passage calling attention to the studio logo, the telescoped format of commercial television put the same or even more attention on the series title. This practice of a recurring theme goes back to 1930s serials—episodic low-budget films, most often 20 to 30 minutes each—but became one of the most familiar characteristics of long-running dramatic television series from the 1950s on.

Meet Me in St. Louis, *Titles and Opening Scene*

Meet Me in St. Louis (1944) is usually taken to be the first characteristic product of what became known as the "Freed Unit" at MGM studios (after Arthur Freed, the producer who ran the unit). This group was well funded by the studio and was able to create a series of musicals with very high production values; their titles include, among others, *Easter Parade* (1948), *An American in Paris* (1951), *Singin' in the Rain* (1952), *Brigadoon* (1954), and *Gigi* (1958). The Freed Unit also was influential because of its focus on the "integrated musical," that is, a musical that drew its performances into the context of a narrative film, or that subordinated the musical's tendency to promote spectacle to the primary emphasis on narrative continuity and clarity of the traditional feature film.

In keeping with this emphasis, *Meet Me in St. Louis* employs what had already become by the late 1930s a conventional musical design for a feature film's opening credits, consisting generally of three or four functionally defined sections (see corresponding images in Figure 7-17): (1) a dramatic gesture begins, quickly announcing a musical theme whose beginning coincides with the main title (that is, the one that gives the film's name); (2) a very brief transition to a

Figure 7-17. *Meet Me in St. Louis* (1944). Titles and establishing sequence.

a	b
c	d

second, more lyrical, and usually quieter theme—this is normally not timed to match any particular title; (3) a slightly longer transition to a dramatic ending flourish or cadence—this normally plays against the credit titles with producer, director, and composer names but only because they are always placed at the end of the main-title sequence; and (4) a transition that "winds down" either to a prologue (with a text-heavy intertitle, voice-over narration, or both) or to an establishing shot for the film's first scene. Depending on how soon the action of the film follows on the director's credit, the functions of parts 3 and 4 may be combined because music is generally timed to go out at the moment of the first significant sound effect or speech.

In *Meet Me in St. Louis*, we hear all parts of this standard, two-theme design: the opening section surrounds the main title with a large orchestra-and-chorus rendition of the title song (1); the second, lyrical section quotes "The Boy Next Door" (2); and the third part tails off to merge with the brass motto that announces the "Summer" title (3). At this point, music winds down to serve as a lyrical background during the establishing shot of Kensington Street, but it continues under the added sound effects and generic speech (4). Music then percolates under the mundane kitchen conversation about ketchup. Everything we have heard thus far (except perhaps the fact that the music did not sneak out under the first line of dialogue) announces a nostalgic costumer, either as romantic comedy or light family melodrama—not a musical. Only when Agnes starts singing several minutes later do the "unreal" traits of a musical start to come to the fore, not because she (or Grandpa shortly after) sings—something natural enough in a high-spirited household—but because the accompaniment is provided by a nondiegetic orchestra (which quickly transitions from providing neutral background music for the kitchen conversation to accompanying Agnes singing). Finally, we recognize this as a "number" when the song is completed after the camera moves outdoors to the street and Esther (Judy Garland) and Rose (Lucille Bremer), amazingly, pick up the song from Grandpa in a perfectly synchronized overlap.

END CREDIT MUSIC

Music for the end credits changed very little over the course of the first two decades of the sound film. As we noted in Chapter 5, a feature film closed with a "The End" card, which may or may not be followed by a cast list. The options for music were as follows: (1) a silent "The End" card, followed by music unrelated to the film for the cast list; (2) unrelated music that begins with a "The End" card; (3) music from the film, whether originally heard diegetically or nondiegetically, that begins with a "The End" card; or (4) music introduced during the last scene that overlaps into "The End" sequence. In Chapter 5, we saw the last of these options used for *The Broadway Melody*. We should also note that, for films throughout the classic studio era, and particularly those in the 1930s, silent cast lists following a "The End" card were very common, but whether those have survived into currently available prints is largely a matter of coincidence.

The "two-part" model for music in the establishing sequence also gave audiences a clue about the film's underscore because the lyrical melody was usually the love theme. In Meet Me in St. Louis *(1944), Judy Garland's character sings "The Boy Next Door" early in the film, thus firmly tying the song not only to her but to her desire for a romantic relationship. (At this point, it is the desire itself that is significant, however, as we know little to nothing about the neighbor who is its object.)*

Three Films from 1933 Starring Katharine Hepburn

As it happens, all three of these early films also use option (4) from the preceding paragraph, which we can understand as a mirror or retrograde of the establishing sequence, where a smooth transition is being aimed for *out* of the film rather than *into* it. In *Christopher Strong*, an organ grinder we saw early in the film playing "Nearer My God to Thee" now (1:16:55) walks past a monument to Lady Cynthia Darrington (Hepburn), who has died in an aviation accident (a long montage of the flight and accident precedes). At 1:17:05, with a cut to an insert (a plaque on the monument), the main-title tango starts up again and continues, rising dramatically, into the end title about 20 seconds later.

In *Morning Glory*, similarly, an introduction (at 1:10:40) leads to a slow version of the main-theme waltz, played as a violin solo in a low register, under dialogue. Almost 2 minutes later this solo leads abruptly to an orchestral end-title up-and-out flourish (still including the waltz melody). The music concludes under an additional card for the studio, and then follows a cast list, which is silent and lasts for 20 seconds.

The ending of *Little Women* offers only a slight variation on the model, in that the music is not the theme heard with the main title but an important associative theme for Jo's mentor, Professor Bhaer: Tchaikovsky's song to a Goethe text "Wer nur die Sehnsucht kennt." This music enters behind their conversation at 1:54:05 and continues into the end title a little over a minute later. An up-and-out flourish is modulated down at last to give a less grandiloquent ending, a nice touch in keeping with the muted nostalgia of the film's final scene.

Films from 1939, End Credits

By the end of the decade of the 1930s, little had changed. The end-credit sequence normally consisted of a "The End" card followed by the cast list. By this time, option (4) was the preferred method: some minimal transition would be made between the final scene and this sequence. In *Intermezzo*, for example, the film closes with Holger (Leslie Howard) entering his house and closing the door, which remains onscreen as the background for the end card and a short rolling cast list. The sequence lasts 25 seconds in all and is accompanied by the film's main theme. The same method is used for *Stagecoach* (1939): as the wagon carrying Claire Trevor and John Wayne's characters rides away into the night, "The End" and then a short cast list are superimposed.

Lower budget films at MGM followed a formula that is a variant of this model. *On Borrowed Time*, for example, separates the end-credits sequence with a short fade to black—then appears an end card with a spare, elegant graphic of a lion (the studio emblem) behind it; after another short fade to black, two cards with the cast list appear. The entire sequence lasts 30 seconds. Music (orchestral underscore) runs continuously from the final scene to the end. *Honolulu* follows exactly the same model but uses the typical bright foxtrot rhythms of earlier films, which we would still expect for a romantic comedy.

In the high-budget production *Gone with the Wind*, the end title is brief, superimposed over a final shot of Scarlett on a hillside looking at Tara. Then a simple card with the legend "Exit Music" appears (Figure 7-18), against which plays a 4-minute composition made up of music heard earlier in the film (this piece is very much like a symphonically developed composition for end credits in contemporary films). There is no cast list. This "Exit Music" balances the Overture that begins the film and the "Entr'acte" between the two parts.

At Warner Bros., Max Steiner continued the practice we saw with the three Hepburn films discussed previously and emphasized continuity between film and credits more strongly than did most other composers. The end-credits sequences he scored are typically a bit longer, too, at 45 to 75 seconds. For *Dust Be My Destiny*, music swells into the "End" card but then shifts to a foxtrot tempo halfway through the shot, overlapping with the first of two cast credits cards. This foxtrot is based on the same theme that Steiner used as the main theme for the film score proper. A brief swell brings the foxtrot, and the film, to an end at 45 seconds. The pattern is almost identical in *They Made Me a Criminal*, another early John Garfield vehicle. For *Confessions of a Nazi Spy*, the design is different: a fade to black precedes "The End," but music actually overlaps into the fade and continues through a rolling cast list to the finish at 75 seconds. The music is "America the Beautiful" played in a foxtrot or moderate march tempo.

Figure 7-18. *Gone with the Wind* (1939). This is an unusual announcement of exit music.

PERFORMANCE SCENE

It is probably not an exaggeration to say that the great majority of dramatic feature films in the classical studio era include at least one performance of some kind, whether neutral or foregrounded, whether "live" or "recorded," whether involved in narrative or simply part of the ambience of a venue, whether the performance is understood as professional or amateur. Generally, the degree to which musical form dictates filmic form depends in great part on the importance of the characters involved and the degree of foregrounding of that performance. Throughout the period, as technology improves and sound editors and music department personnel gradually acquire more skill and experience integrating performances into the sound track, performances achieve both a wider range of application and a greater level of sophistication and subtlety in relation to narrative function. The examples that follow cover the range from an isolated performance (from *To Have and Have Not*) to a collection of performances associated with the ambience of a specific venue (from *Casablanca*) to a theme that wanders back and forth between performance(s) and nondiegetic treatments (from *Laura*).

To Have and Have Not, *"Am I Blue?"*

We look first at a relatively simple example from the best known of the sequels to *Casablanca* (1942): a café number featuring Hoagy Carmichael in *To Have and Have Not* (1944). Carmichael is a secondary character in the film, a hotel pianist nicknamed Cricket. We hear diegetic music in the background in the early minutes of the film, but at 0:14:40, Cricket appears onscreen, plays a short introduction, and then begins to sing the chorus from "Am I Blue?," a song by Harry Akst and Grant Clarke. The chorus is in the standard 32-bar AABA design. Cricket sings and plays the two A phrases solo, and the camera stays focused on him. At the bridge (B), the camera cuts to the band's drummer, who puts down his newspaper and begins a soft accompaniment with brushes. At the reprise of A, the bass and guitar players join in. Lauren Bacall's character (known only as Slim) approaches the piano as the chorus ends and Cricket tells her to "take over," at which they all shift back to the bridge with Slim singing—see Figure 7-19. The reprise comes back one last time with Cricket joining Slim in the singing. The performance ends with audience applause, roughly 1 minute and 40 seconds after it began.

The scene actually begins a few seconds before Cricket starts playing: a dissolve indicates a change from the previous scene (in this case, passage of time, not locale, as both scenes are in the hotel), and we see Harry Morgan (Humphrey Bogart) at a table in a combined lobby-café area. The camera is on him as the piano intro starts offscreen. Cut to a long shot of the orchestra area as Cricket continues to play; cut to a nearby table on a repeated bar of music (Slim and an interested man sit there); cut back to a closer shot of Cricket on the next bar, and he begins to sing. During the two A phrases, cuts back to the tables make it clear that Slim is trying to get Harry's attention, and this is the apparent motivation

Figure 7-19. *To Have and Have Not* (1944). Lauren Bacall sings "Am I Blue?" with Hoagy Carmichael.

for her walking up to the piano (the song's lyrics help, offering lines like "plans with your man falling through"). The end of the performance is clearly the end of the scene segment: we return to Harry's table as the hotel manager approaches and talks about a group of resistance fighters who want to hire Harry's boat to escape—the topic of the conversation in the previous scene.

Thus, we have two simultaneous strands: the musical performance and Slim's efforts to excite Harry's interest. The design of the music may constrain and channel the narrative events, but it does not stop them entirely.

Casablanca, *Music during the First Act*

The first act of *Casablanca* has two components of very different lengths: an opening segment out of doors and the first evening in *Rick's Café Americain*. The exterior segment consists of three short but related scenes: the round-up of Free French sympathizers, conversation of the refugees, and the arrival of Nazi officers at the airport. The evening in the Café, on the other hand, is depicted in a continuously running filmic unit of nearly 30 minutes, with a dissolve into the sign outside the café to begin (at 6:30) and another dissolve just after Rick and Ilsa's reunion defining the end (at 36:06). Time and place are unified by continuous chronological time and the café building itself. It might be possible to refer to this as one enormous scene, but most of us would refer to these 30 minutes as a sequence because of the length and because of the large number of smaller but substantial segments, including the rigged roulette wheel, Ugarte's arrest, at least two song performances, Rick's first encounter with Major Strasser, and the reunion, among others.

During these 30 minutes, we hear all or parts of a dozen songs, culminating in the thirteenth, "As Time Goes By," which appears for the first time when Ilsa (Ingrid Bergman) renders its opening with an understated bit of wordless singing. Table 7-1 gives a complete list, with timings.[6] Virtually all the possibilities for diegetic performance are realized by one or another of these songs. Two highlighted performances are heard in their entirety: no. 4 "Knock on Wood" and no. 11 "Tango delle Rose." No. 1 "It Had to Be You" is heard in progress, offscreen,

Table 7-1 *Casablanca*, Act 1, diegetic music (after Martin Marks).

THAT EVENING AT RICK'S/RICK AND UGARTE

EXT. RICK'S CAFE -- NIGHT

      06:29: music in with shot of sign outside café

1   [song 1] "It Had to Be You" (Gus Kahn, Isham Jones)

      Background/visual vocal: Dooley Wilson

INT. RICK'S CAFE -- MAIN ROOM -- NIGHT

2   connects to: [song 2] "Shine" (Lew Brown, Ford Dabney, Cecil Mack)

      Visual vocal: Dooley Wilson; then instrumental offscreen

      08:20: music fades awkwardly just after cut to casino room

INT. RICK'S CAFE -- GAMBLING ROOM -- NIGHT

      09:12: music in with opening of casino door

3   [song 3] "Crazy Rhythm" (Joseph Meyers, Roger Wolfe Kahn, Irving Caesar)

      Offscreen instrumental

      10:00: music goes out with closing of casino door

BACK IN THE CAFE/RICK, YVONNE, SACHA/RICK TALKS TO RENAULT OUTSIDE

INT. RICK'S CAFE -- MAIN ROOM -- NIGHT

      12:42: music in as a sound advance just before cut to main room

4   [song 4] "Knock on Wood" (M. K. Jerome, Jack Scholl)

      Visual vocal: Dooley Wilson

5   connects to: [song 5] "The Very Thought of You" (Ray Noble)

      Visual instrumental, background instrumental

EXT. RICK'S CAFE -- NIGHT

      17:10: music out

      17:20: music in with cut inside

(Continued)

Table 7-1 (*Continued*)

INT. RICK'S CAFE -- MAIN ROOM -- NIGHT

6 [song 6] "Baby Face" (Benning Davis, Harry Alest)

  Visual instrumental, background instrumental

INT. RICK'S CAFE -- OFFICE-- NIGHT

  18:16: music goes out with office door closing

STRASSER ARRIVES; UGARTE IS ARRESTED; STRASSER INTERVIEWS RICK

INT. RICK'S CAFE -- MAIN ROOM -- NIGHT

  20:32: music in as office door is opened; effect is of a sound advance

7 [song 7] "I'm Just Wild about Harry" (Noble Sissle, Eubie Blake)

  Background instrumental, visual instrumental

INT. RICK'S CAFE -- GAMBLING ROOM -- NIGHT

  22:18: music out under gun shots

INT. RICK'S CAFE -- MAIN ROOM -- NIGHT

  22:45: music in when Rick tells Sam to start playing again

8 [song 8] "Heaven Can Wait" (Eddie DeLange, Jimmy Van Heusen)

  Visual instrumental, background instrumental

  23:55: music goes out as band finishes number

ILSA AND LASZLO ARRIVE

  25:18: music in with the cut: the couple walks into the Café

9 [song 9] "Speak to Me of Love" (= "Parlez moi d'Amour" by Jean Lenoir)

  Visual instrumental, background instrumental

10 connects to: [song 10] "Love for Sale" (Cole Porter)

  Background instrumental

  27:55: music out as Strasser comes to their table

  28:52: applause offscreen; music in with cut to singer 28:59

11 [song 11] "Tango delle Rose" (F. Schreier, A. Bottro, & Carol Raven)

  Visual vocal, background vocal: Corinna Mae

  30:48: music out with end of song

  31:34: music in when Ilsa asks Sam to play

12 [song 12] "Avalon" (Al Jolson, Vincent Rose, & B. G. De Sylva)

  Visual instrumental

  32:04: music out when Sam turns to speak to her

  32:30: music in when Ilsa hums/sings

13 [song 13] "As Time Goes By" (Hermann Hupfeld)

  Visual vocal (Ingrid Bergman, Dooley Wilson

Reel 4,7 connects to: underscore (sketches = 2:34+) 33:32-36:06 = 2:35

  Cue begins in d, ends firmly in D<flat>/d<flat>.

but then finishes onscreen. No. 3 "Crazy Rhythm" is played by the band entirely offscreen. Four move from on- to offscreen as cuts remove the players from the frame: these are nos. 2, 5, 6, 8, and 9. Of all of these songs, only the last one, "As Time Goes By," enters the underscore, at the famous moment when Rick comes out of another room to find Ilsa present and Sam singing the forbidden song.

The range of narrative meanings for song performances in the classical feature film runs the gamut from a simple occasion to a deep and close connection to characters and events. Sometimes, a performance is merely an opportunity for one of the leads to perform—this of course happens in musicals but also seems to be the case with, for example, Lauren Bacall's out-of-character numbers in *The Big Sleep*. In *Casablanca*, "Knock on Wood" and "Tango delle Rose" both would seem to fit this category—they are certainly presented that way—but according to film music scholar Martin Marks, they also have general ties to the narrative.[7] "Knock on Wood" is addressed to the assemblage of refugees in the Café, all of whom hope for exactly the kind of luck promised by the superstitious action. The *flamenco* style of "Tango delle Rose"—markedly different from all the other music in the film—may be a subtle reference to the Spanish Civil War at a moment when Laszlo, the resistance leader, is highlighted in the action. Finally, "As Time Goes By" is as deeply bound in narrative as a song could be—it is even mentioned directly, by Ilsa just before she sings its opening phrase.

Laura, *Performances and Underscore*

In *Casablanca*, the only song to appear in both diegetic and nondiegetic treatments is "As Time Goes By," but its first appearance isn't until more than a quarter of the film is over. After that point, we hear little else until eventually the nondiegetic version entirely takes over the musical component of the sound track. ("La Marseillaise," the French national anthem, also appears in both diegetic and nondiegetic treatments.) In *Laura*, the situation is different. The title song also appears in diegetic and nondiegetic forms, but we hear it immediately and so often thereafter it has become a commonplace to say the film's music is monothematic, that is, that we never hear anything else. Strictly speaking, that is not true: there is a short theme for the film's villain Waldo Lydecker (we hear it when he is first seen onscreen) and a slow ominous theme that signifies danger or mystery and might also be associated with the detective Mark McPherson (it is heard first at the beginning of the "Apartment Scene," when the policeman returns to Laura's apartment at night [40:20]). Waldo's theme, however, is more an instrumental flourish than a melody, although, as film scholar Kathryn Kalinak notes, it is repeatedly used for moments in the narrative that foreshadow Waldo as the murderer. Similarly, the ominous theme is more a product of its slow tempo and distinctive timbre than of a melody—but it does reappear several times in prominent locations and makes an effective foil to the richly lyrical and melodious title theme.

Nevertheless, the title theme is so pervasive that we can say the film *may as well* be monothematic. This is not to say that it is continually present: of the film's

a | b | c **Figure 7-20.** *Laura* (1944). (a) Musicians play the title song in the restaurant. (b) Detective McPherson and Waldo Lydecker at a table. (c) The empty restaurant as Waldo concludes his story (shown to us in flashback).

87-minute runtime, music is present for 48, or a bit over half. Following the establishing sequence, music is absent for 11 minutes, after which the title theme is heard briefly on a phonograph, and music is again absent for another 2 minutes. The long restaurant scene and flashback that follows (from 15:20 to 34:00) is framed by a violinist's performance of the title theme (Figure 7-20a); this reappears several times, as if in progress, as Waldo ends one segment of his story and before he embarks on the next (Figure 7-20b). The final return to present time is punctuated by silence: patrons were gone earlier, now musicians are as well (Figure 7-20c).

To complicate matters, we hear recorded versions of the title theme during some of the flashback scenes, most notably a Latin version during a party (24:00) and a foxtrot version as Laura and her boyfriend Shelby (Vincent Price) talk and then dance in a restaurant (27:30). Both of these, incidentally, reappear as background during the party in Laura's apartment (65:20).

Finally, we should note that, after Laura has returned, the dead woman is identified, and the search for the killer begins in earnest, the title theme is only occasionally present and usually in subdued form (like the recordings for Laura's party). It only reappears in full form at the very end, after Waldo dies, for the film's final "up-and-out" gesture.

The performances, then, function in almost entirely opposite ways. McPherson draws attention to the phonograph when he opens its cover and starts the recording (Figure 7-21a). The tension between the three men is apparent, particularly after Shelby comments that the melody was "Laura's favorite" (at 13:10; see Figure 7-21b). The later phonograph cues, on the other hand, are obviously backgrounded by the party conversation and physical movements of individuals and crowds. The violinist's rendition in the restaurant is strongly motivated in the same way the records were—although of course in both

Figure 7-21. *Laura.* (a) McPherson plays a recording of the title song. (b) Shelby comments that it was Laura's "favorite."

a
b

cases the fact that it is the same melody is at the level of coincidence. But this performance is foregrounded each time the flashback returns to present time, and it therefore strongly frames the whole while firmly imprinting the association between the theme, Laura herself, and Waldo's interest in her.

MONTAGE OR FANTASY SCENE

Gone with the Wind, *Montage Sequence in the Prologue to Part 2*

Like many other aspects of filmmaking, the montage scene to show temporal or spatial movement only becomes more elaborate through the 1930s. At its most extensive, montage style and technique turn into or are embedded in the temporal reversal of the flashback, as in the Paris scene from *Casablanca* or the restaurant flashback in *Laura*. In these cases, however, the term *flashback* is the traditional label; we reserve *montage* for short sequences where rapid or significant movement of time or place is the overriding effect.

The filmic unit of the montage is actually closely related to the prologue, which in its more extended versions takes on the character of a montage, as in the prologue to *Casablanca*, for example, which combines voice-over narration with graphics, newsreel footage, and filmed shots.

The prologue to Part 2 of *Gone with the Wind* (1939) is also a montage in this sense. Part 2 begins with a 90-second overture (it is titled "Entr'acte" after the instrumental music played between the acts of plays or musical theater pieces). Then the background—a stationary graphic image of a vividly covered early evening sky—disappears in a fade to black (while the music continues), but the colors reappear as lurid clouds and smoke in motion; titles are superimposed and so are moving images, of fire first, then silhouettes of soldiers. With a title mentioning Tara, the O'Hara estate, the montage and prologue end. Thus, the entire campaign of Sherman's March to the Sea is compressed into 1 minute. We are given a strong sense of the devastation it caused but we need to know little else than a sense of the passage of time, as none of the lead characters was directly involved in the campaign (at least not after the burning of Atlanta, an episode that occurs near the end of Part 1). The music throughout the Entr'acte is a traditional silent-film "hurry" but with a substantial sense of menace. When the montage begins, the music becomes louder and harsher.

DIALOGUE SCENE

Dialogue underscoring (recall that this means nondiegetic instrumental music played "under" speech) is one of the most characteristic features of film music in the 1930s and 1940s and the one least like any other genre of music. Because it was expected to follow the shifting emotions, associations, and references of conversation, a dialogue cue sacrifices musical form for the sake of conforming to the shape of the scene. Max Steiner, who pioneered the practice in the early 1930s, called this "fitting the film like a glove."[8] It has also been referred to pejoratively as "Mickey-Mousing," from a similar use of close synchronization in cartoons. This style of dialogue underscoring can be compared to "overall scoring," which establishes a mood or tempo for a scene but does not try to follow action closely. In this sense, music acts in a way similar to ambient sound but is not a replacement: one might perhaps say that ambient sound normally establishes or reinforces the "mood" or qualities of a physical space, where a musical cue in the overall scoring manner establishes or reinforces the mood(s) of the characters.

Some of the effects of nondiegetic dialogue underscoring can be achieved using diegetic (or apparently diegetic) music. A song playing in the background of a scene on a phonograph or on a radio can help identify (or intensify) the mood we sense in speakers in a conversation. Neutral or even anempathetic diegetic music played behind conversation, however, is related to but different from overall scoring: a song played by a band or coming from a phonograph in the background is really a third, "negative" style of dialogue underscoring that can contradict or otherwise undermine the speakers, as in *Mildred Pierce* (1945), where a distraught Mildred talking incoherently to Wally while thinking of her spoiled, immoral daughter Veda: behind them and in a corner of the screen, we see a young woman on the lighted club stage singing "You Must Have Been a Beautiful Baby"—see Figure 7-22. At lower sound levels—and without the ironic references—neutral diegetic music has many of the functional qualities of ambient sound.

At the same time, many B-films were lightly scored (probably in good part because of the music production and sound postproduction costs), and it was common in films dominated by dialogue to have very little music (in some romantic comedies but particularly in stage plays translated to cinema). *His Girl Friday* (1939), for example, has a minute-long opening sequence and 1 minute of music for the end credits (it actually sneaks in a few seconds before the final scene ends) in a film that lasts just over 90 minutes. There is no other music of any kind. *Philadelphia Story* (1940) is very similar, although it does include a very few scattered, additional minutes of underscoring. Musicals, also, were less likely to use dialogue underscoring. This genre generally restricted music to the film's framing elements and its performances, although exceptions were made for romantic scenes and in some higher budget productions (such as the MGM Freed Unit's integrated musicals, including *Meet Me in St. Louis*).

Rebecca, *Terrace Scene*

The close pairing of music and continuity in a typical classical dialogue scene is well illustrated by the "terrace scene" in *Rebecca*. This scene occurs early in the film, immediately after the hotel lobby and breakfast scenes discussed earlier. Maxim offers to drive "I" to a spot where she intends to sketch, and the scene changes to an unspecified place on the ocean, a large stone terrace with a low wall and the sea beyond (see Figure 7-23a).

Figure 7-22. *Mildred Pierce* (1945). A singer performs in Wally's tavern. Mildred and Wally are seated at a table offscreen.

The cut to the establishing shot of the terrace brings a pastoral, pleasant, and relaxed music, which continues through their initial conversation (see Figure 7-24). An abrupt shift to several disconnected, playful little musical gestures accompanies the insert of the sketch and Maxim's comments about it. When "I" puts the sketch down and joins Maxim at the terrace wall, they talk amiably; the music returns to the character of the beginning, but now introduces a theme that the composer, Franz Waxman, develops later as the love theme.[9] A sudden but not overly loud chord (labeled a "mild stinger" in Figure 7-24) alerts us to the significance of Manderley, the palatial DeWinter home in Cornwall. As Maxim begins to talk about Manderley, we hear its theme, which has appeared twice earlier in the film and by now is easily associated with the great house. As he continues, Maxim's voice becomes troubled (we hear high tremolo violin chords that bear a suggestion of suspense), and he soon stops speaking. To cover

Figure 7-23. *Rebecca.* Terrace scene, part 1.   a | b / c | d

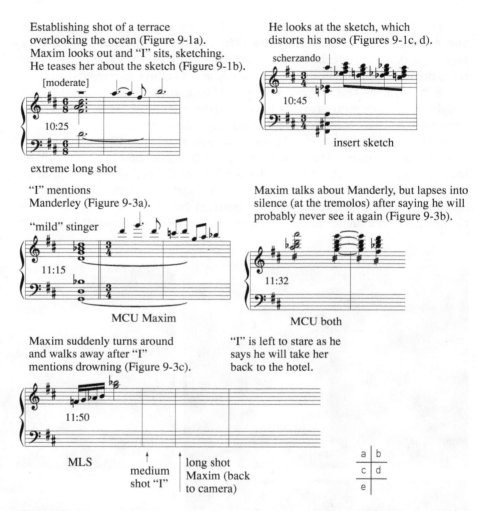

Figure 7-24. *Rebecca.* Terrace scene. Music and action in summary form (transcription from the sound track).

the gap, "I" begins talking about the weather and swimming. Shortly after she mentions drowning, Maxim turns suddenly (to another stinger gesture) and walks away; the music slowly calms down again as we hear him, offscreen, tell "I" that he will take her back to the hotel.

The music changes not according to the conventions and expectations of instrumental music (a musical "logic" that states and develops clearly defined themes) but in a manner that makes clear and expressively intensifies the changes in conversational and emotional interactions of the two characters. Thus, the music guides us carefully in our shifting reactions to the scene. In this it complements the continuity editing. Note that the "neutral" establishing shots (extreme long shot of the terrace, and two long shots, from opposite directions, of the couple) receive pleasant music that is not distinctive; the insert has its own musical "insert"—the brief scherzando (playful) phrase—after which we return to the mood of the beginning, but with just slightly more intensity, as the camera moves in a bit and the "Love" theme is stated.

We move in further with the cut to a medium close-up of "I" as she mentions a postcard of Manderley—this, with the mild stinger, brings us to the central point of the scene, which is Max's mysteriously unsettled relation to Manderley, his own home—see Figure 7-25. From this point until Maxim turns and walks away, the music continues in the same tempo (although with varying figures and instrumentation) as shots alternate in three framings: the medium close-ups of "I" and Maxim and a 2-shot of them at the same distance. The final 12 seconds of the scene are a confusing visual whirl, as Maxim walks out of the frame, then cut to a medium shot of "I", then a long shot of Maxim with his back turned, and finally back to "I"; here the music gives some order to the series of shots as it begins by mirroring Maxim's sudden physical actions but ends by echoing the deflated mood and disappointment that "I" clearly reveals.

As a final note, the terrace scene might indeed be understood to constitute a scene, but the music in fact continues across several similar scenes. Eventually we realize that each of these short scenes is probably better regarded as a segment of a larger sequence, the sequence being a slow-moving montage that, altogether, constitutes the courtship and marriage of Maxim and "I." After the marriage, the location shifts to Manderley, and thus the entire segment—from the beginning to the marriage—constitutes the film's first sequence, or "chapter."

Figure 7-25. *Rebecca.* Terrace scene, part 2.

a
b
c

ACTION SCENE

Music remains mostly obligatory for action scenes in classical feature films, and on terms that are very similar to the hurries and dramatic *allegros* of the silent era. Still, consistent with the trends we saw in the previous placement categories, by the late 1930s one can see a wide variation in practice based for the most part on differences in production budgets and exhibition status. At the extreme of the prestige film, action scenes might be very carefully and minutely scored, as in the famous sword fighting scene from *The Adventures of Robin Hood* (1938) or in the opening scene of *Casablanca*, an action montage of the resistance sympathizers—the "usual suspects"—being rounded up, one of them killed. At the other extreme, low-budget Westerns, which always had several scenes of chases, runaway wagons, and gunfights, typically combined prominent sound effects with a more subdued hurry that was not synchronized. Of literally hundreds of films of this type, we will mention *Lights of Old Santa Fe* (1944), an early

Roy Rogers and Dale Evans vehicle. Following the formula, alternating scenes consist of dialogue with no music and few or no effects, song performances in solo or group arrangements, and action scenes. *Lights of Old Santa Fe* has a chariot race, a fire that stirs a cattle stampede and causes a runaway wagon to head toward a river cliff, and three rides or chases on horseback, with gunfire. In each of these, effects noise dominates and a largely unsynchronized hurry cue adds to the mood. The music is even lacking in one of the chases, the coconut shell imitations of horses hooves—inherited directly from effects-laden performance practices of the 1920s—being quite loud and energetic enough. In none of the action cues is there any thematic connection to the film's songs.

One notable characteristic of the period is that the treatment of action scenes changes little during the years of World War II (1939–1945). All film genres contributed narratives on contemporary war topics. With very few exceptions, A-level feature films used as much symphonic underscoring as did other dramatic films. To a great extent, this is due to the fact that the major American studios were under the authority of the Office of War Information, and the propaganda function of films ruled out any substantial changes that would have resulted in an overly realistic representation of events. The same practices of spectacle and dramatic presentation that served the fictional and historical costume films of the 1930s worked equally well for films on wartime events, among them *Captains of the Clouds, Flying Tigers, Wake Island* (all 1942), *Air Force, Destination Tokyo* (both 1943), *Thirty Seconds Over Tokyo, Wing and a Prayer* (both 1944), *Back to Bataan, God Is My Co-Pilot*, and *Pride of the Marines* (1945).

LOVE SCENE

The most basic form of the romantic scenario creates the couple as the conclusion of the film, the moment where all the plot elements converge (the formula is commonly, if crudely—and often incorrectly—referred to as "boy gets girl"). Most of the Astaire–Rogers musicals work this way—for example, *Swing Time* (1936) and *Top Hat* (1935)—as do many romantic comedies. The possible variants, however, are almost endless. The couple may be formed early in the film and the vicissitudes they endure structure the narrative, as in several early Hitchcock films, including *Young and Innocent* (1937), *Rebecca, Suspicion* (1941), and *Spellbound* (1945). Other films from the classic era include *Made for Each Other* (1939), *The Young in Heart* (1938), and *Now, Voyager* (1942), among many others (especially those, like the three named here, that belong to the genre of melodrama or "women's films"). This variant is particularly suited to stories that end in the breakup of the couple, whether through desertion or death, or, as in *Now, Voyager*, what might be called a retreat from a sexual relationship. Quite often a breakup occurs about midway and the remainder of the film is driven by the consequences, whether it be the two characters trying to establish separate lives (and perhaps new couples) after a breakup (as in *Mildred Pierce*, where Mildred goes through two cycles of divorce), or the surviving person doing the same after a death. It is, of course, also common for a separated couple to succeed in (re)establishing a solid relationship at the end of the film, as in *His Girl Friday* and (somewhat implausibly) *Mildred Pierce*.

As we noted earlier, it was customary for the two-part main title cue to introduce the love theme, though their lyrical character and early association either with the female lead or the male lead's romantic aspirations makes them unmistakable. Despite the ease with which we can identify love themes, their signification is somewhat ambiguous because they generally refer both to the heroine and to the romantic relationship between hero and heroine. The fact that the love theme doubles the signification in this way reinforces the male-dominated point of view that characterizes most narrative film—at least in classical Hollywood. This is especially the case where the male character has a well-defined theme of his own. The love theme defines the heroine in terms of the relationship. In a sense, the music suggests that she *is* essentially identical to that relationship, whereas the theme for the hero establishes a musical identity for him that cannot be reduced in the same way.

We can see something of this process at work in *Captain Blood* (1935), which additionally demonstrates again how effective a means of musical characterization style topics can be. In Figure 7-26, for instance, Peter Blood's themes a and d both have a brash character consistent with the heroic side of his personality. Theme b, on the other hand, is gentler, more flowing and lyrical, consistent with his personality as a caring doctor. (It is also similar to a love theme, which is one reason it dovetails so easily with Arabella's theme (c).) Yet we should note that the musical meaning seems much more specific in the case of the heroic side than the caring side. This is because calls and fanfares, especially those scored for trumpets, have a long history of serving military functions (signals, such as calling to arms) as well as heraldic ones (marking the entrance of nobility). Horns have a similar connection with hunting. These associations were easily imported into theater music—especially opera, operetta, and melodrama—and from there spread to instrumental genres such as program music. In *Captain Blood*, the trumpets give the theme in Figure 7-26a a strong fanfare flavor, despite its somewhat unpredictable rhythmic structure. Played by the horns, Figure 7-26d, by contrast, bears an affinity to hunting calls, perhaps fitting for Peter's new occupation as pirate. "We, the hunted, will now hunt," he declares as he signs the compact with his men (1:03:16). When the bugler plays the theme later in the film, it becomes an explicit call to arms.

The melody in Figure 7-26c is the love theme associated with Arabella. This one is a bit unusual for a love theme in being relatively short. Compare this to the themes for Peter Blood (Figures 7-26a, b, and d). One thing to note is that Peter has three themes, each representing a somewhat different character. Knowing just this much, we can be fairly certain that Peter will receive the bulk of the musical treatment. Another distinction is that, unlike Arabella's theme, where the characteristic part of the motive is presented in the example, then repeated, all of Peter's themes have typical continuations that extend beyond the initial gesture. Peter's themes, in other words, are all fully formed in a way that

a
b
c
d
Figure 7-26. *Captain Blood* (1935). Principal leitmotifs (transcriptions from the sound track).

Arabella's is not. Moreover, throughout the film, Arabella's theme never seems to go to the same place, its continuation being much more determined by context (it is in fact often linked to the end of Peter's theme "b"). This musical treatment suggests that Arabella will be a rather ill-defined character except in terms of her relationship to Peter. (See Figure 7-27 for an image of the composer, Erich Korngold, working.)

As a counter-example, consider the fact that Lauren Bacall's character, "Slim," in *To Have and Have Not* (1944), is never associated with music outside of her performance of "Am I Blue?" (and one other short rehearsal) with Hoagy Carmichael, and that tune is never repeated in the nondiegetic music. What this confirms for the audience is the suspicion gathered early on that Slim might represent the "love interest" but if so she is certainly an unconventional heroine.

Casablanca is certainly rich in music, but compared with *Captain Blood*, the treatment of its love theme is remarkably simple and direct. The evening after their arrival in the city, Ilsa and Laszlo go to Rick's Café; after a while Laszlo walks to the bar to talk with a man who has revealed himself as a resistance fighter, and Ilsa tells a waiter to ask Sam to come over to her table; Sam arrives and she asks him to play "As Time Goes By." From this point, we hear that melody four times in a row: sung by Ilsa, then played and sung by Sam; then heard twice in the nondiegetic orchestra, first as the slow-motion reaction music in the oboe, and then as a slightly distorted waltz when Ilsa refers to Paris. Each time the tune is different in some way—not only in orchestration but also in its signification. The first appearance of this now-famous melody in the film is through Ilsa's humming and brief wordless singing: instantly it becomes the love theme as it is literally embodied in her while we see her in close-up. Sam's repeating it reluctantly but fluently tells us that this melody has a history, something associated with it in Ilsa's—and Sam's—memory. That suggestion is powerfully realized in the "point of view" music that immediately follows the stinger chord, as we "hear" the sudden encounter register in the minds of Rick and Ilsa. Finally, we learn where this history can be localized—in Paris, as Ilsa makes a

Figure 7-27. The composer of *Captain Blood* (1935), Erich Wolfgang Korngold, with fellow composer Franz Waxman (standing). Photo © John W. Waxman Collection. All rights reserved. International copyright secured. Used with permission.

reference to the city and we hear "As Time Goes By" in waltz form. The power of memory builds up during the unusually long close-up on Ingrid Bergman's face while Sam sings: her face changes minimally (a slight glistening in the eyes that might suggest imminent tears), but the music, by its presence and its persistence throughout the close-up, increases the emotional tension significantly.

Timeline

1931	Samuel Goldwyn Company releases *Street Scene*. RCA releases ribbon microphone.
1932	Rerecording becomes normal, allowing for all sound and music except dialogue to be prerecorded or rerecorded.
1933	RKO releases *King Kong, Christopher Strong, Morning Glory,* and *Little Women*.
1935	Warner Bros. releases *Captain Blood*.
1936	RCA develops unidirectional microphone.
1939	Selznick International Pictures releases *Intermezzo* and *Gone with the Wind*. MGM releases *On Borrowed Time* and *Honolulu*. Warner Bros. releases *Dust Be My Destiny, They Made Me a Criminal,* and *Confessions of a Nazi Spy*.

Figure 7-28. *Casablanca.* Rick, Captain Renault, Ilsa, and Victor Laszlo.

When Captain Renault (Claude Rains) intervenes, he, Rick, Ilsa, and her spouse Victor Laszlo (Paul Henreid) sit down for a four-way conversation (Figure 7-28). After a short while, everyone leaves, Rick is left to sit down again dejectedly, and Renault talks briefly to the others outdoors. Given the large number of medium

1940   Selznick International Pictures releases *Rebecca*.

1942   Warner Bros. releases *Casablanca*.

1944   MGM releases *Meet Me in St. Louis*. Twentieth-Century Fox releases *Laura*. Republic Pictures releases *Lights of Old Santa Fe*.

1945   Warner Bros. releases *To Have and to Have Not* and *Mildred Pierce*.

close-ups and close-ups, dialogue synchronization is especially tight. There are very few sound effects and none of substance. The famous stinger chord that accompanies Rick's reaction to seeing Ilsa is not timed with the cut to Rick—it enters 1 second later, on the reaction shot of Ilsa, almost mimicking a sharp intake of breath that might naturally accompany the shock. Dialogue follows expected paths and by and large is quite informative about the emotions behind the speech. Like the music, inflections in the speech throughout follow the shifts in emotion of Rick and Ilsa, not in Captain Renault (who, however, makes plain that he is learning something about his friend Rick's character) and Laszlo (whose speech throughout is guarded).

As for the music, composer Max Steiner said that his ideal for underscoring was that the music "fits the scene like a glove," and "seamless" is undoubtedly the best way to describe this cue: it accompanies, comments on, and amplifies every turn in the action. The stinger chord is a powerful narrative cue ("Look!" "Pay attention!"); "point of view" music immediately follows as we "hear" the sudden encounter register in the minds of Rick and Ilsa; the plaintive oboe suggests sadness, loneliness, isolation; the reinforcement of specific time–place references in quotations of "As Time Goes By" in waltz form as Ilsa make a reference to Paris, then the German national anthem when she mentions the Germans; the "sinking" emotions and movements near the end (Figure 7-29). The only exceptions are the neutral "walking music" (just after Laszlo says that it is time to go) and the unexpectedly loud, formal cadence at the end (we cannot tell from this scene alone, but this is the end of the film's first large section, which has consisted mostly of one evening in Rick's café).

The music does its best to convince us that, appearances aside, we are watching a love scene.

Figure 7-29. *Casablanca*. Rick sits alone after the others leave.

Summary

The sound track of the studio era was codified around developments in the techniques of rerecording. Rerecording allowed studios to cut the cost of sound-film production by making it possible to return to single-camera shooting and by simplifying the work of the production sound team, which could thereby focus on dialogue. Adding music and effects in postproduction offered the filmmakers much needed flexibility as they could build their story through editing the sound track just as they could with editing of the picture.

Mildred Pierce
Writing about Film Sound and Music

Introduction

In Chapter 3 we introduced the film synopsis statement, in its descriptive form and in the modified version intended to ground an interpretive paper that includes music. Chapter 6 expanded on the synopsis to cover the requirements and techniques for carrying out a scene analysis. In this chapter, we use these exercises as starting points for a screening report on an entire film. Like any essay, the screening report may veer in the direction of analytic description or evaluative opinion, or it may strike a balance between the two. For a course in film music or film sound, it is most likely that the instructor will ask that the paper summarize how the sound track as a whole contributes to the narrative point of the film, in which case you should discuss the narrative associations of music or sound effects (speech, too, if there is something unusual about it), the use of music and sound to articulate narrative structure, and the narrative work that the sound track is doing on the more general level of the film as a whole.

Following the latter model (one that emphasizes description more than evaluation), we map out a method to write a short course paper that focuses on the character and treatment of the sound track and on music's narrative functions. Looking ahead, we will develop these analysis and writing tasks into several different types of compare-contrast projects, a paper (Chapters 10 and 12), and finally into two different types of critical essays (Chapter 15).

As our example in this chapter we have chosen *Mildred Pierce*. We have selected this film because it is a well-made feature release from a major studio, because music plays a significant and varied role, because the film raises a number of questions about culture and gender, and because it is often cited and discussed in the film literature. This last one in particular may be of value to you if you wish to extend the reach of the analyses by exploring historical and critical contexts in the scholarly and trade literature (perhaps in connection with writing a critical essay, as in Chapter 15).

Furthermore, to follow up on our historical account in the previous chapter, *Mildred Pierce* is a characteristic product of Warner Bros. in the period before about 1950—it is focused on action and its narrative is fast paced, with an editing style adjusted to match and a large number of relatively short scenes. Nevertheless, its overall design is very clear: two long, chronologically consistent flashbacks embedded in a frame of current time. The studio had long been known for its gangster and detective films, but it had also found a niche by the later 1930s in melodrama or women's films. Starring Joan Crawford in the title role, *Mildred Pierce* combines the two genres: melodrama is evident in the two extended flashbacks that make up the majority of the film's 111-minute runtime; the detective story is the framework of "current" time, from a man's murder in the opening minute to the exposing of the murderer in the final minutes—covering clock time from about 11:00 pm one evening until sunrise the next morning.

Screening Report: Overview and Procedure

A screening report is a short, primarily descriptive paper that demonstrates that you can follow a film's narrative and can analyze and make general statements about some specific aspect of the film (such as comparing plot and story, following character development, observing features of lighting or framing, etc.). Usually an instructor will assign particular features to be analyzed. In our case, of course, the screening report takes as its topic for analysis the sound track as a whole, or some element of it (music, dialogue, or effects).

The screening report is designed to chart the balance and functions of the sound track elements in a film. In other words, what the scene analysis paper in Chapter 6 did for one small section of a film a screening report does at the level of the entire film. There is at least one important difference, however. Whereas the scene analysis is very detailed and specific, the screening report aims to make a number of generalizations about the sound track, its components, and their contribution to the narrative. A screening report still needs to offer concrete examples drawn from the film, but the level of reference will inevitably be much more general.

To write a screening report, it is almost always best to start by taking informal written screening notes from viewing. These notes will often be extensive enough that they themselves can constitute the bulk of the text. We gave guidelines for taking screening notes in Chapter 6, and it would be wise to consult those again. When writing a screening report of this kind, you should also expect to watch the film in its entirety at least twice, and some individual scenes one or more additional times. The design of the screening report is essentially the same as that of the scene analysis paper. In the outline that follows, each of the numbers represents one paragraph in the final paper. The opening paragraph is the synopsis and thesis statement; it should run from 150 to 200 words. The body of the analysis provides details and evaluation, at 300 to 400 words. The summary or concluding paragraph will be 100 to 150 words, making a range of 500 to 800 words (2 to 3 pages) in the entire report document, to which you would probably be asked to append a runtime segmentation at the level of the scene or a list of music cues.

1. A short synopsis of the film (following the steps in Chapter 3) including pertinent background information to serve as an introduction. For an interpretive paper, the end of the synopsis should transition to a short thesis statement making some meaningful (contestable) claim about the sound and music in the film.
2. General description of the sound track elements and their balance. Evaluation of the sound track in terms of one or more of the following: physical sources of sounds, music's narrative functions, musical structure, filmic (or narrative) structure, or sound, music, and representation.
3. Summary statement about the sound track, including a return to the thesis.

Begin by assembling a table of music cues or a scene log that reports the music cues. Table 8-1 presents a detailed runtime segmentation of *Mildred Pierce* that has been adapted to focus on the music cues. The musical themes named in the table are given in Figure 8-1, with their character associations. Although you need to be able to recognize themes when they recur, you do not need to be able to transcribe them in this fashion to write successfully about music in a film. One suitable alternative is to pinpoint the first appearance of each theme, so that a reader can go to the appropriate moment and hear it. In Table 8-1, we have indicated each theme's initial statement by putting it in uppercase letters.

Table 8-1 *Mildred Pierce* (1945). Timeline and cue list.

ESTABLISHING SEQUENCE

    1. 0:00–0:01:38. Logo, main title, and credits, with an overlap into the opening scene (music out under sound of gunfire about 0:01:45). Theme #1 is heard with the main title and throughout the rest of the sequence.

"CURRENT TIME"; LATE EVENING

—Murder 0:01:35 Monty's beach house.

    2. 0:01:48–0:03:20. Music in with the cut inside the beach house; continues into the next scene, till shortly after the policeman raps his baton on the metal railing at 3:15; music is replaced by dialogue and low-level ambient sound.

—Suicide? 0:02:15 cut to wharf; Mildred considers suicide.

—Mildred and Wally 0:03:55 cut to front of Wally's wharf-side cafe; Wally comes out; they go inside to talk; 0:05:57 cut to the beach house; 0:08:46 Wally realizes something is wrong; 0:10:45 police car appears.

    3. 0:03:55–0:06:00. Diegetic cue: band and a singer, "You Must Have Been a Beautiful Baby."

(Continued)

Table 8-1 (*Continued*)

4. 0:08:52–0:14:30. Music in with a soft stinger chord as Wally realizes something is wrong; music continues into the next scene.

—Mildred, Veda, and the police; 0:12:05 Mildred arrives at her house/police/Veda; 0:13:35 at police station; several characters come in and out; 0:16:40 Mildred in Inspector Peterson's office.

(4. continues to 0:14:30, just after Mildred enters the back area of the police station)

FIRST FLASHBACK (DIVORCE THROUGH OPENING THE RESTAURANT)

—Family life. 0:20:15 flashback; real estate office/Bert—Mildred as narrator; 0:25:00 children, outside, then in the house; 0:28:20 Mildred doing bills; 0:29:00 Wally appears; 0:32:00 Mildred talks to Veda upstairs.

5. 0:20:15–0:21:25. Music in with the dissolve to the flashback. Theme #2 is heard the first time.

6. 0:24:25–0:26:07. Music in as conversation ends and Bert resolves to leave. Theme #3 is heard for the first time at 0:25:00, with cut to children playing outdoors. Music out as Kay and Veda enter the house.

7. 0:26:39 and 0:27:25. Veda at the piano plays the opening of Chopin, Waltz in E-flat Major, Op. 18, twice (offscreen, then onscreen).

8. 0:28:13–0:29:04. Music in as Mildred reacts to Veda's spiteful remark; out as Wally arrives at the house.

9. 0:32:05–0:34:40. Music in as Mildred goes upstairs to talk with Veda; music continues into the next scene.

—Mildred; restaurant. 0:34:05 Mildred job hunting; restaurant; 0:39:00 Mildred and Veda argue; 0:40:30 Mildred visits Wally; 0:42:45 Wally/Mildred/visit Beragon beach house.

(9.–continues to 0:34:40, just after Mildred enters the restaurant)

10. 0:36:12–0:37:38. Montage cue as Mildred starts restaurant work. Theme #4 is heard first at the beginning of this cue. Music out as Mildred arrives home, talks to Lottie (Butterfly McQueen).

11. 0:37:38–0:38:12. Diegetic cue slips under the end of cue 10. "South American Way" played and sung by the girls.

12. 0:38:49–0:40:28. Initially, a diegetic cue: Veda briefly plays Chopin, Mazurka in B-flat Major, Op. 7 no. 1; blends into nondiegetic cue from about 0:39:08; music out as Mildred and Veda's argument heats up.

13. 0:42:35–0:43:30. Music in to overlap; out as Monty enters the room.

—Death of Kay. 0:46:05 home, Mildred and Bert talk about divorce—Bert, children, preparing for trip; 0:48:15 new restaurant, Mildred/Monty; 0:49:40 beach house, Mildred/Monty; 0:53:15 home, Bert, rain.

14. 0:48:05–0:48:25. Short transitional cue. Music in as Mildred watches Bert and the children leave; out in the restaurant.

15. 0:49:40–0:50:00. Another transitional cue: in with kiss; out with cut inside the beach house.

16. 0:50:48–0:53:15. Music in for swimming; out under loud waves effect but diegetic cue follows without a break: phonograph plays an arrangement of "It Can't Be Wrong" (this is Theme #5, heard the first time—the song is based on Steiner's main theme for *Now, Voyager* [1942]). The song finishes and we hear noise of the phonograph needle for several seconds.

17. 17. 0:54:08–0:57:40. Music enters as Bert says "pneumonia"; overlaps into the next scene.

—Back to restaurant. 0:57:25 restaurant opening; 01:03:40 Mildred/Monty talk after restaurant, then Bert arrives.

(17. Overlaps for a few seconds into the first scene.)

18. 0:57:45–0:59:05. apparently diegetic cue: low-level music from an unseen sound system; out with cut to the kitchen.

19. 19. 0:59:48–1:02:55. Diegetic cue again with cut back to the restaurant—this time, however, the music continues through a brief cut back to the restaurant; overlaps and fades into nondiegetic cue at 1:01:45; then suddenly back to a diegetic cue with cut to bar area at 1:01:53 ("Please Think of Me" played on foregrounded jukebox, later sung by Wally).

20. 1:03:44–1:05:50. Music in at "Kay died"; out during the whip dissolve to the next scene.

BACK TO CURRENT TIME

1:05:45 Back to Inspector Peterson's office; near the end Mildred says, "I killed him."

SECOND FLASHBACK CONTINUES STORY (SUCCESS THROUGH RE-MARRIAGE)

—Mildred's success in business 1:08:00 to restaurants; success; 1:09:40 Mildred's office; Mildred/Wally argue over Monty; then Mildred/Ida; then Monty and Veda enter; 1:13:00 Veda receives car as present.

21. 1:08:00–1:09:40. Music in with dissolve for montage, overlaps with diegetic dance music cue, which in turn overlaps cut to Mildred and Wally talking in restaurant office.

22. 1:13:25–1:16:00. Music in as Kay goes outside to drive the car, out under the diegetic cue with cut to Wally's club.

—Veda's marriage 1:15:55 Wally's club, with Ted and Veda; 1:16:50 Mildred's office, Mrs. Forrester; 1:18:24 Mildred's house/Wally/Veda; 1:19:50 Forrester lawyer's office.

23. 1:16:00–1:16:52. Diegetic cue (band in background playing "You Must Have Been a Beautiful Baby"); out abruptly with cut to Mildred's office.

24. 1:18:24–1:19:50. Music in with Mildred's return home after conversation with Mrs. Forrester; briefly out at 1:18:51; out with dissolve to lawyer's office.

—Veda leaves 1:21:38 house; Mildred/Veda; they argue; 1:24:35 Mildred returns to restaurant after traveling; 1:27:45 Wally's bar/Bert/Mildred; 1:29:30 dressing room.

25. 1:21:38–1:24:35. Music in with the scene change, continues through argument and brief travel montage, going out as Mildred arrives back at the restaurant.

26. 1:27:45–1:32:08. Diegetic music in (heard from outside Wally's bar, then inside): introduction, then "The Oceana Roll" sung by Veda. Band immediately goes to "Sweet Georgia Brown" when she finishes; heard offscreen during dressing room scene. Music finishes and cut coincides.

—Mildred and Monty; Veda returns; 1:32:08 Monty's large house/Mildred; 1:35:45 marriage; redecorated house/Bert visits; 1:38:00 Veda returns; 1:39:40 Monty enters.

27. 1:35:45–1:36:05. Transitional cue—music in with effect "gag" (music imitates sound of clinking glasses).

28. 1:37:05–1:40:10. Music in when Bert asks if Mildred loves Monty, goes out with change to Veda's birthday party.

(Continued)

Table 8-1 (*Continued*)

—The fatal evening 1:40:00 Veda's birthday party (evening of the "present"); 1:41:10 Mildred calls from the office; 1:42:40 "Monty" (it's revealed that the financial crack-down is his idea); 1:44:03 beach house.

   29. 1:42:40–1:44:15. Music in with quiet stinger chord, builds in intensity till the end, overlapping slightly with return to present time.

CLIMAX AND CONCLUSION

1:44:12 Peterson's office; 1:45:20 beach house/Mildred, then Monty/Veda; 1:49:23 Peterson's office; 1:50:20 outside. Sunrise/Mildred/Bert; end credit in at 1:50:34.

   30. 1:44:36–1:46:00. Music in with the door opening as Veda is brought in; out as Veda speaks when Mildred finds Monty and her together in the beach house.

   31. 1:46:06–1:50:40. Music in with Mildred's reaction, out for a few seconds, then in as Veda is taken away.

Figure 8-1. *Mildred Pierce* (1945). Themes: (a) Mildred. (b) Bert. (c) Children. (d) "Work." (e) "It Can't Be Wrong" (transcriptions from the sound track).

It is also not necessary to have access to formal cue lists or song lists to develop a description of the music in a complete film. Listing entry and exit times, collating these with scenes, and then describing or summarizing the character and function(s) of the music works quite well for most purposes. This can, however, become tedious in films with very large amounts of music, especially when one wants to list and label recurrent themes. We have come close to a reasonable limit in Table 8-1, thanks to the large number of relatively short underscoring cues combined with a dozen diegetic cues. Where the cues segue (transition directly) into one another, we have grouped them together under one number—see, for example, items 16 and 19 in Table 8-1.

As with the musical notation of themes, it can be helpful though it is not necessary to supply specific titles for music reuses (such as the song "You Must Have Been a Beautiful Baby" or the Chopin Waltz in E-flat Major that appear here). A reuse is existing music that is cited in the course of the film—by reproducing the original recording or through a new arrangement. In films since the mid-1980s, these are placed near the end of the credits and are usually listed in order of appearance in the film, a fact that can be very useful in making identifications. (A studio cue sheet—which is the legal document accounting for all music uses and reuses in a film—would resolve all this with precision, but cue sheets are generally not available unless you have a commercial or legal interest in the music licenses.) For older films such as *Mildred Pierce* you will have to go to reference sources for details of credits because early films almost never provide complete music credits. Such information can often be acquired from online sources. The International Movie Database (or IMDb) has generally reliable listings of song uses and reuses under "soundtracks."

Sound track CDs can sometimes help with cue titles and song titles and, of course, music tracks that you can collate with the film's music. Be aware, however, that sound track CDs vary widely in their contents: very few contain all the music in a film, and many do not have the music in the same order that it appears in the film. It is common, for example, to delete popular songs from CDs that highlight the symphonic background music—and vice versa for films with several featured songs. Thus, it can be a difficult and often unrewarding task to collate a sound track CD with the music of a film. Likewise, major online resources rarely have complete sound track listings, but they can serve as good resources for titles of popular songs, standards, and quotations from historical music, as we suggested earlier.

1. *Synopsis*

(1) Directed by Michael Curtiz and with a symphonic underscore by Max Steiner, *Mildred Pierce* (1945) tells the story of a woman who is divorced from her husband, builds a successful chain of restaurants, but is then bankrupted by her second husband and her social-climbing daughter. Despite Monte's (Zachary Scott) philandering and Veda's (Ann Blyth) selfish greed, Mildred (Joan Crawford) cannot deny either of them anything. The story is presented in three main sections: the middle of the night as Mildred is questioned by a policeman about the death of Monte, and two long flashback sequences. The classically modeled sound track emphasizes speech and Steiner's leitmotivic underscore, but also makes good dramatic use of sound effects and of its few diegetic music cues, one of which also passes over into the underscore. Overall, the distinction between past and present is highlighted by an exaggeratedly realistic sound ambience in the police station scenes, which have no music until the murderer is revealed; transitions are effected by Mildred's voice-over narration.

A synopsis paragraph may run from 150 to 200 words—the preceding one is just over 160. We have used all the elements of the template from Chapter 3. The first sentence gives basic background and a central piece of information: the narrative is concerned first and foremost with the title character. The second sentence provides more details about the cause of Mildred's ultimate failure: the behavior of two people who take advantage of her generosity. The third sentence is needed because the film's form is not a simple chronological narrative and because the frame for the narrative is not Mildred herself but the death of her second husband, who has been murdered in his beach house. The fourth and fifth sentences make general statements about the film's sound and music. Throughout this synopsis paragraph, it is important to avoid attempting a blow-by-blow account of the film's narrative.

The final sentence or sentences should constitute the report's thesis, which can be either a mainly descriptive generalization or some interpretive claim. The former is true of the synopsis paragraph presented previously: we assert that both diegetic and nondiegetic musics are effective, and that sound participates in distinguishing past and present segments. The evidence for these is in the details of the film's treatment of the sound track. It may be helpful to think in terms of one of the following templates presented in Chapter 3: "<THEME> is reflected in <COMPOSER>'s handling of the music over the course of the film"; or "<COMPOSER>'s score contributes significantly to representing <THEME>." If we wanted to emphasize interpretation more, we might refashion the final sentence to read something like this: "The sharp contrast between the sound of present and past raises doubts about the reliability of Mildred's story, and [I will argue that] the underscore contributes significantly to that effect." We have obviously used the second of the templates in our example, but the first clause reveals that we are focusing on something that is not readily available in the details or experience of the film but which might be understood as an element of the narration that needs to be uncovered, interpreted. Our sentence needs some further editing, however: the theme remains vague—it is hard to imagine that the film is really about the "unreliability of Mildred's story." Instead, that unreliability suggests that Mildred, even at this late date (she knows that Veda killed Monte), cannot detach herself from her unworthy child and continues to seek to protect her. Thus, we might rewrite the sentence as "The sharp contrast between the sound of present and past raises doubts about the reliability of Mildred's story and suggests that the underscore—but not the diegetic music—is complicit in Mildred's desperate attempt to draw blame on herself in order to protect Veda."

To summarize: The first sentence should introduce the film, give pertinent information and a thematic description of the film. The second sentence (or possibly second and third, as in our example synopsis) should focus on the particulars of the main characters. The next sentence should combine remarks about narrative technique with a sketch of the narrative arc. The paragraph should end with a thesis statement that connects the music to a thematic concern of the film and that can segue to the main body of the text.

2. *General description and evaluation of the sound track elements and their balance, with examples*

(2a) During the establishing sequence and a series of opening scenes, music is almost constantly present (all underscore, except for one diegetic song performance), but then it overlaps into and drops out of the police station scene (at 14:00; music goes out around 14:30). Exaggerated reverberation in the station and a series of accented sound effects emphasize Mildred's nervousness, but in the detective's office the sound flattens out as he and Mildred talk. This same dull ambience is maintained during the first return to present time (at 1:05:55) and the early moments of the second (and final) return at 1:44:20, until the police bring in and identify Veda as the killer, which prompts a flashback of the murder. Music drops out briefly with the final return to present time (1:49:40), quickly reappears as Mildred and Veda talk, the policeman tells Mildred she can leave, and she finds Bert (Bruce Bennett), her first husband, waiting for her outside.

(2b) The burden of music's narrative work is borne by Steiner's orchestral underscoring, which covers about 50 minutes of the film's 111 minutes runtime. The underscore cues consist mostly of variations of themes associated with Mildred and her family. Sound in the flashback scenes may be characterized as alternating between speech with subdued effects and speech or action with underscore. Thus, the film can be said to have three levels of sound: two for the flashbacks, and one for present time.

(2c) Diegetic music occurs in the flashbacks, with one exception—and even that is a reference to performances we will hear in the second flashback. There is no ambiguity about the status of the diegetic music, though one theme does cross over between the diegetic and the nondiegetic.

(2d) Several instances of foregrounded effects are important: loud gun shots, the ring of the policeman's baton hitting the metal railing on the dock, the clock ticking loudly in the police station. All are associated with, and force attention to, the film's "present" time. Along with Mildred's voice-over, they reinforce the separation between the two times of the narration.

This description constitutes a brief statement (at 340 words) that summarizes how the sound track operates, how music works within it, and how these relate to the theme articulated in paragraph 1.

Some questions to consider when writing the second section of your report (not all of them will apply):

- How much of the music is diegetic/nondiegetic? (You can report this as rough percentages, map out the film in terms of scenes, or, if you have access to a copy of the film, a precise count of minutes.) What percentage of the scenes feature sound effects?
- How much ambient sound does the film use? Do certain scenes feature ambient sound more than others? What might be the reasons the filmmakers chose to feature ambient sound?
- What style(s) of music is/are used most often? What types of instrumental ensembles?
- Are there diegetic musical performances? If so, how are they treated? Are there recurring themes in the film? If so, are they attached to any specific characters, places, events, or ideas?

- Are effects used in scenes with dialogue? Which scenes? What do effects seem to be doing in these scenes?
- Are effects used in scenes with music? Which scenes? What do the effects seem to be doing in these scenes?
- Do effects and music seem to be working to establish a mood together or do they seem more in conflict?
- What elements of the sound seem realistic? What elements seem stylized?
- What are the most memorable sounds and/or music of the film?
- Are there any nondiegetic or extradiegetic sound effects? What are the reasons the filmmakers used sound effects this way? Does the film feature any recurring sounds (water, trains, explosions, etc.)? If so, what might be the reasons the filmmakers chose this recurring sound?

One effective strategy is to offer specific contestable statement(s) about the way(s) music and/or sound represents the film's theme. These generally work best when tied to your thesis statement at the end of paragraph 1. Some of the information used for the general description of music and/or sound could be a useful transition into this section. For example:

- Are there recurring musical themes that provide pertinent narrative information about plot and/or character at crucial moments in the film?
- If there are song performances, does their treatment change throughout the course of the film in any significant way? Are musical styles used to distinguish particular characters or settings?
- Are there recurring sounds that provide pertinent narrative information about plot, setting, and/or character at crucial moments in the film?
- Are there any sounds that seem particularly important either narratively or thematically?
- Does the treatment of sound change in any systematic way throughout the course of the film?

You might think about how some specific concepts might intersect with the film's theme. Here are two samples of prompting questions that might apply to individual films:

- How might the film's use of audio dissolve play into a thematic concern that touches on the concept of an idealized world?
- How might the film's use of important sync points (such as explosions) play into a thematic concern that touches on the notion of community and/or personal relationships forged in the film and the threats posed?

In general, you want to be as specific as possible in describing the music and/or sound. It is not enough to say that the music sounds "sad." You want to reflect on that sadness: What musical characteristics make it sound sad? Whose sadness is the music expressing? How can you tell that the music is representing the emotion of a singular character and not the general emotion of the scene? Likewise, it is not enough to say that the effects sound "realistic." What work is such realism (or lack of realism) doing in the film? To what elements of the film do sound effects seem to draw our attention?

   3. *Conclusion*

(3) By the standards of the classical studio system, *Mildred Pierce* has a sophisticated sound track that makes use of all its elements to good narrative effect. The quality of ambient sound helps maintain the distinction between present and past time. The symphonic underscore is applied to the dramatic situations of the film's opening (the murder, Mildred's attempt at suicide, her deception of Wally, the arrival of the police, and her going to the police station), but thereafter its chain of associative themes is linked with the events of memory and, thus, closely to Mildred herself.

The conclusion relates the discussion of the sound track in the second section (paragraphs 2a–2d, preceding) to the narrative theme or plot points or illustrates aspects of characterization. To formulate a conclusion, look back at the details discussed in your second section and try to synthesize them into a summarizing statement. Our summary for *Mildred Pierce* (at just under 100 words) once again emphasizes the full use of the sound track elements and their contribution to the basic narrative frame and progression.

Other Approaches to *Mildred Pierce*

Claudia Gorbman has written an essay on the music for *Mildred Pierce*. That essay appears at the end of a book chapter that delineates "seven rules" for nondiegetic music in the classical Hollywood sound film.[1] Thus, it is not surprising that Gorbman's initial thesis statement announces a descriptive and analytical paper: "I will now emphasize the 'unity' principle [that is, her "rule" 6] by exploring the film's use of musical themes in the context of its narrative." Gorbman adds another sentence, however, with another thesis, one that is clearly interpretive: "I will also suggest ways in which Steiner's compositional style, above and beyond its adequacy to the classical Hollywood model, is paradigmatic for melodrama in particular." In other words, she is making a stylistic claim: that the specific way in which Steiner deploys nondiegetic music is especially appropriate to a particular genre of films, the melodrama or women's film of the 1930s and 1940s. Granted, a generalization like this relies on external knowledge—familiarity with other films in that genre—but Gorbman stays very close to *Mildred Pierce* in working her argument out.

   The essay runs just under 2,500 words. After some introductory background information on Steiner, Gorbman asserts that "only in actively deciding to listen for the music will we realize how structured and repetitive it is, and how central to our emotional reception of the narrated events," and the bulk of the essay then marshals evidence of the presentation, recurrence, and variation of five melodies (associative themes or leitmotifs). At the end, she ties Steiner's Mickey-Mousing and other ways of closely "coordinating [music] with diegetic action" to the "'melodramatic spirit'— a desire to externalize and explicate all inflections of action, from emotional values in a scene to the very rhythms of physical movement. . . . On several levels, . . . the musical score exhibits a pronounced tendency toward hyperexplication. . . . Just as melodrama displays a tendency to use the close-up on the female star's face . . . Steiner's music has a similar effect." Finally, then "the background score has a key function of guiding the spectator-auditor unambiguously into [a] particularly compelling [emotional] identification." Because such emotional identification is fundamental to the film melodrama, a repetitious, "hyperexplicative" music is especially effective and meaningful. (By implication, such music will not be so effective in all genres—but that is another thesis and another essay.)

In terms of the context of Gorbman's argument, her attention to Max Steiner is fully justified. In structuring his underscore almost entirely on themes and their development, Steiner was firmly in the center of a classical tradition that he himself helped to create: "[He] clearly bore in mind the difference between the referential function of a musical theme, 'understanding a melody,' and the theme's emotive function: 'if it gets too decorative, it loses its emotional appeal.' It almost goes without saying that both functions of themes in the film score are 'subordinated . . . to the picture,' to the narrative discourse." (In this quotation from Gorbman, the internal quotes are from Steiner himself.)

We might consider approaching the film's music in an entirely different way. Although the diegetic music cues are few in comparison with the symphonic cues, one could argue that several are highlighted and so bear special significance. If we wanted to base a screening report on this idea, we might write a thesis statement like this: "Against the conventional treatment of the underscore, the diegetic music is carefully placed to emphasize the triangle of Veda, Mildred, and Monte, and thus reinforces the central dramatic tension of the narrative." Table 8-2 isolates the diegetic cues from Table 8-1. The first diegetic cue (no. 3 in the list) would have been appreciated as an insider's joke by those who knew the James Cain novel on which the film is based: a bitter, ironic reference to Veda as we hear "You Must Have Been a Beautiful Baby" from a singer in the scene background while we see Mildred in the foreground. But the viewer who did not catch the reference would realize the connection when Veda performs on the same stage later in the film (no. 26, set up by the band's repetition of "You Must Have Been a Beautiful Baby" in no. 25). This song is the only diegetic music that passes between present time and the flashbacks. Similarly, the only crossover between the diegetic and nondiegetic music is cue no. 16, first heard as the phonograph record playing in the beach house, background for the only romantic scene between Mildred and Monte. Although the music on the phonograph is by Steiner, there is no ambiguity about its status (especially as it is arranged in a popular lyrical style). This theme does appear a few times in the nondiegetic music later (not documented in Table 8-2). Here again the reader of James Cain's novel would appreciate the irony: "It Can't Be Wrong" is hardly the way to characterize the outcome of Mildred and Monte's relationship. Overall, the positive aspects of Mildred's ambitions for Veda are reflected in the two Chopin quotes (nos. 6 and 12), the negative outcomes in the performances in Wally's club. Mildred and Monte are linked through the beach house theme. We might well make a point of the fact that Veda and Monte are never linked musically.

Still another approach would draw particular attention to the many stingers in music and effects. In the sample screening report, we referred to "several instances of foregrounded effects. . . . [that] are associated with, and force attention to, the film's 'present' time." As a variation on the thesis of differences in the sound track as linked to the film's past/present dichotomy, we could trace a hierarchical patterning of stingers through the film, an audiovisual phrasing whose accents are primarily in the present early in the film—gun shots, the ring of the policeman's baton on the metal railing, the loud clock ticking in the police station—but then move mostly into the nondiegetic music in the flashbacks, until past and present are merged in the second iteration of the gun shots (at 1:47:30, just 3 minutes from

Table 8-2 *Mildred Pierce*. **Diegetic music cues.**

"CURRENT TIME"; LATE EVENING

3. 0:03:55–0:06:00. (Diegetic): band and singer, "You Must Have Been a Beautiful Baby"

FIRST FLASHBACK (DIVORCE THROUGH OPENING THE RESTAURANT)

7. 0:26:39, 0:27:25. Veda plays Chopin, Waltz in E-flat Major, Op. 18, twice (offscreen, then onscreen)

11. 0:37:38–0:38:12. Diegetic cue slips in under the end of underscore cue 10. "South American Way" played and sung by the girls

12. 0:38:49–0:40:28. Veda briefly plays Chopin, Mazurka in B-flat Major, Op. 7 no. 1; blends into nondiegetic cue at about 0:39:08

16. 0:50:48–0:53:15. Loud wave effect, then phonograph plays an arrangement of "It Can't Be Wrong" (Theme #5: see Figure 8.1e). The song finishes; noise of the phonograph needle continues for several seconds.

18. 0:57:45–0:59:05. Apparently diegetic cue: low-level music from an unseen sound system; out with cut to the kitchen

19. 0:59:48–1:02:55. Diegetic cue in with cut back to the restaurant, overlaps and fades into nondiegetic cue at 1:01:45; back to a diegetic cue suddenly with cut to bar area at 1:01:53 ("Please Think of Me" on a foregrounded jukebox, later sung by Wally).

SECOND FLASHBACK CONTINUES STORY (SUCCESS THROUGH RE-MARRIAGE)

21. 1:08:00–1:09:40. After a montage, a diegetic dance music cue, which then overlaps the cut to Mildred and Wally talking in restaurant office

22. 1:13:25–1:16:00. Music in as Veda goes outside to drive the car, out under the diegetic cue with cut to Wally's club

23. 1:16:00–1:16:52. Diegetic cue (band in background playing "You Must Have Been a Beautiful Baby"); out abruptly with cut to Mildred's office

26. 1:27:45–1:32:08. Diegetic music in (heard from outside Wally's bar, then inside): introduction, then "Oceana Roll" sung by Veda. Band immediately goes to "Sweet Georgia Brown" when she finishes; heard offscreen during dressing room scene. Music finishes and cut coincides.

the end). If the argument is primarily to the hierarchy, then details might be based on close synchronization. Among a number of such scenes in *Mildred Pierce* one stands out that involves extended Mickey-Mousing. The scene is near the beginning of the film. Wally has been locked inside a beach house after he tries (clumsily) to seduce Mildred; she sneaks out, locking him inside (with a dead body, as it turns out). Wally is basically a comic character who has been duped by Mildred, and he now looks a bit of a fool as he crashes about the house trying to find a way out (Figure 8-2). We learn from this episode that Wally, who has been onscreen nearly from the beginning of the film, is actually a minor character, and we also discover that Mildred is a resourceful risk-taker. The music owes a debt to silent-film era musical topics of the "mysterioso," "the grotesque," or "light agitato," which often played not just to scenes of danger or threat but also to active comedic scenes. Steiner sometimes headed similar cues in his scores with terms like "mysterioso— screwy" or "screwyissimo." A starting point for discussion might be the question of why this scene is so long, surely much longer than it needed to be to make its point.

The last in our list of alternative approaches builds on an unusual feature of the main title cue. As we would expect of a film named after a character (especially a woman), the main title cue is a single theme that is specifically associated with Mildred. This music, however, is not a love theme. It might have been, but its orchestration and volume are too blatant and harsh. Note especially the brass instruments blaring so hard they sometimes go out of tune. This presentation of the theme speaks not to love but instead to the difficult, ultimately tragic circumstances

Figure 8-2. *Mildred Pierce*. Wally is locked in the beach house.

of Mildred's life. The first three notes of the theme, indeed, are a rhythmic mimicking of her name—"Mildred Pierce"—and this motive is used repeatedly in the underscore, reserved particularly for dramatic moments that affect Mildred personally. From this information, we might develop a thesis that focuses, not so much on the underscore as on this particular element of it as point-of-view music, and that involves a leitmotivic tracing through the events of the narrative.

Concluding Comments

Just as in any writing you do, you may bring to bear any specialized knowledge you have: about film production, film history, actor or other personnel biography, the repertoire of a certain film genre or national film tradition, cultural studies, or music theory and history. We have tried to cover modes of description and models that will be useful to most writers, but you could certainly enrich a screening report with transcriptions of the themes in music notation (as we did) or more systematically listed connections between the sound track and continuity editing. Similarly, comments on style and genre can benefit from a broad grasp of the common historical narratives, cultural analyses can be better grounded through a knowledge of critical or music theory, and any study of narrative film can make use of some basic skills in narratology. Nevertheless, as we have tried to demonstrate throughout this book, it is not necessary to have specialized knowledge or terminology to hear music in the sound track and to write about it productively.

At the same time, be careful not to distort your descriptions and interpretations by misjudging the role of music—or other sound track element—or the sound track as a whole. Because you are trying to pay attention to it, music may become decidedly more prominent in your perception of a film than would be the case if you had approached viewing the film in a "normal" way, with typical expectations for narrative films. By paying attention to *any* one element of a film for an extended period of time, you threaten to inadvertently "stylize" that film, to skew its hierarchy and flow of materials and events. (The easy fast forward and recall of the DVD and streaming player only make the problem more acute.) One of the most important skills for film music and film sound study is the ability to alternate—jump back and forth—between a "normal," open but critical mode of film viewing and a biased mode that gives particular attention to music or other elements of the sound track (or to the sound track as a whole). Even the scholarly literature has too many case studies that make exaggerated claims for music's influence and importance in a film because the analyst-author became so focused on the music that he or she was no longer able to position that music appropriately within the context of the film's mode of presentation.

Finally: *always* go back and double-check information you write up from memory. As we said in Chapter 1, films put a great deal of information out at the viewer, and it is extremely difficult to retain an accurate memory of scene details, including the specific interactions of music and action. As a reminder, you might consult Chapter 10 of Michel Chion's book *Audio-Vision*—early in the chapter he discusses two extended examples of faulty memory.[2]

From 1950 to 1975
The Stereo Sound Track and the Post-Classical Era

Introduction

Experimental work on stereo sound had begun already in the 1920s, when research was pursued, primarily by AT&T and RCA, as a means of improving the fidelity of recorded and transmitted sound. The collapse of the recording industry at the outset of the Great Depression and the limited bandwidth for transmitting radio broadcasts combined to discourage the immediate commercial exploitation of stereo sound. Film, on the other hand, was in a better position to exploit stereo than either the recording industry or radio. Studios did experiment with widescreen film and larger area for sound tracks (which offered both higher fidelity and a wider dynamic range) during the early sound era, culminating in the Fox Grandeur system (see Figure 9-1). The film industry, however, was also financially stressed by the Depression, and the studios collectively decided it was in their best interest to consolidate and standardize sound-film production rather than spending money to rewire and re-equip their theaters and production facilities. Although stereo sound was commercially feasible by 1940—Disney deployed such a system for *Fantasia* (see Figure 9-2)—it would not be systematically exploited by the industry until the introduction of Cinemascope in the early 1950s.

Issues of High-Fidelity and Stereo Sound
LEGAL AND ECONOMIC CHALLENGES TO THE INDUSTRY

In a relatively short span of time following World War II, changes in technology, law, and social conditions prompted a move toward stereo sound. Technologically, the development of the long-playing record with a greater frequency response brought vast improvement to music in the home. The introduction of

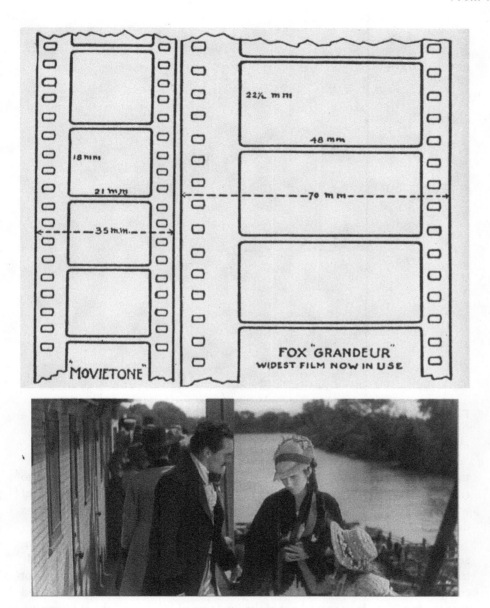

Figure 9-1. (a) A comparison of Movietone and Grandeur formats. Note, in particular, the larger space (between the left sprocket holes and the image) available for the sound track in the Grandeur format. (b) A frame from the Grandeur version of *The Big Trail* (1930), which was also shot in a regular 35 mm version. The Grandeur format was abandoned in the early 1930s due to cost and the limited number of theaters capable of exhibiting films in the format.

a
—
b

Figure 9-2. Sound mixers making a multitrack recording of the Philadelphia Orchestra for use in *Fantasia*. Eight channels were used, and a mixer was required to monitor each channel.

magnetic tape likewise allowed an efficient and relatively inexpensive way to record and mix sound into a number of channels. This also provided an efficient way to provide a variety of mixes, which proved expedient when many theaters decided against installing stereo sound.

The 1948 United States Supreme Court's decision on the Paramount consent decree (1940), which prohibited studios from owning theaters, completely transformed the economics of the film industry. The studios themselves did not collapse, but the traditional production practices of the studio system dissolved over the 1950s. As they moved out of the business of exhibition, the studios substantially reduced their rates of production. Most turned gradually toward a focus on financing and distribution, which was more profitable and seemingly less risky. Production grew increasingly independent, which placed a stronger burden on each film to be profitable because losses on one film could no longer be covered by gains on another. The emphasis on profit also led to a production strategy favoring fewer but more spectacular films because the latter films were more likely to generate a substantial profit. This tactic was by no means unknown during the studio era—in the 1930s, too, prestige films could generate the largest profits—but as an overall strategy it did represent a marked change from the studio era. Formerly, vertical integration, where studios were heavily invested in producing, distributing, and exhibiting films, had ensured that films made by a studio always found an exhibition outlet. This meant that during the studio era, regularity of production was as important to the industry as was turning out films that were considered "events." Over the course of the 1950s, however, more and more films emphasized spectacle and grandeur, and the introduction of the widescreen format and stereo sound furthered this goal. Smaller (and less expensive) films would continue to be made, but there were fewer of them, and production as a whole bifurcated into expensive, spectacular epics for general audiences on the one hand and inexpensive films made for niche audiences (especially the burgeoning youth market) on the other. This distinction was also mirrored in the sound track, where big films would be outfitted with a full symphony orchestra and stereo sound, but smaller films would make do with a small ensemble—if any original music was used at all—and monaural sound.

Finally, the demographic shift to the suburbs after the war moved the American movie audience farther from the central city theaters. Because of the Supreme Court decision, studios were not able to build theaters in the suburbs; but movie attendance was also declining, so the independent theaters did not rush in to service the suburbs either. The result was that the growing suburban population was often located far from theaters. At the same time, the extraordinarily fast dissemination of television meant that film needed to offer something more than was available on the small screen. Television was already having a devastating effect on film attendance. Even the most conservative estimates suggested that attendance by those with televisions had decreased by more than 20 percent in 1950. One study determined that television had caused a 3 percent to 4 percent fall in overall attendance. The erosion of the audience increased over the decade as ownership of televisions rapidly grew. In these circumstances, the only types of films that could reliably draw large audiences into the city were those that could be marketed as events worthy of making a special trip, and grand spectacles fit the bill. The largest central-city theaters were remade in the lavish manner of the old picture palaces in order to bolster the notion of an experience one couldn't have anywhere else.

Ironically, the consent decree insulated the studios from the full effects of the audience decline. The studios could adjust their production to the changes in audience, decreasing production as attendance fell. The theaters, on the other hand, had a fixed number of seats to sell. Moreover, the falling production of film titles generally gave the studios an upper hand in negotiating favorable terms with the theater owners. By the end of the decade, many theater owners had concluded that the consent decree had in fact benefited the studios. The thin to almost nonexistent profits of exhibition meant that only those top theaters specializing in spectacles could afford to invest in maintaining, much less upgrading, their sound systems. The other theaters—prominently among them the new drive-ins—serviced (smaller) local or niche markets and cut costs by retaining monaural sound.

WIDESCREEN AND STEREO FORMATS

Beyond the issue of financial risk, the lack of a standard for stereo hampered its adoption. Widescreen formats suffered from a similar lack of a clear standard, but the investment required for the larger screen, a different sprocket gauge on the projector, and special lenses was relatively modest compared to installing new sound systems, especially because those already available sounded far superior to the small speakers of the television (or radio and phonograph, for that matter). In terms of cost, it is significant that exhibiters were resistant not only to the requirements for stereo but also for the so-called "Miracle Mirror" screen, which produced a brighter, better defined image without the reflections common to other screens. When Twentieth Century Fox introduced Cinemascope, the studio initially demanded that theaters exhibiting films in the format install not only systems for reproducing sound in magnetic stereo but also the special screen. The importance of stereo to the original conception of Cinemascope can be seen in the fact that Twentieth Century Fox continued to insist on stereo installation a full 6 months after the company allowed the exhibition of Cinemascope films without the Miracle Mirror screen. When Twentieth Century Fox finally relented on stereo as well, its release prints contained two sound track formats: four-track magnetic and monaural optical (Figure 9-3).

Introduced commercially in 1952, Cinerama was another widescreen format that used stereo sound, but the system required specially equipped theaters and highly trained projectionists (Figure 9-4). In terms of sound, Cinerama offered a more advanced system, with seven-channel (five front, two rear) magnetic sound tracks. It was also costly, often requiring investments upward of $100,000 for the projection and sound equipment. Labor costs were high as well, requiring about half of the revenues to cover operating expenses. Although it was an attraction in its own right for a number of years—the Cinerama corporation acquired its own theaters for exhibition—it never proved viable for large-scale studio production. In this respect it played a role in film exhibition similar to the one that IMAX theaters play today—although Cinemarama was not as well integrated into feature film presentation as IMAX is.

Cinemascope was developed by Twentieth Century Fox on the model of Cinerama and turned out to be as close to an industry standard as would be possible once the studios decided that the move to widescreen was inevitable. Later in the decade the only two aspect ratios widely in use were 1.85:1 (the familiar 16:9 ratio developed by VistaVision and now the standard for HDTV) and 2.35:1 (the wider ratio of Cinemascope). Like Cinerama, Cinemascope used multitrack sound, with four channels arranged as in the Fantasound system Disney developed for *Fantasia*: center, right, left, and rear (surround; Figure 9-5). VistaVision used an optical track. "Perspecta" sound likewise used an optical track, with encoding to allow some—but not full—stereo separation.

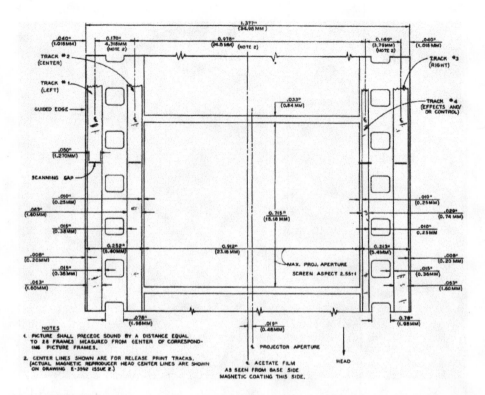

Figure 9-3. Schematic for Cinemascope film. The left channel runs outside the left sprocket, the center channel inside the left sprocket, the right channel outside the right sprocket. The track inside the right sprocket was used for the rear effects. Note that the aspect ratio of the image frame (about 1.27:1) is close to the academy ratio of traditional sound film (1.37:1). The film would be projected into widescreen format (here, 2.55:1) through the use of anamorphic lenses. Later, the format would be changed, allowing space on the print for both optical stereo and a regular monaural optical track, a change that required downsizing the image slightly (2.35:1).

Still another system, Todd-AO, used six tracks: five front speakers and one surround channel; this setup as a whole had a frequency response of 40–12,000 Hz (Figure 9-6). Although it was adopted by only a small group of elite first-run houses, Todd-AO was generally agreed to be an improvement on the sound of Cinemascope because the increased number of speakers reduced the effect of "channeling," the impression that the sound is issuing from a particular set of speakers rather than from the screen. Nevertheless, Todd-AO was employed almost exclusively for films planned for special roadshow exhibition and even then was seldom used because it required a special camera to take full advantage of the system.

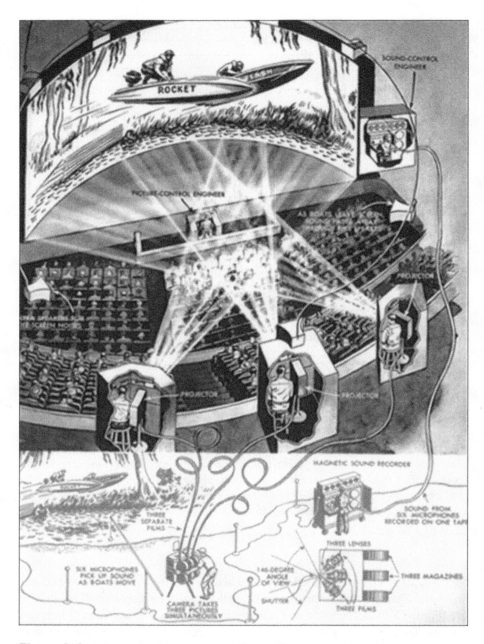

Figure 9-4. Schematic of Cinerama installation. The bottom shows the three-camera-in-one filming process, the top the projection system. The need to abut the images of the three projectors inevitably led to perceptible lines on the screen where the images joined. Consequently, directors avoided placing action at the seams, and indeed often staged the shot in three parts. Many of the shots in the Cinerama version of *How the West Was Won* (1962) were done this way. The system used a seven-track sound system, with five

Figure 9-5. Ad for Cinemascope showing a scene from *The Robe* (1953), the first Cinemascope feature. The huge curved screen was important to the effect of the spectacle, but so was the four-channel stereo. Note the three speaker horns positioned above the screen: left, center, right. Unlike typical theater installations, which hid speakers behind the screen, here the front speakers are clearly visible, like the curved screen, a display of technology. The fourth speaker was located in the rear of the auditorium.

The adoption of widescreen and the limited move to stereo sound along with tentative attempts at 3D film all point to a change in aesthetic sensibilities that were responses to changing consumption patterns of movie audiences in the wake of television and suburbanization. In what one critic calls the "aesthetics of sensation," audio and visual spectacle rose in importance in these films, vying with and sometimes even displacing the narrative needs for dialogue.[1] Such films became "events," precursors to the more standardized blockbuster production that dominates Hollywood filmmaking to this day. The 1960s and early 1970s saw a brief shift away from this mode of production, at least to the extent that the kinds of films that could succeed on the basis of spectacle changed

---

channels across the front and two in the rear. A Sound-Control Engineer (*upper right*) would mix the sound live to the theater according to a script, where, among other things, the two rear channels would be addressed to the proper configuration of rear speakers: right-left, right-center, or center-left.

Figure 9-6. This artist's rendition of an installation of Todd-AO (displaying a scene from *Oklahoma!* [1955]) shows five speakers in front and two on the side. The presence of the horns serves as a display of technology. Experiencing that technology was one of the draws of these shows.

markedly. The extraordinarily expensive *Cleopatra* (1963), the last of the gigantic "sword and sandal" epics until their recent resurrection—most notably in *Gladiator* (2000)—was a monumental flop, as were Twentieth Century Fox's follow-ups to the enormous success of *The Sound of Music* (1965): *Doctor Dolittle* (1967) and *Star!* (1968). The huge losses on these two musicals (more than $25 million) contributed significantly to a marked turn away from the genre. Smaller films with faster editing patterns and music that appealed to youth audiences proved far more profitable. In this environment, the narrower VistaVision aspect ratio came to dominate, especially outside Los Angeles. In the major Hollywood studios, however, Panavision was still favored, because it retained Cinemascope's wider aspect ratio, which filmmakers found encouraged slower editing patterns. Nevertheless, some films aimed at younger audiences, such as *The Graduate* (1967), continued to be released in the wider screen format (in that case Panavision) and with multichannel sound. The aesthetic of sensation and the widescreen would return with a vengeance in the 1970s, with the series of big disaster films, such as *Airport* (1970), *Earthquake* (1974), and *The Towering Inferno* (1974), as well as the New Hollywood "high-concept" blockbusters, such as *Jaws* (1975), *Star Wars* (1977), and *Close Encounters of the Third Kind* (1977). All of these films except *Jaws* were released in widescreen 70mm, and only *Jaws* was released with just a monaural sound track.

MAGNETIC TAPE IN PRODUCTION AND POSTPRODUCTION

Technologically, the biggest changes for the sound track in the 1950s and 1960s concerned the introduction of magnetic recording and stereo reproduction, which affected production and postproduction phases in both music and sound departments. Magnetic sound was the more basic: it was quickly adopted because it offered many advantages over optical sound in production and postproduction. Notably, it was more portable, offered superior fidelity, allowed many generations of rerecording, permitted filmmakers to exploit more dynamic range, especially on the soft end, and did not require further technical development. Its disadvantages arose only in distribution: optical sound was more robust in exhibition (the magnetic striping wore out more quickly than optical tracks) and it was cheaper (magnetic sound required a new sound head for the projector along with rewiring of the theaters because all magnetic striping on film was stereo).

The portability of magnetic tape facilitated location shooting, which became increasingly common over the 1950s and 1960s. Labor costs in particular were much higher in Hollywood, and foreign governments offered filmmakers generous financial incentives to move production overseas. Filmmakers found the foreign settings attractive along with the incentives, but taking full advantage of those settings meant moving the production outside and shooting on location rather than on a sound stage. Even in the United States, location shooting became far more common.

All of this location shooting altered the routine practice of relying on production sound almost exclusively for the capturing of dialogue. This in turn changed the nature of postproduction, especially with respect to the handling of dialogue. Although location shooting was common enough in the studio era, most dialogue continued to be shot in the controlled acoustic environment of the sound stage. On a sound stage, little was left to chance. The sets and lights were soundproofed, the crew was trained to remain silent, and things were arranged to get good microphone coverage. Obviously, an external environment could not be controlled to the same extent. A plane overhead, a police siren, a subway rumbling, a car driving by—these so-called "wild" sounds were captured by the microphone (even a good directional microphone) along with the actors' voices. In and of themselves, such wild sounds could increase the "realism" of the scene, because they placed the scene within an appropriate environment—although an airplane sound for a Western scene, say, would be a problem. Even when appropriate to the film, however, such wild sounds nevertheless severely handicapped the ability to edit a sequence because the exact sound present in one take would not necessarily be present in another.

This issue is an artifact of the way films were (and are) normally shot. Most dialogue scenes used a single camera with changing set-ups. After a master shot of a sequence was filmed, closer shots were taken, especially over-the-shoulder ones designed for shot/reverse-shot editing: first all the lines for one actor, then all the shots for another, and so forth. Note how this arrangement had the potential to pose difficulties for location sound. One actor's lines might have had a siren or subway in the background, whereas the second had an airplane going overhead or a car driving by. The final edit therefore might have to go something like: line 1 (siren in background), line 2 (plane overhead), line 3 (subway rumbles), line 4 (car goes zooming by), and so forth. Moreover, the sound of the siren, plane, subway, or car was unlikely to begin exactly when a line started and ended, so there would be an audible break of that environmental sound on the edit. To control for such problems, recordists usually used a second mike positioned solely for the purpose of capturing wild sounds so they could be added as needed behind other dialogue in editing. The recording of wild sounds thus allowed the impression of continuity in the background, and such continuity would in turn ensure the unity of the action.

Location sound was difficult to control in other ways as well. For example, the environmental noises might simply prove too loud for effective dialogue recording, or the nature of the shot might allow no way to keep a microphone out of sight. (The increasingly common use of wide-angle lenses would help speed the development of effective body mikes.) Such issues would need to be addressed in postproduction either through manipulation of the audio by dialogue and sound editors or through looping (recall our discussion of this method, also known as ADR, in Chapter 4; see Figure 9-7).

In this way, sound work was moved more and more into postproduction, and the production sound—especially the wild environmental sound—simply became another layer to add to the mix. Mixing was often done to make the sound "big," both through compression and by the addition of layers. In general, the result was thinking more in terms of "building" a sound track, where sounds were mixed as much on the basis of inherent aesthetic effect as "naturalism" or even for narrative clarity.

Figure 9-7. *The Good, the Bad, and the Ugly* (1966). Automated dialogue replacement (ADR) became increasingly common during the 1960s. Indeed, the so-called "spaghetti westerns" of Sergio Leone relied exclusively on the technique. Each actor in the international cast would speak lines in his or her own language and the lines would be dubbed in the appropriate language during postproduction.

In this sense the paradoxically constructed realism of location shooting ran to an extent against the more artificial manipulation of the sound track. As the shooting went outside, the recording moved into the studio.

ISSUES OF STEREO

Stereo faced two substantial obstacles: Its slow adoption by the theaters prevented it from affecting filmmaking to the same extent as magnetic sound; and it required significant conceptual adjustments. For stereo changed the terms of representation, destabilizing the narrative hierarchy in the process. In classical sound practice, filmmakers had allied perspective with narrative hierarchy. With monaural sound, the placement of microphones on the basis of shot scale was a relatively subtle technique that principally affected the amount of reflected sound recorded (due to the directionality of the microphone). Such fine gradations of distance did not threaten to overwhelm our sense of the continuity of background, which could be maintained across fairly large shifts in shot scale. Due to the aural perspective permitted by stereo imaging, however, sounds recorded in stereo are much more sensitive to microphone distance; that is, shot scale becomes much more audible. Producer Darryl Zanuck, the head of Twentieth Century Fox studios, advocated image composition and blocking that maximized stereo perspective. "Stereophonic sound," he argued, "is not effective when two people are face to face, unless of course they are in big close-ups or a big 2-shot. The full value of stereophonic sound comes from the distance between the two people who are talking. If one person is planted at one end of the set and the other person is on the other side of the set then the sound has an opportunity to add to the illusion of depth."[2]

One effect of this "illusion of depth" was the so-called "traveling dialogue." As characters moved across the screen—especially across the distances of a wide screen—stereo miking rendered the movement audible: dialogue and other sounds appeared to travel with the moving body. Stereo miking, particularly when coupled with shot scale, was also generally more sensitive to reflected sound, to the "presence" or ambience of the space, which increased with distance and was especially noticeable in reverberant spaces. In such spaces, cuts between shots markedly different in scale seemed audibly jarring to the extent that the audio backgrounds of the two shots were too distinct, threatening the continuity that subjugated the individual shots to the logic of the sequence.

Analysis: The Robe

In *The Robe* (1953), the first feature film shot in Cinemascope, the audio background shifts, sometimes markedly, with the scale of each shot (Figure 9-8). The trial of Marcellus before Caligula concludes the film. In this scene, the disjunctions in audio background continuity are especially acute, emphasized by the relative silence behind the dialogue, despite the presence of a crowd that might have been tapped as a source of ambient sound. The audio background in this scene is therefore carried primarily by room resonance, which varies quite strikingly with shot scale, even within individual speeches (listen, for instance, to Caligula's speech that begins "Senators, Romans" [2:02:57]). Throughout the sequence, crowd sounds appear only intermittently, generally in reaction to a particularly charged bit of dialogue, and music appears only in a quasi-diegetic mode of heralding entrances (brass fanfare representing the power and majesty

Figure 9-8. *The Robe* (1953). Caligula and Gallio exchange dialogue in widescreen space. Each voice is reproduced by a more or less spatially correct speaker. Although filmmakers at the time thought such effects should produce greater "realism," in fact many in the audience found the effect distracting, since it violated the cinematic norms established by monaural sound. The disruption was even more noticeable with changes in shot scale: not only was the reverberation altered, but the voice would jump from one speaker to another.

for Caligula; drums alone representing the fateful march to judgment for Marcellus). The crowd sounds and music therefore only add to the disjunctive quality of
the sound design in the sequence in that they punctuate dialogue. They do not
function as background continuity but as foreground sound effects, which, like
dialogue, simply fill in the silence that dominates the conception of background.

Although not as pronounced as the sound edits in the opening scene of *The
Broadway Melody* (1929), shifts in sound here nevertheless assert, at least on the
surface, the autonomy of the shot in the face of the narrative pressure and need of
the sequence. Only at the very end of the sequence, in response to Caligula's judgment on Marcellus and Diana, does nondiegetic music displace silence as the
figure of background continuity. The music appears here, first of all, to mark the
gravity of the verdict, the muted brass sounding as a transformation of Caligula's
fanfare, indicative of the world awry, an abuse of worldly power. Against the
muted brass, a wordless chorus, which had been introduced over the opening
credits and throughout the film associated with the figure of Christ (particularly
with the entrance into Jerusalem on Palm Sunday), rises up and comes to dominate the orchestration. As Marcellus and Diana recede from Caligula's throne,
the seat of worldly power, toward their execution, the music swells, marking sonically the passage from the rule of Rome to the rule of God. The symbolism here
is emphasized by the way the music is mixed to dominate Caligula's desperately
sarcastic line, "They're going into a better kingdom" (2:12:06) and by the shift to
offscreen sound for Caligula's final line, "They're going to meet their King,"
which renders him completely impotent: His voice, although it speaks the truth
despite itself, simply becomes irrelevant—the music remains wholly indifferent
to his interjections—in the absence of his body, the site of his power as Caesar.

In this respect, it is interesting to compare the treatment of Diana's final line
as she delivers the robe to a Christian in the crowd. Here the music seems to
listen to her dialogue, to make way for her line, "for the big fisherman," suggesting that she, unlike Caligula, has the ear of God. If God thus becomes an audible
presence through the mixing of the sound track, the deployment of sound, especially music, at the end of the sequence allows a somewhat different interpretation
of the seemingly incoherent sound design in the earlier part of the sequence: what
is represented there is the rule of Caligula as God-forsaken. The bodily presence
of Caligula, even his speech, is unable to hold the sound together in a coherent
way. The regal music, which serves to mark his presence and underscore his
power especially in contrast to Marcellus, only works to further the incoherence of
the sound design in the early part of the sequence. Music and sound only come to
serve coherence when they represent divine rather than worldly power.

STEREO AND SPACE

Although stereo sound is used effectively in the final sequence of *The Robe* because its disjunctions were mined for symbolic value, it proved difficult to control
the directionality of dialogue recorded in stereo, with the result that many viewers found traveling dialogue distracting. Audiences were acclimated to monaural

sound, and, however "realistic" it might be, having dialogue move with the characters seemed representationally uncanny and unnatural. The shifts in perspective also tended to underscore the autonomy of the shot at the expense of the integration of the shot into the sequence. These shifts were undermining the narrative hierarchy of foreground and background, and therefore the challenge was, as with the coming of sound, how to construct a consistent aural background against which the foreground sound events could be interpreted.

The solution ultimately adopted was to channel sound according to function. Onscreen dialogue and most foreground sound effects were recorded in monaural sound and played on the center channel (or perhaps slightly panned to location), thus mimicking the standard optical sound track, whereas background (underscoring and ambient sound) was rendered in stereo in the side speakers; offscreen sound would be highly channeled to the appropriate side speaker as well. The rear speaker, little used, was reserved for special "surround" effects such as offscreen cannons in *Battle Cry* (1955), which Darryl Zanuck reported as "a tremendous and realistic thrill when you hear the roar of the cannon coming from behind you and then it seems to pass over your head and land on the screen in the distance."[3]

SILENCE

Given the circumstances of the stereo sound track, it will not be surprising that silence, or the complete absence of effects and ambient sound, was not (and is not) commonly used in films because it tends to instill doubts about the film's physical world. We might make an analogy with the image track, where black or white backgrounds have the effect of destroying all depth cues. In the unusual case of Stanley Kubrick's *2001: A Space Odyssey* (1968), this effect of eliminating depth is mitigated by the fact that silence defines the background of space just as the hum defines that of the space station. In the world of the film, silence *is* the sound of space. More important, it matches the depth-destroying black background of space. Although this can be justified by an appeal to realism—space *is* black and silent—it also serves to define the depth of space as unfathomable. To regress into the "space" of the background is to be removed from and to lose contact with the place of the film, which is constrained by the limits of the station. Every trip to the black silence of space is fraught with the possibility of death. Silence, too, serves as the analogue to death. In terms of sound, this is emphasized in the first instance by the loss of radio contact and in the second by the intense, sound-track consuming breathing of Dave as he returns from silent space and moves through the station to disassemble (and kill) HAL.

Production

PRODUCTION PHASES

Despite the technological changes, the job descriptions in both sound and music departments were largely unchanged from the studio era, although work was done more and more on a freelance basis. In other words, workers were hired by the production company rather than the studio, which was now focused on finance and distribution. This change reduced job security but increased flexibility in that organizational charts, chains of command, and job descriptions could differ markedly from film to film. Increased location shooting paradoxically meant that even more sound track work was moved into postproduction.

MUSIC DEPARTMENT

The dissolution of the studio system had a direct impact on the music department, which had all but disappeared by 1960. In 1958, the studios did not renew their standing contracts with the studio musicians, making all but a few music workers into freelancers. Only the heads of the music departments and a few other managerial personnel were retained. Even the role of the music director was diminished inasmuch as the music personnel were now hired by the production company rather than by the studio.

Aside from the fact that employment was less secure, the basic work of the music department on a film remained much as it had during the studio era. Composers were still the head of the creative team, and they still worked with music editors and orchestrators (Figure 9-9). With all the freelance work that needed to be organized, the music contractor played an increasingly visible supporting role. (The contractor was responsible for hiring the musicians for recording. A similar position had existed in the studio days, but the position assumed new importance when the orchestra had to be assembled from scratch for each production.) Much work was moved out of Hollywood to save money, and more and more existing symphony orchestras would be hired to record scores. (The London Symphony Orchestra was a particular favorite.)

The importance of the soundtrack album as an ancillary product meant that composers (and orchestrators and arrangers) needed to devote time to crafting and recording it in addition to their work on the score for the film. Because the soundtrack album was part of the promotional materials for the film, it also needed to be completed during the postproduction phase—indeed often in advance of the closing of postproduction. The soundtrack album added considerably to the workload of the music department as in many respects it was an entirely separate entity from the film score.

SOUND DEPARTMENT

The trend toward location shooting increased the amount of work done in postproduction, as production sound could no longer be relied on for a clean dialogue recording. Dialogue editing became more complex, as a good deal of dialogue was now rerecorded. ADR (looping) became a regular part of postproduction. The increased fidelity of magnetic tape allowed the regular use of multitrack mixing, which increased the complexity of the sound tracks, even those designed for monaural release. With the ability to make a number of preliminary mixes, sound editors could juggle more sounds at the same time, resulting in livelier sound tracks.

Figure 9-9. Franz Waxman and orchestrator Edward B. Powell during a recording session for *The Virgin Queen* (1955). By the end of the decade, the studio system would have dissolved and composers, orchestrators, and musicians would be working as independent contractors. Waxman himself was among the first composers to make this move from studio staff to freelance. Photo (c) John W. Waxman Collection. All rights reserved. International ©copyright secured. Used with permission.

As with magnetic tape, stereo sound required the development of new techniques and new equipment, but it did not substantively affect the nature of the job.

Stereo Sound, Magnetic Tape, and Elements of Style

ISSUES OF AESTHETICS

Stereo allowed for a number of changes to the sound track, the most important of which was a shift away from thinking of it in terms of tracks (dialogue, music, and effects) arranged hierarchically in foreground and background toward a concept of graduated layers. Among other things, this change allowed for an increased role for ambient sound and a more nuanced and textured sound track. When a dialogue scene needed ambience in the studio era, music had generally been the preferred choice because it was easier to control. With the increased fidelity of magnetic sound and stereo separation, however, ambient sounds could be used much more freely and at much greater volume, and thus it became possible for ambient sound to absorb some of the functions that had traditionally been reserved for music. Music might still perform this function on a stereo sound track, of course, but the tinkling of offscreen cowbells and the twittering of birds in the side channels could evoke the rural pastoral just as easily as music. The decision as to whether to render the ambience of a sequence through music or sound was now precisely that: a decision (Figure 9-10).

Figure 9-10. *2001: A Space Odyssey* (1968). The low noise of magnetic recording allowed a much greater role for silence—or rather the low-level ambient sound characteristic of quiet spaces. The soft wind and nature sounds in the "Dawn of Man" sequence, for instance, serve to underscore the serenity of the landscape, whereas disruptions of this basic quietude serve as figures of violence (but also of life).

SCORING PRACTICES

Music scoring practices in this era did not change markedly with the improvements in technology. Or, to put it another way, the methods of scoring films developed in the studio era remained common choices, especially for the most prestigious pictures. The romantic and post-romantic idiom based on the tradition of the symphony orchestra dominated epic films, such as *Ben-Hur* (1959), *The Ten Commandments* (1956), and the ill-fated *Cleopatra*; and, allowing for differences in genre, the orchestra remained the preferred ensemble in war films (*The Bridge on the River Kwai* [1957], *The Great Escape* [1963], and *Patton* [1970]), horror (*Creature from the Black Lagoon* [1954], *Psycho* [1960], and *The Devils* [1971]), and science fiction (*Fahrenheit 451* [1966], *Planet of the Apes* [1968], *THX 1138* [1971]). The musical language was expanded somewhat with the appropriation of advanced compositional techniques and popular idioms, especially jazz, but even in those cases scoring film remained grounded in the orchestra, and the approach to narrative remained mostly classical in orientation.

If it did not bring a marked change in approach, the new technologies of magnetic tape and stereo reproduction did yield subtle coloristic shifts. Stereo and the higher fidelity of the magnetic sound track made the traditional studio orchestra of twenty-five to thirty players sound anemic—especially compared to the full frequency recordings of orchestras then becoming commercially available for home consumption. The result was a move toward larger orchestras, especially for grand biblical epics such as *The Robe* or *Ben-Hur* or for sweeping westerns such as *The Big Country* (1958) or *The Magnificent Seven* (1960). The sound of the orchestra became an attraction in and of itself, as for instance in the long symphonic prologue to *How to Marry a Millionaire* (1953), which seemingly presents Alfred Newman's main title to *Street Scene* only to show off the quality of the musical reproduction. The stereo separation also allowed the music to be mixed at much higher levels, and for the scoring to be somewhat heavier without affecting the intelligibility of dialogue. Musicals, too, drew on the resources of an expanded orchestra and stereo separation for the orchestral backing to give the scores a more luxuriant sound (Figure 9-11).

The shift away from integrated studio production and exhibition to independent film production also brought with it a strong interest in developing ancillary products, and it was this focus that had the farthest reaching consequences for scoring films. Filmmakers became far more interested in the revenue recordings could generate (and the recording industry in general); and particular recordings, rather than simply songs, increasingly began to be featured in films. Musical tie-ins to films had been long recognized and exploited, and with the need for each film to maximize its profitability music was quickly put to work. Thus, although the basic approach to scoring a film remained relatively unchanged with the dissolution of the studio system, writing music that could be excerpted and marketed as a product in its own right became another part of the composer's task. This practice was in fact already common enough in the studio

Figure 9-11. *Silk Stockings* (1957). The exaggeration of widescreen space and stereo separation is used to humorous effect in Cole Porter's "Stereophonic Sound." The film was, of course, shot in Cinemascope and released with pseudo-stereo Perspecta sound. Perspecta sound, it should be noted, does not possess the wide field of other stereo processes and in that respect is closer to monaural sound.

The recording of songs in musicals generally followed the division of the sound track into foreground and background based on channeling: the singer was recorded and reproduced like dialogue—normally closely miked, resulting in a high degree of direct sound, and placed in the center speaker; the orchestral accompaniment was treated as background—recorded in stereo with some degree of reflected sound for warmth and presence and placed in the side speakers.

era, although it was not done consistently for any genre other than the musical, and there was a special emphasis now on producing commercial recordings rather than saleable sheet music.

According to Ted Wick, music had been used occasionally as a pre-release promotional device since at least 1944, when portions of Max Steiner's score to *Since You Went Away* were sent to radio stations 1 month prior to the release.[4] Moreover, lyrical instrumental themes, particularly love themes, had often enough resembled popular song sufficiently that they could cross over and become hit songs themselves. Essentially these were instrumental themes that would be turned into popular songs through the addition of lyrics after the fact. Joseph Carl Breil's "The Perfect Song" (Figure 4-8) is an early example of this. Also recall Erno Rapee's "Charmaine," mentioned in Chapter 4, and Alfred Newman's theme from *Street Scene*, mentioned a couple of paragraphs ago and in Chapter 7. David Raksin's theme from *Laura* (1944) is a particularly well-known later example, as is Victor Young's "Stella by Starlight" from *The Uninvited* (1944). Indeed, Victor Young, who also contributed to several Broadway shows, was extremely adept at turning out such tunes: "When I Fall in Love" from *One Minute to Zero* (1952) and the title song of *Love Letters* (1945) are two further commercially successful examples. As might be expected, such themes

Epic films of the 1950s featured lavish costume design, exotic locales, and extravagant film scores. Miklós Rózsa, who was especially associated with these films, outlined his scoring process. Epic films often attempted to appear historically accurate through location shooting and costume design, but the scoring was anachronistic, and so, for the film Quo Vadis (1951), a Christian epic set in Rome, Rózsa researched ancient Greek and Roman music. He had period instruments built for scenes with diegetic music, and he also incorporated older styles and ancient modes in his score in an appeal to authenticity.
—See Miklós Rózsa, "Quo Vadis," in Cooke, The Hollywood Film Music Reader.

generally featured prominently in main titles and, like the theme songs of the silent era, appeared frequently in the score, often in both diegetic and nondiegetic forms. Often, such a theme recurred repeatedly, leaving the impression that the score was essentially monothematic (as in *Laura*; see Chapter 7). "Lara's Theme (Somewhere My Love)" from *Doctor Zhivago* (1965) works similarly; indeed, the filmmakers felt sufficiently confident of the appeal of the tune that they replaced many of the underscore cues originally written for the film with repetitions of this theme.

Despite such elegant and effective uses as this, there are certainly dangers in the film manner of thematic treatment. The early film music scholar Frederick Sternfeld described them as follows:

> There are obvious conveniences to [the leitmotif] system that employs the same succession of notes whenever the same character or situation appears. For copyright reasons new tunes must be tagged, and the trick of using the X theme every time X appears on the screen is facile and produces quick results. The proof of the pudding lies, of course, in the eating. If the technique is applied sparingly and thoughtfully, it will seem appropriate—even to the critical observer—besides providing the necessary coherence for the entire fabric. But if used slavishly and mechanically, it will convey a feeling of monotony to the uncritical, while the sensitive listener will be both bored and irritated.[5]

Main Theme from *High Noon*

From the beginning, the producers of *High Noon* (1952) had planned to exploit its theme both to generate ancillary income and as a means of promoting the film. Given this motivation, it is not surprising that the theme is a vocal number sung by Tex Ritter over the main credits. Yet it is interesting to note that in terms of this promotion Ritter's version was only one of six recorded and released at or near the time of the film's premiere. By releasing it in different versions, the thought was that the song would sell more copies and garner more radio airplay because it would appeal to different audience tastes. As film scholar Jeff Smith notes, United Artists (UA) "had no specific expectation for a particular rendition, but Max Youngstein [UA's vice president of marketing] was confident that one of them would reach the Hit Parade's Top Ten within two months of the film's release."[6] Like "Laura" or "Stella by Starlight," the song was conceived as sheet music, and Ritter's performance, although belonging to the film, was understood as only a particular rendition (see Figure 9-12). There was no sense that his would be the only recording of the song.

Like the instrumental theme song used monothematically, "High Noon (Do Not Forsake Me, Oh My Darlin')" served as the primary musical material for the score, but Tex Ritter's vocal rendition of it appeared seven times in addition to the beginning and end of the film. Film music scholar Neil Lerner points to the narrative significance of the title song:

> Since the title song suggests Kane's point of view, and since the film revolves mostly around Kane [played by Gary Cooper], it comes as no surprise to find a

Figure 9-12. Sheet Music, "High Noon" (1952). Notice that Tex Ritter's name is nowhere to be found in the advertising copy, indicating the primacy of the song over the performance.

score dominated by melodies attached to Kane: monothematic as analogue to mono-protagonistic. While Kane's character unquestionably received the most screen time and development, other important characters, namely Helen Ramirez and Frank Miller, actually receive their own melodic motives that are independent from "Do Not Forsake Me." . . . The visual narrative, and the music that synchronously tells the same story, begins with Kane but gradually introduces other characters; musically, the score opens with Kane's ballad but soon adds other character motives, alternating with Kane's music as the film progresses; only at the end of the film does Kane's title ballad reassert itself as the dominant and unchallenged center of the narrative.[7]

It is therefore Ritter's vocal performance of the song that is decisive, and its fragmented appearance at key junctures of the film, according to Lerner's analysis, parallels Kane's situation.

The way *High Noon* challenges the traditional scoring model, then, has to do not only with the use of popular music but also with the use of a particular recording in the course of the film. Although the song also appears in other guises in the score, Ritter's version is always charged with particular narrative significance. The fact that it is a recording is important, as the song often enters and exits mid-phrase, sometimes with a jarring effect, such as when Amy (Grace Kelly) hastily leaves Kane's office.

POPULAR SONG AND THE UNDERSCORE

In *High Noon*, the song is treated rather traditionally as a musical theme, and it is the intermingling of the score and recording that represents the strongest departure from classical practice in the film. The score overall, however, is not reconceived in a popular idiom.

The underscoring in musicals was, by contrast, much more invested in the popular idiom. General stylistic traits as well as the specific material from a romantic ballad, say, would be continued behind dialogue of a subsequent love scene and its presentation (recall the discussion of *Yankee Doodle Dandy* [1942] in the commentary to Figure 7-13), although breaking up, developing, and even moving away from the song's basic material would remain within the style of the song's accompaniment (generally scored like an orchestra for musical theater) rather than being converted over into the traditional film music symphonic idiom.

Through the 1950s, dramatic scores sometimes followed suit. Jazz in particular became an important stylistic possibility, although it was at first restricted to films where the music could be motivated by setting. Film biographies (also known as biopics) of important big-band leaders naturally used this sort of score. Examples include *The Fabulous Dorseys* (1947), *The Glenn Miller Story* (1954), *The Benny Goodman Story* (1956), and *The Gene Krupa Story* (1959). Much the same can be said of biopics of popular song composers. *Rhapsody in Blue* (George Gershwin, 1945), *Night and Day* (Cole Porter, 1946), *Till the Clouds Roll By* (Jerome Kern, 1946), and *Words and Music* (Rodgers and Hart, 1948) are examples of these films. Not only were big-band swing and the closely related popular song necessary elements of the story; such films were also structured closely around the conceits of musical comedy.

Jazz was also frequently used for crime dramas and other films with seedy urban settings, and it was in this capacity that jazz had a decisive impact on

The Russian-born composer Dimitri Tiomkin wrote underscore for several films during a fruitful partnership with filmmaker Frank Capra. These films employed Americana-style music and helped shape Tiomkin's musical vocabulary for Westerns. High Noon *(1951) previewed poorly, and Tiomkin claims—his account is not entirely reliable—that it was only after the commercial success of the ballad "Do Not Forsake Me" that the studio decided on release. Tiomkin did receive two Oscars: for best score and best original song.*
—See Dimitri Tiomkin, "Please Don't Hate Me!," in Cooke, *The Hollywood Film Music Reader.*

scoring practice. *A Streetcar Named Desire* (1951), *The Man with the Golden Arm* (1955), and *Anatomy of a Murder* (1959) are all important examples. Perhaps even more influential was Henry Mancini's work on the television series *Peter Gunn*. (Mancini wrote the theme for the series and scored thirty-eight episodes from 1958 to 1960.) These jazz scores adopted a whole set of stylistic markers. Characteristics such as blue notes, instrumentalization, swinging syncopated rhythms, and improvisatory-like textures set the basic sound of the score. Although elements of jazz extended beyond the theme in such films, jazz hardly attained the level of a neutral style the way the postromantic idiom of the classic film score had earlier. Instead, jazz was mainly used as a musical topic to signify the dangerous world of crime. (This association led to complaints from jazz musicians; see the sidebar.) In this respect, jazz style was appropriated in much the way concert composer Aaron Copland's distinctive style was in the 1950s to signify American nostalgia and, later, the American West. (A good example of the former can be found in *The Best Years of Our Lives* (1946), and of the latter in *The Magnificent Seven* and its sequels.)

Ironically, contemporary romantic comedy proved almost as amenable to scoring with a jazz-influenced idiom as did the crime drama, probably because its plots resembled those of musicals (where "jazziness" often signified urban hipness rather than seediness), and so it was relatively simple to transfer the scoring style from the musical to the romantic comedy. More important, such scores could also be composed to resemble the big-band and jazz-influenced orchestral arrangements of popular song—for instance, the instrumental backings characteristic of recordings by Frank Sinatra, Nat King Cole, and Bing Crosby in the 1950s and 1960s.

Soundtrack Albums

Along with the rising importance of theme songs, the soundtrack album also became an increasingly important format during the 1950s. (We use the compound "soundtrack" to refer specifically to music destined for albums to distinguish it from music in the sound track of the film.) Although portions of scores had occasionally been released to radio stations on transcription disks, and suites had been arranged for orchestral performance at pops concerts or for piano for home consumption, it was the introduction of the LP record after World War II that made possible the large-scale commercial exploitation of the soundtrack album. Although at first these albums consisted of cues taken directly from the recording sessions for the film, by the 1960s they were often crafted as albums, with themes extracted from the score and then arranged as songs appropriate for play on commercial radio.

Jeff Smith argues that Mancini was particularly influential in developing a model for film scoring that could result in a soundtrack album with the potential to produce substantial ancillary revenue.[9] This soundtrack model would persist through the 1970s. First of all, Mancini conceived the album as a musical (and commercial) entity separate from the film. The soundtrack album might not in

I think it may kill jazz. All these [T.V.] crime programs with jazz in the background are setting up in people's mind an association between jazz and crime and slick, cheap women.
—Anonymous jazz pianist, quoted in Down Beat[8]

a | b   **Figure 9-13.** *Breakfast at Tiffany's* (1961). According to Jeff Smith, twenty-seven recordings of "Moon River" were released within a year of the film's premiere. (a) Although Audrey Hepburn's performance of "Moon River" features prominently in the film, her recording of the number was not one of those released. (b) A single featured Hepburn's picture on the cover, but it actually contained Mancini's instrumental version; the song itself—not the performance—was understood as the principal tie-in to the film.

fact be all that representative of the film: Audrey Hepburn's performance of "Moon River" in *Breakfast at Tiffany's* (1961), for instance, was not included on the soundtrack album (nor was it released commercially at the time; see Figure 9-13).[10] The soundtrack album might also take the musical material in completely different directions than it served in the film. Whereas cues in a film necessarily broke the continuity of musical themes to satisfy the needs of the narrative, a soundtrack album need not follow the film in this respect. The album could present fully worked-out themes. Moreover, the most commercially exploitable themes could be arranged to fit into the 3-minute slot favored by radio stations and have lyrics added to them. (Other artists would also be encouraged to record these songs to maximize exposure in as many markets as possible.)

Second, one of the priorities in spotting a film would be to find places where different themes could be introduced unobtrusively because multiple songs—usually about a dozen—would be needed to fill out the album. Because the underscore still needed to work dramatically, much of the soundtrack album material would consist of diegetic music, even if the cues were sometimes used only very briefly in short snippets. In other words, the tunes would be heard at some point in the film—perhaps coming out of a radio in the background. By carefully spotting a film this way, Mancini would have the music he needed for the album.

Besides the additional airplay and sale of singles that went with commercial exploitation in general, Mancini's practice of focusing on creating saleable soundtracks was also to the advantage of the record companies, as LPs returned a greater profit than did singles. This was particularly significant inasmuch as film companies had large holdings in the recording industry, and the sale of soundtrack album rights played an increasingly important role in financing film production.

Mancini was criticized for the way in which he sometimes seemed to go out of his way to introduce tunes unnecessary for the narrative but useful for the profitable soundtrack albums. Nevertheless, his actual scoring practice tended to be quite subtle. In particular, he only rarely respected the structure of the song form when composing for the sound track. When needed, he was fully willing to stretch, compress, break off and develop material provided by his songs to underscore in a rather traditional way. Indeed, Mancini's handling of "Moon River" in *Breakfast at Tiffany's* was not so different from how Max Steiner approached "As Time Goes By" in *Casablanca* (1942) 20 years earlier.

IMPORTANCE OF RECORDINGS

The crafting of soundtrack albums for sale as recordings is a manifestation of a larger sociological and economic trend. Recording had long been the dominant form by which songs were distributed. By the 1960s, however, recording had significantly eclipsed sheet music as the conceptual basis of the song. As we mentioned earlier, "High Noon" was still understood as sheet music. The same can be said for a number of film songs from the 1960s, including "Moon River," "Midnight Lace," "Born Free," and numbers from most musicals.

The same cannot be said of Simon & Garfunkel's contribution to *The Graduate* or the various songs used in *Easy Rider* (1969), *The Last Picture Show* (1971), and *American Graffiti* (1973), to mention only a few films that drew on recorded popular music. In these cases, the recording of the song has become all but synonymous with the song itself, in the sense that any other rendition of, say, Simon & Garfunkel's "The Sound of Silence" is now understood as a "cover," that is, as a derivative of the original recording.

The use of Tex Ritter's recording in *High Noon* reveals an important facet of scoring with recorded popular music: it is a fixed performance that cannot be altered; any edits will generally be "audible," and therefore it is extremely difficult to sneak the music in or out. Consequently, to be effective, its jarring, fragmented appearance must form part of the idea of the film (as is arguably the case with *High Noon*), the music must be motivated diegetically (so that any disruption of the song seems a product of the narrative editing), or, as is commonly the case, the film must be cut to the recording. This last option resembles shooting to playback in musicals, where the music is all prerecorded and so fixed before the scene is filmed and edited.

Popular music has always appeared in films, but a decided marketing shift from sheet music to soundtrack albums occurred in the 1960s. Henry Mancini wrote the title song, "Moon River," for Breakfast at Tiffany's (1961), even though it was still standard practice to bring in a songwriting team. Because the film had a monaural sound track, he had to rerecord all the numbers for the stereo soundtrack LP. The necessary rewriting of the film's dramatic music also led to the replacement of Audrey Hepburn, whose performance Mancini considered the "definitive" version."
—See Henry Mancini, "Did They Mention the Music?" in Cooke, The Hollywood Film Music Reader.

Relation to the Musical

Given this resemblance to the musical, it is probably not surprising that songs synonymous with their recording first began to take root in musicals. This trend had begun already in the 1950s, where such films as the Elvis Presley musicals that aimed at a youth audience were tied to the release of recordings from the film. A good example of this is *Jailhouse Rock* (1957), where the title song was released 2 weeks before the film and also served as the basis of a major production number in the film. The low-budget, "jukebox musicals" that Sam Katzman produced for Columbia, the best known of which are *Rock Around the Clock* (1956) and *Don't Knock the Twist* (1962), likewise appealed to the youth audience drawn to the newly emerging genre of rock and roll. (These Katzman films are the prototype for many later-day musical teenpics such as *Footloose* [1984], *Fast Times at Ridgemont High* [1982], and "Brat Pack" films like *Sixteen Candles* [1984] and *Pretty in Pink* [1986].) Defined particularly by its electric guitar–driven sound, rock and roll— under the shortened rubric "rock"—would prove to be the dominant form of popular music until the commercial success of hip-hop in the second half of the 1980s. The skewing of the audience toward younger viewers in the 1950s and especially the 1960s resulted in the production of more films directed specifically at an adolescent audience; and, as the success of the Katzman musicals demonstrates, music was an important component in attracting this audience.

The Beatles' *A Hard Day's Night* (1964), *Help!* (1965), and *Yellow Submarine* (1968) are familiar, somewhat later examples that tied films directly with recordings. All of these are, like the Elvis films, transitional cases, however, in that the recording continued to be anchored by the presence of the performer(s) in the film. This presence makes the song seem more like a traditional production number in a musical. Yet The Beatles' films often play with—and against—this conceit. The "I Should Have Known Better" sequence from *A Hard Day's Night*, for instance, begins with the band playing cards with Paul's grandfather. The music at first accompanies shots of the game, and the sequence plays silent—we hear only music and no diegetic sound. In a kind of reverse audio dissolve, the music gradually becomes diegetic: Paul mouths a couple of lyrics, John plays the harmonica, and suddenly the entire band is playing. Just prior to the song fading out, the scene then reverts back to the card game as though nothing had happened. In a later set of sequences, "I Wanna Be Your Man," "Don't Bother Me," and "All My Loving" serve as recordings at a dance party. "If I Fell," "And I Love Her," "I'm Happy Just to Dance with You," "Tell Me Why," and the signature "She Loves You" are all played in the TV studio. "Can't Buy Me Love," on the other hand, is entirely nondiegetic the first time it is heard, and treated similarly in the reprise (although one of the instrumental breaks is used under dialogue). Like the card game, the first of these sequences is shot silent (including the use of the fast motion characteristic of silent-film comedy), but here there is no attempt to ground it in performance. Overall, it comes off as a montage reminiscent of music video. The instrumental "This Boy (Ringo's Theme)" serves more or less as underscoring.

The Beatles' music thus functions in several distinct ways in the film: it is used as performance, as recording, as music backing montage, and as underscore. Although *A Hard Day's Night* is related to the backstage musical, none of its songs serve as the basis of a traditional production number of the sort that the "Jailhouse Rock" sequence does in the Elvis movie.

Although music is not simply the product of onscreen performance in *A Hard Day's Night*, the presence of the Beatles clearly motivates and so also contains the music. If "Can't Buy Me Love" offers a kind of nondiegetic commentary on the scene, it nevertheless seems that the band is commenting on itself, much like a character's voice-over narration might in a dramatic film. There is in that sense little separation of the music from the character(s). One consequence of this is that, although *A Hard Day's Night* goes further than *Jailhouse Rock* in scoring with popular music, it remains a special (limited) case. This is because the appearance of the music is rooted in performance (Figure 9-14).

Scoring with Recordings

Particularly with respect to underscoring, *A Hard Day's Night* exemplifies important extensions of scoring with rock-based popular music. Because it remains grounded in the presence of the performers, however, its representational capabilities are somewhat limited. A pronounced loosening of these constraints became increasingly common in the later 1960s. *The Graduate*, for instance, makes no attempt to ground the Simon & Garfunkel songs diegetically (Figure 9-15). Instead, they serve to express Benjamin's inner psychological state: because they are used mainly in meditative sequences, the images can be readily edited to the music. This option avoids those problems mentioned earlier with respect to editing music conceptualized as a recording.

Figure 9-14. *A Hard Day's Night* (1964). The film ends with an extended performance   a | b
sequence (a), and the final song before the credits, "She Loves You," is almost drowned out by screams of the fans (b). The lack of fidelity offers a clear sign of "authentic" performance, rather than a recording, since we expect crowd noise in a live performance but not on a recording.

Timeline

1940   Disney releases *Fantasia*, the first film released commercially in stereo.

1948   Supreme Court issues decision on Paramount consent decree that breaks up vertical integration of industry.

1950   *Rashômon* is released.

1952   *High Noon* is released. Cinerama widescreen process is introduced.

1953   Twentieth Century Fox releases *The Robe*, the first Cinemascope feature.

1955   *Oklahoma!* is released in Todd-AO in some theaters; MGM releases *Blackboard Jungle*.

1956   Twentieth Century Fox releases *D-Day the Sixth of June*.

1960   *Psycho* is released.

1961   *Breakfast at Tiffany's* is released.

Figure 9-15. *The Graduate* (1967). Like underscoring, Simon & Garfunkel's "The Sound of Silence" represents Benjamin's (Dustin Hoffman) emotional state.

The songs in *Easy Rider* function in a similarly meditative way, and the images are likewise edited to the music. The music of both *The Graduate* and *Easy Rider* functions with respect to character or setting the mood of the scene. The use of popular music, however, differs in at least three ways. First, *Easy Rider* uses more songs, which allows the songs to offer more extensive commentary than is the case in *The Graduate*. Second, the music in *Easy Rider* seems to emphasize general mood rather than being restricted to basic inner psychology. Finally, *Easy Rider* has no traditional underscore, which gives its songs a particular prominence.

Another way of conceptualizing the use of rock-based music on the sound track crystallized in the unexpected success of *American Graffiti*, whose score

1962   Twentieth Century Fox releases *The Longest Day.*

1964   *A Hard Day's Night* is released; *Per un pugno di dollari* (**A Fistful of Dollars**) is released.

1965   Twentieth Century Fox releases *The Sound of Music.*

1967   *The Graduate* is released.

1968   MGM releases *2001: A Space Odyssey.*

1969   Columbia releases *Easy Rider.*

1970   Twentieth Century Fox releases *Patton.*

1971   Columbia releases *The Last Picture Show.*

1973   Universal releases *American Graffiti.*

1977   *A Bridge Too Far* is released.

consisted entirely of period songs that served to mark not mood or psychology of character, but rather the time and place of the film's setting. This is not to claim that the use of popular music this way, even recordings, was entirely new. *Blackboard Jungle* (1955), to name just one well-known example, had used Bill Haley and the Comets' "Rock Around the Clock" over its opening titles to situate the urban locale of the film and quickly establish an adolescent culture. That same song was used over the credits of *American Graffiti* as well. This connection is hardly coincidental inasmuch as the use of the song in *Blackboard Jungle* has often been credited with launching the rock and roll era. *American Graffiti* did draw on a set of associations similar to those in *Blackboard Jungle*, the difference being that *American Graffiti* used over forty songs in addition to "Rock Around the Clock" and the songs were employed to evoke not the present, but a particular past era.

As film music scholar Julie Hubbert notes in her discussion of *The Last Picture Show*, the use of recordings in this way was consistent with the values of traditional, studio-era scoring:

> In carefully engineering specific song texts to elide with specific events in [*The Last Picture Show*], [director Peter] Bogdanovich also drew on musical sensibilities more closely affiliated with 1950s filmmaking practices. As several historians have observed, throughout the film Bogdanovich clearly uses song lyrics to both parallel and counterpoint the emotions, actions, and relationships of the character on the screen. . . . At the same time that Bogdanovich displays a stylistic allegiance to the music of the 1950s, however, he also displays an adherence to a more contemporary or [cinema] *vérité* conceptualization of musical realism. In addition to recreating "what" music would have been heard in 1951, Bogdanovich also carefully documents "how" it would have been heard, and in doing so he faithfully imports the *vérité* mandate of "source music only." All the music in the film spills out of visualized sources—radios, jukeboxes, record players,

and even live performing ensembles. All of the music in the film is given careful visual representation on the screen.[11]

The visual representation on screen is a sleight of hand that makes narrative underscoring appear as a function of the diegesis (rather than as an external narrative agent).

Summary

Like film sound in general, stereo began with laboratory research in the 1920s but had to wait several decades before its widespread commercial exploitation. The move to stereo coincided with major changes in the venues of film exhibition, as the maturing of the television industry and legal challenges forced the studios to find new modes of film exhibition. The adoption of widescreen format and stereo sound was the answer. The introduction of the stereo LP record in the later 1950s also gave a kick-start to a practice that had always lingered in the background of film studios' and artists' commercial interests: tie-ins between music for a feature film and soundtrack LP records.

Music and Film Form in the Post-Classical Era

Introduction

Beginning shortly after the end of World War II, the range of production practices for feature films gradually spread outward from the classical model established in the 1930s. While it is true that in the lion's share of mainstream feature films a clear and very gradual continuation and development of the classical model occurs, the 30 years from 1945 to 1975 were also marked by an accommodation to new formats (most notably in television) and to new audiences (most notably the youth audience). Also in this accommodation was an accelerated attention to idiosyncratic practices of individual "auteur" directors and to transnational responses to pre-war and contemporary American film. In this chapter, we augment and fill out the historical narrative by exploring different aspects of a variety of films from the post-classical period. The first section looks at scenes in two representative Hollywood films from the mid-1960s—*The Sound of Music* and *The Graduate*—emphasizing continuity of practices within changing production and exhibition environments. The next section concerns war films, an understandably important genre throughout this period; specifically, we trace the treatment of sound and music in battle scenes. The third section, then, looks at several less conventional films from "auteur" directors: Alfred Hitchcock's *Psycho*, Akira's Kurosawa's *Rashômon* and *Yojimbo*, and Sergio Leone's *A Fistful of Dollars*. The final section returns to the writing exercises of Chapter 8 but now in a form particularly applicable to post-1950 cinema: the compare-contrast essay.

Hollywood Studio Films 1: *The Sound of Music*

Like *My Fair Lady* (1964), *The Sound of Music* (1965) began its life as a highly successful theater musical. It was the last collaboration between Richard Rodgers and Oscar Hammerstein II, as the lyricist died a year after the show premiered on Broadway in

1959. The film version was released in March 1965 and, like many mainstream widescreen features, it came in several different formats, in this case 70 mm image with magnetic stereo sound, 35 mm image with a monaural optical track, and 35 mm image with a mag-optical sound track. (Mag-optical prints had both magnetic and optical sound strips to accommodate different theater sound set-ups. They came into use in the 1950s but were especially common in the 1960s and 1970s.) *The Sound of Music* is also frequently cited as the last of the traditional film musicals. Like many such statements, this is not strictly correct—the British musical *Oliver!* (1968) was very successful and won multiple awards, for example—but it is true that shortly thereafter rock-and-roll musicals came to dominate, starting with the Beatles' film *Yellow Submarine* (1968), and in the early 1970s, with *Jesus Christ Superstar* (1973) and others, both on Broadway and in film. Finally, we should note that the production budget for *The Sound of Music*, at roughly $8 million, was substantial—by comparison *North by Northwest* and *The Apartment* each cost $3 million—but not at the level of the most expensive blockbuster historical films, such as *The Ten Commandments* (1961; $13 million) and *Ben-Hur* (1959; $15 million).

The distinctive traits of earlier musicals are shared by later productions like *The Sound of Music*, but in the context of the 1960s, musicals in general can be regarded as relatively conservative in their treatment of film and sound track aesthetics. In this section, we explore this idea in sequences representing various scene types: the establishing sequence, the end credits, and a dance that doubles as performance and love scene.

OVERTURE AND TITLE SEQUENCE

Beginning in the 1960s, the conventional design of the establishing sequence was frequently compromised, especially in films with popular music underscoring, where the music for an establishing sequence may simply be a recorded song. Occasionally, the establishing sequence was even deleted so as to move immediately to action, but the formal establishing sequence did not entirely disappear—even today, it can be found, with a wide range of variations, in the majority of feature films, and in particular romantic comedies and dramas. More complex variants of the establishing sequence began to appear in the widescreen spectacles of the 1950s, such as historical epics (*Quo Vadis?* [1951], *The Robe* [1953], and *Julius Caesar* [1953]) and lavishly produced musicals such as *Oklahoma!* (1955) and *My Fair Lady* (1964), which open, like theatrical productions, with formal overtures. Overtures, filmed or played to a blackened screen, were occasionally added to films of a variety of types in the 1950s and 1960s, one of the earliest being for *How to Marry a Millionaire* (1953).

The establishing sequence of *The Sound of Music* is a good example of a complex variant. We can describe it most efficiently by means of a timeline:

I. Studio logo
0:02   Twentieth Century Fox studio logo with fanfare.
0:08   Screen fades to black.

II. Prologue A

0:14   (a) Gray clouds appear, mountains with snow, the sound of howling wind; (b) the camera pans over the mountains, and the wind sounds increase.

1:04   As the camera continues to pan, the season changes to spring, birds sing.

1:17   Music enters (Figure 10-1)—an introduction, nebulous, starts quietly and gradually builds, flute and other winds imitate bird sounds with trills and runs, then:

1:43   The first phrase of the title song, "The Sound of Music," enters (played by orchestral horns), then the introductory music, interspersed with bells tolling and occasional phrases from "The Sound of Music" continues to 00:02:44. At 00:01:53, views of Salzburg, the lake, the von Trapp villa. At 00:02:25, a plateau on the mountain, with Maria (Julie Andrews) walking toward the camera from the background.

Figure 10-1. *The Sound of Music* (1965). Establishing sequence. The moment when music enters.

2:44   Maria begins to sing "The Sound of Music" (Figure 10-2).

4:41   She finishes singing; bells toll, she realizes she needs to return to the abbey, begins to run, turns and runs back to pick up her wimple (exclaiming an exasperated "Oh!"), then turns and runs out of sight.

III. Main title and credits sequence

4:58   Credits begin with "A Robert Wise Production" and overture, which plays over various shots of mountains, churches, and steeples from 00:04:58 to 00:07:35.

Figure 10-2. *The Sound of Music.* Establishing sequence. Maria sings.

At 00:05:14, the main title "The Sound of Music" appears. (Credits continue through all this.) At 00:07:25, a final shot of the city of Salzburg during the overture, with a superimposed title: "Salzburg, Austria, in the last Golden Days of the Thirties."

IV. Prologue B—Transition to first scene

7:35   Credits and overture end; new music begins: "Preludium" (three sections: "Dixit Dominus," Morning Hymn, "Alleluia"), with a view of the abbey. At 00:07:43, cut to the courtyard of abbey, nuns walking toward the cloister on way to chapel. At 00:07:56, cut to long shot of nuns walking down the cloister. At 00:08:07, cut to the chapel. At 00:09:27, cut to the cloister, nuns walking. At 00:09:32 comes the first line of dialogue: "Reverend Mother"; conversation among the nuns about Maria ensues.

10:02   "Preludium" ends; the conversation continues, leading after a time to the song performance "Maria."

The typical features are all there, but each has been greatly expanded, and an extra prologue has been inserted before the title and credits sequence. In classical Hollywood sound film, the establishing sequence typically ran to about 1 minute. Even in *Gone with the Wind* (1939), the elaborate opening (which includes a prologue) runs to just a little over 3 minutes. In *The Sound of Music*, the opening would run 5 minutes even if we deleted Prologue A. In keeping with this pattern of expansion, Prologue A itself is at base a simple song performance, but the introduction alone lasts nearly 2½ minutes and includes a variety of visual and aural elements. Finally, note that what would normally be a short transition into the first scene is also very elongated here: the "Preludium" moves along for 30 seconds behind dialogue before it finally ends.

"THE LAENDLER" (1): AS DANCE

Following the familiar patterns of the musical, the Laendler scene in *The Sound of Music* is primarily a performance, a dance by Captain von Trapp (Christopher Plummer) and Maria. It does, however, succeed in contributing in a crucial way to narrative, as the moment in which the two realize they are becoming attracted to one other occurs within (in fact, near the end of) the dance and, one might say, as a result of the dancing itself. In this section, we will concentrate on the scene as a performance. In the next section, we describe its dynamics as a love scene.

Maria, the von Trapp governess, is on a large terrace of the von Trapp villa with the Captain's seven children. They are all looking into the ballroom, watching party guests begin the Laendler, an Austrian folk dance. One of the boys, Kurt, asks Maria to teach him the dance. After a few awkward bars, the Captain appears and cuts in.

To capture the details of the dance, we will again use a timeline. The music has seven clearly defined phrases (in the terminology of the waltz, these are called "strains"), consisting of a first strain (A) that alternates with three others. The entire design, then, can be represented as (introduction)-A-B-A-C-A-D-A. The times given in the following are from the currently available DVD:

1:30:10 Introduction: Indoors, the dance begins; on the terrace, the children ask Maria what the dance is, and Kurt asks her to teach him. At the end of the introduction, Maria and Kurt bow to each other (Figure 10-3).

A: Maria and Kurt dance half the strain, then the Captain cuts in. As Maria takes the Captain's hand, she has a surprised and unsure expression on her face (Figure 10-4).

B: Maria and Captain dance: first a promenade, then a step-hop figure. Maria's face alternates between a social smile and continued uncertainty. [Note: In B through the final full repeat of A, each half of the strain (or each quarter in the case of C and D) is given a specific dance figure.]

Figure 10-3. *The Sound of Music.* Laendler scene.

A: Lady turns (spins), then skaters' arms (holding both hands across the front) (Figure 10-5). In this segment, we cannot see the dancers' faces clearly.

Figure 10-4. *The Sound of Music.* Laendler scene.

C: (This strain is twice as long as the earlier ones, or in musical terms, 16 bars rather than 8) The most complex sequence of the dance, with figures using crossed hands, then 360-degree turns, the lady's turn, and finally a promenade. At first, Maria keeps her eyes demurely down. When they change lanes, the Captain cocks his head and grins in enjoyment and approval. She looks up to his face with a smile of ease as they go into the 360-degree turns.

Figure 10-5. *The Sound of Music.* Laendler scene.

A: He stands and claps while she dances around; then she stands while he walks around, still clapping. Maria smiles as she circles the Captain (Figure 10-6).

D: (Like C, this strain is twice as long) He walks in front of her (Figure 10-7), then brings her around front, moving into hammerlocks (two-handed turns ending in one of the lady's arms behind her back). (In the middle of this strain, cut

Figure 10-6. *The Sound of Music.* Laendler scene.

Figure 10-7. *The Sound of Music.* Laendler scene.

Figure 10-8. *The Sound of Music.* Laendler scene.

away to Baroness Eberfeld looking at them from the terrace door.) The Captain's gaze never waivers, but Maria shifts hers several times; at the end, Maria looks up, mesmerized, and they remain locked in each other's eyes.

A: (at 1:32:14). Still in the second hammerlock, they stop, looking into each other's eyes (Figure 10-8). Maria blinks; the Captain's face has a slightly stunned look, then they release hands and Maria steps back, away.

A: Last half of the strain repeated to end the dance music. Brief speech between Maria and Brigitte, and another of the children.

1:32:34: Music ends.

Both the dance and its narrative elements are highly structured, according to the phrases of the music. The music's introduction and its ending capture the narrative elements: the motivation of the dance and the emotional outcome of the pair's physical contact through the dance. Thus, once again, narrative is able to proceed even within the confines of a performance scene, although in this case the narrative information is part of the dancing itself, not an interruption to a performance.

"THE LAENDLER" (2): AS LOVE SCENE

We have just looked at the formal aspects of the Laendler scene, where we noted that this is the scene in which Maria and Captain von Trapp first realize they are physically attracted to one another. There is no speech during the dance itself, but the narrative is advanced because we are given a number of clues, in their own deportment and facial expressions, in the cutaway to the Baroness, and in the immediate aftermath of the dance (as Maria and the children leave the terrace). All this, of course, is in addition to the cultural convention of erotic potential in a couple dance, particularly when the couple is dancing alone.

The timeline in the previous section includes comments on the changes in their facial expressions: these can be summarized as a progression from uncertainty (on Maria's part, due not only to the stiffness of the Captain's character heretofore but also to her discomfort at the idea of dancing with her employer) to the neutral smile of the courteous social dancer to growing discomposure as they begin to look at each other with more emotion. After one rather intimate figure in the dance, the series of hammerlocks, Maria and the Captain come to a halt, trapped in each other's gaze. Maria becomes flustered and backs away during the last moments of the music, claiming implausibly that she has forgotten the rest of the dance.

One visual clue supplied by the editing and one aural clue provide all the additional information we need to confirm that this was no ordinary dance. During strain D (in the midst of the hammerlock series), we cut away from the dance to the Captain's fiancée, Baroness Eberfeld, who walks onto the terrace and sees the two of them. The look on the Baroness's face makes it clear she is uneasy about what she sees. The aural clue comes after Maria stops dancing and backs away from the Captain. One of the children, Brigitte, suddenly appears onscreen and blurts out "Your face is all red"; Maria barely covers her embarrassment with "Is it? I don't suppose I'm used to dancing."

Managed subtly though it is, the Laendler is unmistakably a love scene, in the limited sense we are using that term here: the moment of realization that creates the couple—even if Maria and the Captain are not quite ready to recognize it openly yet (they do, however, kiss for the first time in the subsequent Gazebo scene). The Laendler is also, appropriately for a story turning on a love relationship, the narrative crux of the film, because their falling in love is the catalyst for many changes: the Captain realizes he is not in love with the Baroness and breaks the engagement, Maria runs away to the Abbey only to confront the fact that the life of a nun is not for her, then Maria and the Captain marry and begin a new life together.

THE SOUND OF MUSIC AND *GREASE*, TWO LARGER PERFORMANCE NUMBERS

In most instances, even large performance numbers are based on one song (or at most two), and each subscene corresponds to a section (verse or chorus of a standard, strophe of a strophic song, A or B of an ABA form). This was prominently the case in the "My Forgotten Man" sequence from *Gold Diggers of 1933*, which we analyzed in detail in Chapter 6. Here, we can observe these traits in the designs of another number from *The Sound of Music* and the finale of the "high school" musical *Grease* (1978).

In the performance scene of "Do Re Mi" from *The Sound of Music*, for example, there are five subscenes based on the two sections (A and B) of the song. The subscenes are as follows:

1. A, repeated three times, while Maria and the children are shown on a field in the mountains.
2. B, repeated three times—they are now on steps and a terrace overlooking the city.
3. A, again—now they are on bicycles.
4. B, in a carriage; and
5. A & B, in the garden and grounds of the villa.

As these brief descriptions suggest, the subscenes are clearly distinguished from one another by their physical settings. (For readers with access to the piano-vocal score of *The Sound of Music*, nos. 1 and 2 in the preceding list correspond to no. 9a "Do-Re-Mi Encore.")

The famous closing scene in *Grease* is more complicated. Based on two songs, "You're the One That I Want" and "We Go Together," it has six subscenes in all, three for each song. These are distributed over verses and choruses but also include an interlude. For "You're the One That I Want":

1. First verse and chorus: Danny (John Travolta) and Sandy (Olivia Newton-John), along with respective groups of friends, on the carnival grounds.
2. Second verse and two choruses: Danny and Sandy in the funhouse.
3. Two more repeats of the chorus: Danny and Sandy with friends, coming out of the funhouse, the friends in photo boards.

At the close of "You're the One That I Want," Danny hammers a "Ring the Bell" game and we hear a bell. Dialogue follows, with the main characters wondering if they will ever see each other after graduation. At the end of this short dialogue transition, Danny hammers the game and the bell is heard again as the next song begins. For "We Go Together" (song in AABA design):

4. AAB: main cast with a few extras added in B.
5. Interludes (chant to nonsense words and instrumental [sax riff]): full cast dancing, pan of carnival rides.
6. A and refrain: full cast in lines with the main cast highlighted, Danny and Sandy drive away.

A central formal feature of both of these song-and-dance numbers is the contrast between the main characters and the full troupe of dancers (the graduating students): we repeatedly cut back and forth between relatively tight shots of the former and wide shots of the entire group.

THE SOUND OF MUSIC, END CREDITS

Contrary to what we might expect of an era that made some substantial departures from the conventions of the establishing sequence, feature-film end credits barely changed throughout the post-classical era. Film scholar Kristin Thompson took timings for ninety films, ten each decade from the 1910s through the 1990s, and her figures show that end titles or credits lists remained well under 1 minute until the 1970s, when a few timed at a minute or more.[1] Only in the 1980s were end credits consistently at 3 minutes or higher; by the 1990s most ran to 4 or 5 minutes. On the other hand, it is true that even in the 1930s, the "end" title and cast list (if there was one) were really just a marker, a signal of the end, and not a part of the film. In fact, the "end" title was normally the last component of a film's epilogue. Recall Thompson's schema for film form as we outlined it in Chapter 6: setup, complicating action, development, and climax. To this she adds "a short epilogue usually follows the climax." Even these epilogues, however, were rarely more than a minute or two in length. In *Casablanca*, for example, it lasts 90 seconds, as Rick and Renault talk and walk off into the night. In *The Robe*, it flows directly out of the final scene, as Marcellus and Diana walk to their deaths, but as they do the background is transformed into a vision of the sky; the "end" card itself lasts 8 seconds. There are, of course, exceptions—*Gone with the Wind* has special "exit music" that lasts 4 minutes after the end title—but, curiously, Thompson's figures show that, even in the 1980s, the length of most epilogues barely changes, even as end credit sequences evolve. Finally, we should note that, like overtures, specially written exit music was included in at least some exhibition prints of larger-scale productions—examples include *Spartacus* (1960), *Lawrence of Arabia* (1962), and *Mutiny on the Bounty* (1962).

The Sound of Music is not adventurous in this respect. The film is nearly 3 hours long, and, as we have seen, its establishing sequence and early scenes are complex. Nevertheless, the end credits consist of "The End" title followed by three cast list cards; the entire lapsed time is 30 seconds. Preceding this is a 1-minute epilogue showing the family walking over mountain-top paths while a chorus sings "Climb Every Mountain" a last time.

Hollywood Studio Films 2: *The Graduate*

The musical style of diegetic music is almost always an obvious marker of time and place: a marching band, a gamelan, a jazz combo, a symphony orchestra—such music is an effective means of quickly establishing a milieu. When we hear a string quartet playing at the Christmas party near the beginning of *Die Hard* (1988), we are not at all surprised to learn that those attending it are upper management of the company. Class is hardly an accidental part of the story, whose romantic strand involves a tension between John (Bruce Willis) and Holly (Bonnie Bedelia): their marriage is strained to the breaking point because of the difference in their respective social classes. As Robynn Stilwell notes, classical music is also associated with the villain in this film, giving him an aristocratic air that darkens the associations of the music in general.[2] The opposite effect is achieved by the association of music-like Australian aboriginal sounds with Paul Hogan's character in *Crocodile Dundee* (1986); as a result, Dundee acquires qualities of mystery and deep-historical rootedness.

The same applies to nondiegetic music, although it must be remembered that the symphony orchestra is not marked as such, except in the most general sense. As noted in the previous chapter, jazz underscoring was frequently used in the 1950s for gritty, urban films such as *The Man with the Golden Arm* (1955) and *Sweet Smell of Success* (1957). Recordings of popular music began appearing nondiegetically in the 1960s, where the style could signify anything from youthful angst, as in *The Graduate* (1967), to social rebellion, as in *Easy Rider* (1969). By the 1980s, romantic comedies would frequently feature compilation scores, where the choice of popular music style was used to delineate character and set the terms of the romantic relationship. *Clueless* (1995) offers a particularly good examples of this device, with Cher (Alicia Silverstone) being associated with synthpop and Josh (Paul Rudd) with grunge.

The topical associations of music have changed over the decades as well. Film scholar Jeff Smith describes what happened at one critical juncture, the early 1950s: "The [traditional] romantic idiom continued as an option throughout the fifties, but it no longer wielded as strong an influence as Hollywood composers began to broaden the classical score's range of styles. At one end of the spectrum, polyphonic textures, modal writing, and atonality surfaced more regularly in the works of Miklos Rózsa, Alex North, Bernard Herrmann, and Leonard Rosenman. At the other end of the spectrum, various jazz and pop elements appeared in the scores of David Raksin, Elmer Bernstein, and Johnny Mandel."[3] (It should also be noted that the new popular music style of rock and roll found its way very quickly into films and film musicals aimed at a teenage audience, such as beach movies and Elvis Presley musicals.) Some composers, especially starting in the 1980s, became specialists in combining different styles, effectively creating a new "cross-over" style; as film music critic and scholar Royal S. Brown describes it, "Many scores by composers such as Jerry Fielding, Lalo Schifrin, and David Shire bring together sophisticated facets of both jazz and classical scoring."[4] Dave Grusin, who is credited with "additional music" for *The Graduate*, is another composer with a broad range of stylistic expertise.

One of the first post-classical mainstream feature films to make distinctive use of popular music as underscore was *The Graduate*. Simon & Garfunkel were already successful recording and touring artists. Their LP album *Parsley, Sage, Rosemary, and Thyme*, released in 1966, became a favorite of the film's director, Mike Nichols, who secured rights to use four songs—"The Sound of Silence," "Scarborough Fair," "April Come She Will," and "The Big Bright Green Pleasure Machine"—and contracted Simon to write three more. Only one song, but an important one—"Mrs. Robinson"—came from that.

Film scholar Kristin Thompson marks out *The Graduate*'s four acts as follows. The set-up begins immediately, as Ben (Dustin Hoffman) comes home for the summer, having graduated from college but unsure of what he wants to do next, and a neighbor, Mrs. Robinson (Anne Bancroft), initiates her seduction of him. The complicating action (beginning at about 25:00 with Ben's phone call) is the affair itself. The development (at 55:00 as Ben's parents talk with him) is the appearance of the Robinson's daughter Elaine (Katharine Ross), Ben and Elaine's dating, the revelation of the affair, and Elaine's rejection of Ben because of it. Thompson places the beginning of the fourth act, the climax, at 1:13:30, but for reasons relating in part to the music we will put it 3 minutes earlier. The action here is Ben's pursuit of Elaine and their eventual escape as Elaine runs away from her wedding. (The often commented-on final minute or two, with the couple sitting at the back of a local bus, Elaine still in her wedding gown, is the epilogue.)

Songs by Simon & Garfunkel are placed in each of the four acts—see the following list. All of these are uncomplicated nondiegetic cues, except for "The Big Bright Green Pleasure Machine," which is diegetic, and the first statement of

"Mrs. Robinson," which is obviously nondiegetic but briefly turns ambiguous when we see (but do not hear) Ben whistling as he leaves the jewelry store.

> Set-up: "The Sound of Silence" 0:55–3:20. Sound track is otherwise silent except for recorded voice giving alerts in the airport.
> Complicating action: "The Sound of Silence" 38:20–41:15, segues to "April Come She Will," which goes out at 43:00.
> Development: "The Big Bright Green Pleasure Machine" 1:02:40–1:03:50.
> Climax and epilogue: (1) "Scarborough Fair/Canticle" 1:10:40 –1:12:25 / 1:13:40–1:16:46 / 1:17:30–1:18:56 / 1:25:45–1:26:10. The second statement is instrumental, the third (incomplete and slow) is solo flute.
> (2) "Mrs. Robinson" 1:30:35–1:31:15 / 1:34:20–1:35:15 / 1:36:40–1:37:38 / 1:38:32–1:41:00. The first statement is whistled; the fourth is just a guitar vamp that slows as the car runs out of gas.
> (3) "The Sound of Silence" 1:44:48 to 1:46:00 (end).

We will discuss each of the nondiegetic song placements in turn. "The Sound of Silence" is the key to the film's audiovisual treatment, a rare instance where a song's lyrics directly influence the style of the sound track. In the establishing sequence, the camera holds steadily on Ben as he passes through and out of the airport terminal. The sound track is sharply bifurcated: there are no environmental noises, either mechanical or human, with the exception of a recorded voice with alerts about the mechanical walkway and, later, about luggage and curbside parking—see Figure 10-9. As a result of the (near) silence and the persistent focus on Ben, the music becomes closely associated with him, perhaps as point of view or, equally, as characterization: the sound track strongly suggests that he is emotionally cut off from his surroundings, a suggestion that is amply confirmed in the subsequent scenes. The irritating recorded voice only increases

Figure 10-9. *The Graduate* (1967). Ben in the airport: action behind the main title.

Figure 10-10. *The Graduate*. Overlap from the establishing sequence: Ben stares at nothing.

the effect: it is human but wholly detached at the same time, and thereby makes sure that the audience does not miss the point about Ben's own self-absorbed loneliness. The final seconds of the song—and the reiteration of the song's title line—overlaps a simple cut to Ben's face seen through the aquarium in his childhood bedroom (Figure 10-10).

Much of the first act is taken up by Ben's attempts to avoid interacting with his parents and their friends, a strategy that falls apart embarrassingly when Mrs. Robinson railroads him into an affair. Sound advances and lags are used throughout the film to soften hard cuts between scenes and to suggest connections (as we saw at the end of the establishing sequence, for example). Music is often involved, but in some cases effects or speech do the work. In one notable example, sound effects take over music's traditional role as accompanimental sound for a scene, and they are tied to a pathetically expressive sound advance. In this scene (starting at 21:15), Ben is decked out in scuba gear that he received as a gift from his parents. As he reluctantly leaves the house to go to the pool to show off the equipment, all we hear is his heavy breathing, a point-of-view sound matched to the image, which also has been matted to give the impression of seeing through a scuba mask (at 23:00). The matched perspective of image and sound continues into the water, separating only when the image changes to an external reverse shot. After the cut, the sound continues with what at first seems to be a return to point of view, but the sound of bubbles gradually dissolves into an externalized perspective as we become aware that a decrescendo in the sound is accompanying a slow tracking back of the camera. As the camera finally comes to rest on Ben in long shot, we hear his voice

Figure 10-11. *The Graduate*. Isolation and inertia versus interaction.   a / b

speaking in normal tones over this image of him isolated in the pool—see Figure 10-11a. With the cut we recognize that he is speaking on the phone with Mrs. Robinson, whom he has agreed to meet for their first rendezvous (Figure 10-11b). The sound bridge here serves to tie these scenes together, his isolation in the pool being literally answered by companionship with Mrs. Robinson.

"The Sound of Silence" reappears—without any intervening music cues—on a cut (not fade) to black, the conventional way to avoid showing all of a sexual encounter (here it is the first assignation between Ben and Mrs. Robinson). This placement was also clearly planned as a reference to darkness in the first line of the lyrics coincides with the blackened screen; the first image after is the pool with bright reflections of sunlight; then follows a cut to a close-up of Ben (see Figure 10-12a). The second act consists of alternating short scenes in the hotel and at Ben's parents' home (prominently including the pool), each change managed with an image match on a close-up of Ben's face, which makes it clear that the song is again to be taken as point of view. The segue to "April Come She Will" shifts the focus away from Ben to a somewhat clumsy reference to the affair.

Figure 10-12. *The Graduate.* Images from the second and third "The Sound of Silence" cues. The first was in the opening credit sequence.

    a
    b

"Scarborough Fair/Canticle" dominates the first half of the climax (fourth act), and "Mrs. Robinson" the second half. Both are treated in the same way: in a series of statements with short scenes intervening. "Scarborough Fair," with its images of travel and of true love, follows Ben in an extended montage, first as he "stalks" Elaine at her home, then drives to Berkeley, where she has returned to college. After an apparently unwelcome encounter on a bus (the music fades out sympathetically to Elaine, as it were—a significant moment), she eventually makes it clear that she is attracted to him but is planning to marry another student. The first two statements are to an otherwise silent sound track, as in earlier cues, but the third includes the sound of the bus. The brief fourth cue is to silence again. The "Mrs. Robinson" cues that follow are not silent—car noise is almost constant throughout. The lyrics are only obliquely relevant to the situation (they seem to imply that Ben has somehow "conquered" the domineering Mrs. Robinson by making Elaine maintain interest in him), but the song's upbeat tempo matches Ben's frenetic rush to Santa Barbara to intervene in Elaine's wedding. After the overloaded sound track of the final action scene, the return to silence—and to "The Sound of Silence"—in the epilogue is all the more striking (a well-known image from a few moments after the song enters is shown in Figure 10-12b). The rapid transformation of Elaine's and Ben's faces from elation to affection to thoughtfulness to serious demeanor turns what was essentially a romantic comedy into something less clear in its outcome, or into what we might call the cosmic comedy of an uncertain, "silent" future.

Battle Scenes from Four War Films
WAR FILMS IN THE TRANSITION AND STUDIO ERA

The sounds of war have been an important source of sonic spectacle since the silent era. Though technically classified as a silent film, *Wings*, the most popular film of 1927, supplemented its musical score with an elaborate set of recorded sound effects that traveled with the road show to enhance the spectacle of the battle sequences through sound reinforcement. As befits the title, the focus was primarily on the sound of the airplanes.

Until the introduction of magnetic sound, battle scenes of modern warfare posed a significant technological challenge. Explosions tended to overwhelm the capabilities of the sound track, essentially masking all other sounds and allowing little distinctiveness to the individual explosions which all sounded with a loud but dull boom. Gunfire likewise quickly lost distinctiveness when many guns were firing at the same time. The machines of war—planes, tanks, trucks, jeeps, and so forth—also produced significant amounts of noise. All of this made for a sound track that was difficult to mix convincingly: the sound technicians often had to choose which of the three elements—explosions, gunfire, or machine noises—they were going to emphasize. In general the sound departments typically followed a strategy of saturation for such scenes.

The battle sequences in *All Quiet on the Western Front* (1930) effectively use saturation this way. By filling the sound track with noises that essentially exceeded the capacity of the medium to record accurately, the filmmakers could represent the awesome destructiveness of the weapons, which seemed to attack the very apparatus of recording. In such contexts, dialogue and music could only appear by mixing the battle noises at lower levels. In *All Quiet on the Western Front*, the battle sequences were shot silent and then had appropriate sound effects synchronized during postproduction, and nondiegetic music was avoided to accord with the film's antiwar theme. But the technological constraints were such that they affected films that did not share that sentiment. It is for this reason that music appears less frequently during battle sequences than might initially be thought given that many of these films border on propaganda. Music certainly appears, and often even during the battle sequences, but it often disappears for the climax of a bombardment.

The firing barrage before the landing in *Guadalcanal Diary* (1943) is a good case in point. The prelude to the barrage focuses on dialogue: men chatting nervously as they prepare to board landing craft. Once the big guns on the ship start firing, the roar essentially obliterates every other sound, and indeed comes across as uncontainable. The sound track is almost completely saturated by the firing of the big guns. The individual big guns, however, are not really distinguishable: flashes indicate individual firing, but there is no attempt to synchronize the booms to those flashes. (In long shot, such synchronization would not be realistic in any case, because sound travels much more slowly than sight, though film sound usually sides with synchronization rather than reality.) A shot of the airplanes preparing to depart from an aircraft carrier motivates the sound of airplane engines, and a shot of a landing craft being placed into the water motivates the squeak of a winch. For these shots the guns are mixed at a lower level (and boom somewhat less frequently) to allow the other sounds to be heard. This then allows space for a brief exchange of dialogue—such snatches of dialogue are common in war films of this era as a way of humanizing the soldiers amidst the awesome sound barrage. Music appears only to accompany the advance of the soldiers from the beachhead to the abandoned village.

In *Halls of Montezuma* (1950), music appears much more prominently during the attack itself. After an initial barrage from the big guns of the ship (without music), music enters for a set of extreme long shots focusing on the formation of the landing craft heading toward shore. The guns continue to fire and we see explosions of the hits (again synchronized), but the sound effects remain well beneath the music, which dominates the sound track during most of the scene (aside from some individual gun blasts that punctuate the music), a strategy that serves to celebrate the violence of the guns and explosions of the bombs. The music exits as the landing craft drive on to land, with the focus of sound shifting to the squeaks of the treads.

D-DAY THE SIXTH OF JUNE

Both strategies of accompanying battle scenes—with and without music—were common during the 1940s, the choice being determined partly by technological capabilities and partly by thematic concerns (e.g., does the film aim to represent awe at the destructive power of violence or to appropriate the spectacle of violence for obvious ideological ends?). Though overtly jingoistic films such as *Halls of Montezuma* are more likely to use music to guide points of identification, even such films were nevertheless required to choose whether to focus on violence or music once the battle was pitched, and this would remain true to some extent even with the improvements of magnetic sound and stereo.

In the landing sequence from *D-Day the Sixth of June* (1956), for instance, music accompanies the assault from the announcement that the landing craft will be departing in 7 minutes through the moment when the German machine guns open fire, at which point the music sneaks out under the barrage. The sound track is then dominated by gunfire and explosions. Unlike *Guadalcanal Diary*, where noises were modulated to get out of the way of dialogue, during this battle, the noises remain relatively high for several of the exchanges to suggest the difficulty of communicating amidst the din (see Figure 10-13). The gunfire itself is also better defined, as different kinds of guns and explosions produce a variety of sounds. The sound of individual bullets is also registered, especially when they hit their mark, as when a sergeant takes a bullet after speaking with Colonel Winter. Music only returns after the battle is completed, as Captain Parker is being moved to a boat to be evacuated.

Fanfares, military calls, hunting calls, and marches are closely associated musical topics. Marches especially are very commonly used as title themes for war films. A good example is The Great Escape *(1963). The themes to both* Star Wars *and* Raiders of the Lost Ark *(1981) are also marches. As leitmotifs, the themes refer to the principal character; as musical topics, they serve much the same function of marking that character as heroic as was the case in* Captain Blood.

Figure 10-13. *D-Day the Sixth of June* (1956). Soldiers have difficulty communicating with surrounding noise.

THE LONGEST DAY

The Longest Day (1962) works similarly to *D-Day the Sixth of June*. After a scene showing preliminary bombardment, music enters for the landing craft attacking Omaha Beach. Music does not sneak out under gunfire, however, but exits with a cut to a German officer reporting that the shelling has stopped. Music does not return for nearly 50 minutes. Although those 50 minutes have a number of battle scenes with a lot of noise, the lack of music in this case does not seem to be primarily a consideration of technology. For one thing, many of the battle scenes are considerably more varied in sound levels. The explosions and gunfire are even better defined than with *D-Day*, and the sounds of guns, bullets, and explosions are more individual. Whereas in *D-Day*, only killing shots were really individualized as sounds, in *The Longest Day* many individual shots ring out, especially as the men initially storm Omaha Beach (see Figure 10-14).

Figure 10-14. *The Longest Day* (1962). Soldiers attempting to cross Omaha Beach.

Still, the emphasis continues to fall on the report of the guns rather than the trajectory of the bullet or what it hits. Rather than a simple whistling falling in pitch to announce the imminent arrival of a shell, the arrival is now heralded with a kind of crackling roar that often sweeps across the stereo field. The stereo field and increased frequency response and dynamic range are evident in the number of additional sounds: engines of the landing craft departing, men yelling, even footsteps as they storm the beach while gunfire and explosions sound around them. Dialogue is also treated more subtly, with no obvious ducking of effects behind the dialogue or the dialogue sounding like it is struggling to be heard.

PATTON

In *Patton* (1970), music plays evocatively behind a sequence of parallel editing that shows the preparation for the Battle of El Guettar, cutting between General Patton waking and getting dressed and local nomadic civilians clearing the area. The music exits with a cut to Patton surveying the approaching German tank column. Initially, the ambient sound track is filled with wind but when Patton tells one of his subordinates to look, the image zooms, which is accompanied by a fade-in of a prominent low rumble of the tanks. This is a curious way to introduce the sound of the tanks, as it suggests counterintuitively that perceiving this low-frequency rumble requires attention. Nevertheless, it does effectively set up an important principle for the sequence: battle sounds will be treated more or less from the point of view of the camera. This helps identify a certain (distanced) sound position with Patton, another (less distanced) with General Bradley, and a third that encompasses the full barrage of sound with shots from the midst of the anonymous soldiers in battle, where it often becomes difficult to distinguish German and American forces once they engage.

Before the guns begin firing, the closer shots of the German tanks also emphasize the detailed sounds of the machines: the pervasive rumble of the engines, of course, but also the sound of the treads running over gravel, and the metallic clanking of the treads as they pass through the mechanism of the tank (Figure 10-15). On shots of the American side, by contrast, the sound is dominated by the (distant) low-frequency rumble of the distant German tanks, but that does not obliterate relatively subtle sounds such as footsteps, the loading of artillery shells, and the moving turret of an American tank. The stereo field is also used to track motion: as a tank moves through the frame, the sounds pan accordingly. When the guns first start firing, the onset of explosions dominates the sound track, initially seeming to follow the saturation strategy common to war films through the 1950s. The focus here is on the power of violence, and it is initially one-sided, with the sound of American cannon firing being matched with a shell exploding among the Germans. When the German infantry initially begins to respond with rifles, the futility is underscored by the sound track, which barely registers their sounds. The sounds of the German tanks—the engines and the treads, as the German tanks have not yet fired—continue to be heard, and

Figure 10-15. *Patton* (1970). Detailed, specific sounds of tanks heard as they move.

when German airplanes arrive, the sounds of their engines and machine guns are also prominent.

Sound, in other words, is a proxy for violent power, and the only thing that stands outside this system is dialogue. The brief bits of dialogue in this sequence are used to draw a distinction between Patton and Bradley: Patton, somewhat removed from the battle, offers commentary and issues orders; Bradley, much closer to the action, speaks only once, after Patton's aide has been killed, ordering that the aide be put in his car. As the battle becomes more intense, rather than continuing the strategy of saturating the sound track, the filmmakers instead develop the stereo field in a manner similar to *The Longest Day*. The gunfire and explosions become more differentiated and are placed into the stereo field. Some shells traverse the field before exploding, and several different kinds of explosions match the variety of artillery and tank guns present. As the forces draw closer together and rifles become effective weapons, their sounds become louder and more defined and occasionally the ricochet of individual bullets is heard.

The sound of the machinery is more prominent, and the sound distinguishes proximity and distance throughout this battle sequence more than in the other films that we have considered. Once the battle is engaged, however, the emphasis remains on gun reports and explosions, but the violence does not take sides, as it were. At the peak of the battle, explosions and gunfire occur indiscriminately—they sound similar no matter who is shooting or dying—and the American and German soldiers are not always clearly distinguished. At such moments, the film represents war as a spectacle of sublime horror, and the significance of Patton's fascination with this spectacle is one of the themes that the film explores.

A BRIDGE TOO FAR

The first major battle scene in *A Bridge Too Far* (1977) is, like the Battle of El Guettar in *Patton*, principally a battle of tanks and artillery. In this scene, the

British XXX Corps runs into German resistance. The scene opens with the sound of idling tanks, followed by a cut to English artillery opening fire. The treatment of the artillery here is quite distinct from all the other scenes we have reviewed thus far. The sound concentrates as much on the process of loading and unloading—the rattling of the shell, the moving of various levers, the sound of the depleted shell being removed—as it does on the explosive discharge (see Figure 10-16). The flight of the artillery fire is also occasionally tracked with precision as the sound crosses the stereo field. Once the firing starts, dialogue, which consists primarily of orders being sent via radio by the British tank commander or yelling of German soldiers under attack, is exceptionally difficult to hear. In the case of the British commander, the lack of intelligibility seems to be the product of rendering the sound from the perspective of the camera, since he seems to have little difficulty communicating his orders.

As with *Patton*, the high-pitched squeak of the tank treads moving through the mechanism figures prominently whenever the tanks are in motion, especially when the camera is placed close to the tanks. The sound level is also quite varied throughout the scene: the sound track never seems to struggle with representing all the explosions, and generally at least one other sound—tank engines, gunfire, trees snapping, men yelling, the artillery shells hitting the ground—is heard even during the explosions. In *Patton*, the battle featured several moments that seemed to follow the strategy of total saturation of the sound track by explosions. That is not the case in *A Bridge Too Far*, even at the height of the battle when planes begin dropping bombs.

Gunfire, when it appears near the end of the sequence, is treated in line with *Patton*: individual bullet ricochets sound occasionally, but the emphasis remains on the gun reports. The machine guns have varied sounds, not simply by distance but also by type of gun. Even at the high point of the battle, the German and the British troops are always kept distinct. Although it cuts freely between shots of British and German forces, the scene exhibits none of the provocative

Figure 10-16. *A Bridge Too Far* (1977). Artillery at work. Both firing and emptying sounds are heard.

confusion of *Patton*. The violence may still be represented as indiscriminate and both sides possess its power, but the effects of the violence are distinguished, and the deaths seem far less arbitrary than is the case in *Patton*.

CONCLUSIONS

The sound track during the era of stereo sound moved quite quickly from a strategy centered on saturation to one focused on increased distinctions in the stereo field. Explosions and gunfire become more varied, and the sounds are carefully positioned in the stereo field to avoid masking. Even as a layered approach to building the sound allowed for a higher density of sound, it also created more space that permitted increased use of dialogue and other ambient sounds such as engines or men yelling, without pushing down the levels on the explosive sounds. Ricochets and other sounds associated with individual bullets are used more frequently, as are the sounds of incoming ordinance sweeping across the stereo field. Throughout this time period, the films worked to supplement the sound of explosions and gunfire with an increased sound of machines: engines of tanks and planes, the treads of a tank as it rolled over ground but also as it squeaked running through the mechanism, the loading and unloading of artillery shells, and so forth. The focus of the sound design remains on the sound of the war machines rather than their effects on men, however. Men yell, issue orders, occasionally banter, and scream melodramatically in agony after being hit, but the sound, though more particularized, has not really moved to a subjective conception of sound. Such subjective sound will become an important feature of subsequent war films, and we return to this issue in Chapter 12.

Nonconventional Hollywood Film: *Psycho*

Even while he was busy generating a distinctive series of mainstream feature films in the 1950s, including *Rear Window, The Trouble with Harry, The Wrong Man, To Catch a Thief, The Man Who Knew Too Much, North by Northwest,* and *Vertigo*, Alfred Hitchcock turned his creative energies and interest toward television. The half-hour series *Alfred Hitchcock Presents* ran from 1955 to 1962, after which the *Alfred Hitchcock Hour* ran another 3 years. After *North by Northwest* achieved blockbuster-level success in 1959, the director was in a strong position to dictate the terms of the last entry in a six-film contract with Paramount Studios. To hold the production budget down, he brought in the crew from his television series and created what in effect is a 110-minute episode of his television show—without the censorship that television would have entailed.

Psycho was provocative on a number of counts—an opening that shows a couple in a cheap hotel after afternoon lovemaking, two brief but gruesome murder scenes, a female lead who dies less than halfway through the film, even a toilet flushing. Its music, too, has its counter-intuitive aspects: rather than the large orchestra of the widescreen feature, for example, we hear a small ensemble made up entirely of string instruments, miked closely in the manner of television sound. (This device of close miking was a carry-over from the 1930s, when it was used to make the usual studio orchestra of twenty to thirty players sound fuller.) On the other hand, Bernard Herrmann's musical cues were familiar from television (and radio) and were thus congenial to the visual and narrative style of the film. A glance at Table 10-1 will confirm that, although *Psycho* has quite a bit of music, it is laid out quite differently from the music in *Mildred Pierce*, the classical studio film we discussed in detail in Chapter 8. The number of music cues is quite large (thirty nine, as opposed to thirty one—including the

Table 10-1 *Psycho* (1960). Timeline and cue list.

ESTABLISHING SEQUENCE

   —main title sequence

      1. 0:00–   (length = 1:50)   (cue title = Psycho Prelude)

   —establishing shots of Phoenix and hotel

      2. segue   (length = 1:02)   (cue title = The City)

MARION CRANE STEALS $40,000 AND FLEES

   —Marion and Sam

      3. 4:25–   (length = :49)   (cue title = Marion)

      4. 5:50–   (length = :40)   (cue title = Marion and Sam)

   —Marion takes the money

      5. 10:44–   (length = 1:45)   (cue title = Temptation)

   —on the road to California (1): overnight

      6. 12:50–   (length = :41)   (cue title = Flight (A))

      7. 16:08–   (length = 1:20)   (cue title = Patrol Car)

   —on the road to California (2): buying a new car

      8. 17:38–   (length = 1:14)   (cue title = The Car Lot)

      9. 21:52–   (length = :55)   (cue title = The Package)

     10. 23:04–   (length = 3:03)   (cue title = The Rainstorm)

THE MOTEL; MURDER

   —arrival; conversation with Norman

     11. 30:28–   (length = 1:28)   (cue title = Hotel Room)

     12. 32:40–   (length = :55)   (cue title = The Window)

     13. segue   (length = 1:32)   (cue title = The Parlor)

     14. 40:25–   (length = 1:45)   (cue title = The Madhouse)

(Continued)

Table 10-1 (*Continued*)

 —Norman contemplates, carries out the murder

  15. 43:05– (length = 2:24) (cue title = The Peephole)

  16. segue   (length = :45) (cue title = The Bathroom)

  17. 47:07– (length = :56) (cue title = The Murder)

 —Norman "finds" the body and cleans up

  18. 49:32– (length = :09) (cue title = The Body)

  19. 50:17– (length = 1:13) (cue title = The Office)

  20. segue   (length = 1:06) (cue title = The Curtain)

  21. 52:45– (length = 1:20) (cue title = The Water)

  22. segue   (length = :48) (cue title = The Car)

  23. 55:42– (length = 1:24) (cue title = The Swamp)

SEARCH & INVESTIGATION

 —Marion's sister talks with Sam, Arbogast; the latter goes to the Bates Motel and is murdered

  24. 63:22– (length = :37) (cue title = The Search (A))

  25. 69:47– (length = :45) (cue title = The Shadow)

  26. 71:24– (length = :48) (cue title = Phone Booth)

  27. 73:35– (length = :58) (cue title = The Porch) ·

  28. segue   (length = 2:17) (cue title = The Stairs)

  29. segue   (length = :14) (cue title = The Knife)

 —Lila and Sam talk; they continue the search (he goes to the motel; they talk to the sheriff); Norman and his mother

  30. 78:09– (length = 1:12) (cue title = The Search (B))

  31. 84:25– (length = 1:51) (cue title = The First Floor)

 —Lila and Sam go to the motel

  32. 88:27– (length = :53) (cue title = Cabin 10)

  33. 91:29– (length = 1:26) (cue title = Cabin 1)

 —Lila goes up to the house; finds Norman's mother

  34. 94:32– (length = :52) (cue title = The Hill)

  35. 96:22– (length = 1:03) (cue title = The Bedroom)

  36. 97:57– (length = 1:00) (cue title = The Toys)

  37. 99:34– (length = 1:36) (cue title = The Cellar)

  38. segue   (length = :10) (cue title = Discovery)

DENOUEMENT

  39. 106:57– (length = 1:16) (cue title = Finale)

  out 108:13

diegetic music—for *Mildred Pierce*), and yet almost all of these cues are relatively short—seventeen are less than 1 minute in length (as opposed to seven such nondiegetic cues in *Mildred Pierce*), and only seven are more than 2 minutes (this number includes combined cues when one cue segues immediately into the next). In *Mildred Pierce,* fourteen diegetic and nondiegetic cues last more than 2 minutes. Furthermore, in *Psycho* there is no diegetic or source music of any kind.

Film music scholar and critic Royal S. Brown explains that the lack of music in everyday circumstances and with familiar styles is one of a number of ways in which "*Psycho* cuts its audience off from normal reality." Because there is no music at all coming from, say, a radio, a phonograph, or via singing or even humming, this absence "has the function of heightening the effect of the film-music convention whereby the appearance of nondiegetic music generally 'means' that something out of the ordinary is happening," or that the emotional or psychological implications of a scene or situation have special significance, that the viewer-listener should pay attention to them. As a result, "since *Psycho* has no diegetic music to somewhat 'rationalize' music's very presence in the film, the nondiegetic music gets an even stronger weighting on the side of the irrational."[5] (For an example of this effect in another film contemporary with *Psycho*, see Figure 10-17.)

Many of the music cues for *Psycho* do offer some kind of emotional enhancement to a scene—for example, Cue 5, which accompanies Marion's mulling over whether to go through with the theft; or Cue 6, which reprises the frenetic music from the main-title sequence to accompany Marion's frantic rush out of town; or, of course, in far more dramatic circumstances, Cue 17, which plays with the murder of Marion and is briefly heard again with the murder of Arbogast (Cue 29). Nevertheless, the cues' formal roles in smoothing transitions between scenes often seem at least as important as their affective qualities. A number of authors have pointed out this trait in Bernard Herrmann's film scores and have traced it to his work in radio during the 1930s. Finally, the whole textures of music cues, not just their themes, are often repeated, and the cues themselves are internally repetitious (an excellent example is the Prelude that accompanies the main-title sequence—for its first few measures, see Figure 10-18). Film music scholar Graham Bruce has called this a "cellular" method of composition, and most writers now consider working with motivic cells as a defining trait of Herrmann's musical style.[6] The technique is not unique to *Psycho*, but, according to film music composer and scholar Fred Steiner, it "assumes special importance" in this score and "[imparts] to it a special, disturbing quality [which contributes] much to its overall effectiveness."[7] Motivic cells and cues built on them can readily serve all the functions of a more traditionally thematic underscore, including motivic unity (where the cells act like themes) and the formal unity imparted by the repetitions. Herrmann's technique had a substantial influence on what are sometimes called "minimalist" orchestral scores in the past 20 years.

The Prelude that accompanies Saul Bass's frenzied, chopped-up graphic images behind the opening credits applies the technique in an obvious parallel

A common theme in film composers' memoirs and interviews is frustration with the subordinate place of the underscore during production and post-production. Occasionally, however, composers have more leeway— or are in a position to choose whom they work with. This was the case for Bernard Herrmann, whose work on Citizen Kane *(1941) with Orson Welles was much more collaborative than most. Herrmann found a similar receptiveness to his work with Alfred Hitchcock, whose directorial style was well suited to Herrmann's dissonant, cell-like music. —See Bernard Herrmann, "A Lecture on Film Music," in Cooke,* The Hollywood Film Music Reader.

Figure 10-17. Ingmar Bergman's early film, *Smultronstället* (Wild Strawberries, 1957), has four substantial scenes that are either dreams or reminiscences with some of the qualities of dream, but these are strikingly different from the classical Hollywood montage or fantasy scene in that music is either absent or plays a secondary role. All are experienced by the protagonist, Isak Borg (Victor Sjöström), an aging doctor who is provoked to review his life and priorities as he travels to another city to receive an honorary degree from its university. The first of the dreams—Borg himself calls it a nightmare—begins immediately after the main-title sequence (at 03:45). A shimmering dreamlike music is heard against Borg's speech and overlaps for a few seconds into the dream itself. Borg finds himself walking through empty city streets, sees a clock without a face, then a man with a strangely pinched face who falls and bleeds profusely when touched, then a hearse from which the coffin drops and in which he not only sees himself but whose occupant catches hold and pulls him forward.

A sinister and insistent music (little more than one high pitch) enters as Borg recognizes his face in the coffin. The majority of the scene, however, has no music: instead, we hear slightly exaggerated footfalls as Borg walks, a repeated drum beat (against the clock), the man's fall, and the horses' hooves and creaking noises from the hearse. Otherwise, the sound track is silent. The absence of music through most of the dream puts the emphasis outside Borg's subjective experience, all the more disconcerting because we understand the dream—including its sounds—as depicting exactly that: Borg's subjective experience. The sound track conveys the sense of a lack of control over events and so allows us to experience the nightmare ourselves, rather than simply empathize with Borg.

Figure 10-18. *Psycho* (1960). Prelude, opening (transcription from the sound track).

to those images: a very small set of musical phrases is repeated several times, sharp accented figures alternating with a brief legato melody. Although the accented figures are significant later—they reappear abruptly when Marion has her first alarm of conscience and flees—the legato melody does not follow the traditional pattern. We expect a theme in the opening credits sequence to become an associative theme later, but nothing like that ever happens. Instead, the Prelude's *agitato* affect is almost completely countermanded in the move to the first scene: a slow-moving series of shots moves in from an establishing shot of Phoenix (identified by a caption), to the side of a hotel, to a window seen from outside, to the inside where we see Marion and her lover Sam (John Gavin). The accompanying music moves, if anything, even more slowly and without motivic profile.

The sense of fragmentation—even bricolage—and of a motivically understated design is characteristic, even in the longer cues that underscore scenes. As one example, Marion is in her room packing before she runs off with $40,000 of her employer's money. (The amount is updated to $400,000 in Gus van Sant's remake of *Psycho* [1998].) In most of the scene she is still uncertain whether she will go through with it. Several cutaways to close-ups of the envelope containing the money confirm for the viewer that the money is the source of her dilemma—see Figure 10-19.

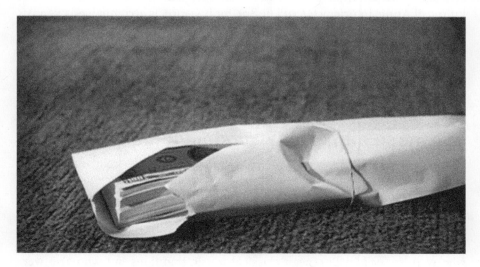

Figure 10-19. *Psycho*. Close-up of the money.

This is not new information—something we could not know without the close-ups—but the redundancy of the close-ups concentrates our attention securely on the money. Normally, attention is drawn to persons in the frame—human characters are naturally foregrounded, and thus we focus on Marion, not the bed, the pictures on the wall, or even the shower that we can see through the open bathroom door (presaging Marion's fate). In this case, however, the money is made to share the foreground with Marion, and everything else (including the quietly nervous orchestral music that accompanies the scene) is in the background. Presence or absence is an aspect of the treatment of each of the sound track elements, but it is perhaps most acutely felt when persons are onscreen and there is no speech. In this scene, there is no speech, and it is left to other elements to guide our evolving understanding: the worried look on Marion's face, the small, repeated hesitations of her body, the cutaways to the money, and the slightly unsettled music.

If the legato melody of the Prelude has no real consequences, the marked accents do, as they are eventually transformed into the most famous musical passage in *Psycho*. The gruesome shower scene also demonstrates that close synchronization of music and action did not disappear after the classical era, but indeed could be intensified for dramatic impact. The percussive hits of the high, screeching violins match the physical gestures of the stabbing and closely follow the sense of shock and fear in Janet Leigh's character. One reason the scene is so terrifying is the way the music couples screaming with physical pounding while also substituting for sound effects. The result seems to shock the scene out of the world into an almost supernatural domain. This potential was realized systematically in slasher films of the late 1970s and later. In these films, the monster's attacks are nearly always associated with music—here, too, music shocks, sets the monster in a supernatural dimension, and in some sense seems to emanate from the monster or even constitute its point of view. The killing of Annie in *Friday the 13th* (1980), for instance, is accompanied by music very reminiscent of *Psycho*, a film that had a strong influence on the horror genre that developed in the 1960s and grew rapidly once the film industry finally dropped the Motion Picture Production Code (known as the "Hays Code") based on censorship and in 1968 moved to the MPAA ratings system that is still in use today.

Japanese Film, Hollywood Style: *Rashômon*

With the enigmatic *Rashômon* (1950), which tells four different versions of a single event without making an ultimate judgment about the veracity of any of them, director Akira Kurosawa won a grand prize at the 1951 Venice Film Festival and immediately became a familiar figure to Western film audiences. Often considered the most "Western" of Japanese directors of his generation (which also includes Mizoguchi and Ozu), Kurosawa worked with musicians who were trained in European classical music traditions but who also were familiar with, and sympathetic to, Japanese traditions. Fumio Hayasaka was trained at a Western-style music conservatory (with strong Russian influence) as a modern European musician, not a traditional Japanese musician; and the means (Western orchestra, piano, and so on) and techniques of his film scores are essentially European. In *Rashômon*, Hayasaka only adds some Japanese features, such as melodies, rhythms, or imitation of traditional instruments or ensembles, for example, in the medieval gagaku (court music) of the main titles and the Priest's music, which the composer himself described as a "study in gagaku rhythm."

Hayasaka was familiar with the scoring conventions of Hollywood films and follows many of them, including the assumption that a film should be heavily underscored with a standard orchestra, that careful plotting of music's functions in relation to narrative is necessary, and that music's presence alone can represent fantasy or, more precisely for this film, the unreliable irrational. The film is just over 87 minutes long and contains roughly 43 minutes of music in fourteen non-diegetic cues (the cue list appears in Table 10-2); there is no diegetic music (although

Table 10-2 *Rashômon* (1950). Timeline and cue list.

MAIN TITLE SEQUENCE

    1. 1. 0:00:25–0:00:58. Music for the titles (beginning with the Main Title).

OPENING SCENE

    —At Rasho Gate. Three men (the Priest, the Woodcutter, and a Thief) talk.

THE FOUR STORIES

    —The Woodcutter's Story (told to the others at the Rasho Gate, then from 0:11:45 to the trial judge).

    2. 0:07:50–0:11:56. Music for the Woodcutter's story; begins immediately; goes out shortly after he begins his testimony before the judge.

    —Testimony of the Priest (0:12:35) and the Policeman (0:14:00) before the judge

    3. 0:12:50–0:13:38. Priest's flashback to encountering the samurai and his wife on the road.

    4. 0:14:25–0:15:15. Policeman's flashback to capturing Tajomaru.

    —Tajomaru's Story (0:15:40)

    5. 0:15:40–0:16:15. Tajomaru's version of his encounter with the Policeman.

    6. 0:17:00–0:20:00. Music starts just before the beginning of the flashback; Tajomaru meets the couple; they pass on; music overlaps with return to Tajomaru speaking to the judge.

    7. 0:20:24–0:21:24. Tajomaru runs after them, talks to husband.

    8. 0:22:10–0:26:50. Music in as the husband looks at a sword Tajomaru shows him, continues through fight with and defeat of the husband and return to the wife; overlaps slightly with cut back to courtyard.

(Continued)

Table 10-2 *(Continued)*

   9. 0:27:10–0:31:10. Tajomaru and the wife run to the husband sitting bound in the woods; she fights Tajomaru and he seizes her; music overlaps slightly with cut back to courtyard.

  10. 0:31:29–0:36:00. Tajomaru and husband fight; husband cries; cut back to courtyard at 0:35:07; music out at 0:36:40 with cut back to Rasho gate.

—Back to Rasho Gate. The three men continue talking; the priest begins to recount the wife's story.

—The Wife's Story

  11. 0:39:07–0:49:00. Music begins immediately with the cut to the wife in the courtyard, continues into the flashback at 40:40 and through the continued courtyard testimony; out with the cut back to Rasho Gate.

—Back to Rasho Gate. The three men continue talking.

—The Husband's Story (told through a medium).

  12. 0:51:00–1:00:10. Percussion only immediately with the cut to the medium in the courtyard; orchestral music at 0:52:40 with the flashback; several cuts back and forth between the medium and the flashback; music out several seconds after the final cut back to the courtyard.

  13. 1:00:23–1:01:17. Final statements of the medium (the husband speaking about the moments after he died); out with abrupt cut back to Rasho Gate.

THE TRUTH?; DENOUEMENT

—Back to Rasho Gate.

—Second version of the Woodcutter's story.

—Back to Rasho Gate; the Thief finds a baby; the Woodcutter takes the baby home.

  14. 1:26:30–1:27:53. Final shots & end title.

the status of drumming at the beginning of the scene with the medium might be considered ambiguous).

The studio logo is silent; music enters with the main title, as we would expect, but behind the credit titles is a series of filmed shots (not stills) showing different angles on the Rashômon gate, the ruins of an historic entrance to the city of Kyoto. (Although still photographs were sometimes used earlier, it was only in the later 1940s that it became common to overlay credits transparently on filmed scenes in title sequences.) We see but do not hear rain as the music and titles continue. After the director's credit, the music stops and, with a very slight audio overlap, a cut to a long shot of the gate brings the sound of rain that takes over the sound track at a loudness level nearly equal to that of the music we have just heard. The image track uses its own (classical) establishing sequence: a series of establishing shots—five of them here—that progressively bring the viewer in from a long shot of the environment to a much tighter shot showing individuals (who typically then begin to speak). The long shot of the gate is followed by a somewhat closer shot of same in which we can barely see two individuals sitting, then two cuts further in, each time with a clearer view of the two (but still at a distance), and finally a medium shot of the two seen from the side, at which point the sound of the rain is reduced somewhat and the man in front (the Woodcutter, played by Takashi Shimura) speaks. The background sound of rain persists throughout the first scene; music enters again when the Woodcutter begins his story and the scene switches to a flashback.

The flashbacks to the trial generally have no music either (nor, by and large, even natural sounds), but music repeatedly comes in under dialogue to smooth over the transitions from the trial to the forest, and vice versa. By using this particular film-scoring convention, Hayasaka helps establish the trial as a kind of secondary "reality": Although it is reached only in flashbacks from the scenes at the gate, the trial is thus more readily accepted as present time, the starting point for flashbacks to the forest. In this context, the presence or absence of music in and of itself has strong narrative connotations, for, as Claudia Gorbman says, "in classical cinema, . . . above and beyond . . . specific emotional connotations, . . . music itself signifies emotion, depth, the obverse of logic."[8] Hayasaka clearly builds his score on this principle—of the 43 minutes of music, 2 minutes and 40 seconds are used for the titles, and all the rest is used in the several forest scenes.

In summary, then, the formal uses of music follow the conventional practices of Hollywood narrative film. Music is used for the titles, beginning and end, and otherwise it follows narrative and dramatic principles, setting up a contrast between reality (or present time) and fantasy (or memory) through its presence or absence and, in most cues, following the turns in action and emotion fairly closely.

The greatest amount of conventional dramatic underscoring occurs in Cues 3 to 10, as the bandit Tajomaru (Toshiro Mifune) tells his version of the story (he is shown at the trial in Figure 10-20). Unlike the music elsewhere, these cues are filled with short passages of varying styles that accompany closely, and reinforce, changing events and actions on the screen—in short, conventional dramatic underscoring in the manner of major Hollywood composers of the 1930s, such as Max Steiner, Alfred Newman, or Franz Waxman. (We should note, however, that Hayasaka also understood conventions of Japanese film perfectly well: as the wife sits quietly on the ground posing for the camera (Cue 8), he introduces an innocuously sweet, otherwise irrelevant tune, exactly in the manner of [silent] Japanese film melodramas

Figure 10-20. *Rashômon* (1950). The bandit Tajomaru tells his story during the trial.

in the 1930s.) Finally, Hayasaka also makes some use of thematic devices. The samurai and his wife, for example, are given two kinds of identifying "walking" music—both "modern" melodies with motives obviously derived from the opening court music, an association that very efficiently confirms the couple's social status. As the bandit and the husband walk back to inspect a fictitious cache of swords the former uses as a ruse, there even reappears about 45 seconds of walking music from the first forest scene (Cue 2). Cue 11 (for the wife's story) stands apart from the others in its melodies and simple tonalities, but its repetitious rhythms are obviously related to those of Cue 2, and the percussion music that opens Cue 13 (to accompany the medium) is clearly a metrically disfigured expansion of the rhythm from Cue 2.

Reciprocal Influence: *Yojimbo* and *Per un Pugno di Dollari* (A Fistful of Dollars)

In immediate post-war Japan and Europe, American films were ubiquitous. This was due in part to the military occupation of Japan and Germany, but also because the American film industry was the only one in the world that continued to produce significant numbers of traditional dramatic and comedic feature films throughout the late 1930s and early 1940s. It was in Japan and France in particular that American films struck a chord, offering a new set of creative possibilities. We have already mentioned Akira Kurosawa in connection with *Rashômon.* In France, a group of young writer-directors in the circle of the critic André Bazin—including Francois Truffaut, Jean-Luc Godard, Agnes Varda, and Eric Rohmer, among others—soon developed what became known as the "New Wave" (*Nouvelle Vague*). In a remarkably short time, the influence moved both ways. As Kurosawa continued to make historical costume films in the 1950s, he sometimes turned toward westerns as models for narrative pace and visual style. In effect, his samurai (medieval Japanese warriors or soldiers) became cowboys. Well-known films in this mold are *Seven Samurai* (1954), *Yojimbo* (1961), and *Sanjuro* (1962). *Seven Samurai* was remade as a western in the United States and became a blockbuster success: *The Magnificent Seven* (1960)—notably, Elmer Bernstein's underscore became the model for the genre for decades thereafter. The path from *Yojimbo* was even longer: it was remade in Italy in 1964 by

Figure 10-21. Parallel Images from *Yojimbo* (1961) a
and *A Fistful of Dollars* (1964; U.S. 1967). b

Sergio Leone as *Per un pugno di dollari*, which was released 3 years later in the United States as *A Fistful of Dollars*, with an English-language dialogue track. The first of the so-called "spaghetti westerns," this film also introduced American audiences to another highly original underscore style in the music of Ennio Morricone.

Yojimbo stars Toshiro Mifune, who was the bandit in *Rashômon*, as a *ronin* (a samurai on his own, not attached to a house or military group). An expert swordsman but enigmatic person, Yojimbo enters a small, isolated village on a whim and, once there, plays off two feuding families against one another. After he resolves the conflict and kills the head of the one of the families, he simply leaves. Substitute Clint Eastwood for Mifune (see Figure 10-21a, b), and an isolated western town for the village, and you have *A Fistful of Dollars*, where, again, the anti-hero simply leaves at the end. As film music scholar Charles Leinberger puts it, "Eventually, the man with no name rides out of town, leaving behind not a restoration of order, but a trail of death and destruction. Unlike the classical Hollywood protagonist, the central character is a stranger who seems to come out of nowhere, only to eventually return to that unknown place in the film's conclusion."[9]

Yojimbo was filmed in black and white but in the 2.35:1 widescreen aspect ratio, the combination giving a sparse, barren effect reminiscent of a ghost town. The sound track is similarly sparse—wind is the most common effect—but is nevertheless often disconcerting because it is sharply punctuated by abrupt speech and, more so, by Masaru Sato's underscore, which relies heavily on percussion and wind instruments and which is placed very high in the mix, in fact generally higher than dialogue. *A Fistful of Dollars*, on the other hand, was filmed in color, and all of its elements represent exaggerations or intensifications of traditional expectations: frequent extreme close-ups of faces (distorted by placement in the center of the widescreen image), narrative pacing that can sometimes become excruciatingly slow, a focus on violence, long and tense silences, and a loud sound track (not just music, as in *Yojimbo*, but dialogue and effects as well).

If Sato's music for *Yojimbo* is distinctive because of its percussion sounds, which evoke historical Japanese instruments and ensembles in their sounds but are presented in a rhythmically marked modern style, Morricone's music for *A Fistful of Dollars* (and for most of his subsequent spaghetti western scores, too) creates a distinctive, elemental "southwestern" sound that highlights instruments other than the violins that are basic to the European orchestra. Not only does Morricone make prominent use of traditional wind instruments, such as the trumpet and English horn, but he also introduces the harmonica, recorder, acoustic and electric guitar, and wordless voices. He grounds these sounds in a simplified tonal scale as well. Charles Leinberger notes that "the use of such a modal scale makes [main-theme] melodies memorable and easy to sing. This unique modality, combined with the composer's eclectic choice of instrumental timbres, aerophones in particular, helps to position his scores as the antithesis of the classic Hollywood western score."[10]

Writing a Compare-Contrast Paper

In Chapter 6, we laid out a method to research and write a screening report, a short paper that integrates analysis and thematic statements about a film's treatment of the sound track, especially including the narrative functions of the sound track and its elements. The device of compare and contrast provides an alternative format for an essay or response paper.

At its most basic level, a compare-contrast essay is a screening report whose thesis makes a general descriptive or evaluative statement that speaks to the comparison. The same elements are required: a synopsis with thesis statement, one or more paragraphs with supportive details, a conclusion, and, depending on the nature of the comparison, appended runtime segmentations for the films or scenes discussed. At this point in a typical semester, you are most likely to be asked to write a compare and contrast study of two scenes, which could be two scenes within a single film or two similar scenes in different films. This was our method in the section on battle scenes earlier in this chapter. We compared the sounds of battle in relation to music in *Guadalcanal Diary* with the similar *Halls of Montezuma*, for example, for *The Longest Day* with *D-Day the Sixth of June*, and for *A Bridge Too Far* with *Patton*.

You could also study two films from the same year, the same studio, with underscore by the same composer, with largely contemporary diegetic music, in the same genre and period, in the same genre but in different decades, or in two genres. Again, we did this earlier in the chapter with two performance scenes from different films in the same genre: "Do Re Mi" from *The Sound of Music* and the finale of *Grease*. We also commented on the placement and function of music in *Mildred Pierce* as opposed to *Psycho*.

You might explore sequels or films that could be considered remakes, such as *Grand Hotel* (1932) and *Hotel Berlin* (1945) or *Sunset Boulevard* (1950) and *Twilight* (1998). In this connection, we characterized the sound tracks of *Yojimbo* and *A Fistful of Dollars*.

In other words, the options are as large as the repertoire. From this diversity of options, it should be apparent that the compare-and-contrast study needs to be governed by what we might call an external motivation to be effective. If you study two scenes within the same film, the goal will be to make very specific remarks about the filmmakers' audiovisual design and rhetoric, to observe parallelisms and try to account for their narrative significance, or to observe highlighted differences and try to assess them. This would be the case, for example, in a film where one scene has continuous dialogue and underscoring while another scene, also with continuous dialogue between the same characters, has clearly presented diegetic music, no music at all, or noticeable effects sounds.

Many of the guiding questions listed under "Screening Report" in Chapter 6 can be readily adapted to fit the compare-and-contrast study as well. Most, in fact, can be taken over directly, for example, "Dialogue will usually dominate most scenes of a film. List any scenes where dialogue is not dominant and the sound track component that is prominent in those scenes. What are the reasons the filmmakers give prominence to music or effects?" Creating the list and then answering the question will provide all the information you need to take a final step, comparing one or more dialogue-dominated scenes in the film with any of those where music or effects are highlighted.

Music and the Sound Track: 1975 to the Present

Introduction to Part III

Changes in the sound track since the mid-1970s have been profound. Techno-logical innovations during the period include the introduction and widespread adoption of Dolby stereo, the appearance of stereo television, the commercial success of VHS tape, and the conversion to digital systems at all levels of produc-tion, postproduction, and exhibition. This last—the digital revolution—on its own has been as significant a development as any in the history of the industry, rivaling and perhaps even surpassing the introduction of synchronized sound. Digital technology has given filmmakers more flexibility, allowed even more work to be moved into postproduction, and significantly altered the workflow and job descriptions in many areas of production and postproduction.

Economically, the breakup of the studio system led to reorganization of the industry, new incentives for filmmakers, and a more diffuse and international system for financing films. The result has been the rise of what has been called "The New Hollywood" system. The label is largely inaccurate—since less and less production and postproduction work is done in Hollywood—but it persists as the mark of a kind of corporate filmmaking that traces its aesthetic roots to the mainstream commercial filmmaking of the studio era. With broad interna-tional financing, increasing numbers of production centers outside Hollywood proper, and films focused on a global rather than national market, this system has increasingly been dominated by large vertically and horizontally organized media companies. The largest of these are reminiscent of the classic Hollywood studios but also quite distinct from them. Companies such as Time Warner, Walt Disney, Viacom, and Fox do not own theaters but instead have focused on acquiring and developing cable and broadcast television stations as well as sepa-rate media and entertainment divisions that can include music, news, sports, publishing, video games, live theater, cruises, and amusement parks. This industrial organization has encouraged the development of blockbusters and franchises as a means of maximizing the value of properties across the various divisions of a company.

Part III continues the plan of Part II, which paired a chapter on technological history, industry organization, and aesthetics with one that provides detailed interpretive readings of scenes and genres that can be used as models for thinking and writing about the sound track from a critical and historical perspective. Chapters 11 and 13 thus present the historical account centered on technological changes and how these affected aesthetic possibilities and reorganized the work of filmmakers. Chapters 12 and 14 focus on individual films and genres. Chapter 15, the final chapter on writing about the soundtrack, offers guidelines for developing a critical essay on a film. It sets out two approaches, one that ties the sound track to thematic criticism, the other that reads the sound track "against the grain" (that is, in terms of what the filmic system tends to suppress or obscure).

From 1975 to 2000
The New Hollywood, Dolby Stereo, and the Emergence of Sound Design

Introduction

Although a working commercial system of stereo had been introduced in 1940 and stereo sound had been a significant component of the various widescreen systems introduced in the 1950s, most theaters did not upgrade their sound systems. Because filmmakers could not be sure that their films would be screened with stereo sound, the result was a decidedly conservative employment of the stereo sound track in film production, a situation that film sound scholar John Belton refers to as a "frozen revolution."[1] Stereo could be used for special effects—and it was—but the sound track also had to be successful in monaural presentation, and therefore the stereo field could contain nothing essential to understanding the film. In other words, the sound track could not be reconceived in stereo (the way, for instance, the almost universal adoption of color film transformed the image track in the 1960s).

Indeed, up through the end of the 1970s, magnetic tape, which significantly reduced the loss of definition in subsequent generations of dubbing, was far more important to changing the nature of sound design in film than was stereo, which would not become an essential component of filmmaking until the wide distribution of Dolby stereo sound around 1980. Such films as *M*A*S*H* (1970), *The Godfather* (1972), *American Graffiti* (1973), *The Exorcist* (1973), and *Jaws* (1975) had strikingly innovative (and award-winning) sound designs, but all were originally released with monaural sound. The striking sound of Godard's *Prénom Carmen* (*First Name: Carmen*, 1983) was likewise executed in mono.

This situation began to change rapidly in the second half of the 1970s, thanks to the introduction of Dolby stereo and to falling prices for audio equipment. Both had the effect of markedly decreasing the cost of installing stereo sound in a theater. In addition, the emergence of the so-called New Hollywood

Figure 11-1. *Star Wars* (1977) proved a much better attraction in theaters equipped for stereo sound. The success of the film was key to convincing theaters to make the transition to Dolby stereo.

brought with it a strong shift to blockbuster production. Like the widescreen spectacles of the 1950s and 1960s, these films were marketed as "events," and many of them focused on special effects. These effects were aural as well as visual, and theaters that had invested in better sound systems soon found that their revenues were significantly outpacing those that had not. The decisive film in this respect was *Star Wars* (1977), where theaters equipped with Dolby Stereo or 70 mm, six-track sound had much higher revenues than monaural ones (Figure 11-1).

Issues of Technology and Economics
THE NEW HOLLYWOOD AND SATURATION BOOKING

By the end of the 1960s, the studio system had ceased to exist. The studios had moved into financing and distributing films (and television programming), and they had either diversified into other leisure and entertainment fields including book, magazine, and music publishing, as well as amusement parks and hotels, or they had been acquired by other diversified corporations. This diversification gave studios strong incentives to find further streams of ancillary income, especially if they could be located within the diversified holdings of the larger corporation.

The result was the emergence of the "New Hollywood," a term that some scholars restrict to the decade between 1965 to 1975, or roughly from the dissolution of the old studio system to the rise of the summer blockbuster. Here, we use the term more broadly to encompass the industrial reorganization into large multinational entertainment conglomerates, a system that remains mostly intact today.[2] The "New Hollywood" was characterized by a marked shift to production centering on what Justin Wyatt calls "high concept" filmmaking.[3] The high concept film banked on the synergy of its underlying concept, which each member of the creative team worked to realize. Generally, a high concept film involved a simple premise that made it easy to market, facilitated ancillary product tie-ins, and offered potential to be turned into a franchise that could be exploited through additional films and related products in other media. The budgets for these films were usually large, and the proliferation of ancillary products (and potential for series exploitation) helped increase profits or at least spread risk.

Like the widescreen spectacles of the 1950s and 1960s, the New Hollywood blockbusters were marketed as events. Unlike the earlier spectacles, however, they were not exhibited first as road shows before moving into the regular theater distribution system. During the studio era and through the 1960s, a film was usually released first to major, downtown theaters, then to the suburbs and finally into rural areas. The film was restricted to a certain class of theater within a zone for a prescribed period of time, and it could take 6 months or longer to work its way through the system. Under this system, relatively few theaters would be showing the same film at any one time. The blockbusters, on the other hand, followed the strategy of saturation booking, a distribution strategy that involved opening a film simultaneously on a large number of screens. This strategy had developed for so-called exploitation films (lower budget films aimed at niche audiences), where films would be released simultaneously on a large number of screens to maximize the effects of closely targeted advertising while minimizing any negative word of mouth. *Jaws*, generally acknowledged as the first mainstream film to use this distribution strategy, opened on just over 400 screens (Figure 11-2); by the 1980s, films would appear on as many as 2,000 screens at the same time. One consequence of this distribution strategy, however, was that

Figure 11-2. *Jaws* (1975) used a national campaign of television advertising and saturation booking in summer release to set a new precedent for how to market a mainstream film. John Williams's short motif for the shark figured prominently in the ads.

John Williams's scores for Jaws *(1975) and the* Star Wars *trilogy are often held up as the archetypal examples of music in the New Hollywood. Williams himself asserted that his traditional orchestral score to the* Star Wars *films helped bring a level of humanity to a film set "far, far away." Character themes exemplify the inter-relationship between musical topics and leitmotifs. The minor mode, brass instru-mentation, and march style help give Darth Vader a dark, militaristic energy while the ascending, heroic, flourishing themes of Luke Skywalker and Han Solo give the charac-ters a sense of righ-teousness and virtue.
—See Craig L. Byrd, "John Williams and Star Wars," in Cooke,* The Hollywood Film Music Reader.

these films would necessarily open in theaters that were not accustomed to showing first-run films and that often had antiquated sound systems. Unlike the lower budget exploitation films, moreover, these films placed far greater demands on the sound systems. With saturation booking making cross-comparisons among theaters relatively easy, it became all the more evident that the sound of many theaters was very poor indeed.

Director Robert Altman complained in the late 1970s that "sound in the theaters—the overwhelming majority of theaters—is just terrible. The acoustics, the speakers, everything."[4] Not only did the sound in most theaters not match the performance of a decent home stereo, but even when it did the sound insulation between auditoria in the large multiplexes that became dominant in the 1970s was often inadequate, and louder sound from one film would often "bleed" over into the room next door.

SOUND IN THE MULTIPLEX

During the 1960s and 1970s, a new type of theater, the multiplex, began rapidly appearing in the suburbs. The multiplex differed quite significantly from the earlier generation of theaters, which had taken the fantasy of the urban picture palace as their ideal. The architecture of the multiplex was by contrast primarily utilitarian, designed above all with an eye to reducing labor and building-maintenance costs. For instance, they contained multiple auditoria and central-ized projection booths, a setup that allowed a single projectionist to service multiple auditoria simultaneously—although at the expense of pronounced dis-tortion (*keystoning*) of the image (Figure 11-3). The multiplex also displayed few ornaments either within or outside the theater. The most prominent architec-tural feature was generally the concession stand. In this respect, the multiplex was also a direct descendant of the drive-in. Like drive-ins, multiplexes were constructed around the idea that the primary commodity was not the film—most of the box office flowed back to the studio—but the concessions. Multiplexes also followed drive-ins in being located primarily in suburban areas, where land was cheap, potential audiences large (with sufficient parking), and theaters rela-tively scarce (due to the 1948 Supreme Court decision, which prevented the ex-isting major chains associated with the studios from following the population shift and building theaters away from city centers). Indeed, many of the firms that first developed multiplexes began in the business of drive-ins.

What drive-ins taught exhibitors, besides the importance of concessions, was that theaters could operate profitably with sound of minimal fidelity. The speak-ers at drive-ins were small, producing a tinny sound hardly even up to the low audio standards of television at the time. So long as the dialogue was minimally intelligible, however, films, even second- and third-rate films, proved sufficient to lure an audience, and, most important, the low cost of admission—drive-ins frequently charged admission by the car rather than by the individual—encouraged group and family attendance with frequent trips to the concession stand.

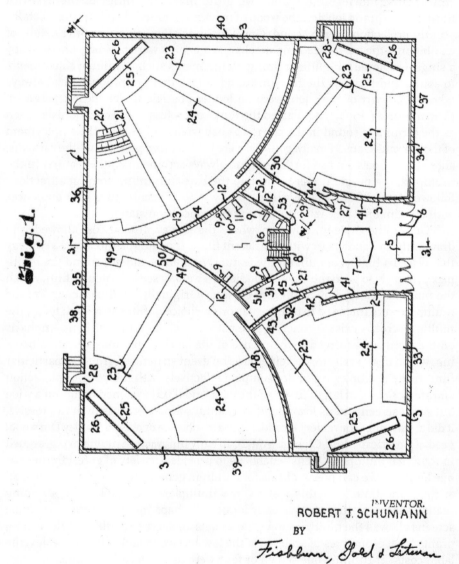

Jan. 6, 1970   R. J. SCHUMANN   3,487,595

ENTERTAINMENT CENTRE WITH MULTIPLE SEPARATE ENTERTAINMENT AREAS

Filed June 7, 1968   3 Sheets—Sheet 1

INVENTOR.
ROBERT J. SCHUMANN

BY

Fishburn, Gold & Litman

ATTORNEYS

Figure 11-3. Patent for a multiplex filed by Robert J. Schumann, who worked for American Multi-Cinema. Note the central projection booth that services all four auditoria. Also note the location of the projectors toward the side walls of the two smaller auditoria, which would result in pronounced keystoning.

With the example of the drive-in, it is hardly surprising that the multiplexes, too, would be constructed with little thought to the sound in the theaters. In general, the multiplex offered what film historian Douglas Gomery calls "minimalist moviegoing."[5] Gone were the many amenities of the first-run theater—the grand lobbies, the troop of ushers, the fanciful architectural details, 70 mm projection, stereo sound. Gone, too, was attention to the finer details of exhibition—the centralized and mechanized booths were now often manned by a single employee with little training. Refinements such as minute adjustments to sound and focus as the film unwound, a task that projectionists had always taken to be part of their job, were no longer possible under these conditions. (The multiplex, in fact, devastated the ranks of professional projectionists much as the coming to sound in the late 1920s had wreaked havoc on the employment of theater musicians.) Finally, gone too were the balanced programs—the cartoons, shorts, newsreels, and so forth, that had always accompanied the feature. In the multiplex, the program was reduced to the bare minimum: coming attractions followed by the feature. The whole point was to efficiently turn over audiences with the aim of maximizing revenue at the concession stand.

Unlike the drive-in, however, where the low admission cost allowed it to draw sufficient audiences with indifferent films, the multiplex followed a strategy that placed a high premium on the feature. Audiences did not attend the multiplex primarily to go to the cinema; audiences went to see a particular film, which the multiplex catered to by offering choices. (Originally, multiple screens of the multiplex were intended to provide patrons a choice of films to attend; today, the multiple screens exist as much to give patrons a choice of time.) This emphasis on the feature conformed to the nature of the blockbuster and saturation booking, which necessarily treated cinema as an event structured around a particular film. If the multiplex could not compete effectively with the 70 mm projection and stereo sound of larger first-run theaters, and if its keystoned image on a wide but small screen and its low-fidelity monaural sound were less than impressive, it did at least offer convenient locations and a semblance of choice. Stanley Durwood, head of American Multi-Cinema (AMC), an early innovator in multiplexing, argued in 1972 that multiple screens "enable us to provide a variety of entertainment in one location. We can present films for children, general audience, and adults, all at the same time."[6] In this respect, the multiplexes resembled the shopping malls near which they were usually located. Perhaps more important, multiple screens allowed the multiplex to hedge its bets on successful films while reaping profits from economies of scale: with the low service model of the multiplex, the labor costs for running one screen or four were by and large the same.

As the number of screens multiplied, the architecture of the multiplex reflected a particular strategy of exhibition: one large main theater with five hundred seats or more was surrounded by several smaller ones of one hundred to two hundred seats. The main screen would show the most popular feature, and the others would be used to service films aimed at smaller but dedicated audiences or to test out new films to see which would have the best drawing power for the main screen. Because as many as half the seats in the multiplex might be in the main auditorium, keeping this theater as full as possible was obviously important to the financial success of the entire operation. As long as most films were released in relatively low-fidelity monaural sound, and so long as stereo sound was limited to a few select films, the multiplex could get away with showing its films, even its feature on the main screen, in monaural sound. The multiplexes increasingly faced uncomfortable choices, however, as Hollywood shifted more and more toward blockbuster production, and as these films placed greater demands on sound systems to differentiate the cinematic experience from television. The climactic sequence of *Earthquake* (1974), for instance, employed Sensurround, a massive subwoofer used to produce a low-frequency rumble that could literally shake the seats in a theater (Figure 11-4). Although technically impressive—Sensurround won several awards, including a Scientific and Technical Award from the Academy of Motion Picture Arts and Sciences—and despite being extremely popular with audiences, Sensurround proved almost unusable in multiplexes because the rumble in the main auditorium disrupted the screenings in all the other auditoria of the complex. The multiplex owners faced the choice of showing the film with Sensurround but alienating their small-theater audiences or forgoing it and risking the loss of audiences to theaters where they could experience the effect.

DOLBY STEREO IN THE THEATERS

Although not as disruptive as Sensurround, the increased dynamic and frequency range of Dolby stereo posed similar challenges to multiplexes. These challenges were in some respects more severe than those of Sensurround. Dolby, with its banks of six-foot speakers, became standard equipment in the main auditorium of the multiplex, but the buildings lacked sufficient acoustical insulation to keep the sound from bleeding into adjacent auditoria, and the cost of retrofitting the buildings to address the issue was often prohibitive. This problem, a source of frequent complaint from audiences throughout the 1980s and 1990s, would remain mostly unaddressed until the building boom of the late 1990s replaced older multiplexes with auditoria specifically designed to handle digital sound.

Figure 11-4. A promotional poster for *Earthquake*. The film was marketed literally as "an event," and a large part of its attraction was the Sensurround system, which promised to make you "*feel* it as well as see it."

Dolby had its origin in noise reduction, in suppressing the hiss and increasing the response of magnetic tape. In the 1970s, Dolby Laboratories began developing products for the film industry, first for use in postproduction, then to increase the frequency and dynamic response of the optical sound track on the release print. Dolby-encoded sound tracks began appearing in feature films in 1974, first in mono (*Callan*) and then 2 years later in stereo (*A Star Is Born*). Stereo had of course been generally available with Cinemascope and Todd-AO, but these systems restricted stereo to magnetic playback. Although the magnetic sound track offered sound that was superior to an optical track, the striping raised the cost of the print by as much as 50 percent, and magnetic striping was also subject to faster wear than optical sound. Dolby stereo therefore offered one great advantage over earlier stereo sound systems: it used optical sound. The original Dolby stereo required two optical tracks on which were encoded four channels worth of information: right, center, left, and surround. In the theater, then, sound was distributed similarly to Cinemascope stereo. This method also offered better definition than traditional optical sound, especially in the high frequencies (above 12,000 Hz), and a wider (but still somewhat limited) dynamic response.

The first films distributed with Dolby stereo were primarily musicals, and prior to 1977 the theaters capable of presenting films in Dolby stereo were few. Consequently, most films continued to be released with only monaural sound tracks, even for first-run theaters. The success of *Close Encounters of the Third Kind* (1977)—and, even more so, *Star Wars*—and markedly higher attendance at theaters equipped with Dolby stereo finally convinced studios and exhibitors to invest in this technology of improved sound reproduction. *Star Wars* has been called "Dolby's *The Jazz Singer*," precisely for the way in which the film served as an impetus for rapid technological change in both production and exhibition.[7]

The rapid dissemination of Dolby stereo into theaters was aided by the modest cost of installation—around $5,000, if the wiring and speakers of the theater were more or less up to date, $20,000 if the theater needed to be completely rewired. By the end of 1977, more than 200 theaters had been equipped with the system. A year later the number was around 800 rising to over 1,200 by the beginning of 1980. By the mid-1980s about a quarter of the screens in the United States—generally the main auditoria in multiplexes—had Dolby, and the vast majority of all films were being released in stereo. Today, even the smallest auditorium of a multiplex has digital stereo sound, and re-releases of older films (such as *The Godfather* in 1997 and *The Exorcist* in 2000) almost always involve remixing the sound tracks in digital surround.

HOME VIDEO AND THE LIMITATIONS OF TELEVISION

Even as blockbusters became the driving force of Hollywood production during the 1980s, pushing toward a more expansive use of the technological resources of the cinema, the small screen of television was a countervailing drag on their full exploitation. Television rights became a large part of the studios' economic thinking in the 1960s, and even with the large revenues produced in a theatrical run, projected television revenue remained fundamental to the financing of films. The rapid development of the market for film on videotape in the 1980s only intensified the incentive to make films television-friendly.

Indeed, it can be argued that, of all the technological transformations over cinema history, none was more significant than the advent of videotape, because it changed fundamentally the way audiences interacted with, and so also understood, film. No longer did audiences have to go to the theater to see a film or wait several years after an initial release for it to appear on broadcast television. By making it possible for the general population to play movies at their convenience, videotape opened the way to transform films into commodities and film audiences into consumers.

In fact, the studios had recognized the transformative effects of videotape in the early 1970s, yet they were resistant to change because that required rethinking the status of their product. They had always treated their film libraries as rental property, receiving payment for use of a film rather than selling it outright. The studios were especially concerned over the recording capabilities of the VCR, which was the most appealing feature of the machine for consumers as it allowed time-shifting of broadcast TV. Because they feared that recordings would allow copies of a film to circulate freely, the studios at first resisted the video market, going so far as to sue Sony over the recording capabilities of Betamax. Even before the 1984 Supreme Court decision finding in favor of Sony, however, the film industry had begun to see the economic potential of the format and had decided to enter the videotape market.

Videotape thus turned movies into a commodity, very similar to a music recording, especially after studios recognized the profits that could be extracted by bypassing video rental shops and "selling through" to consumers directly (Figure 11-5). Once the "sell-through" market was established, the studios found

Figure 11-5. The release of *Raiders of the Lost Ark* (1981) on videotape in 1983 helped establish the viability of the sell-through market for VHS tapes. It grossed $30 million in its first month on the market.

it lucrative to sell video transfers of their films, encouraging customers to buy films rather than renting them. The income from video sales was immense, and video (rather than broadcast television) became the dominant way audiences watched films. Videotape also made the movie seem more tangible and offered something of an archival function for viewers—people could collect favorite TV shows and movies and watch them again and again, at least until the tape degraded from overuse.

As a result of the income generated from video and television, studios were required to calculate both the lack of stereo and the 4:3 ratio of the television screen of the time into their decisions about how to make a film. In general studios solved the problem in a way parallel to the late 1920s, when they had made both silent and sound versions of many titles: now they opted to produce two versions of each film—one for the theaters, one for television. The so-called pan-and-scan technique allowed the widescreen image to be broken down through cuts and pans to fit the smaller television format. This option did not always produce satisfactory results—the more the film was conceived compositionally as widescreen, the more difficult it was to transfer the film to television. Eventually the priorities were reversed, however, and filmmakers necessarily began to shoot with the knowledge that viewers of the film on video would be missing at least a third of the picture available in the theaters. Consequently, this third became largely superfluous in terms of containing essential narrative information. The sound track was similarly affected: the movie had to be intelligible not only in monaural sound but also coming from the small speakers with limited frequency and volume response characteristic of televisions at the time. It would not be until stereo television became ubiquitous in the early 1990s that sound tracks would consistently exploit the resources of stereo—yet another historical delay for stereo sound in film.

CROSS-MARKETING AND PROMOTION

During the 1980s and 1990s, compilation scoring (the use of preexisting musical recordings for the score) solidified as a viable approach to adding music to a film. It was during this period that the music supervisor evolved as a regular position with a particular set of skills—a detailed musical knowledge of recorded popular music and an intricate understanding of music licensing—honed to facilitate the use of music in this way. Many films, particularly blockbusters, continued to follow the convention of instrumental underscoring, sometimes updating the traditional orchestral sound with synthesizers, electric guitars, and drum kits inspired by contemporary popular music. Some films, like *Back to the Future* (1985), offered an effective combination of compilation of period songs (and sound-alikes of period songs) and new songs along with extensive traditional scoring by Alan Silvestri. *Apocalypse Now* (1979) and *American Beauty* (1999) are two very different films that nevertheless combined prominent use of popular music with original score. Some films were scored with a combination of new and preexisting songs, and others used just preexisting songs.

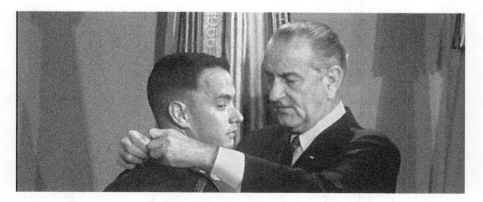

Figure 11-6. *Forrest Gump* (1994). Music serves as an important temporal marker for the film's flashbacks to various periods in the character's life. The compilation score is in some sense simply an expression of the ubiquitous presence of recorded popular music in our life. Like Forrest Gump, many of us measure our personal history by popular music.

The use of popular songs on sound tracks has often come under attack as being motivated solely by the ancillary income they can bring in. Compilation scores take this charge to a new level. Although it is certainly the case that ancillary income was a major consideration in determining scoring decisions during this period, compilation scores are also exceptionally successful at performing certain narrative functions. Indeed, in many situations the compilation score is a better option than traditional scoring, especially now that most audience members have been raised on recorded popular music. Compilations, for instance, are an extremely effective and efficient means to establish time and place—this is the primary reason for the period songs in *Back to the Future*—and it is not surprising that they have frequently been used for this purpose: *The Big Chill* (1983), *Dirty Dancing* (1987), and *Forrest Gump* (1994) are three films from the 1980s and 1990s that employed compilation scores this way (Figure 11-6).

The complaint against compilation scores—or against the presence of popular music in general—acquires more force when the presence of songs seems arbitrary. In these cases, the popular music may seem unmotivated, filling no particular narrative function. Even more egregious to advocates of traditional scoring is the fact that popular music is employed where the narrative functions might be handled as well or better by more traditional scoring methods. In these cases it seems that the scoring decisions are arbitrary because they are being made wholly on the basis of economics. Composer Elmer Bernstein, for instance, offers this assessment:

> Like many things, the business is money-driven, not art-driven. In the past, the function of music was to serve the film. The concerns now have shifted to, "will this music sell outside the film?" At the moment, film scores are mostly song-driven—by pop songs. People are greedy. Everybody hopes some song will jump out and make them a lot of money.[8]

Elmer Bernstein was a well-known advocate for film composers' rights. As president of the Composers and Lyricists Guild of America (CLGA) in the 1970s, he organized a partially successful lawsuit against film studios, television networks, and the Association of Motion Picture and Television Producers. After legal fees bankrupted the CLGA, Bernstein helped establish the Society for Composers and Lyricists to continue their struggle for rights.
—See Elmer Bernstein, "Film Composers vs. the Studios," in Cooke, The Hollywood Film Music Reader.

As we noted in Chapter 9, criticism of the economic (rather than artistic) basis of determining the placement of music in a film is nearly as old as the history of cinema itself. We also noted that the situation is not quite so simple as the criticism makes it seem: economic decisions entered into traditional scoring (even in the silent era) for the purpose of trying to make a hit. As only one example of many, additional repetitions of "Lara's Theme" were added to the orchestral sound track of *Doctor Zhivago* (1965). Undoubtedly, the changing economics of film production placed increasing financial pressures on the sound track to render hit songs. One response to this pressure was to have songs designed for promotion be motivated either diegetically or thematically. "The Morning After" from *The Poseidon Adventure* (1972) is an example of the former; the title songs for the James Bond films are examples of the latter. The need to have a hit could, however, trump narrative considerations, leading to the presence of a sequence out of joint with the narrative (or at least given undue prominence). "Raindrops Keep Falling on My Head" from *Butch Cassidy and the Sundance Kid* (1969) is one well-known example (for a discussion, see Figure 11-7).

Saturday Night Fever (1977) set a new standard for promotion and cross-marketing. Four of the songs were released prior to the film's opening. The success of these singles proved very helpful in promoting the film. Indeed, the success of this promotion can be measured by the fact that the film was re-cut so that it could be re-released with a PG rating suitable for the Bee Gees' new adolescent audience. The success of the film in turn increased demand for the soundtrack album (rather than just the singles) (Figure 11-8). The effectiveness of this strategy can be seen by the sales figures. The initial release of the film

Figure 11-7. *Butch Cassidy and the Sundance Kid* (1969). The song "Raindrops Keep Fallin' on My Head" comes across as an unintegrated musical insert (much like a musical video), which leaves the impression that it was added primarily for the ancillary income it might produce. The song did in fact enjoy great commercial success, spending 4 weeks atop the Billboard Hot 100 chart in 1970. Ironically, perhaps, it also won an Academy Award for Best Original Song.

Figure 11-8. *Saturday Night Fever* (1977). The film and the album enjoyed great success in cross-promotion. The film was well timed to take advantage of the wide popularity of disco.

grossed in the neighborhood of $100 million, a huge return at the time. The album sold more than 850,000 copies prior to the film and then averaged some 500,000 copies per week during the film's run to become by far the best-selling soundtrack album up to that time. Although *Saturday Night Fever* became the standard by which cross-marketing was measured, it proved a difficult formula to follow. Indeed, the sales of its soundtrack album have since been surpassed only by the album for *The Bodyguard* (1992).

In practice, a compilation sound track proved a more effective model. *Saturday Night Fever* placed a large bet on the success of the Bee Gees. (Although one of the songs—"If I Can't Have You"—released prior to the film's premiere was not performed by the group, it was written by them.) If the Bee Gees had not been sufficiently popular, the soundtrack album would certainly have been a flop and it is likely that the film would have suffered as well. In any case, the film would not have received the advance publicity that the extensive airplay of the singles provided. The strategy adopted by *Saturday Night Fever* was in this respect inherently risky. (It also offered high rewards. It is worth noting that *The Bodyguard* featured Whitney Houston to a similar degree and *Purple Rain* [1984], another film with an extremely successful soundtrack album, likewise featured Prince.)

The usual compilation album, by contrast, minimized risk by offering a variety of artists. This was the strategy pursued by *Dirty Dancing*, for instance, which also produced a top-selling soundtrack album, by some accountings the third best-selling soundtrack behind *The Bodyguard* and *Saturday Night Fever*. This strategy, similar to the exploitation of theme songs in the 1950s, attempts to appeal to a wide range of tastes.

Commissioning an artist to write a song for a film (rather than buying a song from a back catalog) is an effective way to promote a film, and it is often done even for films that otherwise rely on traditional underscore. As Geoff King explains,

> Hit records are an ideal form of marketing for films. Radio play and record sales in advance of the release of the film provide what is effectively hours of advertising that is not only free, but for which the company gets paid. Associations with a major blockbuster film and film star, in return, help to sell the music. The sum total is likely to be greater than the parts.[9]

Such songs might be used over the credits, as in James Bond films, or be heard at some point over the end credits. Often the songs bear only a tangential relation to the narrative (as diegetic background, for instance), however, and in such cases the value of the song to the promotion of the film may be minimal no matter how well the song sells on its own. Having such songs on the soundtrack album may, on the other hand, increase the sales of the album. In such cases, the film's use of the song seems to serve as a form of product placement for the soundtrack album because the album will perhaps receive increased sales from the song but the film will not.

This situation was mitigated somewhat by the development of the promotional music video, which coupled shots of the artist with footage from the film, often edited to form a loose narrative suggestive of (although not always identical to) that of the film. A good example of this strategy was Kenny Loggins's "Danger Zone," with a video, directed by Tony Scott, that intercut extensive footage from *Top Gun* (1986), also directed by Scott, with seemingly unconnected shots of Loggins singing to the camera in a bedroom. Playing on MTV, such videos proved an immensely successful means of promoting films. In this respect promotional videos turned out to be a way to realize some of the promised synergies of cross-marketing.

Movie + sound track + video = $$$
—R. Serge Denisoff and George Plasketes[10]

Production
PRODUCTION PHASES

The breakdown of the studio system meant that working conditions became more lucrative for a few in the industry but more precarious for most, since almost every job became a freelance position that lasted only as long as a particular film production. Despite the economic upheaval and ongoing technological change that altered some job descriptions, the work of the sound and music departments retained the outlines that had been established in the studio era. The main addition to the music end was the role of the music supervisor, who managed the placement and licensing of popular music. Indeed, the person in this position would by the 1990s become a dominant player who would frequently be hired during preproduction.

With the rapid adoption of stereo, first by theaters, then by television, the sound department adjusted to the regular production of stereo sound tracks. It also evolved during this period from being primarily a technical department to a fully creative one. This shift is marked by the advent of the title of sound designer, which became a way of designating the creative capacity of the supervising sound editor.

MUSIC DEPARTMENT

By the 1970s, all remnants of the studio system had disappeared. Nevertheless, the basic duties of the composer, orchestrator, and music editor remained much as they had always been, except the work was done freelance rather than as a studio employee. The fee for the composer was based on the production of a score, and other expenses for music—orchestration, copying, musicians, recording, and so forth—were in addition to the basic fee for composition. This standard financial arrangement would begin to change quickly in the late 1990s, when composers began to be required to deliver a recorded music stem instead of a score, a change that shifted much of the cost of music production into the composer's fee.

In music as in other areas of filmmaking, the emergence of the New Hollywood and its emphasis on blockbuster production brought with it a stratification of work and fee structure. John Williams's score to the original *Star Wars* was important in demonstrating that what amounted to an orchestral suite based on the score could sell well as a soundtrack album. The enormous success of the orchestral main title on the singles chart and the album as a whole surprised many in the film industry. Moreover, the themes from the score became fixed properties of the film—the orchestral music seemed to merge with the sound design—in a way that was seldom possible with popular music, so the music from the original film became part of the pre-sold package of any sequel. Music in this way became an essential component of the franchise. All of this elevated a successful composer such as Williams into an important source of revenue for a film, and because most studios released the scores on recording labels owned by the studio's parent company, income from these recordings eventually came back to the studio. As a result, an unofficial "A-list" of composers gradually emerged, with membership shifting and changing depending on the popularity of a composer's recent soundtrack albums. Whereas A-list composers were paid handsomely and had more work than they could handle—indeed, A-list composers frequently ended up overcommitted and had to hand off some of the compositional

Director Sidney Lumet discusses the process of adding music and sound effects, from the initial concept to final dubbing. His description of the creation of some of his films' scores reveals the director's level of involvement. He often has very specific ideas about the musical material and finds that his favorite composers tend to agree with him. He argues that composers "go to work writing for a form that can never belong to them."
—See Sidney Lumet, "Making Movies," in Cooke, The Hollywood Film Music Reader.

tasks to orchestrators and uncredited composers—other composers found work difficult to come by.

Advances in sound synthesis and the rapid development of digital sampling technology during the 1980s made electronic and computer-based composition an increasingly viable alternative, especially for producing effective scores on a highly reduced budget and for creating novel sounds. By the 1990s, as highly specialized digital audio workstation software such as Pro Tools was released, new positions supporting digital musical production—synthesizer and sequencer programmers, midi orchestrators, and experts in editing digital sound files—emerged and quickly became essential to effective and efficient composing for film, television, and increasingly video games, whose music was more and more resembling cinematic underscoring.

With the loss of centralization that studio production offered, the temp track (temporary music track) played an increasingly important part in postproduction. A temp track is a temporary score usually made by the music editor from recordings. These recordings were generally older film scores, production mood music designed for use in documentaries, television and industrial films, or commercial albums in classical, jazz, rock, or any other musical style the filmmakers required. Although the idea of the temp track was not new—the practice dates back to the studio era and in many respects is a descendent of the scoring practice of the silent era—its use did grow more prevalent and became a normal and expected part of the postproduction process. The temp track also began to have a direct bearing on film composition, because composers would often be expected to write pastiches of the temp track.

The temp track served three major purposes. First of all, the filmmakers often wanted to test how editing flowed with music. Already in the 1960s, many picture editors preferred to work with temp tracks to establish a rhythm to the cutting (*A Thousand Clowns* [1965] is one example of a film edited to a temp track). Looking for such a rhythm goes hand in hand with the notion that editing by the 1960s was no longer simply a task of establishing and maintaining narrative continuity but had developed a strong aesthetic component in and of itself, one that may at times even cut against the expected narrative flow. Music was one way to validate this autonomy of editing (and authorize a more complex audiovisual phrasing) because the continuity of music frequently does not coincide with that of the images (or narrative). Second, a temp track could serve as a good starting point when the director and composer spotted a film. James Horner, for instance, finds the temp track productive for this reason:

> Very often when I see the film, the director will ask me if I mind seeing it with temporary music. Temporary music is music he has taken from other movies or whatever and he stuck it in the movie in places to give a sense of flow to the film. I like to see it with that. I must say it gives me a very good starting point with the director from which to either agree and say, "Yeah, I understand what you're doing, that's great," or disagree, be able to say to him, "I don't know why you put that piece of music there, that piece of music does this to me, and the sequence

It takes a very confident director to set aside the temp track and allow the composer to create something new. And a very assertive composer.
—Daniel Schweiger (Music Editor)[11]

doesn't do that to me. I think you're saying two things, one with the music, and one with the sequence, is that really what you want me to do?" So it gives a good point of departure when the composer sees the film with temporary music.[12]

Finally, near the end of postproduction (but before the music was completed) filmmakers often previewed their films before test audiences so they could learn how audiences reacted. Because music significantly affects how an audience responds, this preview version of the film required a temp track to get reliable response from the audience. Temp tracks were already used this way during the studio era.

As mentioned earlier, one important new position emerged in the music department in the early 1980s: the role of music supervisor. The primary responsibility of the music supervisor was identifying and licensing appropriate popular music recordings. By the 1980s, the pressure to incorporate songs into films was sufficiently high to necessitate hiring a specialist to assist the filmmakers in choosing the songs and negotiating the legal and financial contracts. (These specialists were first called "Music Consultants"—not to be confused with ethnic or historic music consultants who are also used in films from time to time—but the nomenclature soon settled on "Music Supervisor.") As studios and their recording affiliates realized the income possibilities that came along with soundtrack compilation recordings (*Saturday Night Fever*, *The Big Chill*, *Dirty Dancing*), experienced music supervisors such as Budd Carr (longtime Oliver Stone collaborator), Bonnie Greenberg (*How the Grinch Stole Christmas* [2000], *Something's Gotta Give* [2003]), Peter Afterman (*The Passion of the Christ* [2004]), Sharon Boyle (*Silence of the Lambs* [1991]), and Karyn Rachtman (longtime Quentin Tarantino collaborator) soon became essential as conduits between filmmakers, bands, and recording and film executives. At first, music supervisors were hired, like the rest of the music department, to assist during postproduction because that was the point at which decisions on music had traditionally been made. Once the position became regularized, however, music supervisors have been hired much earlier in the process, often in preproduction, and have been given much broader responsibilities, from supervising the overall musical content of the film to assisting the director and producers in the selection of composers.

SOUND DEPARTMENT

The shift to Dolby stereo (and digital sound in the 1990s) brought new prominence to the sound department. One indication of this was the appearance of the creative role of the sound designer (or supervising sound editor), responsible for imagining and coordinating the production of the sound track (aside from music) much as the cinematographer does the image. Although the sound design for a film must obviously be made in consultation with the director, the sound designer is the person responsible for making decisions to realize such ideas. As film sound grows in importance, the role of the "sound designer"—a title Walter Murch imported from traditional theater—has become crucial. (The title itself is less common in Hollywood, where the traditional division between mixing and editing remains relatively strict.)

Figure 11-9. *Lara Croft: Tomb Raider* (2001). In this scene (07:34–09:30), Manfred Powell (Iain Glen), who has been charged with finding the Key, stands before the Council of Illuminati to report his progress. Despite a large amount of offscreen dialogue and wide shifts of shot scale, the dialogue remains at a constant level and squarely centered in the stereo field. The large space is cued, however, through the use of pronounced reverb.

Partly due to the reverberant space, the tempo of the dialogue is quite slow, appropriate for the formal setting and the gravity of the discussion. Much of the head of the Council's dialogue is delivered offscreen, which disassociates his voice from his body, allowing the words to transcend the limits of the character. The use of apparently nondiegetic singing voices at the opening and bells tolling periodically throughout reinforce the ecclesiastical setting suggested by the exterior shot of the Santa Maria Della Salute (Venice) in the establishing sequence. The interior, however, is the Painted Hall at the Old Royal Naval College (Greenwich, London), a secular space appropriate to a secret society. The mysterious quality of the quest for the Key is emphasized by brooding strings and a thrice-stated piano figure that displace the voices from the sound track as talk turns to the Key itself. Crackling thunder interspersed with the instrumental music adds to the effect, portending that the Key will unlock something ominous and supernatural.

The digital production and sound synthesis tools available to composers have proved important resources to the sound department as well, since these tools allow the sound team to craft the sound track for the needs of the story. Even during the studio era, sound effects recorded during production were rarely used and filmmakers in fact worked to minimize production sounds other than dialogue, in part because the sound department needed to capture production dialogue as cleanly as possible in order to facilitate editing. Sound effects would then be edited in, like music, during postproduction, and the inclusion of effects was determined primarily by narrative pertinence rather than producing sound that faithfully reproduced the depicted scene. This practice, in turn, led the sound department to evaluate sound precisely according to its effect, and the increasing dynamic and frequency range and the stereo field of improved technology led not to sounds that were more faithful reproductions of "real" sound but to sounds that more effectively clarified the narrative or that could viscerally render the sound it represented. The point was not to more accurately record the sound of a particular punch—how it sounded—but to construct a sound that produced the feeling of that punch—how it felt. Michel Chion calls this practice of constructing sounds and indeed whole soundscapes around the feeling that sound imparts "rendering," and along with symbolic uses of sound, rendering was one of the primary ways sound design developed. (For an example from a recent film, see Figure 11-9.)

The concept of rendering depended on understanding sound as having an affective register very similar to music and indeed on the idea that sound might be molded to characterization and narrative situation much as music has traditionally been. This shift in emphasis led in turn to sound departments moving away from depending largely on sound effects libraries and turning instead to foley, recording sounds specifically for the film, synthesizing sounds, and processing sounds extensively in postproduction. Foley became an art not simply of matching the sounds of the principal bodies but of endowing those bodies with character through sound. As with rendering, foley is less about sonic fidelity than about using sound to tap an affective register that aids in characterization, narrative clarity, and affective investment. ADR (automated dialogue replacement) or looping, which had been used from the earliest days of sound film to fix recording problems in the production dialogue, was increasingly routine, as more location shooting, noisy action scenes, and effects shots made capturing production dialogue ever more precarious, time-consuming, and therefore expensive. In addition, filmmakers learned that worrying less about sound on the set could speed up the shooting schedule considerably, and the increasingly powerful digital editing tools made manipulating sound and synchronizing it to the image much easier. Recording speech in ADR also allowed the actors to be able to concentrate on carefully modulating their vocal performance without needing to worry about the positioning of their bodies, and the actors could also deliver a set of different vocal interpretations that would give the director and dialogue editor more options when editing a scene. We present a full discussion of the transforming effects of digital audio in Chapter 13.

Sound Design and Elements of Style

ISSUES OF AESTHETICS: SOUND DESIGN

Dolby stereo (and later digital sound) represented less a definitive break with earlier stereo sound than a continuation or "thawing" of the frozen revolution that the original introduction of stereo had promised. The advantages of working with the increased frequency response and stereo sound of Dolby came not just from improved definition and fidelity but from the density of sounds it permitted in the mix. Unlike the earlier generation of magnetic stereo for Cinemascope and Todd-AO, where the surround channel in particular was rarely used, the much wider dispersion of Dolby permitted more extensive employment—especially after the success of *Star Wars*. (The surround fields could also be collapsed or eliminated relatively easily when remixing into mono for television.) As Michael Cimino noted in 1978 during work on *The Deer Hunter*, Dolby has "the ability to create a density of detail of sound—a richness so you can demolish the wall separating the viewer from the film."[13]

This density of detail led directly to more careful construction of the sound track. Before Dolby, the sound track remained of secondary concern. Most sound effects, for instance, were not produced specifically for the film, but instead selected from a stock sound library. This basic indifference to the sound track is perhaps best illustrated by the fact that foley artists—specialists in producing synchronized sound effects—were not regularized as part of postproduction until the 1970s. By one account, there were fewer than ten foley artists regularly working in the early 1970s.

The situation began to change with the emergence of the sound designer, who was employed to give significant attention to the overall sound of the film. The rise of the sound designer is correlated with the rise of a generation of film-makers formally trained at film schools rather than through informal mentor-ing. In film schools, the students received training that was as much intellectual as practical. This situation fit with the emergence of the New Hollywood and "high concept" production. Each member of the creative team worked in concert with the director (but also the producer) to realize this concept. (A clear defin-ition of the concept itself through the film was a major concern inasmuch as the clarity of the concept facilitated the ancillary tie-ins.) As the guardian of the con-cept, the director, who already enjoyed a fairly large level of prestige, became an even more important figure, but other members of the creative team gained as well. Because the "look" of the film played a significant role in clearly articulat-ing the concept, the cinematographer enjoyed a particular elevated level of pres-tige, becoming an "auteur" of sorts as well.

Although lagging somewhat behind the trend in cinematography, sound design increasingly also became recognized as a crucial aesthetic component of filmmaking. Composers continued to occupy an important place, as they had for decades, but sound designers now began to be recognized in a similar way for their contribution. Ben Burtt's work on *Star Wars* and Walter Murch's on *Apocalypse Now* (1979) led the way (Figure 11-10), although the importance of sound in terms of the concept did not realize its full potential until the rise of videogames, where sound (in addition to music) could feed directly into that ancillary product.

AESTHETICS AND THE STEREO FIELD

Due no doubt to the experience of Cinemascope and Todd-AO stereo, the implementation of Dolby stereo was understood as an incremental rather than a revolutionary shift in the sound track. As with earlier stereo, Dolby touted its directionality, but now the emphasis really fell on creating a sense of sonic

Figure 11-10. *Apocalypse Now* (1979). The "Helicopter Attack" carefully mixes a recording of Wagner's "Ride of the Valkyries" with wind, bombs, guns, and various helicopter noises. The overall density of noise is controlled by constantly raising the levels of some sounds while lowering those of others. Indeed, Murch says that he rarely if ever used "more than three thematic groupings of sound at the same time" in the film. He continues:

> If I had played the helicopters and the Valkyries *and* the artillery *and* the background voices at full volume at the same time, it would just collapse into a big mush of sound. . . . If you want something to sound loud you have to have a detail in it—especially for a prolonged sequence—and to have detail you have to limit the information to just less than three conceptual levels. . . . What I was doing in the mix was constantly shifting, only keeping two sounds up at any one moment and a third either on the way up or on the way out, depending on the point of view or what you were looking at. My goal throughout the film was to combine density and clarity. If something is clear but isn't dense enough, if it doesn't have any heft to it, I try to find something to make it have heft. If something is as dense as you want it but you can't understand anything in it, what do I have to take out to make it clear? So I'm always looking for that balance point between density and clarity.[14]

continuity with motion and location rather than on registering motion and location accurately. As Robert Warren, a Dolby engineer, explained: "if a sound moves from left to right, the sound field in front is consistent. You simply observe the motion of it moving; you don't hear it changing color or changing timbre as it shifts."[15] The surround channels, on the contrary, functioned as background, that is, as ambient sound. An impression of directionality and location was in fact avoided. Instead, the idea is

> to flood the auditorium with sound from everywhere but the screen, so that you have a very wide natural sound field that really doesn't have any direction or motion to it. Since the surround channel is primarily used from ambiences . . . room tone, and special effects, fly-ins and fly-outs, you don't want the surround

channel to detract or to pull your attention away from the story on the screen. . . . Probably the best way to observe sound that's coming from the surround channel is to turn it off. If you can hear the difference, then it's probably loud enough for ambiences and room tones.[16]

Ambient sound has proven an especially effective way to differentiate intercut story lines. Most of *Sleepless in Seattle* (1993) presents action involving Annie (Meg Ryan) and Sam (Tom Hanks) separately. These scenes, however, are often presented together through parallel editing. Subtle shifts in ambient sound underscore the cuts from Annie to Sam and back. The parallel editing illustrates the connection between the two—although they do not know each other. The difference in ambient sound marks the distance that still remains to be overcome. (For another example with commentary, see Figure 11-11.)

If Robert Warren's description defines the normative functions of the front and surround speakers, more inventive use of sound has tended to devolve from blurring the interpretive clarity that such normative functionality provides. Indeed, one of the hallmarks of filmmaking in the era of Dolby sound has been a willingness to push against the limits set by the classical style, to risk, for instance, clarity of dialogue to capture the spectacle of a particular sonic effect (overlapping dialogue, colliding effects and dialogue, etc.). Stereo certainly raised the potential for blurring interpretive clarity if only because it permitted an increased density of sound. A willingness to risk an erosion of clarity, however, is ultimately an issue of aesthetic commitment. Overlapping dialogue, for instance, had already been used effectively in screwball comedies of the 1930s to

a | b   **Figure 11-11.** In *The Princess Bride* (1987), a grandfather (Peter Falk) reads a story to his sick grandson (Fred Savage). As he does, the story of "The Princess Bride" comes alive. Throughout, however, the story is interrupted occasionally by abrupt returns to the bedroom (a), where the grandson expresses reactions and increasing investment in the story. Background sound is used to separate the bedroom scenes from the world of the story. The bedroom scenes play with silence as a background, whereas the story space (b) is marked with a rich mix of ambient sound and nondiegetic music. Each shift back to the bedroom registers as a sonic disappointment, making the story world seem ever more enchanting by comparison.

give a sense of an unruly and disordered world. Prior to multitrack recording, overlapping dialogue proved somewhat troublesome because it was difficult to fix mistakes in performance and recording. Multitrack recording addressed these problems by recording each actor on a separate track, allowing the voices to be mixed in postproduction. This procedure gave much more control to the filmmakers. Although released in monaural sound, *M*A*S*H* made effective and extensive use of overlapping dialogue (recall Figure 2-9). Indeed, the character of Radar is in many respects defined through his exchanges in overlapping dialogue, as he seems to anticipate the needs of Colonel Blake.

Overlapping dialogue achieved its disorienting effect by treating speech contrapuntally, that is, by putting dialogue into conflict with itself, making it difficult to follow both strands of conversation. In this sense, overlapping dialogue was a particular strategy for increasing the density of sound, but its weakness was that the actors' words frequently became unintelligible in monaural sound. Stereo separation allowed for an increase in density without necessarily imperiling intelligibility, and films produced since 1990 have become increasingly complex in this respect.

The dense sonic texture made possible by the stereo sound track has allowed sound to take on a number of expository functions once reserved for the image track. Establishment is now as likely to be handled aurally as visually. Rich ambient sound allows location to be effectively conveyed without visuals. Rather than showing a shot of a crashing surf and then cutting to a specific location on the beach, filmmakers today are as likely to place the sound of the waves over the end of the previous sequence (as a sound advance) and then use that as a cue to cut straight to the scene on the beach. The idea of using sound to bridge sequences certainly does not require stereo. In the era of monaural sound, music in particular would often overlap changes in location, either heralding the narrative shift with music serving a bridging function or completing a musical thought from the previous sequence as the new sequence is established. As Figure 11-12 suggests, sound bridges today are used much as music bridges were in the monaural period. The main difference is that music bridges typically involve non-diegetic music whereas sound bridges typically use diegetic sound.

Stereo, although not deployed overtly in smaller scale films such as romantic comedies, nevertheless has fundamentally altered the treatment of sound. In the scene from *Sleepless in Seattle* (1993) analyzed in Chapter 1 (recall Figures 1-8 through 1-12), for instance, most of the treatment of sound is made more effective by the presence of stereo. The density of sounds on the road, for instance, would be difficult to convey in monaural sound. Consequently, the magical intimacy of the exchange of "hellos" across the road would be difficult, if not impossible, to render in the absence of stereo sound. It is indeed the reduction of the ambience in the stereo field, the displacement of the street sounds in favor of the dialogue, that gives us this strong sense of a private connection between Sam and Annie. Although it would certainly have been possible to render the "hellos" without stereo sound, it would have been more difficult to achieve the effect of strong

Figure 11-12. *O Brother, Where Art Thou?* (2000). The film opens with ambient insect sounds, bird calls, and the rhythmic fall of pick axes, all this over the Universal logo. Although the opening black-and-white shot has characteristics of establishment—a wide-angle shot of a field and then a slow pan—the falling pick axes and the singing leave the shot uncertain. Indeed, the sound here entirely transforms the signification of the pan, which seems motivated by a need to solve the enigma of the sound source. The camera movement serves not to reveal landscape, as is the typical function of such pans, but to reveal a sound source.

contrast, the juxtaposition of this moment with the surrounding noise. In a sense, the disappearance of the rich sonic detail makes the "hellos" sound enchanted, as if the special intimacy between the two characters is able to shut out the world, here symbolized by the ambient field.

The increased dynamic range was one of the most striking characteristics of theatrical sound in the 1980s and 1990s, but this example from *Sleepless in Seattle* illustrates that it is the ability to control dynamic range precisely that is perhaps of greatest value—the artful use of dynamic contrast is far more effective than absolute volume.

SCORING PRACTICES

After falling somewhat out of disfavor during the 1960s, the orchestral score re-emerged as a usual component of the New Hollywood blockbuster. Credit for revitalizing the orchestral score is often given to John Williams, especially for his work on *Jaws, Close Encounters of the Third Kind,* and especially *Star Wars.* Without discounting Williams's real contributions—among other things, he developed a musical approach capable of integrating smoothly with a richly textured, and often extremely loud and obtrusive, sound design—the return of the orchestral score probably had as much to do with the types of films that New Hollywood favored, many of which consciously reworked genres from the studio era and so drew on attributes, including music, appropriate to those types of films. The use of Dolby stereo was also an important factor, as orchestral music sounded particularly rich on it. (In that sense, much as in the 1950s, the orchestral score was a means of advertising the capabilities of sound technology.)

Popular music, which had only been released regularly in stereo since the end of the 1960s, also sounded good on Dolby sound tracks. The stereo field also meant that popular music could be mixed at a much higher level without masking other sounds, allowing filmmakers to opt for a "wall of sound" approach that was able to highlight the presence of popular music on the sound track. This encouraged the trend, initiated in the 1960s, toward compilation scoring, which became even more prominent in the 1980s, when the emergence of MTV, which began broadcasting in 1981, opened a new outlet for cross-marketing film and music. The period from 1975–2000 was indeed a particularly lucrative one for soundtrack albums.

Composers began using synthesizers and electronic music to score films as early as the 1950s, where these sounds quickly coalesced into a musical topic for the otherworldly, especially in science fiction. But no one at the time could have imagined the extent of the influence that electronics would have upon the creation of the film sound track outside of science fiction. Reductions in the size of the equipment, improvements in mobility, and decreases in cost—as well as quality and quantity of sonic options—began in the 1970s and continued through the 1980s and 1990s. Films that made prominent use of synthesizers during this period include *Chariots of Fire* (1981) and *Blade Runner* (1982) by Vangelis and *Witness* by Maurice Jarre (1985). *Blade Runner* fit loosely with the science fiction connotations of the synthesizer, but neither *Chariots of Fire* nor *Witness* did, as the story line in each of these latter films would have easily accepted a traditional orchestral score.

With the development of high-quality samplers in the 1980s, it also became increasingly possible to make reasonable counterfeits of live acoustic instruments. By substituting synthesizers for some live players—especially strings—composers found they could cut music costs while still retaining the traditional orchestral foundation. Such electronic reinforcement was particularly useful on lower budget films and for work in television. Increasingly, reinforcement was also used for instrumental backings (especially strings) in popular music recording and even to augment the regular small Broadway pit orchestra in such live theater shows as *Les Misérables*. What started out as a way to limit costs through mechanization increasingly turned into an aesthetic value of its own. By 2000, it was not uncommon for composers to reinforce a recording of a full symphony orchestra with synthetic imitations of acoustic instruments for the accrued timbral associations with popular music and because this somewhat hyperbolic sound was increasingly coming to define the cinematic orchestral sound, much as sweetening through overdubbing had done previously.

THE MINIMALIST UNDERSCORE

In some ways responding to the alienating atonality that dominated art music composition through the 1960s and 1970s, a number of young composers at the

Jerry Goldsmith, whose film credits include Alien *(1979) and* Star Trek: The Motion Picture *(1979), partly made his reputation through his skill in writing electronic music, a mode that emerged, via synthesizers, in the 1970s and 1980s. Many composers resisted using electronics, but he thought they gave him more freedom, although he believed that they were meant to enhance and add to the orchestra, not to replace it.*
—See Elmer Bernstein, "A Conversation with Jerry Goldsmith," in Cooke, The Hollywood Film Music Reader.

time pushed in a different direction, one that worked against the inherent complexities of atonal composition. The result was a kind of music built on a high degree of repetition that was termed *minimalism*, and its development was primarily associated with a set of American composers: LaMonte Young, Terry Reilly, Philip Glass, Steve Reich, and later John Adams. Louis Andriessen and Michael Nyman, both of whom composed for film—Nyman extensively—are two Europeans who are often also grouped with these American minimalists. Besides a high degree of repetition, minimalist music also tended to avoid broader patterns of melodic construction in favor of textures created from the repetition of intricately interlocking repeating musical motives. Minimalist music often therefore seems to be without melody, and has become a means of composing a-melodic ambient textures that nevertheless project and sustain a particular range of moods from religious contemplation to anxious pensiveness to the mindless repetitiveness of mass consumer society.

Minimalism quickly became a style that film composers strove to master and assimilate to the film scoring technique, much as in earlier generations film composers had worked to domesticate atonality into a musical topic of psychological disturbance and to turn the simplified pastoral style that Aaron Copland developed in the 1930s and 1940s into the emblematic Hollywood musical topic for the American West (and by extension the embodiment of the ideal of America itself).

In terms of film scoring, Glass and Nyman are the composers associated with minimalism who have worked the most in film. A key score was Glass's music for *Koyaanisqatsi* (1982), which would become one of the most iconic film scores of the decade. Essentially a silent documentary with recorded musical score, *Koyaanisqatsi* uses time-lapse images of natural landscapes, cityscapes, and technology to explore the theme that contemporary life is "unbalanced." (The title is a Hopi word meaning, roughly, "life out of balance.")

The film reaches its crux in the long sequence known as "The Grid," which lasts more than 20 minutes and where the time-lapse technique reveals the various flows that determine and regulate modern urban society. It begins almost peacefully with shots of buildings reflecting the setting sun (44:09) that give way to nighttime imagery of cars floating along roads quite suggestive of a pulsing circulatory system (45:20). Glass's music at first, almost a lullaby, seems to capture the gentle flow and suggest a city resting but alive.

After this introductory phase, which ends with the moon passing behind a building (47:45), the music transitions quickly to a faster, louder, and more insistent pattern (or rather a strict alternation between two patterns distinguished by meter), and the images focus on particular roadways in a way that emphasizes the speed of the transportation flow, especially when the synthesizers enter. With a shift to day (48:53), voices are introduced and the patterns of the accompanying music change somewhat, though the regular metrical alternation continues from the previous section. A closer shot of the street level (49:38) makes individual cars and people distinguishable, but the slow frame rate ensures that everything continues to move at an unnaturally fast pace that emphasizes the pulses and flows. Much as the entry of the synthesizers had suggested that the night-time transportation flow was not sleepy, so too here the return of the fast-pounding synthesizers marks a shift from cars to people. People are first shown scattering through a train station (50:38), but soon they start to organize into queues, and the parallel to the channeling of the rationalized flow of cars along roadways is not easily missed, especially in the few shots that cut back and forth between people and cars.

The final stage of the elaborate comparison is reached with shots of machines of production. The first machine (52:24), part of a sausage producing plant, seemingly produces without the presence of people. Subsequent shots show people operating other kinds of machines, and the full effect of the cutting is to blur lines between people, machines, and products. This purposeful confusion is particularly pronounced in the bald juxtaposition of the sausage casing machine (54:03) with people riding escalators (54:29), especially since the music does not distinguish between them. The remainder of the sequence grows increasingly frenetic, with more and more emphasis on the way people's working, eating, and even leisure service and sustain a social machine whose seemingly insatiable drive only becomes manifest at the scale of the time-lapse photography.

Although Glass's minimalist idiom of "The Grid" has become associated with the excesses and repetitive pressures of mass consumer society, the general style of minimalism has proved surprisingly versatile. Michael Nyman's score for *The Piano* (1993) draws on minimalist textures but adds rudimentary melodic material to give expression to the interiority of the mute pianist Ada (Holly Hunter). Glass's own score for *Kundun* (1997) likewise uses a more subdued version of his own idiom and incorporates throat singing and Tibetan instruments into the orchestration. The result is a score that reflects the complicated intersection of modernity and spirituality as the fourteenth Dalia Lama attempts to steer Tibet through the Chinese invasion before eventually being forced to flee. Thomas Newman deploys minimalist textures to underscore the ennui of American suburban life in *American Beauty* (1999).

MUSIC VIDEO STYLE

Music video did not serve only as an effective promotional tool. The style of the music video also profoundly affected film style during much of the 1980s and 1990s. Given that the MTV audience was one of the most important market segments for film, it should hardly be surprising that filmmakers would turn to the music video for inspiration. Some of the particularly influential traits of music video style were fast, rhythmic editing patterns and the use of music as an underlying continuity to narratively elliptical editing. Films strongly influenced by music video style include *Flashdance* (1983) and *Top Gun* (1986), both high concept films produced by Jerry Bruckheimer and Don Simpson. In *Flashdance* (1983), for instance, the arrival of each song is marked by a pronounced shift to a music video style for the duration of the song. This strategy is somewhat akin to

The film scores of Thomas Newman show the influence of minimalist composers like Philip Glass, but Newman enlivens his scores with allusions to pop, rock, jazz, and folk styles as well as experimental timbres. He believes that the composer's job is to compose music appropriate to each filmic moment, fitting the director's vision. Thus, Newman must at times rely on the "ritual" of traditional orchestral scoring, as in period films like Little Women *(1994), but in films such as* The Rapture *(1991) and* Shawshank Redemption *(1994), he was able to employ more avant-garde instrumental timbres and electronic manipulation.* —See "Thomas Newman on His Film Music," in Cooke, *The Hollywood Film Music Reader.*

the musicals of the studio era, which similarly shifted to highly stylized presentations for musical numbers as characters burst into song, the real world dissolved into the idealized world of romance, and editing, choreography, and camera movement were all subordinated to the music for the length of the song. Instead of bursting into song, a film like *Flashdance* instead bursts into MTV video. The nature of the fantasy space had shifted from the musical's production number rooted in the practice of live theatrical performance to *Flashdance*'s music video rooted in the practice of highly mediated images.

Bruckheimer produced films using this style of editing—especially in action sequences—extensively through the 1980s and 1990s. Indeed, the elliptical, fast-paced rhythmic editing of music video style has now become one of the standard ways of assembling action sequences, which are particularly suitable for the style because such sequences are where spectacle, narrative dislocation, and sensory overload are the rule. This is the case in *Top Gun*, where the flight sequences in particular use this style. (See Figure 11-13.) The extent to which this strategy has become ubiquitous can be seen in a film such as *The Matrix* (1999), where the fight sequences (for example, the Lobby Shootout) follow this strategy. In both these cases, the editing in the action sequences departs significantly from that used elsewhere in the film, which gives these sequences a kind of narrative autonomy: like the musical numbers in *Flashdance*, these action sequences, too, resemble production numbers in musicals that can be easily excerpted as sequences and, to a certain degree, rearranged within the narrative without materially damaging it. In other words, such sequences are "modular" in the sense that Justin Wyatt identifies as a characteristic trait of high concept, New Hollywood cinema.[17] Such modularity is one reason that sequences like these can feel like proto-videogames: indeed, the pounding music, loose narrative integration, and frenetic visuals of the action sequences often serve as the basis for game transfers from

a | b | c   **Figure 11-13.** *Top Gun* (1986). The flight sequences draw extensively on frenetic and rhythmic editing to music. The promotional music videos return the favor by making extensive use of the flight sequences. Kenny Loggins's "Danger Zone" was one of four videos released to help market the film. Typical of these cross-promotional videos, it intercuts (a) shots of the singer or group with (b) flashes of narrative and (c) action from the film.

Figure 11-14. *Lola rennt* (*Run Lola Run*, 1998). Almost all of this film is conceived in music video style, not the modular style of *Top Gun* or *The Matrix*. Lola (Franka Potente) has 20 minutes to find 100,000 Deutschmarks and save her boyfriend, Manni (Moritz Bleibtreu). The film goes through the scenario three times. A slight difference at the beginning of each iteration mushrooms, leading to remarkably different outcomes, only one of which is happy. Each iteration is underscored by its own song, but all are dominated by images of Lola running. The editing makes frequent use of jump cuts, extremely short shot lengths, and other means of narrative dislocation, all of which serve to emphasize by contrast the brief narrative stability of certain recurring events that allow us to measure the slight differences among the iterations on the one hand and to isolate the act of running itself on the other. The music ensures an underlying continuity to each sequence while also expressing Lola's relentless drive that manifests itself in her run.

film narratives. *Lola rennt* (*Run Lola Run*, 1998) is an example of a film that uses music video style in a somewhat less modular fashion—see Figure 11-14.

THE RISE OF RAP

With the rise of rap as a commercial genre in the 1980s, film studios worked to find a way to exploit this music's popularity, and already by the late 1980s it was not unusual to find rap being used on the sound track like any other popular music genre. Diegetically, rap could serve to establish time, place, and character, as in the case of Run DMC's "Christmas in Hollis" in *Die Hard* (1988). Here, near the beginning of the film, Argyle (De'voreaux White) plays the song on the radio of the limo as he drives McClane (Bruce Willis) to the Christmas party. This song is explicitly contrasted to Bach's Third Brandenburg Concerto heard at the party itself, a piece used to characterize the executive class milieu of McClane's wife, Holly (Bonnie Bedelia). Not surprisingly, one of the primary narrative tensions

Timeline

1969   Twentieth Century Fox releases *Butch Cassidy and the Sundance Kid.*

1974   Universal releases *Earthquake,* the first film to use Sensurround; Dolby noise reduction begins to appear on release prints.

1976   *A Star Is Born,* the first film to use the Dolby Stereo matrix for exhibition, is released.

1977   Twentieth Century Fox releases *Star Wars*; *Saturday Night Fever* is released.

1978   *La Cage aux Folles* is released.

1979   *Apocalypse Now* is released.

1981   Paramount releases *Raiders of the Lost Ark. Gallipoli* is released; MTV begins broadcasting.

1982   *Koyaanisqatsi* is released.

1983   Paramount releases *Flashdance.*

of the film turns out to be concern class, which threatens the relationship between McClane and Holly.

Other films have been constructed more consistently around rap and a hip-hop ethos where the sound track is dominated by the music. Predictably, these films are generally set in a contemporary, urban environment, where as a musical genre rap has taken on many of the cultural connotations that jazz held in the 1920s through the 1960s. These films are often divided into two categories: "hip hop" and "hood" films. Generically, these subgenres can be differentiated by whether the presentation of the urban environment is positive (hip hop, the celebration of city life) or negative (the "hood," the alienation and dislocations of urban life). Whereas hip-hop films do not conceal underlying social problems and injustices that press upon the communities in which the films are set, their basic spirit remains comedic or satirical. The films of Spike Lee generally fall in this category. The "hood" films, by contrast, draw on the dystopic iconography of gangsta rap music videos. Although the "hood" films proved the more commercially viable during the 1990s, the valorization of crime in these films has also brought with it critical condemnation similar to what gangsta rap itself suffered, and many of the films remain controversial for this reason. *Boyz n the Hood* (1991) and *Menace II Society* (1993) are the two best known examples of "hood" films.

The gangsta rap of the "hood" films draws on and plays into the musical genre's demonic connotations—similar in some respects to heavy metal—and these connotations were effectively set and exploited already, albeit somewhat

1985   Universal releases *Out of Africa*; regular stereo broadcast of TV begins in the U.S.

1986   Paramount releases *Top Gun*; *Platoon* is released.

1988   Twentieth Century Fox releases *Die Hard*.

1989   MGM releases *When Harry Met Sally*; TriStar releases *Glory*.

1991   *Terminator 2: Judgment Day* is released. Columbia releases *Boyz n the Hood*.

1993   TriStar Pictures releases *Sleepless in Seattle*.

1996   United Artists releases *The Birdcage*.

1998   *Lola rennt (Run Lola Run)* is released; Dreamworks releases *Saving Private Ryan*.

1999   Warner Bros. releases *The Matrix*.

tepidly, in the Fat Boy's "Are You Ready for Freddy," which featured Robert Englund in his guise as Freddy Krueger and was used over the end credits of *A Nightmare on Elm Street 4: The Dream Master* (1988).

Filmmakers have tried to exploit popular music performers as actors since at least Rudy Vallee in the earliest years of the sound film. The same has been true with rap, and commercially the most successful actor in this regard has been Will Smith. His films generally feature some of his own music, at least a title track, which can then be used for cross-promotional videos and as part of a soundtrack album. *Men in Black* (1997) is a good example of this; the title song appears only over the credits.

Summary

Technological, commercial, and cultural changes significantly affected the sound of the feature film in the period from the 1950s into the 1990s: the use of magnetic tape in postproduction, the introduction and gradual adoption of stereo sound reproduction and Dolby stereo, the move to multiplex theaters as the dominant mode of film exhibition, and the emergence of the sound designer, coupled with a greater complexity in the treatment of different musical styles (especially the use of popular music as background scoring) all contributed to changes that mark off older films and their exhibition practices as "classic" and that, if anything, have been intensified and exaggerated into the present day.

Music and Film Form in the New Hollywood

Introduction

As we explained in Chapter 11, "New Hollywood" is useful as a way to distinguish the work of a generation of auteur directors, but it has definite drawbacks as a general term to characterize feature film production in the last quarter of the twentieth century. It would be better to say that the trends starting in the post-classical decades continued and in some respects accelerated: the ongoing con-solidation of finance under conglomerates, multinational production, the gradual rise of transnational cinemas to the world stage, the rise of distinctive directorial personalities and styles, the continuing development of complex and sophisti-cated sound tracks, the continued broadening of the range of musical styles, and the wide variety of functional treatments of music. The foundation of the feature film is still the classical model from earlier in the century, but the historical pat-tern continues toward a more complex image track and a sound track "designed" according to aesthetic choices. In this framework, musical genres are used broadly as referential, but there is still a "universal" or neutral orchestral compo-sitional style.

To emphasize the sense of continuity but also creative development, this chapter has a parallel design to Chapter 10. The first two sections discuss main-stream feature films, a drama and a romantic comedy: *Out of Africa*, one of the top award-winning films of the 1980s, and *When Harry Met Sally*, a characteris-tic early film of writer-director-producer Nora Ephron. The third section picks up the narrative of sound and music in war films, and the fourth looks at action scenes in other genres. The "reciprocal influence" section that follows that one discusses a French classic, *La Cage aux Folles*, and its close American remake starring Robin Williams and Nathan Lane, *The Birdcage*. Finally, we extend the instructions for compare-contrast papers from Chapter 10 to include develop-ment of an historical argument by means of scene comparison from films in different time periods, a method of which there are several exemplars in the main sections of the chapter.

Mainstream Dramatic Film: *Out of Africa*

After the mid-1960s, the historical epics based on the Greek and Roman era had been largely displaced by those situated in more recent history, from the Napoleonic wars through World War II. War films, as we discussed in Chapter 10 (and revisit later in this chapter as well), increasingly took on the form of spectacle. Others, though centered on large historical events, tended more and more to focus on individuals and on romantic and family relationships and thus to overlap with the family melodrama and romantic drama. Among the earliest of this type were *War and Peace* (1956), *Giant* (1956), and *Raintree Country* (1957), but the trend became especially notable in *Shenandoah* (1965), *Doctor Zhivago* (1965), *Nicholas and Alexandra* (1971), and others. The four feature films with the largest numbers of awards in the 1980s were all of this kind: *Gandhi* (1982), *Amadeus* (1984), *The Last Emperor* (1987), and *Out of Africa* (1985).

PROLOGUE AND TITLE SEQUENCE

The film's opening makes it clear that we are going to see more than a simple tale of travel and romance. Like *The Sound of Music* (another memoir-based film), *Out of Africa* begins with a long prologue. Only after 5½ minutes does the main title appear; from that point on, the sequence is conventional; we reach the first scene at 07:30.

The prologue itself is quite complex. It begins ambiguously with a sunrise over an African landscape, the sound of a clarinet, a woman sleeping, a man profiled against the sun. Things gradually become clearer as a woman speaks in voice-over narration, reminiscing about her life in Africa and, in so doing, identifying each of the previous images for us. At about 01:30, cut to a room where the woman is writing: Meryl Streep's character, Karen, the Baroness von Blixen (whose pen name was Isak Dinesen). Her voice-over narration continues and we now understand it to be the text of her memoir, spoken as she writes (Figure 12-1a and b). At a reference to her life in Europe, we see a preliminary scene set there (a flashback, in other words). The main-title sequence follows. The body of the film is thus plainly marked as the staging of the memoir. A text prologue might have accomplished the same thing, but placing the prologue before the titles more forcefully sets the story off from present time, thereby emphasizing a quality of memory, "pastness," or even the sense of unreality or perhaps the mythic that always attends memory.

Voice-over narration is sometimes used as a substitute for stationary or rolling text in prologues. Examples familiar from earlier chapters include the prologues after the main titles and credit sequences in *Rebecca* (1940) and *Casablanca* (1942). Narrated prologues often occur without music, but when music is added it typically supplies an emotional edge that may or may not be obvious in the disembodied voice. That is certainly true in the case of *Casablanca*, where the effect of the serious radio-style announcer is greatly increased by lugubrious music. In *Rebecca*, the dialogue underscoring style is used to emphasize the

A very similar use of the voice-over is when we see an insert of a letter whose text is read in voice-over or by a character momentarily offscreen. The contemporary analogue is an insert of a computer screen—as in You've Got Mail *(1998), the* Matrix *trilogy, and many others—or a cell phone, as in* Casino Royale *(2006), where repetition of such moments gives the cell phone text message the status of a motif.*

a	b
c	d

Figure 12-1. *Out of Africa* (1983). Prologue and establishing sequence.

several shifts in mood in Joan Fontaine's monologue. In *Out of Africa*, the music of the solo clarinet serves two purposes: to add a strong undertone of nostalgia and regret to the speaker's lines, and to introduce a theme that is especially associated with Karen and Denys Finch Hatton (Robert Redford). The point is clinched by the visual motif of the phonograph: see details of the first half of the prologue, following.

00:00	no sound, shot of globe and Universal studio credit
00:15	screen black, no sound
00:18	screen brightens to a view of an African landscape; the sun is just rising, music begins, the solo strains of a clarinet
00:35	cut to a woman's dream, then to her face as she sleeps in bed, then return to the African landscape with the sun just above the horizon, a man silhouetted against the sun
00:41	the woman begins to talk (as voice-over), and reminiscing as we still see views of African landscape
01:17	cut to mid-day, an airplane flying over the landscape
01:31	cut to the woman's room, bed on which a phonograph sits; camera pans over to her sitting at a desk and writing
01:44	cut back to Africa, the woman and man dance, kiss

01:55	cut back to the woman's room
02:00	begin slow pan right toward the window
02:09	the camera stops and holds on the window; it is snowing outside
02:15	gun shots are heard, the music stops, and the woman says, "It really began in Denmark"; from this cut to an outdoor scene of a shooting party.

Once the title sequence begins, action continues in the background as the various credits are shown: behind the text elements, images of the Kenyan land-scape track the progress of a passenger train (see Figures 12-1c and d.) As we would anticipate, the film's main theme starts up and swells at the appearance of the main title. This theme, however, has a definite musical form that continues until music goes out under the noise of the train (which we had previously seen but not heard) and the first scene begins. The form of the theme is the standard AABA design that we have encountered in earlier chapters: a phrase of music (A) is literally repeated with different text, then there is a different phrase (B, or the "bridge"), followed by a final repetition of the first phrase (A) with yet another new line of text. The underscore composer for *Out of Africa*, John Barry, distrib-utes the elements of this design across the credits sequence as follows: the theme phrase and its repetition (A, A) are played in a robust, firmly expressive manner (part 1); the bridge (B) drops back to a quieter, tentative state (part 2); and the reprise of A swells again to provide the dramatic conclusion (part 3), its final mo-ments tapering off as a quiet conclusion/transition (Part 4).

"ON SAFARI": THE SECOND DINNER

After Karen separates from her husband Bror (Klaus Maria Brandauer), she takes time out from managing the coffee plantation to go on safari with Denys, and, during their enforced isolation in the wild, the hint of a possible attraction slowly evolves into a full-blown sexual relationship. Two extended evening dinner scenes are crucial to this. The first begins shortly before 01:30:00, with a cut from a scene in which he assists her in washing her hair. A scene showing the following day's hunting is succeeded (with a simple cut at 01:37:21) by that evening's dinner. Denys puts the needle down on the gramophone (see the top of Figure 12-2), and we hear the first part of the theme for the first move-ment of Mozart's Piano Sonata in A major, K. 331, a pleasant pastoral melody (see Figure 12-3a). The gramophone itself is a motif with special significance, as it was a gift from Denys (recall Figure I-6). The elaborately set dinner table stands apart from its surroundings, as do Karen and Denys with it (the music—traditional European concert music—only reinforces that separation, marking itself as "music for Europeans in Africa").

The music almost appears to choreograph their actions: she comes out of her tent just as the second short phrase starts, then cut back to him standing up and looking toward her as the third short phrase starts, and at the end of the first

a | b
c | d

Figure 12-2. *Out of Africa.* Second safari dinner (love scene).

a
—
b

Figure 12-3. *Out of Africa.* Second safari dinner, musical themes. (a) Mozart, Piano Sonata in A Major, K331, first movement. (b) Eppel, "Missouri Waltz."

part, she sits down. The music is repeated, starting against a cut to the table with him opening wine; and so on. The end of the repeated music overlaps with a sentimental waltz (see Figure 12-3b), to which they dance and that we are presumably to understand as diegetic (as played on the gramophone), although it is obviously far too loud. They finish the dance, return to the table, and start to tell stories; but the waltz only fades slowly under her speaking several seconds later. When finished, she goes to her tent, and he follows after a short interval; they kiss, and we hear a short audio overlap (the film's main-title theme) before a cut to the next day, their third day of safari.

Note that music is used through most of the scene but not for the kiss (or the immediately preceding moment when he unties the strap of her blouse). A stereotypical upswell in the music normally serves a double role as transition or audio overlap if the scene ends, as here, with the kiss. Instead, the roles are kept very distinct: the two pieces on the gramophone (combined with the change from sitting at the table to the physical contact of dancing) gradually raise the emotional level, and the audio overlap is a simple, functional transition played at a low level. The physical contact between Karen and Denys in the tent, then, is separated from its surroundings, the final step in their isolation, as it were: the isolation of a couple making love.

FINAL SCENE AND END CREDITS

The end-credit sequence of *Out of Africa* is an early example of the most common contemporary model. The last chapter (the epilogue in Kristin Thompson's terminology) recounts Karen Blixen's final preparations to leave Africa and has the quality of a slow-moving final scene. There is no music for several minutes. A brief sound advance anticipates an extended shot of the train station as she gives her compass to the farm manager Farah (Malick Bowens); we hear ambient sound behind. When she turns to leave, music enters and the background sound disappears; shortly after—and before she is seen about to enter the train itself—she begins a voice-over that brings us back to the present of the story (that is, her writing her memoirs in Denmark). In these final moments, she recounts (in voice-over; we do not see her) one last nostalgic memory about Denys, then a superimposed legend tells us that she never returned to Africa, and a fade to black brings the credits. There is no "The End" card. The end-credit sequence itself runs just under 3 minutes with the familiar rolling credits against a black background. The music repeats the entire main theme from the beginning of the film, with a final repetition of the reprise phrase.

The two extremes of contemporary musical practices for end credits may be seen in films from 1994: Four Weddings and a Funeral, *where we hear irrelevant pop songs, unconnected to the underscoring music or any of the diegetic music of the film, and* The Shawshank Redemption, *which closes with a several-minute-long symphonic development of the film's main theme growing directly out of the music for the final scene.*

Mainstream Romantic Comedy: *When Harry Met Sally*

In Chapter 7, we noted that romantic comedies during the classical studio era typically used less nondiegetic music, especially dialogue underscore, than did dramatic films. In large part, this was due to the fact that these films were dominated by characters in extended and often fast-paced dialogue, the trademark of Cary Grant, Katharine Hepburn, Irene Dunne, Rosalind Russell, and a host of lesser known actors. We also noted that, by the mid-1940s, the trend of the previous decade started to reverse in all genres, and extensive dialogue underscoring became less and less common: three films from this period that, from a modern perspective, can be said to suffer from overly extensive background scoring are *Double Indemnity* (1944), *Spellbound* (1945), and *The Big Sleep* (1946). The exception to this trend was the heightened emotional environment of spectacles (especially historical films) and melodramas—two heavily scored examples from these genres are *Ben-Hur* (1959) and *Magnificent Obsession* (1954), respectively—and underscoring became more common in musicals as well. In general, this bias toward a limited use of dialogue underscoring except in a few film genres has persisted to the present day, with the very important qualification that, from the early 1970s, multitrack sound has allowed effects to take on some of the functions previously ascribed to background music, including close synchronization (recall instances of this from our discussion of scenes from *Good Will Hunting* in Chapter 1).

In addition to greater use of effects under dialogue, most film genres make more extensive use of voices in connection with offscreen sound and of sound overlaps of various kinds. The film *Emma* (1996), for example, contains several similar examples of the voice-off technique that create a mismatch of sound and image. At 13:58, Emma (Gwyneth Paltrow) and Harriet (Toni Collette) are walking along a creek, where they are presented in an extreme long shot, often even obscured by trees. Nevertheless, their dialogue is rendered with the clarity of a normal 2-shot, into which they eventually move. Another example appears shortly thereafter (15:16). Emma and Harriet are doing embroidery under a canopy. Again, they are first shown in extreme long shot but with the dialogue suggesting much closer proximity. The mismatch encourages a series of cuts that will eventually bring the image in line with the sound. At the end of this sequence, we are once again shown an extreme long shot, but this time the dialogue declines in clarity, moving in tandem with the distance as framed. A pattern of mismatched scale of image and sound continues throughout the film and seems calculated to coincide with the mismatched romantic pairings that Emma attempts to bring about.

In *Lost in Translation* (2003), Bob (Bill Murray) is jetlagged, having just arrived in Tokyo. He is in the hotel bar where a woman is singing. The sound track is filled with ambient chatter, and on the first shot of Bob some of the chatter grows more distinct. Offscreen voices indicate that they have recognized him. As they address him, the camera pans from Bob to reveal two young American businessmen. The two continue talking on a cut back to Bob, where he briefly responds, then gets up while the other voices carry on. The overall effect of the exchange is Bob's refusal to engage the other characters, who remain defined almost entirely by their offscreen voices. The fact that the voices remain offscreen minimizes the importance of these characters, while also suggesting a narrative direction that the film will not follow.

Sound overlaps play an important role in many romantic comedies, especially in situations where the characters are separated from one another or where one character is talking about the other or reminiscing. An especially extended and particularly striking example of diegetic dialogue used as a sound advance occurs in *When Harry Met Sally* (1989). In this sequence, we first hear Harry (Billy Crystal) talking to Sally (Meg Ryan) on the phone (35:29). As they talk, a series of brief scenes shows them apart, then together. Only at the end of the sequence (36:57) do the voices finally synchronize as we see both Harry and

Sally in split screen, each watching *Casablanca* with telephone receivers in their hands—see Figure 12-4. This sound advance is nearly 90 seconds in length!

Apart from its remarkable 1½-minute sound advance, *When Harry Met Sally* treats dialogue largely in the traditional manner of the romantic comedy, but a carefully graduated scheme of changes in framing creates clear visual analogues to the status of the couple's relationship. Much of the film's first half is spent in animated conversations between the two leads, who are only occasionally shown in a shot/reverse shot series—they are more frequently positioned opposite one another, a set-up that emphasizes their constant disagreements (see Figures 12-5a-b).

In the second act, announced by a "Five Years Later" subtitle, the two commiserate over broken relationships in an extended conversation that splices

The device of a plot that plays heavily on physical separation of the couple was common in romantic comedies of the 1930s, and if it was used selectively and to good effect in **When Harry Met Sally,** *in* Sleepless in Seattle *separation is more radical and thorough-going. The couple, Annie and Sam, are only briefly onscreen together before the film's final minutes. Even in those earlier moments, they are visually separated: recall Figure 1-9, where an unusual over-the-shoulder view is done as an ELS and the actors are isolated on screen when they barely manage to speak their intimate "hellos."*

Figure 12-4. *When Harry Met Sally* (1989). Split-screen conversation as the two watch *Casablanca*. Note that they are shown side by side, as if "shoulder to shoulder," not as if looking at one another.

Figure 12-5. *When Harry Met Sally.* (a) The two part after finishing their car trip from Chicago to New York. (b) The two meet several years later and talk while leaving an airport terminal.   a | b

together elements of a slow-moving montage—that is, it is dialogue itself that lends unity to a series of brief scenes (from 30:04 to 34:30). Speech had worked in the same way earlier to connect disparate shots during the long sound advance, but note that the final split-screen segment in Figure 12-4 still has them separated visually. Taken together, these two speech-controlled montages advance Harry and Sally's relationship: the two are now shown in activities together while they tell each other their stories and interact sympathetically. Director Nora Ephron's trademark elements of romantic sentimentality—old standards and old movies—are in full play here. The final minutes of *Casablanca*, of course, were shown on television as the two talked by phone, and during the second-act montage, we can just hear a low-volume phrase from the standard "It Had to Be You"—the song first heard in the main title sequence.

Over the course of the film, more frequent shot/reverse shot series and increasingly close framing follow Harry and Sally's developing relationship until a setback when they have a "one-night stand" they both regret (the scene begins at 1:07:10), after which the entire cycle repeats itself up to their final confrontation during a New Year's Eve party. This time the voice-over montage is delivered by Harry, starting at 1:24:45 as he is alone watching Dick Clark's New Year's Eve show on television. A hard cut with loud music at the party Sally is attending emphasizes the separation and is reinforced by a second hard cut to a quiet and darkened street as Harry walks (1:25:25). A return to the party and then to the street again (at 1:26:15) brings Harry to the place where Sally had dropped him off when they first arrived in New York, and he recalls an early conversation with her, during which we see a series of shots from previous scenes, a simple time-spanning montage. A very quiet, mostly one-line piano rendition of phrases from "It Had to Be You" that accompanied his wandering through the streets continues in the background, turning into a foregrounded vocal performance once he starts running. This performance acts as a sound advance: with another cut, it sounds like diegetic music at the party. When Harry arrives, the two talk, starting in MCU and ending in ECU—see Figures 12-6a-b. Yet another sound advance of the two talking leads to them sitting on a couch talking to the camera about their marriage.

a | b **Figure 12-6.** *When Harry Met Sally.* The two ECUs during the New Year's Eve Party, end of a series of shots that bring the couple together visually.

One can argue that the combination of voice-overs and sound advances guide this final chapter of the film: at first Harry is alone and we are hearing an unconvincing interior monologue about his preference for solitude, then the recall of a conversation brings with it changed feelings and a montage of memories; next the song performance leads to a cut and a shot of Sally—the song reference now as plain as it possibly could be—and, finally, a sound advance of their conversation leads to their joint reminiscence of their wedding.

Battle Scenes from Five War Films: *Apocalypse Now, Platoon, Gallipoli, Glory,* and *Saving Private Ryan*

As we discussed in Chapter 10, war films through the 1970s emphasized the sound of explosions, gunfire, and machines during battle sequences, even as the sound track became more varied and detailed. The detail, however, served to underscore the violence and importance of the guns and machines, and men responded with screams. The violence, especially the killing shots, was rendered with impressive explosions and hails of gunfire or the zing of bullets ricocheting. That is, the war films of this period of the widescreen and introduction of stereo sound continued to correlate the horror of war directly with volume, even as the technological capacities of the sound track expanded and allowed quieter moments. As we will see, the approach to the sound track changed markedly in the war films of the New Hollywood, partly for technological reasons, partly for cultural and aesthetic reasons.

APOCALYPSE NOW

The doubt that was already creeping into war films during the 1970s—*Patton* (1970) and *A Bridge Too Far* (1977), discussed in Chapter 10, are two examples of this trend—no doubt reflected the cultural uncertainty over the wars in Korea and Vietnam. The latter especially was less easy to rationalize and support unreservedly than had been the "good" war in the 1940s, whose melodramatic villains seemed made to order for Hollywood. The shift in cultural perspective was matched, fortuitously or not, by a subjective turn in cinema, which was reinforced by the new immersive possibilities of Dolby surround sound. The opening of *Apocalypse Now* (1979) famously and impressively uses the surround field to bring helicopters circling in from the rear of the theater. Less frequently noted is the fact that these helicopters roving the surround field belong to Captain Willard's dream, memory, or hallucination (see Figure 12-7). The sound is not presented as implicitly objective, in the manner of the heroic representational mode of war films. Instead, it is overtly subjective, stylized in its rendering and in its audacious use of the surround channels to emphasize this fact. The extension into the surround field, in other words, is a means of rendering this "subjectification of sound": it is sound as it feels filtered through Willard's dreaming

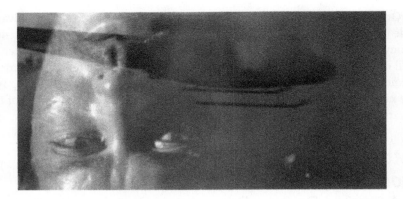

Figure 12-7. *Apocalypse Now* (1979). Helicopters in Captain Willard's dream.

consciousness. The presence of music—The Doors' "This Is the End"—aids this process of subjectification, as does the stylized sound of the helicopter rotors.

The battle sequences of the film are treated more in line with earlier films. With its emphasis on the sounds of gunfire and explosions, we are presented a spectacle of aural violence from an external, that is, apparently "objective" perspective ("objective" because seemingly not filtered through a subjective consciousness). In the helicopter assault on the village (recall Figure 11-10), explosions, gunfire, and the sounds of the helicopters dominate. The scene is accompanied by Richard Wagner's "Ride of the Valkyries," which though ostensibly diegetic is rarely treated as sound coming from speakers mounted on the helicopters and is also faded up and down depending on what explosions and other sounds occupy the sound track. The music, in other words, is effective at allying the violence with myth.

PLATOON

War films from the 1980s continued to feature explosions, gunfire, and the sound of war machines in battle sequences, but at the same time these films followed the trend toward ever more detailed sound design. *Platoon* (1986) is a good case in point. In the initial ambush duty, where the platoon goes into the jungle to flush out enemy patrols, Chris (Charlie Sheen) wakes Junior (Reggie Johnson) to take over guard duty (18:00). Sometime later, mosquitoes wake Chris up. The sound track emphasizes the mosquito buzzing and other nighttime nature sounds along with Chris's breathing and bodily movement. As he is adjusting his hood to protect his neck from the bugs, Chris realizes that Vietcong soldiers are approaching his position. High-pitched strings enter to underscore the rising tension, and when he finally sees a soldier silhouetted in the moonlight, a beating heart sounds, coupled with an extreme close-up on Chris's eyes (Figure 12-8). As the Vietcong soldiers begin to advance, the heartbeat quickens and crescendos, and the music grows increasingly dissonant, with only comparatively slight sounds coming from the soldiers.

Figure 12-8. *Platoon* (1986). Chris's eyes.

The music and heartbeat exit under a set of three explosions, when the sound design changes to an external perspective. Gunfire erupts and fills the sound track in bursts that shift around within the stereo field. The sounds of the various guns are clearly distinguished, and the rattle of the shell casings as they move through the heavy machine gun is clearly audible. Once the shooting begins, the sound design is punctuated: it features explosions, gunfire, and other sounds but it is never saturated. Thus, there can be exceptionally quiet moments, such as when someone throws a grenade and the pulling of the pin and the grenade's landing can be heard. The firefight ends with a soldier writhing in pain, as the Vietcong run off. In this scene, the subjective sound (heartbeat) quickly gave way to the more traditional, objective sound for the combat scene itself, and music disappeared at the moment the shift took place. For the battle proper, the spectacle of violence was aurally explosive, and the sound track recognized the effects of this violence on the men only in their screams.

GALLIPOLI

A somewhat different approach, hewing more closely to subjective sound, is found in *Gallipoli* (1981), a film about an ill-fated attack during the First World War. Near the end of the film, three waves of Australian soldiers attempt to advance on well-defended Turkish bunkers, and each wave is methodically destroyed by machine guns and rifle fire. The sequence begins with the Australian soldiers fixing bayonets on their rifles, followed immediately by a barrage of British artillery fire. The sound design strategy is the traditional one of saturating the sound track with explosions. As the barrage continues, Archy (Mark Lee) writes a letter home in voice-over, with the explosions only barely audible. The scene then returns to the artillery where a British commander is looking at his watch and yelling "cease fire." A cutback to the trenches shows that the Australian commander's watch is behind, and that he is consequently uncertain about when his troops should attack.

After receiving orders that the Australian troops must attack without support of artillery, the commander sends the first wave. The sound of this attack is dominated by the relentless clattering of machine gun fire, but as the focus of the scene falls on the hopelessness of attack, the other important noise is the sound of the bullets hitting and ripping through bodies. Ricocheting bullets are also heard, especially near the end of each wave of attack. After the first wave falters, groaning of injured men serves as a backdrop to the commander barking orders to ready the second wave.

The sound of the second wave is similar except more of the images are located in the trenches and more men are shot just as they exit the trench, so the sound of the bullets hitting the bodies is more pronounced. In addition, several shots focus on the Turkish guns, and the metallic clanging of the shell casings moving through the machine guns is particularly prominent.

A lengthy interlude ensues where Frank (Mel Gibson) runs to headquarters, accompanied by somewhat incongruous synthesizer music, to prevent the third wave from being sent. As the men wait in the trenches, the music changes to Tomaso Albinoni's *Adagio in G Minor*. A call comes ordering the attack. Having obtained a reprieve from the General, Frank rushes back only to arrive as a whistle blows announcing the assault.

The segment depicting the third wave is quite brief, and the sound track again emphasizes the machine guns and bullets hitting bodies. This time, however, we also hear the cries of soldiers falling in pain. The final set of shots shows Archy running top speed without his gun. The sound track focuses on his breathing and his feet hitting the ground until we hear a burst of eight machine gun rounds and his body pummeled by three bullets. The film ends in freeze frame, with Archy still upright and running but having just received the bullets (see Figure 12-9).

Gallipoli's approach to the sound of combat sequences differs from previous films we have considered because it emphasizes rendering violence to the body

Figure 12-9. *Gallipoli* (1981). Archy in freeze frame after being shot.

rather than principally using loudness to saturate the sound track. Rendering of sound in this way does not inspire awe at the power of an unfathomable violence so much as it makes us hear the body that must bear the force of that violence. The sublime horror of war recedes to something arguably far more terrible as the represented body is invaded in this way, and it hardly seems coincidental that these gestures of intense subjectification follow the cultural trauma of the Vietnam War, which like the First World War had come by the 1980s to be understood as a particularly pointless war.

TWO COMBAT SCENES FROM *GLORY*

Films celebrating warfare uncritically continue to be made in the 1980s—*Top Gun* (1986) is a particularly good example. A fundamental skepticism, however, which recognizes that being soldiers often changes men in harmful ways, had become sufficiently widespread by this time that even films about the Civil War and the Second World War frequently borrow these themes.

Sound design focused on impressive explosions do remain common in action films, descendants of the saturation strategy associated with the representation of sublime horror. Films continue to exploit the increased dynamic range for impressively roaring explosions, as when the airplanes bomb the position during the final battle sequence in *Platoon*, or when the sound of the jet engines serves as a complement to the occasional explosion in *Top Gun*. More typical, however, is what we found in the scenes from *Platoon* and *Gallipoli* mentioned previously: use of detailed sound design to render a more intimate, more subjective perspective and to record the damage to the body. In *Glory* (1989), based on an account of the first regular African American combat unit in the Civil War, the initial battle sequence shows the carnage of Antietam. Music continues from the previous scene, which had featured a voice-over of Robert (Matthew Broderick) writing home to his mother confident that the Union army had overpowering strength. The battle sequence opens (3:50) with Union troops advancing across an open field, as Confederate soldiers fire artillery and rifles. Music exits under an artillery blast, but drums continue as the Union troops march forward and the sound becomes increasingly chaotic as the Union line begins to break down. Throughout the sequence, the explosive sound of the artillery is the loudest sound, but it never overwhelms the sound track, which also contains the sound of equipment on the soldiers' bodies, the barking of orders and cursing about the situation, the whinnying of horses, bugle calls and drums used for signaling, the clicks of guns locking and firing, the whoosh of bullets, and even the sound of dirt falling back to earth after an explosion. The sound design gets its energy from being busy and chaotic, with sound moving unpredictably about the stereo field, rather than from the power of sheer loudness. At the same time, the violence is more seen than heard. Bodies simply fall from bullets and blasts, or heads are gruesomely blown apart, but these events are not marked with any particular emphasis on the sound track, and even the groans of downed men are quite limited. This is a killing field, then, but the sound remains focused on anything but the bodies receiving the blows.

A comparison with the final battle sequence—a desperate charge on Battery Wagner outside Charleston, South Carolina—is instructive. Here, the sound design is once again chaotic and busy, but the sounds of injuries to the body are much more prominent, as are the cries of soldiers. The battle sequence proper begins with the men of the 54th Massachusetts Regiment marching forward toward the fort (1:43:10). Music continues from earlier in the scene, where the men had assembled on the beach and Robert had given final instructions. The music sneaks out on a cut to the Confederate soldiers organizing in the fort, where drums are calling the men into formation. A cut back to the beach is accompanied by the sound of artillery shells exploding, and this sound is then mixed in with the dominant sound of the men yelling. The men of the regiment charge, and a bugle sounds. The explosions come in quicker succession, but the sound of sand flying up and falling back down is almost as prominent as the explosion itself. The footsteps of the men and the sounds of their equipment rattling as they move are also quite audible. As the artillery barrage finally scatters the attack, the sound also grows more chaotic—as with the opening battle scene, the filmmakers again intensify the sound design by making it busier and more chaotic, not louder. The troops hunker down in the dunes, where they continue to be harassed by artillery.

The scene picks up again after nightfall. The Confederate artillery is still firing relentlessly into the dunes, and along with the sounds of the exploding shells and the displaced sand raining to the ground, flares sizzle as they float across the stereo field. Robert orders the men to charge, and as they do, men start to fall to gunfire. Now, bullets ripping through bodies become a significant sound, most notably when a group of five soldiers is shot as they go over a dune (Figure 12-10, 1:47:10). Each bullet hitting a body here sounds like a body blow. The sound again becomes increasingly chaotic as the soldiers approach the fort, and the cries of wounded men—a sound that had not been much

Figure 12-10. *Glory* (1989). Bullets hitting men as they charge.

present in the Antietam sequence near the beginning of the film—also become quite prominent.

When they reach the base of the fort, the men come under even heavier attack, but the sound, though perhaps louder, actually seems less chaotic. Robert organizes an attack up the wall of the fort. He is shot almost immediately; the explosive sound of the gunfire rather than the sound of the bullet hitting his body is emphasized. He continues upward, now melodramatically in slow motion, and is immediately hit by two more bullets, again the gunshots rather than the bullets striking the body serving as the principal sound effect. Still in slow motion, he falls heavily, first the sounds of his dropped sword and gun hitting the ground and then his body landing with a thud. Unexpectedly, music enters a beat later with a massive stroke in the chimes and the low orchestra (the inspiration for the music here is Carl Orff's "O Fortuna" from *Carmina Burana*). Inflamed to a desperate rage by Robert's death, the men rally and scale the walls of the fort en masse, overrunning the Confederate positions on the battlements in hand-to-hand combat. The sound throughout this segment is treated in a more stylized fashion: accompanied by this Orff-inspired mythic music that dominates the sound design to the end of the scene, the segment emphasizes yelling, sword and bayonet thrusts into bodies, the use of rifle butts to smash the enemy's heads, and only occasionally the firing of shots (and then only when the shot is central to the action shown). Although the action in this segment is quite frantic and desperate, the sound is focused and never chaotic in the way that every combat sequence had been up to this point. This stylized auditory focus, and not just the presence of music, endows the spectacle of violence in this segment with a grim necessity that the film persuades us to read as courage.

TWO COMBAT SCENES FROM *SAVING PRIVATE RYAN*

When *Saving Private Ryan* appeared in theaters in the summer of 1998, film critics hailed its combat sequences, particularly the Normandy landing, for their realism, their "terrifying reportorial candor," as Janet Maslin of the *New York Times* put it in her review.[1] *Saving Private Ryan* in fact is not so much novel in its approach to sound focused on rendering a subjective experience and feeling— representing the horror of violence through chaotic layering of detail rather than explosive saturation—as it is in consolidating this approach, reclaiming its power for what is actually a rather conventional combat film. The initial minutes of the Normandy landing sequence feature the requisite explosions along the beach and reports of gunfire, especially from German machine guns. But the sound design dwells extensively on the harrowing sounds of bullets hitting sand and water, ricocheting off the landing craft and the metal tripods on the beach, and ripping through flesh of soldiers. As Gary Rydstrom, the sound designer of the film, notes, "The most important element to us sound-wise were bullet impacts because if you are being shot at that's the key sound." The opening minutes of this sequence also effectively use explicit point-of-view sound, first under water, which alters the sound of the bullets but not their lethal effect, and then emulating the effects of shellshock by diminishing the battle sounds and over-laying them with hollow humming to emulate temporary deafness after a con-cussion blast (9:15). With the seeming randomness by which bullets and explosions damage bodies, the sound design here initially emphasizes not just a subjective perspective, but the feeling of disempowerment, as those who survive seem to do so by sheer chance.

In Steven Spielberg's Saving Private Ryan, the battle scenes are shot from the shaky, glancing, and claus-trophobic point of view of a soldier on the ground. There are no sweeping vistas, only the chaos of fighting as it is experienced. The sound for this movie, therefore, had to set the full stage of battle, while putting us squarely in the middle of it. I can honestly say that this film could not have been made in the same way if it were not for the possibili-ties of theatrical surround sound. If sound could not have expressed the scale, orientation, and emotion of a soldier's experience, the camera would have had to show more. Yet it is a point of the movie to show how disorienting the visual experience was. Sound becomes a key storyteller.
—Gary Rydstrom, Sound Designer[2]

The American soldiers' increasing control of the situation, then, is corre-lated with the capacity to make explosive noises of their own, first by using a Bangalore Torpedo to blow a hole in a defensive obstacle protecting German positions and then by their capacity to return gunfire (see Figure 12-11). As the soldiers advance off the beach, the sound design shifts markedly from rendering bullet impacts toward realizing the conventional sounds of war films: gunfire, grenade explosions, flame throwers, and so forth. The ability to act, in other words, moves the sound from a strongly subjective perspective—sound acting on seemingly helpless bodies—to a more impersonal, objective perspective, as sound realizing purposeful action.

Rydstrom notes that the final combat sequence in the village when a small group of American soldiers attempts to hold off an attack by German tanks takes a different perspective on sound than that used in the opening battle. In the vil-lage sequence, he says, the battle "is told from the point of view of the people shooting. So now we're with the guns and we are not so interested in bullet hits and the residuals of war, we are interested in the actual clatter of cartridges through an A4 machine gun, of a Browning automatic rifle and what that sounds like to operate and to shoot."[3] With the exception of the segments focused on Corporal Upham (Jeremy Davies), which underscore his lack of combat experi-ence by following a strategy of subjectified sound design closer to that of the Normandy landing sequence, the sound of the village battle focuses on the command and control of violence, the conventional approach of a more external perspective. The later scene also exploits the traditional strategy of explosive

Figure 12-11. *Saving Private Ryan* (1998). American soldiers return fire.

saturation, with loud blasts from the tanks serving as high points in the spectacle of aural violence. A somewhat frantic and busy sound track carefully distinguishes the sounds of the various types of guns, which often sound impressively explosive in their own right, as the vastly outnumbered and outgunned American troops maneuver to find the most effective lines of attack. This scenario of desperate heroism is a familiar Hollywood trope, and the sound design, though effective, seems inspired by the fantasy of action film—an inspiration that the pun of Captain Miller (Tom Hanks) appearing to blow up the tank with the final round from his pistol explicitly acknowledges.

Overall, then, sound design from the beach to the village maps out a fairly standard Hollywood narrative trajectory from disempowerment to empowerment, from subjective reaction to purposeful action, from intensely subjective rendering of experience to a more impersonal realization of sounds of violence. The passage through the beach, where the violence is horrifying because it is omnipresent, random, mundane, and so fundamentally inscrutable to soldiers and viewers alike, leads to a space among the German battlements where that violence can be confronted and overcome by the American soldiers, who appropriate the power of violence to themselves. This pattern of overcoming the terror of subjectified sound in order to find the power to control sound is confirmed even with Corporal Upham, who is immobilized by fear through much of the final battle in the village, only to overcome his impotence, and the subjectified sound design associated with it, when he shoots a German soldier who insults him after he has taken the soldier prisoner. The subjectified sound design of the Normandy beach sequence does, however, reassert itself quite strongly near the end of the village as the American defense of the bridge collapses and Miller again experiences a shellshock episode just before he is shot and haplessly shoots at the tank with his pistol. But here, too, the subjective rendering of sound for which the film was critically acclaimed serves primarily as an intensified sign of the human weakness and frailty that heroic characters have the courage to master and surmount.

CONCLUSIONS

The war films produced during the era of the New Hollywood benefitted greatly from the vastly improved sound in theaters. Dolby stereo and later digital sound improved both the dynamic range and the frequency response of the sound, allowing not only greater volume but also deeper basses (to give more body to explosive sounds) and improved treble (to give all sorts of sonic details better definition). Along with stereo imaging, these changes allowed for a far more intricate and active sound track, one that could represent the intensity of combat without always resorting to saturating the sound track with explosions. The variety and detail of sounds became as important as impressive volume, and many war films attempted to use sound to capture the chaos, terror, and disorientation of combat. Offscreen sound was particularly good for this, as were trajectories of bullets and bombs whizzing rapidly and unpredictably through the stereo field and the skittering sound of dirt thrown up from explosions raining back to earth or the ghastly dull thud of a bullet hitting a body.

Most characteristic of sound tracks of this era, however, was the development of a repertory of devices for representing the terrifying subjective experience of combat. Because the films tied the horror to a representational aesthetic, music remained uncommon: it appeared only if diegetically motivated or if the mode of representation became more stylized to mark the transformational quality of some event or the intrusion of some external commentative perspective. Although these techniques were developed primarily for a set of critical (if not explicitly antiwar) films that questioned the efficacy of war and the inability of the characters to make sense of their experience, films such as *Glory* and *Saving Private Ryan* that understood war as sometimes necessary but extremely costly also appropriated these devices as a spectacle of verisimilar horror to illustrate the courage and good fortune required to make heroes of men.

That these heroes do not survive the ends of their films is telling. In having the courage to renounce the terror of that subjectified sound, to no longer hear it, they also sacrifice something of their humanity to war. They are made into abstract archetypes placing inhuman demands on the living ("earn it," Captain Miller says to the young James Ryan [Matt Damon] on the village bridge), and doubt haunts the memory of these heroes. "Tell me I've lived a good life," an elderly Ryan implores his wife on visiting Miller's grave in Normandy. "Tell me I'm a good man." A poignant question hangs at the end of *Saving Private Ryan* as to whether the legacy of the Second World War has been good, whether American actions in the years after the war have redeemed the sacrifice. By raising this question of the good in this way, the film obliquely acknowledges the troubled war films, most of them centered on the conflict in Vietnam, that have served as its tacit foil and that had made the combat film a deeply problematic genre by the time of *Saving Private Ryan*.

Action Films and Opening Prologues: Bond Films, *Raiders of the Lost Ark*, *Terminator 2: Judgment Day*, and *The Matrix*

Present in the earliest days of cinema, the chase film is the prototype of the action film. Swashbucklers, adventure serials, cowboy films, spy films, and war films all belong to the same broad category, but it was the New Hollywood reorganization of the film industry around blockbuster production that finally turned the action film into the industry's dominant genre. Although war films can be construed as a subgenre of action film, they are typically committed to some form of historical accuracy, even if as historical fiction, whereas action films appeal more to fantasy, even when they have vaguely historical, wartime settings, such as *Captain America: The First Avenger* (2011), or even when that wartime setting is relatively faithfully reproduced as in *Guns of Navarone* (1961) or (somewhat less plausibly) *Kelly's Heroes* (1970).

Like war films, action films place significant demands on the sound track, and for similar reasons: both genres feature a spectacle of violence with gunshots, physical fights, and explosions. We have noted that combat scenes in war films only rarely use music during the height of the battle, even after technology evolved to allow a shift from saturation to envelopment as the guiding aesthetic for such scenes. Action films, by contrast, are far more likely to underscore their violent episodes with music, because they relate action and destructive chaos to fantasy.

BOND FILMS

The James Bond films codified the dominant template for opening action films with an action prologue. *Goldfinger* (1964), for instance, begins with Bond sneaking into a complex, knocking out a guard, setting a bomb, going to a nearby party, and returning to his hotel room and fighting off a would-be assassin. Only then do the title credits with the well-known song begin. These prologues vary from tense suspense as in *Goldfinger* and *From Russia with Love* (1964) to giving elliptical narrative set-up as in *You Only Live Twice* (1967) and *Live and Let Die* (1971) to full action sequences as in the wild helicopter ride in *For Your Eyes Only* (1981) or in elaborately choreographed ski chases for *The Spy Who Loved Me* (1977) and *A View to a Kill* (1985). All, however, feature significant action before the titles (though the action is not always pertinent to the main narrative of the film), and the scenes always accompany the action with music, usually the famous Bond theme, but sometimes with popular music, frequently used ironically (e.g., The Beach Boys' "California Girls" accompanying Bond as he improvises a snowboard and skis through obstacles during the prologue of *A View to a Kill*). Most action films, including those that open with the title before the first scene, use a similar strategy of starting in the middle of an action scene. Even *Star Wars: A New Hope* (1977), which opens with a broad theme and a very extended title sequence (though it contains few credits), begins its first scene dramatically *in media res*, with two ships flying in over the top of the screen followed by a fight as Storm Troopers and Darth Vader board the Rebel ship.

The Bond films are somewhat unusual for an action film in that they include extensive credits in the title sequence. This arrangement of making credits part of a title sequence was very common in the 1960s (and before) when the template for the series was devised. Because most credits now run at the end, many films today use a very perfunctory title sequence, though some do run the names of the principal actors and creative personnel along with the first scene. Action films, however, have among the sparsest title sequences, often only the logos and/or names of the film production companies and then the title. Occasionally, even the title is deferred to the end of the film.

RAIDERS OF THE LOST ARK

Raiders of the Lost Ark (1981) opens with the Paramount logo in silence. As this logo dissolves into a similarly shaped rock formation, music and ambient sound enter. Credits and titles then appear over the unfolding action for the next 2 minutes. This way of combining the credits with the opening scene has become a relatively common alternative to a classical main credit sequence, and the tense, enigmatic quality of this particular sequence, which begins *in medias res*, allows the names and titles to appear without disturbing the flow of the action. Music and effects dominate and are occasionally difficult to separate (is that a woodblock and part of the music, or a woodpecker and part of the sound?). Throughout the opening segment, the ambient sound of birds, insects, and monkeys is generally given far more prominence than such sounds as footsteps that have a clear source in the image.

The sound design here, which is described in the shot-by-shot scene analysis of Table 12-1, is actually quite reminiscent of horror film, with its emphasis on strange offscreen ambient sound and music that percolates and gestures rather than coalesces into articulate themes. The procedure makes it difficult to decide which sounds are significant (and so portend danger), even as the music unsettles with a continuous foreboding that unpredictably lashes out with stingers. The music and cinematography also make us uncertain about the status of these characters. Indiana Jones (Harrison Ford) is frequently filmed from behind and in the shadows, conventional filmic marks of villains or psychologically troubled protagonists. The aggressively descending brass line that accompanies the close-up of Jones as he steps out of the shadow after having used his whip to disarm one of his party who had drawn a gun on him (see Figure 12-12) is also a musical gesture that is borrowed from the melodramatic depiction of villains. (See the commentary on the final few shots in Table 12-1.)

Table 12-1 contains only the first quarter of the opening action sequence, which runs almost 13 minutes. The part depicted in the table consists of the set-up for the sequence, whose central portion occurs shortly after the table ends, or once Jones and Satipo (Alfred Molina) enter the shrine to loot the golden idol. Music and ambient sound continue to dominate, and the connection of the sound

Figure 12-12. *Raiders of the Lost Ark* (1981). Indiana Jones emerges from the shadows.

Table 12-1 *Raiders of the Lost Ark.*

Time Code	Shot Description	Dialogue	Sound Effects	Music	General Comments
0:00	Paramount logo				Silent
:09	Mountain; figure enters with back to camera at :18; Title at :27; :34 tilt up to follow another character walking through scene; :41 tilt back down	[occasional indistict offscreen chatter] Unidentified man in white hat (mwh): [speaking foreign language]	In: :09 Ambient nature sounds (mostly birds, insects); occasional footsteps, and other body sounds, once people come into view.	In: :09 atmospheric orchestra music; no strong tune but percolating motifs.	Music and ambient sound enter together along with dissolve to shot of mountain matching Paramount logo. Emphasis is on offscreen sound. Nature sounds and music often blur together. Meandering tune in bassoon and flute.
:45	LS, group walking		ambient sounds cont.		
:51	MS, group walking		Add monkey sounds		
:57	MS, Indiana Jones, from behind; camera tracks with him.				
1:01	ELS, group walking from above and through the trees				
1:08	MS, group walking, only feet shown.				
1:12	MS, individual figures pass by camera		Footsteps more prominent; donkey braying; sound of donkey being tied up		
1:24	CU, plants. At end, CU, man using machete				

(Continued)

Table 12-1 (*Continued*)

Time Code	Shot Description	Dialogue	Sound Effects	Music	General Comments
1:26	RS, over-the-shoulder of large stone glyph	**Unidentified man:** [scream]	Chop of machete; scream	Stinger (with scream)	Stinger and scream together mark this as an important moment.
1:28	LS, man and large stone glyph; man runs off screen, Jones enters.		Scream and sound of flapping wings		
1:34	CU, mid-section of Jones as he walks past camera; Satipo in MS at end.				
1:37	LS, Jones in front of glyph.		Bird sounds flying; offscreen birds		
1:43	2-Shot, Satipo and mwh look at each other and then walk forward.				
1:49	ELS, Jones walking along stream		Water and footsteps	Back to percolating ↓	
2:00	LS, Satipo and mwh walking, camera tracks, stops at tree with dart in it. Jones steps into foreground and examines dart (head not shown). Jones exits and Satipo and mwh rush foreward into MCU. As the begin to walk, the camera tracks.	[near end of shot] **Satipo:** The Hovitos are near. . . Poison is still fresh, three days. They're following us. **mwh:** If they knew we were here they would've killed us already. [Indecipherable offscreen chatter]	Sound of dart being pulled out tree and dropped. Heavy footsteps as Sapito and mwh move forward. Spitting sound when Sapito tests dart. Lots of offscreen sound, especially after the dialouge. More prominent body sounds as they move through jungle.	Stinger for dart brass chords then . . . percolating again, but more dramatic	The discovery of the dart here is treated in a similar fashion to the revelation of the glyph, but at a much lower dynamic level. But in both cases the finding disrupts the percolating music with a stinger. The music changes more substantively after the dart.
2:34	LS, Jones through the trees				

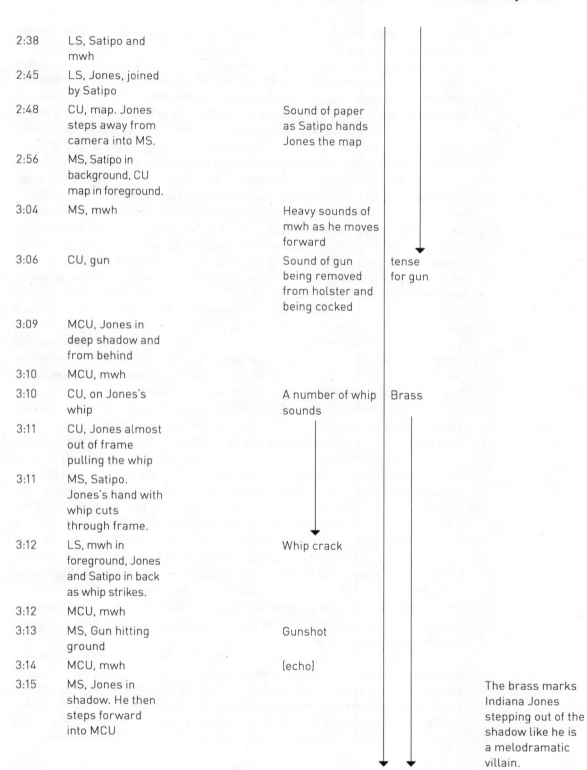

2:38	LS, Satipo and mwh		
2:45	LS, Jones, joined by Satipo		
2:48	CU, map. Jones steps away from camera into MS.	Sound of paper as Satipo hands Jones the map	
2:56	MS, Satipo in background, CU map in foreground.		
3:04	MS, mwh	Heavy sounds of mwh as he moves forward	
3:06	CU, gun	Sound of gun being removed from holster and being cocked	tense for gun
3:09	MCU, Jones in deep shadow and from behind		
3:10	MCU, mwh		
3:10	CU, on Jones's whip	A number of whip sounds	Brass
3:11	CU, Jones almost out of frame pulling the whip		
3:11	MS, Satipo. Jones's hand with whip cuts through frame.		
3:12	LS, mwh in foreground, Jones and Satipo in back as whip strikes.	Whip crack	
3:12	MCU, mwh		
3:13	MS, Gun hitting ground	Gunshot	
3:14	MCU, mwh	(echo)	
3:15	MS, Jones in shadow. He then steps forward into MCU		The brass marks Indiana Jones stepping out of the shadow like he is a melodramatic villain.

design to horror film grows even stronger, as the passage through the narrow corridor plays on associations with the standard suspense scenario of the long, dark hallway. A drone of hollow ambient wind sound early yields to strings that play pizzicato and tremolo derived from the old melodramatic misterioso musical topic, combined with a series of extended techniques that by 1981 had become variants for scoring horror suspense and startles: snap pizzicato, tremolo on the bridge, *col legno battuto*, and glissandos, both normal and across the natural string harmonics. The passage also deploys low, brooding brass and muted horns playing *sforzando*, the latter as an intensified stinger for a moment of startle.

The sound design changes somewhat once they cross the chasm and enter the inner chamber. Here, music and synchronized sound effects are now dominant and ambient sound is more or less absent. Jones's footsteps sound clearly as he carefully winds his way through the maze of stepping stones to reach the altar, and music pivots from horror to suspenseful action, raising tension as Jones moves closer to the idol. The music deftly marks his switching of the bag of sand for the idol with what at first seems a negative stinger that augurs a successful substitution. A careful ear will reveal, however, that a quiet tremolo string remains behind, an expectant tremor. The stone pedestal that had held the idol begins to move, and sound effects begin to take over, first with a scratching sound of the pedestal, then a loud low rumble that quickly obliterates all other sound. Music emerges from a series of crashes and other loud sounds as Jones runs back through the inner chamber, but it only manages to regain control of the soundtrack at the chasm when Satipo strands Jones.

With the accompaniment of tense action music that underscores his desperate plight, Jones struggles across the chasm and squeezes under a closing door, only to discover Satipo has been killed by a trap (this discovery is marked by a sharp but rather ineffectual stinger). Jones then collects the idol only to hear another rumble and recognize that he is not yet out of danger. He scrambles out of the shrine, trying to outrun a giant rolling rock, and jumps to safety. The sound design shifts rapidly from exciting action music and the rumbles of the collapsing shrine to nature sounds, as Jones realizes he is surrounded. (This is also the first extended moment in the film without music.) His rival, Belloq (Paul Freeman), takes the idol, but Jones manages to escape, and music returns as he runs. The music at first is rather inchoate, emphasizing the flight as he races first through the jungle and then across the open meadow pursued by tribesmen, but when Jones begins to swing on a vine out into the river, the Indiana Jones theme sounds for the first time and continues (along with the airplane sound) to the beginning of the next scene.

This whole elaborate sequence plays like an extended action prologue that establishes the ambivalent character of Indiana Jones—he is more a raider of antiquities than a proper archaeologist—and his rivalry with Belloq, but the actual events of the sequence are not closely related to the narrative of the rest of the film. In this respect it is similar to many of the action prologues of Bond films, which also have a mostly tenuous relationship to the main narrative.

TERMINATOR 2: JUDGMENT DAY

Like the Bond films, *Terminator 2* (1991) has both an extended action prologue and an autonomous title sequence. The first Terminator film (1984) also had a prologue and a title sequence, but its prologue, similar to *Terminator 2* in focusing on a combat scene, was very perfunctory and its narration was presented with text on screen rather than in voice-over. *Terminator 2* by contrast is structured as two prologues. The action prologue and Main Titles have the following basic structure:

- Before Skynet (prologue 1)
- After Skynet: battle (prologue 2, part 1)
- After Skynet: John Connor (prologue 2, part 2)
- Main Titles

The film begins in black with a low rumble out of which a unison string pitch emerges. Whether it is orchestral or synthesized is difficult to determine, though given the rest of the score it is most likely synthesized. A sharp string chord is synchronized to a shot of snarled traffic (prologue 1), and music continues in a slow tempo and minor key, creating a pathos-laden affect. A girl is playing on a swing set: her laughter is processed with a very haunting and disturbing echo as a low rumble crescendos and transforms into a nondiegetic "fwish" sound.

As the rumble sounds, the screen dissolves to white, only to be replaced by a sudden silence and a dark screen of blue images, slowly revealed as burned-out cars and skeletons. In this second prologue, music has also disappeared, replaced by a low hollow wind sound and the squeaks of a moving piece of metal on a car. The wind grows more prominent, and a voice-over narrator presents the back story while the camera pans across the destruction. A machine soldier then breaks the relative silence by crushing a skull lying on the ground with a crisp, chilling sound that takes full advantage of the digital sound system. (*Terminator 2* was originally released in the short-lived CDS; see Chapter 13.) This initiates a full-scale futuristic battle, with laser blasts, explosions, tanks, engines (see Figure 12-13), and a machine

Figure 12-13. *Terminator 2: Judgment Day* (1991). Machine soldier.

droning a repeating descending half step that falls halfway between music and noise. The overall effect is chaotic in much the way battle scenes in war films are, although like the films of the 1970s and before, the emphasis falls on the spectacle of violence, a fine distinction in the various sounds of the machines of war but with little to no attention to the damage to bodies (except screams). Like the war films, the combat scene mostly avoids music, though the most significant hits are sweetened with synthetic orchestral stingers.

The voice-over narration returns to relate the narrative premise of the film. The music, at first a heavily synthesized martial drumbeat, takes a heroic turn as John Connor (Edward Furlong) surveys the battlefield; sound effects are low behind narration and music. A shot of John dissolves into a slow motion explosion as the music builds, and a loud metallic clang initiates the title sequence proper.

The title sequence then follows with the Terminator theme played on synthetic strings and a mechanical martial drum pattern sounding underneath. Synthesized male voices appear in a brief middle section, after which the main title theme returns in canon, the second voice played by a trumpet, the only non-percussion instrument so far not to sound overtly synthetic. The close of the main title music returns to the male choir while a loud metallic clank now drives the percussion. The titles end with an out-of-key metallic clank that initiates the action of the film proper.

The opening of *Terminator 2* thus follows the older Bond model of an action prologue followed by a lengthy autonomous title sequence with a theme. Here, however, the action prologue does not simply allow the film to open *in medias res* with action—it also provides crucial back story. In addition, *Terminator 2* has two prologues, one situated just prior to the decisive event that the film's protagonists will struggle to prevent from happening, the other situated in the future, a number years after that event. While the first opens with an arresting but unusual tragic lyrical shot (and sound) of a life cut short, the second provides the typical *in medias res* opening expected of an action film, although this plunge into action was delayed in a provocative way.

Given that the Terminator films develop the theme of conflict between humans and sentient machines, the choice of synthesizers as the dominant sound of the scores is inspired: it ensures that the music cannot map onto the conflict in any simple way, especially if music retains its function of underscoring feeling. This complicated status is particularly relevant to *Terminator 2*, because far more than its predecessor (or indeed its successors) it places the sentient machine at its moral center, and the synthesizer music is frequently mournful, even when, as with the title music, it is also laid over a very mechanical percussion track.

THE MATRIX

With its extremely brief titles, lack of any but corporate credits, and fluid passage from animated corporate logos to storytelling, the opening of *The Matrix* (1999) is quite different from both the Bond template of prologue and titles and the model of integrating the title and credits into the action prologue as was done in *Raiders of the Lost Ark*. Nevertheless, this model plays like a streamlined version of what was done in *Raiders of the Lost Ark* and has become quite common for opening action prologues. The whole segment from the logo sequence for Warner Bros. Pictures to the graphic title sequence, to the intense set of scenes featuring Trinity (a resistance fighter), to the clever transition to Neo's computer after Trinity's escape, about 6 minutes in, serves as an extended action prologue structured in four basic units:

1. Phone call (and credits)
2. Trinity defeats the police
3. Trinity is pursued across the rooftops
4. Phone call

Table 12-2 is a shot-by-shot scene analysis of the bulk of the first two segments, which covers around 3½ minutes. Music enters along with the two studio logos, establishing several distinctive features: the juxtaposition of crashing brass chords along with processed clicks and squeaks that effectively blurs the distinction between music and effects. The music, though distinctive and identifiable, is more gestural than thematic in its organization, and it intensifies (already speeding up to suggest a chase) and overlaps into the main title, whose background green-lit numbers on a computer screen (its frame is not seen) continue into the first voice-over—a phone conversation between Trinity (Carrie-Anne Moss) and Cypher (Joe Pantoliano). Music exits under the conversation, which is accompanied by a recurring beep synchronized to a blinking cursor and other electronic sounds synchronized to screen activity. Near the end of the conversation, music based on the action chase for the title sneaks back in under a set of busy, high, electronic sounds associated with the phone trace, and it crescendos as Trinity expresses growing concern. She hangs up and the music intensifies into a graphical transition to the next scene, the beginning of the second segment, which is marked aurally by a loud, nondiegetic "zap," part music, part sound effect synchronized to a rapid zoom in on a bright light.

This second segment opens with this shot of the light, and as the "zap" is left to resonate in the new reverberant space, the camera moves to reveal first one policeman holding a flashlight and then several others. They move through a corridor accompanied by creepy high-pitched sounds, some seemingly nondiegetic (and so belonging to the score), others like the click of the safety on the gun clearly diegetic. When the officers stop in front of the door, high strings enter softly to underscore the tension. The police kick in the door and dissonant brass chords emerge out of the crash. Trinity is sitting calmly in the room, and she raises her hands as the music crescendos, leading to another heavily punctuated nondiegetic "zap" that emphasizes a dramatic cut outside. Here, diegetic sound of the police gathered outside a ramshackle hotel predominates once the resonance of the "zap" has receded.

Table 12-2 *The Matrix*. Trinity in a jam.

Time Code	Shot Description	Dialogue	Effects	Music	General Notes
0:00	Black				
0:03	LS, aerial shot of Warners sound stage tinted green			Atmospheric. Horns and trumpets in Matrix chords.	Throughout, music and sound effects often blurred.
0:07	Fancy wipe to Warners' logo (dissolve to black)				
0:16	Dissolve to Village Roadshow Pictures (dissolve to black)		High-frequency computer sounds	Strings, short repeated fragments (0:22)	
0:31	Green LED computer characters from top of screen		Buzzes and more high-frequency computer sounds.	Add winds and high strings.	
0:38	Slow dissolve to Title. Zoom then letters disappear to black.		Synchronized high-frequency hits for the title. A modem carrier sound for the zoom, then more sync high-frequency for disappearance of letters.	Decrescndo after title	
0:41	Blinking cursor		Beeps for cursor. Telephone calling tone.	Similar to music at :22, except some winds.	
0:48	Computer lettering	**Cypher**: Yeah. **Trinity**: Is everything in place?	Computer sounds for the lettering.	Music very low.	voice is filtered for telephone.
0:52	New line of lettering	**Male: voice**: You aren't suppose to relieve me. **Trinity**: I know.			
0:54	Full screen of numbers	**Trinity**: But I felt like taking a shift.			
0:56	Multiple columns	**Cypher**: You like him, don't you?			

Time	Visual	Dialogue	Sound Effects	Music
0:59	More columns still (zoom), numbers are sorting out at top. Zoom continues until only three numbers in ECU, then dissolve/ process shot to black.	**Cypher**: You like watching him. **Trinity**: Don't be ridiculous. **Cypher**: We're going to kill him. You understand that? **Trinity**: Morpheus believes he is the One. **Cypher**: Do you? **Trinity**: It doesn't matter what I believe. **Cypher**: You don't, do you? **Trinity**: Did you hear that? **Cypher**: Hear what? **Trinity**: Are you sure this line is clean? **Cypher**: Yeah, of course, I'm sure. **Trinity**: I better go.	Prominent beeps synchronized with numbers begin with 6 at 1:10. At 1:15, a broader, lower boop sound. Electric sci-fi sounds for the process shot.	slow crescendo throughout Trumpets & horns with Matrix chords at 1:19. Crescendo to gong.
1:26	Iris in on light (which looks like a zoom), then slight pan to reveal ECU of policeman. More pan to show other officers. Officer moves through as camera follows.		Zap sync to light. Footsteps of police as they approach door.	Gong on light. Electronic ambient sounds Gong dissipates into ambient background.
1:38	LS, from behind; as police move in, camera tracks.		Movement sounds cont.	
1:45	CU, door. Camera tracks to the side behind police.		Movement sounds cont.	High whistling sound (1:48)

(Continued)

Table 12-2 (*Continued*)

Time Code	Shot Description	Dialogue	Effects	Music	General Notes
1:53	LS, 4 police, one approaches and kicks in door.			↓	
1:54	CU, door		Whack for door being knocked down.	Brass chords	
1:54	RS, door from other side. Police come rushing in.		Door sound continues.		
1:56	ELS, Trinity sitting down, back to camera.	**Police officers**: Freeze,	Guns being cocked.		
1:57	CU, two police in foreground, one behind. Obscured by lights.	Police! Hands on your head.		Wind chord	
1:58	ELS, Trinity sitting down, back to camera.	Do it, do it			
2:00	CU, Trinity looking at camera, which tilts up as she raises her hands.	Now!		Crescendo	
2:05	Exterior building. Camera tilts down along building.		Nondiegetic bang for hardcut outside. Police radio chatter throughout scene. Car sound. Brakes at end.	Sound from hard stinger on cut reverberates into beginning of scene. Dissolves into low string tone	
2:11	Camera tilts up as police car in ECU drives underneath. Ends with ELS of scene outside.		Car sound cont. Brakes at end.	↓	
2:16	MCU, Agents get out of car.	**Smith**: Lieutenant.	Car doors	Low bump with car doors. Low string tremelo afterward.	

2:23	MCU, police officer.	**Lt**: Oh shit.		
2:24	MS, Smith. Moves into over the shoulder RS with officer. Another Smith in background.	**Smith**: Lieutenant, you were given specific orders. **Lt**: Hey, I'm just doing my job.		
2:30	RS, Officer (from above)	You give me this "ain't my jurisdiction" crap, you can cram it up your ass.		Add high strings
2:35	MS, Smith (from below)	**Smith**: The orders were for your protection. [Lt. laughs]		
2:38	RS, Officer (from above)	**Lt.**: I think we can handle one little girl.		
2:42	MS, Smith (from below)			Motives in low instruments.
2:43	RS, Officer (from above)			
2:46	Same shot as Smith before, but the Smiths have left the space and the officer crosses into it. Officer, MS, turns.	I sent two units. They're bringing her down now.	Footsteps	
2:49	CU, Smith (from behind) turns to camera.	**Smith**: No, Lieutenant. You're men are already dead.		Brass chords and crescendo.
2:54	CU, officers gun. Trinity MS and out of focus in background. Rack focus to Trinity when officer pulls out handcuffs.		Nondiegetic thwap for hard cut to sound of handcuffs. Footsteps as officer approaches.	stinger, then high synthesized wind sound.

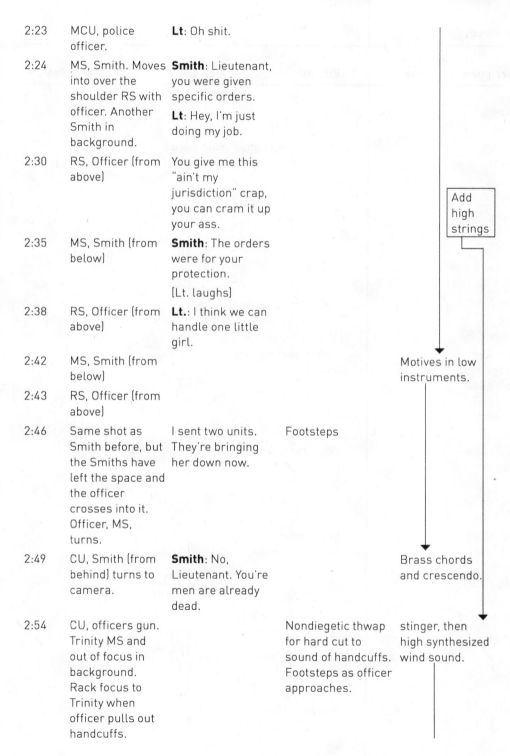

(Continued)

Table 12-2 (*Continued*)

Time Code	Shot Description	Dialogue	Effects	Music	General Notes
2:58	CU, Trinity; Officers MS in background.			↓	
3:00	CU officer, MS Trinity (from behind)		Punches and ughs.	Fast atonal piano.	
3:01	CU Officer				
3:01	Officer from behind, Trinity MCU.				
3:02	CU, Officer and Trinity's hand.		Punch		
3:02	CU, Officer from below		Ugh		
3:03	MCU, Trinity				
3:03	LS, Trinity from side, for elevation shot. Impression of very fast dolly around to other side.		Matrix power sound.	Brass chord ↓	
3:06	CU, Trinity's boot then Officer for kick.		Whap for kick.		
3:07	MS, Officer being kicked.				
3:08	LS, Officer being thrown into two other Officers and hitting wall.		Swish as officers fly back. Crunch for wall.		
3:09	LS, Officer with flashlight			Brass chord	
3:09	MCU, Trinity				
3:10	MS, Trinity	**Trinity**: Hya.	Kicking of chair.	↓	
3:11	MS, Officer shooting		Gun shots		
3:11	MCU, Another Officer		Gun richochets		

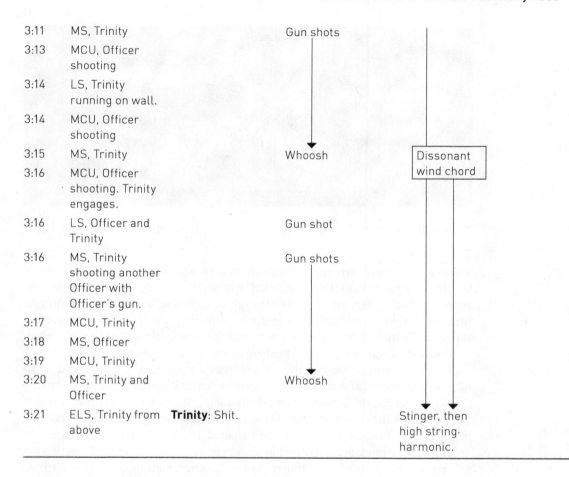

3:11	MS, Trinity	Gun shots	
3:13	MCU, Officer shooting		
3:14	LS, Trinity running on wall.		
3:14	MCU, Officer shooting		
3:15	MS, Trinity	Whoosh	Dissonant wind chord
3:16	MCU, Officer shooting. Trinity engages.		
3:16	LS, Officer and Trinity	Gun shot	
3:16	MS, Trinity shooting another Officer with Officer's gun.	Gun shots	
3:17	MCU, Trinity		
3:18	MS, Officer		
3:19	MCU, Trinity		
3:20	MS, Trinity and Officer	Whoosh	
3:21	ELS, Trinity from above	**Trinity**: Shit.	Stinger, then high string harmonic.

Three special agents arrive and converse with the police lieutenant in charge. When Trinity is obliquely mentioned, an unsettling nondiegetic sound or music sneaks in and slowly crescendos into another "zap" that punctuates a return to Trinity's predicament. She is now standing with her hands behind her head. A policeman approaches with handcuffs as a sound, part way between diegetic ambient wind and nondiegetic music, drones. As he reaches to cuff her, she attacks (see Figure 12-14), with sound effects of physical blows given special prominence. (The detailed sounds of punches and kicks leave a much more powerful impression than the gunshots, which seem somewhat impotent by comparison.) Frenetic music also accompanies the action. She quickly overpowers the policemen. This is where Table 12-2 ends. One of the agents then appears in the hallway with more officers, as Trinity talks by phone with Morpheus (Laurence Fishburne), the leader of her group, about how she can escape.

The third segment begins as Trinity leaves the room, frantically runs out of the building and over rooftops pursued by the agents, and finally flies, spiraling,

Figure 12-14. *The Matrix* (1999). Trinity prepares to attack.

across a substantial gap into the window of another abandoned building. Music is extremely prominent in this segment, which cuts among Trinity running, the agents pursuing her, and officers struggling to follow. The sound design and filmic techniques emphasize the profound difference among these sets of characters, as Trinity and the agents are shown moving in slow motion with sweetened sound effects and music attending to and underscoring the drama of their superhuman feats while the officers are treated with regular film speed, ordinary sound effects, and music that is more or less indifferent to their actions.

The brief fourth segment has Trinity racing to a phone—her portal out of the Matrix—while an agent attempts to run her down. She succeeds, arriving at the phone booth just before it is demolished by the garbage truck. Another graphical transition, accompanied by nondiegetic electronic sounds, overlaps to an extreme close-up of a computer screen, accompanied by diegetic electronic sounds, which marks the beginning of the next scene.

Music plays a prominent role throughout this action prologue, but most of the time it is mixed with—and often indistinguishable from—the sound effects, whose diegetic status is often also nebulous. The prologue is essentially a continuous sequence, but it is articulated into four clear segments, as the action occurs in four concentrated bursts. The latter reinforce but do not coincide completely with the four larger segments that structure the prologue. The bursts do focus on clear stages of Trinity's escape: she defeats the police; she flees across the rooftops; she flies through the window; she gets to the phone. Each time a burst of action starts—usually initiating a chase or fight—it does so abruptly and from a place of relative calm. The music for these bursts of action is also characteristic: repetitious, rhythmically driving with its accents clearly profiled and frequent quick swells in loudness. It is a topically evocative and gestural music but not strongly melodic.

As with the other action films we have examined, *The Matrix* opens with an action sequence *in medias res*. This sequence is also focused on the plight of a secondary character. This is one reason why, despite the fact the sequence is extremely well integrated into the larger narrative, it functions like a prologue that establishes the situation for the main narrative line centered on Neo (Keanu Reeves). This narrative line is only initiated in the next scene.

CONCLUSIONS

It is conventional to begin an action film *in media res* with an action prologue that may or may not be closely integrated with the main narrative. These prologues may precede an autonomous main title sequence (the Bond films, *Terminator 2*), or the titles and credits may be incorporated into the prologue itself (*Raiders of the Lost Ark*, *The Matrix*).

Although action is not reducible to combat as in the war film, violent sounds of explosions, gunfire, and machines of war are frequently encountered in action films, and they are found in each of the action prologues examined in this section. Like war films, action films have also made effective use of the advances in sound technologies, deploying them to craft ever more impressive-sounding explosions, low rumbles that shake the theater, bone-jarring punches, hollow wind sounds, clanking of machinery, the subtle ting of bullet casings hitting the ground amidst a general din, and gunshots that are laden with the sound of doom. Being more focused on using the spectacle of violence to establish the terms of fantasy than to represent the horrific intensity of combat, the combat sequences in action films differ from those in war films in featuring music much more prominently. Action films also effectively blur distinctions between music and effects. Even though action films largely concentrate on moments that violence explodes (literally) into action, their interest in imperiled heroes means that they frequently dwell empathetically on the damage violence inflicts on bodies, especially when the violence involves hitting and punching. Consequently, one of the reasons music and effects are so frequently blurred in action sequences is because filmmakers commit the sound track to rendering the feeling of the violent impact on the body rather than capturing what it sounds like.

A French Film, *La Cage aux Folles*, Remade in America as *The Birdcage*

A runaway hit in the late 1970s, *La Cage aux Folles* (1978) starred two veteran character actors, Ugo Tognazzi and Michel Serrault, playing Renato and Albin, owner and star performer, respectively, of a drag club in Saint-Tropez, an upscale tourist town on the French Riviera. An American remake, *The Birdcage* (1996), was nearly as successful. Closely modeled on the French original, *The Birdcage* moves the scene to Miami Beach but retains nearly all the plot elements and many details of both dialogue and mise-en-scène. Diegetic performances are treated similarly, but nondiegetic music is treated differently: in *The Birdcage*, a variety of musics are heard, many quoted from existing recordings; in *La Cage aux Folles* one hears less music, and almost all of it is a single theme simply repeated or else varied in tempo and arrangement. Table 12-3 lists all the music for

Table 12-3 *The Birdcage* (1996). Timeline and cue list.

[EVENING] [PART 1: "SETUP"]

ESTABLISHING SEQUENCE AND OPENING SCENE

      0:00:00 song [production number] with chorus, possibly nondiegetic at first, eventually revealed
            as diegetic when we see the stage and singers ["We Are Family"]

      0:04:20 trumpet fanfare, followed by an Indian-themed dance [Rossini, William Tell Overture in
            arrangement]

      0:05:40 same, cuts back in

      0:07:28 heard in the background again

      0:10:15 Latin number ["La Virgen Lloraba"]

      0:10:30 orchestra introduces Starina; at 11:00 orchestra plays behind her monologue: the same
            standard that she eventually sings ["Can That Boy Fox Trot"]

Family conversations

    —Val and Armand talk [CF: 0:14:50]

      0:12:30 diegetic Latin music on cut to upstairs (Agador cleaning the kitchen, listens to a radio
            visible in the foreground) ["Conga"] (after about 0:14:00 muffled sounds of the club can be
            heard from downstairs)

    —Barbara talks to her parents (in at 0:17:30) [CF: 0:18:25]

    —cut back to the penthouse

      0:20:00 nondiegetic piano music as Albert looks in on Val, who is sleeping [unidentified]

[NEXT DAY] [PART 2: "COMPLICATING ACTION"]

Morning

    —Albert shops for groceries; breakfast in the penthouse [CF: 0:21:55]

      0:20:50 Latin music, nondiegetic ["Lady Marmalade"]

    —morning in the Keeley house [CF: 0:25:50]

    —cut back to Armand and Albert [CF: 0:28:50]

      0:26:45 on cut, Armand works on "Little Dream" at the piano

    —cut back to Keeley's house (news organization set up outside)

Later that day

    —rehearsal

      0:30:27 rehearsal piano with "Little Dream" [CF: 0:32:30]

    —cut back to the Keeley house at night

      0:38:10 orchestral underscoring (backgrounded) [unidentified]

    —back to the club (after closing) [CF: 0:38:54]

      0:41:15 piano with "Little Dream" (nondiegetic?)

[FOLLOWING DAY]

Early the next day

    —Keeleys on the road; Armand and Albert on the beach; penthouse is cleared out; Armand and Albert return

        0:43:00 orchestral; nondiegetic ["No Pain for Cakes"]—music continues over beach scene, morphing into Latin rhythm, and through subsequent segments; out with Albert's cry

    —Albert and Armand talk outside and in a restaurant [CF: 0:44:00]

        0:47:40 Latin dance music heard faintly in the background—diegetic or nondiegetic? [unidentified]

        0:52:43 orchestral music back in again with cut back to back to Keeleys on the road; goes out just after cut back to Armand and Albert (0:53:15)

BACK TO THE PENTHOUSE [CF: 0:51:40]; DECISION TO ASK VAL'S MOTHER FOR HELP; IN KATHERINE'S OFFICE [CF: 0:52:43]; ARMAND AND ALBERT TALK OUTSIDE [CF: 1:02:20] [PART 3: "DEVELOPMENT"]

        1:00:50 low-level diegetic music (radio) in the office

        1:00:55 Armand and Katherine dance and sing ["Love Is in the Air"] [CF: 0:55:50]

        1:01:20 return to low-level diegetic music in the office

        1:08:25 low-level diegetic music again on cut to the office

Back to the penthouse, the time approaches; the Keeleys arrive; dinner

        1:12:40 Agador sings while working ["She Works Hard for the Money"]

        1:14:45 music outdoors as Keeleys approach the club [CF: 1:10:50]

        1:18:49 same briefly again

        1:20:00 Latin music as Katherine waits in traffic (enters just before the cut) [unidentified]

[PART 4: "CLIMAX AND EPILOGUE"]

        1:27:00 low-level music from the club or from outdoors (as newsmen look at name on the door)

        1:31:07 again, then to piano and singing with cut back to penthouse ["I Could Have Danced All Night"]

Finale: the press arrive; the Keeleys escape; wedding and end credits

        1:47:05 low-level music again with newsmen outside; continues to be heard during subsequent conversation indoors

        1:48:48 Latin performance in the club, goes directly into "We Are Family"; overlaps with Latin music [unidentified] heard outdoors at about 1:53:25 (after cut outside)

        1:53:45 overlaps with Latin music for credits and wedding ["Family Salsa" followed by "Conga"] [CF: 1:34:15]

The Birdcage, along with a sketch of the action. Some parallel actions in *La Cage aux Folles* are marked with "CF" in square brackets.

    The opening sequence of *The Birdcage* moves fluidly through the main titles and an opening stage number—the ambiguously nondiegetic singing over the

Figure 12-15. *The Birdcage* (1996). Exterior shot during the establishing sequence.

titles turns into the singing of the transgendered chorus (although the volume barely changes) as the camera moves over the ocean, onto Miami Beach, lingers on the street outside the club (see Figure 12-15), and then goes inside. Cutaways during the number introduce Robin Williams's character, Armand, and, indirectly through the backstage manager doing a stage call, Albert (Nathan Lane) or Starina (his stage name). Through Armand's walking about the club greeting guests and talking with employees, we are introduced to the physical and cultural environment of the club; through the stage call, we can anticipate the first narrative complication. The stage number ("We Are Family") ends at 04:20, and with it the first scene. In this case, the change of physical environment is minimal and not unequivocal—essentially attention shifts gradually from the club audience and stage to backstage. It takes the conclusion of the musical number and a subsequent narrative complication, the announcement by an assistant, Agador, that Starina/Albert will not perform tonight, to confirm the change. An abrupt shift further into the building—upstairs to the penthouse that Albert shares with Armand—announces another scene shift. Music, stage, and club noise are cut off, but a brief cutaway will confirm that another, Native-American themed, performance has begun.

Whether the backstage segment is a sub-scene of the confrontation between Albert and Armand that follows or whether it is a (transitional) scene unto itself is difficult to say: the motivation for the confrontation comes from backstage, but since the beginning of the film there has also been a steady "geographical" progress from exterior deeper and deeper to and into the interior of the building. In any case, Albert and Agador talk, then with a cut back to the stage area we see Armand heading up the stairs. He bursts in the door (about 05:45) and calls out

"Albert!" There follows a series of yells, screams, and banging on doors, as Albert tries to prevent Armand from entering his dressing room. An exchange of accusations, with Albert doing most of the talking, is interrupted by the stage manager. Through the open door we hear low-level club sounds (including the continuing performance). Confronted with an ultimatum, Albert agrees to go on. Armand instructs the stage manager to insert a mambo number. Agador leaves, and Albert and Armand continue the conversation at a lower level. Close to the end (about 10:00), Albert suddenly interjects a loud word (he is suspicious of Armand), and a bit later another sound accent (his scream as Armand pushes him) abruptly ends the scene as it merges with a sharp cut and loud music for the mambo number.

So far then, an initial scene lasting about 4 minutes was followed by a transitional scene, lasting about a minute and a half, then another scene of about 5 minutes. As the mambo finishes, Armand announces Starina's number (at 10:45) and then goes upstairs shortly after the performance begins: we hear it at a very low level as Armand prepares for his son Val's arrival. At this point, the narrative direction shifts toward the principal driver of the narrative, as we learn that Val (Dan Futterman) wants to get married. One might decide that this starts a second sequence, except that when this last, extended scene ends (at 20:50), an abrupt shift in time and place makes it clear that everything before has belonged to one large segment, a night in the club. The cut is simple, but it does not need to be subtle: Albert is shown outdoors the next day, shopping for groceries.

As its opening sequence suggests by its staged performances and its confusion of the diegetic and nondiegetic realms, *The Birdcage* has a number of affinities with film musicals. Performances are prominent, there is relatively little underscoring, and often diegetic music substitutes for underscoring in backgrounded functions. The nondiegetic music, even the underscoring, is all based on songs or popular Latin dances. In addition, the very prominence of performances and nondiegetic songs and dances accentuates the starkness—or at least the simplicity—of the sound track in scenes or segments without music. Finally, like some traditional musicals, the roles of diegetic and nondiegetic music become more ambiguous—or mixed—as the film proceeds.

La Cage aux Folles, on the other hand, clearly retains its basic character of comedic farce (leavened only slightly by the romance of the young couple). The music corresponds: the signature theme, which is first heard as Renato and Albin talk in their apartment and is thus associated with them, reappears only occasionally to mark particular moments in the narrative. Its bright *chanson* (that is, popular song) character and arrangement mark the film conventionally as comedy as well.

The Birdcage is easily partitioned in terms of time: an evening and two full days—see the headings in Table 12-3—but these do not match the film's four parts except in the first instance: the break from the first evening to the next morning coincides with the end of the set-up. The first evening is dominated by the club, the Birdcage, but parallel narratives also begin here, alternately

*The daytime ana-
logues to crickets
are cicadas. Gener-
ally louder than
crickets, their
sounds are also
more varied, and the
quality of the sound
differs because they
"sing" from trees
and bushes, unlike
the ground-level
sounds of crickets.
An unusually
prominent—and
humorously ironic—
use of cicada noises
occurs in the ceme-
tery scene of* La
Cage aux Folles, *where Renato and
Albin talk on a train-
station bench. The
scene is devoid of
action outside of
their somewhat
subdued conversa-
tion while we hear
the singing of the
(unseen) cicadas.*

showing us family conversations involving Val with Armand and Albert, on the one hand, and Barbara and her parents, on the other. The parallel narratives continue throughout the first full day and into the second, until the families meet.

Music follows a steady path from beginning to end, with clearly divided functions that give way to more complex treatments before resolving suddenly into a framing repeat performance at the end. We hear only diegetic performance in the first 10 minutes, then, briefly, radio sounds. Music, which has been very prominent so far, drops out entirely for the first conversation between Barbara and her parents, thus even further accentuating the divide between the young couple's families—and also the very prosaic character of Barbara's parents. Plainly nondiegetic music appears at 20:00, as Albert looks in on the sleeping Val. With the cut to the next scene (and next day), the status of the Latin music seems only a little less secure (are we hearing it playing from somewhere outdoors and nearby?). Rehearsals involving the song "Little Dream" reassert performance in the sphere of the club, but nondiegetic underscoring appears in the Keeleys' scenes (at 38:10 and 43:00) as the dramatic situation intensifies (they are hounded by reporters and try to escape).

From this point on, the diegetic performances are brief and personal (Armand with his former spouse Katherine at 01:00:55; Agador at 01:12:40; Armand and Mrs. Keeley at 01:31:07), and other diegetic music is decidedly backgrounded until the finale, when Armand and Albert help the Keeleys escape in disguise during a reprise performance of "We Are Family." As a final touch, the diegetic music transforms into (prominent) underscoring for the wedding scene that closes the film—and overlaps with the end credits. For this, arranger Steve Goldstein created an instrumental salsa version of "We Are Family."

The two renditions of "We Are Family" create a powerful frame for the entire film, the recurrence itself being an important factor. The Indian-themed and mambo numbers in the first scene are fragmentary (although we understand clock time to continue) and mostly backgrounded (part of the club's environment), and "Little Dream," although foregrounded, is subverted by narrative as the rehearsal is repeatedly interrupted.

Using Scene Comparison to Construct a Historical Argument

In Chapter 10, we discussed writing a compare-and-contrast paper. Using formal scene analysis to compare and contrast two scenes in the same film can be a useful device to develop an interpretation for a film. This kind of comparison lay behind the interpretations of *Glory* and *Saving Private Ryan* offered earlier in the chapter. Comparing and contrasting scenes from different films can help identify broad stylistic traits if the films are chosen carefully. For instance, the preceding section on treatment of dialogue, the sections on war films in both Chapter 10 and the current chapter, and the section on action films all use comparison and contrast to derive broad inferences about the stylistic traits of sound tracks for a circumscribed set of films.

A good (and accessible) example of a scholarly article that follows this approach to develop a stylistic argument about studio practice of symphonic underscoring is Martin Marks's "Music, Drama, Warner Brothers: The Cases of *Casablanca* and *The Maltese Falcon*."[4] Marks does not choose his two films arbitrarily: they were released within 1 year of each other by the same studio, both involve international intrigue and feature the same (male) actors. Their composers are different, however, and this is Marks's entry point: the background music for *Casablanca* (1942) was composed by Max Steiner; the composer for *The Maltese Falcon* (1941) was Adolf Deutsch. The thesis, then, is "the scores by Deutsch and Steiner follow similar formal schemes, [but] they offer sharp contrasts in style and function, owing partly to the inclinations of the composers, partly to fundamental differences in the filmic narratives." Although the article is generally an appreciation of both works, Marks is critical of details in Deutsch's score, which leads to a broader evaluation: "In summary, we might say that one of these scores [*Casablanca*] sings, the other [*The Maltese Falcon*] doesn't; that one speaks a language we can easily understand, the other whispers secrets; and that, following pathways both parallel and far apart, each finds a different way to move with its film, from beginning to end."[5]

The basic technique of comparing and contrasting a set of films is also one effective way to make a historical argument, and the treatment of music in opening sequences provides a particularly good site to sketch how you might think about this. Although deviations from the standard two-part main title cue or song form cue were possible during the classical studio era, they were understood as exactly that—instances meant to make an unusual, unexpected effect. In the post-classical period, these types of cues were reserved mainly for low-budget or genre films and romantic comedies. In prestige productions, the establishing sequence was more and more often treated in a deliberately nontraditional manner, as a marker of aesthetic quality, and the uses and positioning of music changed accordingly. With "more and more," we are suggesting a difference between the early years of the post-classical era and the final decade, or between the 1950s and the late 1960s and 1970s. We might, then, take this difference as our hypothesis and test it by comparing the openings of two films from the same genres but from opposite ends of the time frame: two "monster thriller" films, such as *Creature from the Black Lagoon* (1954) and *Jaws* (1975); or two sci-fi films, such as *Destination Moon* (1950) or *When Worlds Collide* (1951) and *THX 1138* (1971) or *Slaughterhouse Five* (1972). Another fruitful angle might be to compare openings of studio-era films and similar productions from the post-classical era. Examples might include melodrama, such as *Now, Voyager* (1942) and the similarly themed *Magnificent Obsession* (1954). For the latter title, you could even compare two productions, the earlier one from 1935 and the widescreen version from 1954. You might compare a detective film from the mid-1940s with *Chinatown* (1974). You might examine analogous scenes in *Seven Samurai* (1954) and the American film based on it, *The Magnificent Seven* (1960). This same procedure might be applied to other scene types or indeed extended to entire sound tracks.

We have essentially followed this approach in constructing the sections on war films and action films in the preceding section, and in the section on war films in Chapter 10. Our goal in writing these passages was not simply to abstract stylistic traits of the genre for the period in question but to forge an argument about how the sound track changed in these genres due to technological and aesthetic trends and pressures. It is important in making these sorts of arguments that the corpus of films studied be well chosen for the hypothesis being explored, that the scenes selected for analysis be appropriate to test the hypothesis and develop the argument, and that the claims be properly restricted to the corpus under consideration. Observations about how war films exploited the resources of Dolby Surround, for instance, may have little bearing on how a romantic comedy from the period used the technology.

You should take special care to avoid unwarranted generalizations. Claims about the uniqueness and originality of a film with respect to technological or aesthetic innovation are particularly suspect, and it has been our experience that beginning students are particularly prone to make them. Few students studying sound tracks seriously for the first time will have the deep knowledge of the film repertory required to make such claims. For instance, the sound of bullets hitting the body might seem an especially innovative choice on the part of the sound designers working on *Gallipoli*, but without considerable knowledge of a wide corpus of war films it would be most unwise to claim that the choice is unique or original (which is why we did not make that claim in our discussion). As with most technical matters in art, any sound track technique almost always turns out to have a precursor—or many precursors—if you look hard enough, and most often it is not the technique itself but the particularly arresting context within which the technique does its work that is what is actually fresh and innovative about a particular use of it.

Music and Film Sound Since 2000

Introduction: The Digital Era

Since 2000, the changes in the film industry have been truly remarkable, rivaling the disruptions of the transition to sound. After starting in postproduction, digitization has spread to all facets of film production, distribution, and exhibition. Films are now frequently shot with digital film, the sound is recorded with digital recorders; both image and sound are edited on computers; many scenes are shot in front of blue (or green) screens for chroma key compositing, and dialogue is looped in via ADR (Automated Dialogue Replacement); special effects are built primarily with CGI (Computer-Generated Imagery), again often with the aid of chroma key compositing, and sounds are similarly constructed through synthesizers and samplers with layers of digital effects. Films are now widely distributed as digital files for both images and sound. They are exhibited using state-of-the-art 4K digital projectors, often in 3D or at 48 fps, and with increasingly elaborate surround sound fields extending to seven or more discrete channels. All of this technological change has greatly altered the ways in which films are produced, distributed, and edited, and this has had a profound effect on how we think about the movies, which are no longer "films" in anything but a metaphorical and generic sense.

As noted in previous chapters, magnetic tape and Dolby noise reduction were introduced in postproduction well before they were used on release prints. This is a common path of technological innovation in the film industry, moving from postproduction to production before finally coming to exhibition. Thus, digital sound and images had long held secure places in postproduction by the time they also became standard for prints distributed to theaters. As early as 1979, *Star Trek: The Motion Picture* used digital signal processing for producing and mixing special sound effects, and by the early 1980s, digital recording and rerecording had become common, though not yet standard. Digital sound had definite advantages that made its adoption by the industry nearly inevitable once the cost of the basic technology became manageable: it expanded the dynamic range, it improved the frequency response, especially in the high frequencies crucial to definition, it all but eliminated noise and signal degradation from multiple dubs, and it greatly increased the speed at which sound editors could work and the control they could exercise over the sound track. The use of digital sound in postproduction rerecording thus played much the same role that magnetic tape had in the 1950s and 1960s: It was a means of retaining greater fidelity throughout the process of making multiple dubs during postproduction and, as a result, permitted unprecedented flexibility and new aesthetic options for designing a film's sound track.

Issues of Technology and Economics

DIGITAL SOUND

Broadly speaking, digital sound did not alter the fundamental layout and functional differentiation of the sound track. Nevertheless, significant changes resulted in practice because the ease of producing certain kinds of effects greatly expanded their use. Digital sound also offered unique possibilities through signal processing, including extending a sound, changing its pitch, or adding effects, both subtle and otherwise, via various digital plug-ins and filters. Perhaps the most significant trait of digital sound, however, was that it permitted non-linear editing of the sound track. Prior to such systems as Avid, which was introduced for small-scale editing in 1989 and for feature-length films in 1993, all sound editing and mixing had to be done in sequence within a reel. Digital sound, combined with the easy and relatively inexpensive capability to digitize the image, enabled a non-linear approach to editing the sound track, meaning that sound editors could immediately access and edit the sound track at any point of the film. In terms of sound, the most important aspect of this shift was a new-found ease in layering sound and shaping the sound track over the course of the whole film. It was actually possible to do such sound design and sound editing prior to nonlinear systems, but the work was considerably more time-consuming and therefore much more expensive. Now, rather than dividing sound editing duties according to reels, as was traditionally done before the digital era, sound department personnel can be (and are) assigned tasks according to sound layer and narrative function. The result is a much more consistent treatment of sound across the span of the film, which in turn permits the sound track to be more thoroughly planned or "designed" from the outset.

DIGITAL SOUND FORMATS

The rapidly improving home stereo systems of the late 1960s and 1970s had made the performance of sound systems in the multiplex seem inadequate, and in the 1980s and 1990s the increased frequency and dynamic response of the CD placed similar pressure on theaters to continue upgrading their sound. Although it was a substantial improvement on traditional optical sound, Dolby stereo remained at a disadvantage in noise, frequency, and dynamic response when compared to the CD, and in the second half of the 1980s the CD quickly became the primary form by which music was commercially distributed. In feature films, due to the properties of the optical sound track, Dolby stereo had difficulty distinguishing low-frequency sounds from background hiss, and the restricted space on the optical tracks set an absolute limit to volume control.

To remedy these problems, Dolby Laboratories introduced digital sound for the release of *Batman Returns* in 1992. Ingeniously locating the digital information in the space between the sprocket holes on the film (Figure 13-1), the original 5.1 Dolby Digital carried six channels—left, center, right, two surround channels, and a separate channel for low frequencies. Dolby Digital was not in fact the

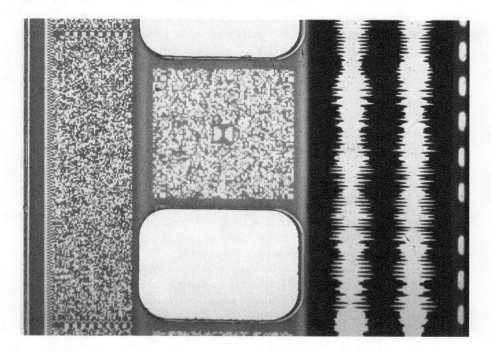

Figure 13-1. Placement of sound track formats on exhibition prints. The space outside the sprocket holes carries part of the SDDS encoding. The rest of the SDDS encoding is placed outside the right-hand sprocket holes (not shown). The space between the sprockets is occupied by the Dolby digital encoding (note the Dolby trademark symbol in the middle of the data field). The two analog optical tracks (variable area) are encoded in Dolby surround and are used primarily for backup. The dashed line along the right edge is the DTS time-code, which ensures synchronization with the special accompanying CD.

first digital format in common distribution. CDS (Cinema Digital Sound), a format developed by Eastman Kodak and Optical Radiation Corporation, appeared in 1990. This, like Dolby Digital, was a 5.1 system, but its information was printed in the space normally occupied by the optical sound track (for 35 mm release prints) and magnetic sound track (for 70 mm release prints), leaving the prints without an analog backup if the digital system failed. This vulnerability left an opening for Dolby Digital, which because the digital sound information of this format was printed between the sprocket holes allowed its prints to also carry a Dolby analog surround sound track as backup. CDS did prove, however, that film stock was sensitive enough to effectively carry a digital sound track. In 1993, DTS (Digital Theater System), with the backing of Steven Spielberg, introduced another competing system for *Jurassic Park*. DTS used a CD synchronized to the film (a distant echo of Warner Bros' Vitaphone system from the 1920s). That same year, the last of the major digital formats, SDDS (Sony Dynamic Digital Sound), appeared. Like Dolby Digital, SDDS was physically encoded on the film, and *Last Action Hero* (1993) was the first film released using the format.

Although these formats were rapidly adopted by studios, branded as superior technologies (especially once DVDs became common), and made into a standard, it was difficult for filmmakers to take full advantage of the improvements offered by digital sound for theatrical releases. As had been the case with stereo, theaters were initially slow to adopt the technology, generally opting to convert only their largest auditorium in order to handle the blockbuster releases. This reluctance on the part of theater owners, along with the continued dominance of the VHS cassette as a primary consumer market for film purchase and rental, placed filmmakers in a bind. Rerecorder mixer Tom Fleischman noted the difficulty that filmmakers and studios have often faced with the uneven dispersion of technological innovation:

> One of the problems we've had in making technological advances in sound is that there's a catch-22 that exists. For us to be able to use something new technologically, it has to be able to be delivered to the public. Dolby Stereo came out in the early seventies and really wasn't widely used until the late seventies because there was an expense involved in converting the theater to be able to play the track. The same thing happened when they went to Dolby SR. They had converted all the theaters to Dolby Stereo, and again there was a cost involved in upgrading to Dolby SR. Until the owners are willing to make that expense to convert their theaters, there's nowhere to play the track. If there's nowhere to play the track, the producer won't want to use that format. The studio that's got the facility doesn't want to make the investment in new equipment that's needed to provide it. It's like the chicken and the egg—what's going to trigger this cycle to begin?[1]

The rapid replacement of older multiplexes by the newer megaplex palaces with raked seating since the late 1990s broke the logjam that Fleischman describes, so that today most theaters are equipped with digital sound.

Recently, theaters have converted to digital projection as well. In 2000 there were just over a dozen theaters in North America equipped for digital projection and roughly the same number elsewhere in the world. Theaters in China rapidly converted to digital, with an estimated fifteen thousand screens by 2005, and cinemas in Great Britain also moved quickly to digital, with a functional base of four hundred theaters with digital projection by 2006. Widespread conversion in the United States came somewhat later, primarily after the onset of the so-called Lesser Depression of 2008, with the enticement of increased revenues for 3D titles and the decreasing number of titles available from distributors in 35mm film format. By 2010, it was estimated that North America already had more than sixteen thousand digital screens, of which about half were equipped for 3D.

This rapid conversion to digital technology resembled the conversion to sound around 1930, which also took place during a period of severe economic upheaval. Now, as then, cinemas in marginal locations—especially those in small towns—could not bear the high capital costs of conversion, which had the effect of squeezing them out of the business. Many venues, such as art museums and libraries, which had acquired 35mm projectors and showed films on an occasional basis, today also find it increasingly difficult to rent even older films in those formats.

THE MULTIPLEX PALACE

In the United States, the indifferent architecture of the multiplex has been largely replaced by a new theater aesthetic, leveraged at least in part by the needs of digital sound. These theaters often have ambitious architecture reminiscent of the old picture palaces, and they often boast as many as fifteen to twenty screens (allowing showings of popular titles to start as close together as every 15 minutes), digital sound and projection, and heavily raked (or stadium) seating. Increasingly, they even have full-service restaurants attached which serve dinner and drinks during a screening. If the exterior is reminiscent of the picture palace, however, the basic structure of the multiplex—especially the concession stand dominating the lobby—remains in place. Although raked seating has made the film-going experience more comfortable for patrons, the needs of sound insulation, especially heavy curtains along the walls to keep reflected sound in the theater to a minimum, have generally kept the architecture of the auditoria themselves more or less nondescript.

A number of factors have driven the building of these new theaters. The most important of these is that the production rate of Hollywood in the past decade or so has increased to the extent that more screens (if not necessarily more seats) are needed. During the summer months especially, prospective blockbusters often open the same weekend as each other. This can result in a severe shortage of screens, not only pushing other films out of the theater but also constraining the gross receipts of the blockbusters themselves (because the gross is limited by the number of available seats). Increasing the number of seats

Figure 13-2. THX is a theater certification standard developed by Tomlinson Holman for Lucasfilm. Unlike Dolby, SDDS, and DTS, THX is not a format for sound reproduction but a technical standard that ensures that all certified theaters (and mixing rooms) will sound alike.

for an individual film maximizes the effects of the saturation advertising used to promote blockbusters (and, increasingly, smaller films as well); the larger number of screens gives exhibitors much greater flexibility in adjusting the number of seats to demand for particular films.

Having been built to exhibit with digital sound, the auditoria of the newer multiplexes, generally speaking, have vastly superior sound characteristics compared to the older generation of theaters. The acoustic insulation between theaters has also been improved. The bleeding over of low-frequency sound from a blockbuster in one auditorium to the romantic comedy next door has been largely mitigated, if not entirely eliminated. And many theaters now undergo THX certification (see Figure 13-2), which guarantees that the auditoria meet certain technical specifications for image projection and sound reproduction. The weak point in this system remains the lack of a dedicated professional staff for projection and sound, because the volume level in particular needs to be adjusted according to the size of the audience.

VIDEO, DVD, AND TELEVISION TECHNOLOGIES

We made the observation in Chapter 11 that stereo could only be fully exploited in the "design" of the sound track when stereo televisions and VCRs became ubiquitous in the early 1990s: the sound track still had to be adequate when heard through the speakers of a television set. Even today, when television sound has vastly improved, filmmakers cannot generally count on more than two-channel stereo with simulated surround in the home setting. Sound tracks therefore cannot take full advantage of the resources of the modern theater—excepting perhaps volume—without risking loss of intelligibility for home viewers, which remain by far the largest audience for any film.

The situation is especially acute with respect to two-channel stereo's lack of center channel, which leaves a "hole" in the stereo field right where the voice is typically placed. This missing channel is why dialogue can seem oddly decentered when listening to television, especially in the wide stereo field of simulated surround. To compensate for this negative result, dialogue is inevitably mixed at a higher level and the music and ambient sound reduced. In point of fact, the same holds true, although to a lesser extent, for 5.1 mixes released on DVD, where dialogue is also boosted compared to the theatrical release mix under the assumption that the conditions and distractions of home viewing tend to impair intelligibility. The situation with television is rapidly changing, however. The 2009 change to digital broadcast in the United States, along with HDTV channels carrying 5.1 sound mixes and the relatively low cost of 5.1 home theater sound systems, has moved the basic DVD (or Blu-Ray) mix closer to those heard in the cinema. Nevertheless, the sheer number of formats and viewing conditions will continue to place a limit on standardization of release mixes. Given various-sized multiplexes, DVDs, in-flight films, and so on, it is simply impossible to prefigure an ideal mix.

Although the DVD did not (at first) have the capacity to record, its relatively quick consumer acceptance was made possible by the fact that it offered far superior sound and picture compared to videotape (although some cineastes complained that it failed to meet the standards of the laserdisc). The DVD also offered digital encoding on a more robust medium than magnetic tape, which meant that the image and sound were not subject to the same degradation over time as was the case with videotape. The large data capacity of the DVD permitted higher fidelity sound with more audio channels and a richer set of mixes, so that it has become standard for films to be released and encoded in 5.1 sound whenever appropriate (and sometimes even when not—see Figure 13-3 for a discussion). Finally, the relative permanence and low cost of DVDs strongly encouraged film purchases and, with that, the creation of personal film libraries, a trend that VHS tapes had already started to a lesser degree. (Streaming services—Netflix, Amazon Instant Video, and Hulu, among others—allow on-demand access to a large library of titles, and these services have in recent years cut considerably into DVD and Blu-Ray purchases.)

Until very recently, filmmakers have not fully utilized the greatly enhanced sound capabilities of the DVD format, but the full frequency sound and wide field spatiality of the surround channels nevertheless played a crucial role in what might be called the "cinematization" of television. To put it bluntly, DVD sound made even a 32" screen look puny by comparison with the sound—the sound engulfed the viewer, while the screen merely contained the picture. Even larger televisions suffered because letterboxing effectively reduces the size of the screen: the wider the aspect ratio of the theatrical release, the smaller the image on the television. The historical point of attraction of the widescreen format had been that it filled the peripheral vision, producing the illusion that we in the audience are in the midst of the film itself. The small image of the letterboxed

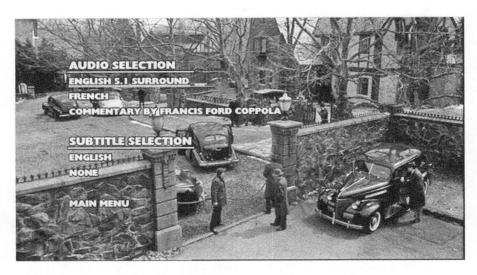

Figure 13-3. Encoding of DVDs in 5.1 surround has become something of a fetish, with the sound tracks of many older monaural films being remixed, often with exaggerated stereo effects. The 5.1 mix of *The Manchurian Candidate* (1962), for instance, contains a significant amount of overtly panned point-of-location sound. Sometimes the remix is presented as having been done under the supervision of the director. The collector's edition of M*A*S*H (1970) advertises: "Director Robert Altman personally oversaw the film restoration for this DVD. The painstaking process included the re-creation of the film negative and a reengineering of the film's original sound track." In this case, the disk includes the original mono sound track as well, but this is not always the case.

The audio menu from the version of *The Godfather* (1972) contained in *The Godfather DVD Collection* is shown above. Note that it contains only the 5.1 surround mix, despite the fact that it was originally released in mono and was nominated for an Academy Award in sound.

Finally, the sound tracks of many older films with monaural optical tracks have often been digitally processed to reduce the background hiss that was present in the original recordings and prints. This processing has allowed these films to sound better than they ever did at the time they were exhibited. The DVD of *The Broadway Melody* (1929), for instance, has not only reduced the characteristic hiss of sound tracks at the time but has also dulled the sharp audio pops between shots in the opening scene.

Clearly we need to be extremely cautious about drawing historical inferences from the sound tracks of DVDs.

version had precisely the opposite effect. Even as television screens became larger, the lack of a commensurate improvement in resolution meant the images lost much of their cinematic sharpness. It would not be too much of a stretch to say that cinematic sound contributed significantly to the obsolescence of analogue television.

FRANCHISES, BRANDING, AND CONVERGENT MEDIA

The rise of iTunes and other forms of digital distribution after 2000 devastated album sales in general. By one count, soundtrack sales dropped more than 30 percent between 1999 and 2004 compared with just over 10 percent for the rest of the record industry. Compilation soundtrack sales were particularly affected by the rise of iTunes and similar services because they allowed consumers to buy the individual songs they wanted. Digital distribution also made the album less effective as film memorabilia since a digital copy lacked the tangibility of a CD or LP. As the ancillary income from soundtrack albums eroded, film producers could no longer rely on soundtrack sales to underwrite costs for any audience but pre-teenage girls (*High School Musical* [2006], *Frozen* [2013]), and this altered to some extent the strategy of selecting music for the film. Exceptions such as *O Brother, Where Art Thou?* (2000), *Garden State* (2004), *Juno* (2007), and *Guardians of the Galaxy* (2014) are increasingly rare and have been difficult to duplicate. Consequently, filmmakers have recently focused more on economizing on basic licensing costs on the one hand and on selecting songs for the meaning they bring to the film on the other. To be sure, these were both major concerns in selecting songs for films before the collapse in the album market in the years after 2000, but they are now by far the dominant factors.

With the emergence of the New Hollywood based on blockbuster production, the shells of the old film studios, which had been incorporated as parts of highly diversified corporations during the 1960s and 1970s, were over the 1980s and 1990s absorbed and consolidated into large media companies that once again worked to achieve a kind of vertical integration that allowed the companies to coordinate production, distribution, and exhibition in a way unparalleled since the consent decree of 1948. These media companies did not rebuild the film production facilities as closed studios or place creative personnel under exclusive long-term contracts as they did in the studio era; and they did not make large investments in theaters (although, as noted earlier, theater chains were also rebuilding, consolidating, and conglomerating during this period). But these media firms did acquire or conglomerate television networks and an ever expanding number of cable channels as well as develop increasingly important home entertainment divisions that specialized in selling films first as VHS tapes and later as DVDs and Blu-Rays and have recently worked toward creating profitable subscription streaming services. They also financed films, acquired broad rights of distribution across various media, and managed these properties in ways that allowed effective exploitation across the divisions of the media firm, which might include book publishing, music labels, toys, video games, network and cable television channels, cable and Internet systems, Internet companies, newspapers and magazines, theme parks, sports teams, retail stores, and so forth. Effective cross-media exploitation required—or at least encouraged—the development of properties that could be easily serialized so that variants appropriate to each medium could be created within a recognizable template of the basic brand. These kinds of media properties have become known as "franchises," which are media properties in the form of a series of films, video games, websites, books, toys, and other ancillary products developed out of a basic unifying concept.

As blockbuster production has turned increasingly to developing and sustaining such franchises, original music—which is typically owned by the company that produced the film and controls its ancillary products—has become a crucial element along with visual style binding the disparate products of the franchise together into a brand. Music is incorporated into many of the media representations of the franchise—film, advertising, video game, website, amusement park ride, and so forth—in a way that establishes the presence of the diegetic world of the franchise. The world of Harry Potter is effectively conjured up by "Hedwig's Theme" composed by John Williams, whether we are watching the film, visiting one of the official Harry Potter websites, walking through the Wizarding World of Harry Potter at the Universal Studios amusement park, or playing "LEGO Harry Potter: Years 1–4" on the Wii or "Harry Potter Spells" for the iPhone. (Jeremy Soule's cinematic scores for the Electronic Arts version of the games for the first four books did not draw on Williams's themes, but James Hannigan's scores for the final four video games in the series used material by both Williams and Soule.) It is telling in this respect that Pottermore.com, the site J. K. Rowling developed for the Harry Potter series with Sony, has suffered from the decision not to use the music from the films, and only to use music in very limited contexts in branding the site. This choice distinguishes the Pottermore brand from the Warner Bros. franchise, which controls the rights to all the music composed for the films, but at the cost of alienating many fans, who have responded by producing their own musical sound tracks drawn from the films and video games and posting them to YouTube.

Establishing continuities among media properties across platforms is, of course, hardly new. Films, books, theater, magazines, and newspapers frequently shared content and freely adapted stories from one another already in the silent era. A film might be based on a play or a book, and the film treatment might then be serialized to a magazine or newspaper as part of the advertising campaign. When first radio, then sound film, and later television became viable commercial media, they too joined in this cycle of adaptation and commercial exploitation. Dramatized radio treatment of film stories was a standard option studios had at their disposal for advertising films during the classical era. These were often fully produced albeit abridged radio dramas based on the film (sometimes including music from the film).

Already in the 1950s, the Walt Disney Company attempted to systematize the interactions among media in order to better exploit its properties. (Disney had been licensing merchandise, especially featuring Mickey Mouse, since 1929.) Although film production remained the center of its activities, the company used its television shows, the anthology show *Disneyland* (later *Walt Disney Presents, Walt Disney's Wonderful World of Color,* and *The Wonderful World of Disney*) and the variety-based *The Mickey Mouse Club*, as a way of keeping its films constantly in front of an audience in order to continue a flow of revenue from ancillary merchandising, including the songs, once the theatrical release had played out. That is, Disney was already managing its films as properties with the aim of maximizing profits over a much longer term and over a wider set of media than was the case with other studios, which rarely handled their back catalogs with any kind of coherent strategy and put much less effort into ancillary merchandising. When the Disneyland theme park opened in 1955, many of the attractions, including most spectacularly the Sleeping Beauty Castle, were adapted from the Disney films, and actors dressed in costumes based on the animated characters roamed Fantasyland putting on shows that surrealistically mixed songs and characters from disparate films. It was the fantasy of a heterogeneous yet congruent Disney universe that then tracked into the individual themed rides, many with appropriate musical numbers, that was key to the idea of the park.

Independent studios like Disney were in the vanguard of such efforts to systematically develop their films into more general properties, and music was one of the principal ways the company did this. Songs from the films, especially "When You Wish Upon a Star" from *Pinocchio*, were key to the early branding of Disney's television series; such uses carried over to the theme park as well, with "The Ballad of Davy Crockett," from the miniseries that aired on the *Disneyland* TV show in 1954, identifying Frontierland and "When You Wish Upon a Star" identifying Fantasyland. These associations were codified through the numerous specials on the park that aired on the *Disneyland* show with appropriate Disney songs and topical underscoring, as well as the album *Walt Disney Takes You to Disneyland* (1956), which presents short narrations of Walt Disney introducing the "realms" of the park and a suite of music inspired by each realm.

Later film franchises, such as *Star Wars,* built on a similar base of merchandising developed by Disney, and music proved especially important to binding the franchise together across the series of six live action films (with a seventh currently in pre-production), a multipart radio drama, an animated film, several animated television series, a theme park attraction, and most if not all of the more than one hundred video games based on the films. Music has served a similar function for unifying such varied film (and television) series as James Bond, *Rocky, Star Trek,* Indiana Jones, and the Muppets, and music was also important to establishing the identity of the three big slasher franchises from the 1980s, *Halloween, Friday the 13th,* and *A Nightmare on Elm Street.*

Since the 1980s blockbuster production has been increasingly predicated on developing such franchises, as the set of sequels and other products allow costs to be amortized so that risk can be spread. Music remains an efficient and cost-effective means of extending the diegetic world of the films to other media and thus imprinting the brand on them.

The medium of cinema itself has become more difficult to distinguish from television, computer video, and even video games, as all of these audiovisual media now share a large set of basic technologies and techniques, and stories, characters, and genres pass almost seamlessly from one medium to the next. If film franchises such as Harry Potter and The Lord of the Rings films are planned to have video games released in close proximity to the theatrical run of the film, successful video game franchises such as Tomb Raider, Final Fantasy, and Mario Bros. have likewise been made into films—though none has yet proved a breakout film hit. This conglomeration of technologies and intellectual properties has led many scholars and observers of the industries to talk about digital media under the term *convergence*, with differences in media often seeming more a property of the screen or device at the site of exhibition and/or consumption than inherent properties of the medium. A television show like *Hannibal* (NBC), *House of Cards* (Netflix), or the new *Dr. Who* (BBC) may look and sound "cinematic," because they are drawing principally on visual and sonic codes historically associated with film rather than with television. Vice versa, a film like the *Blair Witch Project* may look and sound like a combination of documentary and home video, and the so-called "run and gun" techniques of films like the *United 93* (2006), *The Bourne Ultimatum* (2007), and *Argo* (2012)—with highly decentered framings of actors who are even allowed to float unexpectedly out of the frame and sound that is sometimes less than intelligible—seem designed to mimic the rough quality of live, breaking news television reporting, even when such roughness has been carefully planned in production and enhanced in postproduction.

Frequently, action films contain sequences that seem designed primarily to be trailers for the accompanying video game rather than central to the film's immediate action. In this respect, such scenes resemble the popular songs that were often dropped into films during the 1960s and 1970s for ancillary income. The plots of action films, too, are commonly crafted as a series of levels and tests, with clearly delineated enemies and bosses, or, more rarely, even exhibit the characteristic looped structure of video games, as in *Lola rennt* (1998) or *Source Code* (2011). Occasionally films will purposefully play with the boundaries between film and other media. Films such as *Scott Pilgrim vs. the World* (2010) and *Sucker Punch* (2011) borrow freely from video game iconography, sound, and music. Likewise, *The Matrix* (1999) is premised on the immersive possibility of a virtual reality so tangible as to be confused with reality itself.

Production

PRODUCTION PHASES

Digital technologies have transformed film production in all its phases, but nowhere more so than in postproduction. Digital editing offers speed and flexibility over traditional editing practices. The nonlinear editing of digital systems has allowed sound editors in particular to fundamentally change how they approach a film as they are no longer bound to work through the film in the sequence of a reel. Because digital editing is nondestructive, editors also have more freedom to experiment because they know they can always go back to a previous version. On the other hand, the ease and flexibility of digital editing has made it more diffi-cult to "lock" a picture (picture lock is the point in postproduction when picture editing is completed), meaning that components such as music dependent on a locked picture often face even tighter postproduction schedules than in the past.

During the postproduction phase, filmmakers today have remarkable con-trol over the factors that go into the sound track, including directionality (sur-round sound), the music's clarity many generations after the original recording (digital sound systems), and theater sound that is as close to what the filmmak-ers heard in the final dubbing sessions as possible (Tomlinson Holman's THX system for certifying theater sound). The rise of nonlinear editing systems such as Avid, of relatively cheap but powerful film editing software such as Apple's Final Cut Pro or Avid Technology's Media Composer, and of digital audio soft-ware such as Apple's Logic Studio or Avid Technology's Pro Tools has given edi-tors enormously increased flexibility in manipulating sound and picture, and on-board computer recording technology has quickly displaced physical mixing boards. Composers are now generally required to deliver a recorded and fully produced music stem rather than a score, and they often approach their work with an idea of how they might use digital technology to modify the composed recorded sounds with effects processors, time distortion, and mixing techniques. Sound designers work with much the same equipment as composers do, and it is frequently difficult to know whether the music department or sound depart-ment was responsible for producing a particular sound on a sound track.

All these factors have transformed the overall effect films have on audiences. The clean, polished look and sound of films today are in stark contrast to films from years past. In fact, the shift from analogue to digital systems is seen by many to be as monumental a change as the introduction of sound film itself.

In the two sections that follow, we outline the typical work of the music and sound departments in film production today, using the model of the commercial film industry in the United States.

MUSIC DEPARTMENT
Music Production

Depending on the production, the director or the producer is ultimately respon-sible for all decisions about a film, including music. The decisions about music for film are usually delegated either to the music supervisor, who is responsible for uses of preexisting music, or to the composer, who creates an original score. Many films use both existing music and original score—and sometimes music will pass seamlessly from one to the other—in which case the music supervisor and composer will need to coordinate. But whether a music supervisor is select-ing songs or a composer is writing cues, the work in either case is subject to the approval of the director or producer or both. Although the director is generally credited with ultimate creative control of the film, the producer is the one who actually controls the money, and so when the director is not also the producer, it will almost certainly be the producer who is the final arbiter. As film composer

Michael A. Levine reports, it is important for a composer to figure out who has ultimate authority: "I was fired . . . from a film because I jumped through hoops for the director who brought me in while not spending enough time figuring out what the producer—the actual power—wanted. Rather than being sympathetic, Hans [Zimmer] told me I had failed in a fundamental task: determining who was my boss. He was right, and I haven't made that mistake again."[2]

During the studio era, composers were usually brought in relatively late in the film production process. Two important exceptions to this basic procedure were musicals and animated shorts, which followed different production schedules from other common film genres. Composers working today on mainstream commercial films are also only rarely involved at the preproduction planning stage, and they often start getting approval on the basic approach to thematic material during the production stage. The usual practice continues to be for composers to work on actual cues after picture lock—that is, late in the postproduction stage—though for sequels scenes will often be edited to music tracks from earlier films in the series, and these tracks will occasionally be used "as is" or recorded again with only small changes. *The Bourne Ultimatum* (2007), for instance, reuses or only slightly adapts many cues from the first two films of the series. Since the studio era, it has been common to edit the picture and dialogue to what is known as the temp track (temporary music track), and during the studio era a temp track—usually compiled from library music from previous films and from pieces that had been composed as stock cues for use in B productions—was generally deployed for the previews that the studios used to gauge public reception. Even during the studio era, portions of this temp track might make it into the final cut. Since the dissolution of the studio system, some directors and producers have preferred working with pre-existing music (whether from specialty collections of production music or from recordings of concert music) and have essentially scored their films from recordings during the editing process. Stanley Kubrick followed this method for most of his later films. Another procedure sometimes adopted is for the director or producer to commission what is basically a suite of new music, with the composer given only general specifications for particular kinds of moods or situations. This music is then edited to the picture and dialogue (or vice versa) much like a temp track of preexisting music.

Because using popular music involves complicated licensing agreements that can significantly affect the finances, films whose conception depends on the presence of such music will usually need a music supervisor during the preproduction planning stage. Music supervisors are hired for a broad knowledge of recorded music and for legal expertise in negotiating contracts for rights, both for the film itself and for potential exploitation in ancillary markets such as sound-track albums and music videos. Music supervisors work either as freelancers for particular film productions or as employees of studios, production companies, music supervision companies, advertising firms, trailer houses, or video game publishers. As with composers, the most prominent music supervisors today work as freelancers or as heads of firms specializing in music supervision.

Although like other creative personnel most composers during the studio era were under contract with particular studios, the breakup of the studio system after the consent decree in 1948 led increasingly to composers working as free-lancers. This gave the top composers more control over their assignments and the ability to manage their careers but also required them to manage more and more of the music production, including finding potential ways of monetizing the sound track. Until quite recently, the usual financial arrangement for music was the composer's fee plus expenses for music production. That is, the com-poser was paid a fee for delivery of the score and then expenses for the musical production and postproduction of the recording that would actually be used in the film—orchestration, copying, recording, mixing, and so forth—were cov-ered by another budget line. Writing for *Daily Variety* in 2002, Kathy McDonald astutely noted how rapidly conditions of music production for television, advertising, and film had recently changed:

> Composers for film and TV music today must do more than write the score.
>
> Advancements in digital audio technology have made them producers, arrang-ers, engineers and mixers at desktop workstations, capable of delivering a final end product: from a five-second network bumper to an orchestral score.
>
> These days, film and TV producers expect music fees to include creative and production costs. Increasingly, composers work out of one-stop-shop produc-tion music houses.[3]

Today, composers are expected to deliver a recorded and fully produced music stem ready for rerecording into the final mix rather than a score, and this has led composers in turn to economize on production costs, since it now comes directly out of their fee. Big-budget films still tend to use the traditional orchestra—though the score is typically sent to locations, often in Eastern Europe, where recording costs are cheaper—and to augment that sound with electronics and digital processing, but smaller, independent films are routinely created with elec-tronic and so-called "virtual instruments," the latter of which are digital replicas of such instrumental sounds as a violin section playing tremolo, a solo trumpet playing legato, a zither, or even a classic synthesizer like a Minimoog. In such cases, live instruments are brought in merely to color the computer-generated score of electronic and virtual instruments. This practice is even more prevalent in television, where it would be very difficult now to find a show that used only—or even primarily—acoustic instrumentation.

These changes in music production have given rise to firms such as Remote Control Productions, Hans Zimmer's music production company. In some re-spects, these firms resemble the music departments of the old studio system, with a relatively large staff of composers and other musical personnel working under contract and on designated assignments, sometimes for screen credit, sometimes not. In other respects, the organization of work in these firms is quite different, since much of the work involves using computers to edit and manipulate various types of digital sound files. The recording of musicians playing a written score is often not the final (or near final) step in the production process as it was in the studio era; instead, such recording often takes place early in the compositional process, and the recording is used as the basic material to be developed through mixing and signal processing as the music stem takes shape. Composer Michael Levine notes the process Zimmer used for his score to *The Dark Knight*:

> Long before we had footage of the film, Hans asked Heitor Pereira (guitar), Martin Tillman (cello), and me (violin and tenor violin) to separately record some variations on a set of instructions involving 2 notes, C and D. This involved a fair amount of interpretation! For those who are familiar with classical music, it was John Cage meets Phil Glass. We each spent a week making hundreds of snippets. Then we had to listen to each other's work and re-interpret that. The end result was a toolbox of sounds that provided Hans with the attitude of his score.[4]

Zimmer also made an early and particularly large investment in obtaining instrumental samples and building virtual instruments. Like live-action CGI effects, the quality of virtual instruments rose markedly over the 1990s with the increasing processing power of computers, and today an adept composer who understands the limitations of the technology can get even mid-priced professional grade virtual instruments to provide reasonable facsimiles of common instrumental sounds. The quality of these instruments is dependent on a number of factors, but among the most important is the sheer size of the underlying sample library. The sample libraries at Remote Control Productions, which far exceed anything commercially available, are widely recognized to be far ahead of its closest competitor.

Zimmer has been able to effectively exploit this large technological advantage on a number of fronts. First of all, the sample library and other technological resources available at Remote Control Productions have attracted a number of high-quality composers and other musicians and technical personnel to the firm. (Composers associated with Zimmer's studio include Klaus Badelt, John Powell, Harry Gregson-Williams, Henry Jackman, and Jeff Rona.) No single composer at this point could afford to match Zimmer's resources, and anyone wanting to work with the state-of-the-art technology he has assembled must come to Remote Control Productions. Second, the large number of composers and extensive technological resources means that Zimmer can accept much more work than other composers and that he can deliver on time and under very tight deadlines. Given that the time allocated to music in postproduction schedules is only diminishing, this is an extremely important advantage. The fact that Zimmer has lots of work also means that he can keep his staff of composers busy. Third, it has allowed him to create high-quality demos of his work to convince directors and producers of the soundness of his approach. Before virtual instruments, composers had to rely on piano or at most a small ensemble to preview a score. As most directors and producers are not especially well versed in music, the translation from the piano preview to the orchestral score was often fraught, leading to expensive and frantic rewrites on the scoring stage. The high-quality demos that Zimmer's firm is able to produce have largely eliminated this problem. Moreover, when directors and/or producers do not like his approach on a particular cue, he can quickly change directions and deliver an alternative high-quality demo in short order.

With advances in technology for music production and postproduction, especially the wholesale conversion to digital equipment, many of the familiar jobs in both music and sound production have also been transformed. In the music department, for instance, the basic production unit remains the composer and orchestrator, but the duties of each have changed considerably, and many new tasks have appeared, often requiring new expertise and job descriptions. Since the primary contract for music is with the composer, and the contract now usually stipulates delivering a fully produced music stem rather than a score, the position of composer has assumed a fully managerial function. The composer is responsible for spotting the film with the director and producer and coming up with the basic musical approach to the scoring. But the composer is also now generally required to oversee (or at least pay for) the full musical production, including hiring musicians (and/or a musical contactor), orchestrators and additional composers, a synthesizer programmer (if needed), a music editor, and a music preparation supervisor as well as finding appropriate recording space and recording engineers if they do not come along with the recording space. This control over the music budget has the benefit of allowing composers to work with exactly the musicians and other music personnel they want (or can afford). Advances in technology also give composers the ability to record musicians who reside in other cities or countries; by linking studios through digital technology, a composer can sit in a recording studio in Los Angeles and record instrumentalists in New York, hearing them as if they were in the next room. Figure 13-4 shows several photos of highly specialized musicians at work.

Figure 13-4. Because a film orchestra is not a fixed ensemble like a symphony, orchestrations often make use of exotic instruments. (a) Percussionist Emil Richards. (b) Duduk player Arman Gasparian. (c) Pedro Eustache performing custom-created pipes on John Debney's score for *The Ant Bully* (2006) (photos: Dan Goldwasser).   a | b | c

Time spent managing the music budget comes at the expense of time for composing, and accordingly, the role of the principal orchestrator has expanded into the main troubleshooter to whom the composer delegates those difficult last-minute composing tasks and adjustments that the composer cannot handle on his or her own due to needing to attend to managerial (or conducting) responsibilities. The orchestrator often also supervises the score by monitoring the recording in the booth, especially if the composer is conducting, and serves as a conduit between the composer and the director and/or producer. Steve Bartek, Danny Elfman's chief orchestrator, explains his role thus (also see Figure 13-5):

> [Elfman] sits with the director and the director is telling him, This works, this doesn't work, and Danny then deals with me, How can we change this while the orchestra is still rehearsing? I take his notes and we come up with some sort of solution and I call it through the headphones to the conductor to tell the players what to do, to help change it more to what the director wants. So there's a weird chain of command from Danny to me to the conductor to the orchestra.[5]

When the orchestrator is needed for other tasks, someone else will serve as score supervisor and perform the role of monitoring the recording.

Before a score is recorded, the composer previews a demo for the director and producer. Because the stakes of the demo session are so high, composers can spend as much time preparing the demo as writing the score itself, and

Figure 13-5. Music copyist Ron Vermillion, orchestrators Edgardo Simone and Steve Bartek, and *Meet the Robinsons* (2007) composer Danny Elfman (photo: Dan Goldwasser).

Figure 13-6. Composer Hans Zimmer working in his studio. Zimmer is widely recognized for delivering mock-up scores that are exceptionally accurate (photo: Dan Goldwasser).

often the task of producing the demo is assigned to specialists in midi orchestration who are skilled in scoring with virtual instruments. (Figure 13-6 shows a prominent composer at work.)

Similar to the orchestrator and midi orchestrator is the synthesizer programmer, who is hired when the musical conception requires the sound of synthesizers and other electronic sounds but the composer lacks either the time or the technical knowledge to produce the needed sounds. A composer may either order sounds to work with before beginning composition or use presets on available equipment and in software packages or write descriptive phrases such as "pinging choral bells" or "violent winds" as guides for the programmer to create appropriate sounds.

Mundane music production tasks such as making orchestra parts have been profoundly affected by digitalization. *Music preparation* refers to the various activities that entail the creation, organization, and adjustment of the notated music performed during a recording session. For many years, music preparation was the bailiwick of professional "copyists." Parts were created by hand using fountain pens, and although the copyists were spacing everything out by "eye"— without rulers—the resultant works were extremely legible; these craftsmen prided themselves on being artisans of the highest caliber. Beginning in the late 1980s, music notation software applications such as Finale and Sibelius were introduced into the marketplace and by the mid-1990s, the age of hand-written parts in film scores had passed. These software applications allow copyists not only to create engraver-quality scores and parts in a fraction of the time it would take to create them by hand but also to make changes and quickly reprint parts on site as required during a recording session (see Figure 13-7). The shift from hand-written manuscript to digital notation has necessitated a separate sub-group within the music production team that focuses specifically on the various tasks involved in music preparation. Depending on the size of the task, music preparation teams can number anywhere from a handful to twenty or more people, but the tasks they perform can be broken down into four categories.

1. The music preparation supervisor coordinates the entire group and will usually be the point of contact with the composer and orchestrator.
2. Copyists, working under the supervisor, input the handwritten full score into the notation software and create score files for each cue. This work is often no longer necessary, as composers and orchestrators increasingly work directly on computer.
3. Part extractors, using the same software, separate each individual part into separate files and format them for performance.
4. Librarians print out the paper parts, bind them, and organize them into folders destined for the musicians' stands. Several copies of the

Figure 13-7. Global Music Service copyists Jill Streater and Vic Frasier inspect a part engraved with Sibelius notation software during a recording session for *Harry Potter and the Goblet of Fire* (2005) at the Hall at Air Lyndhurst Studios in London, England.

score are also printed out for use by the composer, conductor, orchestrator, and score supervisor. The librarians may also be called upon to edit and reprint parts during the recording session as changes are made.

Often the same person performs more than one of these duties during the production process.

The fact that composers today net as payment the difference between the music fee and the costs of music production means that they now have strong financial incentives to keep music production costs to a minimum. This has in part been responsible for moving the recording of large ensembles to cheaper locations (especially in Eastern Europe) and to encourage greater use of virtual instruments. The scene of a large orchestra playing under the baton of the composer as the film plays behind it (as in Figure 13-8) may be iconic, but it is increasingly rare for all but big-budget films.

Few scores, even those using a full orchestra, are recorded today without some type of electronic reinforcement. This is usually accomplished through a process of *pre-dubbing*, which involves prerecording audio tracks for playback at the recording session. In such cases, the music editor, often assisted by a click-track operator (Figure 13-9), creates click tracks for each cue so that the live and

Figure 13-8. James Horner conducts *Flightplan* (2005) (photo: Dan Goldwasser).

Figure 13-9. Auricle click-track operator (and creator) Richard Grant. In 1984, Ron and Richard Grant invented the Auricle Time Processor, a software application that allowed for the creation and manipulation of a click track that could give the conductor immense control over the tempo of a cue, as well as for the digital imprinting of streamers and punches at the conductor's request onto the displayed film.

pre-dub tracks will be properly synchronized; the click tracks are played into the headphones of the musicians during the session.

Music Postproduction

Once the music has been recorded, the composer and scoring mixer meticulously listen to the different versions or "takes" of each music cue and decide which one to use in the film. After these choices are made, many details still require adjustment within each cue: balance changes, frequency adjustments, fixing mistakes, applying any effects filters, and occasionally even adding new material (Figure 13-10). Once these adjustments are made, the composer can deliver the final music stem.

The final dubbing session (sometimes referred to as the Rerecording Mix Session) combines stems from dialogue, sound effect, and music tracks as rerecording engineers mix them onto the final sound track. Many times this dubbing session will occur in a special dubbing theater that is equipped with an enormous mixing console placed in a central location within the room; this gives the engineers the most accurate idea of what the balances will be in a theater.

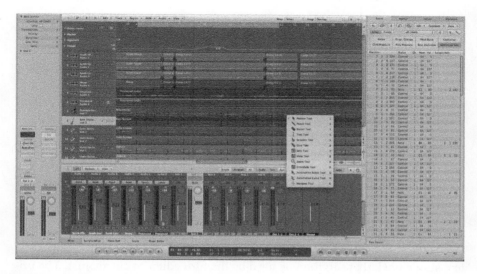

Figure 13-10. Screen shot of Apple's *Logic Studio*, an integrated editing and mixing application often used in music production and postproduction.

The composer will attend these sessions along with the director, producer, and the sound designer and various sound editors who constructed the sound effects and dialogue tracks. Not surprisingly, these sessions can often involve intense discussions among the various parties about the proper balance of sound track elements, even if it is generally agreed that dialogue should have priority.

SOUND DEPARTMENT
Sound Production
Although we used the term *music production* in the previous section, strictly speaking film music is mostly associated with postproduction stage of filmmaking, and in fact with the later phases of that process, after the film is "locked." Work on the other aspects of the sound track, however, is spread across both production and postproduction. The members of the sound team as a whole, especially the composer and the sound designer or supervising sound mixer (who is responsible for conceiving the sound of the film much as the cinematographer is for its look), are often—although not always—hired and consulted during the preproduction phase, but the bulk of their work takes place during the time of postproduction.

Production sound consists of everything that is recorded while the filming is taking place. The production sound mixer is the person in charge of recording while on the set or location. The duties include choosing and placing microphones as well as recording and mixing the sounds from the various microphones. Although the primary concern of production sound is capturing dialogue, the production unit also records ambience, room tone, and some sound effects in order to facilitate both sound and picture editing. All things being

The objective I have as a production sound mixer is to achieve the cleanest dialogue tracks possible with the least amount of background sound.
—Les Larawitz (Production Sound Mixer)[6]

equal, the mixer aims to capture as much direct sound and as little reverberation as possible (see the comment in the sidebar). Reverberation can be easily added in postproduction, but it is much more difficult to reduce or remove.

Besides the production dialogue, the mixer also records "wild" lines. When there is a problem in production sound, particularly if some loud ambient sound on the set or location obscures the dialogue in the original shot, the production mixer will ask the actor or actors to repeat the relevant dialogue, matching the original shot as closely as possible.

The production sound mixer also directs the boom operator, who is the person responsible for following the actors with a boom microphone to ensure a consistent recording of dialogue while keeping the microphone out of the line of sight of the camera. After each day of shooting, the production sound mixer delivers a "mix track," which is used for the daily rushes as well as for film editing in postproduction. Although the various mikes are generally recorded to different tracks, the mix track, as the name implies, mixes down those different tracks to a single track that can then be used by the film editor to cut against. The unmixed tracks are retained for the dialogue editors in making the final cut.

Increasingly, filmmakers are opting to rerecord most dialogue in ADR as it simplifies many tasks during production and postproduction. In these cases, production dialogue is still recorded to be used as a reference track to guide actors during ADR.

Sound Postproduction

Postproduction work on the sound track begins in earnest with a spotting session, which ideally is attended by the director, producer, supervising sound editor, and composer. Here the supervising sound editor (or sound designer) gives a general notion of the effects in the various sequences, and, conversely, the composer can give the sound department a sense of the musical approach. This allows the composer and supervising sound editor to plan their work with a sense of where conflicts are likely to occur between the two components of the sound track.

The basic duty of a sound editor is to choose and place sounds on the sound track, that is, to gather or create sounds and produce instructions (a precise cue sheet) for mixing. Mixers then realize these instructions, creating a series of premixes under the supervision of the appropriate sound editor. (In this sense editors place sound *on* the sound track, whereas mixers place sound *in* it.)

Editors are especially concerned with the principle of continuity. According to the Motion Picture Sound Editors (MPSE), an advocacy group for sound editors, dialogue editors "painstakingly smooth out the production sound recorded on location," whereas "ADR editors help to seamlessly weave the re-recorded dialogue that replaces problematic tracks."[7] The effects department similarly avoids abrupt cuts in room tone and ambient sound in order to maintain a stable definition of space and place within a sequence. They work to create a consistent background that helps maintain the illusion of unity in space and place.

Achieving such continuity is more difficult than it might seem. We need to remember that editors *build* the sound track out of various bits of audio. These bits consist of production dialogue and other production sound, ADR, library effects, foley and effects generated specifically for a film, and different types of music tracks. That is, the sounds of which the sound track consists are anything but continuous. Even production dialogue, which might seem like it should be continuous, is in fact recorded in a series of takes. These include not only those of the master shot but the various close-ups and other cut-ins. So the task of the editors is not only choosing and placing these bits but also combining them in a way that disguises their inherent discontinuity.

The sound department is typically divided into three units—dialogue, foley effects, and sound effects (sfx). Each unit will produce its own track—generally called a "pre-dub" or "stem"—and all of these will be dubbed down or rerecorded into a final mix during the dubbing session (or Rerecording Mix Session) that was described under the "Music Department" heading earlier in the chapter. As the name "final mix" implies, this session occurs very late in postproduction. In fact, a series of final mixes is generally required because each of the various formats requires its own print master.

Dialogue

Dialogue is the responsibility of the dialogue editor, whose general concern is to produce dialogue that can most easily be mixed with other sounds. This means going through the production sound mix, stripping the dialogue tracks of as much background noise as possible, and devising strategies for masking any noise that cannot be cleaned out. In addition, editors try to isolate the dialogue of each actor whenever they can, because this allows each voice to be controlled separately in rerecording the dialogue stem.

One of the first tasks of the dialogue editor is to go through the shots selected by the picture editor, marking any that need fixing. The sound edits are often minor, such as replacing a word or phrase that an actor tripped over or that was obscured by incidental noise on the set or location. Sometimes a longer segment will have an excessive number of these problems; or for some reason the right material is not available to fix the dialogue through simple sound editing; or, after seeing the rushes, an actor (or the director) may decide that his or her recorded voice did not quite capture the emotion in an otherwise acceptable take. In these cases, the dialogue editor will place the segment on list for ADR. On films where filmmakers plan to rerecord all the dialogue in ADR, the production dialogue will only serve as a reference and so the dialogue editor will not spend much time on it.

In ADR, an actor is called back to rerecord portions of dialogue. Carefully watching (and listening to) the segment of film that is to have its dialogue replaced, the actor repeats lines as closely synchronized to the picture as possible. This process is known as "looping." The amount of ADR required is dependent on the quality of sound captured on set and location, the filmmakers' aesthetic priorities, and of course budget. As we noted in Chapter 9, location shooting can pose particular challenges to sound recording due to the presence of unpredictable incidental noises or loud, but otherwise appropriate, environmental noises such as traffic, high winds, rain, waves, waterfalls, and so forth. Production sound teams are highly proficient at figuring out ways to capture a clean recording under the most trying circumstances, but occasionally a location will pose a problem that even the most seasoned pro cannot solve. Another exception is high-budget action films, where the intricate choreography of actors and the noise of special effects make it difficult to record audio clearly. In these cases, dialogue is almost invariably rerecorded in ADR. Indeed, most major commercial films today are shot with the expectation that much if not most of the dialogue will be replaced by ADR. This allows faster work in production (since the crew does not have to concern itself with gathering a high-quality production sound recording).

Directors vary greatly in their attitude toward ADR; most claim to dislike it, but it has become a basic and essential tool in most commercial filmmaking today. A good example of extensive use of ADR is *Apocalypse Now* (1979), where all dialogue was rerecorded in ADR. (The same is true for *Once Upon a Time in America* (1984); see the comments in Figure 13-11.)

Some filmmakers also are indifferent to problems with production sound because they feel the actors can move with less inhibition if they do not have to concern themselves with clearly articulating their words or noting the position of the microphone. Besides fixing mistakes, ADR also allows actors the possibility

Figure 13-11. *Once Upon a Time in America* (1984). As is typical of Sergio Leone films, all of the dialogue on this film was rerecorded in ADR. It took Paul Zydel, the ADR mixer, 10 weeks to do all the rerecording on the film. According to Zydel, the dialogue of an average feature film consists of about 30 percent ADR, although it varies considerably by genre and the amount of location shooting. Most films, however, require some ADR.

of separating voice and bodily action. Although a particular movement may require a lot of exertion, for instance, an actor (or director) may nevertheless want the character to sound relaxed to make a difficult movement seem easy. ADR Supervisor Juno Ellis says, "60 percent of looping is done for technical reasons, and the other 40 percent is done because the director wants to try to get a little different nuance in the scene by changing a reading."[8] Finally, because ADR produces a very dry recording, it gives mixers more flexibility in terms of the volume level of the dialogue with respect to the other elements of the sound track.

Foley Effects

The name "foley" comes from an early practitioner of the art, Jack Foley. These specialized effects originated in the need to separate the dialogue track from the sounds of the actors' bodies because dialogue needed to be dubbed for a film's foreign language distribution; but dubbing the voice also meant removing the sounds of the body unless the two were somehow separated. Analytically, we do not usually distinguish foley from effects in general because both fall into the formal category of "noises." In contemporary filmmaking, the sounds of important bodies, especially the sounds of principal characters, are usually created by a foley artist.

Foley is created much like ADR through a process of looping; that is, it is produced in real time by a foley artist who makes such appropriate noises as the ubiquitous footsteps in synchronization while a segment of film plays (see Figure 13-12 for an example). A foley artist is primarily responsible for non-speech sounds made

The best foley artists learn to be discriminating about what should be heard and what should be ignored. They learn to help focus the scene with the foley, not clutter it.
—Vanessa Theme Ament (Foley Artist)[9]

Figure 13-12. *The Soundscapes of Middle Earth: The Two Towers* (2002). Simon Hewit, a foley artist, works on *The Two Towers* (2002). Foley artists break a scene down, usually recording one character's movements in each pass. Here, Hewit records Aragorn's movements.

by the human characters, and they seek to add sounds that add to the sonic representation of those characters. Because, like speech, foley effects are usually tightly synchronized with the image, they are often mixed to a separate track from the other effects in order to facilitate trimming, slip edits, and other small changes that occur between the rough and final cuts.

The production unit for foley effects consists of the artist (or sometimes a pair of artists), the foley mixer, and the foley editor. As mentioned earlier, the foley artist creates the sounds, often exaggerating or "sweetening" an effect in order to give the impression of being "cinematic." All of the effects of a sequence are not recorded at once, but in a number of passes, which are then layered. The foley mixer is responsible for recording the sounds. As with ADR, the quality of the recording must be sufficiently consistent with that of the rest of the sound, especially the production dialogue, that it can be seamlessly integrated into the sound track. The foley editor is the sound editor who is responsible for processing the sounds in the foley stem, adjusting volume, selecting among takes, and fine-tuning the synchronization.

Sound Effects

Aside from the usual consultations in preproduction, the work of the effects department, like music, takes place almost exclusively in postproduction. The supervising sound editor spots the film along with the director, producer, and composer, making decisions about the sorts of sound effects that will be needed, noting in particular the places that will require so-called "hard" effects. Hard effects are those that require close synchronization, which filmmakers call "hard sync." Many of these will be sent to foley, while others are retained by the effects department. Using this cue list, the assistant sound editor draws on the resource of an effects library to produce a temp track. The temp track is used by the picture editing department to make a rough cut of the film. Working with the supervising sound editor, the sound effects editor then works on fine-tuning the effects, inventing or collecting any sound effects that will be needed, and cutting them into the film.

Sometimes effects departments go to extraordinary lengths to get just the right sound. They may bang on guide wires and use contact mikes to record a distinctive metallic "thwap." They may drop cement slabs from a crane to obtain a suitably impressive "thud." They may work with a synthesizer to produce a sharp laser blast or an ominous rumble. They may layer sounds together, combining the onset of a dog barking with a crow call and a lion roar, producing a cry that is new but characteristically animal-like (see Figure 13-13 for an example of an unusual method to produce a particular sound).

When a sound proves to be useful and distinctive, it will often be recycled. The sound of the bow releasing its arrow from *The Adventures of Robin Hood* (1938) has been called on frequently. Sound designer Ben Burtt was still using it as late as the *Star Wars* films in the 1970s and 1980s. Although the bulk of sounds come from effects libraries, editors must also be careful not to recycle the same effect too often, as the "looping" can become quite noticeable (and therefore sound artificial). (Indeed, avoiding such looping effects is one reason foley

Figure 13-13. *The Soundscapes of Middle Earth: Fellowship of the Ring* (2001). David Farmer, sound designer on *Fellowship of the Ring* (2001), uses a plunger in a stream to make some of the sounds for the Watcher. Wet rubber mats also contributed to the mix. The cry of the Watcher was rendered by an altered recording of a walrus grunt.

is preferred to effects libraries for common human-generated sounds.) If a particular sound occurs often in a film—especially in a scene—a new effect might be needed for almost every occurrence to avoid the perception of reuse.

The creation of the sound effects tracks—typically the track for ambient sound is kept separate from other effects—takes place on approximately the same schedule as the music. Given the tight schedules during postproduction, there is seldom time for any sort of close coordination between the music and effects departments. Consequently, composers often have to write music in anticipation of the effects they imagine will be present, and the effects editors must anticipate decisions composers might make. Both have to be on guard against "frequency masking," which occurs when two sounds, close in frequency, occur at the same time. Stereo can lessen such masking to some extent by placing the sounds in different parts of the stereo field, but the louder sound in a similar frequency range will tend to cover up a softer sound. Frequently, effects, and music come into unexpected conflict, which must be worked out, often awkwardly, in the rerecording session for the final mix.

Digital Sound and Elements of Style
ISSUES OF AESTHETICS

Although nearly all films designed for commercial release today are produced to be screened with digital sound, the consciousness with which the sound track is given emphasis varies considerably by genre. Part of this has to do with the

Figure 13-14. *Shakespeare in Love* (1998). Will (Joseph Fiennes) chases Viola (Gwyneth Paltrow) through the streets. In this sequence music and the ambient sound of the street are both mixed at fairly high levels. Stereo separation mitigates the conflict to a degree, but the sound track retains a sense of competition between these elements, reinforcing the crowd's function as an obstacle in his pursuit.

historical legacy of filmmaking. Spectacular, big-budget films tend to deploy their sound more overtly, seeking to wow their audiences with a display of sound equal to the budget. As we have noted in previous chapters, superior sound reproduction has gone hand in hand with filmic spectacle, a situation that continues, ironically, to make rich, full, highly textured sound a signifier of artifice. For a quite different example, where music and ambient sound are set in conflict with one another, see Figure 13-14 and its commentary.

Digital sound in particular has offered a new take on silence: rather than background hiss, films can make effective use of extremely quiet sounds such as room ambience just above the threshold of hearing. In addition to their use to create varied sonic backgrounds, such silences can prepare explosions of sound. Many of the terrifying "sonic assaults" in David Lynch's films—for example, the ax blow to the television that ends the opening-credits sequence of *Twin Peaks: Fire Walk with Me* (2002)—are achieved through the use of startling and completely gripping dynamic contrasts; it is the unexpected contrast rather than absolute volume that achieves the effect.

Although Dolby stereo greatly increased the definition of sound, digital sound has offered particular opportunities in low and high frequencies. Most of us can easily recall hearing the cinematic crashes and explosions that rumble from the subwoofer in depths unknown on television or even most home stereos, but the use of high-frequency sound has perhaps been even more substantive in changing the way films sound, because high-frequency definition promises proximity and intimacy. It is therefore somewhat ironic that high-frequency sound has become a hallmark of the rendering of violence. Metallic clangs ring out with high-frequency definition and have become a favorite device for displaying the power of digital sound. In *Gladiator* (2000), for instance, sword clashes punctuate the battle sequences, carefully marking the moments of synchronization despite manipulations of film speed. One effect of the relation between sound and image is to make Maximus (Russell Crowe) seem charmed, almost superhuman.

Occasionally a sudden blast of high-frequency sound is used to startle, as when the terminator crushes a human skull with its foot at the opening of *Terminator 2: Judgment Day* (1991). If the sound tracks of recent films seem particularly "live," if the film worlds seem brimming with an almost uncontainable amount of sound, this is due in large measure to the presence of extensive high-frequency sound. When coupled with slow motion, a particular high-frequency sound isolated in the mix can produce the impression of a sort of uncanny hyper-acute hearing. In *The Matrix* (1999), for instance, we hear precisely synchronized tinkling of bullet casings hitting the ground in the midst of a hail of gunfire. (For another example, see Figure 13-15.)

The Fellowship of the Ring (2001), for instance, opens with an impressive mix of sounds. The New Line Cinema logo is accompanied by a synthesized soundscape that moves around the stereo field without settling into a specific place. This synthesized sound then gives way to held string tones positioned traditionally in stereo, and a small choir then begins to chant over the instruments. In this short span, the opening of the film marks out a progression of enchantment: the artificial sounds of the synthesizer give way to the natural tones of the strings, which finally turn into support for the sung voice. Over this music, a voice then begins to whisper in Elvish followed by another voice, in the front of the mix narrating in English. The overall effect is one of disorientation, but one that seems to evoke the idea of epic narration: the world of Middle Earth seems to emerge from the almost magical presence of this voice.

Figure 13-15. *The Fellowship of the Ring* (2001). Contemporary sound design often a | b "sweetens" effects in almost musical fashion for dramatic effect. Both of these frames come from the prologue, and each illustrates a different facet of the sweetened sound effect. In the first case, the sweep of Sauron's scepter is given an artificial, synthetic sound, whereas in the second case, the crash of the helmet is rendered with a very loud metallic clank. In each case, the effect is far larger than life, endowing it with the aura of the supernatural.

SCORING PRACTICES

Instrumentation

Even as digital technology is making synthesizers and virtual instruments a basic part of film composition, the recording of a live symphony orchestra has remained the foundation of the musical score for blockbusters. Howard Shore's score for *The Lord of the Rings* trilogy, for instance, deployed an exceptionally large orchestra supplemented by voices (both individual and choral) and exotic instruments (such as the Hardanger fiddle used for the Rohan theme). Increasingly after 1990, rock rhythm tracks have been combined with orchestral music to give action sequences increased drive. This technique has been especially associated with Hans Zimmer and some of his collaborators; and historically it was sometimes called the "Media Venture" sound, after the studio Zimmer ran until it was dissolved in a legal dispute with his partner. (As noted in Chapter 11, Zimmer has since started a new music production company, organized along similar lines, called Remote Control Productions.) Good examples of this technique can be found in Zimmer's scores to *Pearl Harbor* (2001) and *Blackhawk Down* (2001) and in John Powell's scores to the Bourne trilogy.

While orchestral music has continued to serve as the foundation for scoring blockbusters, the decreasing costs and increasing quality of synthesizers and especially virtual instruments has meant that, for most other films, composers have drawn more and more on the resources of computer-generated music. In general, the convergence of advanced digital technology with the enormous increase of independent filmmaking over the past 30 years has both allowed and forced composers to create scores in innovative ways, including performing and improvising the score themselves, creating a score entirely with electronic synthesizers or samplers, and using personal computers and home recording technology to record a score in the privacy of the composer's own home. Examples of film scores that have utilized various techniques include those created and recorded on synthesizers, composed and improvised to picture (*Dead Man* by Neil Young [1995], parts of *Black Hawk Down*), and even created, recorded, and digitally manipulated in the composer's bedroom studio (*A Scanner Darkly* by Graham Reynolds [2006]). Robert Rodriguez is a contemporary director known for creating his own music (see him at work in Figure 13-16).

New Trends in Action Films

Although orchestra-dominated scores with traditional emphasis on well-articulated thematic material such as Howard Shore's work on the *Lord of the Rings* and *The Hobbit* films, Alan Silvestri's score for *Captain America: The First Avenger* (2011), or John Williams's recent music in films like *The Adventures of Tintin* (2011), *Lincoln* (2012), and *The Book Thief* (2013) continue to be a common approach to film scoring, many composers have adopted a more atmospheric approach, emphasizing mood and affect but without organizing the music into strongly delineated themes. This has been particularly evident in recent action

Figure 13-16. Robert Rodriguez in his home studio.

films, such as Don Davis's music for *The Matrix* (1999), James Newton Howard and Hans Zimmer's moody scores for Christopher Nolan's *Dark Knight* Batman trilogy, John Powell's work on the Bourne trilogy, and Henry Jackman's score for *Captain American: The Winter Soldier* (2014). We can certainly find thematic material in these scores if we go looking for it, but the thematic structure is allusive, and the moody affect almost always overrides thematic articulation. All of these films also feature extensive percussion, often with driving rhythmic grooves, and the close coordination of sound effects with the score, so that it is occasionally hard to determine whether a particular sound belongs to the score or to the sound design.

The opening of *The Matrix*, which was analyzed in detail in the previous chapter, offers an alternation of surging brass chords rather than a well-articulated theme as its basic material. *Batman Begins* (2005) is similar, systematically building cues out of gestures that do not cohere into distinct themes even when recurring motives are clearly evident. The basic motives in Powell's music for the Bourne trilogy, especially the driving string action motive (Figure 13-17a), the mournful bassoon melody associated with Bourne's humanity (Figure 13-17b), and the theme associated with Marie (Figure 13-17c), are by contrast better defined than those of Howard and Zimmer's music for the Batman films. But the musical material in the Bourne films is either highly repetitive (action theme) or somewhat wispy (humanity theme and Marie theme). None of this material is ever really organized into a broader thematic shape even if the musical gestures are themselves strikingly defined. (We analyze scenes from *Batman Begins* and *The Bourne Ultimatum* at greater length in the next chapter.)

Figure 13-17. Themes by John Powell for the Bourne trilogy: (a) action motive; (b) Bourne's humanity; (c) Marie. (Transcriptions from the sound track.)

Jackman's score for *Captain American: The Winter Soldier* is particularly revealing of this tendency toward underarticulated themes because of its relationship to Silvestri's music for *Captain America: The First Avenger*, which developed an extremely well-articulated theme for the title character, an assertive heroic march, typical of the action genre through the 1990s. This theme (shown in Figure 13-18), like the film itself, is a conspicuous throwback, as both film and music seem to dream of a time when and a world where self-certain heroic action could be scored with self-certain music like this. But the ending of the first Captain America film threw the title character out of time, and he awoke to a new world where the clarity of heroic action no longer obtains. In *The Avengers* (2012), Silvestri already began the process of underscoring Captain America's temporal estrangement, all but excising the march from the score. The Captain's powers remain formidable, but his disaffection undermines his confidence that his mode of heroic action is still meaningful and relevant in the modern world. Only the grave threat of alien invasion allows him to put aside his growing doubts and to respond dutifully to the call to action. In *The Winter Soldier*, however, this disaffection is heightened by conspiracy. The line between friend and enemy is no longer clear, and the idea that heroic action serves to protect the world from forces of chaos or to change it for the better becomes increasingly doubtful. The mortal threat now lurks inside the very thing that heroic action is pledged to defend. Jackman underscores the doubt: the power is still there—the music retains its epic tone—but the music is no more certain than Captain America that his actions serve a cause greater than self-preservation.

Figure 13-18. *Captain America: The First Avenger* (2011). Theme for the title character. (Transcription from the sound track.)

Rather than reflecting his heroic being, the music underscores his affect, the suspenseful mood, the impending danger, and the hurried action, but it also promises no social affirmation, no assurance that heroic action is a power for social good. The score's lack of thematic articulation therefore seems to mirror a loss of heroic identity, but that identity was itself compromised, so it is less a loss than an awakening into ambiguity that the theme-less music emphasizes.

Many of the recent action films that have scores with such underarticulated musical themes share a preoccupation with calling into question the self-certainty of modern heroic identity, either by undermining it (as in Bourne or Captain America) or by focusing on origin stories where the mythologizing construction of heroic identity can be ironized (as in Batman, Iron Man, or the recent James Bond reboot). In either case, the musical material remains in an unformed state that reflects the unsettling ambiguities of the heroic action.

However effective and appropriate these scores are in themselves, the trend that they represent has occasionally been criticized for resulting in a slick but somewhat anonymous style that fits seamlessly with risk-averse corporate filmmaking. This criticism has been directed particularly at the work of Zimmer, whose approach to scoring films avoids strongly individualizing stylistic markers even in non-action film and even when he develops a more or less traditional thematic structure. That is, it is hard to discern a distinctive compositional voice in Zimmer's music. Yet the criticism that the anonymity of Zimmer's music suits corporate filmmaking is peculiar, because it ignores the fact that traditional themes and distinctive compositional voices are quite in keeping with important values of corporate filmmaking, in that they allow for more effective branding of franchises and selling of bankable stars. John Williams's Hedwig theme defines the Harry Potter universe (even when Williams is no longer composing for it) in a way that Zimmer's (and Howard's) music for the Dark Knight trilogy never will, because the Dark Knight music captures and displays affective gestures rather than forging a secure thematic identity for Batman. From a corporate standpoint, it may be easier to hire another composer (or several) to work with the atomized modular structure of the affective gestures Zimmer favors, but it is much more difficult to control and monetize such musical material as branded intellectual property. We consider these issues in more detail in the next chapter.

A lack of thematic articulation is one trait that the modern action film shares with minimalist scores. The signification of minimalism broadened from the earlier association with the emptiness of consumer capitalism (*Koyaanisqatsi* [1982]) and spiritualism (*Kundun* [1997]) and was used increasingly to score representations of genius, uncanny rational calculation, and dystopic hyper-rationality (*A Beautiful Mind* [2001], *Proof* [2005], *A.I. Artificial Intelligence* [2001], *Watchmen* [2009], *Star Trek into Darkness* [2013]). As Rebecca Doran Eaton remarks: "While minimalism may have been conceived as a reaction to integral serialism . . . , it has now become an auditory symbol of all that total serialism enjoined itself to be: music of the hyper-rational, of the intellectual elite . . . , of the science lab . . . , even of the academic."[10]

Compilation Scores and Popular Music

With the collapse of the soundtrack market, the precarious sales of popular music in general, and the highly variable licensing fees, the close economic link forged between popular music and film in the 60s, 70s, 80s, and 90s began to quickly erode after 2000. Because it remains such an important part of everyday life, popular music continued to be used, of course, but decisions to include it had a much weaker economic incentive. Music essentially devolved into a cost of production rather than a potential source of additional income.

Beginning during the 1990s and accelerating after 2000, the practices of compilation scoring changed quite markedly. Prior to 1990, recorded popular music was generally used in two basic ways. First, diegetically, a song could appear in a grammatical or ungrammatical snippet depending on the situation. As diegetic sound, the primary purpose of the recording was to establish the time of the film (e.g., the early 1960s) and to signal the musical taste of any character selecting music. Such diegetic background music might also comment on the action, though at the risk of making the world seem somewhat conspiratorial. Second, nondiegetically, a song tended to appear in self-contained modules accompanying lyrical montage sequences or moments of interior contemplation. Generally, a grammatically coherent chunk of the song (a section delimited by a cadence) was used that respected the basic song structure.

Such traditional uses of popular music remain quite common today. An inventive contemporary example occurs in *(500) Days of Summer* (2009). After having broken up with Summer (Zooey Deschanel), Tom (Joseph Gordon-Levitt) meets her at a wedding of a mutual acquaintance. They seem to hit it off again, and she invites him to a party at her apartment. The party scene itself begins with Tom outside the building. As the introduction to Regina Spektor's "Hero" begins to play and Tom enters the gate, the voice-over narrator relates that Tom "believed that this time his expectations would align with reality." The screen then divides in two, the left side marked "Expectations," the right "Reality." With "Hero" playing prominently on the sound track, the scene then unfolds in split screen, as the left side shows Tom and Summer rekindling their relationship, the right presenting Tom's increasing isolation at the party (Figure 13-19a). The crux of the scene comes at the end of the second bridge, as Spektor sings "cheatin', cheatin', cheatin'," the reality half of the split screen widens out to take over, and Tom spots an engagement ring on Summer's hand (Figure 13-19b) just as the opening tune of the song returns with the now clearly ironic lyrics desperately repeating, "I'm the hero of this story." Tom then runs out of the apartment and into the street, where the scene is transformed into a charcoal sketch which is then erased, leaving only his silhouette against a smudged background as the song comes to an end (Figure 13-19c). Here, the scene was quite clearly planned around Spektor's song, with the scene structure following the song structure, and the crux of the scene carefully aligned to form a strong sync point with the final return of the opening musical material.

Although the nondiegetic use of popular music to accompany montages and for moments of introspection remains common, recent compilation practice has also deployed songs in nondiegetic contexts almost as wide as orchestral scoring, such as to link scenes, to back action sequences, to underscore love scenes and even to accompany general dialogue scenes. In *A Serious Man* (2009), for instance, Jimi Hendrix's "Machine Gun" plays behind Rabbi Nachtner's (George Wyner) telling of the story of "The Goy's Teeth." The story is told in Nachtner's voice-over and the nondiegetic playing of Hendrix's song serves as a secondary aural marker to the storytelling. Many films, especially comedies aimed at teen audiences, feature songs in nearly every scene. Short excerpts of well-known songs often appear nondiegetically without respect to grammatical completeness of the excerpt. Before the 1990s, films occasionally drew on such short excerpts for humorous effect, as when the first two phrases of the *Star Wars* theme accompany the parking attendants' reckless joyride in the Ferrari in *Ferris Bueller's Day Off* (1986). Such practice no doubt reflects the old

Figure 13-19. *(500) Days of Summer* (2009). (a) Split-screen conflicting narratives. (b) Tom sees the engagement ring. (c) Silhouette in charcoal as song finishes.

a
b
c

silent film practice of punning with song titles as that practice was carried over to scoring cartoons in the sound era. Once commercial recordings became a common basis for compilation scoring, punning on short song excerpts was occasionally applied as a slapstick gag, but other than for such humorous effects, nondiegetic use of preexisting songs was generally reserved for self-contained modules underscoring lyrical montages or introspective moments. The contemporary practice of compilation scoring frequently moves from one song to the next in response to changes in the narrative and without regard to the integrity of the song. The opening of *Clueless* (1995), for instance, cycles through four songs in about 3½ minutes: 59 seconds of the Muffs' "Kids in America," 29 seconds of David Bowie's "Fashion," 7 seconds of no music, and then 61 seconds of No Doubt's "I'm Just a Girl," 37 seconds of no music, and 20 seconds of Salt-N-Pepa's "Shoop." The primary focus in each case is the delivery title, and in two instances, "Fashion," and "Shoop," the brevity of the excerpt is such that little of the song form remains. Most of "I'm Just a Girl" is buried under dialogue, although it is used nondiegetically. Only "Kids in America," which accompanies the opening montage of supposed teenage activity, is treated in a manner typical of nondiegetic uses of popular song before 1990.

Since 1990, the diegetic/nondiegetic boundary has been breached more regularly with compilation scores. The boundary had never been respected in musicals, and diegetic performances in dramatic films frequently became unanchored from the depicted space and time, such as Rick's flashback in *Casablanca* (1942), the opening of *The Wrong Man* (1956), the performance of "The Boys Are Back in Town" in *48 Hours* (1982), the Diva's performance of "Il dolce suono" from Donizetti's *Lucia di Lammermoor* in *The Fifth Element* (1997), the ball scene where Darcy and Elizabeth first dance in *Pride and Prejudice* (2005), or the Stuttgart Opera scene from *The Avengers* (2012).

Historically, it has been far less common to use recorded music for similar effects. A fine early example occurs at the opening of *Blackboard Jungle* (1955). Bill Haley and the Comets' recording of "Rock Around the Clock" plays under the opening credits and dissolves from nondiegetic to apparently diegetic music for the opening scene through the imposition of a filter. *American Graffiti* (1973) uses the same song for its title sequence, but it applies a filter only for the tuning effects and station ID that sound before the title, and then again after the title, where a filter is again applied for another station ID. Although not particularly evident from this title sequence, *American Graffiti* generally allows its diegetic boundaries to be quite fluid, although the conceit of radio always keeps the music loosely tied to the diegesis.

Recent films frequently achieve similar kinds of effects. The title and opening sequence of *A Serious Man* follows an approach similar to *Blackboard Jungle*, using an undistorted high-fidelity stereo recording of Jefferson Airplane's "Somebody to Love" for the titles and then imposing a severe filter to mimic the diegetic audio leakage of the song from a 1960s transistor radio earpiece once the scene begins after the credits. (The process is then reversed for the ominous ending of the film.) *Iron Man* (2008) exploits a variation of this process for its pre-title sequence. After the corporate titles, a small convoy of vehicles is shown traveling down an isolated road accompanied by wind and the faint sounds of vehicles. On a cut revealing the convoy to be U.S. army vehicles, the introduction to AC/DC's "Back in Black" explodes on the sound track in full stereo, punctuated through several cuts by sound effects of the vehicles. The entrance of the lyrics forms a sync point with a cut inside one of the Humvees, as the song is filtered to suggest that the sound is emanating from a depicted boom box.

Recent uses of recordings have crossed boundaries with impunity. In *Grosse Pointe Blank* (1997), Guns N' Roses' version of "Live and Let Die" plays on the radio as Martin (John Cusack) drives to visit the house he grew up in. The music continues as he gets out of the car and realizes that the site of his childhood home is now occupied by a convenience store. Film scholar Jeff Smith explains this effect as one where music is "spatially displaced." (In this case the spatial displacement obviously also entails a temporal displacement in the form of a sound lag.) These sorts of spatial and temporal displacements are exceptionally common in contemporary film. In *Juno* (2007), Astrud Gilberto's 1965 recording of "Once I Loved," sneaks in as Juno (Ellen Page) selects the couple to adopt her unborn baby. The song continues, with a compression filter added to suggest diegetic sound, as the scene changes to Bleeker (Michael Cera) looking at a year-book on his bed which then segues into a conversation with his mother (Darla Fay). With a scene change to Juno at home, the filter is removed as the song comes to a close on a string trill. Here, the song is (loosely) anchored to the di-egetic space of Bleeker's bedroom (the source of the song is presumably the boom box shown next to the bed), and the lack of filter for both the scene before and the one after indicates spatial (and perhaps temporal) displacement or a shift to nondiegetic status, while knitting the three scenes together.

A similar effect is achieved through a filter in *Suburban Girl* (2007). Archie (Alec Baldwin) is drinking, evidently listening to a recording of Chopin's D-flat Major Prelude, when Brett (Sarah Michelle Gellar) confronts him with his infi-delity. A filter here is applied to the reverb to make it sound like the music is wafting through the house. The music, no longer filtered to suggest a diegetic recording, then continues into the next scene as Brett rides away in a taxi. Here, a simple removal of a filter again indicates a spatial and temporal displacement and perhaps a shift from diegetic to nondiegetic status.

The opening of *Moonrise Kingdom* (2012) offers a similar procedure that cannot be fully explained in terms of such displacements. The film opens with Lionel (Jake Ryan) bringing his portable record player out (Figure 13-20a) and playing a recording of Benjamin Britten's *The Young Person's Guide to the Orchestra*. The music initially sounds highly compressed, appropriate diegetic sound for a record player of that type, as the camera settles on Suzy (Kara Hayward) sitting down to read (Figure 13-20b). Suzy suddenly opens the drapes, prompting a reverse shot of her from outside the house (Figure 13-20c), and the music imme-diately expanding into full stereo and without distortion (her image, however, is distorted by the rain on the window). The shift in aural perspective here removes the stereo sound of the music from the diegesis even if the continuity of the music retains the semblance of a diegetic link. After the title appears, with some ominous thunder claps, the music is once again presented in low-fidelity diegetic sound, but it no longer aligns temporally with the scene, and the record player itself is nowhere in evidence. As the piece plays, the camera moves through the house showing the Bishop family's activities and Suzy's preoccupation with looking through binoculars. The sound of the music does not change with the camera's movements, but only to duck under some dialogue and to open into stereo whenever Suzie moves outside. The scene ends with Lionel interrupting the piece by lifting the needle from the player (Figure 13-20d). Here, the han-dling of music in the scene is evidently largely explained through temporal dis-placement (whether as an advance or a lag), but the moments of spatial displacement are coupled with an increase in fidelity that seems to move the sound into the nondiegetic.

Historically, when compilation scores focused on popular music, the selec-tions tended to be relatively homogenous in terms of style, especially as popular music is one of the principal ways that films signal time period and social milieu. Both *American Graffiti* and *Dirty Dancing*, for instance, draw on music that

Timeline

1979	Digital signal processing used for special effects on *Star Trek: The Movie*.
1982	First commercial CD is released.
1983	THX certification is created by Lucasfilm.
1984	*Once Upon a Time in America* is released.
1988	First version of Finale computer notation software is released.
1989	Warner Bros. releases *Batman*; Avid nonlinear editing system introduced; Hans Zimmer forms Media Ventures.
1990	Eastman Kodak and Optical Radiation Corporation introduce Cinema Digital Sound (CDS).
1991	First version of Pro Tools is released.
1992	Dolby introduces Dolby Digital with the release of *Batman Returns*.
1993	Digital Theater System, Inc. introduces DTS with the release of *Jurassic Park*; Sony introduces SDDS with the release of *Last Action Hero*.
1995	Paramount releases *Clueless*.
1997	*Grosse Point Blank* is released; DVDs begin to be commercially released in U.S.
2000	*Wo Hu Cang Long* (*Crouching Tiger, Hidden Dragon*) is released.

a b
c d

Figure 13-20. *Moonrise Kingdom* (2012). (a) Lionel brings out his portable record player. (b) Suzy sits down to read. (c) Reverse shot from outdoors. (d) Lionel interrupts the music.

2001	New Line Cinema releases *The Fellowship of the Ring*; Miramax releases *Bridget Jones's Diary*; Apple introduces iTunes.
2002	Paramount releases *The Hours*.
2003	Apple introduces iTunes Store.
2004	Hans Zimmer reorganizes Media Ventures as Remote Control Productions.
2005	Warner Bros. releases *Batman Begins*; Focus Features releases *Pride & Prejudice*.
2006	Columbia releases *Marie Antoinette* and *Casino Royale*; Sony introduces commercial Blu-Ray disk system.
2007	Fox Searchlight releases *Juno*; Universal releases *The Bourne Ultimatum*.
2008	Marvel Entertainment releases *Iron Man*; *Joheunnom Nabbeunnom Isanghannom (The Good, the Bad, the Weird)* is released.
2009	Fox Searchlight releases *(500) Days of Summer*; Focus Features releases *A Serious Man*.
2012	*Moonrise Kingdom* is released. Dolby introduces Dolby Atmos with release of *Brave*.
2013	Warner Bros. releases *Gravity*.
2014	Marvel Entertainment releases *Captain America: The Winter Soldier*.

would have been commonly encountered on top 40 radio in the early 1960s, the time both films are set. Films like *Fast Times at Ridgemont High* (1982), *The Breakfast Club* (1984), *Pretty in Pink* (1986), and *Ferris Bueller's Day Off* likewise drew heavily on popular music to establish the contemporary setting, both diegetically in terms of music the characters are listening to and nondiegetically to reflect the mood of particular characters.

Though such recent films as the Coen Brothers' *O Bother, Where Art Thou?* (2000) and *Inside Llewyn Davis* (2013) continue to use songs or soundalikes to establish the setting in this way, many recent films have adopted a much more eclectic compilation practice. Films like Baz Luhrmann's *Moulin Rouge* (2001) and *The Great Gatsby* (2013) freely introduce the sounds of contemporary popular music without any concern for potential anachronisms. Interestingly, in the case of Luhrmann's films these anachronisms are generally restricted to musical performances. In *Marie Antoinette* (2006), by contrast, anachronistic popular music is used even more freely to underscore the young Marie Antoinette's sense of dislocation as a teenager moved suddenly to the court of France. Period eighteenth-century music mixes freely on the sound track with anachronistic popular music. The eighteenth-century music appears in both diegetic and nondiegetic contexts, but the popular music is generally deployed nondiegetically and reserved for the common functions of underscoring lyrical montage and subjective introspection. The masked ball, however, is an exception, since the music here is anachronistic diegetic music (and similar to Luhrmann's use of anachronistic diegetic music).

The thing about the music in [Marie Antoinette] is that there were no rules and no other movies we used as a role model. . . . We didn't do anything for the sake of putting a song in. We always did what felt right to us.
—Brian Reitzell [Music Supervisor][11]

As director Sofia Coppola remarks on the music: "I wanted to use a mixture of eighteenth-century and contemporary music, to use music that had the emotional quality that the scene should have. When [Marie goes] to the ball, she was excited and I picked the music that gives that feeling the most."[12]

Many sound tracks today simply adopt a mix of vocal and instrumental popular music, whether commissioned for the film or compiled from preexisting recordings, in place of orchestral scoring. It is also quite common today to hear a nondiegetic popular song with vocals behind dialogue, though that was generally avoided in earlier periods.

Just as elements of the jazz idiom were abstracted and incorporated into the basic scoring language in the 1950s and 60s, so in the 1990s something similar happened with the rock idiom, and composers with backgrounds in popular music, most notably Danny Elfman and Hans Zimmer, forged prominent careers in the industry. This trend continued after 2000, with percussive rock rhythms becoming a regular part of the basic scoring technique. This has been especially true of contemporary comedies aimed at youth audiences. This trend also allowed composers to merge their scores seamlessly with the hard-driving rock songs that were increasingly used to underscore stylized action scenes, such as the lobby shootout in *The Matrix,* or that musically defined the character, as in *Iron Man.* Other film composers who had prominent careers as musicians in rock bands include Trent Reznor, who won an Academy Award for the score he wrote with Atticus Ross for *The Social Network* (2010), and Johnny Greenwood, who composed the original music for *There Will Be Blood* (2007).

Summary

The ever increasing power of digital technology has continued to alter the sound track in fundamental ways. Sound and music are now recorded, edited, and distributed digitally. More and more, both music and sound are also being produced digitally. These digital tools have given filmmakers, especially composers and sound designers, ever increasing control over the sound track, but they are also highly disruptive to past traditions of filmmaking. The digitization of other commercial domains, such as the distribution of music through iTunes, has also proved to have large effects on film production, which can no longer count on music as a source of substantial ancillary income. This has had the effect of drastically lowering music budgets for films, which has forced most composers and musicians working on film to accept lower rates of compensation. Composers such as Hans Zimmer have responded by organizing work in new ways. Composers today are also no longer focused on delivering a score to be recorded and fitted to the film but rather a fully produced music stem to be mixed with the other primary stems.

Music and Film Form Since 2000

Introduction

The story of dramatic changes over the past 15 years—most of them driven by digital production, platforms, and dissemination—was told in Chapter 13. Here, as in Chapters 10 and 12, we will look at a representative sampling (if such a thing is possible) from three different angles: the individual film, aspects of music and sound in one film genre, and comparison of two related films. *The Hours* is a serious dramatic film with three chronologically separated stories connected by the motif of a novel by Virginia Woolf. Its underscore by the prominent minimalist composer Philip Glass makes a number of adjustments in the style to accommodate the needs of a dramatic film. Next, we update Chapter 12's discussion of action films, which have become ever more important to Hollywood over the past decade, even as they become more internationalized in style and production personnel. Finally, we compare aspects of two quite different versions of a familiar Jane Austen novel, one in contemporary form, the other as a historical costume film. Both are romances. If *Bridget Jones's Diary* leans more to the comedic, even farcical, Joe Wright's rendition of *Pride & Prejudice* emphasizes the various dramas that arise from lovers' conflicts and resolution.

Mainstream Dramatic Film: *The Hours*

The Hours (2002) is based on a novel by Michael Cunningham that self-reflexively focuses on the writing of a novel and the wide-ranging influences of reading it. Three parallel stories play out in the years 1923, 1951, and 2001: during a day in each of these years, respectively, Virginia Woolf (Nicole Kidman) writes a novel, *Mrs. Dalloway,* and ultimately commits suicide; a housewife, Marion Brown (Julianne Moore), reads the novel, contemplates suicide but eventually abandons her family instead; and an editor, Clarissa Vaughan (Meryl Streep), prepares a party honoring a poet (and former lover), who is, coincidentally, Marion Brown's son Richard (Ed Harris) and who commits suicide before the party.

In an interview included among the DVD's special features, composer Philip Glass comments that his task was to try to hold together a film that jumps frequently from one of the parallel stories to another.[1] Whether the film truly required that kind of help at unification is open to question: the mise-en-scène for each period is visually distinctive, the focus on a female lead in each story is obvious, and connections are frequently drawn between the stories, including (among others) the motif of the novel *Mrs. Dalloway* and the themes of lesbian love and of suicide.

Some but not all of Glass's nondiegetic orchestral cues overlap scenes—the simplest and most direct way to tie them together (see especially the cues for the Morning and Lunch segments listed in Table 14-1). Instead, it is the remarkable homogeneity of the music that allows the sound track's musical element to lend a sense of cohesion to the film at the level of the whole. Most of the cues, in fact, can be heard as more or less subtle variants or developments of the first one. Glass's minimalist style emphasizes repetition and small changes within generally homogeneous textures. In a sense, this reduces the "cell" method of Bernard Herrmann, discussed in Chapter 12, to its bare essentials and, usually in slightly less radical forms, has become a common method of film music composition in recent decades (composers who have employed it at one time or another include James Horner, Thomas Newman, Mychael Danna, and Dario Marianelli, among others). At the same time, Glass's cues do satisfy the classical requirements of nondiegetic music, in the formal work of transitions and thematic unification, as mentioned earlier, and also in establishing mood and, in a few instances, even in following shifting moods and circumstances within a scene. For example, a striking—and unique—moment is a "hit" or stinger: a sudden flurry of loud and rapid piano notes as Richard falls out of the window to his death (in scene 15: see Table 14-1). For another example, see cue 10 (in scene 12), which tracks Laura Brown's emotional crescendo as she leaves her son with a babysitter and checks into a hotel, resolved to kill herself—or so she thinks. Glass develops the underscore with the breadth and continuity of a concert piece: a complete movement from the CD suite ("Tearing Herself Away") is the music for this one scene in the film.

We have laid out Table 14-1 so as to show how one can make use of DVD chapter numbers and CD sound track recordings. The film's large segments, its acts, are given as headings, as usual. Within each of these, the DVD chapter numbers are given, along with a description of the chapter's contents. This layout works for *The Hours,* as scene changes coincide well with chapter changes. Musical cues are labeled and numbered ("CUE"), and in parentheses the corresponding CD track is identified by number and title. Note that the CD tracks do not appear in order (three are missing as well): despite titles that evoke the narrative sequence of the film, the CD is not simply a compilation of the recorded cues. Instead, the cues were newly performed and recorded (and some of them

Table 14-1 *The Hours* (2002). Timeline and cue list.

PROLOGUE & CREDITS

> **1.** Virginia Woolf's suicide
>
> > 0:02:00 [CUES 1 & 2] Music in: 1. "The Poet Acts" and segue to 2. "Morning Passages"; continues to 0:09:20
>
> **2.** 0:03:40 Opening credits combined with prologue-style introductions of the three time periods

MORNING

> **3.** 0:08:54 Woolf and her husband Leonard in the morning; "Flowers" parallel between the three periods
>
> > 0:09:20 Music goes out   = 7:20
>
> **4.** 0:11:38 Breakfast in the Browns' house
>
> > 0:13:20 [CUE 3] Music in (6. "'I'm Going to Make a Cake';")
>
> **5.** 0:14:16 Clarissa plans the party; buys flowers; "One day" parallel at the end
>
> > 0:15:30 Music out   = 2:10
> >
> > 0:16:30 [CUE 4] Music in (12. "Escape!")
>
> **6.** 0:17:31 Clarissa visits Richard
>
> > 0:18:53 Music out   = 2:23
> >
> > 0:21:25 [CUE 5] Music in (variant of 1. "The Poet Acts")
> >
> > 0:23:58 Music out   = 2:33
> >
> > 0:26:50 [CUE 6] Music in (6. "'I'm Going to Make a Cake'")

LUNCH

> **7.** 0:27:40 Back to Woolf writing, household, walk ("She's going to die")
>
> > 0:28:14 Music out   = 1:24
> >
> > 0:31:20 [CUE 7] Music in (latter part of 9. "The Kiss")
>
> **8.** 0:32:02 Laura Brown and her son make a cake; Clarissa and Sally talk about the party for Richard
>
> > 0:33:24 Music out   = 2:14
>
> **9.** 0:35:38 Back to Laura Brown working on the cake; a friend Kitty visits

AFTERNOON

> **10.** 0:43:29 Woolf's sister Vanessa and her children arrive early; Woolf and Angelica hold a funeral for a bird; Laura Brown makes a decision
>
> > 0:43:32 Music out
> >
> > 0:45:40 [CUE 8] Music in (8. "Dead Things")
> >
> > 0:50:10 Music out   = 4:30
>
> **11.** 0:50:11 Louis Waters (former lover of Richard's) arrives at Clarissa's apartment, very early for the party

(Continued)

Table 14-1 (*Continued*)

0:50:16 [CUE 9] Music in: diegetic music, recording of Richard Strauss, "Beim Schlafengehen" (from "Four Last Songs")		
0:51:32 Music out		

12. 0:59:25 Laura Brown finishes the cake, then goes to a hotel, intending suicide; back to Woolf with the sister and children, with cuts back and forth to Laura Brown in the hotel; Vanessa and the children leave; Louis leaves; Woolf returns to writing

0:59:25 [CUE 10] Music in (11. "Tearing Herself Away"); 1:04:35 music out	= 5:10
1:05:15 [CUE 11] Music in (3. "Something She Has to Do"); 1:08:23 Music out	= 3:08
1:09:35 [CUE 12] Music in; 1:11:58 music out (from 6. "'I'm Going to Make a Cake'")	= 2:23

13. 1:12:11 Clarissa's daughter Julia arrives

LATE AFTERNOON/EVENING

14. 1:17:02 Virginia Woolf leaves the house; Leonard looks for her, finds her at the train station, they argue

1:23:15 [CUE 13] Music in (4. "'For Your Own Benefit'"); music out 1:26:30	= 3:15

15. 1:25:56 Laura Brown returns; she and Richard talk on the way home; Richard upends his apartment, he jumps to his death; dinner and party at Browns; Clarissa in the hospital; Leonard and Virginia by the fire discuss the book; late night at the Browns and parallel with Leonard and Virginia

1:27:40 [CUE 14] Music in; 1:30:05 music out (variant of 1. "The Poet Acts")	= 2:25
1:31:50 [CUE 15] Music in (12. "Escape"); 1:34:30 music out	= 2:40
1:37:15 [CUE 16] Music in 10. "'Why Does Someone Have to Die?'"	

16. 1:39:42 Taking down the party at Clarissa's; Laura Brown arrives and they talk

1:41:14 Music out	= 3:59
1:44:10 [CUE 17] Music in (13. "Choosing Life"); 1:48:00 music out	= 3:50

EPILOGUE

17. 1:47:59 End of the night; drowning reprise; end credits

1:48:44 [CUE 18] Music in (beginning of 12. "Escape," then 14. "The Hours"); music out 1:54:22

apparently revised as well), with the result that the CD is more like a suite of music from the film than it is a reproduction of the film's music.

The title "suite" has commonly been used for selections of concert music derived from films. The term has been used since the nineteenth century for concert compositions that draw selections of music from larger, usually stage, works—familiar examples are the "Carmen" suite of Georges Bizet (from his opera) and the two "Peer Gynt" suites of Edvard Grieg (drawn from his incidental music for a production of the Ibsen play). In this case, the basic progressions and themes for the film's music cues were in fact derived from *earlier* concert works by Glass. The publication credits for the CD read:

> Music published by Famous Music Corporation (ASCAP), except the following, published by Dunvagen Music Publishers, Inc.: the first section of track 6, "'I'm Going to Make a Cake,'" based on the theme from "Protest" (Act II, Scene 3) from the opera *Satyagraha*; track 11, "Tearing Herself Away," based on "Islands" from the album *Glassworks* (not contained in the motion picture); and track 12, "Escape," based on "Metamorphosis Two" from the album *Solo Piano*.[2]

To complicate matters even further, the reference to track 11 as "not contained in the motion picture" is incorrect: almost the entirety of it, with no orchestrational or other changes, is heard as cue 10.

The DVD and the CD, the film and the "suite," are different artistic works, no matter how much of their material they share. In general, for recent films, a CD recording is not necessary for a study of the film and can, as here, even introduce some obstacles. For classical films, on the other hand, sound track CDs, especially those issued in the past decade or so, frequently *are* compilations of the film's musical cues from the original studio recordings and therefore can often be helpful in sorting out and collating the nondiegetic music.

Action Films Today

In Chapter 12, we discussed a number of prologues and main title sequences from action films of the New Hollywood up to 1999. In this section, we look more generally at action sequences of films after 2000. As a genre, action films have only increased in importance. Economically, they remain the foundational and most lucrative product of the industry, even more so because the international box office now surpasses domestic by some margin. Aesthetically, action films have grown more complex and challenging, with troubled protagonists operating in conspiratorial worlds of gray that often make decisions murky and place characters on morally uncertain ground. Action heroes (and increasingly heroines) remain compelled to act, but increasingly the melodramatic world of good and evil that once assured the moral clarity of action has been sufficiently warped by impersonal forces that discerning the "right" course of action to the particular situation presented by the world is ever in doubt. Characters are moved to action as reaction, and the default legitimation of action as reaction is self-preservation and secondarily the protection of innocents. In Chapter 13, we discussed some changes that have occurred in scoring action films since 2000 and suggested that the shift away from well-articulated themes toward gesture and affect is bound up with these transformations in the genre of the action film and the uncertain status of the action hero.

The Hollywood action film has also been challenged and so influenced by international cinemas, most notably the martial arts tradition of Hong Kong cinema and the grittier action films coming from European cinema. Hollywood has responded to the challenge as it often does: by appropriating ideas and by hiring away key talent. The situation has been made even more complex by the creation of a truly global market for film—a market that now dwarfs the U.S. domestic market—and the entanglements of international financing that now funds large swaths of filmmaking activity, and not just or even primarily American films. This messy situation of film financing makes it more and more difficult to distinguish national cinemas from Hollywood or from each other. Today, the dominant distinguishing factors are the size of the budget and original language of a film more than the source of financing, the sponsoring studio, the place of production, or the personnel involved in the production.

In this section, we discuss a number of action sequences from a variety of different films released in the years since 2000 and explore ways in which the sound tracks of action films have changed due in part to significant shifts in aesthetic priorities.

WO HU CANG LONG (CROUCHING TIGER, HIDDEN DRAGON), THEFT OF THE SWORD

An international co-production, *Wo Hu Cang Long* (2000) is a Chinese-language film that follows the tradition of wuxia cinema, which combines martial arts and fantasy elements with a setting in ancient China to explore moral themes. The film tells the story of Jen Yu (Ziyi Zhang), a young aristocratic woman pledged in an arranged marriage but who loves someone else and has secretly trained as a warrior under the devious Jade Fox (Pei-pei Cheng).

The first action sequence involves the theft of a fabled sword, Green Destiny, which had been brought to the house of Sir Te by Yu Shu Lien, a famed female warrior (Michelle Yeoh). Contemplative flute music accompanied by strings had entered briefly at the end of the previous scene when Jen blew out a candle before apparently settling down for bed (15:05). The action sequence begins with a shot of the city at night. It then cuts to guards patrolling the garden outside the room where the sword is being kept (Figure 14-1a). The music continues and matches the calm but positive mood of the guards. An ominous note suddenly sounds as a dark figure slips quickly over the roof in the background, and the music, though quiet, becomes more percussive and rhythmic as this figure moves through the shadows to the sword, which the masked thief (later revealed to be Jen) bundles up (Figure 14-1b). When a guard enters the room, the thief attacks with a martial arts kick, the loud sound effect being emphasized by a musical change to low-pitched drumming for the subsequent brief fight (Figure 14-1c). From this point on, the music consists of just drumming. Part music, part sound effect, the drumming permits dialogue and physical noises to continue unimpeded. Besides the music, the sound in this portion of the scene is dominated by the guard's clumsy wielding of his weapon. The thief escapes by flying to the roof and throwing tiles at the guards below. The crashing of the tiles and the yelling of the guards attracts the attention of Yu Shu, who then joins the pursuit.

Figure 14-1. *Wo Hu Cang Long* (Crouching Tiger, Hidden Dragon, 2000). The theft of the sword.

a	b
c	d

Yu Shu and the thief fight at three different points in the sequence. The first is brief (Figure 14-1d), but the thief performs one move, given a special sound effect, that reveals knowledge of Wudan, a secret martial art. Confronted, the thief then takes flight, jumping magically across the rooftops with Yu Shu in close pursuit.

The second fight is more extended and occurs in a small courtyard, and the sound emphasizes the hits and blocks in the combat. On one occasion, the thief attempts to execute a Wudan move, which the sound track again marks with a special sound effect, but Yu Shu counters it. The thief manages to escape to the rooftops and Yu Shu again gives chase. As they enter another, larger courtyard, the music intensifies its rhythmic pattern, and Yu Shu manages to catch the thief again.

This results in the third and most intense fight, which becomes very balletic with flips and fights on the walls beyond the hits and kicks of the earlier skirmishes. Yu Shu clearly has the upper hand in this fight, employing Wudan moves on several occasions, but the thief escapes when someone shoots a dart from the rooftop and Yu Shu must break contact with the thief to intercept it. The thief escapes, quickly flying up to the rooftops, and the music stops abruptly as the scene ends with Yu Shu looking inquiringly at the dart.

Music is very important to structuring this sequence. Broadly, it sets, raises, and then maintains the level of physical excitement through instrumentation and the intensity of the rhythmic patterns. Changes in music mark changes in the intensity of the physical action. More locally, music provides continuity, in this case the repeating rhythmic patterns providing a ground that helps ensure that the quick cutting of the image remains intelligible. The movements of the fighters are also tightly choreographed, and the music helps draw out the balletic quality of the fight. This balletic quality is a highly praised characteristic of Hong Kong martial arts cinema that has been frequently imitated by Hollywood. (The martial arts choreographer of *Wo Hu Cang Long* is Yuen Wo Ping, who also worked on the fight scenes of *The Matrix,* among other productions.)

Music makes the design of the theft scene exceptionally clear: the early moment of calm, the theft, the initial battle with ineffective guards, and the much longer series of increasingly dangerous fights with Yu Shu are each given distinctive music, though the change in music is not precisely synchronized with the onset of each of the fights.

"The Theft of the Sword" from *Wo Hu Cang Long* also illustrates the increasingly common technique of accompanying action scenes with a driving percussion groove. Sometimes the music is left almost entirely to the percussion groove, often, as in the case of *Wo Hu Cang Long*, with an ethnic percussion ensemble, but typically this percussion groove is part of a rhythm section in a rock-based scoring as in *Mission: Impossible II* (2000), which uses both rock songs commissioned for the film and similar hard-driving rock-based cues composed by Hans Zimmer.

BATMAN, SHOOTOUT AT THE AXIS CHEMICAL PLANT, AND *BATMAN BEGINS*, INITIATION TO THE LEAGUE OF SHADOWS

A comparison of *Batman* (1989) with *Batman Begins* (2005) illustrates a number of important changes in action film in the intervening 16 years. In general, Danny Elfman scores his film far more thematically than Hans Zimmer and James Newton Howard do theirs. Situations change in *Batman*, whereas the character of Batman does not, and Elfman's music reflects this fact: Batman is inevitably accompanied by his theme, often in the same key and with little variation other than orchestration. The point of the scoring is thematic identity, that is, on establishing who Batman is more than what he does. He is, as film music historian Janet Halfyard pithily puts it, "heroic icon more than heroic agent."[3] In action sequences, the material is developed musically perhaps, but it always ends up back at the same place: the theme.

The Shootout at the Axis Chemical Plant provides a good example. Jack Rapier (Jack Nicholson), the principal villain of the film, has been sent by his boss to rob the plant, but his boss has also arranged for a unit of corrupt police officers to show up and kill him. Police Commissioner Gordon (Pat Hingle) finds out that the corrupt unit is going to the plant and leads a group of officers of his own. Batman (Michael Keaton) overhears Gordon discussing the plan and heads for the plant as well.

The sequence opens (23:56) without music and with the corrupt police unit preparing to kill Jack. As the scene shifts to action, music enters but it remains energetic and mostly nondescript, growing increasingly agitated especially once gunshots begin to be fired. The sound design aims at being chaotic, and gunshots

Figure 14-2. *Batman* (1989). Main theme. (Transcription from the sound track.)

and the sounds of equipment from the plant generally overwhelm the music until Batman appears, announced by his theme (Figure 14-2).

Once Batman arrives, music and sound effects fluctuate in importance, with music's prominence being correlated with Batman's presence and sound effects' prominence being correlated with Jack's actions (turning up the plants' equipment, smashing a storage tank with an ax) until the culminating confrontation between them. Appropriately enough, music dominates the confrontation since Batman overwhelms Jack, although the Batman theme itself appears only when Batman first steps out to challenge Jack (Figure 14-3). The theme then disappears for the bulk of the confrontation, reappearing only in the coda to the sequence after Batman has dropped Jack into a cauldron of chemicals (inadvertently turning him into the Joker). At the end of the sequence, Batman escapes the police, dramatically rising up out of a cloud of smoke as the Batman theme sounds again. Throughout the sequence (and the film), the Batman theme serves to mark the character's power rather than his actions, and the action music is otherwise generic, usually with overtones of a martial musical topic. The action provides the situation, in other words, that allows Batman to assert his power, and the action music provides the setting over which the Batman theme sounds and establishes the musical identity.

Figure 14-3. *Batman.* Batman challenges Jack.

In *Batman Begins*, by contrast, Batman no longer seems a fixed character who responds to a changed situation, and the theme does not provide the same level of identity. Instead, the character seems to evolve along with the situation, and the character's response to and feeling for the situation and its changes seem as important for the music to grasp and articulate as marking thematic identity or underscoring character duality. Action no longer appears as a developmental mask of the thematic material, a situation that puts the theme under stress, breaks it down, and reassembles it to show that it can withstand the rigors of the test that action places before it. Instead, the material develops without ever finding a solid fixed form of identity. Themes are also not placed in affective settings defined generically by topic, as though affect and identity, topic and theme, can be analytically separated without altering the terms of the analysis. Instead, thematic material emerges from and merges with the affect as two sides of the musical gesture that marks the affective state of the body. Bruce Wayne (Christian Bale) is not the false social mask of Batman, and Batman is not the mask that true heroic action must wear in contemporary society. The ego/alter-ego duality that is fundamental to much superhero mythology here dissolves into a singular body moved to action by affect but without achieving a stable place of identity in action. If the Batman of the 1989 film is an icon, the Batman of *Batman Begins* is more of a cipher, the body serving as the ground of intensified feeling but not in order to be channeled into expressing a unified identity.

The first major action sequence of *Batman Begins* occurs when Bruce completes his training with the League of Shadows but fails the final initiation test because he refuses to execute a prisoner. This final test sequence is complex and has the following structure:

1. Flashback to Bruce's Adventures in Crime (31:32)
2. The Test of the Ninja (32:15)
3. The Test of Execution (35:53)
4. Bruce Fights the League (38:42)
5. Bruce Rescues Ducard (39:50)

The whole first part of the film is a complex interleaving of flashbacks of various points in Bruce's life intercut with his training by Henri Ducard (Liam Neeson) for the League of Shadows. In this action sequence, which represents the final test of Bruce's training, music, based on the agitated accompaniment to the main Batman motif (Figure 14-4), continues over from a flashback where Carmine Falcone (Tom Wilkinson), a Gotham crime boss, beats Bruce to killing his parents' murderer, Rachel (Katie Holmes) confronts Bruce about the immorality of his vengeful feelings, and Bruce flees Gotham. The final test sequence begins with Bruce and Ducard speaking in voice-over about Bruce's exploration of the global crime world (part 1 of the five-part structure). The voice-over is then turned into a sound advance as the image shows Ducard mixing a hallucinogenic potion for Bruce (part 2).

Figure 14-4. *Batman Begins* (2005). Basic "Batman" motive. (Transcription from the sound track.)

Once Bruce drinks the potion, both sound and image track begin to distort, suggesting a shift to subjective perspective. A group of ninjas surrounds Ducard and Bruce, as Ducard tests Bruce's reactions and leads him to confront his fear of bats and of himself. The music for this segment consists initially mostly of a low drone, with the subjectified sound effects and Ducard's commentary serving as the foreground events, until Bruce opens the box with the bats, when moody orchestral timbres take over: low, brooding strings and slow majestic swells in the horn build until Ducard misidentifies Bruce, and Bruce passes the test. Music then sneaks out when Ra's al Ghul (Ken Watanabe) begins to speak.

This next segment of the sequence, the test of execution (part 3), is initially accompanied primarily by a soft, hollow wind sound and a fairly extensive amount of reverb. Low, brooding strings enter when the prisoner is brought in, and a horn softly sounds, but without forming a distinctive motive, when Bruce argues in favor of respecting compassion. This orchestral sound then gradually distorts as Ra's al Ghul makes the contrary case for destroying Gotham because the city is too infested with crime and so has become unsalvageable. As Bruce remains resolute in his opposition, the low, brooding strings return. Ducard pleads with him, and Bruce takes up the sword, the music growing dissonant and crescendoing as it appears that Bruce will execute the prisoner.

As the sword comes down, the orchestra registers the hit. Bruce's sword does not strike the prisoner, however, but he instead sticks it into a nearby fire and flings a coal into a pile of explosives (part 4). The music pivots on this unexpected event to the driving percussion rhythms, fiery string lines, heavy orchestra hits, and portentous brass entrances common to action music today. This is music that complements well the sword clashes, punches, and explosions with which it must share the sound track, but the musical gestures are cued to the feeling of the moment rather than asserting anything about thematic identity that might transcend these feelings of the action (Figure 14-5). When Bruce carries the unconscious Ducard from the burning building (part 5), the music grows more lyrical to emphasize a topical shift in the action, but the music remains thematically vague, and something similar happens when Bruce keeps Ducard from tumbling off a cliff at the end of the sequence.

These lyrical moments relate musically to the basic Batman material, but the musical connections are diffuse and what is primary is the affective response

Figure 14-5. *Batman Begins* (2005). Bruce battles Ra's al Ghul.

the music reports, not a thematic identity the music articulates. Because the music in the film never comes into thematic focus—it never coalesces into a distinctive musical shape that exceeds the rudimentary form of its basic material (recall Figure 14-4)—the thematic connections serve only to create variants that circulate around this thematic void, and if we go to the music looking for a clarifying identity, we will find it refusing the terms that would insist on measuring actions and affects according to essential being.

CASINO ROYALE, PROLOGUE

Casino Royale (2006) is the first in a series of Bond films starring Daniel Craig. Craig plays a grittier Bond operating in a world far grayer and more uncertain than the melodramatic world of black and white that has been conventional for the Bond franchise. The basic thematic elements are often the same—a globe-trotting British secret agent working primarily in exotic locales (often former British colonies) to protect the hegemony of Anglo-American Empire from the nefarious plots of evil masterminds seeking either to deploy the forces of chaos so individual power is unchecked by any state power or to impose a utopian world of impossible, inhuman order. But the confidence that this hegemonic order serves good, or that the good that it protects is worth its high costs, is no longer taken for granted, or at least not to the same extent. Craig is also a fallible, more physical, more human Bond, one prone to significant errors of judgment and execution and one who suffers significant bodily injury. The suffering hero has been a strong motif in action films since at least the definitive emergence of the hard-bodied action hero in *Rambo: First Blood* (1982), and Bond films have traditionally featured a scene where Bond has been captured by the villain who has devised some dastardly way for the hero to die. But the torture scene in *Casino Royale* is the first time that this motif of bodily suffering, where the body in pain rather than the threat of death is the immediate focus, has appeared so prominently in the Bond franchise. And throughout the series of three films,

Craig's Bond is far more likely to rely on direct physical violence than his predecessors, who always favored the mediation of modern technologies—guns and other gadgets—when engaging in violence.

Following the Bond formula outlined in Chapter 12, *Casino Royale* opens with an action prologue, and the film begins as if a throwback: it uses black-and-white cinematography, is set in Prague, and borrows iconography from films about the Cold War, such as *The Spy Who Came in from the Cold* (1965). The sound design, like the cinematography, is sparse but stylized, hovering part way between music and effects, with essential foreground sounds like the car door accompanied by a low metallic hum that might be music or might be an overly loud generator, and some unlocalizable indistinct thuds.

The film quickly pivots from the brief initial allusion to the Cold War to an indistinct contemporary setting of high modernism, with a shot of somewhat disorienting architectural angles and glass elevators running up and down the side of an architecturally striking building and then a cut to a lone individual riding inside the elevator. The man exits the elevator and walks through an empty, antiseptic space, suggesting in a most efficient manner that Prague has traded the egalitarian impoverishment of socialism for the modernist alienation of high capitalism. The sound in this segment continues to float between ambience and music, with a disquieting low metallic hum and rumble too loud for the depicted office building space and punctuated by heavy, echoing footsteps once the man leaves the elevator. This soundscape follows the figure into an office, where new sounds, now seeming much more like music, fill the setting with foreboding.

Another figure, as it turns out a young James Bond, is sitting in the dark, and he confronts the man entering the office. This man, we now learn, is Dryden (Malcolm Sinclair), the MI6 section chief in Prague, who has been selling intelligence secrets. Dryden confronts Bond with his operational inexperience, triggering a flashback of Bond attacking another man in a restroom. The image shifts abruptly from dark to an almost oversaturated light, and the sound track explodes with the hits and crashes of physical violence. Orchestral music shadows these violent sounds, sweetening them and adding to their power. A final stinger yanks the scene back to the office, where Dryden has pulled a gun on Bond. The hum now sounds like an electronically manipulated high string tremolo, which continues until Dryden pulls the trigger. When nothing but a click sounds, the music drops in pitch and then shifts to an ominous string figure. Dryden asks how his contact died, and the scene shifts back to the restroom again with extremely loud sound effects, although this time the effects are more widely spaced and the brutal orchestral music paints the extreme violence of the physical action rather than simply adding to the punishing sound of the effects (Figure 14-6). As Dryden's contact collapses to the floor after Bond apparently drowns him, the orchestra mostly drops out, leaving the running water as the dominant sound, an anempathetic auditory mark of a brutal and indifferent world and Bond's entrance into it. Music, however, continues low and uncertain

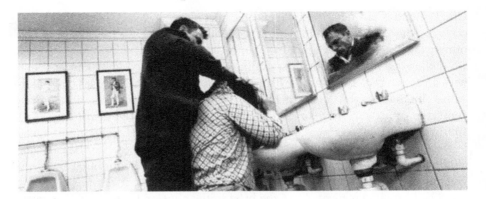

Figure 14-6. *Casino Royale* (2006). Bond fights Dryden's informant in a restroom.

underneath, and this music accompanies the cutback to the office, where Bond now coolly shoots Dryden. The scene then returns to the restroom, where Bond stoops to pick up his gun from the floor. When the seemingly dead contact stirs, Bond wheels and fires, leading directly into the main title credits as the shot reverberates.

Although the action of this prologue is not central to the larger narrative of the film, it does efficiently establish along with Bond's characteristic coolness, his inexperience and his physicality. These latter two traits are significant departures from the Bond franchise, and so the prologue does important work of priming the audience's expectations for a different Bond, one more in keeping with such contemporary action heroes as Christian Bale's Batman. The sound track also signals this departure, as the classic Bond theme (Figure 14-7b) is not even hinted at in this sequence. The opening of the main titles (Figure 14-7d) does recall the explosive gesture of the hits (Figure 14-7a) that initiate the Bond theme and the theme's jazzy riff and brass fanfare that punctuate the tune (Figure 14-7c), but this opening is scored for a rock ensemble and horn, and it is played in the aggressive style of heavy metal, and even when scored for orchestra during later action sequences, this material generally suppresses any jazzy quality (the scoring is typically orchestral horns rather than high jazz trumpets). Indeed, although the characteristic chromatic countermelody to the Bond theme (Figure 14-7b) appears at various points in the film, the theme itself appears only at the very end when Bond claims his identity.

Like *Batman Begins*, *Casino Royale* is an origin story, and the score reflects the fact that the character is in a state of becoming, that the character's fate therefore remains open rather than being predetermined by a theme that fixes an identity the character can accept or resist but never substantively develop. Bond differs from Batman, however, in that when the theme appears at the end, it is as though he has now assumed his proper role so the theme can now confirm his ascension from human to archetypal status.

Figure 14-7. *Casino Royale* (2006). (a) Classic Bond theme: introductory orchestral a hits. (b) Classic Bond theme: main tune. (c) Classic Bond theme: two characteristic b jazzy interjections. (d) *Casino Royale*: opening music for main titles. (Transcriptions c from the sound track.) d

THE BOURNE ULTIMATUM, WATERLOO STATION

Similar to Bond, Jason Bourne is a character based on a best-selling series of spy novels. The Bourne films, however, form a coherent trilogy, with a strong narrative arc that extends across the three films—*The Bourne Identity* (2002), *The Bourne Supremacy* (2004), and *The Bourne Ultimatum* (2007)—as the title character struggles to come to terms with his amnesia. Although the trilogy draws on many of the conventions established by the Bond films (and other spy films and novels), the world of the Bourne trilogy is darker and more conspiratorial than the classic Bond films with the plot revolving around high-level corruption in the intelligence agencies, corruption that has fundamentally subverted their mission. In many respects, Daniel Craig's Bond films can be understood as an attempt by the owners of the Bond franchise to respond to the challenges that the Bourne films posed to the subgenre of the action spy thriller. But even if Craig's Bond resembles the physicality of Matt Damon's Bourne, the Bond films maintain a basic faith in governmental institutions, however much those institutions may suffer from being staffed by fallible people or from being buffeted by seemingly irrational political currents. The Bourne films break with this faith, although *The Bourne Ultimatum* leaves hope that the institutions can eventually be reformed and reconstituted.

John Powell's action music for the Bourne trilogy follows a similar strategy to much contemporary action film in combining a rock-based rhythm section of drums and sometimes guitars, with gestural orchestral music, often based on the action theme (recall Figure 13-17a), layered over top. The action sequences, which are sometimes sustained over more than 15 minutes in these films, are quite elaborate, often involving multiple simultaneous chases with participants using surveillance equipment, computers, cell phones, and radios to observe, guide, and negotiate these chases. The sequences are also internally articulated, with distinct sections, often with discernible narrative functions. The "Waterloo Station" sequence from early in *The Bourne Ultimatum*, for instance, falls into five large sections:

1. Set-Up (Establishes main lines of action, sets goals) 9:45
2. Getting into the Station (Bourne navigates Ross to a place they can meet) 17:04
3. Pursuit through the Station (Bourne navigates Ross through the station) 20:30
4. Failed Flight (Ross is killed by Paz) 24:49
5. Failed Chase (Bourne pursues Paz) 26:21

In this sequence, Simon Ross (Paddy Considine), a reporter for *The Guardian* who has been writing a series of stories on CIA agent Jason Bourne for the paper, lands at Heathrow after a secret meeting with his source. Having read previous articles in the series, Bourne, now on the run from the CIA, contacts Ross and sets up a meeting at Waterloo Station. The sequence follows Ross from the airport to *The Guardian's* headquarters, where he speaks to Bourne on the phone, and then to Waterloo station, where they meet up. Complicating matters is the fact that the CIA is tailing Ross to uncover his source.

The set-up for the sequence is particularly long because it uses parallel editing to introduce Ross, to show Bourne making his way from Paris to London, and to establish the surveillance capabilities of the CIA. Thus, the sequence initially forms three distinct lines of action, and the line of the CIA will multiply repeatedly as its various personnel converge on Waterloo Station. Music plays more or less continuously through this whole sequence, with percussion being a recurring element, and, as with *Wo Hu Cang Long*, drum hits and the introduction of a new percussion pattern in particular register large-scale intensifications in the action.

Table 14-2 gives a shot breakdown and notes on the sound track for the pursuit through the station, the third section, which is essentially a double chase, with agents pursuing Ross on one level and Bourne simultaneously tracking and eliminating the agents on another. In addition, the segment features cuts back to the CIA offices where a team of analysts and executives are following the action through microphones and surveillance cameras. This segment starts with Bourne and Ross meeting face to face, Bourne leading Ross through the station by cell phone to avoid the agents, Ross panicking and being spotted by

Table 14-2 *The Bourne Ultimatum.*

Time Code	Shot Description	Dialogue	Music	Effects
20:30	MS Ross; joined by Bourne	**Bourne**: "Who's your source?	Music bleached back.	Station chatter throughout
20:31	2-CU Ross and Bourne	What's his name? What's your source's name?"		
20:33	MS Ross (over Bourne's shoulder)	**Ross**: "Look, what's going on? Why are these people after me?"		
		Bourne: "Because you found something.		
20:36	RS Bourne (CU framing)	You talked to someone inside Treadstone. Someone who was there at the beginning. Who is it?"		
20:40	MS Ross	**Ross**: "You know I can't tell you that."		
20:42	RS Bourne	**Bourne**: "You have know idea what you are into here. These people will kill you if they have to.		
20:46	MS Ross	**Ross**: "Was it Blackbriar?		
20:47	RS Bourne	Is that what this is?"		
		Bourne: "Blackbriar? What's Blackbriar?"		
		Ross: "Treadstone upgrade. My source		
20:52	MS Ross	told me that it all started with you.		
20:53	RS Bourne	He said that you were square one of a dirty little secret.		
20:56	MS Ross	He said he knows who you are."	String or synth chord to punctuate Ross's line.	
20:58	RS Bourne		Lead into:	
21:00	POV station, with zoom to lock on two agents.		Zoom underscored with drum hits.	
21:02	CU Bourne, then Bourne and Ross walk away.	**Bourne**: "We have to move. Answer your phone." [indecipherable voices]	New music.	
21:07	MCU, Bourne			

(Continued)

Table 14-2 (*Continued*)

Time Code	Shot Description	Dialogue	Music	Effects
21:08	Station ceiling, zoom to surveillance camera			
21:10	Situation room, female analyst	**Offscreen male voice**: "You got visual?" **Female analyst** (overlapping): "coming online."		sound effect for each visual that comes up.
21:11	Screens: banks of surveillance images come up.			sound effect for each visual that comes up.
21:13	Noah and Wills	**Noah**: "Where the hell is he, people?"		
21:15	Station. Zoom to Ross from behind.	[indecipherable voices]		Station chatter throughout
21:17	MS Bourne			Station announcement
21:18	ELS agents running. Whip pan to Ross from behind.	**Bourne**: "Do exactly as I say. Need to move up to your		
21:20	MS Bourne	right. First escalator on the right."		
21:23	MS Ross walking past camera			
21:24	Bourne from behind.			
21:25	LS, agents			
21:27	MS Ross.			
21:28	MS guy standing.			
21:30	MS Ross walking			
21:32	MS Bourne walking			
21:33	LS agent at top of escalator			
21:34	whip pan to different guy coming off of escalator		string trill	
21:37	MS Bourne walking	**Bourne**: "Tie your shoe. Tie your shoe, right now."		
21:38	MS Ross walking	**Ross**: "Shit."		

21:41	MS agent, though at first obscured by crowd.			
21:42	ELS Agent, again obscured by crowd.		Drum hit	
21:45	MS Ross crouching			footsteps
21:48	MS Bourne walking	Bourne: "Wait.		
21:49	MS two agents walking and looking.	Wait.		
21:51	MS Ross crouching from behind.		string trill	
21:52	ELS two agents. Zoom toward end as agents begin to walk.			
21:56	MLS Bourne, whip pan to surveillance camera.	OK, I'm going to walk by you, I want you to move along the far wall		
21:59	MS Ross crouching.	to your left. In		
22:00	RS, CU surveillance camera.	four,		
22:01	MS Bourne	three, two, one—stand		
22:03	MS Ross from behind and above, then picks up Bourne and follows him.	up. That's it."		
22:05	ELS agent in crowd			
22:06	MCU Bourne walking.			
22:07	Situation room. Noah from behind with bank of screens.	[indecipherable voices]		phone ringer. Various office sounds and chatter
22:09	MCU Noah	**Noah**: "Where the hell is he?		
22:09	Whip pan to surveillance cameras on computer screen	We		
22:10	Noah from behind with screens.	cannot afford to lose this		
22:12	MCU Noah	guy, people."		
22:13	ELS Ross, zoom to single out Ross walking.			station announcement

[Continued]

Table 14-2 (*Continued*)

Time Code	Shot Description	Dialogue	Music	Effects
22:14	MS Bourne walking.			Station chatter
22:15	ELS surveillance cameras along wall; pan to show more.			
22:16	MCU Bourne walking.	**Bourne**: "Alright, that line you're on is good.		
22:18	MCU Ross walking, from side.	Stay on that line. Stay		
22:19	MS Ross walking	on that line."		
22:20	ELS trash guy; zoom to MS.			
22:23	MS Ross walking	**Ross**: "Oh, the bin man. I think he's		
22:25	MCU Bourne	one of them."		
22:26	MLS trash guy from Bourne's POV	**Bourne**: "The garbage man?		
22:28	MS Bourne walking, from side.	Negative."		
22:28	MS trash guy	**Ross**: "Oh Jesus, Jesus. He's		
22:30	CU trash guy hand	reaching for something		
22:31	CU Ross	Oh God, he's got a gun,		
22:32	MLS Bourne walking	he's got a gun."		
		Bourne (overlapping): "Stay on the line. Stay on the line your on. Do not deviate."		
22:34	MCU Ross			
22:34	MCU Ross from behind			
22:35	MCU Bourne walking in crowd			
22:36	Whip pan to ELS surveillance cameras. Zoom at end			
22:37	Situation room. Shot of surveillance screen. Zoom on Ross running.			Various office sounds and chatter
22:38	Cheat cut on image.	**Offscreen voice**: "ok [there he is]"		

22:39	MCU Noah	**Noah** (overlapping): "There he is."	
22:40	surveillance images, CU of Ross dominates.	**Wills**: "There he goes.	
22:40	MS Wills	Tell Grab Team A, go."	
22:41	CU Noah	**Noah**: "He's still talking to sombody."	
22:42	2-shot Noah and Wills, then zoom to Wills as he moves.	**Wills**: "Getting instructions. Jimmy, get me the conversation."	
22:44	Analyst in front of screen.	**Analyst**: "Mobile 2, I want subject's [indecipherable]"	
		Wills (overlapping): "Lock the box, lock the box—	
22:46	LS of situation room	move in Grab Team C."	
22:47	Train station. MS two agents walking. Zoom to focus on one until he moves out of frame.		Station chatter
22:49	MS Ross running	**Bourne**: "Hurry, Ross, you gotta move.	Ross breathing.
22:52	MS Ross from behind. LS Bourne	OK, move through this crowd, move	
22:52	MLS Bourne from side and back.	Get under cover right now. Move	
22:54	CU Ross running	through this crowd."	
22:54	MS Asset climbing stairs.		footsteps
22:56	CU Asset's feet coming through door.		footsteps
22:57	CU Asset walking		
22:58	LS Ross walking. Whip pan to agent following.		station chatter
23:02	MS Bourne walking through crowd.		
23:02	CU of agent's hand.		
23:03	MS Bourne walking.	**Bourne**:" Get in the store.	
23:04	MS Ross walking. Agent can be seen pursuing.	There's someone on your tail. Get in the store.	

(Continued)

Table 14-2 (*Continued*)

Time Code	Shot Description	Dialogue	Music	Effects
23:06	ELS crowd. Bourne then steps into frame. Zoom toward end.	You are going to proceed out the east exit. That's to your right		
23:08	Bourne from behind.	as you come into the store."		
23:09	LS Ross, from behind. Agent shown pursuing.			
23:11	CU Ross; agent behind.			
23:11	MS Bourne from behind. Ross passes in front. Bourne intercepts agent.			
23:12	CU Agent's hand.			grunts
23:12	CU Agent's hand.			
23:13	MS Bourne and agent			
23:13	MS Bourne and agent.			
23:15	MS Ross from behind.			
23:16	MCU Bourne from side. Pan to agent, then back to Bourne. Follow Bourne from behind.			
23:19	MCU Bourne	**Bourne**: "Head into the liquor store in front of you		
23:20	Store. Ross enters frame from behind.	Go into the back and lock the door."		
23:22	MS Bourne from side.			
23:24	Situation room. Analyst.	**Analyst**: "Mobile 4 is down."		Various office sounds and chatter
23:25	Noah CU from above and side.			
23:26	screens.	**Noah**: "This guy has got help.		
23:27	MCU Noah	Tell me when the Asset is in the nest."		
23:29	Ross from behind		string trill	station chatter
23:30	Obscured shot. Agents come into frame.			
23:32	store.			door

Time	Shot	Dialogue	Music	Sound
23:33	Bourne from behind. Agents move in background.			
23:34	Agents from behind.			Various office sounds and chatter
23:35	Situation room. MCU Noah and Wills	**Wills**: "Get me a feed in there.		
23:36	Wills from side and below.	I want Grab Team C in there. Tell me what's going on."		
23:40	MS Agents in store.		Bourne theme.	door
23:42	CU Bourne			station chatter
23:42	MS Bourne. Agents pass in front then Bourne and camera follow from behind.			
23:45	MS Bourne walking.			
23:46	LS another agent.	**Agent**: "Team 4's mobile."		
23:48	MS Bourne from behind trailing agents.			
23:49	MCU Bourne from the side.			
23:50	MCU Bourne from opposite side.			door
23:50	MS Ross running		Music changes. Mostly stingers.	footsteps
23:51	MCU Agent			
23:53	MCU Bourne and agent			punches
23:52	MS Ross			
23:54	MS Bourne and agent.			
23:55	MS Bourne			
23:56	MS Ross			
23:57	MS Bourne and agent 2			
23:57	MS agent 2 and Bourne. Whip pan to agent 3			
23:58	MLS Bourne then moves to show agent 3.			
23:58	MS Bourne and agent 3			
23:59	MS Bourne and agent 3 camera moves to show agent 2 as well.			

(Continued)

Table 14-2 (*Continued*)

Time Code	Shot Description	Dialogue	Music	Effects
23:59	MCU Bourne and agents 2 & 3			
24:00	MCU Bourne and agent 2			
24:02	CU Bourne and agent 2			
24:03	CU Bourne and agent 2			
24:04	MS Bourne and agent 2, agent 4 enters through background.			
24:05	CU agent 4			
24:06	MS Bourne agent 2 and 4.			
24:06	CU gun			
24:07	CU Ross from behind. Bourne and agent 2 and 4 in background.			
24:08	MS Bourne and agent 2 and 4			
24:09	MCU Bourne and agent 2. Cut across 180 line.			
24:10	MCU Bourne and agent 2. Cut across 180 line.			
24:12	LS Bourne and agent 2.			
24:17	CU Bourne			
24:20	MS Ross		Music out.	
24:21	MCU Ross from behind, Bourne.			
24:23	CU surveillance camera. Zoom.			
24:24	Wills and Noah from behind. Screen with surveillance image showing Ross and Bourne. Zoom to monitor.			Computer sounds. Typing.
24:27	MCU Noah and Wills	**Noah**: "Jesus Christ. That's Jason Bourne."		

the agents, and Bourne extricating him as the agents close in. The segment ends with Bourne single-handedly taking on and knocking out four agents in a backroom.

Music is minimal at the beginning of this segment for the face-to-face conversation between Bourne and Ross (Figure 14-8). A big drum riff initiates the passage through the station, which is all accompanied with agitated music as Bourne uses a cell phone to direct Ross. Although drawing on the action theme at several points, the music is primarily gestural rather than thematic, punctuating the action and underscoring the rising tension as the agents close in on Ross. Diegetic sounds, many offscreen, are prevalent on the soundtrack and, along with the handheld camera work and rapid cutting, add to the disorienting feeling of the chase. The fight in the backroom concludes the segment, and though music continues until Bourne pistol-whips the last agent, sound effects dominate the fight.

This segment is the most intense of the Waterloo Station sequence, and its treatment is characteristic of a contemporary action sequence in terms of music: repetitive musical rhythms, often with a percussion-based groove but lacking in strong melodic contours, provide energetic continuity. Sound effects, especially offscreen, serve to create a frenetic, frenzied world on the one hand and to produce an aural spectacle of violence on the other. Because the Waterloo Station sequence is structured primarily as a chase, the violence, however, is confined to short bursts when Bourne stealthily takes out agents and the one sustained (but still brief) fight with the four agents in the backroom. Most contemporary action sequences, even chases, feature far more combat than we find here, and so most action sequences will emphasize the sound of punches, gunshots, crashes, and explosions. Dialogue also plays a larger role here than is typical because the scene is structured around Bourne's attempt (and ultimate failure) to steer Ross away from action.

Figure 14-8. *The Bourne Ultimatum* (2007). Conversation between Bourne and Ross.

JOHEUNNOM NABBEUNNOM ISANGHANNOM (THE GOOD, THE BAD, THE WEIRD), THREE ACTION SEQUENCES

An amusing albeit violent remake of Sergio Leone's classic spaghetti western *Il buono, il brutto, il cattivo* (The Good, the Bad, and the Ugly, 1966), *Joheunnom Nabbeunnom Isanghannom* (2008) is an inventive Korean action film. The film commands a large range of international cinematic references, it is purposefully anachronistic (and music participates in this anachronism) in ways that play into a fantasy register that make it difficult to place the film in time or space, and its humor and cartoonish violence are intertwined in provocative ways that recall the best aspects of Quentin Tarantino's work. The film features many action sequences, some with overt cheat cuts to evoke low-budget martial arts films, others spectacularly staged and cleverly choreographed.

The Shootout in the Ghost Market is one of the more elaborate action sequences. The set-up consists of Man-gil (Seung-soo Ryu), a friend of Yoon Tae-goo (the Weird), being taken prisoner and severely beaten and cut up by Park Chang-yi (the Bad; Byung-hun Lee). This segment plays without music, with ambient rain in the background, and the sound effects emphasize the damage of hits and knife cuts to the body.

As Chang-yi attempts to chop off one of Man-gil's fingers, a shot rings out, announcing the arrival of Park Do-won (the Good; Woo-sung Jung) and Tae-goo (Kang-ho Song), which initiates the second segment of the sequence. Do-won and Tae-goo ride through the market, firing on Chang-yi's gang. Although the reports of the gunfire are the most important element of the sound track for most of this segment, the damage of the bullets is also given attention, especially when they hit bodies, as are initially the sounds of Do-won's horse and Tae-goo's motorcycle. The action also frequently stops for dialogue, especially between Do-won and Tae-goo. Music, usually a percussion groove, enters occasionally during the sequence to accompany spectacles like Do-won flying through the air (Figure 14-9). Music grows increasingly frequent and extended as the sequence goes on, but much of the sequence plays with only sound effects and the persistent ambient sound of rain.

Music in this sequence serves primarily to emphasize significant action. The frequent pauses in the shootout where characters wait and reflect on the situation do not use music, even to sustain the tension. In this sequence music belongs to action, not to suspense.

Other action scenes in the film use music much more extensively. Both the train robbery at the beginning of the film and the big chase across the desert plain near the end, for instance, deploy music across multiple lines of action. For the train robbery, the music is also highly eclectic, moving through a series of very disparate exotic musical topics, including Mexican, various oriental, Middle-Eastern, and North African topics, a pop-inspired number and variable scoring ranging from ethnic instruments, voices, and ensembles to synthesizers and even a symphony orchestra. The whole is highly disorienting, but in an amusing and charming rather than incoherent way.

Figure 14-9. *Joheunnom Nabbeunnom Isanghannom* (The Good, the Bad, the Weird, 2008). Do-won flies through the air.

In the chase across the desert, music is omnipresent and used more consistently than in the train robbery. It serves to establish the setting of a grand, epic conflict among primal forces—that is, until the Japanese army shows up and begins firing. Music refuses to accompany the action of the Japanese army, and unlike the epic quality of the chase to that point, the focus of the sound track now splits between registering the Japanese guns on the one hand and the bullets ripping through flesh on the other. Music returns only with fantasy: when Do-won single-handedly and successfully attacks the Japanese army, breaking their formation.

Joheunnom Nabbeunnom Isanghannom differs from the other action films we have considered in often attending to and registering the sound of violence on the body. These sounds of bodily violence are not necessarily loud or prominent, although they can be when someone is punched or sent crashing through a window, and these sounds are not (just) the screams of a consciousness suffering pain. Rather, bullets or knives ripping through flesh are treated as significant inasmuch as they are the mundane (rather than inflated) sounds of physical damage; and to register them is to remind us that violence need not roar to be lethal. As we noted in Chapter 12, such sounds of mundane bodily violence have become familiar in war films, where they are associated with a kind of existential terror of random and seemingly meaningless death, but Hollywood action films have not much embraced these sounds except in physical hand-to-hand combat, where the power of the punch coincides with violence of the hit, so that the sound effect serves as an index of the physical damage of the blow.

GRAVITY

Although lacking in the combat and the sharply defined villain usually associated with the action film genre, *Gravity* (2013) is structured like an action film, with episodes of intense and dangerous action motivated by a strong causal chain—here, literally driven by the force of gravity—and a heroine struggling mightily to master that chain so she can escape her predicament. The film centers on an inexperienced astronaut Ryan Stone (Sandra Bullock), who opens the film securely tethered to the mechanical arm of a space shuttle as she attempts to fix a computer board on the Hubble Space Telescope. She is initially portrayed as essentially passive, suffering from motion sickness and wholly uncomfortable and clumsy moving in space. Her contrary and soon-to-be mentor is Matt Kowalski (George Clooney), who uses a jet pack to playfully and effortlessly move freely around space. When a botched attempt to destroy a spy satellite causes a chain reaction that sends a debris field hurtling toward the shuttle, Ryan is slow to respond. The first action sequence occurs as the debris reaches the shuttle with Ryan still attached to the shuttle's arm (around 11:45).

The sound track to this point had focused on layering background radio chatter with conversations among the astronauts, the shuttle pilot, and the NASA control center, the talk all filtered to sound like radio transmissions and spread among the various channels of the mix. After a brief title sequence that featured a disquieting crescendo ending with a negative stinger synchronized with the first shot of space, music is absent, aside from some brief diegetic country music played by Matt, until Ryan and Matt admire the view, accompanied by ambient synthesizer music, which fades out when they return to work.

Music enters again when NASA control abruptly aborts the mission because the debris field is approaching. Initially sounding like a low growling string tone, the music becomes increasingly electronic, distorted, and unstable as it moves around the stereo field with the background chatter from radios adding to the intensifying effect. When the debris reaches the space around the shuttle, the pitch of the music rises and its tempo quickens considerably. It also adds hints of agitated string figurations that suggest a hurry topic, but they are fragmented, electronically processed, and distributed around the surround field, adding to the confusion.

A musical stinger—really more of an extended zap—marks a piece of debris hitting another astronaut, and when debris strikes the shuttle, sending it spinning, the music responds with a deeper, more hollow-sounding tone (and the music seems for a brief moment slightly less frenetic). The music also adds a new synthetic element that moves through the stereo field loosely synchronized to the rotational speed of the shuttle. The mechanical arm holding Ryan hits another piece of debris, severing the arm from the shuttle and sending her tumbling into space, and the music resumes its previous frenetic pace. The synthetic element is again synchronized to her new rotational speed, and Matt's voice, fading in and out, moves around the stereo field. This continues until Ryan manages to separate from the arm, at which point Matt's voice stabilizes briefly in the center speaker and music recedes into the background as Ryan tumbles alone into the distance (Figure 14-10). The sequence returns to Ryan, as she loses radio contact, and the sound focuses on her breathing and desperate attempts to orient herself and reestablish contact, until she drifts off into space, the music slowly diminishing as her figure recedes into the black screen.

Figure 14-10. *Gravity* (2013). Ryan tumbles into space.

Throughout this sequence, music serves in the place of most of the sound effects, because the debris in space makes no sound as it rips through the parts of the shuttle. Music is in essence performing the function of rendering this impossible sound, relating how the experience feels rather than how it sounds. Underscoring feeling has, of course, long been a common function of film music, but in this case the music seems to mimic the wild kinetic energy of the lethal objects much more than any subject's inner emotional life. That is, the music synchronizes to the movement of the objects rather than to the body except insofar as the body is itself moved by these objects and so set, as an object among objects, within the causal chain of the gravitational force. Everything in the sequence tends to dispersion and entropy, and Ryan's passivity integrates her into this field of objects. She will spend the remainder of the film learning how to act: to use the causal chain of gravity to extract her body from the gravitational pull of the passive object and to return to Earth born anew and able to stand, literally, on her own. (As is often the case with action films, *Gravity* is not at all subtle with its metaphors.) It is only at the end of the film, as Ryan, back on Earth after an emergency reentry, struggles to gain her footing, stand, and then walk that an articulate theme appears and plays into the end titles.

CONCLUSIONS

A common criticism of the action film is that it is a mindless mélange of arresting sounds and kinetic images but that the parts are largely interchangeable. One action sequence can substitute for another, and although the particulars of a scene may advance the plot in clever ways, the situation rarely bears consequences for the archetypal hero, who always simply discovers who he (or she) already is. The conventional score for the action film, with a theme prepared for the hero and literally trumpeted over the titles, reinforces this conception: the theme does not develop, it simply is; and the score uses the narrative situation of the action sequence as a more or less novel setting for the theme to assure us that the hero's identity is not threatened by the action, which is thereby exposed as inconsequential.

Recent action films seem less interested in action heroes who enter their films as archetypes, as fully formed but hardly human characters and virtuosically negotiate situations but are not changed by the action. If action heroes today remain compelled to act, action is the means of their becoming and self-realization; and identity, insofar as the concept is retained as something more than a name for a certain body, belongs to the action, not to the being. One consequence of this shift in emphasis has been the rise of a scoring practice focused on gesture and tone rather than theme, which if one emerges does so at the end of a narrative progression, the articulate result of a series of meaningful actions, rather than being present from the beginning.

The body acts and the body feels; and it becomes what it is by virtue of moving and being moved. But separating action and affect, especially to stabilize identity along an axis of active and passive, misconstrues the power of fantasy and the fantasy of power that lie at the root of the genre's appeal and account for the essential place violence holds in these films. If sound effects mainly register the movement of things—the moment something explodes into action—and music registers the emotion of beings (whether of a character, an external narrator, or the audience), then rendering confuses and crosses them in interesting and provocative ways, and the systemic blurring of music and effects so characteristic of the genre elevates rendering to a principle of stylization that harnesses but also exposes the violent play between fantasy and power.

Two Versions of a Jane Austen Novel: *Bridget Jones's Diary* and *Pride & Prejudice*

The benchmark for romantic novels of the past two centuries, Jane Austen's *Pride & Prejudice* lurks in the background of many romantic comedy films as well. And, of course, a number of film versions of the novel itself have been made over the years, the best known being the 6-hour BBC production for television (1995). Since 2000, two quite different feature films have offered new interpretations of this venerable novel. The first, *Bridget Jones's Diary* (2001), is a contemporary parody based on Helen Fielding's novel of the same name. The plot is still centered on the heroine (played by Renee Zellweger), who tries to maneuver her life around 30-something social and personal issues while—like Austen's Elizabeth Bennet—dealing with two possible lovers, one willing but deceitful (Daniel Cleaver, played by Hugh Grant), the other decent but aloof (Mark Darcy, played by Colin Firth). The heroine's sisters, an important element in Austen's story, are replaced by a chatty and overly helpful group of friends. Joe Wright's *Pride & Prejudice* (2005), on the other hand, is a historical costume drama that maintains the details of the novel's plot and characters but carries out the work in a distinctive and stylized manner—that is to say, it is clearly the work of an auteur director. Both films make effective use of montage scenes, and it is those we will concentrate on here.

In recent decades it has become common to structure a montage as the visual accompaniment to a recorded song (usually nondiegetic and usually very much in the aural foreground, even if on occasion diegetic clues are offered, such as a radio or television at the beginning or just before the montage starts). The consistent beat, voice, and instrumentation, as well as the highly predictable designs and even lengths of popular songs make them excellent devices to structure a montage sequence. In the following examples, the song fades out before it ends, which makes for a smooth transition; a stronger (but possibly more problematic) formal articulation is achieved with a complete song. Using a song performance, as a diegetic performance or as an apparently diegetic music coming from radio or phonograph, to help structure a scene or subscene was already a relatively common device in the classical era. Once popular music began to be used more commonly as nondiegetic music, the function was transferred there as well, making the use for montage both convincing and practical.

Two montage scenes in *Bridget Jones's Diary* use this technique. Of these two, the one in the film's last major sequence is the more straightforward and conventional (1:23:19, DVD ch. 16). Bridget is on a train back to London, having humiliated herself by opening her heart to Mark Darcy and then making a foolish and emotional speech in front of everyone at his parents' anniversary party.

The montage begins with the train ride, over which we hear the introduction to the song, "Out of Reach" (written and performed by Gabrielle) (see Figure 14-11).

Figure 14-11. *Bridget Jones's Diary* (2001). Second montage.

a	b
c	d

The scene changes at the verse, as Bridget, still in a deflated mood, arrives at her apartment. The verse continues as we see Darcy's arrival in New York, his face marked with regret and uncertainty, and the music moves into the first part of the chorus. In the middle of this chorus, cut to Bridget taking out her frustrations by writing in her diary. A single line of the second verse, with its lyrics about despair and drowning, overlaps with a cut to Bridget, dejected, eating out of a jar. Just before the last line, "I know I will be ok," she answers the apartment buzzer: her relentlessly cheerful friends come up to the apartment as the song fades out in the middle of the second chorus. Throughout, lyrics and melody match the mood, which is that of Bridget, emotionally spent and resigned.

In an earlier montage (46:15, DVD ch. 9), Bridget is devastated upon learning that the man she has been dating, her boss Daniel, is in fact engaged to another woman. The montage begins as Bridget decides to write him off and become her own person. During the introduction of "I'm Every Woman," Bridget downs some vodka, passes out, and goes into a dream-like flashback of her time with Daniel. Then, as the first chorus begins, a series of shots shows her attempts at turning over a new leaf as she throws out her empty liquor bottles and a pile of books on how to attract men; she begins exercising, replaces the discarded books with others on empowering women, and looks in the classified ads for a new job.

Through most of the first verse (which follows the chorus here), we see shots of Bridget tumbling off her exercise bike but thereafter walking confidently across a London bridge. The latter part of the montage shifts emphases in the sound track because the dialogue can be heard over the music. During the final lines of the first verse, music fades considerably, and we see the first of three job interviews; this continues through the repeat of the chorus. The second interview starts with the second verse, and music is still low behind the dialogue. The third interview starts with the last line of the second verse and continues over the chorus, which fades out before finishing.

Joe Wright's *Pride & Prejudice* (2005) includes several "out of time" sequences that can be understood as actualizing something in the heroine Elizabeth's imagination. Of these, one is a traditional montage. Two others might be labeled "fantasy montage" as they combine irrational, dream-like elements with the time-distorting devices of montage.

The traditional montage sequence is an attractive variant of the classic "passage-of-time" montage: it shows Elizabeth (Keira Knightley) sitting on a swing and slowly twirling around as the seasons pass, from late November to April. The scene is framed by her friend Charlotte (Claudie Blakley), who challenges Elizabeth for doubting Charlotte's decision to accept a particular suitor. Elizabeth is taken aback, Charlotte leaves, and Elizabeth is left to reflect. She turns slowly in the swing and the camera mimics her point of view as it pans her surroundings in a rapid circular motion. As the fall harvest, winter rains, and early spring renewal pass by her eyes, Elizabeth contemplates the changes in her own life. With spring arrived, the scene ends as she is invited to visit Charlotte's house and she seems grateful for the opportunity. Music in a reflective, contemplative mood accompanies the scene throughout, covering over the all-too-obvious gaps in time and the several cuts. Also corresponding to the method of the classic montage, the music overlaps into the first moments of Elizabeth's arrival at Charlotte's home before it fades out under dialogue. The sound track, however, is complicated by another layer: a voice-over of Elizabeth's reading a letter to Charlotte, accepting her invitation to visit and catching up on news. The scene closes with the reconciling embrace of Charlotte and Elizabeth upon her arrival. Thus, the scene includes (and overlaps) three levels of passage of time: the immediate experience of Elizabeth's reverie, the passing seasons in the background, and the narration of the letter.

The first of the two fantasy montage sequences we will discuss occurs earlier in the film, during the extended Netherfield ball scene, after Darcy (Matthew MacFadyen) asks Elizabeth to dance. She surprises herself by accepting (her sharply negative opinion of him had been formed by his boorishly arrogant behavior during an earlier evening of dancing). In the foreground of two lines of dancers, Elizabeth and Darcy converse awkwardly as the dance begins. A series of visual and aural cues in this scene begins very subtly but mounts toward a decisive disruption of physical space and time: the other dancers are (mostly) in the background, they are in soft focus (or slightly out of focus), and none of them is heard or even depicted as speaking (despite the fact that conversation during country dancing was not only common but expected). The isolation of the couple from the remaining dancers is further emphasized when they stop on the dance floor in a tense verbal exchange, and the dance continues behind and around them; this effect is then taken to its extreme as the other dancers are eliminated from the scene, and Elizabeth and Darcy continue to dance in an emptied room.

Instead of a band of musicians who play for dancing elsewhere in the film, this dance features a solo violin, a sound that reinforces the idea of the couple in their own time and space, but, as the emotional connection between Darcy and Elizabeth advances, more and more instruments are added, as if in an audio dissolve, until a full string orchestra sound is achieved as they finish the dance alone (Figure 14-12). The scene closes as the proper diegesis abruptly returns, the pair bow to each other, and the dance ends.

The second fantasy montage scene is essentially a classical passage-of-time montage, but it is made more complex by layering different levels of time and by superimposing these layers visually. Still visiting Charlotte, Elizabeth reflects on a disastrous first proposal from Darcy and his subsequent letter in which he tries to explain himself. Early in the day Elizabeth is aimless, sitting on her bed, wandering through the hall, glancing at a book; she looks out the window and then stares at herself in a mirror, deep in thought. The light streaming in from the window to her left shifts and changes as day turns to night. The scene becomes dream-like in the dark room: Darcy's voice is heard above a melody in the cello and he appears behind Elizabeth to deposit a letter; she does not react to his presence. Darcy is seen riding away outside, the music continuing as before. Charlotte suddenly appears in daylight, and the scene and music end abruptly

Figure 14-12. *Pride & Prejudice* (2009). Elizabeth and Mr. Darcy dance in a fantasy space.

and unresolved as she speaks to Elizabeth. Four temporal strands overlap here: the compression of passing time in Elizabeth's reverie; the sequence of Darcy's entry, departure, and voice; the implicit time of Elizabeth's reading Darcy's letter; and the actual time emphasized by Charlotte's appearance and voice. The music plays to Elizabeth's reverie, rather than Darcy's actions or the diegetic reality, the score both compressing and suspending time.

The montages in *Bridget Jones's Diary* are traditional passage-of-time figures unified by a nondiegetic popular song recording. In general, romantic comedies tend to be conservative in their treatment of design and in their handling of narrative. *Pride & Prejudice* is also a romantic comedy in the broadest sense that it has a happy ending (the ancient meaning of "comedy," opposed to tragedy), but as we have seen, certain of its stylized elements take on an almost dreamlike quality. Not really point of view of the individual (which the first montage of the swing certainly is), the two fantasy montages are most easily construed as point of view of the couple—shared private experience—and introduce an element of strangeness into the familiar movement of the novel's plot. Wright fulfils the promise of these montages in the film's ending, where Darcy and Elizabeth are finally reconciled not on a daytime walk with others (as in the novel), but early in the morning as they find each other walking alone.

Writing about Film Music
Interpretation

Introduction

In Chapters 6 and 8, we explored the writing of scene analyses and the short papers we called "screening reports." These exercises were concerned mainly with describing how the sound track of a film works. The descriptive language was for the most part put to analytical use to show how the elements of the sound track interact with one another and with the image track to produce particular filmic effects. The goal of the writing—and the bias of interpretation in the thesis statements—was to draw attention to the basic materials of the sound track and to the ways a particular film organizes and uses its materials. In Chapter 12, we extended these techniques to constructing a historical argument.

In this final chapter, we are concerned with developing a critical essay. This type of writing seeks to put observations about a film to a specifically interpretive end—that is, to uncover how a film organizes its meanings and to evaluate the results. The objective is to draw the sound track and music firmly into a thematic reading of a film, especially a reading that shows how these elements support or resist the dominant directions or emphases of the narrative. The critical essay relies primarily on research information gathered by watching a film and making notes on the action, characters, sound track, and music (exactly the same kind of information that formed the core of the screening report). In its most basic form, the critical essay resembles a "long" or more detailed response paper that will typically run to 1,500 to 2,000 words (or six to eight double-spaced pages). A closer focus on argumentation is necessary, however, because the critical essay will be making a case for a particular way of "reading" or understanding a film.

Review of Previous Steps Using *Catch Me If You Can*

To develop the material needed to write a critical essay, we will apply it to *Catch Me If You Can*, the contemporary mainstream Hollywood feature film that we discussed in the general introduction and in Part I. Here we produce a screening report that is inflected toward interpretation and critical evaluation.

1. SYNOPSIS

(1) Directed by Steven Spielberg, *Catch Me If You Can* (2002) tells the story of Frank Abagnale, Jr. (Leonardo DiCaprio), who runs away from home rather than face the trauma of his parents' divorce and his father's (Christopher Walken) slow financial ruin. Frank is a risk-taker, who discovers that he has innate talent for imitating professionals (airline pilots, doctors, and lawyers), and he develops great skill in forging checks. The story, told mostly in flashbacks, is about FBI agent Carl Hanratty's (Tom Hanks) campaign to capture Frank, who spends several years in prison; but eventually Carl persuades the FBI to hire Frank to solve check forgery cases. Aside from the flashbacks, the storytelling is generally straightforward rather than ambitious, and the sound track follows suit in being dominated by speech and music. (131 words)

This was the synopsis we generated in Chapter 3 and which might serve as the basis for a screening report. Notice, however, that the thesis statement is not like that expected of a screening report—in fact, it is pretty much the opposite: instead of looking for a distinctive feature to draw out, describe, and interpret, this thesis statement emphasizes the routine or conventional quality of the film's narrative and the sound track's complicity in it.

1A. RUNTIME SEGMENTATION

See Table 15-1 for a listing of music in *Catch Me If You Can*. The musical themes named in the table are given in Figures 15-1, 15-2, and 15-3. Note that this table only lists the music; it does not include the listing of sequences and acts we would expect of a complete runtime segmentation.

Figure 15-1. *Catch Me If You Can* (2002). Main theme. (Transcription from the sound track.)

Figure 15-2. *Catch Me If You Can.* Frank's theme. (Transcription from the sound track.)

Figure 15-3. *Catch Me If You Can.* Frank's father's theme. (Transcription from the sound track.)

Table 15-1 *Catch Me If You Can.* Music cues.

DVD Track	Scene (Titles in Square Brackets Are from the Sound Track CD)	Timings and Notes
1	Main title sequence ["Catch Me If You Can" theme (Figure 15-1)]	Out 00:03:00. Alternating thirds theme; visual and musical imitation of graphics-based main-title sequences from 1950s–1960s movies; jazz orchestrations mixed with traditional orchestra
1	Song behind *To Tell the Truth* introduction	In 00:03:10; out 00:04:15. "To Tell": Paul Alter and Robert Israel
3	Dance music on phonograph "Embraceable You"	In at 00:11:00 with close-up of phonograph; out 00:12:42 with cut. "Embraceable": Gershwin, sung by Judy Garland
3	Sad music for the move from house to apartment (saxophone solo)	In at 00:16:00; out 00:18:30 under chimes. Shifts mood near the end when Frank is given book of checks—intimation of Frank's theme
4	Phonograph (offscreen; mother and male visitor)—brief: "Put Your Head on My Shoulder"	In at 00:22:50. "Put Your Head": Paul Anka
5–6	He runs from divorce [A Broken Home]; cut to Paris; into Chapter 6 for first check scam	In at 00:26:40; out 00:28:55 with cut to Paris; in again at 00:29:20; out 00:32:55
7–8	He fakes co-pilot (Frank's theme—upper register, undulating [Deadheading] (Figure 15-2)	In at 00:35:00; out in ch. 8 at 00:38:30
8–9	Plane trip (Frank's theme; second section is [The Float])	In at 00:39:45 out 00:040:50; in again at 00:041:15; out in ch. 9 with FBI at 00:42:55

(Continued)

Table 15-1 *(Continued)*

DVD Track	Scene (Titles in Square Brackets Are from the Sound Track CD)	Timings and Notes
9–10	Several pieces in a row: Low-volume neutral diegetic piano music in background under restaurant scene with Frank and father; quick cut to FBI car (big band on radio); to hotel in Hollywood (phonograph? "The Girl From Ipanema"); "Catch Me" theme; Frank escapes	In at 00:44:25; out 00:55:40—Music is continuous; "Girl" enters at 00:51:30, to underscoring ("Catch Me" theme) at 00:52:40; out briefly, back in at 00:55:00. Neutral piano music is "Body and Soul," John Green et al., perf. Errol Garner; "I've Got the World on a String," Harold Arlen, perf. Teddy Wilson. Car radio is "Take the A Train," Billy Strayhorn. "Girl" credits are Antonio Carlos Jobim, performed by Jobim with Stan Getz and Joao Gilberto.
11	"James Bond" sound track in theater; then "The Look of Love" and visual joke with Hanratty in laundromat	In at 00:57:44; "Look" at 00:58:40; out 00:59:45; back in at 01:00:00; segue to next cue. "Bond": Monty Norman. "Look": Burt Bacharach, sung by Dusty Springfield
12	Hanratty and Frank on phone with song ["Mele Kalikimaka"] on radio; cut to restaurant and radio: "He's So Fine"; at word "Flash," the "Catch Me" theme	In at 01:03:30; to underscoring at 01:05:45 (Frank's father's theme [Figure 15-3]); very briefly radio and underscoring together, then to restaurant at 01:06:30; "Flash" at 01:07:02; out 01:07:45. "Molo": Alex Anderson, perf. Bing Crosby. "He's so fine": Ronald Mack
13	"Catch Me" theme (short)	In at 01:09:25; segue
13	Party in Atlanta (rock and roll) "You Really Got Me"	In at 01:10:00; out about 01:10:50. "You Really": Ray Davies
13	Doctor (Frank's theme)	In at 01:13:20; out 01:15:20
13	Father and Hanratty ("Catch Me" theme)	In at 01:19:10; out 01:19:55
13–14	Engaged (Frank's theme changes to "Catch Me" with FBI); Mozart behind dinner with Brenda's family; cut to hospital office ("Catch Me" theme); Frank (Frank's theme)	In at 01:21:05; Mozart at 01:22:20; "Catch Me" at 01:24:50, then back to Mozart; out at 01:27:40 with cut to bar exam. Mozart is the slow movement from Piano Concerto no. 11 in D major
14–15	Frank becomes a lawyer; family watches TV (Mitch Miller: "Anybody Here Seen Kelly?") and phonograph (reprise of "Embraceable You"), continues under meeting of father and son in bar, then "The Way You Look Tonight"; underscoring briefly after father says "You can't stop"; Frank calls Hanratty (lush orchestral setting of "I'll Be Home for Christmas"—recorded, in hotel bar)	In at 01:28:55; lawyer out 01:30:35; then family at TV; "Embraceable" at 01:34:30; "You can't stop" at 01:35:40; phone call at 01:36:00; out 01:37:50. "The Way": Jerome Kern. "I'll be home": Walter Kent

16–17	Background music for engagement party ("I Can't Give You Anything but Love, Baby"; then "I'm Shooting High"); to underscoring, Frank escapes, at 1:44:15 segue to airport (Frank's theme)	In at 01:38:15, to underscoring at 01:42:05; out 01:45:45. "I Can't" and "I'm Shooting": Jimmy McHugh
17	Brief underscoring	01:46:20.
17	Brief diegetic music: "Leaving on a Jet Plane"	01:47:05. "Leaving": John Denver
17	Background voice with piano "Come Fly with Me"	In at 01:47:25; out 01:49:35 under noise of plane taking off (song synchronized to end with scene)
18–19	Hanratty thinks; goes to printer; cut to children's choir in France, then low bass and percussion sounds in printing building	In at 01:50:35; at 01:51:50 "Catch Me"; choir in at 01:52:50, out about 01:53:15; choir in near the end at 01:56:30; out at 01:57:48 with return to the plane. "Angels We Have Heard on High." (Choir credits read "Los angos danos nos campagnos" and "Peuple fideles")
19	After Hanratty says "your father is dead"— theme from divorce scene; "Christmas Song" at mother's house, continues as Frank is placed in jail cell	In at 01:59:00; out at about 2:00:00; song at 2:01:05; out 02:03:40. "The Christmas Song: Mel Tormé, sung by Nat King Cole (song synchronized to end with scene)
20	Frank arrives at FBI office	In at 02:07:10; out 02:09:10
21	FBI Monday morning; music based on Frank's theme; end credits feature "Catch Me"	In at 02:12:25; out 02:13:35; in again at 02:14:10, and into end credits at 02:15:45; ends at 02:20:17.

2. GENERAL DESCRIPTION AND EVALUATION OF THE SOUND TRACK ELEMENTS AND THEIR BALANCE

(2a) This is a sound track dominated by speech and music. Sound effects occasionally play a role (more so in the first part than later), but much of the story takes place indoors in sound-deadened institutional environments. Furthermore, the plot is advanced in considerable part through conversation: Frank's family becomes dysfunctional, Frank tries to maintain his relationship with his father, Frank talks with people to gain information he needs to talk his way through his scams, Carl talks to agents and to Frank as the FBI works through its case. Relatively speaking, the music track is also quite active: music is present in roughly 90 of the film's 141 minutes, although it is only foregrounded on a few occasions. With the conventional exceptions of the main-title cue and end-credits composition, the nondiegetic orchestral music is not foregrounded; it is songs that sometimes receive this treatment, whether they are obviously diegetic (or even a performance, as in the case of the Mitch Miller sing-along), uncertainly diegetic, or nondiegetic.

The evaluation is at the beginning: a short statement of opinion about the effectiveness of the sound track that summarizes it in terms of a satisfying acoustic experience and in terms of success in contributing to the narrative. Our description carries an implied criticism: "This is a sound track dominated by speech and music. Sound effects occasionally play a role. . . ." We could ground a critical essay in an explicit complaint about an over-reliance on speech and music—the under-utilized effects track shortchanges suspense elements in the film, forcing more work onto music, which results in a somewhat romanticized effect overall (an effect considerably exaggerated by the many nostalgic song quotations). We might also connect our evaluation of the sound track with evaluative statements made by film critics. Our complaint about the routine and conventional nature of the sound track fits very well, for example, with Roger Ebert's summary opinion: "This is not a major Spielberg film, although it is an effortlessly watchable one. Spielberg and his writer . . . don't force matters or plumb for deep significance. The story is a good story, directly told, and such meaning as it has comes from the irony that the only person who completely appreciates Abagnale's accomplishments is the man trying to arrest him."[1]

(2b) Music is about equally divided between original orchestral music and reuses, and it passes freely among musical styles and the diegetic and non-diegetic spheres. John Williams's music, which is scored for a small traditional orchestra whose prominent saxophone solos suggest jazz colorings, is heavily dependent on recurrences of three themes: "Catch Me If You Can," the Father's Theme, and Frank's theme. These uniformly function empathetically. The reuses are more complex: (1) simple diegetic cues anchored in their physical spaces by onscreen radios and phonographs; (2) truly neutral diegetic background(ed) music; (3) apparently diegetic cues that continue, at the same volume, through two or even three scenes; and (4) strongly foregrounded non-diegetic cues (such as "Come Fly with Me"). Most of the reuses also serve a definable narrative function—confirming a venue (a diner, an elegant hotel dining room, a mid-60s youth party in an upscale house), acting as the pure code of performance, making culturally coded references to musical styles and genres, and establishing associations within the film (as with the reappearance of "Embraceable You" and the recurring trope of popular Christmas songs, but more often through references in the lyrics or song titles: "Embraceable You" for the two moments when Frank's mother dances; "Come Fly with Me" and "Leaving on a Jet Plane" for Frank's last aerial escape; "I Can't Give You Anything But Love, Baby," when Frank tells his fiancée the truth about himself; etc.).

3. CONCLUSION

(3) The under-utilized effects track shortchanges suspense elements in the film, forcing more work onto the music, a situation that results in a somewhat romanticized effect overall (considerably exaggerated, of course, by the many nostalgic song quotations). Overall, the sound track (and its music) are treated in

an effective but routine and conventional manner, a conclusion that seems to be consistent with Roger Ebert's summary opinion of *Catch Me If You Can*: "This is not a major Spielberg film, although it is an effortlessly watchable one. Spielberg and his writer . . . don't force matters or plumb for deep significance. The story is a good story, directly told, and such meaning as it has comes from the irony that the only person who completely appreciates Abagnale's accomplishments is the man trying to arrest him."[2]

For the conclusion, we drew material out of the comments to step (2) above. The entire essay—that is, paragraphs (1), (2a), (2b), and (3)—is just under 700 words, or within the range of a screening report. Since we have already twisted it in the direction of an interpretive paper, it would be easy to expand into a critical essay.

Before going ahead, a reminder of the warning at the end of Chapter 8: *always* go back and double-check information you write up from memory. As a cautionary example, one of us wrote about the "Christmas Song" scene in *Catch Me If You Can* for Chapter 3, under the heading "counterpoint." A draft version of this text was written from memory of classroom viewing and discussion about 4 months earlier. Memory dictated that all shots but one were from the outside of the house and that the music came from a phonograph visible in the background. Neither of these things is true, and both are significant errors that could result in poorly grounded interpretations of this scene.

Note on the Compare/Contrast Paper

All the possibilities for a compare/contrast paper that we suggested in Chapters 10 and 12 could apply equally well here. For example, you might write a paper that compares *Catch Me If You Can* with another recent film having a score by John Williams, your goal being to articulate common treatment or differences in terms of music's role in the sound track and its narrative functions. (This would be a more descriptive paper in the manner of the screening report.) You can also argue, if you choose, that one film is better suited to Williams's style and methods. (This is more plainly interpretive or critical.) Another possibility would be to make an historical comparison with a Williams score for a similar film—perhaps another dramatic coming-of-age film such as *The Empire of the Sun* (1987). In this case, you might choose to focus on the development of—changes or improvements over time in—Williams's practice. Still another possibility, of course, is to adopt Martin Marks's device of comparing two recent films with scores by different composers (recall *Casablanca* and *The Maltese Falcon* from Chapter 8). It is usually best to use his criteria, too: the films and their scores should show some strong commonalities, so that comparison has a plausible basis—it would be difficult to make much out of a comparison between, for example, *Catch Me If You Can* and *The Lord of the Rings* (2001–2003).

Developing a Reading (1): Finding a Thesis
THESIS OPTIONS FOR *CATCH ME IF YOU CAN*

A thesis is an idea that we want our reader to find true, correct, or plausible thanks to the examples and arguments that we provide in the body of the paper. To arrive at a thesis, ask yourself questions related to your own interest in the film: "What do I find intriguing or disturbing about the film? What broad narrative theme(s) does the film explore? What makes the film noteworthy, in my opinion? Does it illustrate some aspect of filmmaking with special clarity? Does it have an unusual effect on the viewer?"[3] To this list, we can add questions that are directed specifically to film sound, "Are sound track and image track balanced in their effects? How do music and sound influence narrative (through styles, leitmotifs, or empathetic/anempathetic cueing)? Does music—or sound in general—have any subversive effects on narrative?"

In general, the thesis of a critical essay needs to relate to a narrative theme of the film. In the case of *Catch Me If You Can*, one of the primary themes of the film concerns counterfeiting—Frank's talent for passing not only bad checks but for presenting himself as having professional credentials he did not actually earn. A strong interpretative thesis would link the sound track to this theme (or some other). For instance, you might explore how Frank's uncertain professional status relates to the frequently uncertain diegetic status of the music. Another tack might be to consider how, if at all, the sound track differentiates between Frank's reality and his deceptions and what that might tell us about Frank's level of self-understanding. The body of the essay, then, marshals evidence and arguments in favor of the chosen thesis. It is customary to end an essay with a confirming restatement of the thesis, perhaps in a way that casts the thesis in a new light.

Leitmotifs and, more generally, sound motifs also offer good entry points for interpreting a sound track. In the Introduction to Part I, we discussed the scene where Carl receives a call from Frank on Christmas Eve. We noted that at the end of this scene, nondiegetic music appears that was originally associated with Frank's feelings for his father. The recurrence of this music suggests a transference of affection from father to Carl—at the end of the film Carl will assume this father function overtly when he sponsors Frank's social rehabilitation. This connection is strengthened by Bing Crosby's "Mele Kalikimaka" heard on the radio at the beginning of the scene. As we pointed out in our earlier discussion, Christmas music is an important aural motif in the film. Carl and Frank tend to be in contact around Christmas, so this music serves as a temporal marker emphasizing this fact. Yet the motif also plays on the notion that Christmas is a time for family. When Frank, having escaped one last time from the FBI, stands outside his mother's house to the sounds of Nat King Cole's "The Christmas Song," he seems to recognize that he has no place in this family; he asks Carl to put him in the car before his mother has a chance to see him. The parallel use of the Christmas music in these two scenes helps support an interpretation that

Carl's function in the narrative is not so much to be Frank's adversary as to be his surrogate family.

Another useful entry point for interpretation is lyric analysis. For instance, "Mele Kalikimaka" and "The Christmas Song" are obviously Christmas music, but we might ask what makes these particularly good (or not so good) choices for this film. First of all, the two are linked by the fact that each ends with the line "Merry Christmas to you." They are addressed like Christmas cards. This point of commonality also allows us to draw distinctions (in the manner of compare and contrast). The sentiment of "Mele Kalikimaka" is rather abstract and impersonal. Clearly evocative of exoticism and travel, the song emphasizes beauties of the place ("the land where palm trees sway") rather than any kind of personal, familial connection. "The Christmas Song," by contrast, dwells on the figure of the child—"tiny tots," "every mother's child," and "kids from one to ninety-two." The cutting in the sequence underscores these particular lines, drawing out the song's nostalgic portrait of a family Christmas. As intimated in our discussion of this scene in Chapter 3, the song seems particularly poignant here because it underscores the familial relationship that Frank wants but does not have. A fuller interpretation might link this idea to the theme of counterfeiting: outside his mother's house, Frank finally recognizes the relationship that he wants for himself but at the same time the fact that his deceptive life has made that relationship impossible.

EXAMPLES FROM THE PUBLISHED LITERATURE

The academic and tradebook critical literature on film, film music, and film sound has many examples of critical essays that you might use as models for your own work. For that reason, we will not present a completed essay here but instead will provide examples of thesis statements from some published articles and book chapters that focus on music. The first three link music to characterization. Robynn Stilwell argues for music's contributions in *Die Hard* (1988):

> Action films tend to be based on simple juxtapositions of hero and villain. As in musicals, so much of the film's running time is taken up with set pieces— songs and dances, chases and demolitions—that a fairly schematic plot, individualized only by local detail, is essential for narrative clarity. But while the identities of the key players in *Die Hard* are clear, just who is antagonist and who protagonist is not so clear, and music is one of the primary elements undercutting the nominal hero and elevating the "villain" to anti-hero.[4]

Similarly, Miguel Mera, writing about *The Ice Storm* (1997), asserts that the film maintains clear boundaries between diegetic and nondiegetic music and that the former seems to be guided by the characters themselves:

> As it is theoretically owned by the characters, the source music acts primarily as a historical and sociocultural locator, particularly in scenes such as the Carvers' dinner party in reel 1 or the three different "party" locations of reel 4. If "nothing more infallibly classifies than tastes in music," then the choices the

characters have made about the music they wish to hear tells the audience how those characters should be perceived.[5]

Julie Brown applies the idea to the television series *Ally McBeal* (1997–2002), which she says

revels in sound track games. Formally, it flaunts its awareness of the inclusive nature of the sound track as a phenomenon while playing around with several types of musical multimedia: film, music video and staged performance. A musical "sound track" of sorts also invades the diegesis: through various sub-plots and dramatic conceits music, especially a particular type of pop music, is elevated to the role of central plot and series metaphor, above all in relation to Ally's character.[6]

Discussing the role of music in fairy-tale musicals, Rick Altman inventories the musical styles used in one sequence from *Love Me Tonight* (1932) and then extrapolates from that to the thesis that "[The film] is built around an opposition between the idle rich and the working poor—yet paradoxically this very first sequence assures us that contact is possible between penniless Maurice [Chevalier] and loveless Jeanette [MacDonald], but only through the magical continuity provided by music and song."[7]

Finally, in a negative formulation, William Darby and Jack du Bois discuss the music of *Scarface* (1932), a film that, according to them

exhibits some . . . musical sophistication when it presents Tony Camonte (Paul Muni) as a gangland killer who whistles [music by Italian opera composer] Verdi before committing murder. While Camonte's allegiance to Italian opera might well be passed off as simply a national passion, his choice of the "Slaves' Chorus" from *Nabucco* may well offer a discreet comment on his life of violence. Except for this character touch, the musical effects in *Scarface* are obvious, underdeveloped, and schmaltzy.[8]

Developing a Reading (2):
Reading against the Grain

Thus far we have focused on developing interpretive strategies that uncover the way the sound track subtly augments the general narrative theme of the film. We have isolated elements of the sound track that seem more or less harmonious with that theme; the paired Christmas songs in *Catch Me If You Can*, for instance, certainly seem to add a fine aesthetic texture to the narrative of the film, and as such the songs form part of the general class of subsidiary filmic motifs that structure, support, and enable the central narrative.

Here is another example of an opening paragraph for an essay on a film we discussed in Chapter 14. The thesis clearly fits the same approach, as it shows a direct parallel between the changing quality of the sound track and the growing knowledge and power of the principal character.

Directed by Andy and Lana Wachowski, *The Matrix* (1999) tells the story of a renegade group fighting against the Matrix, a computer-generated virtual reality that has imprisoned most of the human population unbeknownst to the humans themselves. Neo (Keanu Reeves), a programmer and hacker, is recruited by the group because the leader, Morpheus (Lawrence Fishburne), feels that Neo has special powers to resist the Matrix. The film follows Neo as he masters his powers through a series of confrontations with the Agents, FBI-like law enforcement officers who are charged with policing violations of the Matrix's virtual reality. When Morpheus is captured by the Agents, Neo and Trinity (Carrie-Anne Moss) enter the Matrix to free him. Morpheus and Trinity escape, but Neo is trapped, leading to a final confrontation with the Agents. Neo is shot but survives, which endows him with new powers, including the ability to terminate an Agent's programming. The difficulty of distinguishing truth from illusion, reality from the virtual world of the Matrix is an important thematic concern of the film, and the sound track, with a score by Don Davis and sound design by Dane A. Davis, contributes significantly to the way that the film frames this issue. In this paper, I argue that the film correlates mastery of the Matrix with a hyperacute sound design. Moments of hyperacuity, which give the impression of point-of-view sound, are a characteristic of those who know and understand the reality of the Matrix as illusion. As Neo's powers increase, the sound track grows ever more acute. Such hyperacuity lays bare the constructed quality of the world: things sound other than they simply are. It also suggests that truth is the perception of the artificiality of the world, that the illusion of natural sound is a lie.

An interpretation need not, however, engage in such direct fashion with the central narrative theme. Indeed, analytical attention toward aspects of the sound track that run counter to, even subvert the dominant narrative theme often produces interpretive readings that reveal important unconscious or at least implicit social assumptions enabling that theme. In other words, an interpretation might avoid taking the film at its word, so to speak, and instead interrogate it for meanings that it does not highlight or that it even seems actively to suppress. This is a common strategy in professional academic writing. An essay in cultural analysis, for instance, might go beyond Gorbman's interpretation of *Mildred Pierce* to question the role of melodrama as a genre in mid-1940s American films, or the ways music is used to characterize (and support or undermine) gender categories and class hierarchies. One could also interrogate the ways the film is used to enforce class and value clusters relating to music—for example, popular music is heard in a seaside dive at the beginning of the film; the proprietor (Wally) even refers to "slumming"; the strong implication, then, is that popular music is both low-class and morally questionable.

Interpretive strategies such as those just described use analysis to approach the film from an angle other than that encouraged or explicitly authorized by the film's narrative. These alternate angles are generally social in nature, and each can be considered to embody a mode of critical theory; common ones are based around gender, sexuality, race, class, and cultural hegemony (for example, colonialism).

Obviously, each mode of critical reading will attend to different social themes of the film and so also to the elements of the sound track that support those themes. Similarly, most films explore more than one important narrative theme, and critical emphasis on one of these themes or the other will draw out somewhat different thematic correspondences in the sound track. It is a mistake, however, to think of the resulting multiplicity of interpretations as a sign of an unwillingness (or inability) to make evaluations, or what is sometimes called "cultural relativism." Although it is true that a particular reading is the product of a certain thematic attention, not everything goes. Some readings are more plausible than others. In all cases, details of the sound track must support the interpretation if the reading is to be convincing; and it is the power to deliver a convincing insight into a film that allows a reading to seem productive rather than forced or even absurd. It is this power to convince and deliver insight that is most important. As a rule of thumb, then, interesting critical readings will be neither forced nor too obvious.

EXAMPLE: *CASABLANCA* AGAINST THE GRAIN

The aim of a critical reading is to uncover something about the film that is not obvious on the surface. Let's take *Casablanca* (1942) as an example. We can begin by noting that the character of Sam is a typical role for African Americans in Hollywood of the period. He is an entertainer and properly deferential toward his "boss," Rick. Although not a surprising representation for the 1940s, such a relationship, needless to say, seems problematic from our standpoint today. If we explored this critical direction further, we might point out the manner in which Rick, as he prepares to leave Casablanca, "sells" Sam's contract to Ferrari, who agrees to Rick's inflated terms because "it wouldn't be Rick's without Sam." This somewhat inadvertent slip "exposes" the exploitative nature of the relationship between Rick and Sam: Ferrari apparently believes that Rick's can survive without Rick but not without Sam—and that Rick had been underpaying him.

The sound track supports this interpretation. Sam appears primarily in the first half of the film, almost exclusively in his role as a singer. He performs a series of upbeat American popular songs, which serve to distract the patrons from the harsh realities of the world. (It is interesting to note that the one song that departs from the generally optimistic tone of the music, "Tango Delle Rose," is also the only one Sam does not sing.) Sam sings so others may forget—not just the patrons but also Rick. This theme of forgetting is underscored by the taboo Rick places on "As Time Goes By," a song he associates with his lost love, Ilsa. For Rick, Sam is both a reminder of Ilsa (because he was in Paris with them) and, through the taboo, a means of forgetting her.

When Ilsa returns and Sam breaks the taboo, playing the song first for Ilsa and then for Rick, Sam's work is done and he is, as it were, discarded by the narrative, a move underscored by the nondiegetic orchestra replacing Sam's diegetic song. No longer an instrument of forgetting, Sam is forgotten, his song silenced.

He reappears substantively only once more during the film, during Rick's negotiation with Ferrari, where he sanctions the sale and expresses his willingness to play for less than he's worth: "I don't have time to spend what I make now." Sam, unlike Rick or even Renault, is incapable of personal growth; of the major characters, only Sam's status remains what it was and where he was at the beginning of the film—an entertainer; and the Black entertainer has no other role to play in this war.

In many respects, this sketch of the underlying work that race does in *Casablanca* is not unlike that of the analysis of *Catch Me If You Can* offered earlier. The difference is primarily one of thematic attention. In the case of *Catch Me If You Can*, the analysis used the central narrative to look for thematic correspondences to that narrative in the details of the sound track. We might think of the theme percolating through the details. In *Casablanca*, on the contrary, the theme of race does not correspond to—or at least seems peripheral to—the central narrative intention and so can appear coincidental or at most subordinate. As the analysis suggests, however, this racial theme runs under the main narrative, articulating it and in many respects enabling it in a substantive way. Here, details have absorbed a theme otherwise repressed by the narrative, and our analysis of the sound track was used to show not only that this repressed theme appeared peripherally in the narrative itself but also that the details of the sound track supported this theme.

Readings that focus on repressed themes such as race, class, and gender are sometimes called "symptomatic readings," and collectively such themes are sometimes referred to as the "political unconscious," with an analogy being drawn from psychoanalysis. One premise shared by most psychological and cognitive theory is that individuals do not react to all stimuli on a conscious level. The concept of the "political unconscious" applies that premise to culture at large: beyond its overt values (such as freedom, justice, diversity, liberty, etc.), cultures are organized by covert values and assumptions (unrecognized or only dimly recognized by individuals) that enable the appearance of those values, that mask the contradictions in the particular social appearance of such values, and that sustain the status quo as the "natural" manifestation of them.

Collectively such overt and covert values are known as "ideology." Understood this way, then, critical readings of a film offer a means of exposing these implicit values and underscoring the contradictions in their appearance. Although such readings are often used in the context of advocacy, it is important to recognize that the adoption of a particular mode of critical reading need not necessarily imply a corresponding political view. For instance, when the late Reverend Jerry Falwell interpreted Tinky Winky of *Teletubbies* (1997–2001) as a homosexual figure, he was tacitly accepting the fundamental validity of the queer interpretive mode—because he required that mode to make the interpretation at all. (*Queer reading* is the academic term given to the interpretive mode of critical theory attentive to themes of homosexuality.) Similarly, the cultural critic who argues against entrenched political structures acknowledges the power of those structures through the very attention given to their analysis; and so on—the "political unconscious" is simply that, an unconscious that structures society; and identifying symptoms point to the location of a social disturbance but do not prescribe a particular "treatment."

Interrogating gender in *Casablanca*, we might point to how Ilsa displaces Sam only to be likewise displaced by Louis at the end. On the sound track this is represented by the replacement of "As Time Goes By" with "La Marseillaise." Ilsa, too, is merely an instrument of Rick's psychological journey from cynicism to idealism. The place of Sam and Ilsa in the narrative may seem to be primarily a result of the fact that this is Rick's story, but one can argue that this is misleading, in the sense that it ignores the way race and gender are terms against which Rick's journey is defined.

Another interpretation might give a queer reading to the one earlier. This reading might suggest that Ilsa is in fact an otherwise superfluous figure who blocks "proper" homosocial camaraderie of the "beautiful friendship" from expressing a latent "improper" homosexuality. In this reading, Rick's affections pass over the course of the film from the eunuch-like Sam to the sexually potent Louis by way of an alluring but obstructing Ilsa, just as cynical and impotent diegetic music turns into an apotheosis of "La Marseillaise" by way of a seductive "As Time Goes By" that can find no end. At the end of the film, both Rick and Louis find a "properly" homosocial bond under the sweet string strains of "La Marseillaise."

A reading emphasizing cultural hegemony, on the other hand, might concentrate on the way the ruling class—Rick, Ferrari, Major Strasser, and especially Louis—are all foreigners, and the way indigenous culture is reflected only in colonialist representations of it. Throughout, Casablanca is portrayed as a characteristic oriental city of danger and illicit love, nowhere more so than in the opening sequence. Musically, this takes form most obviously in the stereotyped melodic arabesques, which are used to give an exotic atmosphere to Ferrari's club, the *Blue Parrot*, every bit as much as Sam's songs give *Rick's Café Américain* its equally exotic, if culturally intrusive, musical accent. In both cases, music represents; it projects a characteristic image.

In terms of class, we might point to the way Rick's benevolent management allows a solidarity to form among his workers despite their otherwise divergent backgrounds. Clearly, this idealized representation is determined by the needs of war-time propaganda, a point that is emphasized by the contrast between Rick and Ferrari. Such benevolent management extends only so far as Rick, which is acknowledged obliquely by his need to negotiate with the profit-minded (and ethnically marked) Ferrari on behalf of his staff when he sells the café. Music marks the difference between Rick and Ferrari in a subtle way: only in the *Blue Parrot* do we hear the stereotypically exotic—"Arabian" or oriental—music of nineteenth-century theater and of silent film.

On a somewhat more abstract plane, we might look at the propaganda work of the sound track. If the basic trajectory of the story is Rick's journey from cynicism to idealism, a path that also traces his growing commitment to the war effort, music in particular helps underscore a progressive shift to melodrama that determines the ideological force of that idealism. As the gray ambiguities of cynicism become the black and white certainties of good and evil, music becomes an agent of demonization and veneration. Music already plays a melodramatic role in the prologue, and the first moment of melodramatic demonization occurs shortly after the return of nondiegetic music, when Ilsa mentions the entry of the German army into Paris and the music responds with a distorted version of "Deutschland über Alles." Over the course of the film, such gestures, especially of demonization, occur more and more frequently, marking the growing clarity of Rick's understanding. (One of the unacknowledged ironies of the film is that, although it associates Rick's trauma with the German arrival in Paris, his relationship with Ilsa is in fact conditioned by Laszlo's absence that was produced by the war.)

Although we have tried to be neutral in our presentation of each previous mode of critical analysis, it is important to recognize that these readings are not uniformly convincing. Whereas each draws our attention to a particular facet of the film, some seem more forced or tangential than others to the larger concerns of the film. Some also find better support in the sound track (and other elements of the film). Nevertheless, even readings unconvincing in themselves might prove useful in projects uncovering, say, unrecognized or repressed cultural assumptions pervading a particular set of films.

Conclusion

This chapter offered strategies for developing and writing an interpretation of a film in terms of its sound track. We presented two different models, one that built an interpretation directly on the overt thematic concerns of the film, the other that worked against the grain of those concerns. In both cases, we stressed the importance of finding suitable evidence because the interpretation will seem convincing only if the evidence does not seem forced.

Although it is possible to produce an excellent critical essay based solely on the evidence of the film itself, you should never be reluctant to use any specialized knowledge you have or can find. Information about film history, music history, cultural history, the production process, or biography all present potential entry points for interpretation, as do, in a somewhat different way, other interpretations of the film.

Glossary

100 percent talkie   In the late 1920s, a film with a complete sound track, including dialogue; to be distinguished from the "synchronized" film and the "part-talkie."

2-Shot   An image frame containing two principal figures. *See* page 19.

Accelerando   Musical term for a smooth and usually gradual speeding up of tempo.

Accent   Sharp or sudden loud sounds in any sound track component; these can range from sounds that stand out only slightly from their surroundings to loud, disruptive noises (such as gun shots); in music, accent is also used to refer to the regularly recurring slight emphases that establish and maintain musical meter. *See also* Stinger.

Acousmêtre   (acoustical being) A special kind of character who exists in the diegetic space but is placed consistently offscreen. Being heard but not seen, such a character is defined wholly in terms of diegetic sound. Michel Chion's term.

Act   Several sequences gathered in a broad narrative grouping, using the same general criterion of unity of time and place as for a scene. Typically, a film would not have more than three or four acts. Alternatively, "chapter."

Added value   The additional information or aesthetic shaping that the sound track brings to the image track (and vice versa). Michel Chion's term.

ADR   (automated dialogue replacement) *See* Dialogue replacement.

Ambient sound   (environmental sound; environmental noise) Background sounds appropriate to the physical space being depicted, such as crickets, water, or birds.

A-melodic texture   Similar to monophony in diminishing the foreground/background distinction, but monophony occupies only a foreground, where an a-melodic texture has only background. *See also* Monophony, Homophony, Polyphony, and Melody and Accompaniment.

Anempathetic   Sounds or music that are emotionally distanced, or not in empathy with the image track. *See also* Empathetic.

Asynchronous sound   (nonsynchronous sound) Any sound that is not synchronized with an image. It may be offscreen or nondiegetic.

Atonality   A style of music, usually highly dissonant, characterized by a lack of centeredness and/or resolution. In film it often connotes states of psychological disturbance and/or the world awry.

Audio dissolve   By analogy to image dissolve, a transition to song and dance in which diegetic accompaniment becomes nondiegetic or is sweetened by nondiegetic elements. Rick Altman's term.

Audiovisual contract   Film viewers intuitively accept the notion that image and sound mutually influence one another. Michel Chion's term.

Audiovisual phrasing   The patterning of sync points in a structured sequence. Michel Chion's term.

Background music   Term often used for nondiegetic music. *See* Underscore.

Background   *See* Foreground/Background.

Cinemascope   Widescreen system introduced by Twentieth Century Fox in the 1950s; initially required a special screen and magnetic stereo sound; used multitrack sound, with four channels arranged center, right, left, and rear (surround). *See also* VistaVision and Cinerama.

Cinerama   Widescreen format that offered the most advanced sound system, with seven-channel (five front, two rear) magnetic sound tracks; required specially equipped theaters and highly trained projectionists. *See also* VistaVision and Cinemascope.

Clarity   Aesthetic priority favoring the film's construction of a world that makes sense to us rather one that is as faithful as possible to the real world. It is usually opposed to fidelity.

Close-up   (CU) *See* page 19.

Commutation   Trying different music or sounds with an image sequence.

Compilation scores   In the silent-film era, most scores were compiled—that is, not original music written specifically for a film, but mostly pre-existing works gathered and ordered for a particular performance. In the 1960s and later, the term refers to underscoring made up from pre-existing recordings, especially of popular music or jazz.

Consonance   Sounds, usually musical, that go together and sound sweet, in harmony, or resolved.

Continuity editing   Film editing for "continuity," that is, where cuts are motivated through matches on action, glances, offscreen sound, etc. and where maintaining narrative clarity is a top priority.

Counterpoint   (not to be confused with the same word used for musical textures: we prefer to reserve "polyphonic" for references to a lively, complex texture) Sound that plays "against" a scene; the failure of temporal synchronizing of image track and sound track elements, and the distancing effect that creates. *See also* Synchronization.

Crescendo   Gradual increase in the volume of sound.

Cross-marketing   Selling products ancillary to a film—and, especially since the 1960s, designing film sound tracks for the purpose of promoting recordings.

Cue sheet   During the silent-film era, lists of compositions, with their placements, sent out by studios or their agents as suggestions for theater musicians. In the sound-film era, a legal document that lists all music that appears on the sound track of a film.

Dialogue   *See* Speech.

Dialogue replacement   (looping) (automated dialogue replacement, or ADR) The rerecording of dialogue to an existing segment of film.

Dialogue underscoring   Music that accompanies speech, playing "under" it. *See also* Underscore.

Diegetic/nondiegetic sound   *Diegetic* was borrowed from literary theory to refer to the world of the narrative, the screen world or world of the film. *Nondiegetic*, then, refers to the level of narration: voice-over narration is nondiegetic—and so is underscoring.

Diminuendo   (or decrescendo) Gradual decrease in the volume of sound.

Dissolve   (lap dissolve) A means of joining two shots, the one briefly overlapping the other so that we momentarily see both shots simultaneously, one fading as the other becomes visible. Commonly used as a transition between scenes. *See also* Audio dissolve.

Dissonance   Sounds, usually musical, that are in tension with one another, often described as "harsh." In traditional music, dissonance leads to resolution in consonance.

Distortion   Manipulation of recorded sound through filters and other devices.

Dolby   In the 1970s, after releasing a noise reduction system for stereo magnetic tape, Dolby Laboratories developed a similar system for the optical sound track to increase the frequency and dynamic response of sound on the release print.

Dolby Digital   The original 5.1 Dolby Digital (from 1992) carried six channels—left, center, right, two surround channels, and a separate channel for low frequencies. Competing systems from the same period include DTS (Digital Theater System) and SDDS (Sony Dynamic Digital Sound).

Dub   *See* Stem.

Empathetic   Empathy or emotional engagement is the default for synchronization of sound and image; the sound track is coordinated with the image track, following and emphasizing the mood of onscreen characters and action—the effect is empathetic or engaged. *See also* Anempathetic and Neutral.

Establishing shot   A general view of the physical space to begin a scene.

Establishing sound   Sound track equivalent of an establishing shot—sounds that characterize the physical space of a scene at its beginning. Rick Altman's term.

Extreme close-up   (ECU) *See* page 19 and Figure I-2.

Extreme long shot   (ELS) *See* page 19.

Fidelity   The principle of recording how something actually sounds. Although rhetoric of sound design often invokes the principle of fidelity as a means of achieving realism, fidelity is rarely the dominant principle.

Film form   The overall design of a film, or the temporal articulations of its running time in relation to the deployment of conventional units such as establishing sequences, scenes, chapters (or acts), and so forth.

Film style   The basis of film style is the collection of techniques, practices, aesthetic preferences, and cultural and cinematic expectations that constitute the distinctive way narrative is "delivered" in any individual film.

Final mix   The rerecording that combines all dialogue, music, and effects stems for a release print of a film.

Foley   Sound effects, usually of important characters and figures, created through looping and added to the sound track.

Foreground/background   A distinction of visual staging carried over to film and affecting the sound track as well: in the classical model, dialogue occupies the sonic foreground and music and effects the background.

Franchise   A set of media properties unified by a fictional world and/or set of characters.

Gaumont Chronophone Sound synchronization system introduced in 1902 and frequently exhibited as a novelty in vaudeville houses before it moved into the nickelodeons; its principal defect was not in synchronization but in amplification.

Generic sound (generic noise) Partially grasped speech of people in groups, such as guests at a party or persons in a crowd. Also called "walla."

Hard cut A simple, direct cut from one shot or scene to the next in which the change in the sound track is as abrupt as it is in the image track. *See also* Sound bridge.

Homophony Texture consisting of more than one line, but each line moves with more or less the same rhythm. *See also* Polyphony, Monophony, Melody and accompaniment, and A-melodic texture.

Hurry A musical topic consisting of fast, agitated music frequently used to accompany scenes of intense action, such as chases, combat, and storms.

Image track The visual component of a film.

Insert A shot (often a close-up and usually still) that interrupts the visual flow of a scene; in silent films, inserts, as intertitles, provided speech or narrative information.

Intertitle An insert that consists of text displayed on the screen.

Kinetoscope Apparatus for watching moving pictures invented by Thomas Edison.

Leitmotif Term derived from nineteenth-century opera and applied to film music; when a musical theme (usually short) is developed (varied, reorchestrated) within a film, the theme acquires some of the properties of a word or symbol, with independent meaning or associations that can be called up when the theme is repeated. The signification of a leitmotif is specific to a particular film (or set of films) and is opposed in that sense to the musical topic, whose signification is more general. Leitmotifs are often also musical topics.

Level *See* Volume.

Link *See* Sound link.

Looping Replacing sound, especially dialogue, through rerecording. *See* Dialogue replacement and Foley.

Masking Watching the image track without audio or listening to the sound track without images.

Medium close-up (MCU) *See* page 19.

Medium long shot (MLS) *See* page 19.

Medium shot (MS) *See* page 19.

Melody and accompaniment Probably the most common texture in music. A tune is supported by its accompaniment, making for a strong functional separation of foreground and background. *See also* Monophony, Polyphony, Homophony, and A-melodic texture.

Meter In music, a regular, recurring unit of time corresponding to groups of beats—in other words, meter is a higher level organization of beats.

Mickey-Mousing Close synchronization within a shot or short series of shots, where music closely mimics screen action, cartoon style, blurring the boundary between music and sound effects. *See also* Sweetening.

Minimalism (music) Style of music characterized by a high degree of repetition and a-melodic textures.

Mise-en-bande The integrated sound track of the classical model analogous to the mise-en-scène. Rick Altman's term.

Mise-en-scène The setting of a film, or the way in which physical space and environments are depicted in a film. A theatrical term commonly used in film studies.

Mix *See* Stem.

Mixing The combination (and usually manipulation) of recorded sounds. Mixing may be done either live to create recorded sound or with previously recorded sounds to produce a rerecorded mix.

Monophony The simplest musical texture; strictly speaking, it consists of a single melodic line; the "background" is absent, consisting only of silence. In film sound, the background is either absent or minimally defined. *See also* Polyphony, Homophony, Melody and accompaniment, and A-melodic texture.

Montage sequence A series of shots or very quick scenes joined together, often with optical effects and music, typically used to show the compression of time.

Motifs In literature, recurring figures; in sound film, these can be either visual or aural; for the musical "motive," *see* Theme and Leitmotif.

Movietone Sound-on-film process developed by Theodor Case; its portability made it especially useful for recording newsworthy events and it became the aural foundation of the newsreel by the mid-1920s. *See also* Vitaphone

Multiplex A type of theater that began rapidly appearing in the suburbs in the 1960s; the architecture was primarily utilitarian (the most prominent feature was generally the concession stand); it contained multiple auditoria and centralized projection booths.

Music In silent-film performance, the principal sound element; in sound film, one of the three components of the sound track.

Musical topic (style topic) Conventional musical figures that evoke, represent, or signify a particular mood, place, emotion, or some other character trait in the narrative. The signification of a musical topic is general and is opposed in that sense to the leitmotif, whose signification belongs to the specific film (or franchise).

Neutral music Music indifferent to the scene, neither significant to its narrative nor emotionally engaged—in other words, music that functions much like ambient or environmental noise.

Nickelodeon Storefront theaters that began appearing in appreciable numbers around 1905 and dominated film exhibition until the mid-1910s; typically held between two hundred and three hundred spectators.

Onscreen/offscreen "Onscreen" refers to the part of the film world that is within the camera's frame at any particular moment. "Offscreen" is whatever part of that filmic world we cannot see in the frame but may already have seen or may imaginatively project from the part that we can see.

Orchestra Musicians performing in a group; normally used for the historical European ensemble in which string instruments (violins and their relatives) are the dominant group, along with sections of wind and percussion instruments. In the silent era, an orchestra is any group of more than two musicians.

Orchestral music *See* Orchestra.

Orchestration (instrumentation) Term musicians use to designate the art of choosing and combining instruments to produce a particular sound.

Parallel editing A sequence of two or more scenes edited together so that shots from one scene interrupt the line of action from another in alternating fashion, producing the effect of crosscutting.

Part-talkie In the late 1920s, a film with a synchronized recorded orchestral accompaniment interspersed with talking sequences; to be distinguished from the "synchronized" film and the "100 percent talkie."

Phrase   (music) More or less aligned with short-term memory, phrases are typically 6- to 10-sec segments articulated by means of devices such as a clichéd cadence, a slight slowing down, a drop downward or stop on a long note in the melodic line, or starting over with the same melodic figure in the immediately following bar. The musical phrase is more like a sentence in language than like a phrase, which usually refers to an incomplete grammatical unit.

Picture palace   In the later 1920s, a large well-appointed theater with a large orchestra and a grand organ such as the Mighty Wurlitzer; dominated film exhibition but only in major metropolitan areas.

Pitch   Musical measure of frequency; pitches are individual musical notes.

"Playing the picture"   After about 1910, nickelodeon musicians were encouraged to coordinate their musical selections more or less closely with the screen action.

Plot   The order in which story events are presented to us in a film. *See also* Story.

Point-of-view sound   Sound rendered from the perspective of a character in the film. "Imagined sound" is a special case of point-of-view sound: the sound track presents what a character is hearing in his or her head. Also called point-of-audition sound.

Polyphony   In music, characterized by an independence of musical lines; exhibits a relatively shallow hierarchy between foreground and background. Polyphonic textures are quite common in sound design. *See also* Monophony, Homophony, Melody and accompaniment, and A-melodic texture.

Rendering   The construction of the sound track around the principle of capturing how something feels rather than how something actually sounds. Michel Chion's term.

Rhythm   Closely connected with the term *meter*, but it usually refers to distinctive groupings of notes rather than to the regular groups of meter.

Ritardando   A smooth and usually gradual slowing down of tempo.

Scene   A number of shots (or, rarely, a single very long shot, or "long take") gathered together in terms of unity of time and space. Scenes, like shots, can vary greatly in length; on average, however, scenes typically last from 1 to 5 min.

Sequence   A series of scenes related as a narrative unit. In common usage, "sequence" is short for "sequence of shots" and thus can refer to any series of shots that are related by some criteria that is important to the person doing the analysis.

Shot   A single strip of film, the basic unit of continuity editing; can vary greatly, from 1 to 100 sec (or more).

Shot/reverse-shot pair   (S/RS) a pair of shots where one shot shows something lacking in the other shot and vice versa. Commonly used in classic cinema for dialogue scenes involving two people where one shot shows one character and the reverse shot shows the other. See discussion and example on page 19.

Silence   Absence of effects and ambient sound; tends to break down foreground/background distinction.

Sound advance   A type of sound bridge where we hear a sound before we see its associated image.

Sound bridge   A smooth transition between shots (or scenes) by means of different kinds of overlaps. *See also* Hard cut, Sound advance, Sound lag, Sound link, and Sound match.

Sound design   Sound editing viewed artistically or aesthetically in terms of the shaping of the sound track in a film; most often associated with complex practices of blending and layering the sound track elements since the early 1970s.

Sound effects   (sfx, effects, fx, or noise) All sounds other than music or speech. *See also* Ambient sound and Foley.

Sound lag   Sound from one scene lingers over as we see images from the next.

Sound link   The use of sound to bridge a series of cuts transforming what might otherwise seem to be unrelated shots.

Sound match   Sound belonging to one scene followed by a similar or identical sound belonging to the next scene.

Sound track   (audio track) The audio component of a sound film. The sound track has taken different physical forms over the course of time.

Sound-off   Short for "sound offscreen." Offscreen sound is localizable as an object that *could* be shown but is not—that is, the sound suggests an object that is more than simply background.

Sound-on-disk   Sound recorded onto a cylinder (Edison), phonograph record, or CD and played in mechanical synchronization with the image track. *See also* Sound-on-film and Vitaphone.

Sound-on-film   Sound imprinted on the film strip itself, in optical, magnetic, or digital form. *See also* Sound-on-disk and Movietone.

Soundtrack album   Music from a film released as a phonograph album or CD. In the 1960s, music from films was often crafted as albums, with themes extracted from the score and then arranged as songs appropriate for play on commercial radio.

Source   Term commonly used for diegetic sound.

Source music   Term commonly used for diegetic music.

Special scores   In the silent-film era, music composed for specific films and distributed by studios along with the film.

Speech   One of the three components of the sound track; human speech in language (non-speech sounds such as grunts are usually considered to be more like noise); also called "dialogue."

Stem   Another name for a component of the sound track. The three most important are Dialogue, Music, and Effects. Foley and Ambient sound often have their own stems. Stems are created through mixing. Also called dub, mix, or premix. *See* Final mix.

Stinger   A sudden and sharp accent; most often applied to music (a loud chord or cymbal crash) but equally appropriate to speech (a shout or loud cry) or effects (gun shot or door slamming). *See also* Accent.

Story   A chronological series of events; "narrative" is a possible synonym. *See also* Plot.

Style topic   *See* Musical topic.

Sweetening   Sound effect rendered so that it seems to violate the conditions of verisimilitude through increasing volume above expected levels, adding unmotivated distortion, and otherwise altering the expected timbre. Also the alteration of sound (or music) through the use of overdubbing. *See also* Mickey-Mousing.

Symphonic underscore   Nondiegetic music played by a traditional European orchestra. *See* Underscore.

Sync point   (also spelled "synch point"; point of synchronization) The temporal coordination of sound and image.

Synchronization   Appropriate temporal linking of sound to image; aids the impression that sound emanates from the world of the screen, an effect that is essential to orienting our relation to the screen. *See also* Counterpoint.

Synchronized film   In the late 1920s, a film with recorded orchestral accompaniment and sound effects; to be distinguished from the "part-talkie" and the "100 percent talkie."

Tempo   Perceived rate (beat or pulse) of sound or musical events. (In non-musical contexts, *tempo* is often used interchangeably with *pace*.)

Tessitura   (Higher or lower) register of the voice (or musical instrument).

Texture   The functional relation of musical lines to one another; the number of musical strands or layers occurring simultaneously. In recording and editing, the creation of sound texture is often called "layering."

Theme   (literature) A concise general statement about a story or poem that says what it is about.

(music) Clearly defined melodies that are "developed" (or altered and commented on) in a composition; for short musical themes, the terms *theme* and *motive* are essentially interchangeable. In film, a musical theme functions like the literary motif, a significant recurring sound element. *See also* Leitmotif and Motif.

Timbre   Distinct coloring of sound.

Topic   *See* Musical topic.

Underscore   Nondiegetic music. Synonym for "background music" (a term we prefer to avoid because it confuses the nondiegetic with background physical space in the image track), "underscoring," "accompaniment," "commentative music," "dramatic scoring," or just "scoring."

Up-and-downer   In the studio era, a device that automatically raised and lowered music levels inversely with the presence of dialogue.

Vaudeville   Middle-class theaters of the later nineteenth and early twentieth centuries; offered mixed programs of music and other acts.

VistaVision   Widescreen format whose aspect ratio eventually became a standard (1.85:1); its sound was coded on an optical track. *See also* Cinerama and Cinemascope.

Vitaphone   Sound-on-disk system developed for Warner Bros. by Western Electric, a subsidiary of AT&T; the first commercially viable system for synchronized sound. The Vitaphone system consisted of a special phonograph mechanically coupled to a projector. Enjoyed superior amplification compared to sound-on-film methods at the time.

Voice-off   A special case of "sound-off" (q.v.); offscreen sound that highlights the voice.

Voice-over narration   (voice-over) A person not seen (and who may not belong to the physical world shown in the film) talks directly to the viewer.

Volume   Physical strength of the sound we perceive, its loudness. Strictly speaking, volume is defined by amplitude, which is the power of sound (normally as measured in decibels). In recording often referred to as levels.

Credits

Notes

INTRODUCTION

1. Robynn Stilwell, "Sound and Empathy: Subjectivity, Gender and the Cinematic Sound-scape," in *Film Music: Critical Approaches*, ed. K. J. Donnelly (Edinburgh: Edinburgh University Press, 2001), 182.
2. http://www.thecityofabsurdity.com/losthighway/lhsound.html.
3. Vincent LoBrutto, *Sound on Film: Interviews with Creators of Film Sound* (Westport, Conn.: Praeger, 1994), xi.
4. Claudia Gorbman, "Film Music," in *Film Studies: Critical Approaches*, ed. John Hill and Pamela Church Gibson (Oxford and New York: Oxford University Press, 2000), 45.
5. Aaron Copland, *What to Listen for in Music*, 2d edition (New York: McGraw-Hill, 1957), 253.
6. Franz Waxman, cited in Tony Thomas, *Film Score: The Art and Craft of Movie Music* (Burbank, Calif.: Riverwood Press, 1991), 39.

INTRODUCTION TO PART I

1. Michel Chion, *Audio-Vision: Sound on Screen*, tr. Claudia Gorbman (New York: Columbia University Press, 1994), 5.
2. Michel Chion, *Audio-Vision: Sound on Screen*, tr. Claudia Gorbman (New York: Columbia University Press, 1994), 1 (title of Part One).

CHAPTER 1

1. Annabel Cohen, "Film Music: Perspectives from Cognitive Psychology," in *Music and Cinema*, ed. James Buhler, Caryl Flinn, and David Neumeyer (Hanover, N.H.: Wesleyan University Press, 2000), 360.
2. Max Steiner Collection, Brigham Young University.
3. Aaron Copland, *What to Listen for in Music*, 2d edition (New York: McGraw-Hill, 1957), 258.
4. Franz Waxman, unpublished document. Used courtesy of John Waxman.

5. Aaron Copland, *What to Listen for in Music,* 2d edition (New York: McGraw-Hill, 1957), 255.

6. Claudia Gorbman, *Unheard Melodies: Narrative Film Music* (Bloomington: Indiana University Press, 1987), 73.

7. Michel Chion, *Audio-Vision: Sound on Screen,* tr. Claudia Gorbman (New York: Columbia University Press, 1994), 205.

8. Michel Chion, *Audio-Vision: Sound on Screen,* tr. Claudia Gorbman (New York: Columbia University Press, 1994), 155.

9. Michel Chion, *Audio-Vision: Sound on Screen,* tr. Claudia Gorbman (New York: Columbia University Press, 1994), 187.

10. Aaron Copland, *What to Listen for in Music,* 2d edition (New York: McGraw-Hill, 1957), 255.

11. Claudia Gorbman, *Unheard Melodies: Narrative Film Music* (Bloomington: Indiana University Press, 1987), 16–18.

12. Michel Chion, *Audio-Vision: Sound on Screen,* tr. Claudia Gorbman (New York: Columbia University Press, 1994), 1 (title of Part One).

CHAPTER 2

1. Quoted in Vincent LoBrutto, *Sound on Film: Interviews with Creators of Film Sound* (Westport, Conn.: Praeger, 1994), 278.

2. Quoted in Vincent LoBrutto, *Sound on Film: Interviews with Creators of Film Sound* (Westport, Conn.: Praeger, 1994), 253.

3. Stanley Cavell, *Must We Mean What We Say?* (New York: Cambridge University Press, 1977 [1969]), 185–6.

4. Quoted in Vincent LoBrutto, *Sound on Film: Interviews with Creators of Film Sound* (Westport, Conn.: Praeger, 1994), 30.

5. Helen Hanson: "Sound Affects: Post-production Sound, Soundscapes and Sound Design in Hollywood's Studio Era," *Music, Sound, and the Moving Image* 1.1 (2007): 41.

6. Quoted in Vincent LoBrutto, *Sound on Film: Interviews with Creators of Film Sound* (Westport, Conn.: Praeger, 1994), 229–30.

7. Michel Chion, *Audio-Vision: Sound on Screen,* tr. Claudia Gorbman (New York: Columbia University Press, 1994), 10–13.

8. Quoted in Vincent LoBrutto, *Sound on Film: Interviews with Creators of Film Sound* (Westport, Conn.: Praeger, 1994), 236.

9. Quoted in Vincent LoBrutto, *Sound on Film: Interviews with Creators of Film Sound* (Westport, Conn.: Praeger, 1994), 99.

10. Quoted in Vincent LoBrutto, *Sound on Film: Interviews with Creators of Film Sound* (Westport, Conn.: Praeger, 1994), 43.

11. Walter Murch, "A Conversation with Walter Murch," *Transom Review* 5.1 (April 2005):46, http://transom.org/guests/review/200504.review.murch3.html (accessed January 28, 2009).

12. Quoted in Vincent LoBrutto, *Sound on Film: Interviews with Creators of Film Sound* (Westport, Conn.: Praeger, 1994), 96.

13. Walter Murch, "Dense Clarity—Clear Density," *Transom Review* 5.1 (April 2005): 7, http://transom.org/guests/review/200504.review.murch2.html (accessed January 28, 2009).

14. Quoted in Vincent LoBrutto, *Sound on Film: Interviews with Creators of Film Sound* (Westport, Conn.: Praeger, 1994), 268.

CHAPTER 3

1. Rick Altman, *The American Film Musical* (Bloomington: Indiana University Press, 1987), 62–74.
2. Alfred Hitchcock, "Direction," in *Footnotes to the Film*, ed. Charles Davy (London: Lovat Dickson and Thompson, 1937); reprinted in *Focus on Hitchcock*, ed. Albert J. LaValley (Englewood Cliffs, N.J.: Prentice-Hall, 1972), 36.
3. Rick Altman, *The American Film Musical* (Bloomington: Indiana University Press, 1987), 63.
4. Michel Chion, *Audio-Vision: Sound on Screen*, tr. Claudia Gorbman (New York: Columbia University Press, 1994), 129.
5. Max Steiner, "Scoring the Film," in *We Make the Movies*, ed. Nancy Naumburg (New York: Norton, 1937), 224–5.

CHAPTER 4

1. Quoted in Max Wilk, *The Wit and Wisdom of Hollywood: From the Squaw Man to the Hatchet Man* (New York: Warner Paperback Library, 1973), 3.
2. Richard Abel, "The Most American of Attractions, the Illustrated Song," in *The Sounds of Early Cinema*, ed. Richard Abel and Rick Altman (Bloomington: Indiana University Press, 2001), 143–55.
3. Wilbur D. Nesbit, "Lizzie Plays for the Pictures," *Moving Picture World*, September 2, 1911, 617.
4. Clyde Martin, "Playing the Pictures," *Film Index*, December 31, 1910, 12.
5. Cited in Charles Hofmann, *Sounds for Silents* (New York: DBS Publications, 1970): 7.
6. Clarence Sinn, "Music for the Picture," *Moving Picture World* 26 (November 1910): 1227.
7. A. W. W., letter to Sinn, "Music for the Picture," *Moving Picture World*, February 14, 1914, 796.
8. S. L. Rothapfel, "Dignity of the Exhibitors' Profession," *Moving Picture World*, February 26, 1910, 289.
9. Erno Rapee, *Encyclopedia of Music for Pictures* ("As Essential as the Picture") (New York: Belwin, 1925), 13.
10. Quoted in Gillian B. Anderson, *Music for Silent Films 1894–1929: A Guide* (Washington, D.C.: Library of Congress, 1988), xxiii.
11. "How the Cinematographer Works," *Moving Picture World*, July 13, 1907, 300.
12. Justin London, "Leitmotifs and Musical Reference in the Classic Film Score," in *Music and Cinema*, ed. James Buhler, Caryl Flinn, and David Neumeyer (Middletown, Conn.: Wesleyan University Press, 2000), 87.
13. Erno Rapee, *Encyclopedia of Music for Pictures* ("As Essential as the Picture") (New York: Belwin, 1925), 13.
14. Erno Rapee, *Encyclopedia of Music for Pictures* ("As Essential as the Picture") (New York: Belwin, 1925), 14.
15. Martin Marks, "About the Music," in *More Treasures from American Film Archives, 1894–1931* (San Francisco: National Film Preservation Foundation, 2004). The quotations in this section are from the DVD's program book, 146–8.
16. Advertisement for J. S. Zamecnik, *Sam Fox Photoplay Edition: Loose Leaf Collections of High-Class Dramatic and Descriptive Motion Picture Music*, vol. 2 of J. S. Zamecnik, *Sam Fox Moving Picture Music* (Cleveland, Ohio: Sam Fox Publishing, 1913), [ii].

CHAPTER 5

1. James Clancy, "The Human Voice as a Factor in the Moving Picture Show," *Motion Picture World,* January 30, 1909, 115.

2. Donald Crafton, *The Talkies: American Cinema's Transition to Sound, 1926–1931* (Berkeley: University of California Press, 1999), 240.

3. K. F. Morgan, "Dubbing Sound Pictures," *Cinematographic Annual* 1 (1930): 425.

4. Rick Altman, with McGraw Jones and Sonia Tatroe, "Inventing the Cinema Sound Track: Hollywood's Multiplane Sound System," in *Music and Cinema,* ed. James Buhler, Caryl Flinn, and David Neumeyer (Middletown, Conn.: Wesleyan University Press, 2000), 356, 358.

5. Quoted in Donald Crafton, *The Talkies: American Cinema's Transition to Sound, 1926–1931* (Berkeley: University of California Press, 1999), 504.

6. Quoted in Donald Crafton, *The Talkies: American Cinema's Transition to Sound, 1926–1931* (Berkeley: University of California Press, 1999), 504.

7. Quoted in Donald Crafton, *The Talkies: American Cinema's Transition to Sound, 1926–1931* (Berkeley: University of California Press, 1999), 504.

8. David Bordwell, Janet Staiger, and Kristin Thompson, *The Classic Hollywood Cinema: Film Style and Mode of Production to 1960* (New York: Columbia University Press, 1985), 54.

9. Leon S. Becker, "Technology in the Art of Producing Motion Pictures," *Journal of the Society of Motion Picture Engineers* 39 (1942): 114.

10. James Lastra, *Sound Technology and the American Cinema* (New York: Columbia University Press, 2000), 160.

11. Erno Rapee, *Encyclopedia of Music for Pictures ("As Essential as the Picture")* (New York: Belwin, 1925), 11.

12. Claudia Gorbman, "Film Music," in *Film Studies: Critical Approaches,* ed. John Hill and Pamela Church Gibson (London/New York: Oxford University Press, 2000), 45.

13. Claudia Gorbman, *Unheard Melodies: Narrative Film Music* (Bloomington: Indiana University Press, 1987), 26.

14. Rick Altman, with McGraw Jones and Sonia Tatroe, "Inventing the Cinema Sound Track: Hollywood's Multiplane Sound System," in *Music and Cinema,* ed. James Buhler, Caryl Flinn, and David Neumeyer (Middletown, Conn.: Wesleyan University Press, 2000), 353.

15. Claudia Gorbman, *Unheard Melodies: Narrative Film Music* (Bloomington: Indiana University Press, 1987), 79.

CHAPTER 6

1. Lawrence Morton, "Film Music of the Quarter," *Hollywood Quarterly* 3–4 (1948): 401–402.

2. Michel Chion, *Audio-Vision: Sound on Screen,* tr. Claudia Gorbman (New York: Columbia University Press, 1994), 58.

CHAPTER 7

1. James Cameron, *Sound Motion Pictures,* 6th ed. (Coral Gables, Fla.: Cameron Pub. Co., 1947), 111.

2. Linda Danly, ed., *Hugo Friedhofer: The Best Years of His Life, A Hollywood Master of Music for the Movies* (Lanham, Md.: Scarecrow Press, 1999), 42.

3. Max Steiner Collection, Brigham Young University.

4. Quoted in Vincent LoBrutto, *Sound on Film: Interviews with Creators of Film Sound* (Westport, Conn.: Praeger, 1994), 32.

5. Sergei Eisenstein, "The Synchronization of the Senses," in *The Film Sense* (New York: Harcourt Brace Jovanovich, 1975), 69–112.

6. Song titles and sequence were taken from Martin Marks, "Music, Drama, Warner Brothers: The Cases of *Casablanca* and the *Maltese Falcon*," in *Music and Cinema*, ed. James Buhler, Caryl Flinn, and David Neumeyer (Middletown, Conn.: Wesleyan University Press, 2000), 165–6.

7. Martin Marks, "Music, Drama, Warner Brothers: The Cases of *Casablanca* and the *Maltese Falcon*," in *Music and Cinema*, ed. James Buhler, Caryl Flinn, and David Neumeyer (Middletown, Conn.: Wesleyan University Press, 2000), 173.

8. Quoted in the Introduction to *Music and Cinema*, ed. James Buhler, Caryl Flinn, and David Neumeyer (Middletown, Conn.: Wesleyan University Press, 2000), 15.

9. See David Neumeyer and Nathan Platte, *Franz Waxman's* Rebecca: *A Film Score Guide* (Lanham, Md.: Scarecrow Press, 2012), 85–87.

CHAPTER 8

1. Quotes in this section are all taken from Gorbman, *Unheard Melodies: Narrative Film Music* (Bloomington: Indiana University Press, 1987), 91–98.

2. Michel Chion, *Audio-Vision: Sound on Screen*, tr. Claudia Gorbman (New York: Columbia University Press, 1994), 192–8.

CHAPTER 9

1. Barbara Kennedy, *Deleuze and Cinema: The Aesthetics of Sensation* (Edinburgh: Edinburgh University Press, 2003).

2. Quoted in John Belton, *Widescreen Cinema* (Cambridge, Mass.: Harvard University Press, 1992), 205.

3. Quoted in John Belton, *Widescreen Cinema* (Cambridge, Mass.: Harvard University Press, 1992), 203.

4. Cited in Jeff Smith, *The Sounds of Commerce: Marketing Popular Film Music* (New York: Columbia University Press, 1998), 58.

5. Frederick Sternfeld, "Music and the Feature Film," *Musical Quarterly* 33.4 (1947): 521.

6. Jeff Smith, *The Sounds of Commerce: Marketing Popular Film Music* (New York: Columbia University Press, 1998), 60.

7. Neil Lerner, "'Look at That Big Hand Move Along': Clocks, Containment, and Music in High Noon," *South Atlantic Quarterly* 104.1 (2005): 163.

8. Fred Binkley, "Mancini's Movie Manifesto," *Down Beat* 5 (March 1970): 16.

9. Jeff Smith, *The Sounds of Commerce: Marketing Popular Film Music* (New York: Columbia University Press, 1998), 69–99.

10. Jeff Smith, *The Sounds of Commerce: Marketing Popular Film Music* (New York: Columbia University Press, 1998), 61.

11. Julie Hubbert, "'Whatever Happened to Great Movie Music?': Cinéma Vérité and Hollywood Film Music of the Early 1970s," *American Music* 21/2 (2003): 197.

CHAPTER 10

1. Kristin Thompson, *Storytelling in the New Hollywood* (Cambridge, Mass.: Harvard University Press, 1999), 355–62.

2. Robynn Stilwell, "'I Just Put a Drone Under Him . . .': Collage and Subversion in the Score of *Die Hard*," *Music & Letters* 78/4 (1997): 551, 563.

3. Jeff Smith, "That Money-Making 'Moon River' Sound: Thematic Organization and Orchestration in the Film Music of Henry Mancini," in *Music and Cinema*, ed. James Buhler, Caryl Flinn, and David Neumeyer (Middletown, Conn.: Wesleyan University Press, 2000), 255.

4. Royal S. Brown, *Overtones and Undertones: Reading Film Music* (Berkeley and Los Angeles: University of California Press, 1994), 347.

5. Royal S. Brown, *Overtones and Undertones: Reading Film Music* (Berkeley and Los Angeles: University of California Press, 1994), 165.

6. Graham Bruce, *Bernard Herrmann: Film Music and Narrative* (Ann Arbor: UMI Research Press, 1985), 35.

7. Fred Steiner, "Herrmann's 'Black-and-White' Music for Hitchcock's Psycho," in *Film Music Notebook* I/1 (1974): 28–36; I/2 (1974-75): 26–46. The quotation is from I/1:34.

8. Claudia Gorbman, *Unheard Melodies: Narrative Film Music* (Bloomington: Indiana University Press, 1987), 79.

9. Charles Leinberger, "The Dollars Trilogy: 'There Are Two Kinds of Western Heroes, My Friend!'," in Kathryn Kalinak, *Music in the Western: Notes from the Frontier* (London/New York: Routledge, 2012), 140.

10. Charles Leinberger, "The Dollars Trilogy: 'There Are Two Kinds of Western Heroes, My Friend!'," in Kathryn Kalinak, *Music in the Western: Notes from the Frontier* (London/New York: Routledge, 2012), 139.

CHAPTER 11

1. John Belton, "1950s Magnetic Sound: The Frozen Revolution," in *Sound Theory, Sound Practice,* ed. Rick Altman (New York: Routledge, 1992), 154–67.

2. See, for instance, Geoff King, *New Hollywood Cinema: An Introduction* (New York: Columbia University Press, 2002), 1–9.

3. Justin Wyatt, *High Concept: Movies and Marketing in Hollywood* (Austin: University of Texas Press, 1994).

4. Quoted in David A. Cook, *Lost Illusions: American Cinema in the Shadow of Watergate and Vietnam, 1970–1979* (Berkeley: The University of California Press, 2000), 386.

5. Douglas Gomery, *Shared Pleasures: A History of Movie Presentation in the United States* (Madison: University of Wisconsin Press, 1992), 100.

6. Quoted in David A. Cook, *Lost Illusions: American Cinema in the Shadow of Watergate and Vietnam, 1970–1979* (Berkeley: The University of California Press, 2000), 404.

7. Quoted in David A. Cook, *Lost Illusions: American Cinema in the Shadow of Watergate and Vietnam, 1970–1979* (Berkeley: The University of California Press, 2000), 386.

8. Quoted in Inga Kiderra, "Scoring Points," *USC Trojan Family Magazine,* Winter 2000 (http://www.usc.edu/dept/pubrel/trojan_family/winter00/FilmScoring/Music_pg2.html).

9. Geoff King, *New Hollywood Cinema: An Introduction* (New York: Columbia University Press, 2002), 165.

10. R. Serge Denisoff and George Plasketes, "Synergy in 1980s Film and Music: Formula for Success or Industry Mythology?," *Film History* 4.3 (1990): 257.

11. Quoted in Edwin Black, "Film Music: Too Much and Not Enough," *Film Score Daily* 16 (April 1998) (http://www.filmscoremonthly.com/articles/1998/16_Apr---Too_Much_and_Not_Enough.asp).

12. "James Horner's Melbourne Seminar," *Soundtrack!* 11.41 (March 1992): 7.

13. Quoted in David A. Cook, *Lost Illusions: American Cinema in the Shadow of Watergate and Vietnam, 1970–1979* (Berkeley: University of California Press, 2000), 390.

14. Quoted in Vincent LoBrutto, *Sound on Film: Interviews with Creators of Film Sound* (Westport, Conn.: Praeger, 1994), 95–96.

15. Quoted in Vincent LoBrutto, *Sound on Film: Interviews with Creators of Film Sound* (Westport, Conn.: Praeger, 1994), 133–4.

16. Quoted in Vincent LoBrutto, *Sound on Film: Interviews with Creators of Film Sound* (Westport, Conn.: Praeger, 1994), 134.

17. Justin Wyatt, *High Concept: Movies and Marketing in Hollywood* (Austin: University of Texas Press, 1994), 144.

CHAPTER 12

1. Janet Maslin, Review of *Saving Private Ryan*, *New York Times*, July 24, 1998, http://www.nytimes.com/movie/review?res=9C01EEDF1239F937A15754C0A96E958260.

2. Gary Rydstrom, "The Use of Surrounds in *Saving Private Ryan*," in Tomlinson Holman, *Surround Sound: Up and Running*, 2d ed. (Burlington, Mass.: Focal Press, 2008), 195.

3. Gary Rydstrom, commentary in "*Saving Private Ryan:* Music and Sound," a documentary included among the special features in the DVD edition "*Saving Private Ryan:* D-Day 60th Anniversary Commemorative Edition," released in 2004 (Universal catalogue 91700). For details, consult http://www.imdb.com/title/tt0493494/.

4. Martin Marks, "Music, Drama, Warner Brothers: The Cases of *Casablanca* and the *Maltese Falcon*," in *Music and Cinema*, ed. James Buhler, Caryl Flinn, and David Neumeyer (Middletown, Conn.: Wesleyan University Press, 2000), 161–86. The quotations are from page 162.

5. Martin Marks, "Music, Drama, Warner Brothers: The Cases of *Casablanca* and the *Maltese Falcon*," in *Music and Cinema*, ed. James Buhler, Caryl Flinn, and David Neumeyer (Middletown, Conn.: Wesleyan University Press, 2000), 181.

CHAPTER 13

1. Quoted in Vincent LoBrutto, *Sound on Film: Interviews with Creators of Film Sound* (Westport, Conn.: Praeger, 1994), 184.

2. Michael A. Levine, "Why Hans Zimmer Got the Job You Wanted (And You Didn't)," http://www.soundtracksandtrailermusic.com/2013/07/hans-zimmer/.

3. Kathy A. McDonald, "Technology Turns Composers into One-Stop Music Shops," *Daily Variety*, July 29, 2002, Section 1, p. A54.

4. Michael A. Levine, "Why Hans Zimmer Got the Job You Wanted (And You Didn't)," http://www.soundtracksandtrailermusic.com/2013/07/hans-zimmer/.

5. Lukas Kendall, "Interview with Steve Bartek," *Film Score Monthly* 64 (December 1995) http://www.boingo.org/articles/FSMBartek.html.

6. Quoted in Vincent LoBrutto, *Sound on Film: Interviews with Creators of Film Sound* (Westport, Conn.: Praeger, 1994), 118.

7. http://www.mpse.org/history/history.html.

8. Quoted in Vincent LoBrutto, *Sound on Film: Interviews with Creators of Film Sound* (Westport, Conn.: Praeger, 1994), 213.

9. Vanessa Theme Ament, *The Foley Grail: The Art of Performing for Films, Games, and Animation*, 2d ed. (Burlington, Mass.: Focal Press, 2014), 24.

10. Rebecca Doran Eaton, "Marking Minimalism: Minimal Music as a Sign of Machines and Mathematics in Multimedia," *Music and the Moving Image* 7, no. 1 (2014): 20.

11. Quoted in "Production Notes: *Marie Antoinette*," http://www.cinemareview.com/production.asp?prodid=3650.

12. Quoted in "Press Conference: *Marie Antoinette*," May 24, 2006, http://www.festival-cannes.fr/fr/theDailyArticle/43408.html.

CHAPTER 14

1. *The Hours* (Paramount Home Entertainment, 2002), catalogue number 33990.

2. Liner notes to Philip Glass, *The Hours: Music from the Motion Picture* (New York: Nonesuch, 2002). Catalogue number 79693-2.

3. Janet Halfyard, "Cue the Big Theme? The Sound of the Superhero," in *Oxford Handbook of New Audiovisual Aesthetics,* ed. John Richardson, Claudia Gorbman, and Carol Vernallis (New York: Oxford, 2013), 176–7.

CHAPTER 15

1. Roger Ebert, "Catch Me If You Can," *Chicago Sun-Times*, December 25, 2002. From the newspaper's archives at http://www.suntimes.com/ebert/ebert_reviews/2002/12/122501.html. Accessed 12/18/2008.

2. Always remember to credit sources for material in course papers. See note 1 for the citation to Ebert's review.

3. All but the second of these questions is quoted from David Bordwell, *The McGraw-Hill Film Viewer's Guide,* supplement to David Bordwell and Kristin Thompson, *Film Art: An Introduction*, 6th ed. (2001), 17.

4. Robynn Stilwell, "Collage and Subversion in the Score of 'Die Hard'," *Music & Letters* 78/4 (Nov 1997): 551.

5. Miguel Mera, *Mychael Danna's The Ice Storm: A Film Score Guide* (Lanham, Md.: Scarecrow Press, 2007), 119.

6. Julie Brown, "Ally McBeal's Postmodern Soundtrack," *Journal of Royal Musical Association* 126 (2001): 275–303.

7. Rick Altman, *The American Film Musical* (Bloomington: Indiana University Press, 1987), 152.

8. William Darby and Jack du Bois, *American Film Music: Major Composers, Techniques, Trends, 1915–1990* (Jefferson, N.C./London: MacFarland, 1990), 13.

Index

Note: page numbers in italics refer to figures or tables.

309; uses of, 13–14, *14–15*, 51–52, *52*.
See also background sound
AMC (American Multi-Cinema), 364
Amélie (Le Fabuleux Destin d'Amélie Poulain)
(2001 film), 69
a-melodic texture, 50–52, *52–53*, *53*, *53–54*
Ament, Vanessa Theme, 459
American Beauty (1999 film), 54, 68,
368, 385
American Federation of Musicians,
155, *156*
American Graffiti (1973 film), 78, 317,
320–21, 359, 470, 471–73
An American in Paris (1951 film), 255
American Multi-Cinema (AMC), 364
American Society of Composers, Authors
and Publishers (ASCAP), 116, 136
Amos 'n' Andy (radio show), *108*
amplification, as early technical issue,
141–42, *143*, 143–44, 145, 146
analysis of sound track(s), using musical
terms, 54–55. *See also* writing
Anatomy of a Murder (1959 film), 315
ancillary products: cross-marketing and
promotion of, 368–72; development of,
310–14; home video market and,
367–68; soundtrack albums as, 307,
311–12, 315–16, 317, 322, 383, 441, 446.
See also sheet music
Anderson, Stephen, *28*
Andriessen, Louis, 384
animation: production schedule for, 446;
sound track for, 237, 238, 239
Annabella, 219
The Ant Bully (2006 film), 449
Antheil, George, 248
The Apartment (1960 film), 64–65, *65*, *66*,
70, 73, 324
Apocalypse Now (1979 film), 368, 378, *379*,
388, 399–400, *400*, 458
Appalachian Spring (Copland), 248
Argo (2012 film), 444
arrangers for studios, 163–64, 238, 239
Arthur, Jean, 241
The Artist (2011 film), 137
Arzner, Dorothy, 252
ASCAP (American Society of Composers,
Authors and Publishers), 116, 136
aspect ratios: standardization of, *148*; for
widescreen film, 296, *297*
L'Assassinat du duc de Guise (1908 film),
106–7, 136
Astaire, Fred, 38, 270
Astor Theatre (New York), 120
Atonement (2007 film), *55*; analysis of sound
track, 54–55; diegetic and nondiegetic
sound in, 56–57, *57–58*; scene transitions
in, 77; sound effects in, 14
AT&T, 144, 146, 292

attendance at movies: Great Depression and,
224, 229; suburbanization and, 295,
299; television and, 295, 299
audio dissolve, 58, 69–72, *71*
audiovisual contract, 4, 98
audiovisual phrasing: and film form, 186; in
musicals, 200, 208; and scene analysis,
199–200, 206, 217; sync points and,
199–200
Auricle Time Processor, 454
Austen, Jane, 504
automated dialogue replacement (ADR),
457–59, *458*; directors' views on, 458–59;
and synchronization, 79; uses of, 302,
303, *307*, 377, 433, 456, *458*
Autry, Gene, 251, *251*
The Avengers (2012 film), 470
Avid system, 434, 445, 472
Avid Technology, 445
Axt, William, *113*, 120, 150, *150*

B

Bacall, Lauren, 46, 62, *63*, 259, *260*,
263, 272
background: in early sound films, 170–71;
as term, 56
background music, 5, 11; benefits *vs.* ambient
sound, 242–43, *243*; and development of
foreground/background distinction,
242; terms for, 18. *See also* nondiegetic
music; underscoring
background sound: and continuity,
11, 241–42, 247, 302; in *Good Will
Hunting*, 27; lack of, as technical
issue, 170–72, 240–41; lack of, digital
sound and, 462; lack of, effects on
viewers, 306; and narrative clarity,
170–72, *172*; narrative function of, 15;
overwhelming, narrative function of,
240, *241*. *See also* ambient sound;
balance of sound track elements;
foreground *vs.* background sound
Back to Bataan (1945 film), 270
Back to the Future (1985 film), 368, 369
Badelt, Klaus, 448
Balaban and Katz Theatre corporation,
110, 111, 137
balance of sound track elements, 21, 22;
and tempo, 36; textures and, 47–54
Baldwin, Alec, 471
Bale, Christian, 81, 484, 488
Bancroft, Anne, 332
Barbier, George, 78
Barry, John, 393
Barrymore, John, 150, *150*
Bartek, Steve, 450, *451*
Bass, Saul, 345–47
Batman (1989 film), 472, 482–83, *483*